P9-BJM-614

America's 101 FASTEST GROWING JOBS

Detailed Information on Major Jobs with the Most Openings and Growth

Eighth Edition

- ★ **Thorough, up-to-date descriptions of the 101 fastest growing jobs**
- ★ **Information on skills needed, education and training required, salaries, growth potential, and much more**
- ★ **Special section providing proven career planning and job-seeking advice**
- ★ **Resume examples by professional resume writers for a variety of fastest growing jobs**
- ★ **Helpful information on labor market trends**

Part of America's Top Jobs™ Series

Michael Farr

jist Works
America's Career Publisher

America's 101 Fastest Growing Jobs, Eighth Edition
Detailed Information on Major Jobs with the Most Openings and Growth

Previous edition was titled *America's Fastest Growing Jobs*

© 2005 by JIST Publishing, Inc.

Published by JIST Works, an imprint of JIST Publishing, Inc.
8902 Otis Avenue
Indianapolis, IN 46216-1033
Phone: 800-648-JIST   Fax: 800-JIST-FAX
E-mail: info@jist.com   Web site: www.jist.com

Some other books by Michael Farr:
The Very Quick Job Search
Same-Day Resume
America's Top Resumes for America's Top Jobs
The Quick Resume & Cover Letter Book
Getting the Job You Really Want
Seven Steps to Getting a Job Fast
Best Jobs for the 21st Century (with database
  work by Laurence Shatkin, Ph.D.)

Other books in the America's Top Jobs™ series:
America's Top 300 Jobs
America's Top 101 Computer and Technical Jobs
America's Top 101 Jobs for People Without a Four-Year Degree
America's Top 101 Jobs for College Graduates
America's Top Military Careers
Career Guide to America's Top Industries

About career materials published by JIST. Our materials encourage people to be self-directed and to take control of their destinies. We work hard to provide excellent content, solid advice, and techniques that get results. If you have questions about this book or other JIST products, call 1-800-648-JIST or visit www.jist.com.

Quantity discounts are available for JIST products. Please call 1-800-648-JIST or visit www.jist.com for a free catalog and more information.

Visit www.jist.com for information on JIST, free job search information, book excerpts, and ordering information on our many products. For free information on 14,000 job titles, visit www.careeroink.com.

Acquisitions Editor: Susan Pines
Editors: Stephanie Koutek, Annie Stalling
Cover and Interior Designer: Aleata Howard
Page Layout Coordinator: Carolyn J. Newland
Proofreaders: David Faust, Jeanne Clark

Printed in Canada

Library of Congress Cataloging-in-Publication data is on file with the Library of Congress.

06 05 04   9 8 7 6 5 4 3 2 1

ISBN 1-59357-070-8

Who Should Use This Book?

This is more than a book of job descriptions. I've spent quite a bit of time thinking about how to make its contents useful for a variety of situations, including

★ **Exploring career options.** The job descriptions in Section One give a wealth of information on many of the most desirable jobs in the labor market.

★ **Considering more education or training.** The information helps you avoid costly mistakes in choosing a career or deciding on additional training or education—and it increases your chances of planning a bright future.

★ **Job seeking.** This book helps you identify new job targets, prepare for interviews, and write targeted resumes. The career planning and job search advice in Section Two has been proven to cut job search time in half!

★ **Career planning.** The job descriptions help you explore your options, and Sections Two and Three provide career planning advice and other useful information.

Source of Information

The occupational descriptions in this book come from the good people at the U.S. Department of Labor, as published in the most recent edition of the *Occupational Outlook Handbook*. The *OOH* is the best source of career information available, and the descriptions include the latest data on earnings, growth, education required, and many other details. So, thank you to all the people at the Labor Department who gather, compile, analyze, and make sense of this information. It's good stuff, and I hope you can make good use of it.

Mike Farr

Mike Farr

Relax—You Don't Have to Read This Whole Book!

*T*his is a big book, but you don't need to read it all. I've organized it into easy-to-use sections so you can browse just the information you want. To get started, simply scan the table of contents, where you'll find brief explanations of the major sections plus a list of the jobs described in this book. Really, this book is easy to use, and I hope it helps you.

Table of Contents

Summary of Major Sections

Introduction. The introduction explains what is included in each job description, gives tips on using the book for career exploration and job seeking, and provides other details. *The introduction begins on page 1.*

Section One: Descriptions of 101 Fastest Growing Jobs. This section presents thorough descriptions of 101 of the fastest growing jobs in the United States. Education and training requirements for these jobs vary from on-the-job training to a four-year college degree or more. Each description gives information on nature of the work, working conditions, employment, training, other qualifications, advancement, job outlook, earnings, related occupations, and sources of additional information. The jobs are presented in alphabetical order. The page numbers where specific descriptions begin are listed here in the table of contents. *Section One begins on page 33.*

Section Two: The Quick Job Search—Seven Steps to Getting a Good Job in Less Time. This brief but important section offers results-oriented career planning and job search techniques. It includes tips on identifying your key skills, defining your ideal job, using effective job search methods, writing resumes, organizing your time, improving your interviewing skills, and following up on leads. The second part of this section features professionally written and designed resumes for some of America's fastest growing jobs. *Section Two begins on page 319.*

Section Three: Important Trends in Jobs and Industries. This section includes two well-written articles and two charts on labor market trends. The articles and charts are short and worth your time. *Section Three begins on page 373.*

Titles of the articles in Section Three are "Tomorrow's Jobs" and "Employment Trends in Major Industries." Titles of the charts are "High-Paying Occupations with Many Openings, Projected 2002–12" and "Large Metropolitan Areas That Had the Fastest Employment Growth, 1998–2003."

★ ★ ★ ★ ★ ★ ★ ★
The 101 Jobs Described in Section One

The titles for the 101 jobs described in Section One are listed below, in alphabetical order. The page number where each description begins is also listed. Simply find jobs that interest you and then read those descriptions. An introduction to Section One begins on page 33 and provides additional information on how to interpret the descriptions.

v

Introduction

This book is about improving your life, not just about selecting a job. The career you choose will have an enormous impact on how you live your life.

A huge amount of information is available on occupations, but most people don't know where to find accurate, reliable facts to help them make good career decisions—or they don't take the time to look. Important choices such as what to do with your career or whether to get additional training or education deserve your time.

If you are considering more training or education—whether technical or job-related training, additional coursework, a college degree, or an advanced degree—this book will help with solid information. The education and training needed for the jobs described in this book vary enormously. You will notice that many of the better-paying jobs may require more training or education than you now have. Some require brief training or on-the-job experience. Many better-paying jobs, however, call for technical training lasting from a few months to a few years. Others require a four-year college degree or more. But some jobs, such as some sales and management jobs, have high pay but do not always require advanced education. This book is designed to give you facts to help you explore your options.

A certain type of work or workplace may interest you as much as a certain type of job. If your interests and values lead you to work in healthcare, for example, you can do so in a variety of work environments, in a variety of industries, and in a variety of jobs. For this reason, I suggest that you begin exploring alternatives by following your interests and finding a career path that allows you to use your talents doing something you enjoy.

Also, remember that money is not everything. The time you spend in career planning can pay off in higher earnings, but being satisfied with your work—and your life—is often more important than the amount you earn. This book can help you find the work that suits you best.

The Fastest Growing Jobs Lists

I think it's important for you to understand how I developed the list of fastest growing jobs used in this book. I started with the most recent projections available from the U.S. Department of Labor. I used data provided for 271 major jobs that cover about 90 percent of the workforce. The most recent data from the Department of Labor provides projections for growth of these jobs through 2012. I started by sorting all 271 of those jobs based on their percent of projected growth, from highest to lowest. I then sorted the 271 jobs based on the projected number of new job openings, also from highest to lowest. From these two lists I created a third list based on the relative position of each job on the first two lists. I did this by adding the score for each job's position on the lists of percentage growth and number of new openings. For example, a job with a high percentage of growth and a high number of new job openings would be listed towards the top of the third list. This third list provides the basis for the jobs I included in this book. The 101 jobs with the most favorable combined scores are presented in Table 1, which follows.

At the end of this introduction are several other lists you may find of interest:

Table 2: 271 Jobs Listed in Order of Percent Growth

Table 3: 271 Jobs Listed in Order of Number of Job Openings

Table 4: 271 Jobs Listed in Order of Combined Scores for Percent Growth and Number of Job Openings

Note: Two job titles, Clergy and Jobs in the Armed Forces, did not have projected growth data available and were therefore excluded from the lists used in this book. Finally, the data for the Engineer job title is presented in the more-specialized engineering-related job titles such as Environmental Engineers.

Table 1: The 101 Fastest Growing Jobs

These are the 101 jobs with the most favorable combined scores for projected percent increase and number of job openings through 2012. Each of these jobs is described in Section One of this book. As you can see, the list includes a wide variety of jobs at all levels of education, training, and interest.

Notice that three of the top 10 fastest growing jobs are computer related and four are in the medical area—two rapidly growing fields that are discussed in Section Three. Another thing to notice is that most of the fastest growing jobs require training or education beyond high school. While job opportunities at all levels of education and training are listed in this table, many better-paying jobs require post-secondary education or training. If you want more information on important labor market trends, consider reading the excellent and brief review of labor market trends in Section Three.

Note that you can find a complete description for each job listed below in Section One, in alphabetical order. You will also find these jobs in the table of contents along with the page number where each job description begins.

Table 1: The 101 Fastest Growing Jobs

	Percent Growth	Numerical Growth			Percent Growth	Numerical Growth
1. Teachers—Postsecondary	38	602,700		11. Receptionists and Information Clerks	29	324,600
2. Computer Systems Analysts, Database Administrators, and Computer Scientists	42	16,000		12. Dental Assistants	42	113,000
3. Computer Software Engineers	45	307,200		13. Management Analysts	30	175,700
4. Medical Assistants	59	214,800		14. Recreation and Fitness Workers	30	143,100
5. Social and Human Service Assistants	49	214,800		15. Customer Service Representatives	24	459,700
6. Nursing, Psychiatric, and Home Health Aides	31	630,400		16. Computer and Information Systems Managers	36	102,600
7. Personal and Home Health Care Aides	40	245,900		17. Teachers—Special Education	30	129,800
8. Security Guards and Gaming Surveillance Officers	32	319,300		18. Medical Records and Health Information Technicians	47	68,700
9. Registered Nurses	27	623,200		19. Advertising, Marketing, Promotions, Public Relations, and Sales Managers	26	185,300
10. Computer Support Specialists and Systems Administrators	33	247,300		20. Teachers—Adult Literacy and Remedial and Self-Enrichment Education	34	96,700

	Percent Growth	Numerical Growth		Percent Growth	Numerical Growth
21. Dental Hygienists	43	63,700	56. Retail Salespersons	15	595,900
22. Teacher Assistants	23	294,100	57. Building Cleaning Workers	15	587,700
23. Human Resources, Training, and Labor Relations Managers and Specialists	25	170,800	58. Veterinary Technologists and Technicians	44	23,200
24. Social Workers	27	127,100	59. Financial Managers	18	109,500
25. Heating, Air-Conditioning, and Refrigeration Mechanics and Installers	32	79,100	60. Firefighting Occupations	20	71,800
26. Counter and Rental Clerks	26	114,400	61. Administrative Services Managers	20	63,500
27. Grounds Maintenance Workers	22	282,500	62. Hotel, Motel, and Resort Desk Clerks	24	42,500
28. Police and Detectives	23	192,700	63. Market and Survey Researchers	25	38,300
29. Pharmacists	30	69,200	64. Maintenance and Repair Workers, General	16	206,800
30. Medical and Health Services Managers	29	71,300	65. Lawyers	17	117,900
31. Emergency Medical Technicians and Paramedics	33	59,300	66. Radiologic Technologists and Technicians	23	40,000
32. Physical Therapists	35	48,300	67. Pipelayers, Plumbers, Pipefitters, and Steamfitters	18	98,800
33. Public Relations Specialists	33	52,100	68. Psychologists	24	33,800
34. Physical Therapist Assistants and Aides	45	39,500	69. Environmental Engineers	38	18,000
35. Electricians	23	154,500	70. Clinical Laboratory Technologists and Technicians	19	57,600
36. Counselors	23	118,900	71. Gaming Services Occupations	21	40,400
37. Top Executives	18	469,300	72. Speech-Language Pathologists	27	25,600
38. Sales Representatives, Wholesale and Manufacturing	19	356,300	73. Hazardous Materials Removal Workers	43	16,200
39. Pharmacy Technicians	29	60,700	74. Cashiers	13	462,100
40. Education Administrators	24	100,800	75. Designers	17	92,700
41. Paralegals and Legal Assistants	29	57,300	76. Loan Counselors and Officers	19	47,600
42. Financial Analysts and Personal Financial Advisors	25	75,800	77. Sheet Metal Workers	20	40,600
43. Accountants and Auditors	19	205,500	78. Drywall Installers, Ceiling Tile Installers, and Tapers	21	37,500
44. Food and Beverage Serving and Related Workers	17	1,133,000	79. Instructional Coordinators	25	25,000
45. Information and Record Clerks	18	913,900	80. Surgical Technologists	28	20,200
46. Teachers—Preschool, Kindergarten, Elementary, Middle, and Secondary	18	665,600	81. Bus Drivers	16	106,300
47. Truck Drivers and Driver/Sales Workers	18	592,200	82. Chefs, Cooks, and Food Preparation Workers	12	366,700
48. Bill and Account Collectors	24	101,000	83. Barbers, Cosmetologists, and Other Personal Appearance Workers	15	111,100
49. Correctional Officers	23	111,100	84. Animal Care and Service Workers	21	31,500
50. Licensed Practical and Licensed Vocational Nurses	20	141,800	85. Cardiovascular Technologists and Technicians	34	14,600
51. Respiratory Therapists	35	38,900	86. Construction Laborers	14	132,700
52. Physician Assistants	49	30,800	87. Cost Estimators	19	35,000
53. Cement Masons, Concrete Finishers, Segmental Pavers, and Terrazzo Workers	26	48,700	88. Taxi Drivers and Chauffeurs	22	28,700
54. Physicians and Surgeons	19	113,500	89. Occupational Therapist Assistants and Aides	40	10,800
55. Occupational Therapists	35	28,700	90. Computer Programmers	15	72,700
			91. Medical Scientists	27	16,800
			92. Library Assistants, Clerical	21	25,900

(continued)

(continued)

Table 1: The 101 Fastest Growing Jobs

	Percent Growth	Numerical Growth		Percent Growth	Numerical Growth
93. Medical Transcriptionists	23	22,800	98. Roofers	19	30,900
94. Office Clerks, General	10	309,600	99. Material Moving Occupations	9	442,600
95. Writers and Editors	16	51,100	100. Welding, Soldering, and Brazing Workers	15	66,700
96. Human Resources Assistants, except Payroll and Timekeeping	19	33,500	101. Athletes, Coaches, Umpires, and Related Workers	18	29,000
97. Childcare Workers	12	141,600			

Some Advice on Using the Tables of Fastest Growing Jobs

Major changes are occurring in our labor market, and they are projected to continue. Section Three describes these changes, and it seems obvious that rapidly growing jobs will often be more attractive career options than jobs that are not growing quickly. Rapidly growing jobs often offer better-than-average opportunities for employment and job security. For this reason, you should certainly pay attention to jobs that are projected to grow rapidly.

But there will always be some openings for new people, even in slower growing or declining jobs. Some slower growing jobs employ large numbers of people and will create many openings due to retirement, people leaving the field, and other reasons. Considering jobs that are generating large numbers of openings but that may not have high percentage growth rates will give you more options to consider.

The best job for you might not be in Table 1 at all because it may not be growing quickly or have large numbers of openings. So look at all jobs that interest you, even if they are not among the fastest growing ones. You can review information on all 271 major jobs provided in Tables 2, 3, and 4 that are included at the end of this introduction.

The more you know about your options, the better your decisions will be. Information on all major occupational and industry groups is provided in Section Three, including those that are growing more slowly than average or even declining.

Keep in Mind That Your Situation Is Probably Not "Average"

Although the employment growth and earnings trends for many occupations and industries are quite positive, the averages in this book will not be true for many individuals. Within any field, for example, some earn much more and some much less. And jobs will be available for good people even in occupations that are projected to decline.

My point here is that your situation is probably not average. Some people do better work than others, and others are willing to accept less pay for a more desirable work environment. Earnings and job opportunities vary enormously in different parts of the country, in different occupations, and in different industries. But this book's solid information is a great place to start. Good information will give you a strong foundation for good decisions.

Four Important Labor Market Trends That Will Affect Your Career

Our economy has changed over the past 10 years, with profound effects on how we work and live. Section Three of this book provides more information on labor market trends, but in case you don't read it, here are four trends that you simply *must* consider in making your career plans.

I. Education Pays

I'm sure you won't be surprised to learn that people with higher levels of education and training have higher average earnings. The data that follows comes from the U.S. Department of Labor and the U.S. Census Bureau. I've selected data to show you the median earnings for people with various levels of education. (The median is the point where half earn more and half earn less.) Based on this information, I computed the earnings advantage of people at various education levels over those who did not graduate from high school. I've also included information showing the average percentage of people at that educational level who are unemployed.

Earnings for Year-Round, Full-Time Workers Age 25 and Over, by Educational Attainment			
Level of Education	Median Annual Earnings	Premium Over High School Dropouts	Unemployment Rate
Master's degree	56,600	34,200	2.8
Bachelor's degree	47,000	24,600	3.1
Associate degree	36,400	14,000	4.0
Some college, no degree	34,300	11,900	4.8
High school graduate	29,200	6,800	5.3
High school dropout	22,400		9.2

Source: Unemployment rate, BLS; annual avg., BLS; earnings, Census

As you can see in the table, the earnings difference between a college graduate and someone with a high school education is $17,800 a year—enough to buy a nice car, make a down payment on a house, or even take a few months' vacation for two to Europe. As you see, over a lifetime, this earnings difference will make an enormous difference in lifestyle.

The table makes it very clear that those with more training and education earn more than those with less and experience lower levels of unemployment. Jobs that require education and training beyond high school are projected to grow significantly faster than jobs that do not. People with higher levels of education and training are less likely to be unemployed and, when they are, they tend to remain unemployed for shorter periods of time. There are always exceptions, but it is quite clear that a college education results in higher earnings and lower rates of unemployment.

2. Knowledge of Computer and Other Technologies Is Increasingly Important

As you look over the list of jobs in the table of contents, you may notice that many require computer or technical skills. Even jobs that do not appear to be technical often call for computer literacy. Managers, for example, are often expected to understand and use spreadsheet, word-processing, and database software.

In most fields, those without job-related technical and computer skills will have a more difficult time finding good opportunities since they are often competing with those who have these skills. Older workers, by the way, often do not have the computer skills that younger workers do. Employers tend to hire people with the skills they need, and people without these abilities won't get the best jobs. So, whatever your age, consider upgrading your job-related computer and technology skills if you need to—and plan to stay up-to-date on your current and future jobs.

3. Ongoing Education and Training Are Essential

School and work once were separate activities, and most people did not go back to school after they began working. But with rapid changes in technology, most people are now required to learn throughout their work lives. Jobs are constantly upgraded, and today's jobs often cannot be handled by people who have only the knowledge and skills that were adequate for workers a few years ago.

To remain competitive, you will need to constantly upgrade your technology and other job-related skills. This may include taking formal courses, reading work-related magazines at home, signing up for on-the-job training, or participating in other forms of education. Upgrading your work-related skills on an ongoing basis is no longer optional for most jobs, and you ignore doing so at your peril.

4. Good Career Planning Is More Important Than Ever

Most people spend more time watching TV in a week than they spend on career planning during an entire year. Yet most people will change their jobs many times and make major career changes five to seven times. For this reason, it is important for you to spend time considering your career options and preparing to advance.

While you probably picked up this book for its information on jobs, it also provides a great deal of information on career planning. For example, Section Two gives good career and job search advice, and Section Three has useful information on labor market trends. I urge you to read these and related materials because career-planning and job-seeking skills are the keys to surviving in this new economy.

Tips on Using This Book

This book is based on information from a variety of government sources and includes the most up-to-date and accurate data available. The job descriptions are well written and pack a lot of information into short descriptions. *America's 101 Fastest Growing Jobs* can be used in many ways, and I've provided tips for four major uses:

- For people exploring career, education, or training alternatives
- For job seekers
- For employers and business people
- For counselors, instructors, and other career specialists

Tips for People Exploring Career, Education, or Training Alternatives

America's 101 Fastest Growing Jobs is an excellent resource for anyone exploring career, education, or training alternatives. Many people do not have a good idea of what they want to do in their careers. They may be considering additional training or education but may not know what sort they should get. If you are one of these people, this book can help in several ways. Here are a few pointers.

Review the list of jobs. Trust yourself. Research studies indicate that most people have a good sense of their interests. Your interests can be used to guide you to career options you should consider in more detail.

Begin by looking over the occupations listed in the table of contents. Look at all the jobs, because you may identify previously overlooked possibilities. If other people will be using this book, please don't mark in it. Instead, on a separate sheet of paper, list the jobs that interest you. Or make a photocopy of the table of contents and use it to mark the jobs that interest you.

Next, look up and carefully read the descriptions of the jobs that most interest you in Section One. A quick review will often eliminate one or more of these jobs based on pay, working conditions, education required, or other considerations. After you have identified the three or four jobs that seem most interesting, research each one more thoroughly before making any important decisions.

Study the jobs and their training and education requirements. Too many people decide to obtain additional training or education without knowing much about the jobs the training will lead to. Reviewing the descriptions in this book is one way to learn more about an occupation before you enroll in an education or training program. If you are currently a student, the job descriptions in this book can also help you decide on a major course of study or learn more about the jobs for which your studies are preparing you.

Do not be too quick to eliminate a job that interests you. If a job requires more education or training than you currently have, you can obtain this training in many ways.

Don't abandon your past experience and education too quickly. If you have significant work experience, training, or education, these should not be abandoned without some thought. Many times, after people carefully consider what they want to do, they change careers and find that the skills they have can still be used.

America's 101 Fastest Growing Jobs can help you explore career options in several ways. First, carefully review descriptions for jobs you have held in the past. On a separate sheet of paper, list the skills needed in those jobs. Then do the same for jobs that interest you now. By comparing the lists, you will be able to identify skills you used in previous jobs that you could also use in jobs that interest you for the future. These "transferable" skills form the basis for moving to a new career.

You can also identify skills you have developed or used in nonwork activities, such as hobbies, family responsibilities, volunteer work, school, military, and extracurricular interests. If you want to stay with your current employer, the job descriptions can also help. For example, you may identify jobs within your organization that offer more rewarding work, higher pay, or other advantages over your present job. Read the descriptions related to these jobs, as you may be able to transfer into another job rather than leave the organization.

Tips for Job Seekers

You can use the job descriptions in this book to give you an edge in finding job openings and in getting job offers—even when you are competing with people who have better credentials. Here are some ways *America's 101 Fastest Growing Jobs* can help you in the job search.

Identify related job targets. You may be limiting your job search to a small number of jobs for which you feel qualified, but by doing so you eliminate many jobs you could do and enjoy. Your search for a new job should be broadened to include more possibilities.

Go through the entire list of jobs in the table of contents and check any that require skills similar to those you have. Look at all the jobs, since doing so sometimes helps you identify targets you would otherwise overlook.

Many people are not aware of the many specialized jobs related to their training or experience. The descriptions in *America's 101 Fastest Growing Jobs* are for major job titles, but a variety of more-specialized jobs may require similar skills. The "Other Major Career Reference Sources" section later in this introduction lists sources you can use to find out about more-specialized jobs.

The descriptions can also point out jobs that interest you but that have higher responsibility or compensation levels. While you may not consider yourself qualified for such jobs now, you should think about seeking jobs that are above your previous levels but within your ability to handle.

Prepare for interviews. This book's job descriptions are an essential source of information to help you prepare for interviews. If you carefully review the description of a job before an interview, you will be much better prepared to emphasize your key skills. You should also review descriptions for past jobs and identify skills needed in the new job.

Negotiate pay. The job descriptions in this book will help you know what pay range to expect. Note that local pay and other details can differ substantially from the national averages in the descriptions.

Tips for Employers and Business People

Employers, human resource professionals, and other business users can use this book's information to write job descriptions, study pay ranges, and set criteria for new employees. The information can also help you conduct more-effective interviews by providing a list of key skills needed by new hires.

Tips for Counselors, Instructors, and Other Career Specialists

Counselors, instructors, and other career specialists will find this book helpful for their clients or students exploring career options or job targets. My best suggestion to professionals is to get this book off the shelf and into the hands of the people who need it. Leave it on a table or desk and show people how the information can help them. Wear this book out—its real value is as a tool used often and well.

Additional Information About the Projections

For more information about employment change, job openings, earnings, unemployment rates, and training requirements by occupation, consult *Occupational Projections and Training Data*, published by the Bureau of Labor Statistics. For occupational information from an industry perspective, including some occupations and career paths that *America's 101 Fastest Growing Jobs* does not cover, consult another BLS publication, *Career Guide to Industries*. This book is also available from JIST under the title *Career Guide to America's Top Industries*.

Other Major Career Information Sources

The information in this book will be very useful, but you may want or need additional information. Keep in mind that the job descriptions here cover major jobs and not the many more-specialized jobs that are often related to them. Each job description in this book provides some sources of information related to that job, but here are additional resources to consider.

The *Occupational Outlook Handbook* (or the *OOH*): Updated every two years by the U.S. Department of Labor, this book provides descriptions for more than 270 major jobs covering more than 85 percent of the workforce. The *OOH* is the source of the job descriptions used in this book, and the book *America's Top 300 Jobs* includes all the *OOH* content plus additional information.

The *Enhanced Occupational Outlook Handbook:* Includes all descriptions in the *OOH* plus descriptions of nearly 8,000 more-specialized jobs that are related to them.

The *O*NET Dictionary of Occupational Titles:* The only printed source of the more than 1,100 jobs described in the U.S. Department of Labor's Occupational Information Network database (O*NET).

Guide for Occupational Exploration: An important career reference that allows you to explore all major O*NET jobs based on your interests.

www.careerOINK.com: This Web site provides more than 14,000 job descriptions, including those mentioned in the previous books, and a variety of useful ways to explore them.

Best Jobs for the 21st Century: Includes descriptions for the 500 jobs (out of more than 1,100) with the best combination of earnings, growth, and number of openings. Useful lists make jobs easy to explore (examples: highest-paying jobs by level of education or training, best jobs overall, and best jobs for different ages, personality types, interests, and many more). Two other books in this series titled *200 Best Jobs for College Graduates* and *300 Best Jobs Without a Four-Year Degree* provide similar information on jobs based on education required.

Exploring Careers—A Young Person's Guide to 1,000 Jobs: For youth exploring career and education opportunities, this book covers 1,000 job options in an interesting and useful format.

Information on the Major Sections of This Book

This book was designed to be easy to use. The table of contents provides brief comments on each section, and that may be all you need. If not, here are some additional details you may find useful in getting the most out of this book.

Section One: Descriptions of 101 Fastest Growing Jobs

Section One is the main part of the book and probably the reason you picked it up. It contains brief, well-written descriptions for 101 of the fastest growing jobs. A list of the jobs is provided in the table of contents as well as in Table 1 in this introduction. The content for each of these job descriptions comes from the U.S. Department of Labor and is considered by many to be the most accurate and up-to-date available. The jobs are presented in alphabetical order.

Together, the jobs in Section One provide an enormous variety at all levels of earnings and interest. One way to explore career options is to go to the table of contents and identify those jobs that seem interesting. If you are interested in medical jobs, for example, you can quickly spot those you will want to learn more about. You may also see other jobs that look interesting, and you should consider these as well.

Your next step would be to read the descriptions for the jobs that interest you and, based on what you learn, identify those that *most* interest you. These are the jobs you should consider, and Sections Two and Three will give you additional information on how you might best do so.

Details on Each Section of the Job Descriptions

Each occupational description in this book follows a standard format, making it easier for you to compare jobs. The following overview describes the kinds of information found in each part of a description and offers tips on how to interpret the information.

Job Title

This is the title used for the job in the *Occupational Outlook Handbook,* published by the U.S. Department of Labor.

O*NET Codes

This section of each job description lists one or more code numbers (for example: 11-9031.00, 11-9032.00) for related jobs in a major occupational information system used by the U.S. Department of Labor. This system, named the Occupational Information Network (or O*NET), is used by a variety of state and federal programs to classify applicants and job openings and by a variety of career information systems. You can use the O*NET code numbers to get additional information on the related O*NET titles on the Internet at www.onetcenter.org or at www.careerOINK.com. Reference books that provide O*NET descriptions include the O*NET Dictionary of Occupational Titles and the Enhanced Occupational Outlook Handbook, both published by JIST Publishing. Your librarian can help you find these books.

Significant Points

The bullet points in this part of a description highlight key characteristics for each job, such as recent trends or education and training requirements.

Nature of the Work

This part of the description discusses what workers typically do in a particular job. Individual job duties may vary by industry or employer. For instance, workers in larger firms tend to be more specialized, whereas those in smaller firms often have a wider variety of duties. Most occupations have several levels of skills and responsibilities through which workers may progress. Beginners may start as trainees performing routine tasks under close supervision. Experienced workers usually undertake more difficult tasks and are expected to perform with less supervision.

In this part of a description, you will also find information about the influence of technological advancements on the way work is done. For example, the Internet enables writers to submit stories from remote locations with just a click of the mouse.

This part also discusses emerging specialties. For instance, Webmasters—who are responsible for all the technical aspects involved in operating a Web site—comprise a specialty within computer systems analysts, database administrators, and computer scientists.

Working Conditions

This part of the description identifies the typical hours worked, the workplace environment, physical activities, risk of injury, special equipment, and the extent of travel required. For example, welding, soldering, and brazing workers are susceptible to injury, while paralegals and legal assistants have high job-related stress. Radiologic technologists and technicians may wear protective clothing or equipment, grounds maintenance workers do physically demanding work, and some top executives travel frequently.

In many occupations, people work regular business hours—40 hours a week, Monday through Friday. In other occupations, they do not. For example, licensed practical and licensed vocational nurses often work evenings and weekends. The work setting can range from a hospital to a mall to an off-shore oil rig.

Information on various worker characteristics, such as the average number of hours worked per week, is obtained from the Current Population Survey (CPS), a survey of households conducted by the U.S. Census Bureau for the Bureau of Labor Statistics (BLS).

Employment

This section reports the number of jobs the occupation recently provided, the key industries where these jobs are found, and the number or proportion of self-employed workers in the occupation, if significant. Self-employed workers accounted for about 8 percent of the workforce in 2002; however, they were concentrated in a small number of occupations, such as farmers and ranchers, childcare workers, lawyers, health practitioners, and the construction trades.

When significant, the geographic distribution of jobs and the proportion of part-time (less than 35 hours a week) workers in the occupation are mentioned.

Training, Other Qualifications, and Advancement

After finding out what a job is all about, it is important to understand how to train for it. This section describes the most significant sources of education and training, including the education or training preferred by employers, the typical length of training, and the possibilities for advancement. Job skills sometimes are acquired through high school, informal on-the-job training, formal training (including apprenticeships), the U.S. Armed Forces, home study, hobbies, or previous work experience. For example, sales experience is particularly important for many sales jobs. Many professional and technical jobs, on the other hand, require formal postsecondary education—postsecondary vocational or technical training or college, postgraduate, or professional education.

This section also mentions desirable skills, aptitudes, and personal characteristics. For some entry-level jobs, personal characteristics are more important than formal training. Employers generally seek people who read, write, and speak well; compute accurately; think logically; learn quickly; get along with others; and demonstrate dependability.

Some occupations require certification or licensing to enter the field, to advance in the occupation, or to practice independently. Certification or licensing generally involves completing courses and passing examinations. Many occupations increasingly are requiring workers to participate in continuing education or training in relevant skills, either to keep up with the changes in their jobs or to improve their advancement opportunities.

Job Outlook

In planning for the future, it is important to consider potential job opportunities. This section describes the factors that will result in employment growth or decline. A number of factors are examined in developing employment projections. One factor is job growth or decline in industries that employ a significant percentage of workers in the occupation. If workers are concentrated in a rapidly growing industry, their employment will likely also grow quickly. For example, the growing need for business expertise is fueling demand for consulting services. Hence, management, scientific, and technical consulting services are projected to be among the fastest growing industries through 2012.

Demographic changes, which affect what services are required, can influence occupational growth or decline. For example, an aging population demands more healthcare workers, from registered nurses to pharmacists. Technological change is another key factor. New technology can either create new job opportunities or eliminate jobs by making workers obsolete. The Internet has increased the demand for workers in the computer and information technology fields, such as computer support specialists and systems administrators. However, the Internet also has adversely affected travel agents, because many people now book tickets, hotels, and rental cars online.

Another factor affecting job growth or decline is changes in business practices, such as the outsourcing of work or the restructuring of businesses. In the past few years, insurance carriers have been outsourcing sales and claims adjuster jobs to large, 24-hour call centers in order to reduce costs. Corporate restructuring also has made many organizations "flatter," resulting in fewer middle management positions.

The substitution of one product or service for another can affect employment projections. For example, consumption of plastic products has grown as they have been substituted for metal goods in many consumer and manufactured products in recent years. The process is likely to continue and should result in stronger demand for machine operators in plastics than in metal.

Competition from foreign trade usually has a negative impact on employment. Often, foreign manufacturers can produce goods more cheaply than they can be produced in the United States, and the cost savings can be passed on in the form of lower prices with which U.S. manufacturers cannot compete. Increased international competition is a major reason for the decline in employment among textile, apparel, and furnishings workers.

In some cases, this book mentions that an occupation is likely to provide numerous job openings or, in others, that an occupation likely will afford relatively few openings. This information reflects the projected change in employment, as well as replacement needs. Large occupations that have high turnover, such as food and beverage serving occupations, generally provide the most job openings, reflecting the need to replace workers who transfer to other occupations or who stop working.

Some job descriptions discuss the relationship between the number of job seekers and the number of job openings. In some occupations, there is a rough balance between job seekers and job openings, resulting in good opportunities. In other occupations, employers may report difficulty finding qualified applicants, resulting in excellent job opportunities. Still other occupations are characterized by a surplus of applicants, leading to keen competition for jobs. On the one hand, limited training facilities, salary regulations, or undesirable aspects of the work—as in the case of private household workers—can result in an insufficient number of entrants to fill all job openings. On the other hand, glamorous or potentially high-paying occupations, such as actors or musicians, generally have surpluses of job seekers. Variation in job opportunities by industry, educational attainment, size of firm, or geographic location also may be discussed. Even in crowded fields, job openings do exist. Good students or highly qualified individuals should not be deterred from undertaking training for, or seeking entry into, those occupations.

Key Phrases Used in the Descriptions	
This table explains how to interpret the key phrases that describe projected changes in employment. It also explains the terms for the relationship between the number of job openings and the number of job seekers.	
Changing Employment Between 2002 and 2012	
If the statement reads:	Employment is projected to:
Grow much faster than average	Increase 36 percent or more
Grow faster than average	Increase 21 to 35 percent
Grow about as fast as average	Increase 10 to 20 percent
Grow more slowly than average	Increase 3 to 9 percent
Little or no change	Increase 0 to 2 percent
Decline	Decrease 1 percent or more
Job Openings Compared	
If the statement reads:	Job openings compared to job seekers may be:
Very good to excellent opportunities	More numerous
Good or favorable opportunities	In rough balance
May face or can expect keen competition	Fewer

Earnings

This section discusses typical earnings and how workers are compensated—by means of annual salaries, hourly wages, commissions, piece rates, tips, or bonuses. Within every occupation, earnings vary by experience, responsibility, performance, tenure, and geographic area. Information on earnings in the major industries in which the occupation is employed may be given. Some statements contain additional earnings data from non-BLS sources. Starting and average salaries of federal workers are based on 2003 data from the U.S. Office of Personnel Management. The National Association of Colleges and Employers supplies information on average salary offers in 2003 for students graduating with a bachelor's, master's, or Ph.D. degree in certain fields. A few statements contain additional earnings information from other sources, such as unions, professional associations, and private companies. These data sources are cited in the text.

Benefits account for a significant portion of total compensation costs to employers. Benefits such as paid vacation, health insurance, and sick leave may not be mentioned because they are so widespread. Although not as common as traditional benefits, flexible hours and profit-sharing plans may be offered to attract and retain highly qualified workers. Less common benefits also include childcare, tuition for dependents, housing assistance, summers off, and free or discounted merchandise or services. For certain occupations, the percentage of workers affiliated with a union is listed.

Related Occupations

Occupations involving similar duties, skills, interests, education, and training are listed here. This allows you to look up these jobs if they also interest you.

Sources of Additional Information

No single publication can describe all aspects of an occupation. Thus, this section lists the mailing addresses of associations, government agencies, unions, and other organizations that can provide occupational information. In some cases, toll-free telephone numbers and Internet addresses also are listed. Free or relatively inexpensive publications offering more information may be mentioned; some of these publications also may be available in libraries, in school career centers, in guidance offices, or on the Internet.

Some Additional Jobs to Consider

The tables at the end of this introduction provide projected growth information on 271 jobs. If a job that interests you is on these lists but its description is not included in Section One of this book, you can find its description in a variety of career information sources, such as those listed in the "Other Major Career Reference Sources" section earlier in this introduction.

Section Two: *The Quick Job Search*—Seven Steps to Getting a Good Job in Less Time

For more than 20 years now, I've been helping people find better jobs in less time. If you have ever experienced unemployment, you know that it is not pleasant. Unemployment is something most people want to get over quickly—in fact, the quicker the better. Section Two will give you some techniques to help.

I know that most of you who read this book want to improve yourselves. You want to consider career and training options that lead to a better job and life in whatever way you define this—better pay, more flexibility, more-enjoyable or more meaningful work, proving to your mom that you really can do anything you set your mind to, and other reasons. That is why I include advice on career planning and job search in Section Two. It's a short section, but it includes the basics that are most important in planning your career and in reducing the time it takes to get a job. I hope it will make you think about what is important to you in the long run.

The second part of Section Two showcases professionally written resumes for some of America's fastest growing jobs. Use these as examples when creating your own resume. I know you will resist completing the activities in Section Two, but consider this: It is often not the best person who gets the job, but the best job seeker. People who do their career planning and job search homework often get jobs over those with better credentials because they have these distinct advantages:

1. **They get more interviews,** including many for jobs that will never be advertised.

2. **They do better in interviews.**

People who understand what they want and what they have to offer employers present their skills more convincingly and are much better at answering problem questions. And, because they have learned more about job search techniques, they are likely to get more interviews with employers who need the skills they have.

Doing better in interviews often makes the difference between getting a job offer and sitting at home. And spending time planning your career can make an enormous difference to your happiness and lifestyle over time. So please consider reading Section Two and completing its activities. I suggest you schedule a time right now to at least read Section Two. An hour or so spent there can help you do just enough better in your career planning, job seeking, and interviewing to make the difference.

One other thing: If you work through Section Two and it helps you in some significant way, I'd like to hear from you. Please write or e-mail me via the publisher, whose contact information appears elsewhere in this book.

Section Three: Important Trends in Jobs and Industries

This section is made up of four very good articles and charts on labor market trends. These articles come directly from U.S. Department of Labor sources and are interesting, well written, and short. One article is on overall trends, with an emphasis on occupational groups; another is on trends in major industry groups; and the two charts present high-paying occupations with many openings and large metropolitan areas with the fastest employment growth. I know they sound boring, but the articles and charts are quick reads and will give you a good idea of factors that will impact your career in the years to come.

The first article is titled "Tomorrow's Jobs." It highlights many important trends in employment and includes information on the fastest-growing jobs, jobs with high pay at various levels of education, and other details.

The second article is titled "Employment Trends in Major Industries." I included this information because you may find that you can use your skills or training in industries you have not considered. The article provides a good review of major trends with an emphasis on helping you make good employment decisions. This information can help you seek jobs in industries that offer higher pay or that are more likely to interest you. Many people overlook one important fact—the industry you work in is as important as the occupation you choose.

The first chart is called "High-Paying Occupations with Many Openings, Projected 2002–12." It shows median earnings for high-paying occupations that also have a large number of openings, many of which are listed in this book.

The second chart, "Large Metropolitan Areas That Had the Fastest Employment Growth, 1998–2003," lists eleven areas of the United States that experienced fast growth during a period when many areas experienced little employment growth or lost jobs.

Overall Lists of Jobs Ranked by Growth and Openings

I used these lists to determine the jobs included in this book.

Table 2: 271 Jobs Listed in Order of Percent Growth

This table presents all 271 major jobs arranged in order of percent growth projected through 2012. It also includes data on the number of projected new job openings through 2012 as well as the total number of people currently employed in each job. Most of the jobs with high growth rates are included in Section One of this book.

As you look at this information, keep in mind that there are other factors to consider in addition to growth projections. Many jobs with lower growth rates will have lots of job openings, particularly those that employ large numbers of people. And, even for jobs with lower or even declining growth rates or small numbers of openings, there are always some opportunities for people who want and are well prepared for these jobs. For example, in occupations with low or even negative growth rates, some jobs will become available as a result of people taking other jobs, retiring, and leaving for other reasons.

Table 2: 271 Jobs Listed in Order of Percent Growth

	Percent Growth	Numerical Growth	Current Employment
1. Medical Assistants	59	214,800	364,600
2. Social and Human Service Assistants	49	148,700	305,200
3. Physician Assistants	49	30,800	63,000
4. Medical Records and Health Information Technicians	47	68,700	146,900
5. Computer Software Engineers	45	307,200	675,200
6. Physical Therapist Assistants and Aides	45	39,500	87,200
7. Veterinary Technologists and Technicians	44	23,200	52,700
8. Dental Hygienists	43	63,700	148,000
9. Hazardous Materials Removal Workers	43	16,200	37,600
10. Computer Systems Analysts, Database Administrators, and Computer Scientists	42	416,000	979,200
11. Dental Assistants	42	113,000	266,000
12. Occupational Therapist Assistants and Aides	40	10,800	26,800
13. Personal and Home Health Care Aides	40	245,900	607,600
14. Environmental Engineers	38	18,000	47,100
15. Teachers—Postsecondary	38	602,700	1,581,200
16. Computer and Information Systems Managers	36	102,600	284,400
17. Occupational Therapists	35	28,700	81,600
18. Physical Therapists	35	48,300	136,900
19. Respiratory Therapists	35	38,900	112,200
20. Teachers—Adult Literacy and Remedial and Self-Enrichment Education	34	96,700	280,400
21. Cardiovascular Technologists and Technicians	34	14,600	43,400
22. Computer Support Specialists and Systems Administrators	33	247,300	758,300
23. Public Relations Specialists	33	52,100	158,100
24. Emergency Medical Technicians and Paramedics	33	59,300	179,100
25. Security Guards and Gaming Surveillance Officers	32	319,300	1,004,400
26. Heating, Air-Conditioning, and Refrigeration Mechanics and Installers	32	79,100	248,700
27. Nursing, Psychiatric, and Home Health Aides	31	630,400	2,014,300
28. Management Analysts	30	175,700	577,400
29. Teachers—Special Education	30	129,800	432,900
30. Pharmacists	30	69,200	230,200
31. Recreation and Fitness Workers	30	143,100	484,800
32. Medical and Health Services Managers	29	71,300	243,600
33. Paralegals and Legal Assistants	29	57,300	199,600
34. Audiologists	29	3,200	10,900
35. Pharmacy Technicians	29	60,700	210,800
36. Desktop Publishers	29	10,200	35,000
37. Receptionists and Information Clerks	29	324,600	1,100,300
38. Surgical Technologists	28	20,200	72,200
39. Medical Scientists	27	16,800	61,700
40. Social Workers	27	127,100	476,600
41. Registered Nurses	27	623,200	2,284,500
42. Speech-Language Pathologists	27	25,600	94,300

	Percent Growth	Numerical Growth	Current Employment
43. Advertising, Marketing, Promotions, Public Relations, and Sales Managers	26	185,300	700,100
44. Biomedical Engineers	26	2,000	7,600
45. Counter and Rental Clerks	26	114,400	435,800
46. Cement Masons, Concrete Finishers, Segmental Pavers, and Terrazzo Workers	26	48,700	190,200
47. Human Resources, Training, and Labor Relations Managers and Specialists	25	170,800	676,700
48. Financial Analysts and Personal Financial Advisors	25	75,800	298,300
49. Market and Survey Researchers	25	38,300	154,700
50. Instructional Coordinators	25	25,000	98,500
51. Veterinarians	25	14,400	57,500
52. Private Detectives and Investigators	25	12,200	48,000
53. Education Administrators	24	100,800	426,600
54. Psychologists	24	33,800	139,100
55. Diagnostic Medical Sonographers	24	8,800	36,500
56. Nuclear Medicine Technologists	24	4,100	17,100
57. Customer Service Representatives	24	459,700	1,894,100
58. Bill and Account Collectors	24	101,000	413,000
59. Hotel, Motel, and Resort Desk Clerks	24	42,500	177,700
60. Counselors	23	118,900	525,900
61. Teacher Assistants	23	294,100	1,276,700
62. Chiropractors	23	11,400	48,900
63. Radiologic Technologists and Technicians	23	40,000	174,100
64. Medical Transcriptionists	23	22,800	100,800
65. Correctional Officers	23	111,100	475,600
66. Police and Detectives	23	192,700	840,100
67. Electricians	23	154,500	659,400
68. Landscape Architects	22	5,100	23,100
69. Interpreters and Translators	22	5,300	24,100
70. Grounds Maintenance Workers	22	282,500	1,310,000
71. Taxi Drivers and Chauffeurs	22	28,700	132,200
72. Animal Care and Service Workers	21	31,500	151,300
73. Gaming Services Occupations	21	40,400	192,000
74. Library Assistants, Clerical	21	25,900	120,400
75. Drywall Installers, Ceiling Tile Installers, and Tapers	21	37,500	176,100
76. Administrative Services Managers	20	63,500	320,500
77. Environmental Scientists and Geoscientists	20	20,300	100,700
78. Broadcast and Sound Engineering Technicians and Radio Operators	20	18,200	93,000
79. Licensed Practical and Licensed Vocational Nurses	20	141,800	701,900
80. Firefighting Occupations	20	71,800	358,900
81. Sales Engineers	20	16,300	81,700
82. Sheet Metal Workers	20	40,600	205,000
83. Accountants and Auditors	19	205,500	1,055,200
84. Cost Estimators	19	35,000	188,000
85. Loan Counselors and Officers	19	47,600	254,600
86. Biological Scientists	19	14,300	75,400

(continued)

(continued)

Table 2: 271 Jobs Listed in Order of Percent Growth

	Percent Growth	Numerical Growth	Current Employment
87. Television, Video, and Motion Picture Camera Operators and Editors	19	8,900	47,500
88. Physicians and Surgeons	19	113,500	583,300
89. Clinical Laboratory Technologists and Technicians	19	57,600	297,400
90. Sales Representatives, Wholesale and Manufacturing	19	356,300	1,857,100
91. Human Resources Assistants, Except Payroll and Timekeeping	19	33,500	173,800
92. Roofers	19	30,900	166,200
93. Small Engine Mechanics	19	12,500	66,900
94. Financial Managers	18	109,500	599,100
95. Top Executives	18	469,300	2,668,600
96. Teachers—Preschool, Kindergarten, Elementary, Middle, and Secondary	18	665,600	3,754,400
97. Actors, Producers, and Directors	18	25,100	139,200
98. Athletes, Coaches, Umpires, and Related Workers	18	29,000	158,400
99. Dietitians and Nutritionists	18	8,700	48,900
100. Opticians, Dispensing	18	11,500	63,200
101. Pharmacy Aides	18	10,600	60,300
102. Information and Record Clerks	18	913,900	5,090,000
103. Pipelayers, Plumbers, Pipefitters, and Steamfitters	18	98,800	550,100
104. Aircraft Pilots and Flight Engineers	18	17,800	100,200
105. Truck Drivers and Driver/Sales Workers	18	592,200	3,220,800
106. Architects, Except Landscape and Naval	17	19,500	113,200
107. Lawyers	17	117,900	695,200
108. Archivists, Curators, and Museum Technicians	17	3,800	22,300
109. Library Technicians	17	20,000	119,300
110. Designers	17	92,700	531,900
111. Optometrists	17	5,500	32,100
112. Food and Beverage Serving and Related Workers	17	1,133,000	6,539,000
113. Pest Control Workers	17	10,400	61,600
114. Demonstrators, Product Promoters, and Models	17	30,300	179,200
115. Carpet, Floor, and Tile Installers and Finishers	17	27,400	163,700
116. Elevator Installers and Repairers	17	3,600	21,000
117. Glaziers	17	8,300	48,500
118. Atmospheric Scientists	16	1,200	7,700
119. Musicians, Singers, and Related Workers	16	34,800	215,400
120. Writers and Editors	16	51,100	318,600
121. Flight Attendants	16	16,600	104,000
122. Insulation Workers	16	8,500	53,500
123. Structural and Reinforcing Iron and Metal Workers	16	17,200	106,700
124. Maintenance and Repair Workers, General	16	206,800	1,265,600
125. Water and Liquid Waste Treatment Plant and System Operators	16	15,900	99,300
126. Bus Drivers	16	106,300	654,400
127. Actuaries	15	2,300	15,300
128. Computer Programmers	15	72,700	498,600

	Percent Growth	Numerical Growth	Current Employment
129. Probation Officers and Correctional Treatment Specialists	15	12,400	84,300
130. Podiatrists	15	2,000	13,300
131. Building Cleaning Workers	15	587,700	3,988,700
132. Barbers, Cosmetologists, and Other Personal Appearance Workers	15	111,100	754,100
133. Retail Salespersons..	15	595,900	4,075,800
134. Gaming Cage Workers	15	2,700	18,300
135. Cargo and Freight Agents	15	9,200	59,100
136. Weighers, Measurers, Checkers, and Samplers, Recordkeeping	15	11,800	80,700
137. Computer, Automated Teller, and Office Machine Repairers	15	23,500	156,300
138. Coin, Vending, and Amusement Machine Servicers and Repairers	15	6,500	42,700
139. Welding, Soldering, and Brazing Workers	15	66,700	451,700
140. Budget Analysts	14	8,700	62,200
141. Claims Adjusters, Appraisers, Examiners, and Investigators	14	33,900	241,400
142. Surveyors, Cartographers, Photogrammetrists, and Surveying Technicians	14	17,500	124,500
143. Artists and Related Workers.......................................	14	21,400	148,700
144. Photographers	14	17,800	130,400
145. Dispatchers	14	36,200	262,200
146. Production, Planning, and Expediting Clerks	14	40,400	287,600
147. Bricklayers, Blockmasons, and Stonemasons	14	23,400	164,900
148. Construction and Building Inspectors..........................	14	11,600	83,700
149. Construction Laborers	14	132,700	937,800
150. Plasterers and Stucco Masons	14	8,000	59,100
151. Diesel Service Technicians and Mechanics	14	37,800	267,200
152. Property, Real Estate, and Community Association Managers	13	37,400	292,900
153. Economists	13	2,200	16,100
154. Science Technicians	13	27,100	208,500
155. Court Reporters	13	2,300	17,800
156. Dancers and Choreographers	13	5,000	37,300
157. Occupational Health and Safety Specialists and Technicians	13	5,400	41,400
158. Cashiers	13	462,100	3,465,100
159. Securities, Commodities, and Financial Services Sales Agents	13	39,000	299,900
160. Automotive Body and Related Repairers.......................	13	28,600	220,100
161. Painting and Coating Workers, Except Construction and Maintenance...	13	24,300	186,600
162. Air Traffic Controllers	13	3,200	25,600
163. Construction Managers	12	46,700	388,800
164. Food Service Managers	12	44,300	385,500
165. Chemists and Materials Scientists	12	11,300	91,300
166. Chefs, Cooks, and Food Preparation Workers	12	366,700	2,968,200
167. Childcare Workers..	12	141,600	1,211,100

(continued)

(continued)

Table 2: 271 Jobs Listed in Order of Percent Growth

	Percent Growth	Numerical Growth	Current Employment
168. Reservation and Transportation Ticket Agents and Travel Clerks	12	21,700	177,300
169. Automotive Service Technicians and Mechanics	12	101,200	818,200
170. Line Installers and Repairers	12	33,000	268,400
171. Urban and Regional Planners	11	3,400	32,200
172. Construction Equipment Operators	11	44,500	415,800
173. Painters and Paperhangers	11	53,100	467,600
174. Engineering and Natural Sciences Managers	10	24,700	257,300
175. Insurance Underwriters	10	10,200	101,800
176. Agricultural Engineers	10	300	2,900
177. Industrial Engineers, Including Health and Safety	10	19,700	193,800
178. Engineering Technicians	10	48,200	478,300
179. Social Scientists, Other	10	1,600	16,500
180. Librarians	10	16,800	167,100
181. Office Clerks, General	10	309,600	2,991,100
182. Carpenters	10	122,400	1,208,600
183. Aircraft and Avionics Equipment Mechanics and Service Technicians	10	15,200	154,000
184. Food-Processing Occupations	10	79,300	756,600
185. Computer-Control Programmers and Operators	10	14,800	151,200
186. Agricultural and Food Scientists	9	1,600	18,000
187. Recreational Therapists	9	2,400	26,700
188. Sales Worker Supervisors	9	204,000	2,395,000
189. Tellers	9	49,800	530,400
190. Electronic Home Entertainment Equipment Installers and Repairers	9	3,700	42,600
191. Heavy Vehicle and Mobile Equipment Service Technicians and Mechanics	9	15,400	175,600
192. Precision Instrument and Equipment Repairers	9	5,500	63,700
193. Ophthalmic Laboratory Technicians	9	3,000	33,100
194. Material Moving Occupations	9	442,600	4,869,400
195. Industrial Production Managers	8	14,300	182,200
196. Purchasing Managers, Buyers, and Purchasing Agents	8	41,300	527,100
197. Civil Engineers	8	18,200	228,100
198. Judges, Magistrates, and Other Judicial Workers	8	4,200	51,400
199. Insurance Sales Agents	8	32,100	381,400
200. Billing and Posting Clerks and Machine Operators	8	40,200	506,600
201. Electrical and Electronics Installers and Repairers	8	14,200	172,200
202. Machinists	8	31,900	386,800
203. Photographic Process Workers and Processing Machine Operators	8	6,500	82,400
204. Funeral Directors	7	1,600	24,300
205. Lodging Managers	7	4,500	68,800
206. Physicists and Astronomers	7	1,000	14,400
207. Financial Clerks	7	260,700	3,725,900
208. Payroll and Timekeeping Clerks	7	12,900	197,700

	Percent Growth	Numerical Growth	Current Employment
209. Office and Administrative Support Worker Supervisors and Managers	7	95,900	1,459,400
210. Operations Research Analysts	6	3,900	61,700
211. Computer Hardware Engineers	6	4,500	73,900
212. Electrical and Electronics Engineers, Except Computer	6	16,700	291,900
213. News Analysts, Reporters, and Correspondents	6	4,100	65,700
214. Industrial Machinery Installation, Repair, and Maintenance Workers, Except Millwrights	6	16,300	289,200
215. Tax Examiners, Collectors, and Revenue Agents	5	3,800	74,800
216. Statisticians	5	1,000	20,000
217. Mechanical Engineers	5	10,300	215,100
218. Real Estate Brokers and Sales Agents	5	19,900	406,800
219. Home Appliance Repairers	5	2,300	42,000
220. Millwrights	5	3,700	69,500
221. Machine Setters, Operators, and Tenders—Metal and Plastic	5	63,400	1,267,400
222. Printing Machine Operators	5	9,100	198,700
223. Woodworkers	5	19,200	373,600
224. Inspectors, Testers, Sorters, Samplers, and Weighers	5	24,100	515,400
225. Materials Engineers	4	1,000	24,300
226. Conservation Scientists and Foresters	4	1,400	32,800
227. Dentists	4	6,300	152,600
228. Interviewers	4	18,700	457,200
229. Couriers and Messengers	4	5,300	132,300
230. Secretaries and Administrative Assistants	4	183,600	4,104,300
231. Agricultural Workers	4	35,600	795,100
232. Dental Laboratory Technicians	4	1,700	46,900
233. Jewelers and Precious Stone and Metal Workers	4	1,800	40,300
234. Drafters	3	6,000	216,100
235. Bookkeeping, Accounting, and Auditing Clerks	3	59,300	1,983,100
236. Shipping, Receiving, and Traffic Clerks	3	24,200	803,000
237. Water Transportation Occupations	3	2,300	68,000
238. Boilermakers	2	400	24,600
239. Material Recording, Scheduling, Dispatching, and Distributing Occupations, Except Postal Workers	1	20,500	4,004,900
240. Chemical Engineers	0	100	32,900
241. Nuclear Engineers	0	-20	15,600
242. File Clerks	0	-700	264,600
243. Tool and Die Makers	0	400	109,500
244. Stationary Engineers and Boiler Operators	0	100	55,400
245. Mathematicians	−1	−30	2,900
246. Power Plant Operators, Distributors, and Dispatchers	−1	−300	50,900
247. Forest, Conservation, and Logging Workers	−2	−1,500	81,100
248. Radio and Telecommunications Equipment Installers and Repairers	−2	−3,500	226,000
249. Mining and Geological Engineers, Including Mining Safety Engineers	−3	−100	5,200
250. Prepress Technicians and Workers	−3	−5,100	147,600

(continued)

(continued)

Table 2: 271 Jobs Listed in Order of Percent Growth

	Percent Growth	Numerical Growth	Current Employment
251. Stock Clerks and Order Fillers	−4	−68,100	1,627,700
252. Postal Service Workers	-4	−28,500	664,200
253. Assemblers and Fabricators	−4	−77,300	2,121,800
254. Aerospace Engineers	−5	−4,100	77,900
255. Bookbinders and Bindery Workers	−5	−4,700	98,000
256. Rail Transportation Occupations	−5	−5,400	101,100
257. Order Clerks	−6	−18,600	329,700
258. Procurement Clerks	−7	−5,200	76,800
259. Credit Authorizers, Checkers, and Clerks	−7	−5,400	79,700
260. Petroleum Engineers	−10	−1,300	13,600
261. Announcers	−10	−7,600	75,700
262. Communications Equipment Operators	−11	−31,900	303,700
263. Semiconductor Processors	−11	−4,900	46,500
264. Travel Agents	−14	−16,400	118,500
265. Meter Readers, Utilities	−14	−7,600	54,000
266. Textile, Apparel, and Furnishings Occupations	−14	−152,500	1,084,700
267. Brokerage Clerks	−15	−11,400	77,900
268. Farmers, Ranchers, and Agricultural Managers	−17	−227,000	1,376,000
269. Computer Operators	−17	−30,400	181,800
270. Data Entry and Information Processing Workers	−18	−114,300	632,800
271. Fishers and Fishing Vessel Operators	−27	−9,800	36,400

Table 3: 271 Jobs Listed in Order of Number of Job Openings

This table presents the 271 major jobs in order of number of net new (additional) job openings projected through 2012. It also includes data on the percent growth rate and the total number of people currently employed in each job.

Occupations projected to have large numbers of new openings tend to be those that also employ large numbers of people. These jobs will often be easier to obtain, although this is not always the case if there are many qualified applicants. In all jobs, the more desirable and higher-paying positions will typically require you to use more-effective job-seeking methods to obtain them, even if you have good credentials.

Some occupations at the bottom of this table are projected to have a net loss of jobs. But even these declining occupations will have job openings as the result of workers retiring or leaving the occupation for other reasons. For example, Stock Clerks and Order Fillers is the 267th job on the list and is projected to lose 4 percent of its jobs, resulting in a net loss of 68,100 positions through 2012. Even so, many new people will be hired to fill open stock clerk and order filler positions during this time to replace people leaving the occupation.

Table 3: 271 Jobs Listed in Order of Number of Job Openings

	Numerical Growth	Percent Growth	Current Employment
1. Food and Beverage Serving and Related Workers	1,133,000	17	6,539,000
2. Information and Record Clerks	913,900	18	5,090,000
3. Teachers—Preschool, Kindergarten, Elementary, Middle, and Secondary	665,600	18	3,754,400
4. Nursing, Psychiatric, and Home Health Aides	630,400	31	2,014,300

	Numerical Growth	Percent Growth	Current Employment
5. Registered Nurses	623,200	27	2,284,500
6. Teachers—Postsecondary	602,700	38	1,581,200
7. Retail Salespersons	595,900	15	4,075,800
8. Truck Drivers and Driver/Sales Workers	592,200	18	3,220,800
9. Building Cleaning Workers	587,700	15	3,988,700
10. Top Executives	469,300	18	2,668,600
11. Cashiers	462,100	13	3,465,100
12. Customer Service Representatives	459,700	24	1,894,100
13. Material Moving Occupations	442,600	9	4,869,400
14. Computer Systems Analysts, Database Administrators, and Computer Scientists	416,000	42	979,200
15. Chefs, Cooks, and Food Preparation Workers	366,700	12	2,968,200
16. Sales Representatives, Wholesale and Manufacturing	356,300	19	1,857,100
17. Receptionists and Information Clerks	324,600	29	1,100,300
18. Security Guards and Gaming Surveillance Officers	319,300	32	1,004,400
19. Office Clerks, General	309,600	10	2,991,100
20. Computer Software Engineers	307,200	45	675,200
21. Teacher Assistants	294,100	23	1,276,700
22. Grounds Maintenance Workers	282,500	22	1,310,000
23. Financial Clerks	260,700	7	3,725,900
24. Computer Support Specialists and Systems Administrators	247,300	33	758,300
25. Personal and Home Health Care Aides	245,900	40	607,600
26. Medical Assistants	214,800	59	364,600
27. Maintenance and Repair Workers, General	206,800	16	1,265,600
28. Accountants and Auditors	205,500	19	1,055,200
29. Sales Worker Supervisors	204,000	9	2,395,000
30. Police and Detectives	192,700	23	840,100
31. Advertising, Marketing, Promotions, Public Relations, and Sales Managers	185,300	26	700,100
32. Secretaries and Administrative Assistants	183,600	4	4,104,300
33. Management Analysts	175,700	30	577,400
34. Human Resources, Training, and Labor Relations Managers and Specialists	170,800	25	676,700
35. Electricians	154,500	23	659,400
36. Social and Human Service Assistants	148,700	49	305,200
37. Recreation and Fitness Workers	143,100	30	484,800
38. Licensed Practical and Licensed Vocational Nurses	141,800	20	701,900
39. Childcare Workers	141,600	12	1,211,100
40. Construction Laborers	132,700	14	937,800
41. Teachers—Special Education	129,800	30	432,900
42. Social Workers	127,100	27	476,600
43. Carpenters	122,400	10	1,208,600
44. Counselors	118,900	23	525,900
45. Lawyers	117,900	17	695,200
46. Counter and Rental Clerks	114,400	26	435,800
47. Physicians and Surgeons	113,500	19	583,300
48. Dental Assistants	113,000	42	266,000
49. Correctional Officers	111,100	23	475,600

(continued)

(continued)

Table 3: 271 Jobs Listed in Order of Number of Job Openings

	Numerical Growth	Percent Growth	Current Employment
50. Barbers, Cosmetologists, and Other Personal Appearance Workers	111,100	15	754,100
51. Financial Managers	109,500	18	599,100
52. Bus Drivers	106,300	16	654,400
53. Computer and Information Systems Managers	102,600	36	284,400
54. Automotive Service Technicians and Mechanics	101,200	12	818,200
55. Bill and Account Collectors	101,000	24	413,000
56. Education Administrators	100,800	24	426,600
57. Pipelayers, Plumbers, Pipefitters, and Steamfitters	98,800	18	550,100
58. Teachers—Adult Literacy and Remedial and Self-Enrichment Education	96,700	34	280,400
59. Office and Administrative Support Worker Supervisors and Managers	95,900	7	1,459,400
60. Designers	92,700	17	531,900
61. Food-Processing Occupations	79,300	10	756,600
62. Heating, Air-Conditioning, and Refrigeration Mechanics and Installers	79,100	32	248,700
63. Financial Analysts and Personal Financial Advisors	75,800	25	298,300
64. Computer Programmers	72,700	15	498,600
65. Firefighting Occupations	71,800	20	358,900
66. Medical and Health Services Managers	71,300	29	243,600
67. Pharmacists	69,200	30	230,200
68. Medical Records and Health Information Technicians	68,700	47	146,900
69. Welding, Soldering, and Brazing Workers	66,700	15	451,700
70. Dental Hygienists	63,700	43	148,000
71. Administrative Services Managers	63,500	20	320,500
72. Machine Setters, Operators, and Tenders—Metal and Plastic	63,400	5	1,267,400
73. Pharmacy Technicians	60,700	29	210,800
74. Emergency Medical Technicians and Paramedics	59,300	33	179,100
75. Bookkeeping, Accounting, and Auditing Clerks	59,300	3	1,983,100
76. Clinical Laboratory Technologists and Technicians	57,600	19	297,400
77. Paralegals and Legal Assistants	57,300	29	199,600
78. Painters and Paperhangers	53,100	11	467,600
79. Public Relations Specialists	52,100	33	158,100
80. Writers and Editors	51,100	16	318,600
81. Tellers	49,800	9	530,400
82. Cement Masons, Concrete Finishers, Segmental Pavers, and Terrazzo Workers	48,700	26	190,200
83. Physical Therapists	48,300	35	136,900
84. Engineering Technicians	48,200	10	478,300
85. Loan Counselors and Officers	47,600	19	254,600
86. Construction Managers	46,700	12	388,800
87. Construction Equipment Operators	44,500	11	415,800
88. Food Service Managers	44,300	12	385,500
89. Hotel, Motel, and Resort Desk Clerks	42,500	24	177,700

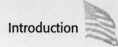

	Numerical Growth	Percent Growth	Current Employment
90. Purchasing Managers, Buyers, and Purchasing Agents	41,300	8	527,100
91. Sheet Metal Workers	40,600	20	205,000
92. Gaming Services Occupations	40,400	21	192,000
93. Production, Planning, and Expediting Clerks	40,400	14	287,600
94. Billing and Posting Clerks and Machine Operators	40,200	8	506,600
95. Radiologic Technologists and Technicians	40,000	23	174,100
96. Physical Therapist Assistants and Aides	39,500	45	87,200
97. Securities, Commodities, and Financial Services Sales Agents	39,000	13	299,900
98. Respiratory Therapists	38,900	35	112,200
99. Market and Survey Researchers	38,300	25	154,700
100. Diesel Service Technicians and Mechanics	37,800	14	267,200
101. Drywall Installers, Ceiling Tile Installers, and Tapers	37,500	21	176,100
102. Property, Real Estate, and Community Association Managers	37,400	13	292,900
103. Dispatchers	36,200	14	262,200
104. Agricultural Workers	35,600	4	795,100
105. Cost Estimators	35,000	19	188,000
106. Musicians, Singers, and Related Workers	34,800	16	215,400
107. Claims Adjusters, Appraisers, Examiners, and Investigators	33,900	14	241,400
108. Psychologists	33,800	24	139,100
109. Human Resources Assistants, Except Payroll and Timekeeping	33,500	19	173,800
110. Line Installers and Repairers	33,000	12	268,400
111. Insurance Sales Agents	32,100	8	381,400
112. Machinists	31,900	8	386,800
113. Animal Care and Service Workers	31,500	21	151,300
114. Roofers	30,900	19	166,200
115. Physician Assistants	30,800	49	63,000
116. Demonstrators, Product Promoters, and Models	30,300	17	179,200
117. Athletes, Coaches, Umpires, and Related Workers	29,000	18	158,400
118. Occupational Therapists	28,700	35	81,600
119. Taxi Drivers and Chauffeurs	28,700	22	132,200
120. Automotive Body and Related Repairers	28,600	13	220,100
121. Carpet, Floor, and Tile Installers and Finishers	27,400	17	163,700
122. Science Technicians	27,100	13	208,500
123. Library Assistants, Clerical	25,900	21	120,400
124. Speech-Language Pathologists	25,600	27	94,300
125. Actors, Producers, and Directors	25,100	18	139,200
126. Instructional Coordinators	25,000	25	98,500
127. Engineering and Natural Sciences Managers	24,700	10	257,300
128. Painting and Coating Workers, Except Construction and Maintenance	24,300	13	186,600
129. Shipping, Receiving, and Traffic Clerks	24,200	3	803,000
130. Inspectors, Testers, Sorters, Samplers, and Weighers	24,100	5	515,400
131. Computer, Automated Teller, and Office Machine Repairers	23,500	15	156,300
132. Bricklayers, Blockmasons, and Stonemasons	23,400	14	164,900

(continued)

(continued)

Table 3: 271 Jobs Listed in Order of Number of Job Openings

	Numerical Growth	Percent Growth	Current Employment
133. Veterinary Technologists and Technicians	23,200	44	52,700
134. Medical Transcriptionists	22,800	23	100,800
135. Reservation and Transportation Ticket Agents and Travel Clerks	21,700	12	177,300
136. Artists and Related Workers	21,400	14	148,700
137. Material Recording, Scheduling, Dispatching, and Distributing Occupations, Except Postal Workers	20,500	1	4,004,900
138. Environmental Scientists and Geoscientists	20,300	20	100,700
139. Surgical Technologists	20,200	28	72,200
140. Library Technicians	20,000	17	119,300
141. Real Estate Brokers and Sales Agents	19,900	5	406,800
142. Industrial Engineers, Including Health and Safety	19,700	10	193,800
143. Architects, Except Landscape and Naval	19,500	17	113,200
144. Woodworkers	19,200	5	373,600
145. Interviewers	18,700	4	457,200
146. Broadcast and Sound Engineering Technicians and Radio Operators	18,200	20	93,000
147. Civil Engineers	18,200	8	228,100
148. Environmental Engineers	18,000	38	47,100
149. Aircraft Pilots and Flight Engineers	17,800	18	100,200
150. Photographers	17,800	14	130,400
151. Surveyors, Cartographers, Photogrammetrists, and Surveying Technicians	17,500	14	124,500
152. Structural and Reinforcing Iron and Metal Workers	17,200	16	106,700
153. Medical Scientists	16,800	27	61,700
154. Librarians	16,800	10	167,100
155. Electrical and Electronics Engineers, Except Computer	16,700	6	291,900
156. Flight Attendants	16,600	16	104,000
157. Sales Engineers	16,300	20	81,700
158. Industrial Machinery Installation, Repair, and Maintenance Workers, Except Millwrights	16,300	6	289,200
159. Hazardous Materials Removal Workers	16,200	43	37,600
160. Water and Liquid Waste Treatment Plant and System Operators	15,900	16	99,300
161. Heavy Vehicle and Mobile Equipment Service Technicians and Mechanics	15,400	9	175,600
162. Aircraft and Avionics Equipment Mechanics and Service Technicians	15,200	10	154,000
163. Computer-Control Programmers and Operators	14,800	10	151,200
164. Cardiovascular Technologists and Technicians	14,600	34	43,400
165. Veterinarians	14,400	25	57,500
166. Biological Scientists	14,300	19	75,400
167. Industrial Production Managers	14,300	8	182,200
168. Electrical and Electronics Installers and Repairers	14,200	8	172,200
169. Payroll and Timekeeping Clerks	12,900	7	197,700
170. Small Engine Mechanics	12,500	19	66,900

	Numerical Growth	Percent Growth	Current Employment
171. Probation Officers and Correctional Treatment Specialists	12,400	15	84,300
172. Private Detectives and Investigators	12,200	25	48,000
173. Weighers, Measurers, Checkers, and Samplers, Recordkeeping	11,800	15	80,700
174. Construction and Building Inspectors........................	11,600	14	83,700
175. Opticians, Dispensing............................	11,500	18	63,200
176. Chiropractors............................	11,400	23	48,900
177. Chemists and Materials Scientists	11,300	12	91,300
178. Occupational Therapist Assistants and Aides............	10,800	40	26,800
179. Pharmacy Aides	10,600	18	60,300
180. Pest Control Workers	10,400	17	61,600
181. Mechanical Engineers	10,300	5	215,100
182. Desktop Publishers	10,200	29	35,000
183. Insurance Underwriters	10,200	10	101,800
184. Cargo and Freight Agents	9,200	15	59,100
185. Printing Machine Operators............................	9,100	5	198,700
186. Television, Video, and Motion Picture Camera Operators and Editors	8,900	19	47,500
187. Diagnostic Medical Sonographers	8,800	24	36,500
188. Dietitians and Nutritionists............................	8,700	18	48,900
189. Budget Analysts	8,700	14	62,200
190. Insulation Workers	8,500	16	53,500
191. Glaziers	8,300	17	48,500
192. Plasterers and Stucco Masons	8,000	14	59,100
193. Coin, Vending, and Amusement Machine Servicers and Repairers	6,500	15	42,700
194. Photographic Process Workers and Processing Machine Operators	6,500	8	82,400
195. Dentists............................	6,300	4	152,600
196. Drafters	6,000	3	216,100
197. Optometrists	5,500	17	32,100
198. Precision Instrument and Equipment Repairers	5,500	9	63,700
199. Occupational Health and Safety Specialists and Technicians	5,400	13	41,400
200. Interpreters and Translators	5,300	22	24,100
201. Couriers and Messengers	5,300	4	132,300
202. Landscape Architects	5,100	22	23,100
203. Dancers and Choreographers	5,000	13	37,300
204. Lodging Managers............................	4,500	7	68,800
205. Computer Hardware Engineers	4,500	6	73,900
206. Judges, Magistrates, and Other Judicial Workers	4,200	8	51,400
207. Nuclear Medicine Technologists............................	4,100	24	17,100
208. News Analysts, Reporters, and Correspondents	4,100	6	65,700
209. Operations Research Analysts............................	3,900	6	61,700
210. Archivists, Curators, and Museum Technicians	3,800	17	22,300
211. Tax Examiners, Collectors, and Revenue Agents............	3,800	5	74,800
212. Electronic Home Entertainment Equipment Installers and Repairers	3,700	9	42,600

(continued)

(continued)

Table 3: 271 Jobs Listed in Order of Number of Job Openings

	Numerical Growth	Percent Growth	Current Employment
213. Millwrights	3,700	5	69,500
214. Elevator Installers and Repairers	3,600	17	21,000
215. Urban and Regional Planners	3,400	11	32,200
216. Audiologists	3,200	29	10,900
217. Air Traffic Controllers	3,200	13	25,600
218. Ophthalmic Laboratory Technicians	3,000	9	33,100
219. Gaming Cage Workers	2,700	15	18,300
220. Recreational Therapists	2,400	9	26,700
221. Actuaries	2,300	15	15,300
222. Court Reporters	2,300	13	17,800
223. Home Appliance Repairers	2,300	5	42,000
224. Water Transportation Occupations	2,300	3	68,000
225. Economists	2,200	13	16,100
226. Biomedical Engineers	2,000	26	7,600
227. Podiatrists	2,000	15	13,300
228. Jewelers and Precious Stone and Metal Workers	1,800	4	40,300
229. Dental Laboratory Technicians	1,700	4	46,900
230. Social Scientists, Other	1,600	10	16,500
231. Agricultural and Food Scientists	1,600	9	18,000
232. Funeral Directors	1,600	7	24,300
233. Conservation Scientists and Foresters	1,400	4	32,800
234. Atmospheric Scientists	1,200	16	7,700
235. Physicists and Astronomers	1,000	7	14,400
236. Statisticians	1,000	5	20,000
237. Materials Engineers	1,000	4	24,300
238. Boilermakers	400	2	24,600
239. Tool and Die Makers	400	0	109,500
240. Agricultural Engineers	300	10	2,900
241. Chemical Engineers	100	0	32,900
242. Stationary Engineers and Boiler Operators	100	0	55,400
243. Nuclear Engineers	−20	0	15,600
244. Mathematicians	−30	−1	2,900
245. Mining and Geological Engineers, Including Mining Safety Engineers	−100	−3	5,200
246. Power Plant Operators, Distributors, and Dispatchers	−300	−1	50,900
247. File Clerks	−700	0	264,600
248. Petroleum Engineers	−1,300	−10	13,600
249. Forest, Conservation, and Logging Workers	−1,500	−2	81,100
250. Radio and Telecommunications Equipment Installers and Repairers	−3,500	−2	226,000
251. Aerospace Engineers	−4,100	−5	77,900
252. Bookbinders and Bindery Workers	−4,700	−5	98,000
253. Semiconductor Processors	−4,900	−11	46,500
254. Prepress Technicians and Workers	−5,100	−3	147,600
255. Procurement Clerks	−5,200	−7	76,800
256. Rail Transportation Occupations	−5,400	−5	101,100

	Numerical Growth	Percent Growth	Current Employment
257. Credit Authorizers, Checkers, and Clerks	−5,400	−7	79,700
258. Announcers	−7,600	−10	75,700
259. Meter Readers, Utilities	−7,600	−14	54,000
260. Fishers and Fishing Vessel Operators	−9,800	−27	36,400
261. Brokerage Clerks	−11,400	−15	77,900
262. Travel Agents	−16,400	−14	118,500
263. Order Clerks	−18,600	−6	329,700
264. Postal Service Workers	−28,500	−4	664,200
265. Computer Operators	−30,400	−17	181,800
266. Communications Equipment Operators	−31,900	−11	303,700
267. Stock Clerks and Order Fillers	−68,100	−4	1,627,700
268. Assemblers and Fabricators	−77,300	−4	2,121,800
269. Data Entry and Information Processing Workers	−114,300	−18	632,800
270. Textile, Apparel, and Furnishings Occupations	−152,500	−14	1,084,700
271. Farmers, Ranchers, and Agricultural Managers	−227,000	−17	1,376,000

Table 4: 271 Jobs Listed in Order of Combined Scores for Percent Growth and Number of Job Openings

This table includes more data than the other tables. It presents all 271 major jobs arranged in order of total score for the combined measures of percent growth and number of job openings through 2012. Three columns include the projected percentage growth, number of new job openings, and total number of people currently employed in each job.

Other columns show where each job ranked on the lists for percent growth and number of new job openings. For example, Teachers—Postsecondary is projected to grow 38 percent and have 602,700 new job openings. The ranking columns show that this job was ranked as number 15 on the percent growth list and number 6 on the number of new openings list. Both of these rankings are very high, and they resulted in this job having the most favorable combined score for percent growth and number of new job openings. The first 101 of these jobs are the ones that are described in Section One, and they are presented in bold type.

Table 4: 271 Jobs Listed in Order of Combined Scores for Percent Growth and Number of Job Openings

	Percent Growth	Rank by Percent Growth	Numerical Growth	Rank by Numerical Growth	Current Employment
1. **Teachers—Postsecondary**	**38**	**15**	**602,700**	**6**	**1,581,200**
2. **Computer Systems Analysts, Database Administrators, and Computer Scientists**	**42**	**10**	**416,000**	**14**	**979,200**
3. **Computer Software Engineers**	**45**	**5**	**307,200**	**20**	**675,200**
4. **Medical Assistants**	**59**	**1**	**214,800**	**26**	**364,600**
5. **Social and Human Service Assistants**	**49**	**2**	**214,800**	**27**	**305,200**
6. **Nursing, Psychiatric, and Home Health Aides**	**31**	**27**	**630,400**	**4**	**2,014,300**
7. **Personal and Home Health Care Aides**	**40**	**13**	**245,900**	**25**	**607,600**
8. **Security Guards and Gaming Surveillance Officers**	**32**	**25**	**319,300**	**18**	**1,004,400**
9. **Registered Nurses**	**27**	**41**	**623,200**	**5**	**2,284,500**
10. **Computer Support Specialists and Systems Administrators**	**33**	**22**	**247,300**	**24**	**758,300**
11. **Receptionists and Information Clerks**	**29**	**37**	**324,600**	**17**	**1,100,300**

(continued)

(continued)

Table 4: 271 Jobs Listed in Order of Combined Scores for Percent Growth and Number of Job Openings

	Percent Growth	Rank by Percent Growth	Numerical Growth	Rank by Numerical Growth	Current Employment
12. Dental Assistants	42	11	113,000	48	266,000
13. Management Analysts	30	28	175,700	34	577,400
14. Recreation and Fitness Workers	30	31	143,100	37	484,800
15. Customer Service Representatives	24	57	459,700	12	1,894,100
16. Computer and Information Systems Managers	36	16	102,600	53	284,400
17. Teachers—Special Education	30	29	129,800	41	432,900
18. Medical Records and Health Information Technicians	47	4	68,700	68	146,900
19. Advertising, Marketing, Promotions, Public Relations, and Sales Managers	26	43	185,300	32	700,100
20. Teachers—Adult Literacy and Remedial and Self-Enrichment Education	34	20	96,700	58	280,400
21. Dental Hygienists	43	8	63,700	70	148,000
22. Teacher Assistants	23	61	294,100	21	1,276,700
23. Human Resources, Training, and Labor Relations Managers and Specialists	25	47	170,800	35	676,700
24. Social Workers	27	40	127,100	42	476,600
25. Heating, Air-Conditioning, and Refrigeration Mechanics and Installers	32	26	79,100	62	248,700
26. Counter and Rental Clerks	26	45	114,400	46	435,800
27. Grounds Maintenance Workers	22	70	282,500	22	1,310,000
28. Police and Detectives	23	66	192,700	31	840,100
29. Pharmacists	30	30	69,200	67	230,200
30. Medical and Health Services Managers	29	32	71,300	66	243,600
31. Emergency Medical Technicians and Paramedics	33	24	59,300	74	179,100
32. Physical Therapists	35	18	48,300	83	136,900
33. Public Relations Specialists	33	23	52,100	79	158,100
34. Physical Therapist Assistants and Aides	45	6	39,500	96	87,200
35. Electricians	23	67	154,500	36	659,400
36. Counselors	23	60	118,900	44	525,900
37. Top Executives	18	95	469,300	10	2,668,600
38. Sales Representatives, Wholesale and Manufacturing	19	90	356,300	16	1,857,100
39. Pharmacy Technicians	29	35	60,700	73	210,800
40. Education Administrators	24	53	100,800	56	426,600
41. Paralegals and Legal Assistants	29	33	57,300	77	199,600
42. Financial Analysts and Personal Financial Advisors	25	48	75,800	63	298,300
43. Accountants and Auditors	19	83	205,500	29	1,055,200
44. Food and Beverage Serving and Related Workers	17	112	1,133,000	1	6,539,000
45. Information and Record Clerks	18	102	913,900	2	5,090,000
46. Teachers—Preschool, Kindergarten, Elementary, Middle, and Secondary	18	96	665,600	3	3,754,400

	Percent Growth	Rank by Percent Growth	Numerical Growth	Rank by Numerical Growth	Current Employment
47. Truck Drivers and Driver/Sales Workers	18	105	592,200	8	3,220,800
48. Bill and Account Collectors	24	58	101,000	55	413,000
49. Correctional Officers	23	65	111,100	49	475,600
50. Licensed Practical and Licensed Vocational Nurses	20	79	141,800	38	701,900
51. Respiratory Therapists	35	19	38,900	98	112,200
52. Physician Assistants	49	3	30,800	115	63,000
53. Cement Masons, Concrete Finishers, Segmental Pavers, and Terrazzo Workers	26	46	48,700	82	190,200
54. Physicians and Surgeons	19	88	113,500	47	583,300
55. Occupational Therapists	35	17	28,700	118	81,600
56. Retail Salespersons	15	133	595,900	7	4,075,800
57. Building Cleaning Workers	15	131	587,700	9	3,988,700
58. Veterinary Technologists and Technicians	44	7	23,200	133	52,700
59. Financial Managers	18	94	109,500	51	599,100
60. Firefighting Occupations	20	80	71,800	65	358,900
61. Administrative Services Managers	20	76	63,500	71	320,500
62. Hotel, Motel, and Resort Desk Clerks	24	59	42,500	89	177,700
63. Market and Survey Researchers	25	49	38,300	99	154,700
64. Maintenance and Repair Workers, General	16	124	206,800	28	1,265,600
65. Lawyers	17	107	117,900	45	695,200
66. Radiologic Technologists and Technicians ..	23	63	40,000	95	174,100
67. Pipelayers, Plumbers, Pipefitters, and Steamfitters	18	103	98,800	57	550,100
68. Psychologists	24	54	33,800	108	139,100
69. Environmental Engineers	38	14	18,000	148	47,100
70. Clinical Laboratory Technologists and Technicians	19	89	57,600	76	297,400
71. Gaming Services Occupations	21	73	40,400	92	192,000
72. Speech-Language Pathologists	27	42	25,600	124	94,300
73. Hazardous Materials Removal Workers	43	9	16,200	159	37,600
74. Cashiers	13	158	462,100	11	3,465,100
75. Designers	17	110	92,700	60	531,900
76. Loan Counselors and Officers	19	85	47,600	85	254,600
77. Sheet Metal Workers	20	82	40,600	91	205,000
78. Drywall Installers, Ceiling Tile Installers, and Tapers	21	75	37,500	101	176,100
79. Instructional Coordinators	25	50	25,000	126	98,500
80. Surgical Technologists	28	38	20,200	139	72,200
81. Bus Drivers	16	126	106,300	52	654,400
82. Chefs, Cooks, and Food Preparation Workers	12	166	366,700	15	2,968,200
83. Barbers, Cosmetologists, and Other Personal Appearance Workers	15	132	111,100	50	754,100
84. Animal Care and Service Workers	21	72	31,500	113	151,300
85. Cardiovascular Technologists and Technicians	34	21	14,600	164	43,400
86. Construction Laborers	14	149	132,700	40	937,800

(continued)

(continued)

Table 4: 271 Jobs Listed in Order of Combined Scores for Percent Growth and Number of Job Openings

	Percent Growth	Rank by Percent Growth	Numerical Growth	Rank by Numerical Growth	Current Employment
87. Cost Estimators	19	84	35,000	105	188,000
88. Taxi Drivers and Chauffeurs	22	71	28,700	119	132,200
89. Occupational Therapist Assistants and Aides	40	12	10,800	178	26,800
90. Computer Programmers	15	128	72,700	64	498,600
91. Medical Scientists	27	39	16,800	153	61,700
92. Library Assistants, Clerical	21	74	25,900	123	120,400
93. Medical Transcriptionists	23	64	22,800	134	100,800
94. Office Clerks, General	10	181	309,600	19	2,991,100
95. Writers and Editors	16	120	51,100	80	318,600
96. Human Resources Assistants, Except Payroll and Timekeeping	19	91	33,500	109	173,800
97. Childcare Workers	12	167	141,600	39	1,211,100
98. Roofers	19	92	30,900	114	166,200
99. Material Moving Occupations	9	194	442,600	13	4,869,400
100. Welding, Soldering, and Brazing Workers	15	139	66,700	69	451,700
101. Athletes, Coaches, Umpires, and Related Workers	18	98	29,000	117	158,400
102. Environmental Scientists and Geoscientists	20	77	20,300	138	100,700
103. Veterinarians	25	51	14,400	165	57,500
104. Sales Worker Supervisors	9	188	204,000	30	2,395,000
105. Desktop Publishers	29	36	10,200	182	35,000
106. Actors, Producers, and Directors	18	97	25,100	125	139,200
107. Automotive Service Technicians and Mechanics	12	169	101,200	54	818,200
108. Broadcast and Sound Engineering Technicians and Radio Operators	20	78	18,200	146	93,000
109. Private Detectives and Investigators	25	52	12,200	172	48,000
110. Carpenters	10	182	122,400	43	1,208,600
111. Musicians, Singers, and Related Workers	16	119	34,800	106	215,400
112. Financial Clerks	7	207	260,700	23	3,725,900
113. Demonstrators, Product Promoters, and Models	17	114	30,300	116	179,200
114. Carpet, Floor, and Tile Installers and Finishers	17	115	27,400	121	163,700
115. Sales Engineers	20	81	16,300	157	81,700
116. Chiropractors	23	62	11,400	176	48,900
117. Production, Planning, and Expediting Clerks	14	146	40,400	93	287,600
118. Diagnostic Medical Sonographers	24	55	8,800	187	36,500
119. Food-Processing Occupations	10	184	79,300	61	756,600
120. Dispatchers	14	145	36,200	103	262,200
121. Claims Adjusters, Appraisers, Examiners, and Investigators	14	141	33,900	107	241,400
122. Construction Managers	12	163	46,700	86	388,800
123. Library Technicians	17	109	20,000	140	119,300

	Percent Growth	Rank by Percent Growth	Numerical Growth	Rank by Numerical Growth	Current Employment
124. Architects, Except Landscape and Naval............	17	106	19,500	143	113,200
125. Audiologists	29	34	3,200	216	10,900
126. Painters and Paperhangers	11	173	53,100	78	467,600
127. Diesel Service Technicians and Mechanics	14	151	37,800	100	267,200
128. Food Service Managers	12	164	44,300	88	385,500
129. Biological Scientists.....................................	19	86	14,300	166	75,400
130. Aircraft Pilots and Flight Engineers................	18	104	17,800	149	100,200
131. Property, Real Estate, and Community Association Managers	13	152	37,400	102	292,900
132. Securities, Commodities, and Financial Services Sales Agents	13	159	39,000	97	299,900
133. Construction Equipment Operators	11	172	44,500	87	415,800
134. Engineering Technicians................................	10	178	48,200	84	478,300
135. Secretaries and Administrative Assistants	4	230	183,600	33	4,104,300
136. Small Engine Mechanics	19	93	12,500	170	66,900
137. Nuclear Medicine Technologists	24	56	4,100	207	17,100
138. Office and Administrative Support Worker Supervisors and Managers	7	209	95,900	59	1,459,400
139. Computer, Automated Teller, and Office Machine Repairers	15	137	23,500	131	156,300
140. Interpreters and Translators	22	69	5,300	200	24,100
141. Tellers	9	189	49,800	81	530,400
142. Landscape Architects....................................	22	68	5,100	202	23,100
143. Biomedical Engineers	26	44	2,000	226	7,600
144. Television, Video, and Motion Picture Camera Operators and Editors	19	87	8,900	186	47,500
145. Structural and Reinforcing Iron and Metal Workers	16	123	17,200	152	106,700
146. Opticians, Dispensing	18	100	11,500	175	63,200
147. Science Technicians......................................	13	154	27,100	122	208,500
148. Flight Attendants...	16	121	16,600	156	104,000
149. Bricklayers, Blockmasons, and Stonemasons	14	147	23,400	132	164,900
150. Artists and Related Workers	14	143	21,400	136	148,700
151. Line Installers and Repairers	12	170	33,000	110	268,400
152. Automotive Body and Related Repairers	13	160	28,600	120	220,100
153. Pharmacy Aides	18	101	10,600	179	60,300
154. Water and Liquid Waste Treatment Plant and System Operators	16	125	15,900	160	99,300
155. Purchasing Managers, Buyers, and Purchasing Agents	8	196	41,300	90	527,100
156. Dietitians and Nutritionists	18	99	8,700	188	48,900
157. Painting and Coating Workers, Except Construction and Maintenance	13	161	24,300	128	186,600
158. Machine Setters, Operators, and Tenders—Metal and Plastic	5	221	63,400	72	1,267,400
159. Surveyors, Cartographers, Photogrammetrists, and Surveying Technicians	14	142	17,500	151	124,500
160. Pest Control Workers....................................	17	113	10,400	180	61,600

(continued)

(continued)

Table 4: 271 Jobs Listed in Order of Combined Scores for Percent Growth and Number of Job Openings

	Percent Growth	Rank by Percent Growth	Numerical Growth	Rank by Numerical Growth	Current Employment
161. Billing and Posting Clerks and Machine Operators	8	200	40,200	94	506,600
162. Photographers	14	144	17,800	150	130,400
163. Probation Officers and Correctional Treatment Specialists	15	129	12,400	171	84,300
164. Engineering and Natural Sciences Managers	10	174	24,700	127	257,300
165. Reservation and Transportation Ticket Agents and Travel Clerks	12	168	21,700	135	177,300
166. Glaziers	17	117	8,300	191	48,500
167. Optometrists	17	111	5,500	197	32,100
168. Weighers, Measurers, Checkers, and Samplers, Recordkeeping	15	136	11,800	173	80,700
169. Bookkeeping, Accounting, and Auditing Clerks	3	235	59,300	75	1,983,100
170. Insurance Sales Agents	8	199	32,100	111	381,400
171. Insulation Workers	16	122	8,500	190	53,500
172. Machinists	8	202	31,900	112	386,800
173. Archivists, Curators, and Museum Technicians	17	108	3,800	210	22,300
174. Industrial Engineers, Including Health and Safety	10	177	19,700	142	193,800
175. Cargo and Freight Agents	15	135	9,200	184	59,100
176. Construction and Building Inspectors	14	148	11,600	174	83,700
177. Budget Analysts	14	140	8,700	189	62,200
178. Elevator Installers and Repairers	17	116	3,600	214	21,000
179. Coin, Vending, and Amusement Machine Servicers and Repairers	15	138	6,500	193	42,700
180. Librarians	10	180	16,800	154	167,100
181. Agricultural Workers	4	231	35,600	104	795,100
182. Chemists and Materials Scientists	12	165	11,300	177	91,300
183. Plasterers and Stucco Masons	14	150	8,000	192	59,100
184. Civil Engineers	8	197	18,200	147	228,100
185. Aircraft and Avionics Equipment Mechanics and Service Technicians	10	183	15,200	162	154,000
186. Computer-Control Programmers and Operators	10	185	14,800	163	151,200
187. Actuaries	15	127	2,300	221	15,300
188. Heavy Vehicle and Mobile Equipment Service Technicians and Mechanics	9	191	15,400	161	175,600
189. Atmospheric Scientists	16	118	1,200	234	7,700
190. Gaming Cage Workers	15	134	2,700	219	18,300
191. Inspectors, Testers, Sorters, Samplers, and Weighers	5	224	24,100	130	515,400
192. Occupational Health and Safety Specialists and Technicians	13	157	5,400	199	41,400
193. Podiatrists	15	130	2,000	227	13,300
194. Insurance Underwriters	10	175	10,200	183	101,800

	Percent Growth	Rank by Percent Growth	Numerical Growth	Rank by Numerical Growth	Current Employment
195. Real Estate Brokers and Sales Agents	5	218	19,900	141	406,800
196. Dancers and Choreographers	13	156	5,000	203	37,300
197. Industrial Production Managers	8	195	14,300	167	182,200
198. Shipping, Receiving, and Traffic Clerks	3	236	24,200	129	803,000
199. Woodworkers	5	223	19,200	144	373,600
200. Electrical and Electronics Engineers, Except Computer	6	212	16,700	155	291,900
201. Electrical and Electronics Installers and Repairers	8	201	14,200	168	172,200
202. Industrial Machinery Installation, Repair, and Maintenance Workers, Except Millwrights	6	214	16,300	158	289,200
203. Interviewers	4	228	18,700	145	457,200
204. Material Recording, Scheduling, Dispatching, and Distributing Occupations, Except Postal Workers	1	239	20,500	137	4,004,900
205. Payroll and Timekeeping Clerks	7	208	12,900	169	197,700
206. Court Reporters	13	155	2,300	222	17,800
207. Economists	13	153	2,200	225	16,100
208. Air Traffic Controllers	13	162	3,200	217	25,600
209. Urban and Regional Planners	11	171	3,400	215	32,200
210. Precision Instrument and Equipment Repairers	9	192	5,500	198	63,700
211. Photographic Process Workers and Processing Machine Operators	8	203	6,500	194	82,400
212. Mechanical Engineers	5	217	10,300	181	215,100
213. Electronic Home Entertainment Equipment Installers and Repairers	9	190	3,700	212	42,600
214. Judges, Magistrates, and Other Judicial Workers	8	198	4,200	206	51,400
215. Printing Machine Operators	5	222	9,100	185	198,700
216. Recreational Therapists	9	187	2,400	220	26,700
217. Lodging Managers	7	205	4,500	204	68,800
218. Social Scientists, Other	10	179	1,600	230	16,500
219. Ophthalmic Laboratory Technicians	9	193	3,000	218	33,100
220. Computer Hardware Engineers	6	211	4,500	205	73,900
221. Agricultural Engineers	10	176	300	240	2,900
222. Agricultural and Food Scientists	9	186	1,600	231	18,000
223. Operations Research Analysts	6	210	3,900	209	61,700
224. News Analysts, Reporters, and Correspondents	6	213	4,100	208	65,700
225. Dentists	4	227	6,300	195	152,600
226. Tax Examiners, Collectors, and Revenue Agents	5	215	3,800	211	74,800
227. Drafters	3	234	6,000	196	216,100
228. Couriers and Messengers	4	229	5,300	201	132,300
229. Millwrights	5	220	3,700	213	69,500
230. Funeral Directors	7	204	1,600	232	24,300
231. Physicists and Astronomers	7	206	1,000	235	14,400
232. Home Appliance Repairers	5	219	2,300	223	42,000

(continued)

(continued)

Table 4: 271 Jobs Listed in Order of Combined Scores for Percent Growth and Number of Job Openings

	Percent Growth	Rank by Percent Growth	Numerical Growth	Rank by Numerical Growth	Current Employment
233. Statisticians	5	216	1,000	236	20,000
234. Conservation Scientists and Foresters	4	226	1,400	233	32,800
235. Water Transportation Occupations	3	237	2,300	224	68,000
236. Jewelers and Precious Stone and Metal Workers	4	233	1,800	228	40,300
237. Dental Laboratory Technicians	4	232	1,700	229	46,900
238. Materials Engineers	4	225	1,000	237	24,300
239. Boilermakers	2	238	400	238	24,600
240. Chemical Engineers	0	240	100	241	32,900
241. Tool and Die Makers	0	243	400	239	109,500
242. Nuclear Engineers	0	241	−20	243	15,600
243. Stationary Engineers and Boiler Operators	0	244	100	242	55,400
244. Mathematicians	−1	245	−30	244	2,900
245. File Clerks	0	242	−700	247	264,600
246. Power Plant Operators, Distributors, and Dispatchers	−1	246	−300	246	50,900
247. Mining and Geological Engineers, Including Mining Safety Engineers	−3	249	−100	245	5,200
248. Forest, Conservation, and Logging Workers	−2	247	−1,500	249	81,100
249. Radio and Telecommunications Equipment Installers and Repairers	−2	248	−3,500	250	226,000
250. Prepress Technicians and Workers	−3	250	−5,100	254	147,600
251. Aerospace Engineers	−5	254	−4,100	251	77,900
252. Bookbinders and Bindery Workers	−5	255	−4,700	252	98,000
253. Petroleum Engineers	−10	260	−1,300	248	13,600
254. Rail Transportation Occupations	−5	256	−5,400	256	101,100
255. Procurement Clerks	−7	258	−5,200	255	76,800
256. Semiconductor Processors	−11	263	−4,900	253	46,500
257. Credit Authorizers, Checkers, and Clerks	−7	259	−5,400	257	79,700
258. Postal Service Workers	−4	252	−28,500	264	664,200
259. Stock Clerks and Order Fillers	−4	251	−68,100	267	1,627,700
260. Announcers	−10	261	−7,600	258	75,700
261. Order Clerks	−6	257	−18,600	263	329,700
262. Assemblers and Fabricators	−4	253	−77,300	268	2,121,800
263. Meter Readers, Utilities	−14	265	−7,600	259	54,000
264. Travel Agents	−14	264	−16,400	262	118,500
265. Brokerage Clerks	−15	267	−11,400	261	77,900
266. Communications Equipment Operators	−11	262	−31,900	266	303,700
267. Fishers and Fishing Vessel Operators	−27	271	−9,800	260	36,400
268. Computer Operators	−17	269	−30,400	265	181,800
269. Textile, Apparel, and Furnishings Occupations	−14	266	−152,500	270	1,084,700
270. Data Entry and Information Processing Workers	−18	270	−114,300	269	632,800
271. Farmers, Ranchers, and Agricultural Managers	−17	268	−227,000	271	1,376,000

Section One

Descriptions of 101 Fastest Growing Jobs

This is the book's main section. It contains descriptions for 101 major occupations that have high projected growth rates and large projected numbers of openings. The jobs are arranged in alphabetical order. Refer to the table of contents for a list of the jobs and the page numbers where their descriptions begin.

The table of contents can also help you identify jobs you want to explore. If you are interested in medical jobs, for example, you can go through the list and quickly find those you want to learn more about. Also, you may spot other jobs that might be interesting, and you should consider those as well. Read the descriptions for any jobs that sound interesting.

While the descriptions in this section are easy to understand, the introduction to this book provides additional information for interpreting them. When reading the descriptions, keep in mind that they present information that is the average for the country. Conditions in your area and with specific employers may be quite different.

(continued)

(continued)

Also, you may come across jobs that sound interesting but require additional training or education. Don't eliminate them too soon. There are many ways to obtain training and education, and most people change jobs and careers many times. You probably have more skills than you realize that can transfer to new jobs, so consider taking some chances. Get out of your rut. Do what it takes to fulfill your dreams. Be creative. You often have more opportunities than barriers, but you have to go out and find the opportunities.

Accountants and Auditors

(O*NET 13-2011.01 and 13-2011.02)

Significant Points

- Most jobs require at least a bachelor's degree in accounting or a related field.

- Overall job opportunities should be favorable, although jobseekers who obtain professional recognition through certification or licensure, a master's degree, proficiency in accounting and auditing computer software, or specialized expertise will have an advantage.

- An increase in the number of businesses, changing financial laws and regulations, and increased scrutiny of company finances will drive growth of accountants and auditors.

Nature of the Work

Accountants and auditors help to ensure that the nation's firms are run efficiently, its public records kept accurately, and its taxes paid properly and on time. They perform these vital functions by offering an increasingly wide array of business and accounting services to their clients. These services include public, management, and government accounting, as well as internal auditing. Beyond the fundamental tasks of the occupation—preparing, analyzing, and verifying financial documents in order to provide information to clients—many accountants now are required to possess a wide range of knowledge and skills. Accountants and auditors are broadening the services they offer to include budget analysis, financial and investment planning, information technology consulting, and limited legal services.

Specific job duties vary widely among the four major fields of accounting: *public, management, government, and internal.*

Public accountants perform a broad range of accounting, auditing, tax, and consulting activities for their clients, who may be corporations, governments, nonprofit organizations, or individuals. For example, some public accountants concentrate on tax matters, such as advising companies of the tax advantages and disadvantages of certain business decisions and preparing individual income tax returns. Others offer advice in areas such as compensation or employee healthcare benefits, the design of accounting and data-processing systems, and the selection of controls to safeguard assets. Still others audit clients' financial statements and report to investors and authorities that the statements have been correctly prepared and reported. Public accountants, many of whom are Certified Public Accountants (CPAs), generally have their own businesses or work for public accounting firms.

Some public accountants specialize in forensic accounting—investigating and interpreting white collar crimes such as securities fraud and embezzlement, bankruptcies and contract disputes, and other complex and possibly criminal financial transactions, such as money laundering by organized criminals. Forensic accountants combine their knowledge of accounting and finance with law and investigative techniques in order to determine if illegal activity is going on. Many forensic accountants work closely with law enforcement personnel and lawyers during investigations and often appear as expert witnesses during trials.

In response to the recent accounting scandals, new federal legislation restricts the nonauditing services that public accountants can provide to clients. If an accounting firm audits a client's financial statements, that same firm cannot provide advice in the areas of human resources, technology, investment banking, or legal matters, although accountants may still advise on tax issues, such as establishing a tax shelter. Accountants may still advise other clients in these areas, or may provide advice within their own firm.

Management accountants—also called cost, managerial, industrial, corporate, or private accountants—record and analyze the financial information of the companies for which they work. Other responsibilities include budgeting, performance evaluation, cost management, and asset management. Usually, management accountants are part of executive teams involved in strategic planning or new-product development. They analyze and interpret the financial information that corporate executives need to make sound business decisions. They also prepare financial reports for nonmanagement groups, including stockholders, creditors, regulatory agencies, and tax authorities. Within accounting departments, they may work in various areas, including financial analysis, planning and budgeting, and cost accounting.

Government accountants and auditors work in the public sector, maintaining and examining the records of government agencies and auditing private businesses and individuals whose activities are subject to government regulations or taxation. Accountants employed by federal, state, and local governments guarantee that revenues are received and expenditures are made in accordance with laws and regulations. Those who are employed by the federal government may work as Internal Revenue Service agents or in financial management, financial institution examination, or budget analysis and administration.

Internal auditors verify the accuracy of their organization's internal records and check for mismanagement, waste, or fraud. Internal auditing is an increasingly important area of accounting and auditing. Internal auditors examine and evaluate their firms' financial and information systems, management procedures, and internal controls to ensure that records are accurate and controls are adequate to protect against fraud and waste. They also review company operations—evaluating their efficiency, effectiveness, and compliance with corporate policies and procedures, laws, and government regulations. There are many types of highly specialized auditors, such as electronic data-processing, environmental, engineering, legal, insurance premium, bank, and healthcare auditors. As computer systems make information timelier, internal auditors help managers to base their decisions on actual data, rather than personal observation. Internal auditors also may recommend controls for their organization's computer system to ensure the reliability of the system and the integrity of the data.

Computers are rapidly changing the nature of the work for most accountants and auditors. With the aid of special software packages, accountants summarize transactions in standard formats for financial records and organize data in special formats for financial analysis. These accounting packages greatly reduce the amount of tedious manual work associated with data management and recordkeeping. Computers enable accountants and auditors to be more mobile and to use their clients' computer systems to extract information from databases and the Internet. As a result, a growing number of accountants and auditors with extensive computer skills specialize in correcting problems with software or in developing software to meet unique data management and analytical needs. Accountants also are beginning to perform more technical duties, such as implementing, controlling, and auditing systems and networks, and developing technology plans and budgets.

Increasingly, accountants also are assuming the role of a personal financial advisor. They not only provide clients with accounting and tax help, but also help them develop personal budgets, manage assets and investments, plan for retirement, and recognize and reduce exposure to risks. This role is a response to client demands for a single trustworthy individual or firm to meet all of their financial needs. However, accountants are restricted from providing these services to clients whose financial statements they also prepare.

Working Conditions

Most accountants and auditors work in a typical office setting. Self-employed accountants may be able to do part of their work at home. Accountants and auditors employed by public accounting firms and government agencies may travel frequently to perform audits at branches of their firm, clients' places of business, or government facilities.

Most accountants and auditors generally work a standard 40-hour week, but many work longer hours, particularly if they are self-employed and have numerous clients. Tax specialists often work long hours during the tax season.

Employment

Accountants and auditors held about 1.1 million jobs in 2002. They worked throughout private industry and government, but 1 out of 5 wage and salary accountants worked for accounting, tax preparation, bookkeeping, and payroll services firms. Approximately 1 out of 10 accountants or auditors were self-employed.

Many accountants and auditors are unlicensed management accountants, internal auditors, or government accountants and auditors; however, a large number are licensed Certified Public Accountants. Most accountants and auditors work in

urban areas, where public accounting firms and central or regional offices of businesses are concentrated.

Some individuals with backgrounds in accounting and auditing are full-time college and university faculty; others teach part time while working as self-employed accountants or employed as accountants for private industry or government.

Training, Other Qualifications, and Advancement

Most accountant and auditor positions require at least a bachelor's degree in accounting or a related field. Beginning accounting and auditing positions in the federal government, for example, usually require 4 years of college (including 24 semester hours in accounting or auditing) or an equivalent combination of education and experience. Some employers prefer applicants with a master's degree in accounting, or with a master's degree in business administration with a concentration in accounting.

Previous experience in accounting or auditing can help an applicant get a job. Many colleges offer students an opportunity to gain experience through summer or part-time internship programs conducted by public accounting or business firms. In addition, practical knowledge of computers and their applications in accounting and internal auditing is a great asset for jobseekers in the accounting field.

Professional recognition through certification or licensure provides a distinct advantage in the job market. CPAs are licensed by a State Board of Accountancy. The vast majority of states require CPA candidates to be college graduates, but a few states substitute a number of years of public accounting experience for a college degree. As of early 2003, based on recommendations made by the American Institute of Certified Public Accountants (AICPA), 42 states and the District of Columbia required CPA candidates to complete 150 semester hours of college coursework—an additional 30 hours beyond the usual 4-year bachelor's degree. Another five states—Arizona, Minnesota, New Mexico, New York, and Virginia—have adopted similar legislation that will become effective between 2004 and 2009. Colorado, Delaware, New Hampshire, and Vermont are the only states that do not require 150 semester hours. Many schools have altered their curricula accordingly with most programs offering masters degrees as part of the 150 hours, and prospective accounting majors should carefully research accounting curricula and the requirements of any states in which they hope to become licensed.

All states use the four-part Uniform CPA Examination prepared by the AICPA. The 2-day CPA examination is rigorous, and only about one-quarter of those who take it each year passes every part they attempt. Candidates are not required to pass all four parts at once, but most states require candidates to pass at least two parts for partial credit and to complete all four sections within a certain period. Most states also require applicants for a CPA certificate to have some accounting experience. In May 2004, the CPA exam will become computerized and offered quarterly at various testing centers throughout the United states.

The AICPA also offers members with valid CPA certificates the option to receive the Accredited in Business Valuation (ABV), Certified Information Technology Professional (CITP), or Personal Financial Specialist (PFS) designations. The addition of these designations to the CPA distinguishes those accountants with a certain level of expertise in the nontraditional areas in which accountants are practicing more frequently. The ABV designation requires a written exam, as well as completion of a minimum of 10 business valuation projects that demonstrate a candidate's experience and competence. The CITP requires payment of a fee, a written statement of intent, and the achievement of a set number of points awarded for business experience and education. Those who do not meet the required number of points may substitute a written exam. Candidates for the PFS designation also must achieve a certain level of points, based on experience and education, and must pass a written exam and submit references.

Nearly all states require CPAs and other public accountants to complete a certain number of hours of continuing professional education before their licenses can be renewed. The professional associations representing accountants sponsor numerous courses, seminars, group study programs, and other forms of continuing education.

Accountants and auditors also can seek to obtain other forms of credentials from professional societies on a voluntary basis. Voluntary certification can attest to professional competence in a specialized field of accounting and auditing. It also can certify that a recognized level of professional competence has been achieved by accountants and auditors who have acquired some skills on the job, without the formal education or public accounting work experience needed to meet the rigorous standards required to take the CPA examination.

The Institute of Management Accountants (IMA) confers the Certified Management Accountant (CMA) designation upon applicants who complete a bachelor's degree or attain a minimum score on specified graduate school entrance exams. Applicants, who must have worked at least 2 years in management accounting, also must pass a four-part examination, agree to meet continuing education requirements, and comply with standards of professional conduct. The CMA program is administered by the Institute of Certified Management Accountants, an affiliate of the IMA.

Graduates from accredited colleges and universities who have worked for 2 years as internal auditors and have passed a four-part examination may earn the Certified Internal Auditor (CIA) designation from the Institute of Internal Auditors (IIA). The IIA recently implemented three new specialty designations—Certification in Control Self-Assessment (CCSA), Certified Government Auditing Professional (CGAP), and Certified Financial Services Auditor (CFSA). Requirements are similar to those of the CIA. The Information Systems Audit and Control Association confers the Certified Information Systems Auditor (CISA) designation upon candidates who pass an examination and have 5 years of experience in auditing information systems. Auditing or data-processing experience and a college education may be substituted for up to 2 years of work experience in this program. For instance, an internal auditor might be a CPA, CIA, and CISA.

The Accreditation Council for Accountancy and Taxation, a satellite organization of the National Society of Public Accountants, confers three designations—Accredited Business Accountant (ABA), Accredited Tax Advisor (ATA), and Accredited Tax Preparer (ATP)—on accountants specializing in tax preparation for small- and medium-sized businesses. Candidates for the ABA must pass an exam, while candidates for the ATA and ATP must complete the required coursework and pass an exam. Often, a practitioner will hold multiple licenses and designations.

The Association of Government Accountants grants the Certified Government Financial Manager (CGFM) designation for accountants, auditors, and other government financial personnel at the federal, state, and local levels. Candidates must have a minimum of a bachelor's degree, 24 hours of study in financial management, and 2 years' experience in government, and must pass a series of three exams. The exams cover topics in governmental environment; governmental accounting, financial reporting, and budgeting; and financial management and control.

Persons planning a career in accounting should have an aptitude for mathematics and be able to analyze, compare, and interpret facts and figures quickly. They must be able to clearly communicate both written and verbally the results of their work to clients and managers. Accountants and auditors must be good at working with people, as well as with business systems and computers. At a minimum, accountants should be familiar with basic accounting software packages. Because financial decisions are made based on their statements and services, accountants and auditors should have high standards of integrity.

Capable accountants and auditors may advance rapidly; those having inadequate academic preparation may be assigned routine jobs and find promotion difficult. Many graduates of junior colleges and business and correspondence schools, as well as bookkeepers and accounting clerks who meet the education and experience requirements set by their employers, can obtain junior accounting positions and advance to positions with more responsibilities by demonstrating their accounting skills on the job.

Beginning public accountants usually start by assisting with work for several clients. They may advance to positions with more responsibility in 1 or 2 years, and to senior positions within another few years. Those who excel may become supervisors, managers, or partners; open their own public accounting firm; or transfer to executive positions in management accounting or internal auditing in private firms.

Management accountants often start as cost accountants, junior internal auditors, or trainees for other accounting positions. As they rise through the organization, they may advance to accounting manager, chief cost accountant, budget director, or manager of internal auditing. Some become controllers, treasurers, financial vice presidents, chief financial officers, or corporation presidents. Many senior corporation executives have a background in accounting, internal auditing, or finance.

In general, public accountants, management accountants, and internal auditors have much occupational mobility. Practitioners often shift into management accounting or internal auditing from public accounting, or between internal auditing and management accounting. However, it is less common for accountants and auditors to move from either management accounting or internal auditing into public accounting.

Job Outlook

Employment of accountants and auditors is expected to grow about as fast as the average for all occupations through the year 2012. An increase in the number of businesses, changing financial laws and regulations, and increased scrutiny of company finances will drive growth. In addition to openings resulting from growth, the need to replace accountants and auditors who retire or transfer to other occupations will produce numerous job openings in this large occupation.

As the economy grows, the number of business establishments will increase, requiring more accountants and auditors to set up books, prepare taxes, and provide management advice. As these businesses grow, the volume and complexity of information developed by accountants and auditors regarding costs, expenditures, and taxes will increase as well. Increased need for accountants and auditors will arise from changes in legislation related to taxes, financial reporting standards, business investments, mergers, and other financial matters. The growth of international business also has led to more demand for accounting expertise and services related to international trade and accounting rules, as well as to international mergers and acquisitions. These trends should create more jobs for accountants and auditors.

As a result of the recent accounting scandals, federal legislation was enacted to increase penalties, and make company executives personally responsible for falsely reporting financial information. These changes should lead to increased scrutiny of company finances and accounting procedures, and should create opportunities for accountants and auditors, particularly Certified Public Accountants, to more thoroughly audit financial records. In order to ensure finances comply with the law before public accountants conduct audits, management accountants and internal auditors will increasingly be needed to discover and eliminate fraud. And, in an effort to make government agencies more efficient and accountable, demand for government accountants should increase.

Increased awareness of financial crimes such as embezzlement, bribery, and securities fraud will also increase the demand for forensic accountants to detect illegal financial activity by individuals, companies, and organized crime rings. Computer technology has made these crimes easier to commit, and it is on the rise. But, development of new computer software and electronic surveillance technology has also made tracking down financial criminals easier, thus increasing the ease and likelihood that forensic accountants will discover their crimes. As success rates of investigations grow, demand will also grow for forensic accountants.

The changing role of accountants and auditors also will spur job growth, although this growth will be limited as a result of financial scandals. In response to demand, some accountants were offering more financial management and consulting services as they assumed a greater advisory role and developed more sophisticated accounting systems. Since federal legislation now prohibits accountants from providing nontraditional services to clients whose books they audit, opportunities for accountants to do non-audit work could be limited. However, accountants will still be able to advise on other financial matters for clients that are not publicly traded companies, and for nonaudit clients, but growth in these areas will be slower than in the past. Also, due to the increasing popularity of tax preparation firms and computer software, accountants will shift away from tax preparation. As computer programs continue to simplify some accounting-related tasks, clerical staff will increasingly handle many routine calculations.

Overall, job opportunities for accountants and auditors should be favorable. After most states instituted the 150-hour rule for CPAs, enrollment in accounting programs declined; however, enrollment is slowly beginning to grow again as more students are attracted to the profession because of the attention from the accounting scandals. Those who pursue a CPA should have excellent job prospects. However, many accounting graduates are instead pursuing other certifications such as the CMA and CIA, so competition could be greater in management accounting and internal auditing than in public accounting. Regardless of specialty, accountants and auditors who have earned professional recognition through certification or licensure should have the best job prospects. Applicants with a master's degree in accounting, or a master's degree in business administration with a concentration in accounting, also will have an advantage. In the aftermath of the accounting scandals, professional certification is even more important in order to ensure that accountants' credentials and ethics are sound.

Proficiency in accounting and auditing computer software, or expertise in specialized areas such as international business, specific industries, or current legislation, may be helpful in landing certain accounting and auditing jobs. In addition, employers increasingly seek applicants with strong interpersonal and communication skills. Because many accountants work on teams with others from different backgrounds, they must be able to communicate accounting and financial information clearly and concisely. Regardless of one's qualifications, however, competition will remain keen for the most prestigious jobs in major accounting and business firms.

Earnings

In 2002, the median wage and salary annual earnings of accountants and auditors were $47,000. The middle half of the occupation earned between $37,210 and $61,630. The top 10 percent of accountants and auditors earned more than $82,730, and the bottom 10 percent earned less than $30,320. In 2002, median annual earnings in the industries employing the largest numbers of accountants and auditors were:

Federal government	$51,070
Accounting, tax preparation, bookkeeping, and payroll services	49,520
Management of companies and enterprises	49,110
Local government	44,690
State government	42,680

According to a salary survey conducted by the National Association of Colleges and Employers, bachelor's degree candidates in accounting received starting offers averaging $40,647 a year in 2003; master's degree candidates in accounting were initially offered $42,241.

According to a 2003 salary survey conducted by Robert Half International, a staffing services firm specializing in accounting and finance, accountants and auditors with up to 1 year of experience earned between $29,500 and $40,500. Those with 1 to 3 years of experience earned between $34,000 and $49,500. Senior accountants and auditors earned between $41,000 and $61,500; managers earned between $47,500 and $78,750; and directors of accounting and auditing earned between $66,750 and $197,500 a year. The variation in salaries reflects differences in size of firm, location, level of education, and professional credentials.

In the federal government, the starting annual salary for junior accountants and auditors was $23,442 in 2003. Candidates who had a superior academic record might start at $29,037, while applicants with a master's degree or 2 years of professional experience usually began at $35,519. Beginning salaries were slightly higher in selected areas where the prevailing local pay level was higher. Accountants employed by the federal government in nonsupervisory, supervisory, and managerial positions averaged $69,370 a year in 2003; auditors averaged $73,247.

Related Occupations

Accountants and auditors design internal control systems and analyze financial data. Others for whom training in accounting is valuable include budget analysts; cost estimators; loan officers; financial analysts and personal financial advisors; tax examiners, collectors, and revenue agents; bill and account collectors; and bookkeeping, accounting, and auditing clerks. Recently, accountants have assumed the role of management analysts and are involved in the design, implementation, and maintenance of accounting software systems. Others who perform similar work include computer programmers, computer software engineers, and computer support specialists and systems administrators.

Sources of Additional Information

Information on accredited accounting programs can be obtained from:

- AACSB International—Association to Advance Collegiate Schools of Business, 600 Emerson Rd., Suite 300, St. Louis, MO 63141. Internet: http://www.aacsb.edu/accreditation/AccreditedMembers.asp

Information about careers in certified public accounting and CPA standards and examinations may be obtained from:

- American Institute of Certified Public Accountants, 1211 Avenue of the Americas, New York, NY 10036. Internet: http://www.aicpa.org

Information on CPA licensure requirements by state may be obtained from:

- National Association of State Boards of Accountancy, 150 Fourth Ave. North, Suite 700, Nashville, TN 37219-2417. Internet: http://www.nasba.org

Information on careers in management accounting and the CMA designation may be obtained from:

- Institute of Management Accountants, 10 Paragon Dr., Montvale, NJ 07645-1760. Internet: http://www.imanet.org

Information on the Accredited in Accountancy, Accredited Business Accountant, Accredited Tax Advisor, or Accredited Tax Preparer designations may be obtained from:

- Accreditation Council for Accountancy and Taxation, 1010 North Fairfax St., Alexandria, VA 22314. Internet: http://www.acatcredentials.org

Information on careers in internal auditing and the CIA designation may be obtained from:

- The Institute of Internal Auditors, 247 Maitland Ave., Altamonte Springs, FL 32701-4201. Internet: http://www.theiia.org

Information on careers in information systems auditing and the CISA designation may be obtained from:

- Information Systems Audit and Control Association, 3701 Algonquin Rd., Suite 1010, Rolling Meadows, IL 60008. Internet: http://www.isaca.org

Information on careers in government accounting and the CGFM designation may be obtained from:

- Association of Government Accountants, 2208 Mount Vernon Ave., Alexandria, VA 22301. Internet: http://www.agacgfm.org

Information on obtaining an accounting or auditing position with the federal government is available from the U.S. Office of Personnel Management (OPM) through a telephone-based system. Consult your telephone directory under U.S. Government for a local number or call (703) 724-1850; Federal Relay Service: (800) 877-8339. The first number is not tollfree, and charges may result. Information also is available from the OPM Internet site: http://www.usajobs.opm.gov.

Administrative Services Managers

(O*NET 11-3011.00)

Significant Points

- Administrative services managers work in private industry and government and have a wide range of responsibilities, experience, earnings, and education.

- Applicants face keen competition due to the substantial supply of competent, experienced workers seeking managerial jobs.

Nature of the Work

Administrative services managers perform a broad range of duties in virtually every sector of the economy. They coordinate and direct support services to organizations as diverse as insurance companies, computer manufacturers, and government offices. These workers manage the many services that allow organizations to operate efficiently, such as secretarial and reception, administration, payroll, conference planning and travel, information and data processing, mail, materials scheduling and distribution, printing and reproduction, records management, telecommunications management, security, parking, and personal property procurement, supply, and disposal.

Specific duties for these managers vary by degree of responsibility and authority. First-line administrative services managers directly supervise a staff that performs various support services. Mid-level managers, on the other hand, develop departmental plans, set goals and deadlines, implement procedures to improve productivity and customer service, and define the responsibilities of supervisory-level managers. Some mid-level administrative services managers oversee first-line supervisors from various departments, including the clerical staff. Mid-level managers also may be involved in the hiring and dismissal of employees, but they generally have no role in the formulation of personnel policy. Some of these managers advance to upper level positions, such as vice president of administrative services.

In small organizations, a single administrative services manager may oversee all support services. In larger ones, however, first-line administrative services managers often report to mid-level managers who, in turn, report to owners or top-level managers. As the size of the firm increases, administrative services managers are more likely to specialize in specific support activities. For example, some administrative services managers work primarily as office managers, contract administrators, or unclaimed property officers. In many cases, the duties of these administrative services managers are similar to those of other managers and supervisors.

Because of the range of administrative services required by organizations, the nature of these managerial jobs also varies significantly. Administrative services managers who work as contract administrators, for instance, oversee the preparation, analysis, negotiation, and review of contracts related to the purchase or sale of equipment, materials, supplies, products, or services. In addition, some administrative services managers acquire, distribute, and store supplies, while others dispose of surplus property or oversee the disposal of unclaimed property.

Administrative services managers who work as facility managers plan, design, and manage buildings and grounds in addition to people. They are responsible for coordinating the physical workplace with the people and work of an organization. This task requires integrating the principles of business administration, architecture, and behavioral and engineering science. Although the specific tasks assigned to facility managers vary substantially depending on the organization, the duties fall into several categories, relating to operations and maintenance, real estate, project planning and management, communication, finance, quality assessment, facility function, technology integration, and management of human and environmental factors. Tasks within these broad categories may include space and workplace planning, budgeting, purchase and sale of real estate, lease management, renovations, or architectural planning and design. Facility managers may suggest and oversee renovation projects for a variety of reasons, ranging from improving efficiency to ensuring that facilities meet government regulations and environmental, health, and security standards. Additionally, facility managers continually monitor the facility to ensure that it remains safe, secure, and well-maintained. Often, the facility manager is responsible for directing staff, including maintenance, grounds, and custodial workers.

Working Conditions

Administrative services managers generally work in comfortable offices. Managers involved in contract administration and personal property procurement, use, and disposal may travel between their home office, branch offices, vendors' offices, and property sales sites. Also, facility managers who are responsible for the design of workspaces may spend time at construction sites and may travel between different facilities while monitoring the work of maintenance, grounds, and custodial staffs. However, new technology has increased the number of managers who telecommute from home or other offices, and teleconferencing has reduced the need for travel.

Most administrative services managers work a standard 40-hour week. However, uncompensated overtime frequently is required to resolve problems and meet deadlines. Facility managers often are "on call" to address a variety of problems that can arise in a facility during nonwork hours.

Employment

Administrative services managers held about 321,000 jobs in 2002. About 9 out of 10 worked in service-providing industries, including federal, state, and local government, health services, financial services, professional, scientific, and technical services, and education. Most of the remaining workers worked in manufacturing industries.

Training, Other Qualifications, and Advancement

Educational requirements for these managers vary widely, depending on the size and complexity of the organization. In small organizations, experience may be the only requirement needed to enter a position as office manager. When an opening in administrative services management occurs, the office manager may be promoted to the position based on past performance. In large organizations, however, administrative services managers normally are hired from outside and each position has formal education and experience requirements. Some administrative services managers have advanced degrees.

Specific requirements vary by job responsibility. For first-line administrative services managers of secretarial, mailroom, and related support activities, many employers prefer an associate degree in business or management, although a high school diploma may suffice when combined with appropriate experience. For managers of audiovisual, graphics, and other technical activities, postsecondary technical school training is preferred. Managers of highly complex services, such as contract administration, generally need at least a bachelor's degree in business, human resources, or finance. Regardless of major, the curriculum should include courses in office technology, accounting, business mathematics, computer applications, human resources, and business law. Most facility managers have an undergraduate or graduate degree in engineering, architecture, construction management, business administration, or facility management. Many have a background in real estate, construction, or interior design, in addition to managerial experience.

Whatever the manager's educational background, it must be accompanied by related work experience reflecting demonstrated ability. For this reason, many administrative services managers have advanced through the ranks of their organization, acquiring work experience in various administrative positions before assuming first-line supervisory duties. All managers who oversee departmental supervisors should be familiar with office procedures and equipment. Managers of personal property acquisition and disposal need experience in purchasing and sales, and knowledge of a variety of supplies, machinery, and equipment. Managers concerned with supply, inventory, and distribution should be experienced in receiving, warehousing, packaging, shipping, transportation, and related operations. Contract administrators may have worked as contract specialists, cost analysts, or procurement specialists. Managers of unclaimed property often have experience in insurance claims analysis and records management.

Persons interested in becoming administrative services managers should have good communication skills and be able to establish effective working relationships with many different people, ranging from managers, supervisors, and professionals, to clerks and blue-collar workers. They should be analytical, detail-oriented, flexible, and decisive. They must also be able to coordinate several activities at once, quickly analyze and resolve specific problems, and cope with deadlines.

Most administrative services managers in small organizations advance by moving to other management positions or to a larger organization. Advancement is easier in large firms that employ several levels of administrative services managers. Attainment of the Certified Administrative Manager (CAM) designation offered by the Institute of Certified Professional Managers, through work experience and successful completion of examinations, can increase a manager's advancement potential. In addition, a master's degree in business administration or related field enhances a first-level manager's opportunities to advance to a mid-level management position, such as director of administrative services, and eventually to a top-level management position, such as executive vice president for administrative services. Those with enough money and experience can establish their own management consulting firm.

Advancement of facility managers is based on the practices and size of individual companies. Some facility managers transfer from other departments within the organization or work their way up from technical positions. Others advance through a progression of facility management positions that offer additional responsibilities. Completion of the competency-based professional certification program offered by the International Facility Management Association can give prospective candidates an advantage. In order to qualify for this Certified Facility Manager (CFM) designation, applicants must meet certain educational and experience requirements.

Job Outlook

Employment of administrative services managers is projected to grow about as fast as the average for all occupations through 2012. Like persons seeking other managerial positions, applicants face keen competition because there are more competent, experienced workers seeking jobs than there are positions available. However, demand should be strong for facility managers because businesses increasingly are realizing the importance of maintaining, securing, and efficiently operating their facilities, which are very large investments for most organizations. Administrative services managers employed in management services and management consulting also should be in demand, as public and private organizations continue to streamline and, in some cases, contract out administrative services functions in an effort to cut costs.

At the same time, continuing corporate restructuring and increasing utilization of office technology should result in a flatter organizational structure with fewer levels of management, reducing the need for some middle management positions. This should adversely affect administrative services managers who oversee first-line mangers. Because many administrative services managers have a wide range of responsibilities, however, the effects of these changes on employment should be less severe than for other middle managers who specialize in only certain functions. In addition to new administrative services management jobs created over the 2002-12 projection period, many job openings will stem from the need to replace workers who transfer to other jobs, retire, or stop working for other reasons.

Earnings

Earnings of administrative services managers vary greatly depending on the employer, the specialty, and the geographic area. In general, however, median annual earnings of administrative services managers in 2002 were $52,500. The middle 50 percent earned between $36,190 and $74,590. The lowest 10 percent earned less than $26,120, and the highest 10 percent earned more than $99,870. Median annual earnings in the industries employing the largest numbers of these managers in 2002 are shown below:

Management of companies and enterprises $66,700
Elementary and secondary schools 59,220
Colleges, universities, and professional schools 56,960
State government...55,710
Local government 51,570

In the federal government, contract specialists in nonsupervisory, supervisory, and managerial positions earned an average of $66,309 a year in 2003. Corresponding averages were $63,509 for facilities operations, $62,552 for industrial property managers, $58,880 for property disposal specialists, $62,751 for administrative officers, and $52,824 for support services administrators.

Related Occupations

Administrative services managers direct and coordinate support services and oversee the purchase, use, and disposal of personal property. Occupations with similar functions include office and administrative support worker supervisors and managers; cost estimators; property, real estate, and community association managers; purchasing managers, buyers, and purchasing agents; and top executives.

Sources of Additional Information

For information about careers and education and degree programs in facility management, as well as the Certified Facility Manager designation, contact:

● International Facility Management Association, 1 East Greenway Plaza, Suite 1100, Houston, TX 77046-0194. Internet: http://www.ifma.org

General information regarding facility management and a list of facility management education and degree programs may be obtained from:

● Association of Higher Education Facilities Officers, 1643 Prince St., Alexandria, VA 22314-2818. Internet: http://www.appa.org

For information about the Certified Manager or Certified Administrative Manager designations, contact:

● Institute of Certified Professional Managers, James Madison University, College of Business, Harrisonburg, VA 22807. Internet: http://cob.jmu.edu/icpm

Advertising, Marketing, Promotions, Public Relations, and Sales Managers

(O*NET 11-2011.00, 11-2021.00, 11-2022.00, and 11-2031.00)

Significant Points

● Keen competition for jobs is expected.

● College graduates with related experience, a high level of creativity, and strong communication skills should have the best job opportunities.

● High earnings, substantial travel, and long hours, including evenings and weekends, are common.

Nature of the Work

The objective of any firm is to market and sell its products or services profitably. In small firms, the owner or chief executive officer might assume all advertising, promotions, marketing, sales, and public relations responsibilities. In large firms, which may offer numerous products and services nationally or even worldwide, an executive vice president directs overall advertising, promotions, marketing, sales, and public relations policies. Advertising, marketing, promotions, public relations, and sales managers coordinate the market research, marketing strategy, sales, advertising, promotion, pricing, product development, and public relations activities.

Managers oversee advertising and promotion staffs, which usually are small, except in the largest firms. In a small firm, managers may serve as a liaison between the firm and the advertising or promotion agency to which many advertising or promotional functions are contracted out. In larger firms, advertising managers oversee in-house account, creative, and media services departments. The *account executive* manages the account services department, assesses the need for advertising, and, in advertising agencies, maintains the accounts of clients. The creative services department develops the subject matter and presentation of advertising. The *creative director* oversees the copy chief, art director, and associated staff. The *media director* oversees planning groups that select the communication media—for example, radio, television, newspapers, magazines, Internet, or outdoor signs—to disseminate the advertising.

Promotions managers supervise staffs of promotion specialists. They direct promotion programs that combine advertising with purchase incentives to increase sales. In an effort to establish closer contact with purchasers—dealers, distributors, or consumers—promotion programs may involve direct mail, telemarketing, television or radio advertising, catalogs, exhibits, inserts in newspapers, Internet advertisements or Web sites, instore displays or product endorsements, and special events. Purchase incentives may include discounts, samples, gifts, rebates, coupons, sweepstakes, and contests.

Marketing managers develop the firm's detailed marketing strategy. With the help of subordinates, including *product development managers* and *market research managers*, they determine the demand for products and services offered by the firm and its competitors. In addition, they identify potential markets—for example, business firms, wholesalers, retailers, government, or the general public. Marketing managers develop pricing strategy with an eye towards maximizing the firm's share of the market and its profits while ensuring that the firm's customers are satisfied. In collaboration with sales, product development, and other managers, they monitor trends that indicate the need for new products and services and oversee product development. Marketing managers work with advertising and promotion managers to promote the firm's products and services and to attract potential users.

Public relations managers supervise public relations specialists. These managers direct publicity programs to a targeted public. They often specialize in a specific area, such as crisis management—or in a specific industry, such as healthcare. They use every available communication medium in their effort to maintain the support of the specific group upon whom their organization's success depends, such as consumers, stockholders, or the general public. For example, public relations managers may clarify or justify the firm's point of view on health or environmental issues to community or special interest groups.

Public relations managers also evaluate advertising and promotion programs for compatibility with public relations efforts and serve as the eyes and ears of top management. They observe social, economic, and political trends that might ultimately affect the firm and make recommendations to enhance the firm's image based on those trends.

Public relations managers may confer with labor relations managers to produce internal company communications—such as newsletters about employee-management relations—and with financial managers to produce company reports. They assist company executives in drafting speeches, arranging interviews, and maintaining other forms of public contact; oversee company archives; and respond to information requests. In addition, some handle special events such as sponsorship of races, parties introducing new products, or other activities the firm supports in order to gain public attention through the press without advertising directly.

Sales managers direct the firm's sales program. They assign sales territories, set goals, and establish training programs for the sales representatives. Managers advise the sales representatives on ways to improve their sales performance. In large, multiproduct firms, they oversee regional and local sales managers and their staffs. Sales managers maintain contact with dealers and distributors. They analyze sales statistics gathered by their staffs to determine sales potential and inventory requirements and monitor the preferences of customers. Such information is vital to develop products and maximize profits.

Working Conditions

Advertising, marketing, promotions, public relations, and sales managers work in offices close to those of top managers. Long hours, including evenings and weekends are common. About 44 percent of advertising, marketing, and public relations managers worked more than 40 hours a week in 2002. Working under pressure is unavoidable when schedules change and problems arise, but deadlines and goals must still be met.

Substantial travel may be involved. For example, attendance at meetings sponsored by associations or industries often is mandatory. Sales managers travel to national, regional, and local offices and to various dealers and distributors. Advertising and promotions managers may travel to meet with clients or representatives of communications media. At times, public relations managers travel to meet with special interest groups or government officials. Job transfers between headquarters and regional offices are common, particularly among sales managers.

Employment

Advertising, marketing, promotions, public relations, and sales managers held about 700,000 jobs in 2002. The following tabulation shows the distribution of jobs by occupational specialty.

Sales managers	343,000
Marketing managers	203,000
Advertising and promotions managers	85,000
Public relations managers	69,000

These managers were found in virtually every industry. Sales managers held almost half of the jobs; most were employed in manufacturing, wholesale and retail trade, and finance and insurance industries. Marketing managers held more one-fourth of the jobs; manufacturing, and professional, scientific, and technical services industries employed more than one-third of marketing managers. More than one-third of advertising and promotions managers worked in professional, scientific, and technical services, and information industries, including advertising and related services, and publishing industries. Most public relations managers were employed in services industries, such as other services (except government), professional, scientific, and technical services, finance and insurance, health care and social assistance services, and educational services.

Training, Other Qualifications, and Advancement

A wide range of educational backgrounds is suitable for entry into advertising, marketing, promotions, public relations, and sales managerial jobs, but many employers prefer those with experience in related occupations plus a broad liberal arts background. A bachelor's degree in sociology, psychology, literature, journalism, or philosophy, among other subjects, is acceptable. However, requirements vary, depending upon the particular job.

For marketing, sales, and promotions management positions, some employers prefer a bachelor's or master's degree in business administration with an emphasis on marketing. Courses in business law, economics, accounting, finance, mathematics, and statistics are advantageous. In highly technical industries, such as computer and electronics manufacturing, a bachelor's degree in engineering or science, combined with a master's degree in business administration, is preferred.

For advertising management positions, some employers prefer a bachelor's degree in advertising or journalism. A course of study should include marketing, consumer behavior, market research, sales, communication methods and technology, and visual arts-for example, art history and photography.

For public relations management positions, some employers prefer a bachelor's or master's degree in public relations or journalism. The applicant's curriculum should include courses in advertising, business administration, public affairs, public speaking, political science, and creative and technical writing.

For all these specialties, courses in management and completion of an internship while in school are highly recommended. Familiarity with word processing and database applications also is important for many positions. Computer skills are vital because marketing, product promotion, and advertising on the Internet are increasingly common. The ability to communicate in a foreign language may open up employment opportunities in many rapidly growing areas around the country, especially in cities with large Spanish-speaking populations.

Most advertising, marketing, promotions, public relations, and sales management positions are filled by promoting experienced staff or related professional personnel. For example, many managers are former sales representatives, purchasing agents, buyers, or product, advertising, promotions, or public relations specialists. In small firms, where the number of positions is limited, advancement to a management position usually comes slowly. In large firms, promotion may occur more quickly.

Although experience, ability, and leadership are emphasized for promotion, advancement can be accelerated by participation in management training programs conducted by many large firms. Many firms also provide their employees with continuing education opportunities, either in-house or at local colleges and universities, and encourage employee participation in seminars and conferences, often provided by professional societies. In collaboration with colleges and universities, numerous marketing and related associations sponsor national or local management training programs. Course subjects include brand and product management, international marketing, sales management evaluation, tele-marketing and direct sales, interactive marketing, promotion, marketing communication, market research, organizational communication, and data processing systems procedures and management. Many firms pay all or part of the cost for those who successfully complete courses.

Some associations offer certification programs for these managers. Certification-a sign of competence and achievement in this field-is particularly important in a competitive job market. While relatively few advertising, marketing, promotions, public relations, and sales managers currently are certified, the number of managers who seek certification is expected to grow. For example, Sales and Marketing Executives International offers a management certification program based on education and job performance. The Public Relations Society of America offers a certification program for public relations practitioners based on years of experience and performance on an examination.

Persons interested in becoming advertising, marketing, promotions, public relations, and sales managers should be mature, creative, highly motivated, resistant to stress, flexible, and decisive. The ability to communicate persuasively, both orally and in writing, with other managers, staff, and the public is vital. These managers also need tact, good judgment, and exceptional ability to establish and maintain effective personal relationships with supervisory and professional staff members and client firms.

Because of the importance and high visibility of their jobs, advertising, marketing, promotions, public relations, and sales managers often are prime candidates for advancement to the highest ranks. Well-trained, experienced, successful managers may be promoted to higher positions in their own, or other, firms. Some become top executives. Managers with extensive experience and sufficient capital may open their own businesses.

Job Outlook

Advertising, marketing, promotions, public relations, and sales manager jobs are highly coveted and will be sought by other managers or highly experienced professionals, resulting in keen competition. College graduates with related experience, a high level of creativity, and strong communication skills should have the best job opportunities. Employers will particularly seek those who have the computer skills to conduct advertising, marketing, promotions, public relations, and sales activities on the Internet.

Employment of advertising, marketing, promotions, public relations, and sales managers is expected to grow faster than the average for all occupations through 2012, spurred by intense domestic and global competition in products and services offered to consumers. However, projected employment growth varies by industry. For example, employment is projected to grow much faster than average in scientific, professional, and related services such as computer systems design and related services and advertising and related services, as businesses increasingly hire contractors for these services instead of additional full-time staff. On the other hand, little or no change in employment is expected in many manufacturing industries.

Earnings

Median annual earnings in 2002 were $57,130 for advertising and promotions managers, $78,250 for marketing managers, $75,040 for sales managers, and $60,640 for public relations managers. Earnings ranged from less than $30,310 for the lowest 10 percent of advertising and promotions managers, to more than $145,600 for the highest 10 percent of marketing and sales managers.

Median annual earnings advertising and promotions managers in 2002 in the advertising and related services industry were $72,630.

Median annual earnings in the industries employing the largest numbers of marketing managers in 2002 were as follows:

Computer systems design and related services	$96,440
Management of companies and enterprises	90,750
Depository credit intermediation	65,960

Median annual earnings in the industries employing the largest numbers of sales managers in 2002 were as follows:

Computer systems design and related services	$102,520
Automobile dealers	91,350
Management of companies and enterprises	87,800
Insurance carriers	80,540
Traveler accommodation	44,560

Median annual earnings of public relations managers in 2002 in colleges, universities, and professional schools were $55,510.

According to a National Association of Colleges and Employers survey, starting salaries for marketing majors graduating in 2003 averaged $34,038; starting salaries for advertising majors averaged $29,495.

Salary levels vary substantially, depending upon the level of managerial responsibility, length of service, education, firm size, location, and industry. For example, manufacturing firms usually pay these managers higher salaries than do nonmanufacturing firms. For sales managers, the size of their sales territory is another important determinant of salary. Many managers earn bonuses equal to 10 percent or more of their salaries.

Related Occupations

Advertising, marketing, promotions, public relations, and sales managers direct the sale of products and services offered by their firms and the communication of information about their firms' activities. Other workers involved with advertising, marketing, promotions, public relations, and sales include actors, producers, and directors; artists and related workers; demonstrators, product promoters, and models; market and survey researchers; public relations specialists; sales representatives, wholesale and manufacturing; and writers and editors.

Sources of Additional Information

For information about careers in advertising management, contact:

- American Association of Advertising Agencies, 405 Lexington Ave., New York, NY 10174-1801. Internet: http://www.aaaa.org

Information about careers and professional certification in public relations management is available from:

- Public Relations Society of America, 33 Irving Place, New York, NY 10003-2376. Internet: http://www.prsa.org

Animal Care and Service Workers

(O*NET 39-2011.00 and 39-2021.00)

Significant Points

- Animal lovers get satisfaction in this occupation, but the work can be unpleasant and physically and emotionally demanding.

- Most workers are trained on the job, but advancement depends on experience, formal training, and continuing education.

- Good employment opportunities are expected for most positions; however, keen competition is expected for jobs as zookeepers.

- Starting salaries are significantly lower than those in many other fields.

Nature of the Work

Many people like animals. But, as pet owners can attest, taking care of them is hard work. Animal care and service workers—which include animal caretakers and animal trainers—train, feed, water, groom, bathe, and exercise animals, and clean, disinfect, and repair their cages. They also play with the animals, provide companionship, and observe behavioral changes that could indicate illness or injury. Boarding kennels, animal shelters, veterinary hospitals and clinics, stables, laboratories, aquariums, and zoological parks all house animals and employ animal care and service workers. Job titles and duties vary by employment setting.

Kennel attendants care for pets while their owners are working or traveling out of town. Beginning attendants perform basic tasks, such as cleaning cages and dog runs, filling food and water dishes, and exercising animals. Experienced attendants may provide basic animal healthcare, as well as bathe animals, trim nails, and attend to other grooming needs. Attendants who work in kennels also may sell pet food and supplies, assist in obedience training, help with breeding, or prepare animals for shipping.

Animal caretakers who specialize in grooming or maintaining a pet's—usually a dog's or cat's—appearance are called *groomers*. Some groomers work in kennels, veterinary clinics, animal shelters, or pet-supply stores. Others operate their own grooming business, typically at a salon, or sometimes by making house calls. Groomers answer telephones, schedule appointments, discuss pets' grooming needs with clients, and collect information on the pet's disposition and its veterinarian. Groomers often are the first to notice a medical problem, such as an ear or skin infection, that requires veterinary care.

Grooming the pet involves several steps: an initial brush-out is followed by an initial clipping of hair or fur using electric clippers, combs, and grooming shears; the groomer then cuts the nails, cleans the ears, bathes, and blow-dries the animal, and ends with a final clipping and styling.

Animal caretakers in animal shelters perform a variety of duties and work with a wide variety of animals. In addition to attending to the basic needs of the animals, caretakers also must keep records of the animals received and discharged and any tests or treatments done. Some vaccinate newly admitted animals under the direction of a veterinarian or veterinary technician, and euthanize (painlessly put to death) seriously ill, severely injured, or unwanted animals. Animal caretakers in animal shelters also interact with the public, answering telephone inquiries, screening applicants for animal adoption, or educating visitors on neutering and other animal health issues.

Caretakers in stables are called *grooms*. They saddle and unsaddle horses, give them rubdowns, and walk them to cool them off after a ride. They also feed, groom, and exercise the horses; clean out stalls and replenish bedding; polish saddles; clean and organize the tack (harness, saddle, and bridle) room; and store supplies and feed. Experienced grooms may help train horses.

In zoos, animal care and service workers, called *keepers*, prepare the diets and clean the enclosures of animals, and sometimes assist in raising them when they are very young. They watch for any signs of illness or injury, monitor eating patterns or any changes in behavior, and record their observations. Keepers also may answer questions and ensure that the visiting public behaves responsibly toward the exhibited animals. Depending on the zoo, keepers may be assigned to work with a broad group of animals such as mammals, birds, or reptiles, or they may work with a limited collection of animals such as primates, large cats, or small mammals.

Animal trainers train animals for riding, security, performance, obedience, or assisting persons with disabilities. Animal trainers do this by accustoming the animal to human voice and contact, and conditioning the animal to respond to commands. Trainers use several techniques to help them train animals. One technique, known as a bridge, is a stimulus that a trainer uses to communicate the precise moment an animal does something correctly. When the animal responds correctly, the trainer gives positive reinforcement in a variety of ways: food, toys, play, rubdowns, or speaking the word "good." Animal training takes place in small steps, and often takes months and even years of repetition. During the conditioning process, trainers provide animals mental stimulation, physical exercise, and husbandry care. In addition to their hands-on work with the animals, trainers often oversee other aspects of the animal's care, such as diet preparation. Trainers often work in competitions or shows, such as the circus or marine parks. Trainers who work in shows also may participate in educational programs for visitors and guests.

Working Conditions

People who love animals get satisfaction from working with and helping them. However, some of the work may be unpleasant, physically and emotionally demanding, and sometimes dangerous. Most animal care and service workers have to clean animal cages and lift, hold, or restrain animals, risking exposure to bites or scratches. Their work often involves kneeling, crawling, repeated bending, and lifting heavy supplies like bales of hay or bags of feed. Animal caretakers must take precautions when treating animals with germicides or insecticides. The work setting can be noisy. Caretakers of show and sports animals travel to competitions.

Animal care and service workers who witness abused animals or who assist in the euthanizing of unwanted, aged, or hopelessly injured animals may experience emotional stress. Those working for private humane societies and municipal animal shelters often deal with the public, some of whom might react with hostility to any implication that the owners are neglecting or abusing their pets. Such workers must maintain a calm and professional demeanor while they enforce the laws regarding animal care.

Animal care and service workers may work outdoors in all kinds of weather. Hours are irregular. Animals must be fed every day, so caretakers often work weekend and holiday shifts. In some animal hospitals, research facilities, and animal shelters, an attendant is on duty 24 hours a day, which means night shifts.

Employment

Animal care and service workers held 151,000 jobs in 2002. Over 80 percent worked as nonfarm animal caretakers; the remainder worked as animal trainers. Nonfarm animal caretakers worked primarily in boarding kennels, animal shelters, stables, grooming shops, animal hospitals, and veterinary offices. A significant number also worked for animal humane societies, racing stables, dog and horse racetrack operators, zoos, theme parks, circuses, and other amusement and recreations services. In 2002, 1 out of every 4 nonfarm animal caretakers was self-employed.

Employment of animal trainers was concentrated in animal services that specialize in training horses, pets, and other animal specialties; and in commercial sports, training racehorses and dogs. Over 2 in 5 animal trainers were self-employed.

Training, Other Qualifications, and Advancement

Most animal care and service workers are trained on the job. Employers generally prefer to hire people with some experience with animals. Some training programs are available for specific types of animal caretakers, such as groomers, but formal training is usually not necessary for entry-level positions. Animal trainers often need to possess a high school diploma or GED equivalent. However, some animal training jobs may require a bachelor's degree and additional skills. For example, a marine mammal trainer usually needs a bachelor's degree in biology, marine biology, animal science, psychology, zoology, or related field, plus strong swimming skills and SCUBA certification. All animal trainers need patience, sensitivity, and experience with problem-solving and animal obedience. Certification is not mandatory for animal trainers, but several organizations offer training programs and certification for prospective animal trainers.

Most pet groomers learn their trade by completing an informal apprenticeship, usually lasting 6 to 10 weeks, under the guidance of an experienced groomer. Prospective groomers also may attend one of the 50 state-licensed grooming schools throughout the country, with programs varying in length from 2 to 18 weeks. The National Dog Groomers Association of America certifies groomers who pass a written examination consisting of 400 questions, including some on cats, with a separate part testing practical skills. Beginning groomers often start by taking on one duty, such as bathing and drying the pet. They eventually assume responsibility for the entire grooming process, from the initial brush-out to the final clipping. Groomers who work in large retail establishments or kennels may, with experience, move into supervisory or managerial positions. Experienced groomers often choose to open their own shops.

Beginning animal caretakers in kennels learn on the job, and usually start by cleaning cages and feeding and watering animals. Kennel caretakers may be promoted to kennel supervisor, assistant manager, and manager, and those with enough capital and experience may open up their own kennels. The American Boarding Kennels Association (ABKA) offers a three-stage, home-study program for individuals interested in pet care. The first two stages address basic and advanced principles of animal care, while the third stage focuses on indepth animal care and good business procedures. Those who complete the third stage and pass oral and written examinations administered by the ABKA become Certified Kennel Operators (CKO).

Some zoological parks may require their caretakers to have a bachelor's degree in biology, animal science, or a related field. Most require experience with animals, preferably as a volunteer or paid keeper in a zoo. Zookeepers may advance to senior keeper, assistant head keeper, head keeper, and assistant curator, but very few openings occur, especially for the higher-level positions.

Animal caretakers in animal shelters are not required to have any specialized training, but training programs and workshops are increasingly available through the Humane Society of the United States, the American Humane Association, and the National Animal Control Association. Workshop topics include cruelty investigations, appropriate methods of euthanasia for shelter animals, proper guidelines for capturing animals, and techniques for preventing problems with wildlife. With experience and additional training, caretakers in animal shelters may become adoption coordinators, animal control officers, emergency rescue drivers, assistant shelter managers, or shelter directors.

Job Outlook

Good job opportunities are expected for most positions because many workers leave this occupation each year. The need to replace workers leaving the field will create the overwhelming majority of job openings. Many animal caretaker jobs require little or no training and have flexible work schedules, attracting people seeking their first job, students, and others looking for temporary or part-time work. The outlook for caretakers in zoos, however, is not favorable due to slow growth in zoo capacity and keen competition for the few positions. Job opportunities for animal care and service workers may vary from year to year, because the strength of the economy affects demand for these workers. Pet owners tend to spend more on animal services when the economy is strong.

In addition to replacement needs, employment of animal care and service workers is expected to grow faster than the average for all occupations through 2012. The pet population—which drives employment of animal caretakers in kennels, grooming shops, animal shelters, and veterinary clinics and hospitals—is expected to increase. Pet owners—including a large number of baby boomers, whose disposable income is expected to increase as they age— are expected to increasingly take advantage of grooming services, daily and overnight boarding services, training services, and veterinary services, resulting in more jobs for animal care and service workers. As many pet owners increasingly consider their pet as part of the family, their demand for luxury animal services and willingness to spend greater amounts of money on their pet will continue to grow.

Demand for animal care and service workers in animal shelters is expected to remain steady. Communities are increasingly recognizing the connection between animal abuse and abuse toward humans, and will probably continue to commit funds to animal shelters, many of which are working hand-in-hand with social service agencies and law enforcement teams. Employment growth of personal and group animal trainers will stem from an increased number of animal owners seeking training services for their pets, including behavior modification and feline behavior training.

Earnings

Median hourly earnings of nonfarm animal caretakers were $8.21 in 2002. The middle 50 percent earned between $6.95 and $10.26. The bottom 10 percent earned less than $6.13, and the top 10 percent earned more than $13.39. Median hourly earnings in the industries employing the largest numbers of nonfarm animal caretakers in 2002 were as follows:

Other personal services	$8.39
Spectator sports	8.24
Social advocacy organizations	7.79
Other miscellaneous store retailers	7.62
Other professional, scientific, and technical services	7.55

Median hourly earnings of animal trainers were $11.03 in 2002. The middle 50 percent earned between $8.21 and $15.96. The lowest 10 percent earned less than $6.87, and the top 10 percent earned more than $21.65.

Related Occupations

Others who work extensively with animals include farmers, ranchers, and agricultural managers; agricultural workers; veterinarians; veterinary technologists and technicians; veterinary assistants; biological scientists; and medical scientists.

Sources of Additional Information

For more information on jobs in animal caretaking and control, and the animal shelter and control personnel training program, write to:

- The Humane Society of the United States, 2100 L St. NW, Washington, DC 20037-1598. Internet: http://www.hsus.org

For career information and information on training, certification, and earnings of animal control officers at federal, state, and local levels, contact:

- National Animal Control Association, P.O. Box 480851, Kansas City, MO 64148-0851. Internet: http://www.nacanet.org

To obtain a listing of state-licensed grooming schools, send a stamped, self-addressed, business-size envelope to:

- National Dog Groomers Association of America, P.O. Box 101, Clark, PA 16113. For information on certification, see the following Internet site: http://www.nauticom.net/www/ndga

For information on becoming an advanced pet care technician at a kennel, contact:

- The American Boarding Kennels Association, 1702 East Pikes Peak Ave., Colorado Springs, CO 80909.

Athletes, Coaches, Umpires, and Related Workers

(O*NET 27-2021.00, 27-2022.00, and 27-2023.00)

Significant Points

- Work hours are often irregular; travel may be extensive.

- Career-ending injuries are always a risk for athletes.

- Job opportunities for coaches, sports instructors, umpires, referees, and sports officials will be best in high school and other amateur sports.

- Competition for professional athlete jobs will continue to be extremely intense; athletes who seek to compete professionally must have extraordinary talent, desire, and dedication to training.

Nature of the Work

We are a nation of sports fans and sports players. Interest in watching sports continues at a high level and recreational participation in sports continues to grow. Some of those who participate in amateur sports dream of becoming paid professional athletes, coaches, or sports officials but very few beat the long and daunting odds of making a full-time living from professional athletics. Those athletes who do make it to professional levels find that careers are short and jobs are insecure. Even though the chances of employment as a professional athlete are slim, there are many opportunities for at least a part-time job related to athletics as a coach, instructor, referee, or umpire in amateur athletics and in high schools, colleges, and universities.

Athletes and *sports competitors* compete in organized, officiated sports events to entertain spectators. When playing a game, athletes are required to understand the strategies of their game while obeying the rules and regulations of the sport. The events in which they compete include both team sports—such as baseball, basketball, football, hockey, and soccer—and individual sports—such as golf, tennis, and bowling. As the type of sport varies, so does the level of play, ranging from unpaid high school athletics to professional sports, in which the best from around the world compete before international television audiences.

In addition to competing in athletic events, athletes spend many hours practicing skills and teamwork under the guidance of a coach or sports instructor. Most athletes spend hours in hard practices every day. They also spend additional hours viewing video tapes, in order to critique their own performances and techniques and to scout their opponents' tendencies and weaknesses to gain a competitive advantage. Some athletes may also be advised by *strength trainers* in an effort to gain muscle and stamina, while also preventing injury. Competition at all levels is extremely intense and job security is always precarious. As a result, many athletes train year round to maintain excellent form, technique, and peak physical condition. Very little downtime from the sport exists at the professional level. Athletes also must conform to regimented diets during the height of their sports season to supplement any physical training program. Many athletes push their bodies to the limit during both practice and play, so career-ending injury always is a risk. Even minor injuries to an athlete may put the player at risk of replacement.

Coaches organize, instruct, and teach amateur and professional athletes in fundamentals of individual and team sports. In individual sports, *instructors* may sometimes fill this role. Coaches train athletes for competition by holding practice sessions to perform drills and improve the athlete's skills and stamina. Using their expertise in the sport, coaches instruct the athlete on proper form and technique in beginning and, later, in advanced exercises attempting to maximize the players' physical potential. Along with overseeing athletes as they refine their individual skills, coaches also are responsible for managing the team during both practice sessions and competitions, and for instilling good sportsmanship, a competitive spirit, and teamwork. They may also select, store, issue, and inventory equipment, materials, and supplies. During competitions, for example, coaches substitute players for optimum team chemistry and success. In addition, coaches direct team strategy and may call specific plays during competition to surprise or overpower the opponent. To choose the best plays, coaches evaluate or "scout" the opposing team prior to the competition, allowing them to determine game strategies and practice specific plays.

Many coaches in high schools are primarily teachers of academic subjects who supplement their income by coaching part time. College coaches consider coaching a full-time discipline and may be away from home frequently as they travel to scout and recruit prospective players.

Sports instructors teach professional and nonprofessional athletes on an individual basis. They organize, instruct, train, and lead athletes of indoor and outdoor sports such as bowling, tennis, golf, and swimming. Because activities are as diverse as weight lifting, gymnastics, and scuba diving, and may include self-defense training such as karate, instructors tend to specialize in one or a few types of activities. Like coaches, sports instructors also may hold daily practice sessions and be responsible for any needed equipment and sup-

plies. Using their knowledge of their sport, physiology, and corrective techniques, they determine the type and level of difficulty of exercises, prescribe specific drills, and correct the athlete's techniques. Some instructors also teach and demonstrate use of training apparatus, such as trampolines or weights, while correcting athletes' weaknesses and enhancing their conditioning. Using their expertise in the sport, sports instructors evaluate the athlete and the athlete's opponents to devise a competitive game strategy.

Coaches and sports instructors sometimes differ in their approach to athletes because of the focus of their work. For example, while coaches manage the team during a game to optimize its chance for victory, sports instructors—such as those who work for professional tennis players—often are not permitted to instruct their athletes during competition. Sports instructors spend more of their time with athletes working one-on-one, which permits them to design customized training programs for each individual. Motivating athletes to play hard challenges most coaches and sports instructors but is vital for the athlete's success. Many coaches and instructors derive great satisfaction working with children or young adults, helping them to learn new physical and social skills and to improve their physical condition, as well as helping them to achieve success in their sport.

Umpires, referees, and other sports officials officiate at competitive athletic and sporting events. They observe the play, detect infractions of rules, and impose penalties established by the sports' rules and regulations. Umpires, referees, and sports officials anticipate play and position themselves to best see the action, assess the situation, and determine any violations. Some sports officials, such as boxing referees, may work independently, while others such as umpires—the sports officials of baseball—work in groups. Regardless of the sport, the job is highly stressful because officials are often required to make a decision in a matter of a split second, sometimes resulting in strong disagreement among competitors, coaches, or spectators.

Professional *scouts* evaluate the skills of both amateur and professional athletes to determine talent and potential. As a sports intelligence agent, the scout's primary duty is to seek out top athletic candidates for the team he or she represents, ultimately contributing to team success. At the professional level, scouts typically work for scouting organizations, or as freelance scouts. In locating new talent, scouts perform their work in secrecy so as to not "tip off" their opponents about their interest in certain players. At the college level, the head scout is often an assistant coach, although freelance scouts may aid colleges by providing reports about exceptional players to coaches. Scouts at this level seek talented high school athletes by reading newspapers, contacting high school coaches and alumni, attending high school games, and studying videotapes of prospects' performances.

Working Conditions

Irregular work hours are the trademark of the athlete. They also are common for the coach, as well as umpires, referees, and other sports officials. Athletes, coaches, umpires, and related workers often work Saturdays, Sundays, evenings, and holidays. Athletes and full-time coaches usually work more than 40 hours a week for several months during the sports season, if not most of the year. Some coaches in educational institutions may coach more than one sport, particularly at the high school level.

Athletes, coaches, and sports officials who participate in competitions that are held outdoors may be exposed to all weather conditions of the season; those involved in events that are held indoors tend to work in climate-controlled comfort, often in arenas, enclosed stadiums, or gymnasiums. Athletes, coaches, and some sports officials frequently travel to sporting events by bus or airplane. Scouts also travel extensively in locating talent, often by automobile.

Employment

Athletes, coaches, umpires, and related workers held about 158,000 jobs in 2002. Coaches and scouts held 130,000 jobs; athletes, 15,000; and umpires, referees, and other sports officials, 14,000. Large proportions of athletes, coaches, umpires, and related workers worked part time—about 37 percent, while 17 percent maintained variable schedules. Many sports officials and coaches receive such a small and irregular payment for their services (occasional officiating at club games, for example) that they may not consider themselves employed in these occupations, even part time.

About 27 percent of workers in this occupation were self-employed, earning prize money or fees for lessons, scouting, or officiating assignments, and many other coaches and sports officials, although technically not self-employed, have such irregular or tenuous working arrangements that their working conditions resemble self-employment.

Among those employed in wage and salary jobs, 20 percent held jobs in private educational services. About 12 percent worked in amusement, gambling, and recreation industries, including golf and tennis clubs, gymnasiums, health clubs, judo and karate schools, riding stables, swim clubs, and other sports and recreation-related facilities. Another 7 percent worked in the spectator sports industry.

Training, Other Qualifications, and Advancement

Education and training requirements for athletes, coaches, umpires, and related workers vary greatly by the level and type of sport. Regardless of the sport or occupation, jobs require immense overall knowledge of the game, usually acquired through years of experience at lower levels. Athletes usually begin competing in their sports while in elementary or middle school and continue through high school and sometimes college. They play in amateur tournaments and on high school and college teams, where the best attract the attention of professional scouts. Most schools require that participating athletes maintain specific academic standards to remain eligible to play. Becoming a pro-

fessional athlete is the culmination of years of effort. Athletes who seek to compete professionally must have extraordinary talent, desire, and dedication to training.

For high school coach and sports instructor jobs, schools usually prefer to hire teachers willing to take on the jobs part time. If no one suitable is found, they hire someone from outside. Some entry-level positions for coaches or instructors require only experience derived as a participant in the sport or activity. Many coaches begin their careers as assistant coaches to gain the necessary knowledge and experience needed to become a head coach. Head coaches at larger schools that strive to compete at the highest levels of a sport require substantial experience as a head coach at another school or as an assistant coach. To reach the ranks of professional coaching, it usually takes years of coaching experience and a winning record in the lower ranks.

Public secondary school head coaches and sports instructors at all levels usually must have a bachelor's degree. Those who are not teachers must meet state requirements for certification in order to become a head coach. Certification, however, may not be required for coach and sports instructor jobs in private schools. Degree programs specifically related to coaching include exercise and sports science, physiology, kinesiology, nutrition and fitness, physical education, and sports medicine.

For sports instructors, certification is highly desirable for those interested in becoming a tennis, golf, karate, or any other kind of instructor. Often, one must be at least 18 years old and CPR certified. There are many certifying organizations specific to the various sports, and their training requirements vary depending on their standards. Participation in a clinic, camp, or school usually is required for certification. Part-time workers and those in smaller facilities are less likely to need formal education or training.

Each sport has specific requirements for umpires, referees, and other sports officials. Referees, umpires, and other sports officials often begin their careers by volunteering for intramural, community, and recreational league competitions. For college refereeing, candidates must be certified by an officiating school and be evaluated during a probationary period. Some larger college conferences require officials to have certification and other qualifications, such as residence in or near the conference boundaries along with previous experience that typically includes several years officiating at high school, community college, or other college conference games.

Standards are even more stringent for officials in professional sports. For umpire jobs in professional baseball, for example, a high school diploma or equivalent is usually sufficient, plus 20/20 vision and quick reflexes. To qualify for the professional ranks, however, prospective candidates must attend professional umpire training school. Currently, there are two schools whose curriculums have been approved by the Professional Baseball Umpires Corporation (PBUC) for training. Top graduates are selected for further evaluation while officiating in a rookie minor league. Umpires then usually need 8 to 10 years of experience in various minor leagues before being considered for major league jobs. Football also is competitive, as candidates must have at least 10 years of officiating experience, with 5 of them at a collegiate varsity or minor professional level. For the National Football League (NFL), prospects are interviewed by clinical psychologists to determine levels of intelligence and ability to handle extremely stressful situations. In addition, the NFL's security department conducts thorough background checks. Potential candidates are likely to be interviewed by a panel from the NFL officiating department and are given a comprehensive examination on the rules of the sport.

Jobs as scouts require experience playing a sport at the college or professional level that enables them to spot young players who possess extraordinary athletic abilities and skills. Most beginning scout jobs are as part-time talent spotters in a particular area or region. Hard work and a record of success often lead to full-time jobs responsible for bigger territories. Some scouts advance to scouting director jobs or various administrative positions in sports.

Athletes, coaches, umpires, and related workers must relate well to others and possess good communication and leadership skills. Coaches also must be resourceful and flexible to successfully instruct and motivate individuals or groups of athletes.

Job Outlook

Employment of athletes, coaches, umpires, and related workers is expected to increase about as fast as the average for all occupations through the year 2012. Employment will grow as the general public continues to increasingly participate in organized sports as a form of entertainment, recreation, and physical conditioning. Job growth also will be driven by the increasing numbers of baby boomers approaching retirement, during which they are expected to become more active participants of leisure-time activities, such as golf and tennis, and require instruction. The large numbers of the children of baby boomers in high schools and colleges also will be active participants in athletics and require coaches and instructors.

Expanding opportunities are expected for coaches and instructors, as a higher value is being placed upon physical fitness in our society. Americans of all ages are engaging in more physical fitness activities, such as participating in amateur athletic competition and joining athletic clubs, and are being encouraged to participate in physical education. Employment of coaches and instructors also will increase with expansion of school and college athletic programs and growing demand for private sports instruction. Sports-related job growth within education also will be driven by the decisions of local school boards. Population growth dictates the construction of additional schools, particularly in the expanding suburbs. However, funding for athletic programs is often one of the first areas to be cut when budgets become tight, but the popularity of team sports often enables shortfalls to be offset somewhat by assistance from

fundraisers, booster clubs, and parents. Persons who are state-certified to teach academic subjects in addition to physical education are likely to have the best prospects for obtaining coach and instructor jobs. The need to replace many high school coaches also will provide some coaching opportunities.

Competition for professional athlete jobs will continue to be extremely intense. Opportunities to make a living as a professional in individual sports such as golf or tennis may grow as new tournaments are established and prize money distributed to participants increases. Most professional athletes' careers last only several years due to debilitating injuries and age, so a large proportion of the athletes in these jobs is replaced every year, creating some job opportunities. However, a far greater number of talented young men and women dream of becoming a sports superstar and will be competing for a very limited number of job openings.

Opportunities should be best for persons seeking part-time umpire, referee, and other sports official jobs at the high school level, but competition is expected for higher paying jobs at the college level, and even greater competition for jobs in professional sports. Competition should be very keen for jobs as scouts, particularly for professional teams, as the number of available positions is limited.

Earnings

Median annual earnings of athletes were $45,320 in 2002. The lowest 10 percent earned less than $14,090, and the highest 10 percent earned more than $145,600. However, the highest paid professional athletes earn salaries far in excess of these estimates.

Median annual earnings of umpires and related workers were $20,540 in 2002. The middle 50 percent earned between $16,210 and $29,490. The lowest 10 percent earned less than $13,760, and the highest 10 percent earned more than $40,350.

Median annual earnings of coaches and scouts were $27,880 in 2002. The middle 50 percent earned between $17,890 and $42,250. The lowest 10 percent earned less than $13,370, and the highest 10 percent earned more than $60,230. Median annual earnings in the industries employing the largest numbers of coaches and scouts in 2002 were as follows:

Colleges, universities, and professional schools	$36,170
Other amusement and recreation industries	25,900
Elementary and secondary schools	24,740
Other schools and instruction	22,570

Earnings vary by education level, certification, and geographic region. Some instructors and coaches are paid a salary, while others may be paid by the hour, per session, or based on the number of participants.

Related Occupations

Athletes and coaches have extensive knowledge of physiology and sports, and instruct, inform, and encourage participants. Other workers with similar duties include dietitians and nutritionists; physical therapists; recreation and fitness workers; recreational therapists; and teachers—preschool, kindergarten, elementary, middle, and secondary.

Sources of Additional Information

For general information on coaching, contact:

- National High School Athletic Coaches Association, P.O. Box 4342, Hamden, CT 06514. Internet: http://www.hscoaches.org

For information about sports officiating for team and individual sports, contact:

- National Association of Sports Officials, 2017 Lathrop Ave., Racine, WI 53405. Internet: http://www.naso.org

Barbers, Cosmetologists, and Other Personal Appearance Workers

(O*NET 39-5011.00, 39-5012.00, 39-5091.00, 39-5092.00, 39-5093.00, and 39-5094.00)

Significant Points

- Job opportunities generally should be good, but competition is expected for jobs and clients at higher paying salons; opportunities will be best for those licensed to provide a broad range of services.

- Barbers, cosmetologists, and most other personal appearance workers must be licensed.

- Almost half of all barbers, cosmetologists, and other personal appearance workers are self-employed; many also work flexible schedules.

Nature of the Work

Barbers and cosmetologists, also called hairdressers and hairstylists, help people look neat and well-groomed. Other personal appearance workers, such as manicurists and pedicurists, shampooers, and skin care specialists provide specialized services that help clients look and feel their best.

Barbers cut, trim, shampoo, and style hair. Also, they fit hairpieces and offer scalp treatments and facial massages. In many states, barbers are licensed to color, bleach, or highlight hair and offer permanent-wave services. Many barbers also provide skin care and nail treatments.

Hairdressers, hairstylists, and cosmetologists provide beauty services, such as shampooing, cutting, coloring, and styling hair. They may advise clients on how to care for their hair, straighten hair or give it a permanent wave, or lighten or darken hair color. Additionally, cosmetologists may train to give manicures, pedicures, and scalp and facial treatments; provide makeup analysis; and clean and style wigs and hairpieces.

A number of workers offer specialized services. *Manicurists and pedicurists*, called *nail technicians* in some states, work exclusively on nails and provide manicures, pedicures, coloring, and nail extensions to clients. Another group of specialists is *skin care specialists*, or *estheticians*, who cleanse and beautify the skin by giving facials, full-body treatments, and head and neck massages and by removing hair through waxing. *Electrologists* use an electrolysis machine to remove hair. Finally, in some larger salons, *shampooers* specialize in shampooing and conditioning clients' hair.

In addition to their work with clients, personal appearance workers are expected to maintain clean work areas and sanitize all work implements. They may make appointments and keep records of hair color and permanent-wave formulas used by their regular clients. A growing number actively sell hair products and other cosmetic supplies. Barbers, cosmetologists, and other personal appearance workers who operate their own salons have managerial duties that include hiring, supervising, and firing workers, as well as keeping business and inventory records, ordering supplies, and arranging for advertising.

Working Conditions

Barbers, cosmetologists, and other personal appearance workers usually work in clean, pleasant surroundings with good lighting and ventilation. Good health and stamina are important, because these workers are on their feet for most of their shift. Because prolonged exposure to some hair and nail chemicals may cause irritation, special care is taken to use protective clothing, such as plastic gloves or aprons.

Most full-time barbers, cosmetologists, and other personal appearance workers put in a 40-hour week, but longer hours are common in this occupation, especially among self-employed workers. Work schedules may include evenings and weekends, the times when beauty salons and barbershops are busiest. Because barbers and cosmetologists generally will be working on weekends and during lunch and evening hours, they may arrange to take breaks during less popular times. About 30 percent of cosmetologists and 19 percent of barbers work part time and 14 percent of cosmetologists and 13 percent of barbers have variable schedules.

Employment

Barbers, cosmetologists, and other personal appearance workers held about 754,000 jobs in 2002. Of these, barbers, hairdressers, hairstylists, and cosmetologists held 651,000 jobs; manicurists and pedicurists, 51,000; skin care specialists, 25,000; and shampooers, 25,000.

Most of these workers are employed in beauty salons or barber shops, but they are also found in nail salons, department stores, nursing and other residential care homes, and drug and cosmetics stores. Nearly every town has a barbershop or beauty salon, but employment in this occupation is concentrated in the most populous cities and states.

Almost half of all barbers, cosmetologists, and other personal appearance workers are self-employed. Many own their own salon, but a growing number lease booth space or a chair from the salon's owner.

Training, Other Qualifications, and Advancement

All states require barbers, cosmetologists, and most other personal appearance workers to be licensed. Qualifications for a license, however, vary. Generally, a person must have graduated from a state-licensed barber or cosmetology school and be at least 16 years old. A few states require applicants to pass a physical examination. Some states require graduation from high school while others require as little as an eighth-grade education. In a few states, the completion of an apprenticeship can substitute for graduation from a school, but very few barbers or cosmetologists learn their skills in this way. Applicants for a license usually are required to pass a written test and demonstrate an ability to perform basic barbering or cosmetology services.

Some states have reciprocity agreements that allow licensed barbers and cosmetologists to obtain a license in a different state without additional formal training. Other states do not recognize training or licenses obtained in another state; consequently, persons who wish to work in a particular state should review the laws of that state before entering a training program.

Public and private vocational schools offer daytime or evening classes in barbering and cosmetology. Full-time programs in barbering and cosmetology usually last 9 to 24 months, but training for manicurists and pedicurists, skin care specialists, and electrologists requires significantly less time. An apprenticeship program can last from 1 to 3 years. Shampooers generally do not need formal training or a license. Formal training programs include classroom study, demonstrations, and practical work. Students study the basic services—cutting hair, shaving customers, providing facial massages, and giving hair and scalp treatments—and, under supervision, practice on customers in school "clinics." Most schools also teach unisex hairstyling and chemical styling. Students attend lectures on the use and care of instruments, sanitation and hygiene, chemistry, anatomy, physiology, and the recognition of simple skin ailments. Instruction also is provided in communication, sales, and general business practices. Experienced barbers and cosmetologists may take advanced courses in hairstyling, coloring, and the sale and service of hairpieces.

After graduating from a training program, students can take the state licensing examination, which consists of a written test and, in some cases, a practical test of styling skills based on established performance criteria. A few states include an oral examination in which the applicant is asked to explain the procedures he or she is following while taking the practical test. In many states, cosmetology training may be credited toward a barbering license, and vice versa. A few states combine the two licenses into one hairstyling license. Many states require separate licensing examinations for manicurists, pedicurists, and skin care specialists.

For many barbers, cosmetologists, and other personal appearance workers, formal training and a license are only the first steps in a career that requires years of continuing education. Because hairstyles change, new products are developed, and services expand to meet clients' needs, personal appearance workers must keep abreast of the latest fashions and beauty techniques. They attend training at salons, cosmetology schools, or product shows. Through workshops and demonstrations of the latest techniques, industry representatives introduce cosmetologists to a wide range of products and services. As retail sales become an increasingly important part of salons' revenue, the ability to be an effective salesperson becomes vital for salon workers.

Successful personal appearance workers should have an understanding of fashion, art, and technical design. They should enjoy working with the public and be willing and able to follow clients' instructions. Communication, image, and attitude play an important role in career success. Some cosmetology schools consider "people skills" to be such an integral part of the job that they require coursework in this area. Business skills are important for those who plan to operate their own salons.

During their first months on the job, new workers are given relatively simple tasks or are assigned the simpler hairstyling patterns. Once they have demonstrated their skills, they are gradually permitted to perform more complicated tasks, such as coloring hair or applying a permanent wave. As they continue to work in the field, more training is usually required to learn the techniques used in each salon and to build on the basics learned in cosmetology school.

Advancement usually takes the form of higher earnings as barbers and cosmetologists gain experience and build a steady clientele. Some barbers and cosmetologists manage large salons or open their own after several years of experience. Others teach in barber or cosmetology schools, or provide training through vocational schools. Still others advance to become sales representatives, image or fashion consultants, or examiners for state licensing boards.

Job Outlook

Overall employment of barbers, cosmetologists, and other personal appearance workers is projected to grow about as fast as the average for all occupations through 2012, because of increasing population, incomes, and demand for personal appearance services. In addition to those arising from job growth, numerous job openings will arise from the need to replace workers who transfer to other occupations, retire, or leave the labor force for other reasons. As a result, job opportunities generally should be good. However, competition is expected for jobs and clients at higher paying salons, as applicants compete with a large pool of licensed and experienced cosmetologists for these positions. Opportunities will be best for those licensed to provide a broad range of services.

Employment trends are expected to vary among the different specialties within this grouping of occupations. For example, more slowly than average growth is expected in employment of barbers due to a large number of retirements and the relatively small number of cosmetology school graduates opting to obtain barbering licenses. On the other hand, employment of hairdressers, hairstylists, and cosmetologists should grow about as fast as average, because many now cut and style both men's and women's hair and because the demand for coloring services and other hair treatments, such as permanent waves, by teens and aging baby boomers is expected to remain steady or even grow.

Continued growth in the number of nail salons and full-service day spas will generate numerous job openings for manicurists, pedicurists, skin care specialists, and shampooers. Nail salons specialize in providing manicures and pedicures. Day spas typically provide a full range of services, including beauty wraps, manicures and pedicures, facials, and massages.

Earnings

Barbers, cosmetologists, and other personal appearance workers receive income from a variety of sources. They may receive commissions based on the price of the service or a salary based on number of hours worked. All receive tips, and many receive commissions on the products they sell. In addition, some salons pay bonuses to employees who bring in new business.

Median annual earnings in 2002 for salaried hairdressers, hairstylists, and cosmetologists, including tips and commission, were $18,960. The middle 50 percent earned between $15,010 and $25,600. The lowest 10 percent earned less than $13,020, and the highest 10 percent earned more than $35,240.

Median annual earnings in 2002 for salaried barbers, including tips, were $19,550. The middle 50 percent earned between $14,540 and $27,290. The lowest 10 percent earned less than $12,720, and the highest 10 percent earned more than $37,370.

Among skin care specialists, median annual earnings, including tips, were $22,450; for manicurists and pedicurists, $17,330; and $14,360 for shampooers.

A number of factors determine the total income of barbers, cosmetologists, and other personal appearance workers, including the size and location of the salon, the number of hours worked, clients' tipping habits, and competition from other barber shops and salons. Cosmetologists or barber's initiative and ability to attract and hold regular clients also

are key factors in determining his or her earnings. Earnings for entry-level workers are usually low; however, for those who stay in the profession, earnings can be considerably higher.

Although some salons offer paid vacations and medical benefits, many self-employed and part-time workers in this occupation do not enjoy such common benefits.

Related Occupations

Other workers who provide a personal service to clients and usually must be professionally licensed or certified include massage therapists and fitness workers.

Sources of Additional Information

A list of licensed training schools and licensing requirements for cosmetologists may be obtained from:

- National Accrediting Commission of Cosmetology Arts and Sciences, 4401 Ford Ave., Suite 1300, Alexandria, VA 22302. Internet: http://www.naccas.org

Information about a career in cosmetology is available from:

- National Cosmetology Association, 401 N. Michigan Ave., 22nd floor, Chicago, IL 60611. Internet: http://www.salonprofessionals.org

For details on state licensing requirements and approved barber or cosmetology schools, contact the state boards of barber or cosmetology examiners in your state capital.

Bill and Account Collectors

(O*NET 43-3011.00)

Significant Points

- Most jobs require only a high school diploma.

- Numerous job opportunities should arise due to high turnover.

- Slower-than-average growth is expected in overall employment, reflecting the spread of computers and other office automation, as well as organizational restructuring.

Nature of the Work

Bill and account collectors, called simply *collectors*, keep track of accounts that are overdue and attempt to collect payment on them. Some are employed by third-party collection agencies, while others—known as "in-house collectors"—work directly for the original creditors, such as department stores, hospitals, or banks.

The duties of bill and account collectors are similar in the many different organizations in which they are employed. First, collectors are called upon to locate and notify customers of delinquent accounts, usually over the telephone, but sometimes by letter. When customers move without leaving a forwarding address, collectors may check with the post office, telephone companies, credit bureaus, or former neighbors to obtain the new address. The attempt to find the new address is called "skip tracing."

Once collectors find the debtor, they inform him or her of the overdue account and solicit payment. If necessary, they review the terms of the sale, service, or credit contract with the customer. Collectors also may attempt to learn the cause of the delay in payment. Where feasible, they offer the customer advice on how to pay off the debts, such as by taking out a bill consolidation loan. However, the collector's prime objective is always to ensure that the customer pays the debt in question.

If a customer agrees to pay, collectors record this commitment and check later to verify that the payment was indeed made. Collectors may have authority to grant an extension of time if customers ask for one. If a customer fails to respond, collectors prepare a statement indicating the customer's action for the credit department of the establishment. In more extreme cases, collectors may initiate repossession proceedings, disconnect the customer's service, or hand the account over to an attorney for legal action. Most collectors handle other administrative functions for the accounts assigned to them, including recording changes of addresses and purging the records of the deceased.

Collectors use computers and a variety of automated systems to keep track of overdue accounts. Typically, collectors work at video display terminals that are linked to computers. In sophisticated predictive dialer systems, a computer dials the telephone automatically, and the collector speaks only when a connection has been made. Such systems eliminate time spent calling busy or nonanswering numbers. Many collectors use regular telephones, but others wear headsets like those used by telephone operators.

Working Conditions

Bill and account collectors typically are employed in an office environment. Bill collectors who work for third-party collection agencies may spend most of their days on the phone in a call-center environment. However, a growing number work at home, and many work part time.

Because the majority of collectors use computers on a daily basis, these workers may experience eye and muscle strain, backaches, headaches, and repetitive motion injuries. Also, collectors who review detailed data may have to sit for extended periods.

Many collectors work regular business hours. However, collectors often have to work evenings and weekends, when it usually is easier to reach people.

Employment

Bill and account collectors held about 413,000 jobs in 2002. About 1 in 5 collectors works for collection agencies. Many others work in banks, retail stores, government, hospitals, and other institutions that lend money and extend credit.

Training, Other Qualifications, and Advancement

Most bill and account collectors are required to have at least a high school diploma. However, having completed some college is becoming increasingly important. Some collectors have bachelor's degrees in business, accounting, or liberal arts. Although a degree is rarely required, many graduates accept entry-level clerical positions to get into a particular company or to enter the finance or accounting field with the hope of being promoted to professional or managerial positions. Some companies have a set plan of advancement that tracks college graduates from entry-level clerical jobs into managerial positions. Workers with bachelor's degrees are likely to start at higher salaries and advance more easily than those without degrees.

Experience in a related job also is recommended. For example, telemarketing experience is useful for bill and account collectors. Experience working in an office environment or in customer service is always beneficial. Regardless of the type of work, most employers prefer workers with good communication skills who are computer literate; knowledge of word-processing and spreadsheet software is especially valuable.

Once hired, bill and account collectors usually receive on-the-job training. Under the guidance of a supervisor or some other senior worker, new employees learn company procedures. Some formal classroom training also may be necessary, such as training in specific computer software. Bill and account collectors generally receive training in telephone techniques, negotiation skills, and the laws governing the collection of debt. Collectors must be careful, orderly, and detail oriented in order to avoid making errors and to recognize errors made by others. These workers also should be discreet and trustworthy, because they frequently come in contact with confidential material. In addition, all bill and account collectors should have a strong aptitude for numbers.

Bill and account collectors usually advance by taking on more duties in the same occupation for higher pay or by transferring to a closely related occupation. Most companies fill office and administrative support supervisory and managerial positions by promoting individuals from within the organization, so collectors who acquire additional skills, experience, and training improve their advancement opportunities. With appropriate experience and education, some may become accountants, human resource specialists, or buyers.

Job Outlook

Employment of bill and account collectors is expected to grow faster than the average for all occupations through 2012. Cash flow is becoming increasingly important to companies, which are now placing greater emphasis on collecting bad debts sooner. Thus, the workload for collectors is up as they seek to collect, not only debts that are relatively old, but ones that are more recent. Also, as more companies in a wide range of industries get involved in lending money and issuing their own credit cards, they will need to hire collectors, because debt levels will inevitably rise. Hospitals and physicians' offices are two of the fastest-growing areas requiring collectors. With insurance reimbursements not keeping up with cost increases, the health-care industry is seeking to recover more money from patients. Government agencies also are making more use of collectors to collect on everything from parking tickets to child-support payments and past-due taxes. Finally, the Internal Revenue Service (IRS) is looking into outsourcing the collection of overdue federal taxes to third-party collection agencies. If the IRS does outsource, more collectors will be required for this large job.

Despite the increasing demand for bill collectors, an increasing number of mergers between collection agencies may result in fewer collectors being hired. Small, less automated agencies are being bought by larger, more computerized firms, resulting in greater productivity. Contrary to the pattern in most occupations, employment of bill and account collectors tends to rise during recessions, reflecting the difficulty that many people have in meeting their financial obligations. However, collectors usually have more success at getting people to repay their debts when the economy is good.

Earnings

Salaries of bill and account collectors vary considerably. The region of the country, size of the city, and type and size of the establishment all influence salary levels. Also, the level of expertise required and the complexity and uniqueness of a collector's responsibilities may affect earnings. Median hourly earnings of full-time bill and account collectors in 2002 were 12.88.

In addition to earning their salaries, some bill and account collectors receive commissions or bonuses based on the number of cases they close.

Related Occupations

Bill and account colelctors enter data into a computer, handle cash, and keep track of business and other financial transactions. Higher-level collectors can generate reports and analyze the data. Other occupations that perform these duties include brokerage clerks; cashiers; credit authorizers, checkers, and clerks; loan interviewers and clerks; new-accounts clerks; order clerks; and secretaries and administrative assistants.

Sources of Additional Information

Career information on bill and account collectors is available from:

- Association of Credit and Collection Professionals, P.O. Box 39106, Minneapolis, MN 55439. Internet: http://www.acainternational.org

Building Cleaning Workers

(O*NET 37-1011.01, 37-1011.02, 37-2011.00, and 37-2012.00)

Significant Points

- This very large occupation requires few skills to enter and has one of the largest numbers of job openings of any occupation each year.

- Most job openings result from the need to replace the many workers who leave these jobs due to their limited opportunities for training or advancement, low pay, and high incidence of only part-time or temporary work.

- Businesses providing janitorial and cleaning services on a contract basis are expected to be one of the fastest-growing employers of these workers.

Nature of the Work

Building cleaning workers—including janitors, maids, housekeeping cleaners, window washers, and rug shampooers—keep office buildings, hospitals, stores, apartment houses, hotels, and residences clean and in good condition. Some only do cleaning, while others have a wide range of duties.

Janitors and cleaners perform a variety of heavy cleaning duties, such as cleaning floors, shampooing rugs, washing walls and glass, and removing rubbish. They may fix leaky faucets, empty trash cans, do painting and carpentry, replenish bathroom supplies, mow lawns, and see that heating and air-conditioning equipment works properly. On a typical day, janitors may wet- or dry-mop floors, clean bathrooms, vacuum carpets, dust furniture, make minor repairs, and exterminate insects and rodents. They also clean snow or debris from sidewalks in front of buildings and notify management of the need for major repairs. While janitors typically perform most of the duties mentioned, cleaners tend to work for companies that specialize in one type of cleaning activity, such as washing windows.

Maids and housekeeping cleaners perform any combination of light cleaning duties to maintain private households or commercial establishments, such as hotels, restaurants, and hospitals, clean and orderly. In hotels, aside from cleaning and maintaining the premises, maids and housekeeping cleaners may deliver ironing boards, cribs, and rollaway beds to guests' rooms. In hospitals, they also may wash bed-frames, brush mattresses, make beds, and disinfect and sterilize equipment and supplies with germicides and sterilizing equipment.

Janitors, maids, and cleaners use various equipment, tools, and cleaning materials. For one job they may need a mop and bucket, for another an electric polishing machine and a special cleaning solution. Improved building materials, chemical cleaners, and power equipment have made many tasks easier and less time consuming, but cleaning workers must learn the proper use of equipment and cleaners to avoid harming floors, fixtures, and themselves.

Cleaning supervisors coordinate, schedule, and supervise the activities of janitors and cleaners. They assign tasks and inspect building areas to see that work has been done properly, issue supplies and equipment, and inventory stocks to ensure that an adequate amount of supplies is present. They also screen and hire job applicants, train new and experienced employees, and recommend promotions, transfers, or dismissals. Supervisors may prepare reports concerning the occupancy of rooms, hours worked, and department expenses. Some also perform cleaning duties.

Cleaners and servants in private households dust and polish furniture; sweep, mop, and wax floors; vacuum; and clean ovens, refrigerators, and bathrooms. They also may wash dishes, polish silver, and change and make beds. Some wash, fold, and iron clothes; a few wash windows. General houseworkers also may take clothes and laundry to the cleaners, buy groceries, and perform many other errands.

Working Conditions

Because most office buildings are cleaned while they are empty, many cleaning workers work evening hours. Some, however, such as school and hospital custodians, work in the daytime. When there is a need for 24-hour maintenance, janitors may be assigned to shifts. Most full-time building cleaners work about 40 hours a week. Part-time cleaners usually work in the evenings and on weekends.

Building cleaning workers in large office and residential buildings often work in teams consisting of workers who specialize in vacuuming, picking up trash, and cleaning rest rooms, among other things. Supervisors conduct inspections to ensure that the building is cleaned properly and the team is functioning efficiently.

Building cleaning workers usually work inside heated, well-lighted buildings. However, they sometimes work outdoors, sweeping walkways, mowing lawns, or shoveling snow. Working with machines can be noisy, and some tasks, such as cleaning bathrooms and trash rooms, can be dirty and unpleasant. Janitors may suffer cuts, bruises, and burns from machines, handtools, and chemicals. They spend most of their time on their feet, sometimes lifting or pushing heavy furniture or equipment. Many tasks, such as dusting or sweeping, require constant bending, stooping, and stretching. As a result, janitors also may suffer back injuries and sprains.

Employment

Building cleaning workers held nearly 4 million jobs in 2002. More than 6 percent were self-employed.

Janitors and cleaners work in nearly every type of establishment and held about 2.3 million jobs. They accounted for about 57 percent of all building cleaning workers. About 28 percent worked for firms supplying building maintenance services on a contract basis, 21 percent were employed in educational institutions, and 2 percent worked in hotels. Other employers included hospitals, restaurants, religious institutions, manufacturing firms, government agencies, and operators of apartment buildings, office buildings, and other types of real estate.

First-line supervisors of housekeeping and janitorial workers held about 230,000 jobs. Approximately 22 percent worked in firms supplying building maintenance services on a contract basis, 14 percent were employed in hotels, 7 percent held jobs in nursing and other residential care facilities, and 5 percent worked in hospitals. Other employers included educational institutions and amusement and recreation facilities.

Maids and housekeepers held about 1.5 million jobs. Hotels, motels, and other traveler accommodations employed the most maids and housekeepers—27 percent—while private households employed the second most: 25 percent. Eight percent were employed in hospitals; and, a similar percentage worked in nursing and other residential care facilities. Although cleaning jobs can be found in all cities and towns, most are located in highly populated areas where there are many office buildings, schools, apartment houses, nursing homes, and hospitals.

Training, Other Qualifications, and Advancement

No special education is required for most janitorial or cleaning jobs, but beginners should know simple arithmetic and be able to follow instructions. High school shop courses are helpful for jobs involving repair work.

Most building cleaners learn their skills on the job. Usually, beginners work with an experienced cleaner, doing routine cleaning. As they gain more experience, they are assigned more complicated tasks.

In some cities, programs run by unions, government agencies, or employers teach janitorial skills. Students learn how to clean buildings thoroughly and efficiently, how to select and safely use various cleansing agents, and how to operate and maintain machines, such as wet and dry vacuums, buffers, and polishers. Students learn to plan their work, to follow safety and health regulations, to interact positively with people in the buildings they clean, and to work without supervision. Instruction in minor electrical, plumbing, and other repairs also may be given. Those who come in contact with the public should have good communication skills. Employers usually look for dependable, hard-working individuals who are in good health, follow directions well, and get along with other people.

Building cleaners usually find work by answering newspaper advertisements, applying directly to organizations where they would like to work, contacting local labor unions, or contacting state employment service offices.

Advancement opportunities for workers usually are limited in organizations where they are the only maintenance worker. Where there is a large maintenance staff, however, cleaning workers can be promoted to supervisor and to area supervisor or manager. A high school diploma improves the chances for advancement. Some janitors set up their own maintenance or cleaning businesses.

Supervisors usually move up through the ranks. In many establishments, they are required to take some inservice training to improve their housekeeping techniques and procedures and to enhance their supervisory skills.

A small number of cleaning supervisors and managers are members of the International Executive Housekeepers Association, which offers two kinds of certification programs to cleaning supervisors and managers: Certified Executive Housekeeper (CEH) and Registered Executive Housekeeper (REH). The CEH designation is offered to those with a high school education, while the REH designation is offered to those who have a 4-year college degree. Both designations are earned by attending courses and passing exams, and both must be renewed every 2 years to ensure that workers keep abreast of new cleaning methods. Those with the REH designation usually oversee the cleaning services of hotels, hospitals, casinos, and other large institutions that rely on well-trained experts for their cleaning needs.

Job Outlook

Overall employment of building cleaning workers is expected to grow about as fast as the average for all occupations through 2012, as more office complexes, apartment houses, schools, factories, hospitals, and other buildings requiring cleaning are built to accommodate a growing population and economy. As many firms reduce costs by contracting out the cleaning and maintenance of buildings, businesses providing janitorial and cleaning services on a contract basis are expected to be one of the faster growing employers of these workers. Although there have been some improvements in productivity in the way buildings are cleaned and maintained—using teams of cleaners, for example, and better cleaning supplies—it is still very much a labor-intensive job. Average growth is expected among janitors and cleaners and among cleaning supervisors, but less-than-average growth is projected for maids and housekeeping cleaners. In addition to job openings arising due to growth, numerous openings should result from the need to replace those who leave this very large occupation each year. Limited formal education and training requirements, low pay, and numerous part-time and temporary jobs induce many to leave the occupation, thereby contributing to the number of job openings and the need to replace these workers.

Much of the growth in these occupations will come from cleaning residential properties. As families become more pressed for time, they increasingly are hiring cleaning and handyman services to perform a variety of tasks in their homes. Also, as the population ages, older people will need to hire cleaners to help maintain their houses. In addition, housekeeping cleaners will be needed to clean the growing number of residential care facilities for the elderly. These facilities, including assisted-living arrangements, generally provide housekeeping services as part of the rent.

Earnings

Median annual earnings of janitors and cleaners, except maids and housekeeping cleaners, were $18,250 in 2002. The middle 50 percent earned between $14,920 and $23,650. The lowest 10 percent earned less than $12,920, and the highest 10 percent earned more than $30,700. Median annual earnings in 2002 in the industries employing the largest numbers of janitors and cleaners, except maids and housekeeping cleaners, were as follows:

Elementary and secondary schools	$22,820
Local government	22,770
Colleges, universities, and professional schools	21,540
Lessors of real estate	20,240
Services to buildings and dwellings	16,370

Median annual earnings of maids and housekeepers were $16,440 in 2002. The middle 50 percent earned between $14,210 and $19,400. The lowest 10 percent earned less than $12,560, and the highest 10 percent earned more than $23,750. Median annual earnings in 2002 in the industries employing the largest numbers of maids and housekeepers were as follows:

General medical and surgical hospitals	$18,050
Community care facilities for the elderly	16,470
Nursing care facilities	16,440
Services to buildings and dwellings	16,210
Traveler accommodation	15,740

Median annual earnings of first-line supervisors and managers of housekeeping and janitorial workers were $28,140 in 2002. The middle 50 percent earned between $21,520 and $36,940. The lowest 10 percent earned less than $17,490, and the highest 10 percent earned more than $46,570. Median annual earnings in 2002 in the industries employing the largest numbers of first-line supervisors and managers of housekeeping and janitorial workers were as follows:

Elementary and secondary schools	$33,080
General medical and surgical hospitals	29,000
Nursing care facilities	26,960
Services to buildings and dwellings	25,410
Traveler accommodation	22,710

Related Occupations

Workers who specialize in one of the many job functions of janitors and cleaners include pest control workers; industrial machinery installation, repair, and maintenance workers; and grounds maintenance workers.

Sources of Additional Information

Information about janitorial jobs may be obtained from state employment service offices.

For information on certification in executive housekeeping, contact:

- International Executive Housekeepers Association, Inc., 1001 Eastwind Dr., Suite 301, Westerville, OH 43081-3361. Internet: http://www.ieha.org

Bus Drivers

(O*NET 53-3021.00 and 53-3022.00)

Significant Points

- Opportunities should be good, particularly for school-bus driver jobs.

- A commercial driver's license is required to operate a bus.

- Work schedules vary considerably among various types of bus drivers.

- Bus drivers must possess strong customer service skills, including communication skills and the ability to manage large groups of people with varying needs.

Nature of the Work

Every day, millions of Americans every day leave the driving to bus drivers. Bus drivers are essential in providing passengers with an alternative to their automobiles or other forms of transportation. Intercity bus drivers transport people between regions of a state or of the country; local-transit bus drivers do so within a metropolitan area or county; motor coach drivers take customers on charter excursions and tours; and schoolbus drivers take children to and from schools and related events.

Drivers pick up and drop off passengers at bus stops, stations, or, in the case of students, at regularly scheduled neighborhood locations based on strict time schedules. Drivers must operate vehicles safely, especially when traffic is heavier than normal. However, they cannot let light traffic put them ahead of schedule so that they miss passengers.

Local-transit and *intercity bus drivers* report to their assigned terminal or garage, where they stock up on tickets or trans-

fers and prepare trip report forms. In some transportation firms, maintenance departments are responsible for keeping vehicles in good condition. In others, drivers may check their vehicle's tires, brakes, windshield wipers, lights, oil, fuel, and water supply before beginning their routes. Drivers usually verify that the bus has safety equipment, such as fire extinguishers, first aid kits, and emergency reflectors in case of an emergency.

During the course of their shift, local-transit and intercity bus drivers collect fares; answer questions about schedules, routes, and transfer points; and sometimes announce stops. Intercity bus drivers may make only a single one-way trip to a distant city or a round trip each day. They may stop at towns just a few miles apart or only at large cities hundreds of miles apart. Local-transit bus drivers may make several trips each day over the same city and suburban streets, stopping as frequently as every few blocks.

Local-transit bus drivers submit daily trip reports with a record of trips, significant schedule delays, and mechanical problems. Intercity drivers who drive across state or national boundaries must comply with U.S. Department of Transportation regulations. These include completing vehicle inspection reports and recording distances traveled and the periods they spend driving, performing other duties, and off duty.

Motorcoach drivers transport passengers on charter trips and sightseeing tours. Drivers routinely interact with customers and tour guides to make the trip as comfortable and informative as possible. They are directly responsible for keeping to strict schedules, adhering to the guidelines of the tours' itinerary, and ensuring the overall success of the trip. These drivers act as customer service representative, tour guide, program director, and safety guide. Trips frequently last more than 1 day. The driver may be away for more than a week if assigned to an extended tour. As with all drivers who drive across state or national boundaries, motorcoach drivers must comply with Department of Transportation regulations.

Schoolbus drivers usually drive the same routes each day, stopping to pick up pupils in the morning and return them to their homes in the afternoon. Some schoolbus drivers also transport students and teachers on field trips or to sporting events. In addition to driving, some schoolbus drivers work part time in the school system as janitors, mechanics, or classroom assistants when not driving buses.

Bus drivers must be alert in order to prevent accidents, especially in heavy traffic or in bad weather, and to avoid sudden stops or swerves that jar passengers. Schoolbus drivers must exercise particular caution when children are getting on or off the bus. They must maintain order on their bus and enforce school safety standards by allowing only students to board. In addition, they must know and enforce rules regarding student conduct used throughout the school system.

Schoolbus drivers do not always have to report to an assigned terminal or garage. In some cases, they have the choice of taking their bus home or parking it in a more convenient area. Schoolbus drivers do not collect fares. Instead, they prepare weekly reports on the number of students, trips or "runs," work hours, miles, and fuel consumption. Their supervisors set time schedules and routes for the day or week.

Working Conditions

Driving a bus through heavy traffic while dealing with passengers is more stressful and fatiguing than physically strenuous. Many drivers enjoy the opportunity to work without direct supervision, with full responsibility for their bus and passengers. To improve working conditions and retain drivers, many buslines provide ergonomically designed seats and controls for drivers.

Intercity bus drivers may work nights, weekends, and holidays and often spend nights away from home, during which they stay in hotels at company expense. Senior drivers with regular routes have regular weekly work schedules, but others do not have regular schedules and must be prepared to report for work on short notice. They report for work only when called for a charter assignment or to drive extra buses on a regular route. Intercity bus travel and charter work tends to be seasonal. From May through August, drivers may work the maximum number of hours per week that regulations allow. During winter, junior drivers may work infrequently, except for busy holiday travel periods, and may be furloughed at times.

Schoolbus drivers work only when school is in session. Many work 20 hours a week or less, driving one or two routes in the morning and afternoon. Drivers taking field or athletic trips, or who also have midday kindergarten routes, may work more hours a week. As more students with a variety of physical and behavioral disabilities assimilate into mainstream schools, schoolbus drivers must learn how to accommodate their special needs.

Regular local-transit bus drivers usually have a 5-day workweek; Saturdays and Sundays are considered regular workdays. Some drivers work evenings and after midnight. To accommodate commuters, many work "split shifts," for example, 6 a.m. to 10 a.m. and 3 p.m. to 7 p.m., with time off in between.

Tour and charter bus drivers may work any day and all hours of the day, including weekends and holidays. Their hours are dictated by the charter trips booked and the schedule and prearranged itinerary of tours. However, like all bus drivers, their weekly hours must be consistent with the Department of Transportation's rules and regulations concerning hours of service. For example, a driver may drive for 10 hours and work for up to 15 hours—including driving and nondriving duties—before having 8 hours off-duty. A driver may not drive after having worked for 70 hours in the past 8 days. Most drivers are required to document their time in a logbook.

Employment

Bus drivers held about 654,000 jobs in 2002. Over one-third worked part time. More than two-thirds of all bus drivers were schoolbus drivers working primarily for school systems or for companies providing schoolbus services under contract. Most of the remainder worked for private and local government transit systems; some also worked for intercity and charter buslines.

Training, Other Qualifications, and Advancement

Bus driver qualifications and standards are established by state and federal regulations. All drivers must comply with federal regulations and with any state regulations that exceed federal requirements. Federal regulations require drivers who operate commercial motor vehicles to hold a commercial driver's license (CDL) from the state in which they live.

To qualify for a commercial driver's license, applicants must pass a written test on rules and regulations and then demonstrate that they can operate a bus safely. A national databank permanently records all driving violations incurred by persons who hold commercial licenses. A state may not issue a commercial driver's license to a driver who has already had a license suspended or revoked in another state. A driver with a CDL must accompany trainees until the trainees get their own CDL. Information on how to apply for a commercial driver's license may be obtained from state motor vehicle administrations.

While many states allow those who are 18 years of age and older to drive buses within state borders, the Department of Transportation establishes minimum qualifications for bus drivers engaged in interstate commerce. Federal Motor Carrier Safety Regulations require drivers to be at least 21 years old and to pass a physical examination once every 2 years. The main physical requirements include good hearing, at least 20/40 vision with or without glasses or corrective lenses, and a 70-degree field of vision in each eye. Drivers must not be colorblind. They must be able to hear a forced whisper in one ear at not less than 5 feet, with or without a hearing aide. Drivers must have normal use of arms and legs and normal blood pressure. They may not use any controlled substances, unless prescribed by a licensed physician. Persons with epilepsy or diabetes controlled by insulin are not permitted to be interstate bus drivers. Federal regulations also require employers to test their drivers for alcohol and drug use as a condition of employment, and require periodic random tests of the drivers while they are on duty. In addition, a driver must not have been convicted of a felony involving the use of a motor vehicle; a crime involving drugs; driving under the influence of drugs or alcohol; or hit-and-run driving that resulted in injury or death. All drivers must be able to read and speak English well enough to read road signs, prepare reports, and communicate with law enforcement officers and the public. In addition, drivers must take a written examination on the Motor Carrier Safety Regulations of the U.S. Department of Transportation.

Many employers prefer high school graduates and require a written test of ability to follow complex bus schedules. Many intercity and public transit bus companies prefer applicants who are at least 24 years of age; some require several years of experience driving a bus or truck. In some states, schoolbus drivers must pass a background investigation to uncover any criminal record or history of mental problems.

Because bus drivers deal with passengers, they must be courteous. They need an even temperament and emotional stability because driving in heavy, fast-moving, or stop-and-go traffic and dealing with passengers can be stressful. Drivers must have strong customer service skills, including communication skills and the ability to coordinate and manage large groups of people.

Most intercity bus companies and local-transit systems give driver trainees 2 to 8 weeks of classroom and "behind-the-wheel" instruction. In the classroom, trainees learn Department of Transportation and company work rules, safety regulations, state and municipal driving regulations, and safe driving practices. They also learn to read schedules, determine fares, keep records, and deal courteously with passengers.

Schoolbus drivers also are required to obtain a commercial driver's license from the state in which they live. Many persons who become schoolbus drivers have never driven any vehicle larger than an automobile. They receive between 1 and 4 weeks of driving instruction plus classroom training on state and local laws, regulations, and policies of operating schoolbuses; safe driving practices; driver-pupil relations; first aid; special needs of disabled and emotionally troubled students; and emergency evacuation procedures. Schoolbus drivers also must be aware of the school system's rules for discipline and conduct for bus drivers and the students they transport.

During training, bus drivers practice driving on set courses. They practice turns and zigzag maneuvers, backing up, and driving in narrow lanes. Then, they drive in light traffic and, eventually, on congested highways and city streets. They also make trial runs, without passengers, to improve their driving skills and learn the routes. Local-transit trainees memorize and drive each of the runs operating out of their assigned garage. New drivers begin with a "break-in" period. They make regularly scheduled trips with passengers, accompanied by an experienced driver who gives helpful tips, answers questions, and evaluates the new driver's performance.

New intercity and local-transit drivers are usually placed on an "extra" list to drive charter runs, extra buses on regular runs, and special runs (for example, during morning and evening rush hours and to sports events). They also substitute for regular drivers who are ill or on vacation. New drivers remain on the extra list, and may work only part time, for perhaps several years, until they have enough seniority to be given a regular run.

Senior drivers may bid for the runs that they prefer, such as those with more work hours, lighter traffic, weekends off, or, in the case of intercity bus drivers, higher earnings or fewer workdays per week.

Opportunities for promotion are generally limited. However, experienced drivers may become supervisors or dispatchers, assigning buses to drivers, checking whether drivers are on schedule, rerouting buses to avoid blocked streets or other problems, and dispatching extra vehicles and service crews to scenes of accidents and breakdowns. In transit agencies with rail systems, drivers may become train operators or station attendants. A few drivers become managers. Promotion in publicly owned bus systems is often by competitive civil service examination. Some motorcoach drivers purchase their own equipment and open their own business.

Job Outlook

Persons seeking jobs as bus drivers should encounter good opportunities. Individuals who have good driving records and who are willing to work a part-time or irregular schedule should have the best job prospects. Schoolbus driving jobs, particularly in rapidly growing suburban areas, should be easiest to acquire because most are part-time positions with high turnover and minimal training requirements. Those seeking higher paying intercity and public transit bus driver positions may encounter competition. Employment prospects for motorcoach drivers will fluctuate with the cyclical nature of the economy, as demand for motorcoach services is very dependent on tourism.

Employment of bus drivers is expected to increase about as fast as the average for all occupations through the year 2012, primarily to meet the transportation needs of the growing general population and the school-age population. Many additional job openings are expected to occur each year because of the need to replace workers who take jobs in other occupations or who retire or leave the occupation for other reasons.

The number of schoolbus drivers is expected to increase as a result of growth in elementary and secondary school enrollments. In addition, more schoolbus drivers will be needed as more of the nation's population is concentrated in suburban areas, where students generally ride schoolbuses, and less in central cities, where transportation is not provided for most pupils.

Employment growth of local-transit bus drivers will be spurred by increases in the number of passengers and in funding levels. Funding levels for public transit may fluctuate as the public's interest in transportation changes. There may be competition for positions with more regular hours and steady driving routes.

Competition from other modes of transportation—airplane, train, or automobile—will temper job growth among intercity bus drivers. Most growth in intercity bus transportation will occur in group charters to locations not served by other modes of transportation. Like automobiles, buses have a far greater number of possible destinations than airplanes or trains. Due to greater cost savings and convenience over automobiles, buses usually are the most economical option for tour groups traveling to out-of-the-way destinations.

Full-time bus drivers are rarely laid off during recessions. However, employers might reduce hours of part-time local-transit and intercity bus drivers if the number of passengers decreases, because fewer extra buses would be needed. Seasonal layoffs are common. Many intercity bus drivers with little seniority, for example, are furloughed during the winter when regular schedule and charter business declines; schoolbus drivers seldom work during the summer or school holidays.

Earnings

Median hourly earnings of transit and intercity bus drivers were $14.22 in 2002. The middle 50 percent earned between $10.51 and $18.99 an hour. The lowest 10 percent earned less than $8.37, and the highest 10 percent earned more than $22.51 an hour. Median hourly earnings in the industries employing the largest numbers of transit and intercity bus drivers in 2002 were as follows:

Local government	$16.95
Interurban and rural bus transportation	15.15
Urban transit systems	15.02
School and employee bus transportation	11.29
Charter bus industry	10.64

Median hourly earnings of schoolbus drivers were $10.77 in 2002. The middle 50 percent earned between $7.73 and $13.53 an hour. The lowest 10 percent earned less than $6.24, and the highest 10 percent earned more than $16.44 an hour. Median hourly earnings in the industries employing the largest numbers of schoolbus drivers in 2002 were as follows:

School and employee bus transportation	$11.44
Local government	11.09
Elementary and secondary schools	10.50
Other transit and ground passenger transportation	9.79
Individual and family services	8.27

The benefits bus drivers receive from their employers vary greatly. Most intercity and local-transit bus drivers receive paid health and life insurance, sick leave, vacation leave, and free bus rides on any of the regular routes of their line or system. Schoolbus drivers receive sick leave, and many are covered by health and life insurance and pension plans. Because they generally do not work when school is not in session, they do not get vacation leave. In a number of states, local-transit and schoolbus drivers employed by local governments are covered by a statewide public employee pension system. Increasingly, school systems extend benefits to drivers who supplement their driving by working in the school system during off hours.

Most intercity and many local-transit bus drivers are members of the Amalgamated Transit Union. Local-transit bus drivers in New York and several other large cities belong to the Transport Workers Union of America. Some drivers belong to the United Transportation Union or the International Brotherhood of Teamsters.

Related Occupations

Other workers who drive vehicles on highways and city streets include taxi drivers and chauffeurs and truck drivers and driver/sales workers.

Sources of Additional Information

For information on employment opportunities, contact local-transit systems, intercity buslines, school systems, or the local offices of the state employment service.

General information on schoolbus driving is available from:

- National School Transportation Association, 625 Slaters Lane, Suite 205, Alexandria, VA 22314.

General information on local-transit bus driving is available from:

- American Public Transportation Association, 1666 K St. NW, Suite 1100, Washington, DC 20006.

General information on motorcoach driving is available from:

- United Motorcoach Association, 113 S. West St., 4th Floor, Alexandria, VA 22314.

Cardiovascular Technologists and Technicians

(O*NET 29-2031.00)

Significant Points

- Employment will grow faster than the average, but the number of job openings created will be low because the occupation is small.

- Employment of most specialties will grow, but fewer EKG technicians will be needed.

- About 3 out of 4 jobs were in hospitals.

Nature of the Work

Cardiovascular technologists and technicians assist physicians in diagnosing and treating cardiac (heart) and peripheral vascular (blood vessel) ailments. Cardiovascular technologists may specialize in three areas of practice—invasive cardiology, echocardiography, and vascular technology. Cardiovascular technicians who specialize in electrocardiograms (EKGs), stress testing, and Holter monitors are known as *cardiographic*, or *EKG technicians*.

Cardiovascular technologists specializing in invasive procedures are called *cardiology technologists*. They assist physicians with cardiac catheterization procedures in which a small tube, or catheter, is wound through a patient's blood vessel from a spot on the patient's leg into the heart. The procedure can determine whether a blockage exists in the blood vessels that supply the heart muscle. The procedure also can help to diagnose other problems. Part of the procedure may involve balloon angioplasty, which can be used to treat blockages of blood vessels or heart valves without the need for heart surgery. Cardiology technologists assist physicians as they insert a catheter with a balloon on the end to the point of the obstruction.

Technologists prepare patients for cardiac catheterization and balloon angioplasty by first positioning them on an examining table and then shaving, cleaning, and administering anesthesia to the top of their leg near the groin. During the procedures, they monitor patients' blood pressure and heart rate with EKG equipment and notify the physician if something appears to be wrong. Technologists also may prepare and monitor patients during open-heart surgery and the implantation of pacemakers.

Cardiovascular technologists who specialize in echocardiography or vascular technology often run noninvasive tests using ultrasound instrumentation, such as Doppler ultrasound. Tests are called "noninvasive" if they do not require the insertion of probes or other instruments into the patient's body. The ultrasound instrumentation transmits high-frequency sound waves into areas of the patient's body and then processes reflected echoes of the sound waves to form an image. Technologists view the ultrasound image on a screen, and may record the image on videotape or photograph it for interpretation and diagnosis by a physician. As the instrument scans the image, technologists check the image on the screen for subtle differences between healthy and diseased areas, decide which images to include in the report to the physician, and judge if the images are satisfactory for diagnostic purposes. They also explain the procedure to patients, record any additional medical history the patient relates, select appropriate equipment settings, and change the patient's position as necessary.

Those who assist physicians in the diagnosis of disorders affecting the circulation are known as *vascular technologists* or *vascular sonographers*. They perform a medical history and evaluate pulses by listening to the sounds of the arteries for abnormalities. Then, they perform a noninvasive procedure using ultrasound instrumentation to record vascular information, such as vascular blood flow, blood pressure, limb volume changes, oxygen saturation, cerebral circulation, peripheral circulation, and abdominal circulation. Many of these tests are performed during or immediately after surgery.

Technologists who use ultrasound to examine the heart chambers, valves, and vessels are referred to as *cardiac sonographers*, or *echocardiographers*. They use ultrasound instrumentation to create images called echocardiograms. An echocardiogram may be performed while the patient is either resting or physically active. Technologists may administer medication to physically active patients to assess their heart function. Cardiac sonographers may also assist physicians who perform transesophageal echocardiography, which involves placing a tube in the patient's esophagus to obtain ultrasound images.

Cardiovascular technicians who obtain EKGs are known as *electrocardiograph (*or *EKG) technicians*. To take a basic EKG, which traces electrical impulses transmitted by the heart, technicians attach electrodes to the patient's chest, arms, and legs, and then manipulate switches on an EKG machine to obtain a reading. A printout is made for interpretation by the physician. This test is done before most kinds of surgery or as part of a routine physical examination, especially for persons who have reached middle age or who have a history of cardiovascular problems.

EKG technicians with advanced training perform Holter monitor and stress testing. For Holter monitoring, technicians place electrodes on the patient's chest and attach a portable EKG monitor to the patient's belt. Following 24 or more hours of normal activity by the patient, the technician removes a tape from the monitor and places it in a scanner. After checking the quality of the recorded impulses on an electronic screen, the technician usually prints the information from the tape so that a physician can interpret it later. Physicians use the output from the scanner to diagnose heart ailments, such as heart rhythm abnormalities or problems with pacemakers.

For a treadmill stress test, EKG technicians document the patient's medical history, explain the procedure, connect the patient to an EKG monitor, and obtain a baseline reading and resting blood pressure. Next, they monitor the heart's performance while the patient is walking on a treadmill, gradually increasing the treadmill's speed to observe the effect of increased exertion. Like vascular technologists and cardiac sonographers, cardiographic technicians who perform EKG, Holter monitor, and stress tests are known as "noninvasive" technicians.

Some cardiovascular technologists and technicians schedule appointments, type doctors' interpretations, maintain patient files, and care for equipment.

Working Conditions

Technologists and technicians generally work a 5-day, 40-hour week that may include weekends. Those in catheterization labs tend to work longer hours and may work evenings. They also may be on call during the night and on weekends.

Cardiovascular technologists and technicians spend a lot of time walking and standing. Those who work in catheterization labs may face stressful working conditions because they are in close contact with patients with serious heart ailments. Some patients, for example, may encounter complications from time to time that have life-or-death implications.

Employment

Cardiovascular technologists and technicians held about 43,000 jobs in 2002. About 3 out 4 jobs were in hospitals, primarily in cardiology departments. The remaining jobs were mostly in offices of physicians, including cardiologists; or in medical and diagnostic laboratories, including diagnostic imaging centers.

Training, Other Qualifications, and Advancement

Although a few cardiovascular technologists, vascular technologists, and cardiac sonographers are currently trained on the job, most receive training in 2- to 4-year programs. Cardiovascular technologists, vascular technologists, and cardiac sonographers normally complete a 2-year junior or community college program. The first year is dedicated to core courses and is followed by a year of specialized instruction in either invasive, noninvasive cardiovascular, or noninvasive vascular technology. Those who are qualified in an allied health profession need to complete only the year of specialized instruction.

Graduates from the 29 programs accredited by the Joint Review Committee on Education in Cardiovascular Technology are eligible to obtain professional certification in cardiac catheterization, echocardiography, vascular ultrasound, and cardiographic techniques from Cardiovascular Credentialing International. Cardiac sonographers and vascular technologists also may obtain certification from the American Registry of diagnostic medical sonographers.

For basic EKGs, Holter monitoring, and stress testing, 1-year certification programs exist, but most EKG technicians are still trained on the job by an EKG supervisor or a cardiologist. On-the-job training usually lasts about 8 to 16 weeks. Most employers prefer to train people already in the healthcare field—nursing aides, for example. Some EKG technicians are students enrolled in 2-year programs to become technologists, working part time to gain experience and make contact with employers.

Cardiovascular technologists and technicians must be reliable, have mechanical aptitude, and be able to follow detailed instructions. A pleasant, relaxed manner for putting patients at ease is an asset.

Job Outlook

Employment of cardiovascular technologists and technicians is expected to grow faster than the average for all occupations through the year 2012. Growth will occur as the population ages, because older people have a higher incidence of heart problems. Employment of vascular technolo-

gists and echocardiographers will grow as advances in vascular technology and sonography reduce the need for more costly and invasive procedures. However, fewer EKG technicians will be needed, as hospitals train nursing aides and others to perform basic EKG procedures. Individuals trained in Holter monitoring and stress testing are expected to have more favorable job prospects than are those who can perform only a basic EKG.

Some job openings for cardiovascular technologists and technicians will arise from replacement needs, as individuals transfer to other jobs or leave the labor force. However, job growth and replacement needs will produce relatively few job openings because the occupation is small.

Earnings

Median annual earnings of cardiovascular technologists and technicians were $36,430 in 2002. The middle 50 percent earned between $26,730 and $46,570. The lowest 10 percent earned less than $20,920, and the highest 10 percent earned more than $56,080. Median annual earnings of cardiovascular technologists and technicians in 2002 were $36,420 in offices of physicians and $35,800 in general medical and surgical hospitals.

Related Occupations

Cardiovascular technologists and technicians operate sophisticated equipment that helps physicians and other health practitioners to diagnose and treat patients. So do diagnostic medical sonographers, nuclear medicine technologists, radiation therapists, radiologic technologists and technicians, and respiratory therapists.

Sources of Additional Information

For general information about a career in cardiovascular technology, contact:

- Alliance of Cardiovascular Professionals, 4456 Thalia Landing Offices, Bldg. 2, 4356 Bonney Rd., Suite 103, Virginia Beach, VA 23452-1200. Internet: http://www.acp-online.org

For a list of accredited programs in cardiovascular technology, contact:

- Committee on Accreditation for Allied Health Education Programs, 39 East Wacker Dr., Chicago, IL 60601. Internet: http://www.caahep.org

- Joint Review Committee on Education in Cardiovascular Technology, 3525 Ellicott Mills Dr., Suite N, Ellicott City, MD 21043-4547.

For information on vascular technology, contact:

- Society of Vascular Ultrasound, 4601 Presidents Dr., Suite 260, Lanham, MD 20706-4381. Internet: http://www.svunet.org

For information on echocardiography, contact:

- American Society of Echocardiography, 1500 Sunday Dr., Suite 102, Raleigh, NC 27607. Internet: http://www.asecho.org

For information regarding registration and certification, contact:

- Cardiovascular Credentialing International, 1500 Sunday Dr., Suite 102, Raleigh, NC 27607. Internet: http://www.cci-online.org

- American Registry of Diagnostic Medical Sonographers, 51 Monroe St., Plaza East One, Rockville, MD 20850-2400. Internet: http://www.ardms.org

Cashiers

(O*NET 41-2011.00 and 41-2012.00)

Significant Points

- Cashiers are trained on the job; this occupation provides opportunities for many young people with no previous work experience.

- Nearly one-half of all cashiers work part time.

- Good employment opportunities are expected because of the large number of workers who leave this occupation each year.

- Many cashiers start at the federal minimum wage.

Nature of the Work

Supermarkets, department stores, gasoline service stations, movie theaters, restaurants, and many other businesses employ cashiers to register the sale of their merchandise. Most cashiers total bills, receive money, make change, fill out charge forms, and give receipts.

Although specific job duties vary by employer, cashiers usually are assigned to a register at the beginning of their shifts and are given drawers containing a specific amount of money with which to start—their "banks." They must count their banks to ensure that they contain the correct amount of money and adequate supplies of change. At the end of their shifts, they once again count the drawers' contents and compare the totals with sales data. An occasional shortage of small amounts may be overlooked but, in many establishments, repeated shortages are grounds for dismissal.

In addition to counting the contents of their drawers at the end of their shifts, cashiers usually separate and total charge forms, return slips, coupons, and any other noncash items. Cashiers also handle returns and exchanges. They must ensure that returned merchandise is in good condition, and determine where and when it was purchased and what type of payment was used.

After entering charges for all items and subtracting the value of any coupons or special discounts, cashiers total the customer's bill and take payment. Acceptable forms of payment include cash, personal checks, credit cards, and debit cards. Cashiers must know the store's policies and procedures for each type of payment the store accepts. For checks and charges, they may request additional identification from the customer or call in for an authorization. They must verify the age of customers purchasing alcohol or tobacco. When the sale is complete, cashiers issue a receipt to the customer and return the appropriate change. They may also wrap or bag the purchase.

Cashiers traditionally have totaled customers' purchases using cash registers—manually entering the price of each product bought. However, most establishments now use more sophisticated equipment, such as scanners and computers. In a store with scanners, a cashier passes a product's Universal Product Code over the scanning device, which transmits the code number to a computer. The computer identifies the item and its price. In other establishments, cashiers manually enter codes into computers, and descriptions of the items and their prices appear on the screen.

Depending on the type of establishment, cashiers may have other duties as well. In many supermarkets, for example, cashiers weigh produce and bulk food, as well as return unwanted items to the shelves. In convenience stores, cashiers may be required to know how to use a variety of machines other than cash registers, and how to furnish money orders and sell lottery tickets. Operating ticket-dispensing machines and answering customers' questions are common duties for cashiers who work at movie theaters and ticket agencies. In casinos, *gaming change persons* and *booth cashiers* exchange coins and tokens and may issue payoffs. They may also operate a booth in the slot-machine area and furnish change persons with a money bank at the start of the shift, or count and audit money in drawers

Working Conditions

Nearly one-half of all cashiers work part time. Hours of work often vary depending on the needs of the employer. Generally, cashiers are expected to work weekends, evenings, and holidays to accommodate customers' needs. However, many employers offer flexible schedules. For example, full-time workers who work on weekends may receive time off during the week. Because the holiday season is the busiest time for most retailers, many employers restrict the use of vacation time from Thanksgiving through the beginning of January.

Most cashiers work indoors, usually standing in booths or behind counters. In addition, they often are unable to leave their workstations without supervisory approval because they are responsible for large sums of money. The work of cashiers can be very repetitive, but improvements in workstation design are being made to combat problems caused by repetitive motion. In addition, the work can sometimes be dangerous; cashiers' risk from workplace homicides is much higher than that of the total workforce.

Employment

Cashiers held about 3.5 million jobs in 2002. Although cashiers are employed in almost every industry, 26 percent of all jobs were in food and beverage stores. Gasoline stations, department stores, other retail establishments, and restaurants also employed large numbers of these workers. Outside of retail establishments, many cashiers worked in amusement, gambling, and recreation industries, local government, and personal and laundry services. Because cashiers are needed in businesses and organizations of all types and sizes, job opportunities are found throughout the country.

Training, Other Qualifications, and Advancement

Cashier jobs tend to be entry-level positions requiring little or no previous work experience. Although there are no specific educational requirements, employers filling full-time jobs often prefer applicants with high school diplomas.

Nearly all cashiers are trained on the job. In small businesses, an experienced worker often trains beginners. The trainee spends the first day observing the operation and becoming familiar with the store's equipment, policies, and procedures. After this, trainees are assigned to a register—frequently under the supervision of an experienced worker. In larger businesses, trainees spend several days in classes before being placed at cash registers. Topics typically covered in class include a description of the industry and the company, store policies and procedures, equipment operation, and security.

Training for experienced workers is not common, except when new equipment is introduced or when procedures change. In these cases, the employer or a representative of the equipment manufacturer trains workers on the job.

Persons who want to become cashiers should be able to do repetitive work accurately. They also need basic mathematics skills and good manual dexterity. Because cashiers deal constantly with the public, they should be neat in appearance and able to deal tactfully and pleasantly with customers. In addition, some businesses prefer to hire persons who can operate specialized equipment or who have business experience, such as typing, selling, or handling money.

Advancement opportunities for cashiers vary. For those working part time, promotion may be to a full-time position. Others advance to head cashier or cash-office clerk. In addition, this job offers a good opportunity to learn about an employer's business and can serve as a steppingstone to a more responsible position.

Job Outlook

Opportunities for full-time and part-time cashier jobs should continue to be good, because of employment growth and the need to replace the large number of workers who transfer to other occupations or leave the labor force. There is substantial movement into and out of the occupation because education and training requirements are minimal, and the predominance of part-time jobs is attractive to people seeking a short-term source of income rather than a full-time career. Historically, workers under the age of 25 have

filled many of the openings in this occupation—in 2002, one-half of all cashiers were 24 years of age or younger. Some establishments have begun hiring elderly and disabled persons to fill some of their job openings.

Cashier employment is expected to grow about as fast as the average for all occupations through the year 2012 because of expanding demand for goods and services by a growing population. The rising popularity of electronic commerce, which does not require a cashier to complete a transaction or accept payment, may reduce the employment growth of cashiers. However, electronic commerce will have a limited impact on this large occupation, as many consumers lack Internet access or still prefer the traditional method of purchasing goods at stores. The growing use of self-service check-out systems in retail trade, especially at grocery stores, may also have an adverse effect on employment of cashiers. This trend, however, will largely depend on the public's acceptance of the new self-service technology.

Job opportunities may vary from year to year, because the strength of the economy affects demand for cashiers. Companies tend to hire more persons for such jobs when the economy is strong. Seasonal demand for cashiers also causes fluctuations in employment.

Earnings

Many cashiers start at the federal minimum wage, which was $5.15 an hour in 2003. Some state laws set the minimum wage higher, and establishments must pay at least that amount. Wages tend to be higher in areas in which there is intense competition for workers.

Median hourly earnings of cashiers, except gaming in 2002 were $7.41. The middle 50 percent earned between $6.51 and $8.73 an hour. The lowest 10 percent earned less than $5.86, and the highest 10 percent earned more than $10.97 an hour. Median hourly earnings in the industries employing the largest numbers of cashiers in 2002 were as follows:

Grocery stores $7.57

Department stores 7.55

Other general merchandise stores 7.27

Gasoline stations 7.18

Health and personal care stores................................7.08

Benefits for full-time cashiers tend to be better than those for cashiers working part time. In addition to typical benefits, those working in retail establishments often receive discounts on purchases, and cashiers in restaurants may receive free or low-cost meals. Some employers also offer employee stock-option plans and education-reimbursement plans.

Related Occupations

Cashiers accept payment for the purchase of goods and services. Other workers with similar duties include tellers, counter and rental clerks, food and beverage serving and related workers, gaming cage workers, Postal Service workers, and retail salespersons.

Sources of Additional Information

General information on retailing is available from:

● National Retail Federation, 325 7th St. NW, Suite 1100, Washington, DC 20004.

For information about employment opportunities as a cashier, contact:

● National Association of Convenience Stores, 1605 King St., Alexandria, VA 22314-2792.

● United Food and Commercial Workers International Union, Education Office, 1775 K St. NW, Washington, DC 20006-1502.

Cement Masons, Concrete Finishers, Segmental Pavers, and Terrazzo Workers

(O*NET 47-2051.00, 47-2053.00, and 47-4091.00)

Significant Points

● Job opportunities are expected to be favorable.

● Most learn on the job, either through formal 3-year or 4-year apprenticeship programs or by working as helpers.

Nature of the Work

Cement masons, concrete finishers, and terrazzo workers all work with concrete, one of the most common and durable materials used in construction. Once set, concrete—a mixture of Portland cement, sand, gravel, and water—becomes the foundation for everything from decorative patios and floors to huge dams or miles of roadways.

Cement masons and *concrete finishers* place and finish the concrete. They also may color concrete surfaces; expose aggregate (small stones) in walls and sidewalks; or fabricate concrete beams, columns, and panels. In preparing a site for placing concrete, cement masons first set the forms for holding the concrete and properly align them. They then direct the casting of the concrete and supervise laborers who use shovels or special tools to spread it. Masons then guide a straightedge back and forth across the top of the forms to "screed," or level, the freshly placed concrete. Immediately after leveling the concrete, masons carefully smooth the concrete surface with a "bull float," a long-handled tool

about 8 by 48 inches that covers the coarser materials in the concrete and brings a rich mixture of fine cement paste to the surface.

After the concrete has been leveled and floated, concrete finishers press an edger between the forms and the concrete and guide it along the edge and the surface. This produces slightly rounded edges and helps prevent chipping or cracking. Concrete finishers use a special tool called a "groover" to make joints or grooves at specific intervals that help control cracking. Next, they trowel the surface using either a powered or hand trowel, a small, smooth, rectangular metal tool.

Sometimes, cement masons perform all the steps of laying concrete, including the finishing. As the final step, they retrowel the concrete surface back and forth with powered and hand trowels to create a smooth finish. For a coarse, nonskid finish, masons brush the surface with a broom or stiff-bristled brush. For a pebble finish, they embed small gravel chips into the surface. They then wash any excess cement from the exposed chips with a mild acid solution. For color, they use colored premixed concrete. On concrete surfaces that will remain exposed after the forms are stripped, such as columns, ceilings, and wall panels, cement masons cut away high spots and loose concrete with hammer and chisel, fill any large indentations with a Portland cement paste, and smooth the surface with a carborundum stone. Finally, they coat the exposed area with a rich Portland cement mixture, using either a special tool or a coarse cloth to rub the concrete to a uniform finish.

Throughout the entire process, cement masons must monitor how the wind, heat, or cold affects the curing of the concrete. They must have a thorough knowledge of concrete characteristics so that, by using sight and touch, they can determine what is happening to the concrete and take measures to prevent defects.

Segmental pavers lay out, cut, and install pavers, which are flat pieces of masonry usually made from compacted concrete or brick. Pavers are used to pave paths, patios, playgrounds, driveways, and steps. They are manufactured in various textures and often interlock together to form an attractive pattern. Segmental pavers first prepare the site by removing the existing pavement or soil. They grade the remaining soil to the proper depth and determine the amount of base material that is needed, which depends on the local soil conditions. They then install and compact the base material, a granular material that compacts easily, and lay the pavers from the center out, so that any trimmed pieces will be on the outside rather than in the center. Then, they install edging materials to prevent the pavers from shifting and fill the spaces between the pavers with dry sand.

Terrazzo workers create attractive walkways, floors, patios, and panels by exposing marble chips and other fine aggregates on the surface of finished concrete. Much of the preliminary work of terrazzo workers is similar to that of cement masons. Attractive, marble-chip terrazzo requires three layers of materials. First, cement masons or terrazzo workers build a solid, level concrete foundation that is 3 to 4 inches deep. After the forms are removed from the foundation, workers add a 1-inch layer of sandy concrete. Before this layer sets, terrazzo workers partially embed metal divider strips in the concrete wherever there is to be a joint or change of color in the terrazzo. For the final layer, terrazzo workers blend and place into each of the panels a fine marble chip mixture that may be color-pigmented. While the mixture is still wet, workers toss additional marble chips of various colors into each panel and roll a lightweight roller over the entire surface.

When the terrazzo is thoroughly dry, helpers grind it with a terrazzo grinder, which is somewhat like a floor polisher, only much heavier. Slight depressions left by the grinding are filled with a matching grout material and hand-troweled for a smooth, uniform surface. Terrazzo workers then clean, polish, and seal the dry surface for a lustrous finish.

Working Conditions

Concrete, segmental paving, or terrazzo work is fast-paced and strenuous, and requires continuous physical effort. Because most finishing is done at floor level, workers must bend and kneel often. Many jobs are outdoors, and work is generally halted during inclement weather. The work, either indoors or outdoors, may be in areas that are muddy, dusty, or dirty. To avoid chemical burns from uncured concrete and sore knees from frequent kneeling, many workers wear kneepads. Workers usually also wear water-repellent boots while working in wet concrete.

Employment

Cement masons, concrete finishers, segmental pavers, and terrazzo workers held about 190,000 jobs in 2002; segmental pavers and terrazzo workers accounted for only a small portion of the total. Most cement masons and concrete finishers worked for concrete contractors or for general contractors on projects such as highways; bridges; shopping malls; or large buildings such as factories, schools, and hospitals. A small number were employed by firms that manufacture concrete products. Most segmental pavers and terrazzo workers worked for special trade contractors who install decorative floors and wall panels.

Only about 1 out of 20 cement masons, concrete finishers, segmental pavers, and terrazzo workers were self-employed, a smaller proportion than in other building trades. Most self-employed masons specialized in small jobs, such as driveways, sidewalks, and patios.

Training, Other Qualifications, and Advancement

Most cement masons, concrete finishers, segmental pavers, and terrazzo workers learn their trades either through on-the-job training as helpers, or through 3-year or 4-year apprenticeship programs. Many masons and finishers first gain experience as construction laborers.

When hiring helpers and apprentices, employers prefer high school graduates who are at least 18 years old and in good physical condition, and who have a driver's license. The ability to get along with others also is important because cement masons frequently work in teams. High school courses in general science, vocational-technical subjects, mathematics, blueprint reading, or mechanical drawing provide a helpful background.

On-the-job training programs consist of informal instruction, in which experienced workers teach helpers to use the tools, equipment, machines, and materials of the trade. Trainees begin with tasks such as edging, jointing, and using a straightedge on freshly placed concrete. As training progresses, assignments become more complex, and trainees can usually do finishing work within a short time.

Three-year or four-year apprenticeship programs, usually jointly sponsored by local unions and contractors, provide on-the-job training in addition to a recommended minimum of 144 hours of classroom instruction each year. A written test and a physical exam may be required. In the classroom, apprentices learn applied mathematics, blueprint reading, and safety. Apprentices generally receive special instruction in layout work and cost estimation. Some workers learn their jobs by attending trade or vocational-technical schools.

Cement masons, concrete finishers, segmental pavers, and terrazzo workers should enjoy doing demanding work. They should take pride in craftsmanship and be able to work without close supervision.

With additional training, cement masons, concrete finishers, segmental pavers, or terrazzo workers may become supervisors for masonry contractors. Some eventually become owners of businesses employing many workers and may spend most of their time as managers rather than practicing their original trade. Others move into closely related areas such as construction management, building inspection, or contract estimation.

Job Outlook

Opportunities for cement masons, concrete finishers, segmental pavers, and terrazzo workers are expected to be favorable as the demand meets the supply of workers trained in this craft. In addition, many potential workers may prefer work that is less strenuous and has more comfortable working conditions.

Employment of cement masons, concrete finishers, segmental pavers, and terrazzo workers is expected to grow faster than the average for all occupations through 2012. These workers will be needed to build highways, bridges, subways, factories, office buildings, hotels, shopping centers, schools, hospitals, and other structures. In addition, the increasing use of concrete as a building material will add to the demand. More cement masons also will be needed to repair and renovate existing highways, bridges, and other structures. In addition to job growth, other openings will become available as experienced workers transfer to other occupations or leave the labor force.

Employment of cement masons, concrete finishers, segmental pavers, and terrazzo workers, like that of many other construction workers, is sensitive to the fluctuations of the economy. Workers in these trades may experience periods of unemployment when the overall level of construction falls. On the other hand, shortages of these workers may occur in some areas during peak periods of building activity.

Earnings

In 2002, the median hourly earnings of cement masons and concrete finishers were $14.74. The middle 50 percent earned between $11.52 and $20.02. The top 10 percent earned over $26.02, and the bottom 10 percent earned less than $9.31.

In 2002, the median hourly earnings of terrazzo workers and finishers were $13.42. The middle 50 percent earned between $10.46 and $17.72. The top 10 percent earned over $23.70, and the bottom 10 percent earned less than $8.94.

Like those of other construction trades workers, earnings of cement masons, concrete finishers, segmental pavers, and terrazzo workers may be reduced on occasion because poor weather and downturns in construction activity limit the amount of time they can work. Cement masons often work overtime, with premium pay, because once concrete has been placed, the job must be completed.

Many cement masons, concrete finishers, segmental pavers, and terrazzo workers belong to the Operative Plasterers' and Cement Masons' International Association of the United States and Canada, or to the International Union of Bricklayers and Allied Craftworkers. Some terrazzo workers belong to the United Brotherhood of Carpenters and Joiners of the United States. Nonunion workers generally have lower wage rates than do union workers. Apprentices usually start at 50 to 60 percent of the rate paid to experienced workers.

Related Occupations

Cement masons, concrete finishers, segmental pavers, and terrazzo workers combine skill with knowledge of building materials to construct buildings, highways, and other structures. Other occupations involving similar skills and knowledge include brickmasons, blockmasons, and stonemasons; carpet, floor, and tile installers and finishers; drywall installers, ceiling tile installers, and tapers; and plasterers and stucco masons.

Sources of Additional Information

For information about apprenticeships and work opportunities, contact local concrete or terrazzo contractors, locals of

unions previously mentioned, a local joint union-management apprenticeship committee, or the nearest office of the state employment service or apprenticeship agency.

For general information about cement masons, concrete finishers, segmental pavers, and terrazzo workers, contact:

- Associated Builders and Contractors, Workforce Development Department, 4250 North Fairfax Dr., 9th Floor, Arlington, VA 22203.

- Associated General Contractors of America, Inc., 333 John Carlyle St., Alexandria, VA 22314. Internet: http://www.agc.org

- International Union of Bricklayers and Allied Craftworkers, International Masonry Institute, The James Brice House, 42 East St., Annapolis, MD 21401. Internet: http://www.imiweb.org

- Operative Plasterers' and Cement Masons' International Association of the United States and Canada, 14405 Laurel Place, Suite 300, Laurel, MD 20707. Internet: http://www.opcmia.org

- National Terrazzo and Mosaic Association, 110 E. Market St., Suite 200 A, Leesburg, VA 20176.

- Portland Cement Association, 5420 Old Orchard Rd., Skokie, IL 60077. Internet: http://www.portcement.org

- United Brotherhood of Carpenters and Joiners of America, 50 F St. NW, Washington, DC 20001. Internet: http://www.Carpenters.org

For general information about cement masons and concrete finishers, contact:

- National Concrete Masonry Association, 13750 Sunrise Valley Dr., Herndon, VA 20171-3499. Internet: http://www.ncma.org

There are more than 500 occupations registered by the U.S. Department of Labor's National Apprenticeship system. For more information on the Labor Department's registered apprenticeship system and links to state apprenticeship programs, check their Web site: http://www.doleta.gov/.

Chefs, Cooks, and Food Preparation Workers

(O*NET 35-1011.00, 35-2011.00, 35-2012.00, 35-2013.00, 35-2014.00, 35-2015.00, and 35-2021.00)

Significant Points

- Many young people worked as cooks and food preparation workers—almost 20 percent were between 16 and 19 years old.

- More than 2 out of 5 food preparation workers were employed part time.

- Job openings are expected to be plentiful, primarily reflecting substantial replacement needs in this large occupation.

Nature of the Work

Chefs, cooks, and food preparation workers prepare, season, and cook a wide range of foods—from soups, snacks, and salads to entrees, side dishes, and desserts—in a variety of restaurants and other food services establishments. Chefs and cooks create recipes and prepare meals, while food preparation workers peel and cut vegetables, trim meat, prepare poultry, and perform other duties such as keeping work areas clean and monitoring temperatures of ovens and stovetops.

In general, *chefs* and *cooks* measure, mix, and cook ingredients according to recipes, using a variety of pots, pans, cutlery, and other equipment, including ovens, broilers, grills, slicers, grinders, and blenders. Chefs and head cooks also are responsible for directing the work of other kitchen workers, estimating food requirements, and ordering food supplies.

Larger restaurants and food services establishments tend to have varied menus and larger kitchen staffs. They often include several chefs and cooks, sometimes called assistant or line cooks, along with other lesser skilled kitchen workers, such as *food preparation workers*. Each chef or cook works an assigned station that is equipped with the types of stoves, grills, pans, and ingredients needed for the foods prepared at each station. Job titles often reflect the principal ingredient prepared or the type of cooking performed—*vegetable cook, fry cook, or grill cook.*

Executive chefs and *head cooks* coordinate the work of the kitchen staff and direct the preparation of meals. They determine serving sizes, plan menus, order food supplies, and oversee kitchen operations to ensure uniform quality and presentation of meals. The terms chef and cook often are used interchangeably, but generally reflect the different types of chefs and the organizational structure of the kitchen staff. For example, an *executive chef* is in charge of all food service operations and also may supervise the many kitchens of a hotel, restaurant group, or corporate dining operation. A *chef de cuisine* reports to an executive chef and is responsible for the daily operations of a single kitchen. A *sous chef*, or sub chef, is the second-in-command and runs the kitchen in the absence of the chef. Chefs tend to be more highly skilled and better trained than cooks. Many chefs earn fame both for themselves and for their kitchens because of the quality and distinctive nature of the food they serve.

The specific responsibilities of most cooks are determined by a number of factors, including the type of restaurant in which they work. *Institution and cafeteria cooks*, for example, work in the kitchens of schools, cafeterias, businesses, hospitals, and other institutions. For each meal, they prepare a large quantity of a limited number of entrees, vegetables, and desserts. *Restaurant cooks* usually prepare a wider selection of dishes, cooking most orders individually. *Short-order cooks* prepare foods in restaurants and coffee shops that emphasize fast service and quick food preparation. They grill and garnish hamburgers, prepare sandwiches, fry eggs, and cook French fries, often working on several orders at the same time. *Fast-food cooks* prepare a limited selection of menu items in fast-food restaurants. They cook and package batches of food, such as hamburgers and fried chicken, to be kept warm until served. *Private household cooks* plan and prepare meals in private homes according to the client's tastes or dietary needs. They order groceries and supplies, clean the kitchen and wash dishes and utensils. They also may serve meals.

Food preparation workers perform routine, repetitive tasks such as readying ingredients for complex dishes, slicing and dicing vegetables, and composing salads and cold items, under the direction of chefs and cooks. They weigh and measure ingredients, go after pots and pans, and stir and strain soups and sauces. Food preparation workers may cut and grind meats, poultry, and seafood in preparation for cooking. Their responsibilities also include cleaning work areas, equipment, utensils, dishes, and silverware.

The number and types of workers employed in kitchens depends on the type of establishment. For example, fast-food establishments offer only a few items, which are prepared by fast-food cooks. Small, full-service restaurants offering casual dining often feature a limited number of easy-to-prepare items supplemented by short-order specialties and ready-made desserts. Typically, one cook prepares all the food with the help of a short-order cook and one or two other kitchen workers.

Grocery and specialty food stores employ chefs, cooks, and food preparation workers to develop recipes and prepare meals to go. Typically, entrees, side dishes, salads, or other items are prepared in large quantities and stored at an appropriate temperature. Servers portion and package items according to customer orders for serving at home.

Working Conditions

Many restaurant and institutional kitchens have modern equipment, convenient work areas, and air conditioning, but kitchens in older and smaller eating places are often not as well designed. Kitchens must be well ventilated, appropriately lit, and properly equipped with sprinkler systems to protect against fires. Kitchen staffs invariably work in small quarters against hot stoves and ovens. They are under constant pressure to prepare meals quickly, while ensuring quality is maintained and safety and sanitation guidelines are observed.

Working conditions vary with the type and quantity of food prepared and the local laws governing food service operations. Workers usually must withstand the pressure and strain of standing for hours at a time, lifting heavy pots and kettles, and working near hot ovens and grills. Job hazards include slips and falls, cuts, and burns, but injuries are seldom serious.

Work hours in restaurants may include early mornings, late evenings, holidays, and weekends. Work schedules of chefs, cooks and other kitchen workers in factory and school cafeterias may be more regular. In 2002, about 33 percent of cooks and 45 percent of food preparation workers had part-time schedules, compared to 16 percent of workers throughout the economy.

The wide range in dining hours and the need for fully-staffed kitchens during all open hours creates work opportunities for individuals seeking supplemental income, flexible work hours, or variable schedules. For example, almost 20 percent of cooks and food preparation workers were 16-19 years old in 2002, and almost 10 percent had variable schedules. Kitchen workers employed by schools may work during the school year only, usually for 9 or 10 months. Similarly, resort establishments usually only offer seasonal employment.

Employment

Chefs, cooks and food preparation workers held nearly 3.0 million jobs in 2002. The distribution of jobs among the various types of chefs, cooks, and food preparation workers was as follows:

Food preparation workers 850,000

Cooks, restaurant 727,000

Cooks, fast food 588,000

Cooks, institution and cafeteria 436,000

Cooks, short order 227,000

Chefs and head cooks 132,000

Cooks, private household 8,000

More than three-fifths of all chefs, cooks, and food preparation workers were employed in restaurants and other food services and drinking places. Nearly one-fifth worked in institutions such as schools, universities, hospitals, and nursing care facilities. Grocery stores, hotels, gasoline stations with convenience stores, and other organizations employed the remainder.

Training, Other Qualifications, and Advancement

Most fast-food or short-order cooks and food preparation workers require little education or training; most skills are learned on the job. Training generally starts with basic sanitation and workplace safety subjects and continues with instruction on food handling, preparation, and cooking procedures.

A high school diploma is not required for beginning jobs, but it is recommended for those planning a career as a cook or chef. High school or vocational school programs may offer courses in basic food safety and handling procedures and general business and computer classes for those who want to manage or open their own place. Many school districts, in cooperation with state departments of education, provide on-the-job training and summer workshops for cafeteria kitchen workers who aspire to become cooks. Large corporations in the food services and hospitality industries also offer paid internships and summer jobs to those just starting out in the field. Internships provide valuable experience and can lead to placement in more formal chef training programs.

Executive chefs and head cooks who work in fine restaurants require many years of training and experience and an intense desire to cook. Some chefs and cooks may start their training in high school or post-high school vocational programs. Others may receive formal training through independent cooking schools, professional culinary institutes, or 2- or 4-year college degree programs in hospitality or culinary arts. In addition, some large hotels and restaurants operate their own training and job-placement programs for chefs and cooks. Most formal training programs require some form of apprenticeship, internship, or outplacement program that are jointly offered by the school and affiliated restaurants. Professional culinary institutes, industry associations, and trade unions also may sponsor formal apprenticeship programs in coordination with the U.S. Department of Labor. Many chefs are trained on the job, receiving real work experience and training from chef mentors in the restaurants where they work.

People who have had courses in commercial food preparation may start in a cook or chef job without spending a lot of time in lower-skilled kitchen jobs. Their education may give them an advantage when looking for jobs in better restaurants. Some vocational programs in high schools may offer training, but employers usually prefer training given by trade schools, vocational centers, colleges, professional associations, or trade unions. Postsecondary courses range from a few months to 2 years or more. Degree-granting programs are open only to high school graduates. Chefs also may compete and test for certification as master chefs. Although certification is not required to enter the field, it can be a measure of accomplishment and lead to further advancement and higher-paying positions. The U.S. Armed Forces also are a good source of training and experience.

Although curricula may vary, students in formal culinary training programs spend most of their time in kitchens learning to use the appropriate equipment and to prepare meals through actual practice. They learn good knife techniques, safe food-handling procedures, and proper use and care of kitchen equipment. Training programs often include courses in nutrition, menu planning, portion control, purchasing and inventory methods, proper food storage procedures, and use of leftover food to minimize waste. Students also learn sanitation and public health rules for handling food. Training in food service management, computer accounting and inventory software, and banquet service are featured in some training programs.

The number of formal and informal culinary training programs continues to increase to meet demand. Formal programs, which may offer training leading to a certificate or a 2- or 4-year degree, are geared more for training chefs for fine-dining or upscale restaurants. They offer a wider array of training options and specialties, such as advanced cooking techniques or foods and cooking styles from around the world.

The American Culinary Federation accredits over 100 formal training programs and sponsors apprenticeship programs around the country. Typical apprenticeships last three years and combine classroom training and work experience.

Accreditation is an indication that a culinary program meets recognized standards regarding course content, facilities, and quality of instruction. The American Culinary Federation also certifies pastry professionals and culinary educators in addition to various levels of chefs. Certification standards are based primarily on experience and formal training.

Vocational or trade-school programs typically offer more basic training in preparing food, such as food handling and sanitation procedures, nutrition, slicing and dicing methods for various kinds of meats and vegetables, and basic cooking methods, such as baking, broiling, and grilling.

Important characteristics for chefs, cooks, and food preparation workers include working well as part of a team, having a keen sense of taste and smell, and working efficiently to turn out meals rapidly. Personal cleanliness is essential, because most states require health certificates indicating that workers are free from communicable diseases. Knowledge of a foreign language may improve communication with other restaurant staff, vendors, and the restaurant's clientele.

Advancement opportunities for chefs, cooks, and food preparation workers depend on their training, work experience, and ability to perform more responsible and sophisticated tasks. Many food preparation workers, for example, may move into assistant or line cook positions. Chefs and cooks who demonstrate an eagerness to learn new cooking skills and to accept greater responsibility may move up within the kitchen and take on responsibility for training or supervising newer or lesser skilled kitchen staff. Others may move from one kitchen or restaurant to another.

Some chefs and cooks go into business as caterers or open their own restaurant. Others become instructors in culinary training programs. A number of cooks and chefs advance to executive chef positions or food service management positions, particularly in hotels, clubs, or larger, more elegant restaurants.

Job Outlook

Job openings for chefs, cooks, and food preparation workers are expected to be plentiful through 2012; however, competition for jobs in the top kitchens of higher-end restaurants should be keen. While job growth will create new positions, the overwhelming majority of job openings will stem from the need to replace workers who leave this large occupational group. Minimal education and training requirements, combined with a large number of part-time positions, make employment as chefs, cooks, and food preparation workers attractive to people seeking first-time or short-term employment, a source of additional income, or a flexible schedule. Many of these workers will transfer to other occupations or stop working, creating numerous openings for those entering the field.

Overall employment of chefs, cooks, and food preparation workers is expected to increase about as fast as the average for all occupations over the 2002-12 period. Employment growth will be spurred by increases in population, house-

hold income, and leisure time that will allow people to dine out and take vacations more often. In addition, growth in the number of two-income households will lead more families to opt for the convenience of dining out.

Projected employment growth, however, varies by specialty. The number of higher-skilled chefs and cooks working in full-service restaurants—those that offer table service and more varied menus—is expected to increase about as fast as the average. Much of the increase in this segment, however, will come from more casual rather than up-scale full-service restaurants. Dining trends suggest increasing numbers of meals eaten away from home, growth in family dining restaurants, and greater limits on expense-account meals.

Employment of fast-food cooks is expected to grow more slowly than the average. Duties of cooks in fast-food restaurants are limited; most workers are likely to be combined food preparation and serving workers, rather than fast-food cooks. Employment of short-order cooks is expected to increase about as fast as the average. Short-order cooks may work a grill or sandwich station in a full-line restaurant, but also may work in lunch counters or coffee shops that specialize in meals served quickly.

Employment of institution and cafeteria chefs and cooks will show little or no growth. Their employment will not keep pace with the rapid growth in the educational and health services industries—where their employment is concentrated. In an effort to make "institutional food" more attractive to office workers, students, staff, visitors, and patients, offices, schools and hospitals increasingly contract out their food services. Many of the contracted food service companies emphasize simple menu items and employ short-order cooks, instead of institution and cafeteria cooks, reducing the demand for these workers.

Employment of chefs, cooks, and food preparation workers who prepare meals-to-go, such as those who work in the prepared foods sections of grocery or specialty food stores, should increase faster than the average as people continue to demand quality meals and convenience.

Earnings

Wages of chefs, cooks, and food preparation workers vary greatly according to region of the country and the type of food services establishment in which they work. Wages usually are highest in elegant restaurants and hotels, where many executive chefs are employed, and in major metropolitan areas.

Median hourly earnings of chefs and head cooks were $13.43 in 2002. The middle 50 percent earned between $9.86 and $19.03. The lowest 10 percent earned less than $7.66, and the highest 10 percent earned more than $25.86 per hour. Median hourly earnings in the industries employing the largest number of head cooks and chefs in 2002 were:

Other amusement and recreation industries $18.31

Traveler accommodation 17.03

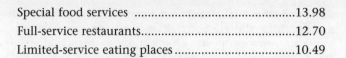

Special food services 13.98

Full-service restaurants.............................12.70

Limited-service eating places 10.49

Median hourly earnings of restaurant cooks were $9.16 in 2002. The middle 50 percent earned between $7.64 and $10.93. The lowest 10 percent earned less than $6.58, and the highest 10 percent earned more than $13.21 per hour. Median hourly earnings in the industries employing the largest number of restaurant cooks in 2002 were:

Traveler accommodation $10.49

Other amusement and recreation industries 10.45

Special food services 9.77

Full-service restaurants.............................9.14

Drinking places (alcoholic beverages) 9.03

Limited-service eating places....................8.08

Median hourly earnings of institution and cafeteria cooks were $8.72 in 2002. The middle 50 percent earned between $7.06 and $10.83. The lowest 10 percent earned less than $6.10, and the highest 10 percent earned more than $13.34 per hour. Median hourly earnings in the industries employing the largest number of institution and cafeteria cooks in 2002 were:

General medical and surgical hospitals.................$10.01

Special food services 9.89

Community care facilities for the elderly 9.10

Nursing care facilities.............................8.95

Elementary and secondary schools 7.89

Median hourly earnings of food preparation workers were $7.85 in 2002. The middle 50 percent earned between $6.72 and $9.43. The lowest 10 percent earned less than $5.96, and the highest 10 percent earned more than $11.37 per hour. Median hourly earnings in the industries employing the largest number of food preparation workers in 2002 were:

Elementary and secondary schools $8.74

Grocery stores 8.43

Nursing care facilities.............................7.94

Full-service restaurants.............................7.66

Limited-service eating places 7.07

Median hourly earnings of short-order cooks were $7.82 in 2002. The middle 50 percent earned between $6.69 and $9.59. The lowest 10 percent earned less than $5.93, and the highest 10 percent earned more than $11.25 per hour. Median hourly earnings in the industries employing the largest number of short-order cooks in 2002 were:

Full-service restaurants.............................$8.29

Drinking places (alcoholic beverages) 7.85

Other amusement and recreation industries 7.74

Gasoline stations 7.04

Limited-service eating places 6.97

Median hourly earnings of fast-food cooks were $6.90 in 2002. The middle 50 percent earned between $6.16 and $8.03. The lowest 10 percent earned less than $5.68, and the highest 10 percent earned more than $9.13 per hour. Median hourly earnings in the industries employing the largest number of fast-food cooks in 2002 were:

Special food services $7.79

Full-service restaurants.............................7.19

Gasoline stations 7.02

Limited-service eating places 6.84

Some employers provide employees with uniforms and free meals, but federal law permits employers to deduct from their employees' wages the cost or fair value of any meals or lodging provided, and some employers do so. Chefs, cooks, and food preparation workers who work full time often receive typical benefits, but part-time workers usually do not.

In some large hotels and restaurants, kitchen workers belong to unions. The principal unions are the Hotel Employees and Restaurant Employees International Union and the Service Employees International Union.

Related Occupations

Workers who perform tasks similar to those of chefs, cooks, and food preparation workers include food processing occupations, such as butchers and meat cutters, and bakers. Many executive chefs have primary responsibility for selecting menu items and share other tasks with food service managers.

Sources of Additional Information

Information about job opportunities may be obtained from local employers and local offices of the state employment service.

Career information about chefs, cooks, and other kitchen workers, as well as a directory of 2- and 4-year colleges that offer courses or programs that prepare persons for food service careers, is available from:

● National Restaurant Association, 1200 17th St. NW, Washington, DC 20036-3097. Internet: http://www.restaurant.org

For information on the American Culinary Federation's apprenticeship and certification programs for cooks, as well as a list of accredited culinary programs, send a self-addressed, stamped envelope to:

● American Culinary Federation, 180 Center Place Way, St. Augustine, FL 32095. Internet: http://www.acfchefs.org

For general information on hospitality careers, contact:

● International Council on Hotel, Restaurant, and Institutional Education, 2613 North Parham Rd., 2nd Floor, Richmond, VA 23294. Internet: http://www.chrie.org

Childcare Workers

(O*NET 39-9011.00)

Significant Points

- About 2 out of 5 childcare workers are self-employed; most of these are family childcare providers.

- A high school diploma and little or no experience are adequate for many jobs, but training requirements vary from a high school diploma to a college degree.

- Large numbers of workers leave these jobs every year, creating good job opportunities.

Nature of the Work

Childcare workers nurture and teach children of all ages in childcare centers, nursery schools, preschools, public schools, private households, family childcare homes, and before- and afterschool programs. These workers play an important role in a child's development by caring for the child when parents are at work or away for other reasons. Some parents enroll their children in nursery schools or childcare centers primarily to provide them with the opportunity to interact with other children. In addition to attending to children's basic needs, these workers organize activities that stimulate the children's physical, emotional, intellectual, and social growth. They help children to explore their interests, develop their talents and independence, build self-esteem, and learn how to get along with others.

Private household workers who are employed on an hourly basis usually are called *babysitters*. These childcare workers bathe, dress, and feed children; supervise their play; wash their clothes; and clean their rooms. They also may put them to bed and waken them, read to them, involve them in educational games, take them for doctors' visits, and discipline them. Those who are in charge of infants, sometimes called infant nurses, also prepare bottles and change diapers.

Nannies generally take care of children from birth to age 10 or 12, tending to the child's early education, nutrition, health, and other needs. They also may perform the duties of a general housekeeper, including general cleaning and laundry duties.

Childcare workers spend most of their day working with children. However, they do maintain contact with parents or guardians through informal meetings or scheduled conferences to discuss each child's progress and needs. Many childcare workers keep records of each child's progress and suggest ways in which parents can stimulate their child's learning and development at home. Some preschools, childcare centers, and before- and after-school programs actively recruit parent volunteers to work with the children and participate in administrative decisions and program planning.

Most childcare workers perform a combination of basic care and teaching duties. Through many basic care activities, childcare workers provide opportunities for children to learn. For example, a worker who shows a child how to tie a shoelace teaches the child while also providing for that child's basic care needs. Childcare programs help children to learn about trust and to gain a sense of security.

Young children learn mainly through play. Recognizing the importance of play, childcare workers build their program around it. They capitalize on children's play to further language development (storytelling and acting games), improve social skills (working together to build a neighborhood in a sandbox), and introduce scientific and mathematical concepts (balancing and counting blocks when building a bridge or mixing colors when painting). Thus, a less structured approach is used to teach preschool children, including small-group lessons, one-on-one instruction, and learning through creative activities, such as art, dance, and music.

Interaction with peers is an important part of a child's early development. Preschool children in childcare centers have an opportunity to engage in conversation and discussions, and to learn to play and work cooperatively with their classmates. Childcare workers play a vital role in preparing children to build the skills they will need in school.

Childcare workers in preschools greet young children as they arrive, help them to remove outer garments, and select an activity of interest. When caring for infants, they feed and change them. To ensure a well-balanced program, childcare workers prepare daily and long-term schedules of activities. Each day's activities balance individual and group play, and quiet and active time. Children are given some freedom to participate in activities in which they are interested.

Concern over school-age children being home alone before and after school has spurred many parents to seek alternative ways for their children to constructively spend their time. The purpose of before- and after-school programs is to watch over school-age children during the gap between school hours and their parents' work hours. These programs also may operate during the summer and on weekends. Workers in before- and after-school programs may help students with their homework or engage them in other extracurricular activities. These activities may include field trips, learning about computers, painting, photography, and participating in sports. Some childcare workers may be responsible for taking children to school in the morning and picking them up from school in the afternoon. Before- and after-school programs may be operated by public school systems, local community centers, or other private organizations.

Helping to keep young children healthy is an important part of the job. Childcare workers serve nutritious meals and snacks and teach good eating habits and personal hygiene. They ensure that children have proper rest periods. They identify children who may not feel well or who show signs of emotional or developmental problems and discuss these matters with their supervisor and the child's parents. In some cases, childcare workers help parents to locate programs that will provide basic health services.

Early identification of children with special needs—such as those with behavioral, emotional, physical, or learning disabilities—is important to improve their future learning ability. Special education teachers often work with these preschool children to provide the individual attention they need.

Working Conditions

Preschool or childcare facilities include private homes, schools, religious institutions, workplaces in which employers provide care for employees' children, and private buildings. Individuals who provide care in their own homes generally are called family childcare providers.

Nannies and babysitters usually work in the pleasant and comfortable homes or apartments of their employers. Most are day workers who live in their own homes and travel to work. Some live in the home of their employer, generally with their own room and bath. They often become part of their employer's family, and may derive satisfaction from caring for them.

Watching children grow, learn, and gain new skills can be very rewarding. While working with children, childcare workers often improve the child's communication, learning, and other personal skills. The work is sometimes routine; however, new activities and challenges mark each day. Childcare can be physically and emotionally taxing, as workers constantly stand, walk, bend, stoop, and lift to attend to each child's interests and problems.

To ensure that children receive proper supervision, state or local regulations may require a certain ratio of workers to children. The ratio varies with the age of the children. Child development experts generally recommend that a single caregiver be responsible for no more than 3 or 4 infants (less than 1 year old), 5 or 6 toddlers (1 to 2 years old), or 10 preschool-age children (between 2 and 5 years old). In before- and after-school programs, workers may be responsible for many school-age children at one time.

The work hours of childcare workers vary widely. Childcare centers usually are open year round, with long hours so that parents can drop off and pick up their children before and after work. Some centers employ full-time and part-time staff with staggered shifts to cover the entire day. Some workers are unable to take regular breaks during the day due to limited staffing. Public and many private preschool programs operate during the typical 9- or 10-month school year, employing both full-time and part-time workers. Family childcare providers have flexible hours and daily routines, but may work long or unusual hours to fit parents' work schedules. Live-in nannies usually work longer hours than do those who have their own homes. However, if they work evenings or weekends, they may get other time off.

Replacement needs in this occupation are high. Many childcare workers leave the occupation temporarily to fulfill family responsibilities, to study, or for other reasons. Some workers leave permanently because they are interested in pursuing other occupations or because of dissatisfaction with hours, low pay and benefits, and stressful conditions.

Employment

Childcare workers held about 1.2 million jobs in 2002. Many worked part time. About 2 out of 5 childcare workers were self-employed; most of these were family childcare providers.

Sixteen percent of all childcare workers are found in child daycare services, and about 14 percent work for private households. The remainder worked primarily in local government educational services, nursing and residential care facilities, religious organizations, other amusement and recreation industries, private educational services, civic and social organizations, individual and family services, and local government, excluding education and hospitals. Some childcare programs are for-profit centers; some of these are affiliated with a local or national chain. Religious institutions, community agencies, school systems, and state and local governments operate nonprofit programs. Only a very small percentage of private industry establishments operate onsite childcare centers for the children of their employees.

Training, Other Qualifications, and Advancement

The training and qualifications required of childcare workers vary widely. Each state has its own licensing requirements that regulate caregiver training; these range from a high school diploma, to community college courses, to a college degree in child development or early-childhood education. Many states require continuing education for workers in this field. However, state requirements often are minimal. Childcare workers generally can obtain employment with a high school diploma and little or no experience. Local governments, private firms, and publicly funded programs may have more demanding training and education requirements.

Some employers prefer to hire childcare workers with a nationally recognized childcare development credential, secondary or postsecondary courses in child development and early childhood education, or work experience in a childcare setting. Other employers require their own specialized training. An increasing number of employers require an associate degree in early childhood education. Schools for nannies teach early childhood education, nutrition, and childcare.

Childcare workers must anticipate and prevent problems, deal with disruptive children, provide fair but firm discipline, and be enthusiastic and constantly alert. They must communicate effectively with the children and their parents, as well as other teachers and childcare workers. Workers should be mature, patient, understanding, and articulate, and have energy and physical stamina. Skills in music, art, drama, and storytelling also are important. Self-employed childcare workers must have business sense and management abilities.

Opportunities for advancement are limited. However, as childcare workers gain experience, some may advance to supervisory or administrative positions in large childcare centers or preschools. Often, these positions require additional training, such as a bachelor's or master's degree. Other workers move on to work in resource and referral agencies, consulting with parents on available child services. A few workers become involved in policy or advocacy work related to childcare and early childhood education. With a bachelor's degree, workers may become preschool teachers or become certified to teach in public or private schools. Some workers set up their own childcare businesses.

Job Outlook

High replacement needs should create good job opportunities for childcare workers. Many childcare workers must be replaced each year as they leave the occupation to take other jobs, to meet family responsibilities, or for other reasons. Qualified persons who are interested in this work should have little trouble finding and keeping a job. Opportunities for nannies should be especially good, as many workers prefer not to work in other people's homes.

Employment of childcare workers is projected to grow about as fast as the average for all occupations through the year 2012. The number of women of childbearing age (widely considered to be ages 15 to 44) in the labor force and the number of children under 5 years of age is expected to rise gradually over the projected 2002-12 period. Also, the proportion of youngsters enrolled full or part time in childcare and preschool programs is likely to continue to increase, spurring demand for additional childcare workers.

Changes in perceptions of preprimary education may lead to increased public and private spending on childcare. If more parents believe that some experience in center-based care and preschool is beneficial to children, enrollment will increase. Concern about the behavior of school-age children during nonschool hours should increase demand for before- and after-school programs. In addition, the difficulty of finding suitable nannies or private household workers also may force many families to seek out alternative childcare arrangements in centers and family childcare programs. Government policy often favors increased funding of early childhood education programs, and that trend will probably continue. Government funding for before- and after-school programs also is expected to be steady over the projection period. The growing availability of government-funded center-based care and preschool programs may induce some parents to enroll their children who otherwise would not do so. Some states also are increasing subsidization of the child daycare services industry in response to welfare reform legislation. This reform might cause some mothers to enter the workforce during the projection period as their welfare benefits are reduced or eliminated.

Earnings

Pay depends on the educational attainment of the worker and the type of establishment. Although the pay generally is very low, more education usually means higher earnings. Median hourly earnings of wage and salary childcare workers were $7.86 in 2002. The middle 50 percent earned between $6.66 and $9.65. The lowest 10 percent earned less than $5.91, and the highest 10 percent earned more than $11.46. Median hourly earnings in the industries employing the largest numbers of childcare workers in 2002 were as follows:

Other residential care facilities $9.51
Elementary and secondary schools 9.04
Civic and social organizations....................................7.25
Child daycare services 7.18
Other amusement and recreation industries..............7.09

Earnings of self-employed childcare workers vary depending on the hours worked, the number and ages of the children, and the location.

Benefits vary, but are minimal for most childcare workers. Many employers offer free or discounted childcare to employees. Some offer a full benefits package, including health insurance and paid vacations, but others offer no benefits at all. Some employers offer seminars and workshops to help workers learn new skills. A few are willing to cover the cost of courses taken at community colleges or technical schools. Live-in nannies get free room and board.

Related Occupations

Childcare work requires patience; creativity; an ability to nurture, motivate, teach, and influence children; and leadership, organizational, and administrative skills. Others who work with children and need these qualities and skills include teacher assistants; teachers—preschool, kindergarten, elementary, middle, and secondary; and teachers—special education.

Sources of Additional Information

For an electronic question-and-answer service on childcare, information on becoming a childcare provider, and other resources for persons interested in childcare work, contact:

- National Child Care Information Center, 243 Church St. NW, 2nd floor, Vienna, VA 22180. Telephone (tollfree): 800-424-4310. Internet: http://www.nccic.org

For information on becoming a family childcare provider, send a stamped, self-addressed envelope to:

- The Children's Foundation, 725 15th St. NW, Suite 505, Washington, DC 20005-2109. Internet: http://www.childrensfoundation.net

For eligibility requirements and a description of the Child Development Associate credential, contact:

- Council for Professional Recognition, 2460 16th St. NW, Washington, DC 20009-3575. Internet: http://www.cdacouncil.org

For eligibility requirements and a description of the Certified Childcare Professional designation, contact:

- National Childcare Association, 1016 Rosser St., Conyers, GA 30012. Internet: http://www.nccanet.org

For information about a career as a nanny, contact:

- International Nanny Association, 191 Clarksville Rd., Princeton Junction, NJ 08550-3111. Telephone (tollfree): 888-878-1477. Internet: http://www.nanny.org

State Departments of Human Services or Social Services can supply state regulations and training requirements for child-care workers.

Clinical Laboratory Technologists and Technicians

(O*NET 29-2011.00 and 29-2012.00)

Significant Points

- Clinical laboratory technologists usually have a bachelor's degree with a major in medical technology or in one of the life sciences; clinical laboratory technicians generally need either an associate degree or a certificate.

- Average employment growth is expected as the volume of laboratory tests increases with both population growth and the development of new types of tests.

- Job opportunities are expected to be excellent.

Nature of the Work

Clinical laboratory testing plays a crucial role in the detection, diagnosis, and treatment of disease. Clinical laboratory technologists, also referred to as clinical laboratory scientists or medical technologists, and clinical laboratory technicians, also known as medical technicians or medical laboratory technicians, perform most of these tests.

Clinical laboratory personnel examine and analyze body fluids, tissues, and cells. They look for bacteria, parasites, and other microorganisms; analyze the chemical content of fluids; match blood for transfusions; and test for drug levels in the blood to show how a patient is responding to treatment. These technologists also prepare specimens for examination, count cells, and look for abnormal cells. They use automated equipment and instruments capable of performing a number of tests simultaneously, as well as microscopes, cell counters, and other sophisticated laboratory equipment. Then they analyze the results and relay them to physicians. With increasing automation and the use of computer technology, the work of technologists and technicians has become less hands-on and more analytical.

The complexity of tests performed, the level of judgment needed, and the amount of responsibility workers assume depend largely on the amount of education and experience they have.

Clinical laboratory technologists generally have a bachelor's degree in medical technology or in one of the life sciences, or they have a combination of formal training and work experience. They perform complex chemical, biological, hematological, immunologic, microscopic, and bacteriological tests. Technologists microscopically examine blood, tissue, and other body substances. They make cultures of body fluid and tissue samples, to determine the presence of bacteria, fungi, parasites, or other microorganisms. Clinical laboratory technologists analyze samples for chemical content or a chemical reaction and determine blood glucose and cholesterol levels. They also type and cross match blood samples for transfusions.

Clinical laboratory technologists evaluate test results, develop and modify procedures, and establish and monitor programs, to ensure the accuracy of tests. Some clinical laboratory technologists supervise clinical laboratory technicians.

Technologists in small laboratories perform many types of tests, whereas those in large laboratories generally specialize. Technologists who prepare specimens and analyze the chemical and hormonal contents of body fluids are called clinical chemistry technologists. Those who examine and identify bacteria and other microorganisms are microbiology technologists. Blood bank technologists, or immunohematology technologists, collect, type, and prepare blood and its components for transfusions. Immunology technologists examine elements of the human immune system and its response to foreign bodies. Cytotechnologists prepare slides of body cells and examine these cells microscopically for abnormalities that may signal the beginning of a cancerous growth. Molecular biology technologists perform complex protein and nucleic acid testing on cell samples.

Clinical laboratory technicians perform less complex tests and laboratory procedures than technologists perform. Technicians may prepare specimens and operate automated analyzers, for example, or they may perform manual tests in accordance with detailed instructions. Like technologists, they may work in several areas of the clinical laboratory or specialize in just one. Histotechnicians cut and stain tissue specimens for microscopic examination by pathologists, and phlebotomists collect blood samples. They usually work under the supervision of medical and clinical laboratory technologists or laboratory managers.

Working Conditions

Hours and other working conditions of clinical laboratory technologists and technicians vary with the size and type of employment setting. In large hospitals or in independent laboratories that operate continuously, personnel usually work the day, evening, or night shift and may work weekends and holidays. Laboratory personnel in small facilities may work on rotating shifts, rather than on a regular shift. In some facilities, laboratory personnel are on call several nights a week or on weekends, in case of an emergency.

Clinical laboratory personnel are trained to work with infectious specimens. When proper methods of infection control and sterilization are followed, few hazards exist. Protective masks, gloves, and goggles are often necessary to ensure the safety of laboratory personnel.

Laboratories usually are well lighted and clean; however, specimens, solutions, and reagents used in the laboratory sometimes produce fumes. Laboratory workers may spend a great deal of time on their feet.

Employment

Clinical laboratory technologists and technicians held about 297,000 jobs in 2002. More than half of jobs were in hospitals. Most of the remaining jobs were in offices of physicians and in medical and diagnostic laboratories. A small proportion was in educational services; other ambulatory healthcare services, including blood and organ banks; outpatient care centers; and scientific research and development services.

Training, Other Qualifications, and Advancement

The usual requirement for an entry-level position as a clinical laboratory technologist is a bachelor's degree with a major in medical technology or in one of the life sciences, although it is possible to qualify through a combination of education, on-the-job, and specialized training. Universities and hospitals offer medical technology programs.

Bachelor's degree programs in medical technology include courses in chemistry, biological sciences, microbiology, mathematics, and statistics, as well as specialized courses devoted to knowledge and skills used in the clinical laboratory. Many programs also offer or require courses in management, business, and computer applications. The Clinical Laboratory Improvement Act requires technologists who perform highly complex tests to have at least an associate degree.

Medical and clinical laboratory technicians generally have either an associate degree from a community or junior college or a certificate from a hospital, a vocational or technical school, or one of the U.S. Armed Forces. A few technicians learn their skills on the job.

The National Accrediting Agency for Clinical Laboratory Sciences (NAACLS) fully accredits 467 programs for medical and clinical laboratory technologists, medical and clinical laboratory technicians, histotechnologists and histotechnicians, cytogenetic technologists, and diagnostic molecular scientists. NAACLS also approves 57 programs in phlebotomy and clinical assisting. Other nationally recognized accrediting agencies that accredit specific areas for clinical laboratory workers include the Commission on Accreditation of Allied Health Education Programs and the Accrediting Bureau of Health Education Schools.

Some states require laboratory personnel to be licensed or registered. Information on licensure is available from state departments of health or boards of occupational licensing. Certification is a voluntary process by which a nongovernmental organization, such as a professional society or certifying agency, grants recognition to an individual whose professional competence meets prescribed standards. Widely accepted by employers in the health industry, certification is a prerequisite for most jobs and often is necessary for advancement. Agencies certifying medical and clinical laboratory technologists and technicians include the Board of Registry of the American Society for Clinical Pathology, the American Medical Technologists, the National Credentialing Agency for Laboratory Personnel, and the Board of Registry of the American Association of Bioanalysts. These agencies have different requirements for certification and different organizational sponsors.

Clinical laboratory personnel need good analytical judgment and the ability to work under pressure. Close attention to detail is essential, because small differences or changes in test substances or numerical readouts can be crucial for patient care. Manual dexterity and normal color vision are highly desirable. With the widespread use of automated laboratory equipment, computer skills are important. In addition, technologists in particular are expected to be good at problem solving.

Technologists may advance to supervisory positions in laboratory work or may become chief medical or clinical laboratory technologists or laboratory managers in hospitals. Manufacturers of home diagnostic testing kits and laboratory equipment and supplies seek experienced technologists to work in product development, marketing, and sales. A graduate degree in medical technology, one of the biological sciences, chemistry, management, or education usually speeds advancement. A doctorate is needed to become a laboratory director; however, federal regulation allows directors of moderately complex laboratories to have either a master's degree or a bachelor's degree, combined with the appropriate amount of training and experience. Technicians can become technologists through additional education and experience.

Job Outlook

Job opportunities are expected to be excellent, because the number of job openings is expected to continue to exceed the number of job seekers. Employment of clinical laboratory workers is expected to grow about as fast as the average for all occupations through the year 2012, as the volume of laboratory tests increases with both population growth and the development of new types of tests.

Technological advances will continue to have two opposing effects on employment through 2012. On the one hand, new, increasingly powerful diagnostic tests will encourage additional testing and spur employment. On the other hand, research and development efforts targeted at simplifying routine testing procedures may enhance the ability of nonlaboratory personnel—physicians and patients in particular—to perform tests now conducted in laboratories. Although hospitals are expected to continue to be the major employer of clinical laboratory workers, employment is expected to grow faster in medical and diagnostic laboratories, offices of physicians, and other ambulatory health care services, including blood and organ banks.

Although significant, job growth will not be the only source of opportunities. As in most occupations, many openings will result from the need to replace workers who transfer to other occupations, retire, or stop working for some other reason.

Earnings

Median annual earnings of medical and clinical laboratory technologists were $42,910 in 2002. The middle 50 percent earned between $36,400 and $50,820. The lowest 10 percent earned less than $30,530, and the highest 10 percent earned more than $58,000. Median annual earnings in the industries employing the largest numbers of medical and clinical laboratory technologists in 2002 were as follows:

General medical and surgical hospitals	$43,340
Medical and diagnostic laboratories	42,020
Offices of physicians	38,690

Median annual earnings of medical and clinical laboratory technicians were $29,040 in 2002. The middle 50 percent earned between $23,310 and $35,840. The lowest 10 percent earned less than $19,070, and the highest 10 percent earned more than $43,960. Median annual earnings in the industries employing the largest numbers of medical and clinical laboratory technicians in 2002 were as follows:

General medical and surgical hospitals	$30,500
Colleges, universities, and professional schools	30,350
Offices of physicians	27,820
Medical and diagnostic laboratories	27,550
Other ambulatory health care services	26,710

According to the American Society for Clinical Pathology, median annual wages of staff clinical laboratory technologists and technicians in 2002 varied by specialty as follows:

	Lowest	Average	Highest
Cytotechnologist	$41,454	$49,920	$54,600
Histotechnologist	33,280	41,122	45,760
Medical technologist	33,280	40,186	45,760
Histotechnician	28,413	34,549	38,667
Medical laboratory technician	27,040	31,928	35,776
Phlebotomist	18,720	21,944	25,168

Related Occupations

Clinical laboratory technologists and technicians analyze body fluids, tissue, and other substances, using a variety of tests. Similar or related procedures are performed by chemists and materials scientists, science technicians, and veterinary technologists and technicians.

Sources of Additional Information

For a list of accredited and approved educational programs for clinical laboratory personnel, contact:

- National Accrediting Agency for Clinical Laboratory Sciences, 8410 W. Bryn Mawr Ave., Suite 670, Chicago, IL 60631. Internet: http://www.naacls.org

Information on certification is available from the following organizations:

- American Association of Bioanalysts, Board of Registry, 917 Locust St., Suite 1100, St. Louis, MO 63101. Internet: http://www.aab.org
- American Medical Technologists, 710 Higgins Rd., Park Ridge, IL 60068.
- American Society for Clinical Pathology, Board of Registry, 2100 West Harrison St., Chicago, IL 60612. Internet: http://www.ascp.org/bor
- National Credentialing Agency for Laboratory Personnel, P.O. Box 15945-289, Lenexa, KS 66285. Internet: http://www.nca-info.org

Additional career information is available from the following sources:

- American Association of Blood Banks, 8101 Glenbrook Rd., Bethesda, MD 20814-2749. Internet: http://www.aabb.org
- American Society for Clinical Laboratory Science, 6701 Democracy Blvd., Suite 300, Bethesda, MD 20817. Internet: http://www.ascls.org
- American Society for Clinical Pathology, 2100 West Harrison St., Chicago, IL 60612. Internet: http://www.ascp.org
- American Society for Cytopathology, 400 West 9th St., Suite 201, Wilmington, DE 19801. Internet: http://www.cytopathology.org
- Clinical Laboratory Management Association, 989 Old Eagle School Rd., Wayne, PA 19087. Internet: http://www.clma.org

Computer and Information Systems Managers

(O*NET 11-3021.00)

Significant Points

- Projected job growth stems primarily from rapid growth among computer-related occupations.
- Employers prefer managers with formal education and advanced technical knowledge acquired through computer-related work experience.

- Job opportunities should be best for applicants with a master's degree in business administration or management information systems with technology as a core component.

Nature of the Work

The need for organizations to incorporate existing and future technologies in order to remain competitive has become a more pressing issue over the last several years. As electronic commerce becomes more common, how and when companies use technology are critical issues. Computer and information systems managers play a vital role in the technological direction of their organizations. They do everything from constructing the business plan to overseeing network security to directing Internet operations.

Computer and information systems managers plan, coordinate, and direct research and design the computer-related activities of firms. They help determine both technical and business goals in consultation with top management, and make detailed plans for the accomplishment of these goals. For example, working with their staff, they may develop the overall concepts of a new product or service, or may identify how an organization's computing capabilities can effectively aid project management.

Computer and information systems managers direct the work of systems analysts, computer programmers, support specialists, and other computer-related workers. These managers plan and coordinate activities such as installation and upgrading of hardware and software, programming and systems design, development of computer networks, and implementation of Internet and intranet sites. They are increasingly involved with the upkeep and maintenance and security of networks. They analyze the computer and information needs of their organization, from an operational and strategic perspective, and determine immediate and long-range personnel and equipment requirements. They assign and review the work of their subordinates, and stay abreast of the latest technology in order to assure the organization does not lag behind competitors.

The duties of computer and information systems managers vary with their specific titles. *Chief technology officers*, for example, evaluate the newest and most innovative technologies and determine how these can help their organization. The chief technology officer, who often reports to the organization's chief information officer, manages and plans technical standards and tends to the daily information technology issues of the firm. Because of the rapid pace of technological change, chief technology officers must constantly be on the lookout for developments that could benefit their organization. They are responsible for demonstrating to a company how information technology can be used as a competitive tool that not only cuts costs, but also increases revenue and maintains or increases competitive advantage.

Management information systems (MIS) directors manage information systems and computing resources for their entire organization. They may also work under the chief informa-
tion officer and plan and direct the work of subordinate information technology employees. These managers oversee a variety of user services such as an organization's help desk, which employees can call with questions or problems. MIS directors also may make hardware and software upgrade recommendations based on their experience with an organization's technology. Helping to assure the availability, continuity, and security of data and information technology services are key responsibilities for these workers.

Project managers develop requirements, budgets, and schedules for their firm's information technology projects. They coordinate such projects from development through implementation, working with internal and external clients, vendors, consultants, and computer specialists. These managers are increasingly involved in projects that upgrade the information security of an organization.

LAN/WAN (Local Area Network/Wide Area Network) *managers* provide a variety of services, from design to administration, of an organization's local area network, which connects staff within an organization. These managers direct the network, and its related computing environment, including hardware, systems software, applications software, and all other computer-related configurations.

Computer and information system managers need strong communication skills. They coordinate the activities of their unit with those of other units or organizations. They confer with top executives; financial, production, marketing, and other managers; and contractors and equipment and materials suppliers.

Working Conditions

Computer and information systems managers spend most of their time in an office. Most work at least 40 hours a week and may have to work evenings and weekends to meet deadlines or solve unexpected problems. Some computer and information systems managers may experience considerable pressure in meeting technical goals within short timeframes or tight budgets. As networks continue to expand and more work is done remotely, computer and information system managers have to communicate with and oversee offsite employees using modems, laptops, e-mail, and the Internet.

Like other workers who sit continuously in front of a keyboard, computer and information system managers are susceptible to eyestrain, back discomfort, and hand and wrist problems such as carpal tunnel syndrome.

Employment

Computer and information systems managers held about 284,000 jobs in 2002. About 2 in 5 works in service-providing industries, mainly in computer systems design and related services. This industry provides services related to the commercial use of computers on a contract basis, including custom computer programming services; computer systems integration design services; computer facilities management services, including computer systems or data-processing facilities support services for clients; and other computer-related services, such as disaster recovery services and software installation. Other large employers include insurance and financial services firms, government agencies, and manufacturers.

Training, Other Qualifications, and Advancement

Strong technical knowledge is essential for computer and information systems managers, who must understand and guide the work of their subordinates, yet also explain the work in nontechnical terms to senior management and potential customers. Therefore, these management positions usually require work experience and formal education similar to that of other computer occupations.

Many computer and information systems managers have experience as systems analysts; others may have experience as computer support specialists, programmers, or other information technology professionals. A bachelor's degree usually is required for management positions, although employers often prefer a graduate degree, especially a master's degree in business administration (MBA) with technology as a core component. This degree differs from a traditional MBA in that there is a heavy emphasis on information technology in addition to the standard business curriculum. This is becoming important because more computer and information systems managers are making important technology decisions as well as business decisions for their organizations. Some universities specialize in offering degrees in management information systems, which blend technical core subjects with business, accounting, and communications courses. A few computer and information systems managers may have only an associate degree if they have sufficient experience and were able to learn additional skills on the job. To aid their professional advancement, though, many managers with an associate degree eventually earn a bachelor's or master's degree while working.

Computer and information systems managers need a broad range of skills. In addition to technical skills, employers also seek managers with strong business skills. Employers want managers who have experience with the specific software or technology to be used on the job, as well as a background in either consulting or business management. The expansion of electronic commerce has elevated the importance of business insight, because many managers are called upon to make important business decisions. Managers need a keen understanding of people, management processes, and customers' needs.

Computer and information systems managers must possess strong interpersonal, communication, and leadership skills because they are required to interact not only with their staff, but also with other people inside and outside their organization. They also must possess team skills to work on group projects and other collaborative efforts. Computer and information systems managers increasingly interact with persons outside their organization, reflecting their emerging role as vital parts of their firm's executive team.

Computer and information systems managers may advance to progressively higher leadership positions in their field. Some may become managers in non-technical areas such as marketing, human resources, or sales. In high technology firms, managers in non-technical areas often must possess the same specialized knowledge as do managers in technical areas.

Job Outlook

Employment of computer and information systems managers is expected to grow much faster than the average for all occupations through the year 2012. Technological advancements will boost the employment of computer-related workers; as a result, the demand for managers to direct these workers also will increase. In addition, job openings will result from the need to replace managers who retire or move into other occupations. Opportunities for obtaining a management position will be best for workers possessing an MBA with technology as a core component or a management information systems degree, advanced technical knowledge, and strong communication and administrative skills.

Despite the recent downturn in the economy, especially in technology-related sectors, the outlook for computer and information systems managers remains strong. In order to remain competitive, firms will continue to install sophisticated computer networks and set up more complex Internet and intranet sites. Keeping a computer network running smoothly is essential to almost every organization. Firms will be more willing to hire managers who can accomplish that.

The security of computer networks will continue to increase in importance as more business is conducted over the Internet. The security of the nation's entire electronic infrastructure has come under renewed focus in light of recent threats. Organizations need to understand how their systems are vulnerable and how to protect their infrastructure and Internet sites from hackers, viruses, and other acts of cyber-terrorism. The emergence of "cyber-security" as a key issue facing most organizations should lead to strong growth for computer managers. Firms will increasingly hire cyber-security experts to fill key leadership roles in their information technology departments, because the integrity of their computing environment is of the utmost concern. As a result, there will be a high demand for managers proficient in computer security issues.

Due to the explosive growth of electronic commerce and the capacity of the Internet to create new relationships with customers, the role of computer and information systems managers will continue to evolve in the future. Persons in these jobs will continue to become more vital to their companies. The expansion of the wireless Internet will spur the need for computer and information systems managers with both business savvy and technical proficiency.

Opportunities for those who wish to become computer and information systems managers should be closely related to the growth of the occupations they supervise and the industries in which they are found.

Earnings

Earnings for computer and information systems managers vary by specialty and level of responsibility. Median annual earnings of these managers in 2002 were $85,240. The middle 50 percent earned between $64,150 and $109,950. The lowest 10 percent earned less than $47,440, and the highest 10 percent earned more than $140,440. Median annual earnings in the industries employing the largest numbers of computer and information systems managers in 2002 were:

Computer systems design and related services $94,240

Management of companies and enterprises 91,710

Insurance carriers..89,920

Depository credit intermediation 75,160

Colleges, universities, and professional schools 68,100

According to Robert Half International, average starting salaries in 2003 for high-level information technology managers ranged from $82,750 to $151,500. According to a 2003 survey by the National Association of Colleges and Employers, starting salary offers for those with an MBA, a technical undergraduate degree, and 1 year or less of experience averaged $54,643; for those with a master's degree in management information systems/business data processing, the starting salary averaged $43,750.

In addition, computer and information systems managers, especially those at higher levels, often receive more employment-related benefits—such as expense accounts, stock option plans, and bonuses—than do non-managerial workers in their organizations.

Related Occupations

The work of computer and information systems managers is closely related to that of computer programmers; computer software engineers; computer systems analysts, database administrators, and computer scientists; and computer support specialists and systems administrators. Computer and information systems managers also have some high-level responsibilities similar to those of top executives.

Sources of Additional Information

Further information about computer careers is available from:

- Association for Computing Machinery (ACM), 1515 Broadway, New York, NY 10036. Internet: http://www.acm.org

- Institute of Electrical and Electronics Engineers Computer Society, Headquarters Office, 1730 Massachusetts Ave. NW, Washington, DC 20036-1992. Internet: http://www.computer.org

- National Workforce Center for Emerging Technologies, 3000 Landerholm Circle SE, Bellevue, WA 98007. Internet: http://www.nwcet.org

Computer Programmers

(O*NET 15-1021.00)

Significant Points

- Nearly half of all computer programmers held a bachelor's degree in 2002; about 1 in 5 held a graduate degree.

- Employment is expected to grow much more slowly than that of other computer specialists.

- Prospects should be best for college graduates with knowledge of a variety of programming languages and tools; those with less formal education or its equivalent in work experience should face strong competition for programming jobs.

Nature of the Work

Computer programmers write, test, and maintain the detailed instructions, called programs, that computers must follow to perform their functions. They also conceive, design, and test logical structures for solving problems by computer. Many technical innovations in programming—advanced computing technologies and sophisticated new languages and programming tools—have redefined the role of a programmer and elevated much of the programming work done today. Job titles and descriptions may vary, depending on the organization. In this occupational statement, *computer programmer* refers to individuals whose main job function is programming; this group has a wide range of responsibilities and educational backgrounds.

Computer programs tell the computer what to do—which information to identify and access, how to process it, and what equipment to use. Programs vary widely depending upon the type of information to be accessed or generated. For example, the instructions involved in updating financial records are very different from those required to duplicate conditions on board an aircraft for pilots training in a flight simulator. Although simple programs can be written in a few hours, programs that use complex mathematical formulas, whose solutions can only be approximated, or that draw data from many existing systems may require more than a year of work. In most cases, several programmers work together as a team under a senior programmer's supervision.

Programmers write programs according to the specifications determined primarily by computer software engineers and systems analysts. After the design process is complete, it is the job of the programmer to convert that design into a logical series of instructions that the computer can follow. The programmer then codes these instructions in a conventional programming language, such as COBOL; an artificial intelligence language, such as Prolog; or one of the most advanced object-oriented languages, such as Java, C++, or Smalltalk. Different programming languages are used depending on the purpose of the program. COBOL, for example, is commonly used for business applications, whereas Fortran (short for "formula translation") is used in science and engineering. C++ is widely used for both scientific and business applications. Many programmers at the enterprise level are also expected to know platform-specific languages used in database programming. Programmers generally know more than one programming language and, because many languages are similar, they often can learn new languages relatively easily. In practice, programmers often are referred to by the language they know, as are Java programmers, or the type of function they perform or environment in which they work, which is the case for database programmers, mainframe programmers, or Web programmers.

Many programmers update, repair, modify, and expand existing programs. When making changes to a section of code, called a *routine*, programmers need to make other users aware of the task that the routine is to perform. They do this by inserting comments in the coded instructions, so that others can understand the program. Many programmers use computer-assisted software engineering (CASE) tools to automate much of the coding process. These tools enable a programmer to concentrate on writing the unique parts of the program, because the tools automate various pieces of the program being built. CASE tools generate whole sections of code automatically, rather than line by line. Programmers also utilize libraries of pre-written code, which can then be modified or customized for a specific application. This also yields more reliable and consistent programs and increases programmers' productivity by eliminating some routine steps.

Programmers test a program by running it to ensure that the instructions are correct and that the program produces the desired outcome. If errors do occur, the programmer must make the appropriate change and recheck the program until it produces the correct results. This process is called testing and debugging. Programmers may continue to fix these problems throughout the life of a program. Programmers working in a mainframe environment, which involves a large centralized computer, may prepare instructions for a computer operator who will run the program. They also may contribute to a manual for persons who will be using the program.

Programmers often are grouped into two broad types—applications programmers and systems programmers. *Applications programmers* write programs to handle a specific job, such as a program to track inventory within an organization. They may also revise existing packaged software or customize generic applications called middleware. *Systems programmers*, on the other hand, write programs to maintain and control computer systems software, such as operating systems, networked systems, and database systems. These workers make changes in the sets of instructions that determine how the network, workstations, and central processing unit of the system handle the various jobs they have been given, and how they communicate with peripheral equipment such as terminals, printers, and disk drives. Because of their knowledge of the entire computer system, systems programmers

often help applications programmers to determine the source of problems that may occur with their programs.

Programmers in software development companies may work directly with experts from various fields to create software—either programs designed for specific clients or packaged software for general use—ranging from games and educational software to programs for desktop publishing and financial planning. Much of this type of programming takes place in the preparation of packaged software, which constitutes one of the most rapidly growing segments of the computer services industry.

In some organizations, particularly small ones, workers commonly known as *programmer-analysts* are responsible for both the systems analysis and the actual programming work. Advanced programming languages and new object-oriented programming capabilities are increasing the efficiency and productivity of both programmers and users. The transition from a mainframe environment to one that is based primarily on personal computers (PCs) has blurred the once rigid distinction between the programmer and the user. Increasingly, adept end-users are taking over many of the tasks previously performed by programmers. For example, the growing use of packaged software, such as spreadsheet and database management software packages, allows users to write simple programs to access data and perform calculations.

Computer programmers write programs according to the specifications determined by software engineers or systems analysts.

Working Conditions

Programmers generally work in offices in comfortable surroundings. Many programmers may work long hours or weekends to meet deadlines or fix critical problems that occur during off hours. Given the technology available, telecommuting is becoming common for a wide range of computer professionals, including computer programmers. As computer networks expand, more programmers are able to make corrections or fix problems remotely by using modems, e-mail, and the Internet to connect to a customer's computer.

Like other workers who spend long periods in front of a computer terminal typing at a keyboard, programmers are susceptible to eyestrain, back discomfort, and hand and wrist problems, such as carpal tunnel syndrome.

Employment

Computer programmers held about 499,000 jobs in 2002. Programmers are employed in almost every industry, but the largest concentrations are in computer systems design and related services and in software publishers, which includes firms that write and sell software. Large numbers of programmers also can be found in management of companies and enterprises, telecommunications companies, manufacturers of computer and electronic equipment, financial institutions, insurance carriers, educational institutions, and government agencies.

A large number of computer programmers are employed on a temporary or contract basis or work as independent consultants, as companies demand expertise with new programming languages or specialized areas of application. Rather than hiring programmers as permanent employees and then laying them off after a job is completed, employers can contract with temporary help agencies, consulting firms, or directly with programmers themselves. A marketing firm, for example, may require the services of several programmers only to write and debug the software necessary to get a new customer resource management system running. This practice also enables companies to bring in people with a specific set of skills—usually in one of the latest technologies—as it applies to their business needs. Bringing in an independent contractor or consultant with a certain level of experience in a new or advanced programming language, for example, enables an establishment to complete a particular job without having to retrain existing workers. Such jobs may last anywhere from several weeks to a year or longer. There were 18,000 self-employed computer programmers in 2002.

Training, Other Qualifications, and Advancement

While there are many training paths available for programmers, mainly because employers' needs are so varied, the level of education and experience employers seek has been rising, due to the growing number of qualified applicants and the specialization involved with most programming tasks. Bachelor's degrees are commonly required, although some programmers may qualify for certain jobs with 2-year degrees or certificates. The associate degree is an increasingly attractive entry-level credential for prospective computer programmers. Most community colleges and many independent technical institutes and proprietary schools offer an associate degree in computer science or a related information technology field.

Employers are primarily interested in programming knowledge, and computer programmers can become certified in a programming language such as C++ or Java. College graduates who are interested in changing careers or developing an area of expertise also may return to a 2-year community college or technical school for additional training. In the absence of a degree, substantial specialized experience or expertise may be needed. Even when hiring programmers with a degree, employers appear to be placing more emphasis on previous experience.

Some computer programmers hold a college degree in computer science, mathematics, or information systems, whereas others have taken special courses in computer programming to supplement their degree in a field such as accounting, inventory control, or another area of business. As the level of education and training required by employers continues to rise, the proportion of programmers with a college degree should increase in the future. As indicated by the following tabulation, 65 percent of computer programmers had a bachelor's or higher degree in 2002.

TABLE 1

Highest level of school completed or degree received, computer programmers, 2002

Level	Percent
High school graduate or equivalent or less	7.7
Some college, no degree	15.2
Associate degree	11.6
Bachelor's degree	48.6
Graduate degree	16.7

Required skills vary from job to job, but the demand for various skills generally is driven by changes in technology. Employers using computers for scientific or engineering applications usually prefer college graduates who have degrees in computer or information science, mathematics, engineering, or the physical sciences. Graduate degrees in related fields are required for some jobs. Employers who use computers for business applications prefer to hire people who have had college courses in management information systems (MIS) and business and who possess strong programming skills. Although knowledge of traditional languages still is important, employers are placing increasing emphasis on newer, object-oriented programming languages and tools, such as C++ and Java. Additionally, employers are seeking persons familiar with fourth- and fifth-generation languages that involve graphic user interface (GUI) and systems programming. Employers also prefer applicants who have general business skills and experience related to the operations of the firm. Students can improve their employment prospects by participating in a college work-study program or by undertaking an internship.

Most systems programmers hold a 4-year degree in computer science. Extensive knowledge of a variety of operating systems is essential for such workers. This includes being able to configure an operating system to work with different types of hardware and having the skills needed to adapt the operating system to best meet the needs of a particular organization. Systems programmers also must be able to work with database systems, such as DB2, Oracle, or Sybase.

When hiring programmers, employers look for people with the necessary programming skills who can think logically and pay close attention to detail. The job calls for patience, persistence, and the ability to work on exacting analytical work, especially under pressure. Ingenuity, creativity, and imagination also are particularly important when programmers design solutions and test their work for potential failures. The ability to work with abstract concepts and to do technical analysis is especially important for systems programmers, because they work with the software that controls the computer's operation. Because programmers are expected to work in teams and interact directly with users, employers want programmers who are able to communicate with nontechnical personnel.

Entry-level or junior programmers may work alone on simple assignments after some initial instruction, or they may be assigned to work on a team with more experienced programmers. Either way, beginning programmers generally must work under close supervision. Because technology changes so rapidly, programmers must continuously update their knowledge and skills by taking courses sponsored by their employer or by software vendors, or offered through local community colleges and universities.

For skilled workers who keep up to date with the latest technology, the prospects for advancement are good. In large organizations, programmers may be promoted to lead programmer and be given supervisory responsibilities. Some applications programmers may move into systems programming after they gain experience and take courses in systems software. With general business experience, programmers may become programmer-analysts or systems analysts or be promoted to a managerial position. Other programmers, with specialized knowledge and experience with a language or operating system, may work in research and development on multimedia or Internet technology, for example. As employers increasingly contract out programming jobs, more opportunities should arise for experienced programmers with expertise in a specific area to work as consultants.

Certification is a way to demonstrate a level of competence, and may provide a jobseeker with a competitive advantage. In addition to language-specific certificates that a programmer can obtain, product vendors or software firms also offer certification and may require professionals who work with their products to be certified. Voluntary certification also is available through other various organizations.

Job Outlook

Employment of programmers is expected to grow about as fast as the average for all occupations through 2012. Jobs for both systems and applications programmers should be most plentiful in data processing service firms, software houses, and computer consulting businesses. These types of establishments are part of computer systems design and related services and software publishers, which are projected to be among the fastest growing industries in the economy over the 2002-12 period. As organizations attempt to control costs and keep up with changing technology, they will need programmers to assist in conversions to new computer languages and systems. In addition, numerous job openings will result from the need to replace programmers who leave the labor force or transfer to other occupations such as manager or systems analyst.

Employment of programmers, however, is expected to grow much more slowly than that of other computer specialists. With the rapid gains in technology, sophisticated computer software now has the capability to write basic code, eliminating the need for more programmers to do this routine work. The consolidation and centralization of systems and applications, developments in packaged software, advances in programming languages and tools, and the growing ability of users to design, write, and implement more of their own programs means that more of the programming functions can be transferred from programmers to other types of workers. Furthermore, as the level of technological innovation and sophistication increases, programmers are likely to face increasing competition from programming businesses overseas, to which much routine work can be contracted out at a lower cost.

Nevertheless, employers will continue to need programmers who have strong technical skills and who understand an employer's business and its programming requirements. This means that programmers will have to keep abreast of changing programming languages and techniques. Given the importance of networking and the expansion of client/server, Web-based, and wireless environments, organizations will look for programmers who can support data communications and help to implement electronic commerce and Intranet strategies. Demand for programmers with strong object-oriented programming capabilities and technical specialization in areas such as client/server programming, wireless applications, multimedia technology, and graphic user interface (GUI) should arise from the expansion of intranets, extranets, and Internet applications. Programmers also will be needed to create and maintain expert systems and embed these technologies in more products. Finally, growing emphasis on cyber-security will lead to increased demand for programmers who are familiar with digital security issues and skilled in using appropriate security technology.

As programming tasks become increasingly sophisticated and additional levels of skill and experience are demanded by employers, graduates of 2-year programs and people with less than a 2-year degree or its equivalent in work experience should face strong competition for programming jobs. Competition for entry-level positions, however, also can affect applicants with a bachelor's degree. Prospects should be best for college graduates with knowledge of, and experience working with, a variety of programming languages and tools—including C++ and other object-oriented languages such as Java, as well as newer, domain-specific languages that apply to computer networking, database management, and Internet application development. Obtaining vendor-specific or language-specific certification also can provide a competitive edge. Because demand fluctuates with employers' needs, jobseekers should keep up to date with the latest skills and technologies. Individuals who want to become programmers can enhance their prospects by combining the appropriate formal training with practical work experience.

Earnings

Median annual earnings of computer programmers were $60,290 in 2002. The middle 50 percent earned between $45,960 and $78,140 a year. The lowest 10 percent earned less than $35,080; the highest 10 percent earned more than $96,860. Median annual earnings in the industries employing the largest numbers of computer programmers in 2002 were:

Professional and commercial equipment and supplies merchant wholesalers	$70,440
Software publishers	66,870
Computer systems design and related services	65,640
Management of companies and enterprises	59,850
Data processing, hosting, and related services	59,300

According to the National Association of Colleges and Employers, starting salary offers for graduates with a bachelor's degree in computer programming averaged $45,558 a year in 2003.

According to Robert Half International, a firm providing specialized staffing services, average annual starting salaries in 2003 ranged from $51,500 to $80,500 for applications development programmers/analysts, and from $55,000 to $87,750 for software developers. Average starting salaries for mainframe systems programmers ranged from $53,250 to $68,750 in 2003.

Related Occupations

Other professional workers who deal extensively with data include computer software engineers; computer systems analysts, database administrators, and computer scientists; statisticians; mathematicians; engineers; financial analysts and personal financial advisors; accountants and auditors; actuaries; and operations research analysts.

Sources of Additional Information

State employment service offices can provide information about job openings for computer programmers. Municipal chambers of commerce are an additional source of information on an area's largest employers.

Further information about computer careers is available from:

- Association for Computing Machinery (ACM), 1515 Broadway, New York, NY 10036. Internet: http://www.acm.org

- Institute of Electrical and Electronics Engineers Computer Society, Headquarters Office, 1730 Massachusetts Ave. NW, Washington, DC 20036-1992. Internet: http://www.computer.org

- National Workforce Center for Emerging Technologies, 3000 Landerholm Circle SE, Bellevue, WA 98007. Internet: http://www.nwcet.org

Computer Software Engineers

(O*NET 15-1031.00 and 15-1032.00)

Significant Points

- Computer software engineers are projected to be one of the fastest growing occupations over the 2002–12 period.

- Highly favorable opportunities are expected for college graduates with at least a bachelor's degree in computer engineering or computer science and with practical work experience.

- Computer software engineers must continually strive to acquire new skills in conjunction with the rapid changes in computer technology.

Nature of the Work

The explosive impact of computers and information technology on our everyday lives has generated a need to design and develop new computer software systems and to incorporate new technologies in a rapidly growing range of applications. The tasks performed by workers known as computer software engineers evolve quickly, reflecting new areas of specialization or changes in technology, as well as the preferences and practices of employers. Computer software engineers apply the principles and techniques of computer science, engineering, and mathematical analysis to the design, development, testing, and evaluation of the software and systems that enable computers to perform their many applications.

Software engineers working in applications or systems development analyze users' needs and design, construct, test, and maintain computer applications software or systems. Software engineers can be involved in the design and development of many types of software, including software for operating systems and network distribution, and compilers, which convert programs for execution on a computer. In programming, or coding, software engineers instruct a computer, line by line, how to perform a function. They also solve technical problems that arise. Software engineers must possess strong programming skills, but are more concerned with developing algorithms and analyzing and solving programming problems than with actually writing code.

Computer applications software engineers analyze users' needs and design, construct, and maintain general computer applications software or specialized utility programs. These workers use different programming languages, depending on the purpose of the program. The programming languages most often used are C, C++, and Java, with Fortran and COBOL used less commonly. Some software engineers develop both packaged systems and systems software or create customized applications.

Computer systems software engineers coordinate the construction and maintenance of a company's computer systems and plan their future growth. Working with a company, they coordinate each department's computer needs—ordering, inventory, billing, and payroll recordkeeping, for example—and make suggestions about its technical direction. They also might set up the company's intranets—networks that link computers within the organization and ease communication among the various departments.

Systems software engineers work for companies that configure, implement, and install complete computer systems. They may be members of the marketing or sales staff, serving as the primary technical resource for sales workers and customers. They also may be involved in product sales and in providing their customers with continuing technical support.

Computer software engineers often work as part of a team that designs new hardware, software, and systems. A core team may comprise engineering, marketing, manufacturing, and design people who work together until the product is released.

Working Conditions

Computer software engineers normally work in well-lighted and comfortable offices or computer laboratories in which computer equipment is located. Most software engineers work at least 40 hours a week; however, due to the project-oriented nature of the work, they also may have to work evenings or weekends to meet deadlines or solve unexpected technical problems. Like other workers who sit for hours at a computer, typing on a keyboard, software engineers are susceptible to eyestrain, back discomfort, and hand and wrist problems such as carpal tunnel syndrome.

As they strive to improve software for users, many computer software engineers interact with customers and coworkers. Computer software engineers who are employed by software vendors and consulting firms, for example, spend much of their time away from their offices, frequently traveling overnight to meet with customers. They call on customers in businesses ranging from manufacturing plants to financial institutions.

As networks expand, software engineers may be able to use modems, laptops, e-mail, and the Internet to provide more technical support and other services from their main office, connecting to a customer's computer remotely to identify and correct developing problems.

Employment

Computer software engineers held about 675,000 jobs in 2002. About 394,000 were computer applications software engineers, and about 281,000 were computer systems software engineers. Although they are employed in most industries, the largest concentration of computer software engineers, about 30 percent, is in computer systems design and related services. Many computer software engineers also work for establishments in other industries, such as government agencies, manufacturers of computers and related electronic equipment, and colleges and universities.

Employers of computer software engineers range from startup companies to established industry leaders. The proliferation of Internet, e-mail, and other communications systems expands electronics to engineering firms traditionally associated with unrelated disciplines. Engineering firms specializing in building bridges and power plants, for example, hire computer software engineers to design and develop new geographic data systems and automated drafting systems. Communications firms need computer software engineers to tap into growth in the personal communications market. Major communications companies have many job openings for both computer software applications and computer systems engineers.

An increasing number of computer software engineers are employed on a temporary or contract basis, with many being self-employed, working independently as consultants. Some consultants work for firms that specialize in developing and maintaining client companies' Web sites and intranets. Consulting opportunities for software engineers should grow as businesses need help managing, upgrading, and customizing increasingly complex computer systems. About 21,000 computer software engineers were self-employed in 2002.

Training, Other Qualifications, and Advancement

Most employers prefer to hire persons who have at least a bachelor's degree and broad knowledge of, and experience with, a variety of computer systems and technologies. Usual degree concentrations for applications software engineers are computer science or software engineering; for systems software engineers, usual concentrations are computer science or computer information systems. Graduate degrees are preferred for some of the more complex jobs.

Academic programs in software engineering emphasize software and may be offered as a degree option or in conjunction with computer science degrees. Increasing emphasis on computer security suggests that software engineers with advanced degrees that include mathematics and systems design will be sought after by software developers, government agencies, and consulting firms specializing in information assurance and security. Students seeking software engineering jobs enhance their employment opportunities by participating in internship or co-op programs offered through their schools. These experiences provide the students with broad knowledge and experience, making them more attractive candidates to employers. Inexperienced college graduates may be hired by large computer and consulting firms that train new hires in intensive, company-based programs. In many firms, new employees are mentored, and their mentors have an input into the new hires' evaluations.

For systems software engineering jobs that require workers who have a college degree, a bachelor's degree in computer science or computer information systems is typical. For systems engineering jobs that place less emphasis on workers having a computer-related degree, computer training programs leading to certification are offered by systems software vendors, including Microsoft, Novell, and Oracle. These programs usually last from 1 to 4 weeks, but the worker is not required to attend classes in order to sit for a certification exam; several study guides also are available to help prepare for the exams. Nonetheless, many training authorities feel that program certification alone is not sufficient for most software engineering jobs.

Professional certification is now offered by the Institute of Electrical and Electronics Engineers (IEEE) Computer Society. To be classified as a Certified Software Development Professional, individuals need a bachelor's degree and work experience that demonstrates that they have mastered a relevant body of knowledge, and they must pass a written exam.

Persons interested in jobs as computer software engineers must have strong problem-solving and analytical skills. They also must be able to communicate effectively with team members, other staff, and the customers they meet. Because they often deal with a number of tasks simultaneously, they must be able to concentrate and pay close attention to detail.

As is the case with most occupations, advancement opportunities for computer software engineers increase with experience. Entry-level computer software engineers are likely to test and verify ongoing designs. As they become more experienced, computer software engineers may be involved in designing and developing software. Eventually, they may advance to become a project manager, manager of information systems, or chief information officer. Some computer software engineers with several years of experience or expertise find lucrative opportunities working as systems designers or independent consultants or starting their own computer consulting firms.

As technological advances in the computer field continue, employers demand new skills. Computer software engineers must continually strive to acquire such skills if they wish to remain in this extremely dynamic field. To help them keep up with the changing technology, continuing education and professional development seminars are offered by employers and software vendors, colleges and universities, private training institutions, and professional computing societies.

Job Outlook

Computer software engineers are projected to be one of the fastest growing occupations from 2002 to 2012. Rapid employment growth in the computer systems design and related services industry, which employs the greatest number of computer software engineers, should result in highly favorable opportunities for those college graduates with at least a bachelor's degree in computer engineering or computer science and practical experience working with computers. Employers will continue to seek computer professionals with strong programming, systems analysis, interpersonal, and business skills.

Despite the recent downturn in information technology, employment of computer software engineers is expected to increase much faster than the average for all occupations, as businesses and other organizations adopt and integrate new technologies and seek to maximize the efficiency of their computer systems. Job growth will not be as rapid as growth

during the previous decade as the software industry begins to mature and as routine software engineering work is increasingly outsourced overseas. Competition among businesses will continue to create an incentive for increasingly sophisticated technological innovations, and organizations will need more computer software engineers to implement these changes. In addition to jobs created through employment growth, many job openings will result annually from the need to replace workers who move into managerial positions, transfer to other occupations, or leave the labor force.

Despite the recent downturn among firms specializing in information technology, demand for computer software engineers will increase as computer networking continues to grow. For example, the expanding integration of Internet technologies and the explosive growth in electronic commerce—doing business on the Internet—have resulted in rising demand for computer software engineers who can develop Internet, intranet, and World Wide Web applications. Likewise, expanding electronic data-processing systems in business, telecommunications, government, and other settings continue to become more sophisticated and complex. Growing numbers of systems software engineers will be needed to implement, safeguard, and update systems and resolve problems. Consulting opportunities for computer software engineers also should continue to grow as businesses seek help to manage, upgrade, and customize their increasingly complex computer systems.

New growth areas will continue to arise from rapidly evolving technologies. The increasing uses of the Internet, the proliferation of Web sites, and "mobile" technology such as the wireless Internet have created a demand for a wide variety of new products. As individuals and businesses rely more on hand-held computers and wireless networks, it will be necessary to integrate current computer systems with this new, more mobile technology. Also, information security concerns have given rise to new software needs. Concerns over "cyber security" should result in businesses and government continuing to invest heavily in security software that protects their networks and vital electronic infrastructure from attack. The expansion of this technology in the next 10 years will lead to an increased need for computer engineers to design and develop the software and systems to run these new applications and that will allow them to be integrated into older systems.

As with other information technology jobs, employment growth of computer software engineers may be tempered somewhat by an increase in contracting out of software development abroad. Firms may look to cut costs by shifting operations to foreign countries with highly educated workers who have strong technical skills.

Earnings

Median annual earnings of computer applications software engineers who worked full time in 2002 were about $70,900. The middle 50 percent earned between $55,510 and $88,660. The lowest 10 percent earned less than $44,830, and the highest 10 percent earned more than $109,800.

Median annual earnings in the industries employing the largest numbers of computer applications software engineers in 2002 were:

Software publishers $76,450

Navigational, measuring, electromedical,
and control instruments manufacturing..............75,890

Computer systems design and related services 71,890

Architectural, engineering, and related services 70,090

Management of companies and enterprises 67,260

Median annual earnings of computer systems software engineers who worked full time in 2002 were about $74,040. The middle 50 percent earned between $58,500 and $91,160. The lowest 10 percent earned less than $45,890, and the highest 10 percent earned more than $111,600. Median annual earnings in the industries employing the largest numbers of computer systems software engineers in 2002 are shown below:

Scientific research and development services $82,270

Software publishers 77,120

Navigational, measuring, electromedical,
and control instruments manufacturing..............76,200

Computer systems design and related services 73,460

Wired telecommunications carriers........................68,510

According to the National Association of Colleges and Employers, starting salary offers for graduates with a bachelor's degree in computer engineering averaged $51,343 in 2003, and those with a master's degree averaged $64,200. Starting salary offers for graduates with a bachelor's degree in computer science averaged $47,109.

According to Robert Half International, starting salaries for software engineers in software development ranged from $64,250 to $97,000 in 2003.

In addition to typical benefits, computer software engineers may be provided with profit sharing, stock options, and a company car with a mileage allowance.

Related Occupations

Other workers who use mathematics and logic extensively include computer systems analysts, database administrators, and computer scientists; computer programmers; financial analysts and personal financial advisors; computer hardware engineers; computer support specialists and systems administrators; statisticians; mathematicians; management analysts; actuaries; and operations research analysts.

Sources of Additional Information

Additional information on a career in computer software engineering is available from any of the following sources:

● Association for Computing Machinery (ACM), 1515 Broadway, New York, NY 10036. Internet: http://www.acm.org

● Institute of Electronics and Electrical Engineers Computer Society, Headquarters Office, 1730 Massachusetts Ave. NW, Washington, DC 20036-1992. Internet: http://www.computer.org

● National Workforce Center for Emerging Technologies, 3000 Landerholm Circle SE, Bellevue, WA 98007. Internet: http://www.nwcet.org

Computer Support Specialists and Systems Administrators

(O*NET 15-1041.00 and 15-1071.00)

Significant Points

● Computer support specialists and systems administrators are projected to be among the fastest growing occupations over the 2002-12 period.

● There are many paths of entry to these occupations.

● Job prospects should be best for college graduates who are up to date with the latest skills and technologies; certifications and practical experience are essential for persons without degrees.

Nature of the Work

In the last decade, computers have become an integral part of everyday life, used for a variety of reasons at home, in the workplace, and at schools. And almost every computer user encounters a problem occasionally, whether it is the disaster of a crashing hard drive or the annoyance of a forgotten password. The explosion of computer use has created a high demand for specialists to provide advice to users, as well as day-to-day administration, maintenance, and support of computer systems and networks.

Computer support specialists provide technical assistance, support, and advice to customers and other users. This occupational group includes *technical support specialists* and *help-desk technicians*. These troubleshooters interpret problems and provide technical support for hardware, software, and systems. They answer telephone calls, analyze problems using automated diagnostic programs, and resolve recurrent difficulties. Support specialists may work either within a company that uses computer systems or directly for a computer hardware or software vendor. Increasingly, these specialists work for help-desk or support services firms, where they provide computer support to clients on a contract basis.

Technical support specialists are troubleshooters, providing valuable assistance to their organization's computer users. Because many nontechnical employees are not computer experts, they often run into computer problems that they cannot resolve on their own. Technical support specialists install, modify, clean, and repair computer hardware and software. They also may work on monitors, keyboards, printers, and mice.

Technical support specialists answer telephone calls from their organizations' computer users and may run automatic diagnostics programs to resolve problems. They also may write training manuals and train computer users how to properly use new computer hardware and software. In addition, technical support specialists oversee the daily performance of their company's computer systems and evaluate software programs for usefulness.

Help-desk technicians assist computer users with the inevitable hardware and software questions not addressed in a product's instruction manual. Help-desk technicians field telephone calls and e-mail messages from customers seeking guidance on technical problems. In responding to these requests for guidance, help-desk technicians must listen carefully to the customer, ask questions to diagnose the nature of the problem, and then patiently walk the customer through the problem-solving steps.

Help-desk technicians deal directly with customer issues, and companies value them as a source of feedback on their products. These technicians are consulted for information about what gives customers the most trouble, as well as other customer concerns. Most computer support specialists start out at the help desk.

Network or *computer systems administrators* design, install, and support an organization's LAN (local-area network), WAN (wide-area network), network segment, Internet, or intranet system. They provide day-to-day onsite administrative support for software users in a variety of work environments, including professional offices, small businesses, government, and large corporations. They maintain network hardware and software, analyze problems, and monitor the network to ensure its availability to system users. These workers gather data to identify customer needs and then use that information to identify, interpret, and evaluate system and network requirements. Administrators also may plan, coordinate, and implement network security measures.

Systems administrators are the information technology employees responsible for the efficient use of networks by organizations. They ensure that the design of an organization's computer site allows all of the components, including computers, the network, and software, to fit together and work properly. Furthermore, they monitor and adjust performance of existing networks and continually survey the current computer site to determine future network needs. Administrators also troubleshoot problems as reported by users and automated network monitoring systems and make recommendations for enhancements in the implementation of future servers and networks.

In some organizations, *computer security specialists* may plan, coordinate, and implement the organization's information security. These workers may be called upon to educate users on computer security, install security software, monitor the network for security breaches, respond to cyber attacks, and

in some cases, gather data and evidence to be used in prosecuting cyber crime. This and other growing specialty occupations reflect the increasing emphasis on client-server applications, the expansion of Internet and intranet applications, and the demand for more end-user support.

Working Conditions

Computer support specialists and systems administrators normally work in well-lit, comfortable offices or computer laboratories. They usually work about 40 hours a week, but that may include being "on call" via pager or telephone for rotating evening or weekend work if the employer requires computer support over extended hours. Overtime may be necessary when unexpected technical problems arise. Like other workers who type on a keyboard for long periods, computer support specialists and systems administrators are susceptible to eyestrain, back discomfort, and hand and wrist problems such as carpal tunnel syndrome.

Due to the heavy emphasis on helping all types of computer users, computer support specialists and systems administrators constantly interact with customers and fellow employees as they answer questions and give valuable advice. Those who work as consultants are away from their offices much of the time, sometimes spending months working in a client's office.

As computer networks expand, more computer support specialists and systems administrators may be able to connect to a customer's computer remotely, using modems, laptops, e-mail, and the Internet, to provide technical support to computer users. This capability would reduce or eliminate travel to the customer's workplace. Systems administrators also can administer and configure networks and servers remotely, although this practice is not as common as it is with computer support specialists.

Employment

Computer support specialists and systems administrators held about 758,000 jobs in 2002. Of these, about 507,000 were computer support specialists and about 251,000 were network and computer systems administrators. Although they worked in a wide range of industries, 35 percent of all computer support specialists and systems administrators were employed in professional and business services industries, principally in computer systems design and related services. Other organizations that employed substantial numbers of these workers include banks, government agencies, insurance companies, educational institutions, and wholesale and retail vendors of computers, office equipment, appliances, and home electronic equipment. Many computer support specialists also worked for manufacturers of computers, semiconductors, and other electronic components.

Employers of computer support specialists and systems administrators range from startup companies to established industry leaders. With the continued development of the Internet, telecommunications, and e-mail, industries not typically associated with computers—such as construction—increasingly need computer-related workers. Small and large firms across all industries are expanding or developing computer systems, creating an immediate need for computer support specialists and systems administrators.

Training, Other Qualifications, and Advancement

Due to the wide range of skills required, there are many paths of entry to a job as a computer support specialist or systems administrator. While there is no universally accepted way to prepare for a job as a computer support specialist, many employers prefer to hire persons with some formal college education. A bachelor's degree in computer science or information systems is a prerequisite for some jobs; however, other jobs may require only a computer-related associate degree. For systems administrators, many employers seek applicants with bachelor's degrees, although not necessarily in a computer-related field.

Many companies are becoming more flexible about requiring a college degree for support positions because of the explosive demand for specialists. However, certification and practical experience demonstrating these skills will be essential for applicants without a degree. Completion of a certification training program, offered by a variety of vendors and product makers, may help some people to qualify for entry-level positions. Relevant computer experience may substitute for formal education.

Beginning computer support specialists usually work for organizations that deal directly with customers or in-house users. Then, they may advance into more responsible positions in which they use what they have learned from customers to improve the design and efficiency of future products. Job promotions usually depend more on performance than on formal education. Eventually, some computer support specialists become applications developers, designing products rather than assisting users. Computer support specialists at hardware and software companies often enjoy great upward mobility; advancement sometimes comes within months of initial employment.

Entry-level network and computer systems administrators are involved in routine maintenance and monitoring of computer systems, typically working behind the scenes in an organization. After gaining experience and expertise, they often are able to advance into more senior-level positions, in which they take on more responsibilities. For example, senior network and computer systems administrators may present recommendations to management on matters related to a company's network. They also may translate the needs of an organization into a set of technical requirements, based on the available technology. As with support specialists, administrators may become software engineers, actually involved in the designing of the system or network and not just the day-to-day administration.

Persons interested in becoming a computer support specialist or systems administrator must have strong problem-solving, analytical, and communication skills because troubleshooting and helping others are vital parts of the job. The constant interaction with other computer personnel, customers, and employees requires computer support specialists and systems administrators to communicate effectively on paper, via e-mail, or in person. Strong writing skills are useful when preparing manuals for employees and customers.

As technology continues to improve, computer support specialists and systems administrators must keep their skills current and acquire new ones. Many continuing education programs are offered by employers, hardware and software vendors, colleges and universities, and private training institutions. Professional development seminars offered by computing services firms also can enhance one's skills and advancement opportunities.

Job Outlook

Employment of computer support specialist is expected to increase faster than the average for all occupations through 2012, as organizations continue to adopt and integrate increasingly sophisticated technology. Job growth will continue to be driven by the continued expansion of the computer system design and related services industry, which is projected to remain one of the fastest growing industries in the U.S. economy, despite recent job losses. Job growth will not be as explosive as growth during the previous decade as these jobs are being increasingly outsourced overseas.

Employment growth among computer support specialists reflects the rapid pace of improved technology. As computers and software become more complex, support specialists will be needed to provide technical assistance to customers and other users. New mobility technologies, such as the wireless Internet, will continue to create a demand for these workers to familiarize and educate computer users. Consulting opportunities for computer support specialists also should continue to grow as businesses increasingly need help managing, upgrading, and customizing more complex computer systems. However, growth in employment of support specialists may be tempered somewhat as firms continue to cut costs by shifting more routine work abroad to countries where workers are highly skilled but labor costs are lower. Physical location is not as important for these workers as it is for others, because computer support specialists can provide assistance remotely and support services can be provided around the clock.

Employment of systems administrators is expected to increase much faster than average as firms will continue to invest heavily in securing computer networks. Companies are looking for workers knowledgeable about the function and administration of networks. Such employees have become increasingly hard to find as systems administration has moved from being a separate function within corporations to one that forms a crucial element of business in an increasingly high-technology economy. Also, demand for computer security specialists will grow as businesses and government continue to invest heavily in "cyber-security," protecting vital computer networks and electronic infrastructure from attack.

The growth of electronic commerce means that more establishments use the Internet to conduct their business online. This translates into a need for information technology specialists who can help organizations use technology to communicate with employees, clients, and consumers. Explosive growth in these areas also is expected to fuel demand for specialists knowledgeable about network, data, and communications security.

Job prospects should be best for college graduates who are up to date with the latest skills and technologies, particularly if they have supplemented their formal education with some relevant work experience. Employers will continue to seek computer specialists who possess a strong background in fundamental computer skills, combined with good interpersonal and communication skills. Due to the rapid growth in demand for computer support specialists and systems administrators, those who have strong computer skills but do not have a bachelor's degree should continue to qualify for some entry-level positions. However, certifications and practical experience are essential for persons without degrees.

Earnings

Median annual earnings of computer support specialists were $39,100 in 2002. The middle 50 percent earned between $29,760 and $51,680. The lowest 10 percent earned less than $23,060, and the highest 10 percent earned more than $67,550. Median annual earnings in the industries employing the largest numbers of computer support specialists in 2002 were:

Professional and commercial equipment and supplies merchant wholesalers	$46,740
Software publishers	42,870
Computer systems design and related services	41,110
Management of companies and enterprises	40,850
Elementary and secondary schools	33,480

Median annual earnings of network and computer systems administrators were $54,810 in 2002. The middle 50 percent earned between $43,290 and $69,530. The lowest 10 percent earned less than $34,460, and the highest 10 percent earned more than $86,440. Median annual earnings in the industries employing the largest numbers of network and computer systems administrators in 2002 were:

Wired telecommunications carriers	$59,710
Computer systems design and related services	58,790
Management of companies and enterprises	58,610
Data processing, hosting, and related services	56,140
Elementary and secondary schools	48,350

According to Robert Half International, starting salaries in 2003 ranged from $27,500 to $56,500 for help-desk support staff, and from $51,000 to $67,250 for more senior technical support specialists. For systems administrators, starting salaries in 2003 ranged from $49,000 to $70,250.

Related Occupations

Other computer-related occupations include computer programmers; computer software engineers; and computer systems analysts, database administrators, and computer scientists.

Sources of Additional Information

For additional information about a career as a computer support specialist, contact:

- Association of Computer Support Specialists, 218 Huntington Rd., Bridgeport, CT 06608. Internet: http://www.acss.org
- Association of Support Professionals, 122 Barnard Ave., Watertown, MA 02472.

For additional information about a career as a systems administrator, contact:

- System Administrators Guild, 2560 9th St., Suite 215, Berkeley, CA 94710. Internet: http://www.sage.org

Further information about computer careers is available from:

- National Workforce Center for Emerging Technologies, 3000 Landerholm Circle SE, Bellevue, WA 98007. Internet: http://www.nwcet.org

Computer Systems Analysts, Database Administrators, and Computer Scientists

(O*NET 15-1011.00, 15-1051.00, 15-1061.00, 15-1081.00, and 15-1099.99)

Significant Points

- Education requirements range from a 2-year degree to a graduate degree.

- Employment is expected to increase much faster than the average as organizations continue to adopt increasingly sophisticated technologies.

- Job prospects are favorable.

Nature of the Work

The rapid spread of computers and information technology has generated a need for highly trained workers to design and develop new hardware and software systems and to incorporate new technologies. These workers—computer systems analysts, database administrators, and computer scientists—include a wide range of computer specialists. Job tasks and occupational titles used to describe these workers evolve rapidly, reflecting new areas of specialization or changes in technology, as well as the preferences and practices of employers.

Systems analysts solve computer problems and apply computer technology to meet the individual needs of an organization. They help an organization to realize the maximum benefit from its investment in equipment, personnel, and business processes. Systems analysts may plan and develop new computer systems or devise ways to apply existing systems' resources to additional operations. They may design new systems, including both hardware and software, or add a new software application to harness more of the computer's power. Most systems analysts work with specific types of systems—for example, business, accounting, or financial systems, or scientific and engineering systems—that vary with the kind of organization. Some systems analysts also are known as *systems developers* or *systems architects*.

Systems analysts begin an assignment by discussing the systems problem with managers and users to determine its exact nature. Defining the goals of the system and dividing the solutions into individual steps and separate procedures, systems analysts use techniques such as structured analysis, data modeling, information engineering, mathematical model building, sampling, and cost accounting to plan the system. They specify the inputs to be accessed by the system, design the processing steps, and format the output to meet users' needs. They also may prepare cost-benefit and return-on-investment analyses to help management decide whether implementing the proposed technology will be financially feasible.

When a system is accepted, systems analysts determine what computer hardware and software will be needed to set the system up. They coordinate tests and observe the initial use of the system to ensure that it performs as planned. They prepare specifications, flow charts, and process diagrams for computer programmers to follow; then, they work with programmers to "debug," or eliminate, errors from the system. Systems analysts who do more indepth testing of products may be referred to as *software quality assurance analysts*. In addition to running tests, these individuals diagnose problems, recommend solutions, and determine whether program requirements have been met.

In some organizations, *programmer-analysts* design and update the software that runs a computer. Because they are responsible for both programming and systems analysis, these workers must be proficient in both areas. As this dual proficiency becomes more commonplace, these analysts increasingly work with databases, object-oriented programming languages, as well as client–server applications development and multimedia and Internet technology.

One obstacle associated with expanding computer use is the need for different computer systems to communicate with each other. Because of the importance of maintaining up-to-date information—accounting records, sales figures, or budget projections, for example—systems analysts work on making the computer systems within an organization, or among organizations, compatible so that information can be shared among them. Many systems analysts are involved with "networking," connecting all the computers internally—in an individual office, department, or establishment—or externally, because many organizations now rely on e-mail or the Internet. A primary goal of networking is to allow users to retrieve data from a mainframe computer or a server and use it on their desktop computer. Systems analysts must design the hardware and software to allow the free exchange of data, custom applications, and the computer power to process it all. For example, analysts are called upon to ensure the compatibility of computing systems between and among businesses to facilitate electronic commerce.

Networks come in many variations, so *network systems and data communications analysts* are needed to design, test, and evaluate systems such as local area networks (LANs), wide area networks (WANs), the Internet, intranets, and other data communications systems. Systems can range from a connection between two offices in the same building to globally distributed networks, voice mail, and e-mail systems of a multinational organization. Network systems and data communications analysts perform network modeling, analysis, and planning; they also may research related products and make necessary hardware and software recommendations. *Telecommunications specialists* focus on the interaction between computer and communications equipment. These workers design voice and data communication systems, supervise the installation of those systems, and provide maintenance and other services to clients after the system is installed.

The growth of the Internet and the expansion of the World Wide Web (the graphical portion of the Internet) have generated a variety of occupations related to the design, development, and maintenance of Web sites and their servers. For example, *webmasters* are responsible for all technical aspects of a Web site, including performance issues such as speed of access, and for approving the content of the site. *Internet developers* or *Web developers*, also called *Web designers*, are responsible for day-to-day site design and creation.

Computer scientists work as theorists, researchers, or inventors. Their jobs are distinguished by the higher level of theoretical expertise and innovation they apply to complex problems and the creation or application of new technology. Those employed by academic institutions work in areas ranging from complexity theory, to hardware, to programming-language design. Some work on multidisciplinary projects, such as developing and advancing uses of virtual reality, extending human-computer interaction, or designing robots. Their counterparts in private industry work in areas such as applying theory, developing specialized languages or information technologies, or designing programming tools, knowledge-based systems, or even computer games.

With the Internet and electronic business generating large volumes of data, there is a growing need to be able to store, manage, and extract data effectively. *Database administrators* work with database management systems software and determine ways to organize and store data. They identify user requirements, set up computer databases, and test and coordinate modifications to the systems. An organization's database administrator ensures the performance of the system, understands the platform on which the database runs, and adds new users to the system. Because they also may design and implement system security, database administrators often plan and coordinate security measures. With the volume of sensitive data generated every second growing rapidly, data integrity, backup systems, and database security have become increasingly important aspects of the job of database administrators.

Working Conditions

Computer systems analysts, database administrators, and computer scientists normally work in offices or laboratories in comfortable surroundings. They usually work about 40 hours a week—the same as many other professional or office workers do. However, evening or weekend work may be necessary to meet deadlines or solve specific problems. Given the technology available today, telecommuting is common for computer professionals. As networks expand, more work can be done from remote locations through modems, laptops, electronic mail, and the Internet.

Like other workers who spend long periods in front of a computer terminal typing on a keyboard, computer systems analysts, database administrators, and computer scientists are susceptible to eyestrain, back discomfort, and hand and wrist problems such as carpal tunnel syndrome or cumulative trauma disorder.

Employment

Computer systems analysts, database administrators, and computer scientists held about 979,000 jobs in 2002; including about 89,000 who were self-employed. Employment was distributed among the following detailed occupations:

Computer systems analysts	468,000
Network systems and data communications analysts	186,000
Database administrators	110,000
Computer and information scientists, research	23,000
All other computer specialists	192,000

Although they are increasingly employed in every sector of the economy, the greatest concentration of these workers is in the computer systems design and related services industry.

Firms in this industry provide services related to the commercial use of computers on a contract basis, including custom computer programming services; computer systems integration design services; computer facilities management services, including computer systems or data-processing facilities support services for clients; and other computer-related services, such as disaster recovery services and software installation. Many computer systems analysts, database administrators, and computer scientists are employed by Internet service providers, Web search portals, and data-processing, hosting, and related services firms. Others work for government, manufacturers of computer and electronic products, insurance companies, financial institutions, and universities.

A growing number of computer specialists, such as systems analysts and network and data communications analysts, are employed on a temporary or contract basis; many of these individuals are self-employed, working independently as contractors or consultants. For example, a company installing a new computer system may need the services of several systems analysts just to get the system running. Because not all of the analysts would be needed once the system is functioning, the company might contract for such employees with a temporary help agency or a consulting firm or with the systems analysts themselves. Such jobs may last from several months up to 2 years or more. This growing practice enables companies to bring in people with the exact skills the firm needs to complete a particular project, rather than having to spend time or money training or retraining existing workers. Often, experienced consultants then train a company's in-house staff as a project develops.

Training, Other Qualifications, and Advancement

Rapidly changing technology requires an increasing level of skill and education on the part of employees. Companies look for professionals with an ever-broader background and range of skills, including not only technical knowledge, but also communication and other interpersonal skills. This shift from requiring workers to possess solely sound technical knowledge emphasizes workers who can handle various responsibilities. While there is no universally accepted way to prepare for a job as a systems analyst, computer scientist, or database administrator, most employers place a premium on some formal college education. A bachelor's degree is a prerequisite for many jobs; however, some jobs may require only a 2-year degree. Relevant work experience also is very important. For more technically complex jobs, persons with graduate degrees are preferred.

For systems analyst, programmer-analyst, and database administrator positions, many employers seek applicants who have a bachelor's degree in computer science, information science, or management information systems (MIS). MIS programs usually are part of the business school or college and differ considerably from computer science programs, emphasizing business and management-oriented course work and business computing courses. Employers are increasingly seeking individuals with a master's degree in business administration (MBA), with a concentration in information systems, as more firms move their business to the Internet. For some network systems and data communication analysts, such as webmasters, an associate's degree or certificate is sufficient, although more advanced positions might require a computer-related bachelor's degree. For computer and information scientists, a doctoral degree generally is required due to the highly technical nature of their work.

Despite employers' preference for those with technical degrees, persons with degrees in a variety of majors find employment in these computer occupations. The level of education and type of training that employers require depend on their needs. One factor affecting these needs is changes in technology. Employers often scramble to find workers capable of implementing "hot" new technologies. Those workers with formal education or experience in information security, for example, are in demand because of the growing need for their skills and services. Another factor driving employers' needs is the timeframe during which a project must be completed.

Most community colleges and many independent technical institutes and proprietary schools offer an associate's degree in computer science or a related information technology field. Many of these programs may be more geared toward meeting the needs of local businesses and are more occupation specific than are 4-year degree programs. Some jobs may be better suited to the level of training that such programs offer. Employers usually look for people who have broad knowledge and experience related to computer systems and technologies, strong problem-solving and analytical skills, and good interpersonal skills. Courses in computer science or systems design offer good preparation for a job in these computer occupations. For jobs in a business environment, employers usually want systems analysts to have business management or closely related skills, while a background in the physical sciences, applied mathematics, or engineering is preferred for work in scientifically oriented organizations. Art or graphic design skills may be desirable for webmasters or Web developers.

Jobseekers can enhance their employment opportunities by participating in internship or co-op programs offered through their schools. Because many people develop advanced computer skills in a non-computer-related occupation and then transfer those skills to a computer occupation, a background in the industry in which the person's job is located, such as financial services, banking, or accounting, can be important. Others have taken computer science courses to supplement their study in fields such as accounting, inventory control, or other business areas. For example, a financial analyst who is proficient in computers might become a computer support specialist in financial systems development, while a computer programmer might move into a systems analyst job.

Computer systems analysts, database administrators, and computer scientists must be able to think logically and have good communication skills. Because they often deal with a number of tasks simultaneously, the ability to concentrate and pay close attention to detail is important. Although these computer specialists sometimes work independently, they frequently work in teams on large projects. They must be able to communicate effectively with computer personnel, such as programmers and managers, as well as with users or other staff who may have no technical computer background.

Computer scientists employed in private industry may advance into managerial or project leadership positions. Those employed in academic institutions can become heads of research departments or published authorities in their field. Systems analysts may be promoted to senior or lead systems analyst. Those who show leadership ability also can become project managers or advance into management positions such as manager of information systems or chief information officer. Database administrators may advance into managerial positions, such as chief technology officer, on the basis of their experience managing data and enforcing security. Computer specialists with work experience and considerable expertise in a particular subject or a certain application may find lucrative opportunities as independent consultants or may choose to start their own computer consulting firms.

Technological advances come so rapidly in the computer field that continuous study is necessary to keep one's skills up to date. Employers, hardware and software vendors, colleges and universities, and private training institutions offer continuing education. Additional training may come from professional development seminars offered by professional computing societies.

Certification is a way to demonstrate a level of competence in a particular field. Some product vendors or software firms offer certification and require professionals who work with their products to be certified. Many employers regard these certifications as the industry standard. For example, one method of acquiring enough knowledge to get a job as a database administrator is to become certified in a specific type of database management. Voluntary certification also is available through various organizations associated with computer specialists. Professional certification may afford a jobseeker a competitive advantage.

Job Outlook

Computer systems analysts, database administrators, and computer scientists are expected to be among the fastest growing occupations through 2012. Employment of these computer specialists is expected to grow much faster than the average for all occupations as organizations continue to adopt and integrate increasingly sophisticated technologies. Job increases will be driven by very rapid growth in computer system design and related services, which is projected to be one of the fastest-growing industries in the U.S. economy. In addition, many job openings will arise annually from the need to replace workers who move into managerial positions or other occupations or who leave the labor force. Job growth will not be as rapid as growth during the previous decade, however, as the information technology sector begins to mature and as routine work is increasingly outsourced overseas.

Despite the recent economic downturn among information technology firms, workers in the occupation should still enjoy favorable job prospects. The demand for networking to facilitate the sharing of information, the expansion of client–server environments, and the need for computer specialists to use their knowledge and skills in a problem-solving capacity will be major factors in the rising demand for computer systems analysts, database administrators, and computer scientists. Moreover, falling prices of computer hardware and software should continue to induce more businesses to expand their computerized operations and integrate new technologies into them. In order to maintain a competitive edge and operate more efficiently, firms will keep demanding computer specialists who are knowledgeable about the latest technologies and are able to apply them to meet the needs of businesses.

Increasingly, more sophisticated and complex technology is being implemented across all organizations, which should fuel the demand for these computer occupations. There is a growing demand for system analysts to help firms maximize their efficiency with available technology. Expansion of electronic commerce—doing business on the Internet—and the continuing need to build and maintain databases that store critical information on customers, inventory, and projects are fueling demand for database administrators familiar with the latest technology. Also, the increasing importance being placed on "cybersecurity"—the protection of electronic information—will result in a need for workers skilled in information security.

The development of new technologies usually leads to demand for various kinds of workers. The expanding integration of Internet technologies into businesses, for example, has resulted in a growing need for specialists who can develop and support Internet and intranet applications. The growth of electronic commerce means that more establishments use the Internet to conduct their business online. The introduction of the wireless Internet, known as WiFi, creates new systems to be analyzed and new data to be administered. The spread of such new technologies translates into a need for information technology professionals who can help organizations use technology to communicate with employees, clients, and consumers. Explosive growth in these areas also is expected to fuel demand for specialists who are knowledgeable about network, data, and communications security.

As technology becomes more sophisticated and complex, employers demand a higher level of skill and expertise from their employees. Individuals with an advanced degree in computer science or computer engineering or with an MBA with a concentration in information systems should enjoy highly favorable employment prospects. College graduates with a bachelor's degree in computer science, computer engineering, information science, or MIS also should enjoy favorable prospects for employment, particularly if they have supplemented their formal education with practical experience. Because employers continue to seek computer specialists who can combine strong technical skills with good interpersonal and business skills, graduates with non-computer-science degrees, but who have had courses in computer programming, systems analysis, and other information technology areas, also should continue to find jobs in these computer fields. In fact, individuals with the right experience and training can work in these computer occupations regardless of their college major or level of formal education.

Earnings

Median annual earnings of computer systems analysts were $62,890 in 2002. The middle 50 percent earned between $49,500 and $78,350 a year. The lowest 10 percent earned less than $39,270, and the highest 10 percent earned more than $93,400. Median annual earnings in the industries employing the largest numbers of computer systems analysts in 2002 were as follows:

Federal government	$68,370
Computer systems design and related services	67,690
Data processing, hosting, and related services	64,560
Management of companies and enterprises	63,390
Insurance carriers	59,510

Median annual earnings of database administrators were $55,480 in 2002. The middle 50 percent earned between $40,550 and $75,100. The lowest 10 percent earned less than $30,750, and the highest 10 percent earned more than $92,910. In 2002, median annual earnings of database administrators employed in computer system design and related services were $66,650, and, for those in management of companies and enterprises, earnings were $59,620.

Median annual earnings of network systems and data communication analysts were $58,420 in 2002. The middle 50 percent earned between $44,850 and $74,290. The lowest 10 percent earned less than $34,880, and the highest 10 percent earned more than $92,110. Median annual earnings in the industries employing the largest numbers of network systems and data communications analysts in 2002 were as follows:

Computer systems design and related services	$65,800
Management of companies and enterprises	63,050
State government	45,110

Median annual earnings of computer and information scientists, research, were $77,760 in 2002. The middle 50 percent earned between $58,630 and $98,490. The lowest 10 percent earned less than $42,890, and the highest 10 percent earned more than $121,650. Median annual earnings of computer and information scientists employed in computer systems design and related services in 2002 were $78,730.

Median annual earnings of all other computer specialists were $54,070 in 2002. Median annual earnings of all other computer specialists employed in computer system design and related services were $49,590, and, for those in scientific research and development services, earnings were $70,150 in 2002.

According to the National Association of Colleges and Employers, starting offers for graduates with a master's degree in computer science averaged $62,806 in 2003. Starting offers averaged $47,109 for graduates with a bachelor's degree in computer science; $45,346 for those with a degree in computer programming; $41,118 for those with a degree in computer systems analysis; $40,556 for those with a degree in management information systems; and $38,282 for those with a degree in information sciences and systems.

According to Robert Half International, starting salaries in 2003 ranged from $69,750 to $101,750 for database administrators. Salaries for networking and Internet-related occupations ranged from $45,500 to $65,750 for LAN administrators and from $51,250 to $73,750 for Intranet developers. Starting salaries for security professionals ranged from $62,500 to $91,750 in 2003.

Related Occupations

Other workers who use logic and creativity to solve business and technical problems are computer programmers, computer software engineers, computer and information systems managers, financial analysts and personal financial advisors, urban and regional planners, engineers, mathematicians, statisticians, operations research analysts, management analysts, and actuaries.

Sources of Additional Information

Further information about computer careers is available from any of the following organizations:

- Association for Computing Machinery (ACM), 1515 Broadway, New York, NY 10036. Internet: http://www.acm.org

- Institute of Electrical and Electronics Engineers Computer Society, Headquarters Office, 1730 Massachusetts Ave. NW, Washington, DC 20036-1992. Internet: http://www.computer.org

- National Workforce Center for Emerging Technologies, 3000 Landerholm Circle SE, Bellevue, WA 98007. Internet: http://www.nwcet.org

Construction Laborers

(O*NET 47-2061.00)

Significant Points

- Job opportunities should be good.

- The work can be physically demanding and sometimes dangerous.

- Most construction laborers learn through informal on-the-job training, but formal apprenticeship programs provide more thorough preparation.

- Like many other construction occupations, employment opportunities are affected by the cyclical nature of the construction industry and can vary greatly by state and locality.

Nature of the Work

Construction laborers perform a wide range of physically demanding tasks involving building and highway construction, tunnel and shaft excavation, hazardous waste removal, environmental remediation, and demolition. Although the term "laborer" implies work that requires relatively little skill or training, many tasks that these workers perform require a fairly high level of training and experience. Construction laborers clean and prepare construction sites to eliminate possible hazards, dig trenches, mix and place concrete, and set braces to support the sides of excavations. They load, unload, identify, and distribute building materials to the appropriate location according to project plans and specifications on building construction projects. They also tend machines; for example, they may mix concrete using a portable mixer or tend a machine that pumps concrete, grout, cement, sand, plaster, or stucco through a spray gun for application to ceilings and walls. Construction laborers often help other craftworkers, including carpenters, plasterers, operating engineers, and masons.

At heavy and highway construction sites, construction laborers clear and prepare highway work zones and rights of way; install traffic barricades, cones, and markers; and control traffic passing near, in, and around work zones. They also install sewer, water, and storm drain pipes, and place concrete and asphalt on roads.

At hazardous waste removal sites, construction laborers prepare the site and safely remove asbestos, lead, radioactive waste, and other hazardous materials. They operate, read, and maintain air monitoring and other sampling devices in confined and/or hazardous environments. They also safely sample, identify, handle, pack, and transport hazardous and/or radioactive materials and clean and decontaminate equipment, buildings, and enclosed structures. Other highly specialized tasks include operating laser guidance equipment to place pipes, operating air, electric, and pneumatic drills, and transporting and setting explosives for tunnel, shaft, and road construction.

Construction laborers operate a variety of equipment including pavement breakers; jackhammers; earth tampers; concrete, mortar, and plaster mixers; electric and hydraulic boring machines; torches; small mechanical hoists; laser beam equipment; and surveying and measuring equipment. They may use computers and other high-tech input devices to control robotic pipe cutters and cleaners. To perform their jobs effectively, construction laborers must be familiar with the duties of other craftworkers and with the materials, tools, and machinery they use. Construction laborers often work as part of a team with other skilled craftworkers, jointly carrying out assigned construction tasks. At other times, construction laborers may work alone, reading and interpreting instructions, plans, and specifications with little or no supervision.

While most construction laborers tend to specialize in a type of construction, such as highway or tunnel construction, they are generalists who perform many different tasks during all stages of construction. However, construction laborers who work in underground construction (such as in tunnels) or in demolition are more likely to specialize in only those areas.

Working Conditions

Most laborers do physically demanding work. They may lift and carry heavy objects, and stoop, kneel, crouch, or crawl in awkward positions. Some work at great heights, or outdoors in all weather conditions. Some jobs expose workers to harmful materials or chemicals, fumes, odors, loud noise, or dangerous machinery. To avoid injury, workers in these jobs wear safety clothing, such as gloves, hardhats, protective chemical suits, and devices to protect their eyes, respiratory system, or hearing. While working in underground construction, construction laborers must be especially alert to safely follow procedures and must deal with a variety of hazards.

Construction laborers generally work 8-hour shifts, although longer shifts also are common. They may work only during certain seasons, when the weather permits construction activity.

Employment

Construction laborers held about 938,000 jobs in 2002. They worked throughout the country but, like the general population, were concentrated in metropolitan areas. Almost all construction laborers work in the construction industry and almost one-third work for special trade contractors. About 14 percent were self-employed in 2002.

Training, Other Qualifications, and Advancement

Many construction laborer jobs require no experience or training related to the occupation. Although many workers enter the occupation with few skill, training is encourage and available through apprenticeships and laborer training centers. However, the work requires more strength and stamina than do most occupations, as well as a basic education. The willingness to work outdoors or in confined spaces also is needed. Basic literacy is a must if a worker is to read and comprehend warning signs and labels and understand instructions and specifications.

Most construction laborers learn their skills informally, observing and learning from experienced workers. Individuals who learn the trade on the job usually start as helpers.

These workers perform routine tasks, such as cleaning and preparing the worksite and unloading materials. When the opportunity arises, they learn how to do more difficult tasks, such as operating tools and equipment, from experienced craftworkers. Becoming a fully skilled construction laborer by training on the job normally takes longer than the 2 to 4 years required to complete a construction craft laborer apprenticeship program.

Formal apprenticeship programs provide more thorough preparation for jobs as construction laborers than does on-the-job training. Local apprenticeship programs are operated under guidelines established by the Laborers-Associated General Contractors of America Education and Training Fund. These programs typically require at least 4,000 hours of supervised on-the-job training and approximately 400 hours of classroom training. Depending on the availability of work and on local training schedules, it can take an individual from 2 to 4 years to complete the apprenticeship. A core curriculum consisting of basic construction skills such as blueprint reading, the correct use of tools and equipment, and knowledge of safety and health procedures comprises the first 200 hours. The remainder of the curriculum consists of specialized skills training in three of the largest segments of the construction industry: Building construction, heavy/highway construction, and environmental remediation (cleaning up debris, landscaping, and restoring the environment to its original state). Workers who use dangerous equipment or handle toxic chemicals usually receive specialized training in safety awareness and procedures. Apprentices must complete a minimum 144 hours of classroom work each year.

Most apprenticeship programs require workers to be at least 18 years old and physically able to perform the work. Many apprenticeship programs require a high school diploma or equivalent. High school and junior college courses in science, physics, chemistry, and mathematics are helpful. Vocational classes in welding, construction, and other general building skills can give anyone wishing to become a construction laborer a significant head start.

Experience and training is helpful but usually is not necessary to obtain a job. Relevant work experience that provides construction-related job skills can often reduce or eliminate a wide range of training and apprenticeship requirements. Finally, most apprenticeship programs, local unions, and employers look very favorably on military service and/or service in the Job Corps, as veterans and Job Corps graduates have already demonstrated a high level of responsibility and reliability and may have gained many valuable job skills.

Construction laborers need good manual dexterity, hand-eye coordination, and balance. They also need the ability to read and comprehend all warning signs and labels on a construction site and reading skills sufficient to understand and interpret plans, drawings, and written instructions and specifications. They should be capable of working as a member of a team and have basic problem-solving and math skills. Employers want workers who are hard-working, reliable, and diligent about being on time. Additionally, construction laborers who wish to work in environmental remediation must pass a physical test that measures the ability to wear protective equipment such as respirators. Computer skills also are important as construction becomes increasingly mechanized and computerized.

Experience in many construction laborer jobs may allow some workers to advance to positions such as supervisor or construction superintendent. Some construction laborers become skilled craftworkers, either through extensive on the job training or apprenticeships in a craft. A few become independent contractors.

Job Outlook

Job opportunities for construction laborers are expected to be good due to the numerous openings arising each year as laborers leave the occupation. In addition, many potential workers are not attracted to the occupation because they prefer work that is less strenuous and has more comfortable working conditions. Opportunities will be best for workers who are willing to relocate to different worksites.

Employment of construction laborers is expected to grow about as fast as the average for all occupations through the year 2012. New jobs will arise from a continuing emphasis on environmental remediation and on rebuilding infrastructure—roads, airports, bridges, tunnels, and communications facilities, for example. However, employment growth will be adversely affected by automation as some jobs are replaced by new machines and equipment that improve productivity and quality.

Employment of construction laborers, like that of many other construction workers, can be variable or intermittent due to the limited duration of construction projects and the cyclical nature of the construction industry. Employment opportunities can vary greatly by state and locality. During economic downturns, job openings for construction laborers decrease as the level of construction activity declines.

Earnings

Median hourly earnings of construction laborers in 2002 were $11.90. The middle 50 percent earned between $9.33 and $17.06. The lowest 10 percent earned less than $7.58, and the highest 10 percent earned more than $23.36. Median hourly earnings in the industries employing the largest number of construction laborers in 2002 were as follows:

Highway, street, and bridge construction	$14.48
Nonresidential building construction	12.97
Other specialty trade contractors	12.35
Foundation, structure, and building exterior contractors	11.89
Residential building construction	11.42

Earnings for construction laborers can be reduced by poor weather or by downturns in construction activity, which sometimes result in layoffs.

Apprentices or helpers usually start at about 50 percent of the wage rate paid to experienced workers. Pay increases as apprentices gain experience and learn new skills.

Some laborers belong to the Laborers' International Union of North America.

Related Occupations

The work of construction laborers is closely related to other construction occupations. Other workers who perform similar physical work include persons in material-moving occupations; forest, conservation, and logging workers; and grounds maintenance workers.

Sources of Additional Information

For information about jobs as construction laborers, contact local building or construction contractors, local joint labor-management apprenticeship committees, apprenticeship agencies, or the local office of your state Employment Service.

For general information about the work of construction laborers, contact:

- Laborers' International Union of North America, 905 16th St. NW, Washington, DC 20006. Internet: http://www.liuna.org

For information on education programs for laborers, contact:

- Laborers-AGC Education and Training Fund, 37 Deerfield Road, P.O. Box 37, Pomfret Center, CT 06259. Internet: http://www.laborerslearn.org

- National Center for Construction Education and Research, P.O. Box 141104, Gainesville FL 32614-1104. Internet: http://www.nccer.org

There are more than 500 occupations registered by the U.S. Department of Labor's National Apprenticeship system. For more information on the Labor Department's registered apprenticeship system and links to state apprenticeship programs, check their Web site: http://www.doleta.gov.

Correctional Officers

(O*NET 33-1011.00, 33-3011.00, and 33-3012.00)

Significant Points

- The work can be stressful and hazardous.

- Most correctional officers work in institutions located in rural areas with smaller inmate populations than those in urban jails.

- Job opportunities are expected to be excellent.

Nature of the Work

Correctional officers are responsible for overseeing individuals who have been arrested and are awaiting trial or who have been convicted of a crime and sentenced to serve time in a jail, reformatory, or penitentiary. They maintain security and inmate accountability to prevent disturbances, assaults, or escapes. Officers have no law enforcement responsibilities outside the institution where they work.

Police and sheriffs' departments in county and municipal jails or precinct station houses employ many correctional officers, also known as *detention officers*. Most of the approximately 3,300 jails in the United States are operated by county governments, with about three-quarters of all jails under the jurisdiction of an elected sheriff. Individuals in the jail population change constantly as some are released, some are convicted and transferred to prison, and new offenders are arrested and enter the system. Correctional officers in the U.S. jail system admit and process more than 11 million people a year, with about half a million offenders in jail at any given time. When individuals are first arrested, the jail staff may not know their true identity or criminal record, and violent detainees may be placed in the general population. This is the most dangerous phase of the incarceration process for correctional officers.

Most correctional officers are employed in large jails or state and federal prisons, watching over the approximately one million offenders who are incarcerated at any given time. In addition to jails and prisons, a relatively small number of correctional officers oversee individuals being held by the U.S. Immigration and Naturalization Service before they are released or deported, or they work for correctional institutions that are run by private for-profit organizations. While both jails and prisons can be dangerous places to work, prison populations are more stable than jail populations, and correctional officers in prisons know the security and custodial requirements of the prisoners with whom they are dealing.

Regardless of the setting, correctional officers maintain order within the institution and enforce rules and regulations. To help ensure that inmates are orderly and obey rules, correctional officers monitor the activities and supervise the work assignments of inmates. Sometimes, it is necessary for officers to search inmates and their living quarters for contraband like weapons or drugs, settle disputes between inmates, and enforce discipline. Correctional officers periodically inspect the facilities, checking cells and other areas of the institution for unsanitary conditions, contraband, fire hazards, and any evidence of infractions of rules. In addition, they routinely inspect locks, window bars, grilles, doors, and gates for signs of tampering. Finally, officers inspect mail and visitors for prohibited items.

Correctional officers report orally and in writing on inmate conduct and on the quality and quantity of work done by inmates. Officers also report security breaches, disturbances, violations of rules, and any unusual occurrences. They usually keep a daily log or record of their activities. Correctional officers cannot show favoritism and must report any inmate who violates the rules. Should the situation arise, they help the responsible law enforcement authorities investigate crimes committed within their institution or search for escaped inmates.

In jail and prison facilities with direct supervision cellblocks, officers work unarmed. They are equipped with communications devices so that they can summon help if necessary. These officers often work in a cellblock alone, or with another officer, among the 50 to 100 inmates who reside there. The officers enforce regulations primarily through their interpersonal communications skills and the use of progressive sanctions, such as loss of some privileges.

In the highest security facilities where the most dangerous inmates are housed, correctional officers often monitor the activities of prisoners from a centralized control center with the aid of closed-circuit television cameras and a computer tracking system. In such an environment, the inmates may not see anyone but officers for days or weeks at a time and only leave their cells for showers, solitary exercise time, or visitors. Depending on the offender's security classification within the institution, correctional officers may have to restrain inmates in handcuffs and leg irons to safely escort them to and from cells and other areas to see authorized visitors. Officers also escort prisoners between the institution and courtrooms, medical facilities, and other destinations outside the institution.

Working Conditions

Working in a correctional institution can be stressful and hazardous. Every year, a number of correctional officers are injured in confrontations with inmates. Correctional officers may work indoors or outdoors. Some correctional institutions are well lighted, temperature controlled, and ventilated, while others are old, overcrowded, hot, and noisy. Correctional officers usually work an 8-hour day, 5 days a week, on rotating shifts. Prison and jail security must be provided around the clock, which often means that officers work all hours of the day and night, weekends, and holidays. In addition, officers may be required to work paid overtime.

Employment

Correctional officers held about 476,000 jobs in 2002. About 3 of every 5 jobs were in state correctional institutions such as prisons, prison camps, and youth correctional facilities. Most of the remaining jobs were in city and county jails or other institutions run by local governments. About 16,000 jobs for correctional officers were in federal correctional institutions, and about 16,000 jobs were in privately owned and managed prisons.

There are 118 jail systems in the United States that house over 1,000 inmates, all of which are located in urban areas. A significant number work in jails and other facilities located in law enforcement agencies throughout the country. However, most correctional officers work in institutions located in rural areas with smaller inmate populations than those in urban jails.

Training, Other Qualifications, and Advancement

Most institutions require correctional officers to be at least 18 to 21 years of age and a U.S. citizen; have a high school education or its equivalent; demonstrate job stability, usually by accumulating two years of work experience; and have no felony convictions. Promotion prospects may be enhanced through obtaining a postsecondary education.

Correctional officers must be in good health. Candidates for employment are generally required to meet formal standards of physical fitness, eyesight, and hearing. In addition, many jurisdictions use standard tests to determine applicant suitability to work in a correctional environment. Good judgment and the ability to think and act quickly are indispensable. Applicants are typically screened for drug abuse, subject to background checks, and required to pass a written examination.

Federal, state, and some local departments of corrections provide training for correctional officers based on guidelines established by the American Correctional Association and the American Jail Association. Some states have regional training academies which are available to local agencies. All states and local correctional agencies provide on-the-job training at the conclusion of formal instruction, including legal restrictions and interpersonal relations. Many systems require firearms proficiency and self-defense skills. Officer trainees typically receive several weeks or months of training in an actual job setting under the supervision of an experienced officer. However, specific entry requirements and on-the-job training vary widely from agency to agency.

Academy trainees generally receive instruction on a number of subjects, including institutional policies, regulations, and operations, as well as custody and security procedures. As a condition of employment, new federal correctional officers must undergo 200 hours of formal training within the first year of employment. They also must complete 120 hours of specialized training at the U.S. Federal Bureau of Prisons residential training center at Glynco, Georgia within the first 60 days after appointment. Experienced officers receive annual in-service training to keep abreast of new developments and procedures.

Some correctional officers are members of prison tactical response teams, which are trained to respond to disturbances, riots, hostage situations, forced cell moves, and other potentially dangerous confrontations. Team members receive training and practice with weapons, chemical agents, forced entry methods, crisis management, and other tactics.

With education, experience, and training, qualified officers may advance to correctional sergeant. Correctional sergeants supervise correctional officers and usually are responsible for maintaining security and directing the activities of other officers during an assigned shift or in an assigned area. Ambitious and qualified correctional officers can be promoted to supervisory or administrative positions all the way up to warden. Officers sometimes transfer to related areas, such as probation officer, parole officer, or correctional treatment specialist.

Job Outlook

Job opportunities for correctional officers are expected to be excellent. The need to replace correctional officers who transfer to other occupations, retire, or leave the labor force, coupled with rising employment demand, will generate thousands of job openings each year. In the past, some local and state corrections agencies have experienced difficulty in attracting and keeping qualified applicants, largely due to relatively low salaries and the concentration of jobs in rural locations. This situation is expected to continue.

Employment of correctional officers is expected to grow faster than the average for all occupations through 2012, as additional officers are hired to supervise and control a growing inmate population. The adoption of mandatory sentencing guidelines calling for longer sentences and reduced parole for inmates will continue to spur demand for correctional officers. Moreover, expansion and new construction of corrections facilities also are expected to create many new jobs for correctional officers, although state and local government budgetary constraints could affect the rate at which new facilities are built and staffed. Some employment opportunities also will arise in the private sector as public authorities contract with private companies to provide and staff corrections facilities.

Layoffs of correctional officers are rare because of increasing offender populations. While officers are allowed to join bargaining units, they are not allowed to strike.

Earnings

Median annual earnings of correctional officers and jailers were $32,670 in 2002. The middle 50 percent earned between $25,950 and $42,620. The lowest 10 percent earned less than $22,010, and the highest 10 percent earned more than $52,370. Median annual earnings in the public sector were $40,900 in the federal government, $33,260 in state government, and $31,380 in local government. In the management and public relations industry, where the relatively small number of officers employed by privately operated prisons are classified, median annual earnings were $21,390. According to the Federal Bureau of Prisons, the starting salary for federal correctional officers was about $23,000 a year in 2003. Starting federal salaries were slightly higher in selected areas where prevailing local pay levels were higher.

Median annual earnings of first-line supervisors/managers of correctional officers were $44,940 in 2002. The middle 50 percent earned between $33,730 and $59,160. The lowest 10 percent earned less than $29,220, and the highest 10 percent earned more than $69,370. Median annual earnings were $43,240 in state government and $49,120 in local government.

Median annual earnings of bailiffs were $32,710 in 2002. The middle 50 percent earned between $22,960 and

$44,280. The lowest 10 percent earned less than $16,870, and the highest 10 percent earned more than $55,270. Median annual earnings were $27,470 in local government.

In addition to typical benefits, correctional officers employed in the public sector usually are provided with uniforms or a clothing allowance to purchase their own uniforms. Civil service systems or merit boards cover officers employed by the federal government and most state governments. Their retirement coverage entitles them to retire at age 50 after 20 years of service or at any age with 25 years of service.

Related Occupations

A number of options are available to those interested in careers in protective services and security. Security guards and gaming surveillance officers protect people and property against theft, vandalism, illegal entry, and fire. Police and detectives maintain law and order, prevent crime, and arrest offenders. Probation officers and correctional treatment specialists monitor and counsel offenders in the community and evaluate their progress in becoming productive members of society.

Sources of Additional Information

Information about correctional jobs in a jail setting is available from:

- American Jail Association, 1135 Professional Ct., Hagerstown, MD 21740.

Information on entrance requirements, training, and career opportunities for correctional officers at the federal level may be obtained from the Federal Bureau of Prisons. Internet: http://www.bop.gov

Information on obtaining a position as a correctional officer with the federal government is available from the Office of Personnel Management (OPM) through a telephone-based system. Consult your telephone directory under U.S. Government for a local number or call (703) 724-1850; Federal Relay Service: (800) 877-8339. The first number is not toll-free, and charges may result. Information also is available from the OPM Internet site: http://www.usajobs.opm.gov.

Cost Estimators

(O*NET 13-1051.00)

Significant Points

- Over half work in the construction industry and another 20 percent are employed in manufacturing industries.

- Growth of the construction industry will be the driving force behind the demand for cost estimators.

- In construction and manufacturing, job prospects should be best for those with industry work experience and a bachelor's degree in a related field.

Nature of the Work

Accurately forecasting the cost of future projects is vital to the survival of any business. Cost estimators develop the cost information that business owners or managers need to make a bid for a contract or to determine if a proposed new product will be profitable. They also determine which endeavors are making a profit.

Regardless of the industry in which they work, estimators compile and analyze data on all of the factors that can influence costs—such as materials, labor, location, and special machinery requirements, including computer hardware and software. Job duties vary widely depending on the type and size of the project.

The methods of and motivations for estimating costs can differ greatly by industry. On a construction project, for example, the estimating process begins with the decision to submit a bid. After reviewing various preliminary drawings and specifications, the estimator visits the site of the proposed project. The estimator needs to gather information on access to the site and availability of electricity, water, and other services, as well as on surface topography and drainage. The information developed during the site visit usually is recorded in a signed report that is included in the final project estimate.

After the site visit is completed, the estimator determines the quantity of materials and labor the firm will need to furnish. This process, called the quantity survey or "takeoff," involves completing standard estimating forms, filling in dimensions, number of units, and other information. A cost estimator working for a general contractor, for example, will estimate the costs of all items the contractor must provide. Although subcontractors will estimate their costs as part of their own bidding process, the general contractor's cost estimator often analyzes bids made by subcontractors as well. Also during the takeoff process, the estimator must make decisions concerning equipment needs, sequence of operations, crew size, and physical constraints at the site. Allowances for the waste of materials, inclement weather, shipping delays, and other factors that may increase costs also must be incorporated in the estimate.

On completion of the quantity surveys, the estimator prepares a cost summary for the entire project, including the costs of labor, equipment, materials, subcontracts, overhead, taxes, insurance, markup, and any other costs that may affect the project. The chief estimator then prepares the bid proposal for submission to the owner.

Construction cost estimators also may be employed by the project's architect or owner to estimate costs or to track actual costs relative to bid specifications as the project develops. In large construction companies employing more than one estimator, it is common practice for estimators to specialize. For example, one may estimate only electrical work and another may concentrate on excavation, concrete, and forms.

In manufacturing and other firms, cost estimators usually are assigned to the engineering, cost, or pricing departments. The estimators' goal in manufacturing is to accurately estimate the costs associated with making products. The job may begin when management requests an estimate of the costs associated with a major redesign of an existing product or the development of a new product or production process. When estimating the cost of developing a new product, for example, the estimator works with engineers, first reviewing blueprints or conceptual drawings to determine the machining operations, tools, gauges, and materials that would be required for the job. The estimator then prepares a parts list and determines whether it is more efficient to produce or to purchase the parts. To do this, the estimator must initiate inquiries for price information from potential suppliers. The next step is to determine the cost of manufacturing each component of the product. Some high-technology products require a tremendous amount of computer programming during the design phase. The cost of software development is one of the fastest growing and most difficult activities to estimate. Some cost estimators now specialize in estimating only computer software development and related costs.

The cost estimator then prepares time-phase charts and learning curves. Time-phase charts indicate the time required for tool design and fabrication, tool "debugging"—finding and correcting all problems—manufacturing of parts, assembly, and testing. Learning curves graphically represent the rate at which performance improves with practice. These curves are commonly called "cost reduction" curves because many problems—such as engineering changes, rework, parts shortages, and lack of operator skills—diminish as the number of parts produced increases, resulting in lower unit costs.

Using all of this information, the estimator then calculates the standard labor hours necessary to produce a predetermined number of units. Standard labor hours are then converted to dollar values, to which are added factors for waste, overhead, and profit to yield the unit cost in dollars. The estimator then compares the cost of purchasing parts with the firm's cost of manufacturing them to determine which is cheaper.

Computers play an integral role in cost estimation because estimating often involves complex mathematical calculations and requires advanced mathematical techniques. For example, to undertake a parametric analysis (a process used to estimate project costs on a per unit basis, subject to the specific requirements of a project), cost estimators use a computer database containing information on costs and conditions of many other similar projects. Although computers cannot be used for the entire estimating process, they can relieve estimators of much of the drudgery associated with routine, repetitive, and time-consuming calculations. Computers also are used to produce all of the necessary documentation with the help of word-processing and spreadsheet software, leaving estimators more time to study and analyze projects.

Operations research, production control, cost, and price analysts who work for government agencies may do significant amounts of cost estimating in the course of their regular duties. In addition, the duties of construction managers also may include estimating costs.

Working Conditions

Although estimators spend most of their time in an office, construction estimators must make visits to project worksites that can be dusty, dirty, and occasionally hazardous. Likewise, estimators in manufacturing must spend time on the factory floor, where it also can be noisy and dirty. In some industries, frequent travel between a firm's headquarters and its subsidiaries or subcontractors may be required.

Although estimators normally work a 40-hour week, overtime is common. Cost estimators often work under pressure and stress, especially when facing bid deadlines. Inaccurate estimating can cause a firm to lose out on a bid or to lose money on a job that was not accurately estimated.

Employment

Cost estimators held about 188,000 jobs in 2002. About 53 percent were in the construction industry, and another 20 percent were in manufacturing industries. The remainder worked in a wide range of other industries.

Cost estimators work throughout the country, usually in or near major industrial, commercial, and government centers, and in cities and suburban areas undergoing rapid change or development.

Training, Other Qualifications, and Advancement

Job entry requirements for cost estimators vary by industry. In the construction industry, employers increasingly prefer individuals with a degree in building construction, construction management, construction science, engineering, or architecture. However, most construction estimators also have considerable construction experience, gained through work in the industry, internships, or cooperative education programs. Applicants with a thorough knowledge of construction materials, costs, and procedures in areas ranging from heavy construction to electrical work, plumbing systems, or masonry work have a competitive edge.

In manufacturing industries, employers prefer to hire individuals with a degree in engineering, physical science, operations research, mathematics, or statistics; or in accounting, finance, business, economics, or a related subject. In most industries, great emphasis is placed on experience involving quantitative techniques.

Cost estimators should have an aptitude for mathematics, be able to quickly analyze, compare, and interpret detailed and sometimes poorly defined information, and be able to make sound and accurate judgments based on this knowledge. Assertiveness and self-confidence in presenting and supporting their conclusions are important, as are strong communications and interpersonal skills, because estimators may work as part of a project team alongside managers, owners, engineers, and design professionals. Cost estimators also need knowledge of computers, including word-processing and spreadsheet packages. In some instances, familiarity with special estimation software or programming skills also may be required.

Regardless of their background, estimators receive much training on the job because every company has its own way of handling estimates. Working with an experienced estimator, they become familiar with each step in the process. Those with no experience reading construction specifications or blueprints first learn that aspect of the work. They then may accompany an experienced estimator to the construction site or shop floor, where they observe the work being done, take measurements, or perform other routine tasks. As they become more knowledgeable, estimators learn how to tabulate quantities and dimensions from drawings and how to select the appropriate material prices.

For most estimators, advancement takes the form of higher pay and prestige. Some move into management positions, such as project manager for a construction firm or manager of the industrial engineering department for a manufacturer. Others may go into business for themselves as consultants, providing estimating services for a fee to government or to construction or manufacturing firms.

Many colleges and universities include cost estimating as part of bachelor's and associate degree curriculums in civil engineering, industrial engineering, and construction management or construction engineering technology. In addition, cost estimating is a significant part of many master's degree programs in construction science or construction management. Organizations representing cost estimators, such as the Association for the Advancement of Cost Engineering (AACE International) and the Society of Cost Estimating and Analysis (SCEA), also sponsor educational and professional development programs. These programs help students, estimators-in-training, and experienced estimators stay abreast of changes affecting the profession. Specialized courses and programs in cost estimating techniques and procedures also are offered by many technical schools, community colleges, and universities.

Voluntary certification can be valuable to cost estimators because it provides professional recognition of the estimator's competence and experience. In some instances, individual employers may even require professional certification for employment. Both AACE International and SCEA administer certification programs. To become certified, estimators usually must have between 2 and 8 years of estimating experience and must pass an examination. In addition, certification requirements may include publication of at least one article or paper in the field.

Job Outlook

Overall employment of cost estimators is expected to grow about as fast as the average for all occupations through the year 2012. In addition to openings created by growth, some job openings will arise from the need to replace workers who transfer to other occupations or leave the labor force. In construction and manufacturing—the primary employers of cost estimators—job prospects should be best for those with industry work experience and a bachelor's degree in a related field.

Growth of the construction industry, in which 53 percent of all cost estimators are employed, will be the driving force behind the demand for these workers. Construction and repair of highways, streets, and bridges, as well as construction of more subway systems, airports, water and sewage systems, and electric power plants and transmission lines, will stimulate demand for many more cost estimators. The increasing population and its changing demographics that will boost the demand for residential construction and remodeling also will spur demand for cost estimators. As the population ages, the demand for nursing and extended care facilities will increase. School construction and repair also will add to the demand for cost estimators. Job prospects in construction should be best for cost estimators with a degree in construction management or construction science, engineering, or architecture, and who have practical experience in various phases of construction or in a specialty craft area.

Employment of cost estimators in manufacturing will also grow, but not as fast as in construction as firms continue to use their services to identify and control operating costs. Experienced estimators with degrees in engineering, science, mathematics, business administration, or economics should have the best job prospects in manufacturing.

Earnings

Salaries of cost estimators vary widely by experience, education, size of firm, and industry. Median annual earnings of cost estimators in 2002 were $47,550. The middle 50 percent earned between $36,440 and $62,040. The lowest 10 percent earned less than $28,670, and the highest 10 percent earned more than $79,240. Median annual earnings in the industries employing the largest numbers of cost estimators in 2002 were:

Nonresidential building construction	$53,820
Building equipment contractors	50,240
Foundation, structure, and building exterior contractors	47,630
Residential building construction	47,180
Building finishing contractors	45,630

College graduates with degrees in fields that provide a strong background in cost estimating, such as engineering or construction management, could start at a higher level. According to a 2003 salary survey by the National Association of

Colleges and Employers, bachelor's degree candidates with degrees in construction science/management received job offers averaging $42,229 a year.

Related Occupations

Other workers who quantitatively analyze information include accountants and auditors; budget analysts; claims adjusters, appraisers, examiners, and investigators; economists; financial analysts and personal financial advisors; insurance underwriters; loan counselors and officers; market and survey researchers; and operations research analysts. In addition, the duties of industrial production managers and construction managers also may involve analyzing costs.

Sources of Additional Information

Information about career opportunities, certification, educational programs, and cost estimating techniques may be obtained from:

- Association for the Advancement of Cost Engineering (AACE International), 209 Prairie Ave., Suite 100, Morgantown, WV 26501. Internet: http://www.aacei.org

- Society of Cost Estimating and Analysis, 101 S. Whiting St., Suite 201, Alexandria, VA 22304. Internet: http://www.sceaonline.net

Counselors

(O*NET 21-1011.00, 21-1012.00, 21-1013.00, 21-1014.00, and 21-1015.00)

Significant Points

- A master's degree is often required to be licensed or certified as a counselor.

- All but three states require some form of licensure or certification for practice outside of schools; all states require school counselors to hold a state school counseling certification.

Nature of the Work

Counselors assist people with personal, family, educational, mental health, and career decisions and problems. Their duties depend on the individuals they serve and on the settings in which they work.

Educational, vocational, and school counselors provide individuals and groups with career and educational counseling. In school settings—elementary through postsecondary—they are usually called school counselors and they work with students, including those considered to be at risk and those with special needs. They advocate for students and work with other individuals and organizations to promote the academic, career, and personal and social development of children and youths. School counselors help students evaluate their abilities, interests, talents, and personality characteristics in order to develop realistic academic and career goals. Counselors use interviews, counseling sessions, tests, or other methods in evaluating and advising students. They also operate career information centers and career education programs. High school counselors advise students regarding college majors, admission requirements, entrance exams, financial aid, trade or technical schools, and apprenticeship programs. They help students develop job search skills such as resume writing and interviewing techniques. College career planning and placement counselors assist alumni or students with career development and job-hunting techniques.

Elementary school counselors observe younger children during classroom and play activities and confer with their teachers and parents to evaluate the children's strengths, problems, or special needs. They also help students develop good study habits. Elementary school counselors do less vocational and academic counseling than do secondary school counselors.

School counselors at all levels help students understand and deal with social, behavioral, and personal problems. These counselors emphasize preventive and developmental counseling to provide students with the life skills needed to deal with problems before they occur and to enhance the student's personal, social, and academic growth. Counselors provide special services, including alcohol and drug prevention programs and conflict resolution classes. Counselors also try to identify cases of domestic abuse and other family problems that can affect a student's development. Counselors work with students individually, with small groups, or with entire classes. They consult and collaborate with parents, teachers, school administrators, school psychologists, medical professionals, and social workers in order to develop and implement strategies to help students be successful in the education system.

Vocational counselors who provide mainly career counseling outside the school setting are also referred to as *employment counselors* or *career counselors*. Their chief focus is helping individuals with their career decisions. Vocational counselors explore and evaluate the client's education, training, work history, interests, skills, and personality traits, and arrange for aptitude and achievement tests to assist in making career decisions. They also work with individuals to develop their job search skills, and they assist clients in locating and applying for jobs. In addition, career counselors provide support to persons experiencing job loss, job stress, or other career transition issues.

Rehabilitation counselors help people deal with the personal, social, and vocational effects of disabilities. They counsel people with disabilities resulting from birth defects, illness or disease, accidents, or the stress of daily life. They evaluate the strengths and limitations of individuals, provide personal and vocational counseling, and arrange for medical care, vocational training, and job placement. Rehabilitation counselors interview both individuals with disabilities and their families, evaluate school and medical reports, and confer and plan with physicians, psychologists, occupational therapists, and employers to determine the capabilities and skills of the individual. Conferring with the client, they develop a rehabilitation program that often includes training to help the person develop job skills. Rehabilitation counselors also work toward increasing the client's capacity to live independently.

Mental health counselors work with individuals, families, and groups to address and treat mental and emotional disorders and to promote optimum mental health. They are trained in a variety of therapeutic techniques used to address a wide range of issues, including depression, addiction and substance abuse, suicidal impulses, stress management, problems with self-esteem, issues associated with aging, job and career concerns, educational decisions, issues related to mental and emotional health, and family, parenting, and marital or other relationship problems. Mental health counselors often work closely with other mental health specialists, such as psychiatrists, psychologists, clinical social workers, psychiatric nurses, and school counselors.

Substance abuse and behavioral disorder counselors help people who have problems with alcohol, drugs, gambling, and eating disorders. They counsel individuals who are addicted to drugs, helping them identify behaviors and problems related to their addiction. These counselors hold sessions for one person, for families, or for groups of people.

Marriage and family therapists apply principles, methods, and therapeutic techniques to individuals, family groups, couples, or organizations for the purpose of resolving emotional conflicts. In doing so, they modify people's perceptions and behaviors, enhance communication and understanding among all family members, and help to prevent family and individual crises. Marriage and family therapists also may engage in psychotherapy of a nonmedical nature, with appropriate referrals to psychiatric resources, and in research and teaching in the overall field of human development and interpersonal relationships.

Other counseling specialties include gerontological, multicultural, and genetic counseling. A gerontological counselor provides services to elderly persons who face changing lifestyles because of health problems; the counselor helps families cope with the changes. A multicultural counselor helps employers adjust to an increasingly diverse workforce. Genetic counselors provide information and support to families who have members with birth defects or genetic disorders and to families who may be at risk for a variety of inherited conditions. These counselors identify families at risk, investigate the problem that is present in the family, interpret information about the disorder, analyze inheritance patterns and risks of recurrence, and review available options with the family.

Working Conditions

Most school counselors work the traditional 9- to 10-month school year with a 2- to 3-month vacation, although increasing numbers are employed on 10½- or 11-month contracts.

They usually work the same hours that teachers do. College career planning and placement counselors work long and irregular hours during student recruiting periods.

Rehabilitation counselors usually work a standard 40-hour week. Self-employed counselors and those working in mental health and community agencies, such as substance abuse and behavioral disorder counselors, frequently work evenings to counsel clients who work during the day. Both mental health counselors and marriage and family therapists also often work flexible hours, to accommodate families in crisis or working couples who must have evening or weekend appointments.

Counselors must possess high physical and emotional energy to handle the array of problems they address. Dealing daily with these problems can cause stress. Because privacy is essential for confidential and frank discussions with clients, counselors usually have private offices.

Employment

Counselors held about 526,000 jobs in 2002. Employment was distributed among the counseling specialties as follows:

Educational, vocational, and school counselors	228,000
Rehabilitation counselors	122,000
Mental health counselors	85,000
Substance abuse and behavioral disorder counselors	67,000
Marriage and family therapists	23,000

Educational, vocational, and school counselors work primarily in elementary and secondary schools and colleges and universities. Other types of counselors work in a wide variety of public and private establishments, including health care facilities; job training, career development, and vocational rehabilitation centers; social agencies; correctional institutions; and residential care facilities, such as halfway houses for criminal offenders and group homes for children, the elderly, and the disabled. Some substance abuse and behavioral disorder counselors work in therapeutic communities where addicts live while undergoing treatment. Counselors also work in organizations engaged in community improvement and social change and work as well in drug and alcohol rehabilitation programs and state and local government agencies. A growing number of counselors are self-employed and working in group practices or private practice. This growth has been helped by laws allowing counselors to receive payments from insurance companies and the growing recognition that counselors are well-trained professionals.

Training, Other Qualifications, and Advancement

All states require school counselors to hold state school counseling certification and to have completed at least some graduate course work; most require the completion of a master's degree. Some states require public school counselors to have both counseling and teaching certificates and to have had some teaching experience before receiving certification. For counselors based outside of schools, 47 states and the District of Columbia had some form of counselor credentialing, licensure, certification, or registration that governed their practice of counseling. Requirements typically include the completion of a master's degree in counseling, the accumulation of 2 years or 3,000 hours of supervised clinical experience beyond the master's degree level, the passage of a state-recognized exam, adherence to ethical codes and standards, and the satisfaction of annual continuing education requirements.

Counselors must be aware of educational and training requirements that are often very detailed and that vary by area and by counseling specialty. Prospective counselors should check with state and local governments, employers, and national voluntary certification organizations in order to determine which requirements apply.

As mentioned, a master's degree is typically required to be licensed or certified as a counselor. A bachelor's degree often qualifies a person to work as a counseling aide, rehabilitation aide, or social service worker. Some states require counselors in public employment to have a master's degree; others accept a bachelor's degree with appropriate counseling courses. Counselor education programs in colleges and universities usually are in departments of education or psychology. Fields of study include college student affairs, elementary or secondary school counseling, education, gerontological counseling, marriage and family counseling, substance abuse counseling, rehabilitation counseling, agency or community counseling, clinical mental health counseling, counseling psychology, career counseling, and related fields. Courses are grouped into eight core areas: Human growth and development, social and cultural diversity, relationships, group work, career development, assessment, research and program evaluation, and professional identity. In an accredited master's degree program, 48 to 60 semester hours of graduate study, including a period of supervised clinical experience in counseling, are required for a master's degree.

In 2003, 176 institutions offered programs in counselor education—including career, community, gerontological, mental health, school, student affairs, and marriage and family counseling—that were accredited by the Council for Accreditation of Counseling and Related Educational Programs (CACREP). CACREP also recognizes many counselor education programs, apart from those in the 176 accredited institutions, that use alternative instruction methods, such as distance learning. Programs that use such alternative instruction methods are evaluated on the basis of the same standards for accreditation that CACREP applies to programs that employ the more traditional methods. Another organization, the Council on Rehabilitation Education (CORE), accredits graduate programs in rehabilitation counseling. Accredited master's degree programs include a minimum of 2 years of full-time study, including 600 hours of supervised clinical internship experience.

Many counselors elect to be nationally certified by the National Board for Certified Counselors, Inc. (NBCC), which grants the general practice credential "National Certified Counselor." To be certified, a counselor must hold a master's or higher degree, with a concentration in counseling, from a regionally accredited college or university; must have at least 2 years of supervised field experience in a counseling setting (graduates from counselor education programs accredited by CACREP are exempted); must provide two professional endorsements, one of which must be from a recent supervisor; and must have a passing score on the NBCC's National Counselor Examination for Licensure and Certification (NCE). This national certification is voluntary and is distinct from state certification. However, in some states, those who pass the national exam are exempted from taking a state certification exam. NBCC also offers specialty certification in school, clinical mental health, and addiction counseling. Beginning January 1, 2004, new candidates for NBCC's National Certified School counselor (NCSC) credential must pass a practical simulation examination in addition to fulfilling the current requirements. To maintain their certification, counselors retake and pass the NCE or complete 100 hours of acceptable continuing education credit every 5 years.

Another organization, the Commission on Rehabilitation Counselor Certification, offers voluntary national certification for rehabilitation counselors. Many employers require rehabilitation counselors to be nationally certified. To become certified, rehabilitation counselors usually must graduate from an accredited educational program, complete an internship, and pass a written examination. (Certification requirements vary according to an applicant's educational history. Employment experience, for example, is required for those with a counseling degree in a specialty other than rehabilitation.) After meeting these requirements, candidates are designated "Certified Rehabilitation Counselors." To maintain their certification, counselors must successfully retake the certification exam or complete 100 hours of acceptable continuing education credit every 5 years.

Other counseling organizations also offer certification in particular counseling specialties. Usually these are voluntary, but having one may enhance one's job prospects.

Some employers provide training for newly hired counselors. Others may offer time off or provide help with tuition if it is needed to complete a graduate degree. Counselors must participate in graduate studies, workshops, and personal studies to maintain their certificates and licenses.

Persons interested in counseling should have a strong interest in helping others and should possess the ability to inspire respect, trust, and confidence. They should be able to work independently or as part of a team. Counselors must follow the code of ethics associated with their respective certifications and licenses.

Prospects for advancement vary by counseling field. School counselors can move to a larger school; become directors or supervisors of counseling, guidance, or pupil personnel services; or, usually with further graduate education, become counselor educators, counseling psychologists, or school administrators. Some counselors choose to work for a state's department of education. For marriage and family therapists, doctoral education in family therapy emphasizes the training of supervisors, teachers, researchers, and clinicians in the discipline.

Counselors can become supervisors or administrators in their agencies. Some counselors move into research, consulting, or college teaching or go into private or group practice.

Job Outlook

Overall employment of counselors is expected to grow faster than the average for all occupations through 2012, and job opportunities should be very good because there are usually more job openings than graduates of counseling programs. In addition, numerous job openings will occur as many counselors retire or leave the profession.

Employment of educational, vocational, and school counselors is expected to grow as fast as the average for all occupations as a result of: increasing student enrollments, particularly in secondary and postsecondary schools; state legislation requiring counselors in elementary schools; and an expansion in the responsibilities of counselors. For example, counselors are becoming more involved in crisis and preventive counseling, helping students deal with issues ranging from drug and alcohol abuse to death and suicide. Although schools and governments realize the value of counselors in achieving academic success in their students, budget constraints at every school level will dampen job growth of school counselors. However, federal grants and subsidies may fill in the gaps and allow the current ongoing reduction in student-to-counselor ratios to continue.

Demand for vocational or career counselors should grow as the notion of staying in one job over a lifetime continues to be rejected and replaced by the concept of managing one's own career and taking responsibility for it. In addition, changes in welfare laws that require beneficiaries to work will continue to create demand for counselors by state and local governments. Other opportunities for employment counselors will arise in private job-training centers that provide training and other services to laid-off workers, as well as to those seeking a new or second career or wanting to upgrade their skills.

Demand is expected to be strong for substance abuse and behavioral, mental health, and marriage and family therapists and for rehabilitation counselors, for a variety of reasons. For one, California and a few other states have recently passed laws requiring substance abuse treatment instead of jail for people caught possessing a drug. This shift will require more substance abuse counselors in those states. Second, the increasing availability of funds to build statewide networks to improve services for children and adolescents with serious emotional disturbances and for their family members should increase employment opportunities for counselors. Under managed care systems, insurance companies are increasingly providing for reimbursement of counselors as a less costly alternative to psychiatrists and psychologists. Also, legislation is pending that may provide counseling services to Medicare recipients.

The number of people who will need rehabilitation counseling is expected to grow as the population continues to age and as advances in medical technology continue to save lives that only a few years ago would have been lost. In addition, legislation requiring equal employment rights for people with disabilities will spur demand for counselors, who not only will help these people make a transition into the workforce, but also will help companies comply with the law.

Employment of mental health counselors and marriage and family therapists will grow as the nation becomes more comfortable seeking professional help for a variety of health and personal and family problems. Employers also are increasingly offering employee assistance programs that provide mental health and alcohol and drug abuse services. More people are expected to use these services as society focuses on ways of developing mental well-being, such as controlling stress associated with job and family responsibilities.

Earnings

Median annual earnings of educational, vocational, and school counselors in 2002 were $44,100. The middle 50 percent earned between $33,160 and $56,770. The lowest 10 percent earned less than $24,930, and the highest 10 percent earned more than $70,320. School counselors can earn additional income working summers in the school system or in other jobs. Median annual earnings in the industries employing the largest numbers of educational, vocational, and school counselors in 2002 were as follows:

Elementary and secondary schools $49,530

State government...45,480

Junior colleges 43,250

Colleges, universities, and professional schools 36,990

Individual and family services...............................26,910

Median annual earnings of substance abuse and behavioral disorder counselors in 2002 were $30,180. The middle 50 percent earned between $24,350 and $37,520. The lowest 10 percent earned less than $19,540, and the highest 10 percent earned more than $45,570.

Median annual earnings of mental health counselors in 2002 were $29,940. The middle 50 percent earned between $23,950 and $39,160. The lowest 10 percent earned less than $19,760, and the highest 10 percent earned more than 50,170.

Median annual earnings of rehabilitation counselors in 2002 were $25,840. The middle 50 percent earned between $20,350 and $34,000. The lowest 10 percent earned less than

$16,840, and the highest 10 percent earned more than $44,940.

For substance abuse, mental health, and rehabilitation counselors, government employers generally pay the highest wages, followed by hospitals and social service agencies. Residential care facilities often pay the lowest wages.

Median annual earnings of marriage and family therapists in 2002 were $35,580. The middle 50 percent earned between $26,790 and $44,620. The lowest 10 percent earned less than 20,960, and the highest 10 percent earned more than $59,030. Median annual earnings in 2002 were $29,160 in individual and family social services, the industry employing the largest numbers of marriage and family therapists.

Self-employed counselors who have well-established practices, as well as counselors employed in group practices, usually have the highest earnings.

Related Occupations

Counselors help people evaluate their interests, abilities, and disabilities and deal with personal, social, academic, and career problems. Others who help people in similar ways include teachers, social and human service assistants, social workers, psychologists, physicians and surgeons, registered nurses, members of the clergy, occupational therapists, and human resources, training, and labor relations managers and specialists.

Sources of Additional Information

For general information about counseling, as well as information on specialties such as school, college, mental health, rehabilitation, multicultural, career, marriage and family, and gerontological counseling, contact:

- American Counseling Association, 5999 Stevenson Ave., Alexandria, VA 22304-3300. Internet: http://www.counseling.org

For information on accredited counseling and related training programs, contact:

- Council for Accreditation of Counseling and Related Educational Programs, American Counseling Association, 5999 Stevenson Ave., 4th floor, Alexandria, VA 22304. Internet: http://www.counseling.org/cacrep

For information on national certification requirements for counselors, contact:

- National Board for Certified Counselors, Inc., 3 Terrace Way, Suite D, Greensboro, NC 27403-3660. Internet: http://www.nbcc.org

State departments of education can supply information on those colleges and universities which offer guidance and counseling training that meets state certification and licensure requirements.

State employment service offices have information about job opportunities and about entrance requirements for counselors.

Counter and Rental Clerks

(O*NET 41-2021.00)

Significant Points

- Jobs are primarily entry-level and require little or no experience and minimal formal education.

- Faster-than-average employment growth is expected as businesses strive to improve customer service.

- Part-time employment opportunities should be plentiful.

Nature of the Work

Whether renting videotapes, air compressors, or moving vans or dropping off clothes to be drycleaned or appliances to be serviced, we rely on counter and rental clerks to handle these transactions efficiently. Although the specific duties of these workers vary by establishment, counter and rental clerks answer questions involving product availability, cost, and rental provisions. Counter and rental clerks also take orders, calculate fees, receive payments, and accept returned merchandise.

Regardless of where they work, counter and rental clerks must be knowledgeable about the company's services, policies, and procedures. Depending on the type of establishment, counter and rental clerks use their special knowledge to give advice on a wide variety of products and services, ranging from hydraulic tools to shoe repair. For example, in the car rental industry, these workers inform customers about the features of different types of automobiles, as well as daily and weekly rental costs. They also ensure that customers meet age and other requirements for renting cars, and they indicate when and in what condition the cars must be returned. Those in the equipment rental industry have similar duties, but must also know how to operate and care for the machinery rented. In drycleaning establishments, counter clerks inform customers when items will be ready and what the effects, if any, of the chemicals used on garments are. In video rental stores, counter clerks advise customers about the use of video and game players and the length of a rental, scan returned movies and games, restock shelves, handle money, and log daily reports.

When taking orders, counter and rental clerks use various types of equipment. In some establishments, they write out tickets and order forms, although most use computers or bar-code scanners. Most of these computer systems are user friendly, require very little data entry, and are customized for the firm. Scanners read the product code and display a description of the item on a computer screen. However, clerks must ensure that the data on the screen pertain to the product.

Working Conditions

Firms employing counter and rental clerks usually operate nights and weekends for the convenience of their customers. However, many employers offer flexible schedules. Some counter and rental clerks work 40-hour weeks, but about half are on part-time schedules—usually during rush periods, such as weekends, evenings, and holidays.

Working conditions usually are pleasant; most stores and service establishments are clean, well lighted, and temperature controlled. However, clerks are on their feet much of the time and may be confined behind a small counter area or be exposed to harmful chemicals. The job requires constant interaction with the public and can be stressful, especially during busy periods.

Employment

Counter and rental clerks held 436,000 jobs in 2002. About 21 percent of clerks worked in consumer goods rental, which includes video rental stores. Other large employers included drycleaning and laundry services; automotive equipment rental and leasing services; automobile dealers; amusement, gambling, and recreation industries; and grocery stores.

Counter and rental clerks are employed throughout the country, but are concentrated in metropolitan areas, where personal services and renting and leasing services are in greater demand.

Training, Other Qualifications, and Advancement

Counter and rental clerk jobs are primarily at the entry level and require little or no experience and minimal formal education. However, many employers prefer workers with at least a high school diploma.

In most companies, counter and rental clerks are trained on the job, sometimes through the use of videotapes, brochures, and pamphlets. Clerks usually learn how to operate a firm's equipment and become familiar with the firm's policies and procedures under the observation of a more experienced worker. However, some employers have formal classroom training programs lasting from a few hours to a few weeks. Topics covered in this training include the nature of the industry, the company and its policies and procedures, operation of equipment, sales techniques, and customer service. Counter and rental clerks also must become familiar with the different products and services rented or provided by their company in order to give customers the best possible service.

Counter and rental clerks should enjoy working with people and should have the ability to deal tactfully with difficult customers. They also should be able to handle several tasks at once, while continuing to provide friendly service. In addition, good oral and written communication skills are essential.

Advancement opportunities depend on the size and type of company. Many establishments that employ counter or rental clerks tend to be small businesses, making advancement difficult. But in larger establishments with a corporate structure, jobs such as counter and rental clerks offer good opportunities for workers to learn about their company's products and business practices. These jobs can lead to more responsible positions. It is common in many establishments to promote counter and rental clerks to event planner, assistant manager, or salesperson. Workers may choose to pursue related positions, such as mechanic, or even establish their own business.

In certain industries, such as equipment repair, counter and rental jobs may be an additional or alternative source of income for workers who are unemployed or semiretired. For example, retired mechanics could prove invaluable at tool rental centers because of their knowledge of, and familiarity with, tools.

Job Outlook

Employment of counter and rental clerks is expected to grow faster than the average for all occupations through the year 2012, as all types of businesses strive to improve customer service by hiring more clerks. In addition, some industries employing counter and rental clerks—for example, rental and leasing services and amusement and recreation industries—are expected to grow rapidly. Nevertheless, most job openings will arise from the need to replace experienced workers who transfer to other occupations or leave the labor force. Part-time employment opportunities are expected to be plentiful.

Earnings

Counter and rental clerks typically start at the minimum wage, which, in establishments covered by federal law, was $5.15 an hour in 2003. In some states, the law sets the minimum wage higher, and establishments must pay at least that amount. Wages also tend to be higher in areas where there is intense competition for workers. In addition to wages, some counter and rental clerks receive commissions, based on the number of contracts they complete or services they sell.

Median hourly earnings of counter and rental clerks in 2002 were $8.31. The middle 50 percent earned between $6.89 and $10.91 an hour. The lowest 10 percent earned less than $6.03 an hour, and the highest 10 percent earned more than $15.10 an hour. Median hourly earnings in the industries employing the largest number of counter and rental clerks in 2002 were as follows:

Automobile dealers	$16.09
Automotive equipment rental and leasing	9.69
Lessors of real estate	9.19
Drycleaning and laundry services	7.34
Amusement and recreation services	7.30

Full-time workers typically receive health and life insurance, paid vacation, and sick leave. Benefits for counter and rental clerks who work part time or for independent stores tend to be significantly less than for those who work full time. Many companies offer discounts to both full-time and part-time employees on the services they provide.

Related Occupations

Counter and rental clerks take orders and receive payment for services rendered. Other workers with similar duties include tellers, cashiers, food and beverage serving and related workers, gaming cage workers, Postal Service workers, and retail salespersons.

Sources of Additional Information

For general information on employment in the equipment rental industry, contact:

- American Rental Association, 1900 19th St., Moline, IL 61265. Internet: http://www.ararental.org

For more information about the work of counter clerks in drycleaning and laundry establishments, contact:

- International Fabricare Institute, 12251 Tech Rd., Silver Spring, MD 20904. Internet: http://www.ifi.org

Customer Service Representatives

(O*NET 43-4051.01 and 43-4051.02)

Significant Points

- Job prospects are expected to be excellent.

- Most jobs require only a high school diploma.

- Strong verbal communication and listening skills are important.

Nature of the Work

Customer service representatives are employed by many different types of companies throughout the country to serve as a direct point of contact for customers. They are responsible for ensuring that their company's customers receive an adequate level of service or help with their questions and concerns. These customers may be individual consumers or other companies, and the nature of their service needs can vary considerably.

All customer service representatives interact with customers to provide information in response to inquiries about products or services and to handle and resolve complaints. They communicate with customers through a variety of means— either in person; by telephone, e-mail or regular mail correspondence, or fax; or even over the Internet. Some customer service representatives handle general questions and complaints, whereas others specialize in a particular area.

Many customer inquiries involve routine questions and requests. For example, customer service representatives may be asked to provide a customer with a bank account balance, or to check on the status of an order that has been placed. Obtaining the answers to such questions usually requires simply looking up information on their computer. Other questions are more involved, and may call for additional research or further explanation on the part of the customer service representative. In handling customers' complaints, customer service representatives must attempt to resolve the problem according to guidelines established by the company. These procedures may involve asking questions to determine the validity of a complaint, offering possible solutions, or providing customers with refunds, exchanges, or other offers such as discounts or coupons. In some cases, customer service representatives are required to follow up with an individual customer until a question is answered or an issue is resolved.

Some customer service representatives help people decide what types of products or services would best suit their needs. They may even aid customers in completing purchases or transactions. Although the primary function of customer service representatives is not sales, some may spend a part of their time with customers attempting to convince them to purchase additional products or services. Customer service representatives may also make changes or updates to a customer's profile or account information. They may keep records of transactions and update and maintain databases of information.

Most customer service representatives use computers and telephones extensively in their work. Customer service representatives frequently enter information into a computer as they are speaking to customers. Often, companies have large amounts of data, such as account information, that can be pulled up on a computer screen while the representative is talking to a customer so that he or she can answer specific questions relating to the account. Customer service representatives also may have access to information such as answers to the most common customer questions, or guidelines for dealing with complaints. In the event that they encounter a question or situation to which they do not know how to respond, workers consult with a supervisor to determine the best course of action. Customer service representatives use multiline telephones systems, which often route calls directly to the most appropriate representative. However, at times, a customer service representative will need to transfer a call to someone who may be better able to respond to the customer's needs.

In some organizations, customer service representatives spend their entire day on the telephone. In others, they may spend part of their day answering e-mails and the remainder of the day taking calls. For some, most of their contact with the customer is face to face. Customer service representatives need to remain aware of the amount of time spent with each customer in order to fairly distribute their time among the people who require their assistance. This is particularly important for customer service representatives whose primary activities are answering telephone calls, and conversations often are required to be kept within set time limits. For customer service representatives working in call centers, there is usually very little time between telephone calls; as soon as they have finished with one call they must immediately move on to another. When working in call centers, customer service representatives are likely to be under close supervision. Telephone calls may be taped and reviewed by supervisors to ensure that company policies and procedures are being followed, or a supervisor may listen in on conversations.

Job responsibilities can differ, depending on the industry in which a customer service representative is employed. For example, a customer service representative working in the branch office of a bank may assume the responsibilities of other workers, such as teller or new account clerk, as needed. In insurance agencies, a customer service representative interacts with agents, insurance companies, and policyholders. These workers handle much of the paperwork related to insurance policies, such as policy applications and changes and renewals to existing policies. They answer questions regarding issues such as policy coverage, help with reporting claims, and do anything else that may need to be done. Although they must know as much as insurance agents about insurance products, and usually must have credentials equal to those of an agent in order to sell products and make changes to policies, the duties of a customer service representative differ from those of an agent in that customer service representatives are not responsible for actively seeking potential customers. Customer service representatives employed by communications and utilities companies assist individuals interested in opening accounts for various utilities such as electricity and gas, or for communication services such as cable television and telephone. They explain various options and receive orders for services to be installed, turned on, turned off, or changed. They may also look into and resolve complaints about billing and service provided by telephone, cable television, and utility companies.

Working Conditions

Although customer service representatives can work in a variety of settings, most work in areas that are clean and well lit. Many work in call or customer contact centers. In this type of environment, workers generally have their own workstation or cubicle space and are equipped with a telephone, headset, and computer. Because many call centers are open extended hours, beyond the traditional 9-to-5 business day, or are staffed around the clock, these positions may require workers to take on early morning, evening, or late night shifts. Weekend or holiday work also may be necessary. As a result, the occupation is well-suited to flexible work schedules. About 1 out of 7 customer service representatives work part time. The occupation also offers the oppor-

tunity for seasonal work in certain industries, often through temporary help agencies.

Call centers may be crowded and noisy, and work may be repetitive and stressful, with little time in between calls. Workers usually must attempt to minimize the length of each call, while still providing excellent service. To ensure that these procedures are followed, conversations may be monitored by supervisors, which can be stressful. Also, long periods spent sitting, typing, or looking at a computer screen may cause eye and muscle strain, backaches, headaches, and repetitive motion injuries.

Customer service representatives working outside of a call center environment may interact with customers through several different means. For example, workers employed by an insurance agency or in a grocery store may have customers approach them in person or contact them by telephone, computer, mail, or fax. Many of these customer service representatives will work a standard 40-hour week; however, their hours generally will depend on the hours of operation of the establishment in which they are employed. Work environments outside of a call center also will vary accordingly. Most customer service representatives will work either in an office or at a service or help desk.

For virtually all types of customer service representatives, dealing with difficult or irate customers can be a trying task; however, the ability to directly help and resolve customers' problems has the potential to be very rewarding.

Employment

Customer service representatives held about 1.9 million jobs in 2002. Although they were found in a variety of industries, more than 1 in 4 customer service representatives worked in finance and insurance. The largest numbers were employed by insurance carriers, insurance agencies and brokerages, and banks and credit unions.

Nearly 1 in 8 customer service representatives were employed in administrative and support services. These workers were concentrated in the industries business support services—which includes telephone call centers—and employment services—which includes temporary help services and employment placement agencies. Another 1 in 8 customer service representatives were employed in retail trade establishments such as general merchandise stores, food and beverage stores, or nonstore retailers. Other industries that employ significant numbers of customer service representatives include information, particularly the telecommunications industry; manufacturing, such as printing and related support activities; and wholesale trade.

Although they are found in all states, customer service representatives who work in call centers tend to be concentrated geographically. Four states make up over 30 percent of total employment—California, Texas, Florida, and New York. Delaware, South Dakota, Utah, and Arizona have the highest concentration of workers in this occupation, with customer service representatives comprising over 2 percent of total employment in these states.

Training, Other Qualifications, and Advancement

A high school diploma or the equivalent is the most common educational requirement for customer service representatives. Basic computer knowledge and good interpersonal skills also are important qualities for people who wish to be successful in the field. Because customer service representatives constantly interact with the public, strong communication and problem-solving skills are a must, particularly strong verbal communication and listening skills. Additionally, for those workers who communicate through e-mail, good typing, spelling, and written communication skills are necessary. High school courses in computers, English, or business are helpful in preparing for a job in customer service.

Customer service representatives play a critical role in providing an interface between the customer and the company that employs them, and for this reason employers seek out people who are able to come across in a friendly and professional manner. The ability to deal patiently with problems and complaints and to remain courteous when faced with difficult or angry people is very important. Also, a customer service representative needs to be able to work independently within specified time constraints. Workers should have a clear and pleasant speaking voice and be fluent in the English language. However, the ability to speak a foreign language is becoming increasingly necessary, and bilingual skills are considered a plus.

Training requirements vary by industry. Almost all customer service representatives are provided with some training prior to beginning work and training continues once on the job. This training generally will cover four primary components: Training on customer service and phone skills, training on products and services or common customer problems, training on the use or operation of the telephone and/or computer systems, and training on company policies and regulations. Length of training varies, but it usually lasts at least several weeks. Because of a constant need to update skills and knowledge, most customer service representatives continue to receive instruction and training throughout their career. This is particularly true of workers in industries such as banking, in which regulations and products are continually changing.

Although some positions may require previous industry, office, or customer service experience, many customer service jobs are entry level. Customer service jobs are often good introductory positions into a company or an industry. In some cases, experienced workers can move up within the company into supervisory or managerial positions or they may move into areas such as product development, in which they can use their knowledge to improve products and services.

Within insurance agencies and brokerages, however, a customer service representative job is usually not an entry-level position. Workers must have previous experience in insurance and are often required by state regulations to be licensed like insurance sales agents. A variety of designations are available to demonstrate that a candidate has sufficient knowledge and skill, and continuing education and training are often offered through the employer. As they gain more knowledge of industry products and services, customer service representatives in insurance may advance to other, higher level positions, such as insurance sales agent.

Job Outlook

Prospects for obtaining a job in this field are expected to be excellent, with more job openings than jobseekers. Bilingual jobseekers, in particular, may enjoy favorable job prospects. In addition to many new openings occurring as businesses and organizations expand, numerous job openings will result from the need to replace experienced customer service representatives who transfer to other occupations or leave the labor force. Replacement needs are expected to be significant in this large occupation because many young people work as customer service representatives before switching to other jobs. This occupation is well-suited to flexible work schedules, and many opportunities for part-time work will continue to be available, particularly as organizations attempt to cut labor costs by hiring more temporary workers.

Employment of customer service representatives is expected to grow faster than the average for all occupations through the year 2012. Beyond growth stemming from expansion of the industries in which customer service representatives are employed, a need for additional customer service representatives is likely to result from heightened reliance on these workers. Customer service is critical to the success of any organization that deals with customers, and strong customer service can build sales and visibility as companies try to distinguish themselves from competitors. In many industries, the need to gain a competitive edge and retain customers will become increasingly important over the next decade. This is particularly true in industries such as financial services, communications, and utilities that already employ numerous customer service representatives. As the trend towards consolidation within industries continues, centralized call centers will provide an effective method for delivering a high level of customer service. As a result, employment of customer service representatives may grow at a faster rate in call centers than in other areas; however, this growth may be tempered as a variety of factors, including technological improvements, make it increasingly feasible and cost-effective for call centers to be built or relocated outside of the United States. Technology is impacting the occupation in many ways. Advancements such as the Internet and automated teller machines have provided customers with means of obtaining information and conducting transactions that do not entail interacting with another person. Technology also allows for a greater streamlining of processes, while at the same time increasing the productivity of workers. Use of computer software to filter e-mails, generating automatic responses or directing messages to the appropriate representative, and use of similar systems to answer or route telephone inquiries are likely to become more prevalent in the future.

Despite such developments, the need for customer service representatives is expected to remain strong. In many ways, technology has heightened consumers' expectations for information and services, and availability of information online seems to have generated more need for customer service representatives, particularly to respond to e-mail. Also, technology cannot replace the need for human skills. As more sophisticated technologies are able to resolve many customers' questions and concerns, the nature of the inquiries to be handled by customer service representatives is likely to become increasingly complex.

Furthermore, the job responsibilities of customer service representatives are expanding. As companies downsize or look to increase profitability, workers are being trained to perform additional duties such as opening bank accounts or cross-selling products. As a result, employers may increasingly prefer customer service representatives who have education beyond high school, such as some college or even a college degree.

While jobs in some industries, such as retail trade, may be impacted by economic downturns, the occupation is generally resistant to major fluctuations in employment.

Earnings

In 2002, median annual earnings for wage and salary customer service representatives were $26,240. The middle 50 percent earned between $20,960 and $33,540. The lowest 10 percent earned less than $17,230, and the highest 10 percent earned more than $42,990.

Earnings for customer service representatives vary according to level of skill required, experience, training, location, and size of firm. Median annual earnings in the industries employing the largest numbers of these workers in 2002 are shown below:

Wired telecommunications carriers	$38,980
Insurance carriers	28,560
Agencies, brokerages, and other insurance related activities	28,270
Management of companies and enterprises	27,990
Nondepository credit intermediation	25,600
Depository credit intermediation	24,850
Employment services	22,510
Electronic shopping and mail-order houses	21,530
Business support services	21,130
Grocery stores	17,230

In addition to receiving an hourly wage, full-time customer service representatives who work evenings, nights, weekends, or holidays may receive shift differential pay. Also, because call centers are often open during extended hours, or even 24 hours a day, some customer service representatives have the benefit of being able to work a schedule that does not conform to the traditional workweek. Other bene-

fits can include life and health insurance, pensions, bonuses, employer-provided training, or discounts on the products and services the company offers.

Related Occupations

Customer service representatives interact with customers to provide information in response to inquiries about products and services and to handle and resolve complaints. Other occupations in which workers have similar dealings with customers and the public are information and record clerks; financial clerks, such as tellers and new-account clerks; insurance sales agents; securities, commodities, and financial services sales agents; retail salespersons; computer support specialists; and gaming services workers.

Sources of Additional Information

State employment service offices can provide information about employment opportunities for customer service representatives.

Dental Assistants

(O*NET 31-9091.00)

Significant Points

- Job prospects should be excellent.

- Dentists are expected to hire more assistants to perform routine tasks so that they may devote their own time to more profitable procedures.

- Most assistants learn their skills on the job, although an increasing number are trained in dental-assisting programs; most programs take 1 year or less to complete.

Nature of the Work

Dental assistants perform a variety of patient care, office, and laboratory duties. They work chairside as dentists examine and treat patients. They make patients as comfortable as possible in the dental chair, prepare them for treatment, and obtain their dental records. Assistants hand instruments and materials to dentists and keep patients' mouths dry and clear by using suction or other devices. Assistants also sterilize and disinfect instruments and equipment, prepare trays of instruments for dental procedures, and instruct patients on postoperative and general oral health care.

Some dental assistants prepare materials for impressions and restorations, take dental x rays, and process x-ray film as directed by a dentist. They also may remove sutures, apply topical anesthetics to gums or cavity-preventive agents to teeth, remove excess cement used in the filling process, and place rubber dams on the teeth to isolate them for individual treatment.

Those with laboratory duties make casts of the teeth and mouth from impressions, clean and polish removable appliances, and make temporary crowns. Dental assistants with office duties schedule and confirm appointments, receive patients, keep treatment records, send bills, receive payments, and order dental supplies and materials.

Dental assistants should not be confused with dental hygienists, who are licensed to perform different clinical tasks.

Working Conditions

Dental assistants work in a well-lighted, clean environment. Their work area usually is near the dental chair so that they can arrange instruments, materials, and medication and hand them to the dentist when needed. Dental assistants must wear gloves, masks, eyewear, and protective clothing to protect themselves and their patients from infectious diseases. Following safety procedures also minimizes the risks associated with the use of x-ray machines.

About half of dental assistants have a 35- to 40-hour workweek, which may include work on Saturdays or evenings.

Employment

Dental assistants held about 266,000 jobs in 2002. Almost all jobs for dental assistants were in offices of dentists. A small number of jobs were in offices of physicians, educational services, and hospitals. About a third of dental assistants worked part time, sometimes in more than one dental office.

Training, Other Qualifications, and Advancement

Most assistants learn their skills on the job, although an increasing number are trained in dental-assisting programs offered by community and junior colleges, trade schools, technical institutes, or the Armed Forces. Assistants must be a second pair of hands for a dentist; therefore, dentists look for people who are reliable, can work well with others, and have good manual dexterity. High school students interested in a career as a dental assistant should take courses in biology, chemistry, health, and office practices.

The American Dental Association's Commission on Dental Accreditation approved 259 dental-assisting training programs in 2002. Programs include classroom, laboratory, and preclinical instruction in dental-assisting skills and related theory. In addition, students gain practical experience in dental schools, clinics, or dental offices. Most programs take 1 year or less to complete and lead to a certificate or diploma. Two-year programs offered in community and junior colleges lead to an associate degree. All programs require a high school diploma or its equivalent, and some require

science or computer-related courses for admission. A number of private vocational schools offer 4- to 6-month courses in dental assisting, but the Commission on Dental Accreditation does not accredit these programs.

Most states regulate the duties that dental assistants are allowed to perform through licensure or registration. Licensure or registration may require passing a written or practical examination. States offering licensure or registration have a variety of schools offering courses—approximately 10 to 12 months in length—that meet their state's requirements. Many states require continuing education to maintain licensure or registration. A few states allow dental assistants to perform any function delegated to them by the dentist.

Individual states have adopted different standards for dental assistants who perform certain advanced duties, such as radiological procedures. The completion of the Radiation Health and Safety examination offered by the Dental Assisting National Board (DANB) meets those standards in more than 30 states. Some states require the completion of a state-approved course in radiology as well.

Certification is available through DANB and is recognized or required in more than 30 states. Other organizations offer registration, most often at the state level. Certification is an acknowledgment of an assistant's qualifications and professional competence and may be an asset when one is seeking employment. Candidates may qualify to take the DANB certification examination by graduating from an accredited training program or by having 2 years of full-time, or 4 years of part-time, experience as a dental assistant. In addition, applicants must have current certification in cardiopulmonary resuscitation. For annual recertification, individuals must earn continuing education credits.

Without further education, advancement opportunities are limited. Some dental assistants become office managers, dental-assisting instructors, or dental product sales representatives. Others go back to school to become dental hygienists. For many, this entry-level occupation provides basic training and experience and serves as a steppingstone to more highly skilled and higher paying jobs.

Job Outlook

Job prospects for dental assistants should be excellent. Employment is expected to grow much faster than the average for all occupations through the year 2012. In fact, dental assistants is expected to be one of the fastest growing occupations through the year 2012.

In addition to job openings due to employment growth, numerous job openings will arise out of the need to replace assistants who transfer to other occupations, retire, or leave the labor force for other reasons. Many opportunities are for entry-level positions offering on-the-job training.

Population growth and greater retention of natural teeth by middle-aged and older people will fuel demand for dental services. Older dentists, who have been less likely to employ assistants, are leaving the occupation and will be replaced by recent graduates, who are more likely to use one or even two assistants. In addition, as dentists' workloads increase, they are expected to hire more assistants to perform routine tasks, so that they may devote their own time to more profitable procedures.

Earnings

Median hourly earnings of dental assistants were $13.10 in 2002. The middle 50 percent earned between $10.35 and $16.20 an hour. The lowest 10 percent earned less than $8.45, and the highest 10 percent earned more than $19.41 an hour.

Benefits vary substantially by practice setting and may be contingent upon full-time employment. According to the American Dental Association, almost all full-time dental assistants employed by private practitioners received paid vacation time. The ADA also found that 9 out of 10 full-time and part-time dental assistants received dental coverage.

Related Occupations

Other workers supporting health practitioners include medical assistants, occupational therapist assistants and aides, pharmacy aides, pharmacy technicians, and physical therapist assistants and aides.

Sources of Additional Information

Information about career opportunities and accredited dental assistant programs is available from:

- Commission on Dental Accreditation, American Dental Association, 211 E. Chicago Ave., Suite 1814, Chicago, IL 60611. Internet: http://www.ada.org

For information on becoming a Certified Dental Assistant and a list of state boards of dentistry, contact:

- Dental Assisting National Board, Inc., 676 North Saint Clair, Suite 1880, Chicago, IL 60611. Internet: http://www.danb.org

For more information on a career as a dental assistant and general information about continuing education, contact:

- American Dental Assistants Association, 35 East Wacker Drive, Suite 1730, Chicago, IL 60601. Internet: http://www.dentalassistant.org

For more information about continuing education courses, contact:

- National Association of Dental Assistants, 900 S. Washington Street, Suite G-13, Falls Church, VA 22046.

Dental Hygienists

(O*NET 29-2021.00)

Significant Points

- Most dental hygiene programs grant an associate degree; others offer a certificate, a bachelor's degree, or a master's degree.

- Job prospects are expected to remain excellent.

- Opportunities for part-time work and flexible schedules are common.

Nature of the Work

Dental hygienists remove soft and hard deposits from teeth, teach patients how to practice good oral hygiene, and provide other preventive dental care. Hygienists examine patients' teeth and gums, recording the presence of diseases or abnormalities. They remove calculus, stains, and plaque from teeth; perform root planing as a periodontal therapy; take and develop dental x rays; and apply cavity-preventive agents such as fluorides and pit and fissure sealants. In some States, hygienists administer anesthetics; place and carve filling materials, temporary fillings, and periodontal dressings; remove sutures; and smooth and polish metal restorations. Although hygienists may not diagnose diseases, they can prepare clinical and laboratory diagnostic tests for the dentist to interpret. Hygienists sometimes work chairside with the dentist during treatment.

Dental hygienists also help patients develop and maintain good oral health. For example, they may explain the relationship between diet and oral health or inform patients how to select toothbrushes and show them how to brush and floss their teeth.

Dental hygienists use hand and rotary instruments and ultrasonics to clean and polish teeth, x-ray machines to take dental pictures, syringes with needles to administer local anesthetics, and models of teeth to explain oral hygiene.

Working Conditions

Flexible scheduling is a distinctive feature of this job. Full-time, part-time, evening, and weekend schedules are widely available. Dentists frequently hire hygienists to work only 2 or 3 days a week, so hygienists may hold jobs in more than one dental office.

Dental hygienists work in clean, well-lighted offfices. Important health safeguards include strict adherence to proper radiological procedures, and the use of appropriate protective devices when administering anesthetic gas. Dental hygienists also wear safety glasses, surgical masks, and gloves to protect themselves and patients from infectious diseases.

Employment

Dental hygienists held about 148,000 jobs in 2002. Because multiple jobholding is common in this field, the number of jobs exceeds the number of hygienists. More than half of all dental hygienists worked part time—less than 35 hours a week.

Almost all jobs for dental hygienists were in offices of dentists. A very small number worked for employment services or in offices of physicians.

Training, Other Qualifications, and Advancement

Dental hygienists must be licensed by the state in which they practice. To qualify for licensure, a candidate must graduate from an accredited dental hygiene school and pass both a written and clinical examination. The American Dental Association Joint Commission on National Dental Examinations administers the written examination, which is accepted by all states and the District of Columbia. State or regional testing agencies administer the clinical examination. In addition, most states require an examination on the legal aspects of dental hygiene practice. Alabama allows candidates to take its examinations if they have been trained through a state-regulated on-the-job program in a dentist's office.

In 2002, the Commission on Dental Accreditation accredited about 265 programs in dental hygiene. Most dental hygiene programs grant an associate degree, although some also offer a certificate, a bachelor's degree, or a master's degree. A minimum of an associate degree or certificate in dental hygiene is required for practice in a private dental office. A bachelor's or master's degree usually is required for research, teaching, or clinical practice in public or school health programs.

About half of the dental hygiene programs prefer applicants who have completed at least 1 year of college. However, requirements vary from one school to another. Schools offer laboratory, clinical, and classroom instruction in subjects such as anatomy, physiology, chemistry, microbiology, pharmacology, nutrition, radiography, histology (the study of tissue structure), periodontology (the study of gum diseases), pathology, dental materials, clinical dental hygiene, and social and behavioral sciences.

Dental hygienists should work well with others and must have good manual dexterity, because they use dental instruments within a patient's mouth, with little room for error. High school students interested in becoming a dental hygienist should take courses in biology, chemistry, and mathematics.

Job Outlook

Employment of dental hygienists is expected to grow much faster than the average for all occupations through 2012, in response to increasing demand for dental care and the greater utilization of hygienists to perform services previously performed by dentists. Job prospects are expected to remain excellent. In fact, dental hygienists is expected to be one of the fastest growing occupations through the year 2012.

Population growth and greater retention of natural teeth will stimulate demand for dental hygienists. Older dentists, who have been less likely to employ dental hygienists, are leaving the occupation and will be replaced by recent graduates, who are more likely to employ one or even two hygienists. In addition, as dentists' workloads increase, they are expected to hire more hygienists to perform preventive dental care, such as cleaning, so that they may devote their own time to more profitable procedures.

Earnings

Median hourly earnings of dental hygienists were $26.59 in 2002. The middle 50 percent earned between $21.96 and $32.48 an hour. The lowest 10 percent earned less than $17.34, and the highest 10 percent earned more than $39.24 an hour.

Earnings vary by geographic location, employment setting, and years of experience. Dental hygienists may be paid on an hourly, daily, salary, or commission basis.

Benefits vary substantially by practice setting and may be contingent upon full-time employment. According to the American Dental Association, almost all full-time dental hygienists employed by private practitioners received paid vacation. The ADA also found that 9 out of 10 full-time and part-time dental hygienists received dental coverage. Dental hygienists who work for school systems, public health agencies, the federal government, or state agencies usually have substantial benefits.

Related Occupations

Other workers supporting health practitioners in an office setting include dental assistants, medical assistants, occupational therapist assistants and aides, physical therapist assistants and aides, physician assistants, and registered nurses.

Sources of Additional Information

For information on a career in dental hygiene, including educational requirements, contact:

● Division of Education, American Dental Hygienists' Association, 444 N. Michigan Ave., Suite 3400, Chicago, IL 60611. Internet: http://www.adha.org

For information about accredited programs and educational requirements, contact:

● Commission on Dental Accreditation, American Dental Association, 211 E. Chicago Ave., Suite 1814, Chicago, IL 60611. Internet: http://www.ada.org

The State Board of Dental Examiners in each state can supply information on licensing requirements.

Designers

(O*NET 27-1021.00, 27-1022.00, 27-1023.00, 27-1024.00, 27-1025.00, 27-1026.00, 27-1027.01, and 27-1027.02)

Significant Points

- Nearly one-third of designers were self-employed—almost five times the proportion for all professional and related occupations.

- Creativity is crucial in all design occupations; most designers need a bachelor's degree, and candidates with a master's degree hold an advantage.

- Keen competition is expected for most jobs, despite average projected employment growth, because many talented individuals are attracted to careers as designers.

Nature of the Work

Designers are people with a desire to create. They combine practical knowledge with artistic ability to turn abstract ideas into formal designs for the merchandise we buy, the clothes we wear, the Web sites we use, the publications we read, and the living and office space we inhabit. Designers usually specialize in a particular area of design, such as automobiles, industrial or medical equipment, home appliances, clothing and textiles, floral arrangements, publications, Web sites, logos, signage, movie or TV credits, interiors of homes or office buildings, merchandise displays, or movie, television, and theater sets.

The first step in developing a new design or altering an existing one is to determine the needs of the client, the ultimate function for which the design is intended, and its appeal to customers or users. When creating a design, designers often begin by researching the desired design characteristics, such as size, shape, weight, color, materials used, cost, ease of use, fit, and safety.

Designers then prepare sketches or diagrams—by hand or with the aid of a computer—to illustrate the vision for the design. After consulting with the client, a creative director, or a product development team, designers create detailed designs, using drawings, a structural model, computer simulations, or a full-scale prototype. Many designers use computer-aided design (CAD) tools to create and better visualize the final product. Computer models allow ease and flexibility in exploring a greater number of design alternatives, thus reducing design costs and cutting the time it takes to deliver a product to market. Industrial designers use computer-aided industrial design (CAID) tools to create designs and machine-readable instructions that communicate with automated production tools.

Designers sometimes supervise assistants who carry out their creations. Designers who run their own businesses also may devote a considerable amount of time to developing new business contacts, examining equipment and space needs, and performing administrative tasks, such as reviewing catalogues and ordering samples. The need for up-to-date computer and communications equipment is an ongoing consideration for many designers, especially those in industrial and graphic design.

Design encompasses a number of different fields. Many designers specialize in a particular area of design, whereas others work in more than one area.

Commercial and industrial designers develop countless manufactured products, including airplanes; cars; children's toys; computer equipment; furniture; home appliances; and medical, office, and recreational equipment. They combine artistic talent with research on the use of a product, on customer needs, and on marketing, materials, and production methods to create the most functional and appealing design that will be competitive with others in the marketplace. Industrial designers typically concentrate in a subspecialty such as kitchen appliances, auto interiors, or plastic-molding machinery.

Fashion designers design clothing and accessories. Some high-fashion designers are self-employed and design for individual clients. Other high-fashion designers cater to specialty stores or high-fashion department stores. These designers create original garments, as well as clothing that follows established fashion trends. Most fashion designers, however, work for apparel manufacturers, creating designs of men's, women's, and children's fashions for the mass market.

Floral designers cut and arrange live, dried, or artificial flowers and foliage into designs, according to the customer's order. They design arrangements by trimming flowers and arranging bouquets, sprays, wreaths, dish gardens, and terrariums. They may either meet with customers to discuss the arrangement or work from a written order. Floral designers make note of the occasion, the customer's preference with regard to the color and type of flower involved, the price of the completed order, the time at which the floral arrangement or plant is to be ready, and the place to which it is to be delivered. The variety of duties performed by floral designers depends on the size of the shop and the number of designers employed. In a small operation, floral designers may own their shops and do almost everything, from growing and purchasing flowers to keeping financial records.

Graphic designers plan, analyze, and create visual solutions to communications problems. They use a variety of print, electronic, and film media and technologies to execute a design that meet clients' communication needs. They consider cognitive, cultural, physical, and social factors in planning and executing designs appropriate for a given context. Graphic designers use computer software to develop the overall layout and production design of magazines, newspapers, journals, corporate reports, and other publications. They also produce promotional displays and marketing brochures for products and services, design distinctive logos for products and businesses, and develop signs and signage systems—called environmental graphics—for business and government. An increasing number of graphic designers are developing material for Internet Web pages, computer interfaces, and multimedia projects. Graphic designers also produce the credits that appear before and after television programs and movies.

Interior designers enhance the function, safety, and quality of interior spaces of private homes, public buildings, and business or institutional facilities, such as offices, restaurants, retail establishments, hospitals, hotels, and theaters. They also plan the interiors of existing structures that are undergoing renovation or expansion. Most interior designers specialize. For example, some may concentrate on residential design, while others focus on business design. Still others may specialize further by focusing on particular rooms, such as kitchens or baths. With a client's tastes, needs, and budget in mind, interior designers prepare drawings and specifications for non-load-bearing interior construction, furnishings, lighting, and finishes. Increasingly, designers are using computers to plan layouts, because computers make it easy to change plans to include ideas received from the client. Interior designers also design lighting and architectural details—such as crown molding, built-in bookshelves, or cabinets—coordinate colors, and select furniture, floor coverings, and window treatments. Interior designers must design space to conform to federal, state, and local laws, including building codes. Designs for public areas also must meet accessibility standards for the disabled and the elderly.

Merchandise displayers and window dressers, or *visual merchandisers*, plan and erect commercial displays, such as those in windows and interiors of retail stores or at trade exhibitions. Those who work on building exteriors erect major store decorations, including building and window displays and lights. Those who design store interiors outfit store departments, arrange table displays, and dress mannequins. In large retail chains, store layouts typically are designed corporately, through a central design department. To retain the chain's visual identity and ensure that a particular image or theme is promoted in each store, designs are distributed to individual stores by e-mail, downloaded to computers equipped with the appropriate design software, and adapted to meet the size and dimension requirements of each individual store.

Set and exhibit designers create sets for movie, television, and theater productions and design special exhibition displays. Set designers study scripts, confer with directors and other designers, and conduct research to determine the historical period, fashion, and architectural styles appropriate for the production on which they work. They then produce sketches or scale models to guide in the construction of the actual sets or exhibit spaces. Exhibit designers work with curators, art and museum directors, and trade-show sponsors to determine the most effective use of available space.

Working Conditions

Working conditions and places of employment vary. Designers employed by manufacturing establishments, large corporations, or design firms generally work regular hours in well-lighted and comfortable settings. Designers in smaller design consulting firms, or those who freelance, generally work on a contract, or job, basis. They frequently adjust their workday to suit their clients' schedules and deadlines, meeting with the clients during evening or weekend hours when necessary. Consultants and self-employed designers tend to work longer hours and in smaller, more congested, environments.

Designers may transact business in their own offices or studios or in clients' homes or offices. They also may travel to other locations, such as showrooms, design centers, clients' exhibit sites, and manufacturing facilities. Designers who are paid by the assignment are under pressure to please clients and to find new ones in order to maintain a steady income. All designers sometimes face frustration when their designs are rejected or when their work is not as creative as they wish. With the increased speed and sophistication of computers and advanced communications networks, designers may form international design teams, serve a geographically more dispersed clientele, research design alternatives by using information on the Internet, and purchase supplies electronically, all with the aid of a computer in their workplace or studio.

Occasionally, industrial designers may work additional hours to meet deadlines. Similarly, graphic designers usually work regular hours, but may work evenings or weekends to meet production schedules. In contrast, set and exhibit designers work long and irregular hours; often, they are under pressure to make rapid changes. Merchandise displayers and window trimmers may spend much of their time designing displays in their office or studio, but those who also construct and install the displays may have to move lumber and heavy materials and perform some carpentry and painting. Fashion designers may work long hours to meet production deadlines or prepare for fashion shows. In addition, fashion designers may be required to travel to production sites across the United States and overseas. Interior designers generally work under deadlines and may put in extra hours to finish a job. Also, they typically carry heavy, bulky sample books to meetings with clients. Floral designers generally work regular hours in a pleasant work environment, but holiday, wedding, and funeral orders often require overtime.

Employment

Designers held about 532,000 jobs in 2002. Approximately one-third were self-employed. Employment was distributed as follows:

Graphic designers	212,000
Floral designers	104,000
Merchandise displayers and window trimmers	77,000
Interior designers	60,000
Commercial and industrial designers	52,000
Fashion designers	15,000
Set and exhibit designers	12,000

Salaried designers worked in a number of different industries, depending on their design specialty. Graphic designers, for example, worked primarily in specialized design services; newspaper, periodical, book, and directory publishers; and advertising and related services. Floral designers were concentrated in retail florists or floral departments of grocery stores. Merchandise displayers and window trimmers were dispersed across a variety of retailers and wholesalers. Interior designers generally worked in specialized design services or in retail furniture stores. Most commercial and industrial designers were employed in manufacturing or architectural, engineering, and related services. Fashion designers generally worked in apparel manufacturing or wholesale distribution of apparel, piece goods, and notions. Set and exhibit designers worked primarily for performing arts companies, movie and video industries, and radio and television broadcasting.

In 2002, a large proportion of designers were self-employed and did freelance work—full time or part time—in addition to holding a salaried job in design or in another occupation.

Training, Other Qualifications, and Advancement

Creativity is crucial in all design occupations. People in this field must have a strong sense of the esthetic—an eye for color and detail, a sense of balance and proportion, and an appreciation for beauty. Designers also need excellent communication and problem-solving skills. Despite the advancement of computer-aided design, sketching ability remains an important advantage in most types of design, especially fashion design. A good portfolio—a collection of examples of a person's best work—often is the deciding factor in getting a job.

A bachelor's degree is required for most entry-level design positions, except for floral design and visual merchandising. Esthetic ability is important in floral design and visual merchandising, but formal preparation typically is not necessary. Many candidates in industrial design pursue a master's degree to increase their chances of selection for open positions.

Interior design is the only design field subject to government regulation. According to the American Society of Interior Designers, 22 states and the District of Columbia register or license interior designers. Passing the National Council for Interior Design qualification examination is required for registration or licensure in these jurisdictions. To be eligible to take the exam, an applicant must have at least 6 years of combined education and experience in interior design, of which at least 2 years constitute postsecondary education in design. Because registration or licensure is not mandatory in all states, membership in a professional association is an indication of an interior designer's qualifications and professional standing—and can aid in obtaining clients.

In fashion design, employers seek individuals with a 2- or 4-year degree who are knowledgeable in the areas of textiles, fabrics, and ornamentation and about trends in the fashion world. Set and exhibit designers typically have college degrees in design. A Master of Fine Arts degree from an accredited university program further establishes one's design credentials. For set designers, membership in the United Scenic Artists, Local 829, is recognized nationally as the attainment of professional standing in the field.

Most floral designers learn their skills on the job. When employers hire trainees, they generally look for high school graduates who have a flair for arranging and a desire to learn. The completion of formal design training, however, is an asset for floral designers, particularly those interested in advancing to chief floral designer or in opening their own businesses. Vocational and technical schools offer programs in floral design, usually lasting less than a year, while 2- and 4-year programs in floriculture, horticulture, floral design, or ornamental horticulture are offered by community and junior colleges, colleges, and universities. The American Institute of Floral Designers offers an accreditation examination to its members as an indication of professional achievement in floral design.

Formal training for some design professions also is available in 2- and 3-year professional schools that award certificates or associate degrees in design. Graduates of 2-year programs normally qualify as assistants to designers, or they may enter a formal bachelor's degree program. The Bachelor of Fine Arts degree is granted at 4-year colleges and universities. The curriculum in these schools includes art and art history, principles of design, designing and sketching, and specialized studies for each of the individual design disciplines, such as garment construction, textiles, mechanical and architectural drawing, computerized design, sculpture, architecture, and basic engineering. A liberal arts education or a program that includes training in business or project management, together with courses in merchandising, marketing, and psychology, along with training in art, is recommended for designers who want to freelance. In addition, persons with training or experience in architecture qualify for some design occupations, particularly interior design.

Employers increasingly expect new designers to be familiar with computer-aided design software as a design tool. For example, industrial designers use computers extensively in the aerospace, automotive, and electronics industries. Interior designers use computers to create numerous versions of interior space designs—images can be inserted, edited, and replaced easily and without added cost—making it possible for a client to see and choose among several designs.

The National Association of Schools of Art and Design accredits more than 200 postsecondary institutions with programs in art and design. Most of these schools award a degree in art, and some award degrees in industrial, interior, textile, graphic, or fashion design. Many schools do not allow formal entry into a bachelor's degree program until a student has successfully finished a year of basic art and design courses. Applicants may be required to submit sketches and other examples of their artistic ability.

The Foundation for Interior Design Education Research also accredits interior design programs that lead to a bachelor's degree. There are about 120 accredited professional programs in the United States, located primarily in schools of art, architecture, and home economics.

Individuals in the design field must be creative, imaginative, and persistent and must be able to communicate their ideas in writing, visually, and verbally. Because tastes in style and fashion can change quickly, designers need to be well read, open to new ideas and influences, and quick to react to changing trends. Problem-solving skills and the ability to work independently and under pressure are important traits. People in this field need self-discipline to start projects on their own, to budget their time, and to meet deadlines and production schedules. Good business sense and sales ability also are important, especially for those who freelance or run their own business.

Beginning designers usually receive on-the-job training and normally need 1 to 3 years of training before they can advance to higher level positions. Experienced designers in large firms may advance to chief designer, design department head, or other supervisory positions. Some designers leave the occupation to become teachers in design schools or in colleges and universities. Many faculty members continue to consult privately or operate small design studios to complement their classroom activities. Some experienced designers open their own firms.

Job Outlook

Overall employment of designers is expected to grow about as fast as the average for all occupations through the year 2012 as the economy expands and consumers, businesses, and manufacturers continue to rely on the services provided by designers. However, designers in most fields—with the exception of floral design—are expected to face keen competition for available positions. Many talented individuals are attracted to careers as designers. Individuals with little or no formal education in design, as well as those who lack creativity and perseverance, will find it very difficult to establish and maintain a career in the occupation.

Among the design specialties, graphic designers are projected to provide the most new jobs. Demand for graphic designers should increase because of the rapidly expanding market for Web-based information and expansion of the video entertainment market, including television, movies, video, and made-for-Internet outlets.

Rising demand for interior design of private homes, offices, restaurants and other retail establishments, and institutions that care for the rapidly growing elderly population should spur employment growth of interior designers. New jobs for floral designers are expected to stem mostly from the relatively high replacement needs in retail florists that result from comparatively low starting pay and limited opportunities for advancement. The majority of new jobs for merchandise displayers and window trimmers will also result from the need to replace workers who retire, transfer to other occupations, or leave the labor force for other reasons.

Increased demand for industrial designers will stem from continued emphasis on the quality and safety of products, demand for new products that are easy and comfortable to use, and the development of high-technology products in medicine, transportation, and other fields. Demand for fashion designers should remain strong, because many consumers continue to seek new fashions and fresh styles of apparel. Employment growth for fashion designers will be slowed, however, by declines in the apparel manufacturing industries. Despite faster-than-average growth for set and exhibit designers, few job openings will result because the occupation is small.

Earnings

Median annual earnings for commercial and industrial designers were $52,260 in 2002. The middle 50 percent earned between $39,240 and $67,430. The lowest 10 percent earned less than $28,820, and the highest 10 percent earned more than $82,130. Median annual earnings were $61,530 in architectural, engineering, and related services.

Median annual earnings for fashion designers were $51,290 in 2002. The middle 50 percent earned between $35,550 and $75,970. The lowest 10 percent earned less than $25,350, and the highest 10 percent earned more than $105,280.

Median annual earnings for floral designers were $19,480 in 2002. The middle 50 percent earned between $15,880 and $23,560. The lowest 10 percent earned less than $13,440, and the highest 10 percent earned more than $29,830. Median annual earnings were $21,610 in grocery stores and $18,950 in florists.

Median annual earnings for graphic designers were $36,680 in 2002. The middle 50 percent earned between $28,140 and $48,820. The lowest 10 percent earned less than $21,860, and the highest 10 percent earned more than $64,160. Median annual earnings in the industries employing the largest numbers of graphic designers were as follows:

Advertising and related services	$39,510
Specialized design services	38,710
Printing and related support activities	31,800
Newspaper, periodical, book, and directory publishers	31,670

Median annual earnings for interior designers were $39,180 in 2002. The middle 50 percent earned between $29,070 and $53,060. The lowest 10 percent earned less than $21,240, and the highest 10 percent earned more than $69,640. Median annual earnings in the industries employing the largest numbers of interior designers were as follows:

Architectural, engineering, and related services	$41,680
Specialized design services	39,870
Furniture stores	36,320

Median annual earnings of merchandise displayers and window dressers were $22,550 in 2002. The middle 50 percent earned between $18,320 and $29,070. The lowest 10 percent earned less than $15,100, and the highest 10 percent earned more than $40,020. Median annual earnings were $22,130 in department stores.

Median annual earnings for set and exhibit designers were $33,870 in 2000. The middle 50 percent earned between $24,780 and $46,350. The lowest 10 percent earned less than $17,830, and the highest 10 percent earned more than $63,280.

The American Institute of Graphic Arts reported 2002 median annual earnings for graphic designers with increasing levels of responsibility. Staff-level graphic designers earned $40,000, while senior designers, who may supervise junior staff or have some decisionmaking authority that reflects their knowledge of graphic design, earned $55,000. Solo designers, who freelanced or worked under contract to another company, reported median earnings of $55,000. Design directors, the creative heads of design firms or in-house corporate design departments, earned $85,000. Graphic designers with ownership or partnership interests in a firm or who were principals of the firm in some other capacity earned $93,000.

Related Occupations

Workers in other occupations who design or arrange objects, materials, or interiors to enhance their appearance and function include artists and related workers; architects, except landscape and naval; engineers; landscape architects; and photographers. Some computer-related occupations, including computer software engineers and desktop publishers, require design skills.

Sources of Additional Information

For general information about art and design and a list of accredited college-level programs, contact:

● National Association of Schools of Art and Design, 11250 Roger Bacon Dr., Suite 21, Reston, VA 20190. Internet: http://nasad.arts-accredit.org

For information about graphic, communication, or interaction design careers, contact:

● American Institute of Graphic Arts, 164 Fifth Ave., New York, NY 10010. Internet: http://www.aiga.org

For information on degree, continuing education, and licensure programs in interior design and interior design research, contact:

● American Society for Interior Designers, 608 Massachusetts Ave. NE, Washington, DC 20002-6006. Internet: http://www.asid.org

For a list of schools with accredited programs in interior design, contact:

● Foundation for Interior Design Education Research, 146 Monroe Center NW, Suite 1318, Grand Rapids, MI 49503. Internet: http://www.fider.org

For information on careers, continuing education, and certification programs in the interior design specialty of residential kitchen and bath design, contact:

● National Kitchen and Bath Association, 687 Willow Grove St., Hackettstown, NJ 07840. Internet: http://www.nkba.org/student

For information about careers in floral design, contact:

● Society of American Florists, 1601 Duke St., Alexandria, VA 22314. Internet: http://www.safnow.org

★ ★ ★ ★ ★ ★ ★ ★ ★ ★ ★ ★

Drywall Installers, Ceiling Tile Installers, and Tapers

(O*NET 47-2081.01, 47-2081.02, and 47-2082.00)

Significant Points

● Most workers learn the trade on the job, either by working as helpers or through a formal apprenticeship.

● Job prospects are expected to be good.

● Inclement weather seldom interrupts work, but workers may be idled when downturns in the economy slow new construction activity.

Nature of the Work

Drywall consists of a thin layer of gypsum between two layers of heavy paper. It is used for walls and ceilings in most buildings today because it is both faster and cheaper to install than plaster.

There are two kinds of drywall workers—installers and tapers—although many workers do both types of work. Installers, also called *applicators* or *hangers*, fasten drywall panels to the inside framework of residential houses and other buildings. *Tapers*, or *finishers*, prepare these panels for painting by taping and finishing joints and imperfections.

Because drywall panels are manufactured in standard sizes—usually 4 feet by 8 or 12 feet—drywall installers must measure, cut, and fit some pieces around doors and windows. They also saw or cut holes in panels for electrical outlets, air-conditioning units, and plumbing. After making these alterations, installers may glue, nail, or screw the wallboard panels to the wood or metal framework. Because drywall is heavy and cumbersome, a helper generally assists the installer in positioning and securing the panel. Workers often use a lift when placing ceiling panels.

After the drywall is installed, tapers fill joints between panels with a joint compound. Using the wide, flat tip of a special trowel, they spread the compound into and along each side of the joint with brush-like strokes. They immediately use the trowel to press a paper tape—used to reinforce the drywall and to hide imperfections—into the wet compound and to smooth away excess material. Nail and screw depressions also are covered with this compound, as are imperfections caused by the installation of air-conditioning vents and other fixtures. On large projects, finishers may use automatic taping tools that apply the joint compound and tape in one step. Tapers apply second and third coats of the compound, sanding the treated areas where needed after each coat to make them as smooth as the rest of the wall surface. This results in a very smooth and almost perfect surface. Some tapers apply textured surfaces to walls and ceilings with trowels, brushes, or spray guns.

Ceiling tile installers, or *acoustical carpenters*, apply or mount acoustical tiles or blocks, strips, or sheets of shock-absorbing materials to ceilings and walls of buildings to reduce reflection of sound or to decorate rooms. First, they measure and mark the surface according to blueprints and drawings. Then, they nail or screw moldings to the wall to support and seal the joint between the ceiling tile and the wall. Finally, they mount the tile, either by applying a cement adhesive to the back of the tile and then pressing the tile into place, or by nailing, screwing, stapling, or wire-tying the lath directly to the structural framework.

Lathers also are included in this occupation. Lathers fasten metal or rockboard lath to walls, ceilings, and partitions of buildings. Lath forms the support base for plaster, fireproofing, or acoustical materials. At one time, lath was made of wooden strips. Now, lathers work mostly with wire, metal mesh, or rockboard lath. Metal lath is used where the plaster application will be exposed to weather or water or for curved or irregular surfaces for which drywall is not a practical material. Using handtools and portable power tools, lathers nail, screw, staple, or wire-tie the lath directly to the structural framework.

Working Conditions

As in many other construction trades, the work sometimes is strenuous. Drywall installers, ceiling tile installers, and tapers spend most of the day on their feet, either standing, bending, or kneeling. Some tapers use stilts to tape and finish ceiling and angle joints. Installers have to lift and maneuver heavy panels. Hazards include falls from ladders and scaffolds and injuries from power tools and from working with sharp materials. Because sanding a joint compound to a smooth finish creates a great deal of dust, some finishers wear masks for protection.

Employment

Drywall installers, ceiling tile installers, and tapers held about 176,000 jobs in 2002. Most worked for contractors specializing in drywall and ceiling tile installation; others worked for contractors doing many kinds of construction. About 33,000 were self-employed independent contractors.

Most installers and tapers are employed in populous areas. In other areas, where there may not be enough work to keep a drywall or ceiling tile installer employed full time, carpenters and painters usually do the work.

Training, Other Qualifications, and Advancement

Most drywall installers, ceiling tile installers, and tapers start as helpers and learn their skills on the job. Installer helpers start by carrying materials, lifting and holding panels, and cleaning up debris. Within a few weeks, they learn to measure, cut, and install materials. Eventually, they become fully experienced workers. Taper apprentices begin by taping joints and touching up nail holes, scrapes, and other imperfections. They soon learn to install corner guards and to conceal openings around pipes. At the end of their training, drywall installers, ceiling tile installers, and tapers learn to estimate the cost of installing and finishing drywall.

Some drywall installers, ceiling tile installers, and tapers learn their trade in an apprenticeship program. The United Brotherhood of Carpenters and Joiners of America, in cooperation with local contractors, administers an apprenticeship program both in drywall installation and finishing and in acoustical carpentry. Apprenticeship programs consist of at least 3 years, or 6,000 hours, of on-the-job training and 144 hours a year of related classroom instruction. In addition, local affiliates of the Associated Builders and Contractors and the National Association of Home Builders conduct training programs for nonunion workers. The International Union of Painters and Allied Trades conducts an apprenticeship program in drywall finishing that lasts 2 to 3 years.

Employers prefer high school graduates who are in good physical condition, but they frequently hire applicants with less education. High school or vocational school courses in carpentry provide a helpful background for drywall work. Regardless of educational background, installers must be good at simple arithmetic. Other useful high school courses include English, wood shop, metal shop, blueprint reading, and mechanical drawing.

Drywall installers, ceiling tile installers, and tapers with a few years of experience and with leadership ability may become supervisors. Some workers start their own contracting businesses.

Job Outlook

Job opportunities for drywall installers, ceiling tile installers, and tapers are expected to be good. Many potential workers are not attracted to this occupation because they prefer work that is less strenuous and has more comfortable working conditions. Experienced workers will have especially favorable opportunities.

Employment is expected to grow faster than the average for all occupations over the 2002-12 period, reflecting increases in the numbers of new construction and remodeling projects. In addition to jobs involving traditional interior work, drywall workers will find employment opportunities in the installation of insulated exterior wall systems, which are becoming increasingly popular.

Besides those resulting from job growth, many jobs will open up each year because of the need to replace workers who transfer to other occupations or leave the labor force. Some drywall installers, ceiling tile installers, and tapers with limited skills leave the occupation when they find that they dislike the work or fail to find steady employment.

Despite the growing use of exterior panels, most drywall installation and finishing is done indoors. Therefore, drywall workers lose less worktime because of inclement weather than do some other construction workers. Nevertheless, they may be unemployed between construction projects and during downturns in construction activity.

Earnings

In 2002, the median hourly earnings of drywall and ceiling tile installers were $16.21. The middle 50 percent earned between $12.43 and $21.50. The lowest 10 percent earned less than $9.76, and the highest 10 percent earned more than $28.03. The median hourly earnings in the industries employing the largest numbers of drywall and ceiling tile installers in 2002 were:

Building finishing contractors................................$16.50
Nonresidential building construction 14.66

In 2002, the median hourly earnings of tapers were $18.75. The middle 50 percent earned between $14.57 and $24.68. The lowest 10 percent earned less than $11.07, and the highest 10 percent earned more than $29.32.

Trainees usually started at about half the rate paid to experienced workers and received wage increases as they became more highly skilled.

Some contractors pay these workers according to the number of panels they install or finish per day; others pay an hourly rate. A 40-hour week is standard, but the workweek may sometimes be longer. Workers who are paid hourly rates receive premium pay for overtime.

Related Occupations

Drywall installers, ceiling tile installers, and tapers combine strength and dexterity with precision and accuracy to make materials fit according to a plan. Other occupations that require similar abilities include carpenters; carpet, floor, and tile installers and finishers; insulation workers; and plasterers and stucco masons.

Sources of Additional Information

For information about work opportunities in drywall application and finishing and ceiling tile installation, contact local drywall installation and ceiling tile installation contractors, a local of the unions previously mentioned, a local joint union-management apprenticeship committee, a state or local chapter of the Associated Builders and Contractors, or the nearest office of the state employment service or apprenticeship agency.

For details about job qualifications and training programs in drywall application and finishing and ceiling tile installation, contact:

- Associated Builders and Contractors, 1300 N. 17th St., Arlington, VA 22209.

- National Association of Home Builders, 1201 15th St. NW, Suite 800, Washington, DC 20005. Internet: http://www.nahb.org

- Home Builders Institute, 1201 15th St. NW, Washington, DC 20005. Internet: http://www.hbi.org

- International Union of Painters and Allied Trades, 1750 New York Ave. NW, Washington, DC 20006. Internet: http://www.iupat.org

- United Brotherhood of Carpenters and Joiners of America, 50 F St. NW, Washington, DC 20001. Internet: http://www.carpenters.org

There are more than 500 occupations registered by the U.S. Department of Labor's National Apprenticeship system. For more information on the Labor Department's registered apprenticeship system and links to state apprenticeship programs, check their Web site: http://www.doleta.gov.

Education Administrators

(O*NET 11-9031.00, 11-9032.00, 11-9033.00, and 11-9039.99)

Significant Points

- Many jobs require a master's or doctoral degree and experience in a related occupation, such as a teacher or admissions counselor.

- Strong interpersonal and communication skills are essential because much of an administrator's job involves working and collaborating with others.

- Job outlook is expected to be excellent because a large proportion of education administrators are expected to retire over the next 10 years.

Nature of the Work

Smooth operation of an educational institution requires competent administrators. *Education administrators* provide instructional leadership as well as manage the day-to-day activities in schools, preschools, daycare centers, and colleges and universities. They also direct the educational programs of businesses, correctional institutions, museums, and job training and community service organizations. Education administrators set educational standards and goals and establish the policies and procedures to carry them out. They also supervise managers, support staff, teachers, counselors, librarians, coaches, and others. They develop academic programs; monitor students' educational progress; train and motivate teachers and other staff; manage guidance and other student services; administer recordkeeping; prepare budgets; handle relations with parents, prospective and current students, employers, and the community; and perform many other duties. In an organization such as a small daycare center, one administrator may handle all these functions. In universities or large school systems, responsibilities are divided among many administrators, each with a specific function.

Those who manage elementary, middle, and secondary schools are called *principals*. They set the academic tone and hire, evaluate, and help improve the skills of teachers and other staff. Principals confer with staff to advise, explain, or answer procedural questions. They visit classrooms, observe teaching methods, review instructional objectives, and examine learning materials. They actively work with teachers to develop and maintain high curriculum standards, develop mission statements, and set performance goals and objectives. Principals must use clear, objective guidelines for teacher appraisals, because pay often is based on performance ratings.

Principals also meet and interact with other administrators, students, parents, and representatives of community organizations. Decisionmaking authority has increasingly shifted from school district central offices to individual schools. Thus, parents, teachers, and other members of the community play an important role in setting school policies and goals. Principals must pay attention to the concerns of these groups when making administrative decisions.

Principals prepare budgets and reports on various subjects, including finances and attendance, and oversee the requisition and allocation of supplies. As school budgets become tighter, many principals have become more involved in public relations and fundraising to secure financial support for their schools from local businesses and the community.

Principals must take an active role to ensure that students meet national, state, and local academic standards. Many principals develop school/business partnerships and school-to-work transition programs for students. Increasingly, principals must be sensitive to the needs of the rising number of non-English speaking and culturally diverse students. Growing enrollments, which are leading to overcrowding at many existing schools, also are a cause for concern. When addressing problems of inadequate resources, administrators serve as advocates for the building of new schools or the repair of existing ones. During summer months, principals are responsible for planning for the upcoming year, overseeing summer school, participating in workshops for teachers and administrators, supervising building repairs and improvements, and working to be sure the school has adequate staff for the school year.

Schools continue to be involved with students' emotional welfare as well as their academic achievement. As a result, principals face responsibilities outside the academic realm. For example, in response to the growing numbers of dual-

income and single-parent families and teenage parents, schools have established before- and after-school childcare programs or family resource centers, which also may offer parenting classes and social service referrals. With the help of community organizations, some principals have established programs to combat increases in crime, drug and alcohol abuse, and sexually transmitted diseases among students.

Assistant principals aid the principal in the overall administration of the school. Some assistant principals hold this position for several years to prepare for advancement to principal jobs; others are career assistant principals. They are primarily responsible for scheduling student classes, ordering textbooks and supplies, and coordinating transportation, custodial, cafeteria, and other support services. They usually handle student discipline and attendance problems, social and recreational programs, and health and safety matters. They also may counsel students on personal, educational, or vocational matters. With the advent of site-based management, assistant principals are playing a greater role in ensuring the academic success of students by helping to develop new curriculums, evaluating teachers, and dealing with school-community relations—responsibilities previously assumed solely by the principal. The number of assistant principals that a school employs may vary, depending on the number of students.

In preschools and childcare centers, education administrators are the director or supervisor of the school or center. Their job is similar to that of other school administrators in that they oversee daily activities and operation of the schools, hire and develop staff, and make sure that the school meets required regulations.

Administrators in school district central offices oversee public schools under their jurisdiction. This group includes those who direct subject-area programs such as English, music, vocational education, special education, and mathematics. They supervise instructional coordinators and curriculum specialists, and work with them to evaluate curriculums and teaching techniques and improve them. Administrators also may oversee career counseling programs and testing that measures students' abilities and helps to place them in appropriate classes. Others may also direct programs such as school psychology, athletics, curriculum and instruction, and professional development. With site-based management, administrators have transferred primary responsibility for many of these programs to the principals, assistant principals, teachers, instructional coordinators, and other staff in the schools.

In colleges and universities, *academic deans, deans of faculty, provosts*, and *university deans* assist presidents, make faculty appointments, develop budgets, and establish academic policies and programs. They also direct and coordinate the activities of deans of individual colleges and chairpersons of academic departments. Fundraising also is becoming an essential part of their job.

College or university department heads or *chairpersons* are in charge of departments that specialize in particular fields of study, such as English, biological science, or mathematics. In addition to teaching, they coordinate schedules of classes and teaching assignments; propose budgets; recruit, interview, and hire applicants for teaching positions; evaluate faculty members; encourage faculty development; serve on committees; and perform other administrative duties. In overseeing their departments, chairpersons must consider and balance the concerns of faculty, administrators, and students.

Higher education administrators also direct and coordinate the provision of student services. *Vice presidents of student affairs or student life, deans of students, and directors of student services* may direct and coordinate admissions, foreign student services, health and counseling services, career services, financial aid, and housing and residential life, as well as social, recreational, and related programs. In small colleges, they may counsel students. In larger colleges and universities, separate administrators may handle each of these services. *Registrars* are custodians of students' records. They register students, record grades, prepare student transcripts, evaluate academic records, assess and collect tuition and fees, plan and implement commencement, oversee the preparation of college catalogs and schedules of classes, and analyze enrollment and demographic statistics. *Directors of admissions* manage the process of recruiting, evaluating, and admitting students, and work closely with *financial aid directors*, who oversee scholarship, fellowship, and loan programs. Registrars and admissions officers at most institutions need computer skills because they use electronic student information systems. For example, for those whose institutions present information—such as college catalogs and schedules—on the Internet, knowledge of online resources, imaging, and other computer skills is important. *Athletic directors* plan and direct intramural and intercollegiate athletic activities, seeing to publicity for athletic events, preparation of budgets, and supervision of coaches. Other increasingly important administrators direct fundraising, public relations, distance learning, and technology.

Working Conditions

Education administrators hold leadership positions with significant responsibility. Most find working with students extremely rewarding, but as the responsibilities of administrators have increased in recent years, so has the stress. Coordinating and interacting with faculty, parents, students, community members, business leaders, and state and local policymakers can be fast-paced and stimulating, but also stressful and demanding. Principals and assistant principals, whose varied duties include discipline, may find working with difficult students challenging. The pressures associated with education administrator jobs have multiplied in recent years, as workers in these positions are increasingly being held accountable for ensuring that their schools meet recently imposed state and federal guidelines for student performance and teacher qualifications, and as they must cope with the additional challenges presented by current budget shortfalls.

Many education administrators work more than 40 hours a week, often including school activities at night and on weekends. Most administrators work 11 or 12 months out of the year. Some jobs include travel.

Employment

Education administrators held about 427,000 jobs in 2002. About 2 in 10 worked for private education institutions, and 6 in 10 worked for state and local governments, mainly in schools, colleges and universities, and departments of education. Less than 5 percent were self-employed. The rest worked in child daycare centers, religious organizations, job training centers, and businesses and other organizations that provided training for their employees.

Training, Other Qualifications, and Advancement

Most education administrators begin their careers in related occupations, and prepare for a job in education administration by completing a master's or doctoral degree. Because of the diversity of duties and levels of responsibility, their educational backgrounds and experience vary considerably. Principals, assistant principals, central office administrators, academic deans, and preschool directors usually have held teaching positions before moving into administration. Some teachers move directly into principal positions; others first become assistant principals or gain experience in other central office administrative jobs at either the school or district level in positions such as department head, curriculum specialist, or subject matter advisor. In some cases, administrators move up from related staff jobs such as recruiter, guidance counselor, librarian, residence hall director, or financial aid or admissions counselor.

To be considered for education administrator positions, workers must first prove themselves in their current jobs. In evaluating candidates, supervisors look for leadership, determination, confidence, innovativeness, and motivation. The ability to make sound decisions and to organize and coordinate work efficiently is essential. Because much of an administrator's job involves interacting with others—such as students, parents, teachers, and the community— a person in such a position must have strong interpersonal skills and be an effective communicator and motivator. Knowledge of leadership principles and practices, gained through work experience and formal education, is important. A familiarity with computer technology is a necessity for principals, who are required to gather information and coordinate technical resources for their students, teachers, and classrooms.

In most public schools, principals, assistant principals, and school administrators in central offices need a master's degree in education administration or educational supervision. Some principals and central office administrators have a doctorate or specialized degree in education administration. In private schools, which are not subject to state licensure requirements, some principals and assistant principals hold only a bachelor's degree; however, the majority have a master's or doctoral degree. Most states require principals to be licensed as school administrators. License requirements vary by state. National standards for school leaders, including principals and supervisors, have been developed by the Interstate School Leaders Licensure Consortium. Many states use these national standards as guidelines to assess beginning principals for licensure. Increasingly, on-the-job training, often with a mentor, is required for new school leaders. Some states require administrators to take continuing education courses to keep their license, thus ensuring that administrators have the most up-to-date skills. The number and types of courses required to maintain licensure vary by state.

Educational requirements for administrators of preschools and childcare centers vary depending on the setting of the program and the state of employment. Administrators who oversee school-based preschool programs are often required to have at least a bachelor's degree. Child care directors are generally not required to have a degree; however, most states require a credential such as the Child Development Associate credential (CDA) sponsored by the Council for Professional Recognition or other credential specifically designed for administrators. The National Child Care Association, offers a National Administration Credential, which some recent college graduates voluntarily earn to better qualify for positions as childcare center directors.

Academic deans and chairpersons usually have a doctorate in their specialty. Most have held a professorship in their department before advancing. Admissions, student affairs, and financial aid directors and registrars sometimes start in related staff jobs with bachelor's degrees—any field usually is acceptable—and obtain advanced degrees in college student affairs, counseling, or higher education administration. A Ph.D. or Ed.D. usually is necessary for top student affairs positions. Computer literacy and a background in accounting or statistics may be assets in admissions, records, and financial work.

Advanced degrees in higher education administration, educational supervision, and college student affairs are offered in many colleges and universities. The National Council for Accreditation of Teacher Education and the Educational Leadership Constituent Council accredit these programs. Education administration degree programs include courses in school leadership, school law, school finance and budgeting, curriculum development and evaluation, research design and data analysis, community relations, politics in education, and counseling. Educational supervision degree programs include courses in supervision of instruction and curriculum, human relations, curriculum development, research, and advanced teaching courses.

Education administrators advance through promotion to more responsible administrative positions or by transferring to more responsible positions at larger schools or systems. They also may become superintendents of school systems or presidents of educational institutions.

Job Outlook

Employment of education administrators is projected to grow faster than the average for all occupations through 2012. As education and training take on greater importance in everyone's lives, the need for people to administer education programs will grow. Job opportunities for many of these positions should also be excellent because a large proportion of education administrators are expected to retire over the next 10 years.

A significant portion of growth will stem from growth in the private and for-profit segments of education. Many of these schools cater to working adults, many of whom might not ordinarily participate in postsecondary education. These schools allow students to earn a degree, receive job-specific training or update their skills, in a convenient manner, such as through part-time programs or distance learning. As the number of these schools continues to grow, more administrators ill be needed to oversee them.

Enrollments of school-age children will also have an impact on the demand for education administrators. The U.S. Department of Education projects enrollment of elementary and secondary school students to grow between 5 and 7 percent over the next decade. Preschool and childcare center administrators are expected to experience substantially more growth as enrollments in formal child care programs continues to expand as fewer private households care for young children. Additionally, if mandatory preschool becomes more widespread more preschool directors will be needed. The number of postsecondary school students is projected to grow more rapidly than other student populations, creating significant demand for administrators at that level. In addition, enrollments are expected to increase the fastest in the West and South, where the population is growing, and to decline or remain stable in the Northeast and the Midwest. School administrators also are in greater demand in rural and urban areas, where pay is generally lower than in the suburbs.

Principals and assistant principals should have favorable job prospects. A sharp increase in responsibilities in recent years has made the job more stressful and has discouraged teachers from taking positions in administration. Principals are now being held more accountable for the performance of students and teachers, while at the same time they are required to adhere to a growing number of government regulations. In addition, overcrowded classrooms, safety issues, budgetary concerns, and teacher shortages in some areas all are creating additional stress for administrators. The increase in pay is often not high enough to entice people into the field.

Job prospects also are expected to be favorable for college and university administrators, particularly those seeking nonacademic positions. Colleges and universities may be subject to funding shortfalls during economic downturns, but increasing enrollments over the projection period will require that institutions replace the large numbers of administrators who retire, and even hire additional administrators.

While competition among faculty for prestigious positions as academic deans and department heads is likely to remain keen, fewer applicants are expected for nonacademic administrative jobs, such as director of admissions or student affairs. Furthermore, many people are discouraged from seeking administrator jobs by the requirement that they have a master's or doctoral degree in education administration—as well as by the opportunity to earn higher salaries in other occupations.

Earnings

In 2002, elementary and secondary school administrators had median annual earnings of $71,490; postsecondary school administrators had median annual earnings of $64,640, while preschool and childcare center administrators earned a median of $33,340 per year. Salaries of education administrators depend on several factors, including the location and enrollment level in the school or school district. According to a survey of public schools, conducted by the Educational Research Service, average salaries for principals and assistant principals in the 2002-03 school year were as follows:

Directors, managers, coordinators, and
supervisors, finance and business $81,451
Principals:
Elementary school $75,291
Jr. high/middle school 80,708
Senior high school 86,452
Assistant principals:
Elementary school $62,230
Jr. high/middle school 67,288
Senior high school 70,874

According to the College and University Professional Association for Human Resources, median annual salaries for selected administrators in higher education in 2001-02 were as follows:

Academic deans:
Business $107,414
Graduate programs 100,391
Education 100,227
Arts and sciences 98,780
Health-related professions 89,234
Nursing...88,386
Continuing education 84,457
Occupational or vocational education 73,595
Other administrators:
Dean of students $70,012
Director, admissions and registrar.........................61,519
Director, student financial aid...............................57,036
Director, annual giving 49,121
Director, student activities.....................................41,050

Benefits for education administrators are generally very good. Many get 4 or 5 weeks vacation every year and have generous health and pension packages. Many colleges and universities offer free tuition to employees and their families.

Related Occupations

Education administrators apply organizational and leadership skills to provide services to individuals. Workers in related occupations include administrative services managers; office and administrative support worker supervisors and managers; human resource, training, and labor relations managers and specialists; and archivists, curators, and museum technicians. Education administrators also work with students and have backgrounds similar to those of counselors; librarians; instructional coordinators; teachers—preschool, kindergarten, elementary, middle, and secondary; and teachers—postsecondary.

Sources of Additional Information

For information on principals and other management staff in public schools, contact:

● Educational Research Service, 2000 Clarendon Boulevard, Arlington, VA 22201-2908. Internet: http://www.ers.org

For information on principals, contact:

● The National Association of Elementary School Principals, 1615 Duke St., Alexandria, VA 22314-3483. Internet: http://www.naesp.org

● The National Association of Secondary School Principals, 1904 Association Drive, Reston, VA 20191-1537. Internet: http://www.nassp.org

For information on collegiate registrars and admissions officers, contact:

● American Association of Collegiate Registrars and Admissions Officers, One Dupont Circle NW, Suite 520, Washington, DC 20036-1171. Internet: http://www.aacrao.org

For information on professional development and graduate programs for college student affairs administrators, contact:

● NASPA, Student Affairs Administrators in Higher Education, 1875 Connecticut Ave. NW, Suite 418, Washington, DC 20009. Internet: http://www.naspa.org

Electricians

(O*NET 47-2111.00)

Significant Points

● Job opportunities are expected to be good.

● Most electricians acquire their skills by completing an apprenticeship program lasting 3 to 5 years.

● More than one-quarter of wage and salary electricians work in industries other than construction.

Nature of the Work

Electricity is essential for light, power, air-conditioning, and refrigeration. Electricians install, connect, test, and maintain electrical systems for a variety of purposes, including climate control, security, and communications. They also may install and maintain the electronic controls for machines in business and industry. Although most electricians specialize in construction or maintenance, a growing number do both.

Electricians work with blueprints when they install electrical systems in factories, office buildings, homes, and other structures. Blueprints indicate the locations of circuits, outlets, load centers, panel boards, and other equipment. Electricians must follow the National Electric Code and comply with state and local building codes when they install these systems. In factories and offices, they first place conduit (pipe or tubing) inside designated partitions, walls, or other concealed areas. They also fasten to the walls small metal or plastic boxes that will house electrical switches and outlets. They then pull insulated wires or cables through the conduit to complete circuits between these boxes. In lighter construction, such as residential, plastic-covered wire usually is used instead of conduit.

Regardless of the type of wire used, electricians connect it to circuit breakers, transformers, or other components. They join the wires in boxes with various specially designed connectors. After they finish the wiring, they use testing equipment, such as ohmmeters, voltmeters, and oscilloscopes, to check the circuits for proper connections, ensuring electrical compatibility and safety of components.

Electricians also may install low voltage wiring systems in addition to wiring a building's electrical system. Low voltage wiring involves voice, data, and video wiring systems, such as those for telephones, computers and related equipment, intercoms, and fire alarm and security systems. Electricians also may install coaxial or fiber optic cable for computers and other telecommunications equipment and electronic controls for industrial equipment.

Maintenance work varies greatly, depending on where the electrician is employed. Electricians who specialize in residential work may rewire a home and replace an old fuse box with a new circuit breaker box to accommodate additional appliances. Those who work in large factories may repair motors, transformers, generators, and electronic controllers on machine tools and industrial robots. Those in office buildings and small plants may repair all types of electrical equipment.

Maintenance electricians spend much of their time doing preventive maintenance. They periodically inspect equipment, and locate and correct problems before breakdowns occur. Electricians may also advise management whether continued operation of equipment could be hazardous. When needed, they install new electrical equipment. When breakdowns occur, they must make the necessary repairs as quickly as possible in order to minimize inconvenience. Electricians may replace items such as circuit breakers, fuses, switches, electrical and electronic components, or wire. When working with complex electronic devices, they may work with engineers, engineering technicians, or industrial machinery installation, repair, and maintenance workers.

Electricians use handtools such as screwdrivers, pliers, knives, hacksaws, and wire strippers. They also use a variety of power tools as well as testing equipment such as oscilloscopes, ammeters, and test lamps.

Working Conditions

Electricians' work is sometimes strenuous. They bend conduit, stand for long periods, and frequently work on ladders and scaffolds. Their working environment varies, depending on the type of job. Some may work in dusty, dirty, hot, or wet conditions, or in confined areas, ditches, or other uncomfortable places. Electricians risk injury from electrical shock, falls, and cuts; to avoid injuries, they must follow strict safety procedures. Some electricians may have to travel great distances to jobsites.

Most electricians work a standard 40-hour week, although overtime may be required. Those in maintenance work may work nights or weekends, and be on call. Maintenance electricians may also have periodic extended overtime during scheduled maintenance or retooling periods. Companies that operate 24 hours a day may employ three shifts of electricians.

Employment

Electricians held about 659,000 jobs in 2002. More than one-quarter of wage and salary workers were employed in the construction industry; while the remainder worked as maintenance electricians employed outside the construction industry. In addition, about one in ten electricians were self-employed.

Because of the widespread need for electrical services, jobs for electricians are found in all parts of the country.

Training, Other Qualifications, and Advancement

Most people learn the electrical trade by completing an apprenticeship program lasting 3 to 5 years. Apprenticeship gives trainees a thorough knowledge of all aspects of the trade and generally improves their ability to find a job. Although electricians are more likely to be trained through apprenticeship than are workers in other construction trades, some still learn their skills informally on the job. Others train to be residential electricians in a 3-year program.

Apprenticeship programs may be sponsored by joint training committees made up of local unions of the International Brotherhood of Electrical Workers and local chapters of the National Electrical Contractors Association; company management committees of individual electrical contracting companies; or local chapters of the Associated Builders and

Contractors and the Independent Electrical Contractors Association. Because of the comprehensive training received, those who complete apprenticeship programs qualify to do both maintenance and construction work.

The typical large apprenticeship program provides at least 144 hours of classroom instruction and 2,000 hours of on-the-job training each year. In the classroom, apprentices learn blueprint reading, electrical theory, electronics, mathematics, electrical code requirements, and safety and first aid practices. They also may receive specialized training in welding, communications, fire alarm systems, and cranes and elevators. On the job, under the supervision of experienced electricians, apprentices must demonstrate mastery of the electrician's work. At first, they drill holes, set anchors, and set up conduit. Later, they measure, fabricate, and install conduit, as well as install, connect, and test wiring, outlets, and switches. They also learn to set up and draw diagrams for entire electrical systems.

After finishing an apprenticeship, journeymen often continue to learn about related electrical systems, such as low voltage voice, data, and video systems. Many builders and owners want to work with only one contractor who can install or repair both regular electrical systems and low voltage systems.

Those who do not enter a formal apprenticeship program can begin to learn the trade informally by working as helpers for experienced electricians. While learning to install conduit, connect wires, and test circuits, helpers also learn safety practices. Many helpers supplement this training with trade school or correspondence courses.

Regardless of how one learns the trade, previous training is very helpful. High school courses in mathematics, electricity, electronics, mechanical drawing, science, and shop provide a good background. Special training offered in the U.S. Armed Forces and by postsecondary technical schools also is beneficial. All applicants should be in good health and have at least average physical strength. Agility and dexterity also are important. Good color vision is needed because workers frequently must identify electrical wires by color.

Most apprenticeship sponsors require applicants for apprentice positions to be at least 18 years old, have a high school diploma or its equivalent, and be able to pass a skills test. For those interested in becoming maintenance electricians, a background in electronics is increasingly important because of the growing use of complex electronic controls on manufacturing equipment.

Most localities require electricians to be licensed. Although licensing requirements vary from area to area, electricians usually must pass an examination that tests their knowledge of electrical theory, the National Electrical Code, and local electric and building codes. Electricians periodically take courses offered by their employer or union to keep abreast of changes in the National Electrical Code, materials, or methods of installation.

Experienced electricians can become supervisors and then superintendents. Those with sufficient capital and management skills may start their own contracting business, although this may require an electrical contractor's license. Many electricians become electrical inspectors.

Job Outlook

Job opportunities for electricians are expected to be good. Numerous openings will arise each year as experienced electricians leave the occupation. In addition, many potential workers may choose not to enter training programs because they prefer work that is less strenuous and has more comfortable working conditions.

Employment of electricians is expected to grow faster than the average for all occupations through the year 2012. As the population and economy grow, more electricians will be needed to install and maintain electrical devices and wiring in homes, factories, offices, and other structures. New technologies also are expected to continue to stimulate the demand for these workers. For example, buildings will be prewired during construction to accommodate use of computers and telecommunications equipment. More factories will be using robots and automated manufacturing systems. Additional jobs will be created by rehabilitation and retrofitting of existing structures.

In addition to jobs created by increased demand for electrical work, many openings will occur each year as electricians transfer to other occupations, retire, or leave the labor force for other reasons. Because the training for this occupation is long and difficult and the earnings are relatively high, a smaller proportion of electricians than of other craftworkers leave the occupation each year. The number of retirements is expected to rise, however, as more electricians reach retirement age.

Employment of construction electricians, like that of many other construction workers, is sensitive to changes in the economy. This results from the limited duration of construction projects and the cyclical nature of the construction industry. During economic downturns, job openings for electricians are reduced as the level of construction activity declines. Apprenticeship opportunities also are less plentiful during these periods.

Although employment of maintenance electricians is steadier than that of construction electricians, those working in the automotive and other manufacturing industries that are sensitive to cyclical swings in the economy may be laid off during recessions. Also, efforts to reduce operating costs and increase productivity through the increased use of contracting out for electrical services may limit opportunities for maintenance electricians in many industries. However, this should be partially offset by increased job opportunities for electricians in electrical contracting firms.

Job opportunities for electricians also vary by area. Employment opportunities follow the movement of people and businesses among states and local areas, and reflect differences in local economic conditions. The number of job opportunities in a given year may fluctuate widely from area to area.

Earnings

In 2002, median hourly earnings of electricians were $19.90. The middle 50 percent earned between $14.95 and $26.50. The lowest 10 percent earned less than $11.81, and the highest 10 percent earned more than $33.21. Median hourly earnings in the industries employing the largest numbers of electricians in 2002 are shown below:

Motor vehicle parts manufacturing	$28.72
Local government	21.15
Building equipment contractors	19.54
Nonresidential building construction	19.36
Employment services	15.46

Depending on experience, apprentices usually start at between 40 and 50 percent of the rate paid to fully trained electricians. As apprentices become more skilled, they receive periodic increases throughout the course of their training. Many employers also provide training opportunities for experienced electricians to improve their skills.

Many construction electricians are members of the International Brotherhood of Electrical Workers. Among unions organizing maintenance electricians are the International Brotherhood of Electrical Workers; the International Union of Electronic, Electrical, Salaried, Machine, and Furniture Workers; the International Association of Machinists and Aerospace Workers; the International Union, United Automobile, Aircraft and Agricultural Implement Workers of America; and the United Steelworkers of America.

Related Occupations

To install and maintain electrical systems, electricians combine manual skill and knowledge of electrical materials and concepts. Workers in other occupations involving similar skills include heating, air-conditioning, and refrigeration mechanics and installers; line installers and repairers; electrical and electronics installers and repairers; electronic home entertainment equipment installers and repairers; and elevator installers and repairers.

Sources of Additional Information

For details about apprenticeships or other work opportunities in this trade, contact the offices of the state employment service, the state apprenticeship agency, local electrical contractors or firms that employ maintenance electricians, or local union-management electrician apprenticeship committees. This information also may be available from local chapters of the Independent Electrical Contractors, Inc.; the National Electrical Contractors Association; the Home Builders Institute; the Associated Builders and Contractors; and the International Brotherhood of Electrical Workers.

For information about union apprenticeship programs, contact:

- National Joint Apprenticeship Training Committee (NJATC), 301 Prince George's Blvd., Upper Marlboro, MD 20774. Internet: http://www.njatc.org

- National Electrical Contractors Association (NECA), 3 Metro Center, Suite 1100, Bethesda, MD 20814. Internet: http://www.necanet.org

- International Brotherhood of Electrical Workers (IBEW), 1125 15th St. NW, Washington, DC 20005. Internet: http://www.ibew.org

For information about independent apprenticeship programs, contact:

- Associated Builders and Contractors, Workforce Development Department, 4250 North Fairfax Dr., 9th Floor, Arlington, VA 22203.

- Independent Electrical Contractors, Inc., 4401 Ford Ave., Suite 1100, Alexandria, VA 22302. Internet: http://www.ieci.org

- National Association of Home Builders, 1201 15th St. NW, Washington, DC 20005. Internet: http://www.nahb.org

- Home Builders Institute, 1201 15th St. NW, Washington, DC 20005. Internet: http://www.hbi.org

There are more than 500 occupations registered by the U.S. Department of Labor's National Apprenticeship system. For more information on the Labor Department's registered apprenticeship system and links to state apprenticeship programs, check their Web site: http://www.doleta.gov.

Emergency Medical Technicians and Paramedics

(O*NET 29-2041.00)

Significant Points

- Job stress is common because hours of work are irregular and workers often must treat patients in life-or-death situations.

- Formal training and certification are required, but state requirements vary.

- Employment is projected to grow faster than average as paid emergency medical technician positions replace unpaid volunteers.

- Competition will be greater for jobs in local fire, police, and rescue squad departments than in private ambulance services; opportunities will be best for those who have advanced certification.

Nature of the Work

People's lives often depend on the quick reaction and competent care of emergency medical technicians (EMTs) and paramedics—EMTs with additional advanced training to perform more difficult prehospital medical procedures. Incidents as varied as automobile accidents, heart attacks, drownings, childbirth, and gunshot wounds all require immediate medical attention. EMTs and paramedics provide this vital attention as they care for and transport the sick or injured to a medical facility.

In an emergency, EMTs and paramedics typically are dispatched to the scene by a 911 operator, and often work with police and fire department personnel.Once they arrive, they determine the nature and extent of the patient's condition while trying to ascertain whether the patient has preexisting medical problems. Following strict rules and guidelines, they give appropriate emergency care and, when necessary, transport the patient. Some paramedics are trained to treat patients with minor injuries on the scene of an accident or at their home without transporting them to a medical facility. Emergency treatment for more complicated problems is carried out under the direction of medical doctors by radio preceding or during transport.

EMTs and paramedics may use special equipment, such as backboards, to immobilize patients before placing them on stretchers and securing them in the ambulance for transport to a medical facility. Usually, one EMT or paramedic drives while the other monitors the patient's vital signs and gives additional care as needed. Some EMTs work as part of the flight crew of helicopters that transport critically ill or injured patients to hospital trauma centers.

At the medical facility, EMTs and paramedics help transfer patients to the emergency department, report their observations and actions to emergency room staff, and may provide additional emergency treatment. After each run, EMTs and paramedics replace used supplies and check equipment. If a transported patient had a contagious disease, EMTs and paramedics decontaminate the interior of the ambulance and report cases to the proper authorities.

Beyond these general duties, the specific responsibilities of EMTs and paramedics depend on their level of qualification and training. To determine this, the National Registry of Emergency Medical Technicians (NREMT) registers emergency medical service (EMS) providers at four levels: First Responder, EMT-Basic, EMT-Intermediate, and EMT-Paramedic. Some states, however, do their own certification and use numeric ratings from 1 to 4 to distinguish levels of proficiency.

The lowest-level workers—First Responders—are trained to provide basic emergency medical care because they tend to be the first persons to arrive at the scene of an incident. Many firefighters, police officers, and other emergency workers have this level of training. The EMT-Basic, also known as EMT-1, represents the first component of the emergency medical technician system. An EMT-1 is trained to care for patients at the scene of an accident and while transporting patients by ambulance to the hospital under medical direction. The EMT-1 has the emergency skills to assess a patient's condition and manage respiratory, cardiac, and trauma emergencies.

The EMT-Intermediate (EMT-2 and EMT-3) has more advanced training that allows the administration of intravenous fluids, the use of manual defibrillators to give lifesaving shocks to a stopped heart, and the application of advanced airway techniques and equipment to assist patients experiencing respiratory emergencies. EMT-Paramedics (EMT-4) provide the most extensive prehospital care. In addition to carrying out the procedures already described, paramedics may administer drugs orally and intravenously, interpret electrocardiograms (EKGs), perform endotracheal intubations, and use monitors and other complex equipment.

Working Conditions

EMTs and paramedics work both indoors and outdoors, in all types of weather. They are required to do considerable kneeling, bending, and heavy lifting. These workers risk noise-induced hearing loss from sirens and back injuries from lifting patients. In addition, EMTs and paramedics may be exposed to diseases such as hepatitis-B and AIDS, as well as violence from drug overdose victims or mentally unstable patients. The work is not only physically strenuous, but also stressful, involving life-or-death situations and suffering patients. Nonetheless, many people find the work exciting and challenging and enjoy the opportunity to help others.

EMTs and paramedics employed by fire departments work about 50 hours a week. Those employed by hospitals frequently work between 45 and 60 hours a week, and those in private ambulance services, between 45 and 50 hours. Some of these workers, especially those in police and fire departments, are on call for extended periods. Because emergency services function 24 hours a day, EMTs and paramedics have irregular working hours that add to job stress.

Employment

EMTs and paramedics held about 179,000 jobs in 2002. Most career EMTs and paramedics work in metropolitan areas. There are many more volunteer EMTs and paramedics, especially in smaller cities, towns, and rural areas. These individuals volunteer for fire departments, emergency medical services (EMS), or hospitals, and may respond to only a few calls for service per month or may answer the majority of calls, especially in smaller communities. EMTs and paramedics work closely with firefighters, who often are certified as EMTs as well and act as first responders.

Full-time and part-time paid EMTs and paramedics were employed in a number of industries. About 4 out of 10 worked as employees of private ambulance services. About 3 out of 10 worked in local government for fire departments, public ambulance services, and EMS. Another 2 out 10 were found in hospitals, working full time within the medical facility or responded to calls in ambulances or helicopters to transport critically ill or injured patients. The remainder worked in various industries providing emergency services.

Training, Other Qualifications, and Advancement

Formal training and certification is needed to become an EMT or paramedic. All 50 states have a certification procedure. In most states and the District of Columbia, registration with the NREMT is required at some or all levels of certification. Other states administer their own certification examination or provide the option of taking the NREMT examination. To maintain certification, EMTs and paramedics must reregister, usually every 2 years. In order to reregister, an individual must be working as an EMT or paramedic and meet a continuing education requirement.

Training is offered at progressive levels: EMT-Basic, also known as EMT-1; EMT-Intermediate, or EMT-2 and EMT-3; and EMT-Paramedic, or EMT-4. EMT-Basic coursework typically emphasizes emergency skills, such as managing respiratory, trauma, and cardiac emergencies, and patient assessment. Formal courses are often combined with time in an emergency room or ambulance. The program also provides instruction and practice in dealing with bleeding, fractures, airway obstruction, cardiac arrest, and emergency childbirth. Students learn how to use and maintain common emergency equipment, such as backboards, suction devices, splints, oxygen delivery systems, and stretchers. Graduates of approved EMT basic training programs who pass a written and practical examination administered by the state certifying agency or the NREMT earn the title "Registered EMT-Basic." The course also is a prerequisite for EMT-Intermediate and EMT-Paramedic training.

EMT-Intermediate training requirements vary from state to state. Applicants can opt to receive training in EMT-Shock Trauma, wherein the caregiver learns to start intravenous fluids and give certain medications, or in EMT-Cardiac, which includes learning heart rhythms and administering advanced medications. Training commonly includes 35 to 55 hours of additional instruction beyond EMT-Basic coursework, and covers patient assessment as well as the use of advanced airway devices and intravenous fluids. Prerequisites for taking the EMT-Intermediate examination include registration as an EMT-Basic, required classroom work, and a specified amount of clinical experience.

The most advanced level of training for this occupation is EMT-Paramedic. At this level, the caregiver receives additional training in body function and learns more advanced skills. The Technology program usually lasts up to 2 years and results in an associate degree in applied science. Such education prepares the graduate to take the NREMT examination and become certified as an EMT-Paramedic. Extensive related coursework and clinical and field experience is required. Due to the longer training requirement, almost all EMT-Paramedics are in paid positions, rather than being volunteers. Refresher courses and continuing education are available for EMTs and paramedics at all levels.

EMTs and paramedics should be emotionally stable, have good dexterity, agility, and physical coordination, and be able to lift and carry heavy loads. They also need good eyesight (corrective lenses may be used) with accurate color vision.

Advancement beyond the EMT-Paramedic level usually means leaving fieldwork. An EMT-Paramedic can become a supervisor, operations manager, administrative director, or executive director of emergency services. Some EMTs and paramedics become instructors, dispatchers, or physician assistants, while others move into sales or marketing of emergency medical equipment. A number of people become EMTs and paramedics to assess their interest in healthcare, and then decide to return to school and become registered nurses, physicians, or other health workers.

Job Outlook

Employment of emergency medical technicians and paramedics is expected to grow faster than the average for all occupations through 2012. Population growth and urbanization will increase the demand for full-time paid EMTs and paramedics rather than for volunteers. In addition, a large segment of the population—the aging baby boomers—will further spur demand for EMT services as they become more likely to have medical emergencies. There will still be demand for part-time, volunteer EMTs and paramedics in rural areas and smaller metropolitan areas. In addition to those arising from job growth, openings will occur because of replacement needs; some workers leave the occupation because of stressful working conditions, limited potential for advancement, and the modest pay and benefits in private-sector jobs.

Most opportunities for EMTs and paramedics are expected to found in private ambulance services. Competition will be greater for jobs in local government, including fire, police, and independent third-service rescue squad departments, in which salaries and benefits tend to be slightly better. Opportunities will be best for those who have advanced certifications, such as EMT-Intermediate and EMT-Paramedic, as clients and patients demand higher levels of care before arriving at the hospital.

Earnings

Earnings of EMTs and paramedics depend on the employment setting and geographic location as well as the individual's training and experience. Median annual earnings of EMTs and paramedics were $24,030 in 2002. The middle 50 percent earned between $19,040 and $31,600. The lowest 10 percent earned less than $15,530, and the highest 10 percent earned more than $41,980. Median annual earnings in the industries employing the largest numbers of EMTs and paramedics in 2002 were:

Local government $27,440
General medical and surgical hospitals..................24,760
Other ambulatory health care services 22,180

Those in emergency medical services who are part of fire or police departments receive the same benefits as firefighters or police officers. For example, many are covered by pension plans that provide retirement at half pay after 20 or 25 years of service or if the worker is disabled in the line of duty.

Related Occupations

Other workers in occupations that require quick and level-headed reactions to life-or-death situations are air traffic controllers, firefighting occupations, physician assistants, police and detectives, and registered nurses.

Sources of Additional Information

General information about emergency medical technicians and paramedics is available from:

- National Association of Emergency Medical Technicians, P.O. Box 1400, Clinton, MS 39060-1400. Internet: http://www.naemt.org

- National Registry of Emergency Medical Technicians, Rocco V. Morando Bldg., 6610 Busch Blvd., P.O. Box 29233, Columbus, OH 43229. Internet: http://www.nremt.org

- National Highway Transportation Safety Administration, EMS Division, 400 7th St. SW, NTS-14, Washington, DC 20590. Internet: http://www.nhtsa.dot.gov/people/injury/ems

Environmental Engineers

(O*NET 17-2081.00)

Significant Points

- Overall, job opportunities in engineering are expected to be good, but will vary by specialty.

- A bachelor's degree is required for most entry-level jobs.

- Starting salaries are significantly higher than those of college graduates in other fields.

- Continuing education is critical to keep abreast of the latest technology.

Nature of the Work

Using the principles of biology and chemistry, environmental engineers develop solutions to environmental problems. They are involved in water and air pollution control, recycling, waste disposal, and public health issues. Environmental engineers conduct hazardous-waste management studies in which they evaluate the significance of the hazard, offer analysis on treatment and containment, and develop regulations to prevent mishaps. They design municipal water supply and industrial wastewater treatment systems. They

conduct research on proposed environmental projects, analyze scientific data, and perform quality control checks.

Environmental engineers are concerned with local and worldwide environmental issues. They study and attempt to minimize the effects of acid rain, global warming, automobile emissions, and ozone depletion. They also are involved in the protection of wildlife.

Many environmental engineers work as consultants, helping their clients to comply with regulations and to clean up hazardous sites.

Working Conditions

Most engineers work in office buildings, laboratories, or industrial plants. Others may spend time outdoors at construction sites and oil and gas exploration and production sites, where they monitor or direct operations or solve onsite problems. Some engineers travel extensively to plants or worksites.

Many engineers work a standard 40-hour week. At times, deadlines or design standards may bring extra pressure to a job, sometimes requiring engineers to work longer hours.

Employment

Environmental engineers held about 47,000 jobs in 2002. Almost half worked in professional, scientific, and technical services and about 15,000 were employed in federal, state, and local government agencies. Most of the rest worked in various manufacturing industries.

Training, Other Qualifications, and Advancement

A bachelor's degree in engineering is required for almost all entry-level engineering jobs. College graduates with a degree in a physical science or mathematics occasionally may qualify for some engineering jobs, especially in specialties in high demand. Most engineering degrees are granted in electrical, electronics, mechanical, or civil engineering. However, engineers trained in one branch may work in related branches. This flexibility allows employers to meet staffing needs in new technologies and specialties in which engineers may be in short supply. It also allows engineers to shift to fields with better employment prospects or to those that more closely match their interests.

Most engineering programs involve a concentration of study in an engineering specialty, along with courses in both mathematics and science. Most programs include a design course, sometimes accompanied by a computer or laboratory class or both.

In addition to the standard engineering degree, many colleges offer 2- or 4-year degree programs in engineering technology. These programs, which usually include various hands-on laboratory classes that focus on current issues, prepare students for practical design and production work rather than for jobs that require more theoretical and scientific knowledge. Graduates of 4-year technology programs may get jobs similar to those obtained by graduates with a bachelor's degree in engineering. Engineering technology graduates, however, are not qualified to register as professional engineers under the same terms as graduates with degrees in engineering. Some employers regard technology program graduates as having skills between those of a technician and an engineer.

Graduate training is essential for engineering faculty positions and many research and development programs, but is not required for the majority of entry-level engineering jobs. Many engineers obtain graduate degrees in engineering or business administration to learn new technology and broaden their education. Many high-level executives in government and industry began their careers as engineers.

About 340 colleges and universities offer bachelor's degree programs in engineering that are accredited by the Accreditation Board for Engineering and Technology (ABET), and about 240 colleges offer accredited bachelor's degree programs in engineering technology. ABET accreditation is based on an examination of an engineering program's student achievement, program improvement, faculty, curricular content, facilities, and institutional commitment. Although most institutions offer programs in the major branches of engineering, only a few offer programs in the smaller specialties. Also, programs of the same title may vary in content. For example, some programs emphasize industrial practices, preparing students for a job in industry, whereas others are more theoretical and are designed to prepare students for graduate work. Therefore, students should investigate curricula and check accreditations carefully before selecting a college.

Admissions requirements for undergraduate engineering schools include a solid background in mathematics (algebra, geometry, trigonometry, and calculus) and science (biology, chemistry, and physics), and courses in English, social studies, humanities, and computer and information technology. Bachelor's degree programs in engineering typically are designed to last 4 years, but many students find that it takes between 4 and 5 years to complete their studies. In a typical 4-year college curriculum, the first 2 years are spent studying mathematics, basic sciences, introductory engineering, humanities, and social sciences. In the last 2 years, most courses are in engineering, usually with a concentration in one branch. Some programs offer a general engineering curriculum; students then specialize in graduate school or on the job.

Some engineering schools and 2-year colleges have agreements whereby the 2-year college provides the initial engineering education, and the engineering school automatically admits students for their last 2 years. In addition, a few engineering schools have arrangements whereby a student spends 3 years in a liberal arts college studying pre-engineering subjects and 2 years in an engineering school studying core subjects, and then receives a bachelor's degree from each school. Some colleges and universities offer 5-year master's degree programs. Some 5-year or even 6-year cooperative plans combine classroom study and practical work, permitting students to gain valuable experience and to finance part of their education.

All 50 states and the District of Columbia require licensure for engineers who offer their services directly to the public. Engineers who are licensed are called Professional Engineers (PE). This licensure generally requires a degree from an ABET-accredited engineering program, 4 years of relevant work experience, and successful completion of a state examination. Recent graduates can start the licensing process by taking the examination in two stages. The initial Fundamentals of Engineering (FE) examination can be taken upon graduation. Engineers who pass this examination commonly are called Engineers in Training (EIT) or Engineer Interns (EI). After acquiring suitable work experience, EITs can take the second examination, the Principles and Practice of Engineering exam. Several states have imposed mandatory continuing education requirements for relicensure. Most states recognize licensure from other states provided that the manner in which the initial license was obtained meets or exceeds their licensure requirements.

Engineers should be creative, inquisitive, analytical, and detail-oriented. They should be able to work as part of a team and to communicate well, both orally and in writing. Communication abilities are important because engineers often interact with specialists in a wide range of fields outside engineering.

Beginning engineering graduates usually work under the supervision of experienced engineers and, in large companies, also may receive formal classroom or seminar-type training. As new engineers gain knowledge and experience, they are assigned more difficult projects with greater independence to develop designs, solve problems, and make decisions. Engineers may advance to become technical specialists or to supervise a staff or team of engineers and technicians. Some may eventually become engineering managers or enter other managerial or sales jobs.

Job Outlook

Environmental engineering graduates should have favorable job opportunities. Employment of environmental engineers is expected to increase much faster than the average for all occupations through 2012. Much of the expected growth will be due to the emergence of this occupation as a widely recognized engineering specialty rather than as an area that other engineering specialties, such as civil engineers, specialize in. More environmental engineers will be needed to comply with environmental regulations and to develop methods of cleaning up existing hazards. A shift in emphasis toward preventing problems rather than controlling those that already exist, as well as increasing public health concerns, also will spur demand for environmental engineers. However, political factors determine the job outlook for environmental engineers more than that for other engineers. Looser environmental regulations would reduce job opportunities; stricter regulations would enhance opportunities.

Even though employment of environmental engineers should be less affected by economic conditions than that of most other types of engineers, a significant economic downturn could reduce the emphasis on environmental protection, reducing employment opportunities. Environmental engineers need to keep abreast of a range of environmental issues to ensure their steady employment because their area of focus may change frequently—for example, from hazardous waste cleanup to the prevention of water pollution.

Earnings

Median annual earnings of environmental engineers were $61,410 in 2002. The middle 50 percent earned between $47,650 and $77,360. The lowest 10 percent earned less than $38,640, and the highest 10 percent earned more than $91,510. Median annual earnings in the industries employing the largest numbers of environmental engineers in 2002 were:

Architectural, engineering, and related services	$58,620
Management, scientific, and technical consulting services	57,800
State government	54,160

According to a 2003 salary survey by the National Association of Colleges and Employers, bachelor's degree candidates in environmental/environmental health engineering received starting offers averaging $44,702 a year.

Related Occupations

Environmental engineers apply the principles of physical science and mathematics in their work. Other workers who use scientific and mathematical principles include architects, except landscape and naval; engineering and natural sciences managers; computer and information systems managers; mathematicians; drafters; engineering technicians; sales engineers; science technicians; and physical and life scientists, including agricultural and food scientists, biological scientists, conservation scientists and foresters, atmospheric scientists, chemists and materials scientists, environmental scientists and geoscientists, and physicists and astronomers.

Sources of Additional Information

Further information about environmental engineering careers, training, and certification can be obtained from:

● American Academy of Environmental Engineers, 130 Holiday Court, Suite 100, Annapolis, MD 21401. Internet: http://www.aaee.net

Financial Analysts and Personal Financial Advisors

(O*NET 13-2051.00 and 13-2052.00)

Significant Points

● A college degree and good interpersonal skills are among the most important qualifications for these workers.

● Although both occupations will benefit from an increase in investing by individuals, personal financial advisors will benefit more.

● Financial analysts will face keen competition for jobs, especially at top securities firms, where pay can be lucrative.

Nature of the Work

Financial analysts and personal financial advisors provide analysis and guidance to businesses and individuals to help them with their investment decisions. Both types of specialist gather financial information, analyze it, and make recommendations to their clients. However, their job duties differ because of the type of investment information they provide and the clients they work for. *Financial analysts* assess the economic performance of companies and industries for firms and institutions with money to invest. *Personal financial advisors* generally assess the financial needs of individuals, providing them a wide range of options.

Financial analysts, also called *securities analysts* and *investment analysts*, work for banks, insurance companies, mutual and pension funds, securities firms, and other businesses, helping these companies or their clients make investment decisions. Financial analysts read company financial statements and analyze commodity prices, sales, costs, expenses, and tax rates in order to determine a company's value and project future earnings. They often meet with company officials to gain a better insight into a company's prospects and to determine the company's managerial effectiveness. Usually, financial analysts study an entire industry, assessing current trends in business practices, products, and industry competition. They must keep abreast of new regulations or policies that may affect the industry, as well as monitor the economy to determine its effect on earnings.

Financial analysts use spreadsheet and statistical software packages to analyze financial data, spot trends, and develop forecasts. On the basis of their results, they write reports and make presentations, usually making recommendations to buy or sell a particular investment or security. Senior analysts may actually make the decision to buy or sell for the company or client if they are the ones responsible for managing the assets. Other analysts use the data to measure the financial risks associated with making a particular investment decision.

Financial analysts in investment banking departments of securities or banking firms often work in teams, analyzing the future prospects of companies that want to sell shares to the public for the first time. They also ensure that the forms and written materials necessary for compliance with Securities and Exchange Commission regulations are accurate and complete. They may make presentations to prospective investors about the merits of investing in the new company. Financial analysts also work in mergers and acquisitions departments, preparing analyses on the costs and benefits of a proposed merger or takeover.

Some financial analysts, called *ratings analysts*, evaluate the ability of companies or governments that issue bonds to repay their debt. On the basis of their evaluation, a management team assigns a rating to a company's or government's bonds. Other financial analysts perform budget, cost, and credit analysis as part of their responsibilities.

Personal financial advisors, also called *financial planners* or *financial consultants*, use their knowledge of investments, tax laws, and insurance to recommend financial options to individuals in accordance with their short-term and long-term goals. Some of the issues that planners address are retirement and estate planning, funding for college, and general investment options. While most planners offer advice on a wide range of topics, some specialize in areas such as retirement and estate planning or risk management.

An advisor's work begins with a consultation with the client, from whom the advisor obtains information on the client's finances and financial goals. The advisor then develops a comprehensive financial plan that identifies problem areas, makes recommendations for improvement, and selects appropriate investments compatible with the client's goals, attitude toward risk, and expectation or need for a return on the investment. Sometimes this plan is written, but, more often, it is in the form of verbal advice. Financial advisors usually meet with established clients at least once a year to update them on potential investments and to determine whether the clients have been through any life changes— such as marriage, disability, or retirement—that might affect their financial goals. Financial advisors also answer questions from clients regarding changes in benefit plans or the consequences of a change in their job or career.

Some advisors buy and sell financial products, such as mutual funds or insurance, or refer clients to other companies for products and services—for example, the preparation of taxes or wills. A number of advisors take on the responsibility of managing the clients' investments for them.

Finding clients and building a customer base is one of the most important parts of a financial advisor's job. Referrals from satisfied clients are an important source of new business. Many advisors also contact potential clients by giving seminars or lectures or meet clients through business and social contacts.

Working Conditions

Financial analysts and personal financial advisors usually work indoors in safe, comfortable offices or their own homes. Many of these workers enjoy the challenge of helping firms or people make financial decisions. However, financial analysts may face long hours, frequent travel to visit companies and talk to potential investors, and the pressure of deadlines. Much of their research must be done after office hours, because their day is filled with telephone calls and meetings. Personal financial advisors usually work standard business hours, but they also schedule meetings with clients in the evenings or on weekends. Many teach evening classes or hold seminars in order to bring in more clients.

Employment

Financial analysts and personal financial advisors held 298,000 jobs in 2002; financial analysts accounted for almost 6 in 10 of the total. Many financial analysts work at the headquarters of large financial companies, several of which are based in New York City. Nineteen percent of financial analysts work for securities and commodity brokers, exchanges, and investment services firms; and 17 percent work for depository and nondepository institutions, including banks, savings institutions, and mortgage bankers and brokers. The remainder work primarily for insurance carriers; accounting, tax preparation, bookkeeping, and payroll services; management, scientific, and technical consulting services; and state and local government agencies.

Approximately 38 percent of personal financial advisors are self-employed, operating small investment advisory firms, usually in urban areas. About 31 percent of personal financial advisors are employed by securities and commodity brokers, exchanges, and investment services firms. Another 14 percent are employed by depository and nondepository institutions, including banks, savings institutions, and credit unions. A small number work for insurance carriers and insurance agents, brokers, and services.

Training, Other Qualifications, and Advancement

A college education is required for financial analysts and is strongly preferred for personal financial advisors. Most companies require financial analysts to have at least a bachelor's degree in business administration, accounting, statistics, or finance. Coursework in statistics, economics, and business is required, and knowledge of accounting policies and procedures, corporate budgeting, and financial analysis methods is recommended. A master of business administration is desirable. Advanced courses in options pricing or bond valuation and knowledge of risk management also are suggested.

Employers usually do not require a specific field of study for personal financial advisors, but a bachelor's degree in accounting, finance, economics, business, mathematics, or law provides good preparation for the occupation. Courses in investments, taxes, estate planning, and risk management also are helpful. Programs in financial planning are becoming more widely available in colleges and universities. However, many financial planners enter the field after working in a related occupation, such as accountant, auditor, insurance sales agent, lawyer, or securities, commodities, and financial services sales agent.

Mathematical, computer, analytical, and problem-solving skills are essential qualifications for financial analysts and personal financial advisors. Good communication skills also are necessary, because these workers must present complex financial concepts and strategies in easy-to-understand language to clients and other professionals. Self-confidence, maturity, and the ability to work independently are important as well.

Financial analysts must be detail oriented, motivated to seek out obscure information, and familiar with the workings of the economy, tax laws, and money markets. Strong interpersonal skills and sales ability are crucial to the success of both financial analysts and personal financial advisors.

Although not required for financial analysts or personal financial advisors to practice, certification can enhance one's professional standing and is strongly recommended by many financial companies. Financial analysts may receive the title Chartered Financial Analyst (CFA), sponsored by the Association of Investment Management and Research. To qualify for CFA designation, applicants must hold a bachelor's degree, must have 3 years of work experience in a related field, and must pass a series of three examinations. The essay exams, administered once a year for 3 years, cover subjects such as accounting, economics, securities analysis, asset valuation, and portfolio management.

Personal financial advisors may obtain the Certified Financial Planner credential, often referred to as CFP (R), demonstrating to potential customers that a planner has extensive training and competency in the area of financial planning. The CFP (R) certification, issued by the Certified Financial Planner Board of Standards, Inc., requires relevant experience, the completion of education requirements, the passage of a comprehensive examination, and adherence to an enforceable code of ethics. Personal financial advisors may also obtain the Chartered Financial Consultant (ChFC) designation, issued by the American College in Bryn Mawr, Pennsylvania, which requires experience and the completion of an eight-course program of study. Both designations have a continuing education requirement.

A license is not required to work as a personal financial advisor, but advisors who sell stocks, bonds, mutual funds, insurance, or real estate may need licenses to perform these additional services. Also, if legal advice is provided, a license to practice law may be required. Financial advisors who do not provide these additional services often refer clients to those qualified to provide them.

Financial analysts may advance by becoming portfolio managers or financial managers, directing the investment portfolios of their companies or of clients. Personal financial advisors who work in firms also may move into managerial positions, but most advisors advance by accumulating clients and managing more assets.

Job Outlook

Increased investment by businesses and individuals is expected to result in faster-than-average employment growth of financial analysts and personal financial advisors through 2012. Both occupations will benefit as baby boomers save for retirement and as a generally better educated and wealthier population requires investment advice. In addition, people are living longer and must plan to finance more years of retirement. The globalization of the securities markets will increase the need for analysts and advisors to help investors make financial choices.

Deregulation of the financial services industry is also expected to spur demand for financial analysts and personal financial advisors. Since 1999, banks, insurance companies, and brokerage firms have been allowed to broaden their financial services. Many firms are adding investment advice to their list of services and are expected to increase their hiring of personal financial advisors. Numerous banks are now entering the securities brokerage and investment banking fields and will increasingly need the skills of financial analysts in these areas.

Employment of personal financial advisors is expected to grow faster than the average for all occupations through the year 2012. The rapid expansion of self-directed retirement plans, such as 401(k) plans, is expected to continue. As the number and complexity of investments rises, more individuals will look to financial advisors to help manage their money. Financial advisors who have either the CFP (R) certification or ChFC designation are expected to have the best opportunities.

Employment of financial analysts is expected to grow about as fast as the average for all occupations through the year 2012. As the number of mutual funds and the amount of assets invested in the funds increase, mutual-fund companies will need increased numbers of financial analysts to recommend which financial products the funds should buy or sell.

Financial analysts also will be needed in the investment banking field, where they help companies raise money and work on corporate mergers and acquisitions. However, growth in demand for financial analysts to do company research will be constrained by the implementation of reform proposals calling for investment firms to subsidize independent research boutiques and separate research from investment banking. Firms may try to contain the costs of reform by eliminating research jobs.

Demand for financial analysts in investment banking fluctuates because investment banking is sensitive to changes in the stock market. In addition, further consolidation in the financial services industry may eliminate some financial analyst positions, dampening overall employment growth somewhat. Competition is expected to be keen for these highly lucrative positions, with many more applicants than jobs.

Earnings

Median annual earnings of financial analysts were $57,100 in 2002. The middle 50 percent earned between $43,660 and $76,620. The lowest 10 percent earned less than $34,570, and the highest 10 percent earned more than $108,060. Median annual earnings in the industries employing the largest numbers of financial analysts in 2002 were as follows:

Other financial investment activities	$74,860
Management of companies and enterprises	60,670
Securities and commodity contracts intermediation and brokerage	58,540
Nondepository credit intermediation	51,700
Depository credit intermediation	51,570

Median annual earnings of personal financial advisors were $56,680 in 2002. The middle 50 percent earned between $36,180 and $100,540. Median annual earnings in the industries employing the largest number of personal financial advisors in 2002 were as follows:

Other financial investment activities	$74,260
Securities and commodity contracts intermediation and brokerage	68,110
Depository credit intermediation	51,030

Many financial analysts receive a bonus in addition to their salary, and the bonus can add substantially to their earnings. Usually, the bonus is based on how well their predictions compare to the actual performance of a benchmark investment. Personal financial advisors who work for financial services firms are generally paid a salary plus bonus. Advisors who work for financial-planning firms or who are self-employed either charge hourly fees for their services or charge one set fee for a comprehensive plan, based on its complexity. Advisors who manage a client's assets usually charge a percentage of those assets. A majority of advisors receive commissions for financial products they sell, in addition to charging a fee.

Related Occupations

Other jobs requiring expertise in finance and investment or in the sales of financial products include accountants and auditors; financial managers; insurance sales agents; real estate brokers and sales agents; and securities, commodities, and financial services sales representatives.

Sources of Additional Information

For information on a career in financial planning, contact:

- The Financial Planning Association, 4100 E. Mississippi Ave., Denver, CO 80246-3053. Internet: http://www.fpanet.org

For information about the Certified Financial Planner, CFP (R), certification, contact:

- Certified Financial Planner Board of Standards, Inc., 1670 Broadway, Suite 600, Denver, CO 80202-4809. Internet: http://www.cfp.net/become

For information about the Chartered Financial Consultant (ChFC) designation, contact:

- The American College, 270 South Bryn Mawr Ave., Bryn Mawr, PA 19010. Internet: http://www.amercoll.edu

For information on a career as a financial analyst, contact:

- American Academy of Financial Management, 102 Beverly Dr., Metairie, LA 70001. Internet: http://www.financialanalyst.org
- Association of Investment Management and Research, P.O. Box 3668, 560 Ray C. Hunt Dr., Charlottesville, VA 22903. Internet: http://www.aimr.org

Financial Managers

(O*NET 11-3031.01 and 11-3031.02)

Significant Points

- A bachelor's degree in finance, accounting, or a related field is the minimum academic preparation, but many employers increasingly seek graduates with a master's degree.

- Employment will grow as the economy expands and increases the need for workers with financial expertise.

Nature of the Work

Almost every firm, government agency, and organization has one or more financial managers who oversee the preparation of financial reports, direct investment activities, and implement cash management strategies. As computers are increasingly used to record and organize data, many financial managers are spending more time developing strategies and implementing the long-term goals of their organization.

The duties of financial managers vary with their specific titles, which include controller, treasurer or finance officer, credit manager, cash manager, and risk and insurance manager. *Controllers* direct the preparation of financial reports that summarize and forecast the organization's financial position, such as income statements, balance sheets, and analyses of future earnings or expenses. Controllers also are in charge of preparing special reports required by regulatory authorities. Often, controllers oversee the accounting, audit, and budget departments. *Treasurers* and *finance officers* direct the organization's financial goals, objectives, and budgets. They oversee the investment of funds and manage associated risks, supervise cash management activities, execute capital-raising strategies to support a firm's expansion, and deal with mergers and acquisitions. *Credit managers* oversee the firm's issuance of credit. They establish credit-rating criteria, determine credit ceilings, and monitor the collections of past-due accounts. Managers specializing in international finance develop financial and accounting systems for the banking transactions of multinational organizations.

Cash managers monitor and control the flow of cash receipts and disbursements to meet the business and investment needs of the firm. For example, cashflow projections are needed to determine whether loans must be obtained to meet cash requirements or whether surplus cash should be invested in interest-bearing instruments. *Risk and insurance managers* oversee programs to minimize risks and losses that might arise from financial transactions and business operations undertaken by the institution. They also manage the organization's insurance budget.

Financial institutions, such as commercial banks, savings and loan associations, credit unions, and mortgage and finance companies, employ additional financial managers who oversee various functions, such as lending, trusts, mortgages, and investments, or programs, including sales, operations, or electronic financial services. These managers may be required to solicit business, authorize loans, and direct the investment of funds, always adhering to federal and state laws and regulations

Branch managers of financial institutions administer and manage all of the functions of a branch office, which may include hiring personnel, approving loans and lines of credit, establishing a rapport with the community to attract business, and assisting customers with account problems. Financial managers who work for financial institutions must keep abreast of the rapidly growing array of financial services and products.

In addition to the general duties described above, all financial managers perform tasks unique to their organization or industry. For example, government financial managers must be experts on the government appropriations and budgeting processes, whereas healthcare financial managers must be knowledgeable about issues surrounding healthcare financing. Moreover, financial managers must be aware of special tax laws and regulations that affect their industry.

Financial managers play an increasingly important role in mergers and consolidations, and in global expansion and related financing. These areas require extensive, specialized knowledge on the part of the financial manager to reduce risks and maximize profit. Financial managers increasingly are hired on a temporary basis to advise senior managers on these and other matters. In fact, some small firms contract out all accounting and financial functions to companies that provide these services.

The role of the financial manager, particularly in business, is changing in response to technological advances that have significantly reduced the amount of time it takes to produce financial reports. Financial managers now perform more data analysis and use it to offer senior managers ideas on how to maximize profits. They often work on teams, acting as business advisors to top management. Financial managers need to keep abreast of the latest computer technology in order to increase the efficiency of their firm's financial operations.

Working Conditions

Financial managers work in comfortable offices, often close to top managers and to departments that develop the financial data these managers need. They typically have direct access to state-of-the-art computer systems and information services. Financial managers commonly work long hours, often up to 50 or 60 per week. They generally are required to attend meetings of financial and economic associations and may travel to visit subsidiary firms or to meet customers.

Employment

Financial managers held about 599,000 jobs in 2002. While the vast majority is employed in private industry, nearly 1 in 10 work for the different branches of government. In addition, although they can be found in every industry, approximately 1 out of 4 are employed by insurance and finance establishments, such as banks, savings institutions, finance companies, credit unions, and securities dealers.

Training, Other Qualifications, and Advancement

A bachelor's degree in finance, accounting, economics, or business administration is the minimum academic preparation for financial managers. However, many employers now seek graduates with a master's degree, preferably in business administration, economics, finance, or risk management. These academic programs develop analytical skills and provide knowledge of the latest financial analysis methods and technology.

Experience may be more important than formal education for some financial manager positions—notably, branch managers in banks. Banks typically fill branch manager positions by promoting experienced loan officers and other professionals who excel at their jobs. Other financial managers may enter the profession through formal management training programs offered by the company.

Continuing education is vital for financial managers, who must cope with the growing complexity of global trade, changes in federal and state laws and regulations, and the proliferation of new and complex financial instruments. Firms often provide opportunities for workers to broaden their knowledge and skills by encouraging employees to take graduate courses at colleges and universities or attend conferences related to their specialty. Financial management, banking, and credit union associations, often in cooperation with colleges and universities, sponsor numerous national and local training programs. Persons enrolled prepare extensively at home and then attend sessions on subjects such as accounting management, budget management, corporate cash management, financial analysis, international banking, and information systems. Many firms pay all or part of the costs for employees who successfully complete courses. Although experience, ability, and leadership are emphasized for promotion, advancement may be accelerated by this type of special study.

In some cases, financial managers also may broaden their skills and exhibit their competency by attaining professional certification. There are many different associations that offer professional certification programs. For example, the Association for Investment Management and Research confers the Chartered Financial Analyst designation on investment professionals who have a bachelor's degree, pass three sequential examinations, and meet work experience requirements. The Association for Financial Professionals (AFP) confers the Certified Cash Manager credential to those who pass a computer-based exam and have a minimum of 2 years of relevant experience. The Institute of Management Accountants offers a Certified in Financial Management designation to members with a BA and at least 2 years of work experience who pass the institute's four-part examination and fulfill continuing education requirements. Also, financial managers who specialize in accounting may earn the Certified Public Accountant (CPA) or Certified Management Accountant (CMA) designations.

Candidates for financial management positions need a broad range of skills. Interpersonal skills are important because these jobs involve managing people and working as part of a team to solve problems. Financial managers must have excellent communication skills to explain complex financial data. Because financial managers work extensively with various departments in their firm, a broad overview of the business is essential.

Financial managers should be creative thinkers and problem-solvers, applying their analytical skills to business. They must be comfortable with the latest computer technology. As financial operations increasingly are affected by the global economy, financial managers must have knowledge of international finance. Proficiency in a foreign language also may be important.

Because financial management is critical for efficient business operations, well-trained, experienced financial managers who display a strong grasp of the operations of various departments within their organization are prime candidates for promotion to top management positions. Some financial managers transfer to closely related positions in other industries. Those with extensive experience and access to sufficient capital may start their own consulting firms.

Job Outlook

Employment of financial managers is expected to grow about as fast as the average for all occupations through 2012. Growth is expected to be steady and will increase in line with the growth of the economy as a whole. However, jobseekers are likely to face keen competition for jobs, as the number of job openings is expected to be less than the number of applicants. Candidates with expertise in accounting and finance, particularly those with a master's degree, should enjoy the best job prospects. Strong computer skills and knowledge of international finance are important; so are excellent communication skills, because financial management jobs involve working on strategic planning teams.

As the economy expands, job growth for financial managers will stem from both the expansion of established companies and from the creation of new businesses. Over the short term, employment in this occupation is negatively impacted by economic downturns, during which companies are more likely to close departments, or even go out of business—decreasing the need for financial managers. Mergers, acquisitions, and corporate downsizing also are likely to adversely affect employment of financial managers. However, the growing need for financial expertise as the economy expands will ensure job growth over the next decade.

The banking industry, which employs more than 1 out of 10 financial managers, will continue to consolidate, although at a slower rate than in previous years. In spite of this trend, employment of bank branch managers is expected to increase as banks begin to refocus on the importance of their existing branches and as new branches are created to service a growing population. As banks expand the range of products and services they offer to include insurance and investment products, branch managers with knowledge in these areas will be needed. As a result, candidates who are licensed to sell insurance or securities will have the most favorable prospects.

Despite the current downturn in the securities and commodities industry, the long-run prospects for financial managers in that industry should be favorable, as more will be needed to handle increasingly complex financial transactions and manage a growing amount of investments. Financial managers also will be needed to handle mergers and acquisitions, raise capital, and assess global financial transactions. Risk managers, who assess risks for insurance and investment purposes, also will be in demand.

Some companies may hire financial managers on a temporary basis, to see the organization through a short-term crisis or to offer suggestions for boosting profits. Other companies may contract out all accounting and financial operations. Even in these cases, however, financial managers may be needed to oversee the contracts.

Computer technology has reduced the time and staff required to produce financial reports. As a result, forecasting earnings, profits, and costs, and generating ideas and creative ways to increase profitability will become a major role of corporate financial managers over the next decade. Financial managers who are familiar with computer software that can assist them in this role will be needed.

Earnings

Median annual earnings of financial managers were $73,340 in 2002. The middle 50 percent earned between $52,490 and $100,660. The lowest 10 percent had earnings of less than $39,120, while the top 10 percent earned over $142,260. Median annual earnings in the industries employing the largest numbers of financial managers in 2002 were as follows:

Securities and commodity contracts intermediation and brokerage	$125,220
Management of companies and enterprises	88,310
Nondepository credit intermediation	78,400
Local government	63,090
Depository credit intermediation	58,790

According to a 2002 survey by Robert Half International, a staffing services firm specializing in accounting and finance professionals, directors of finance earned between $75,000 and $204,500, and corporate controllers earned between $54,000 and $138,750.

The Association for Financial Professionals' 14th annual compensation survey showed that financial officers' average total compensation in 2002, including bonuses and deferred compensation, was $130,900. Selected financial manager positions had average total compensation as follows:

Vice president of finance	$183,500
Treasurer	150,600
Assistant vice president-finance	141,300
Controller/comptroller	134,300
Director	113,600
Assistant treasurer	111,900
Assistant controller/comptroller	115,500
Manager	84,500
Cash manager	64,700

Large organizations often pay more than small ones, and salary levels also can depend on the type of industry and location. Many financial managers in both public and private industry receive additional compensation in the form of bonuses, which also vary substantially by size of firm. Deferred compensation in the form of stock options is becoming more common, especially for senior level executives.

Related Occupations

Financial managers combine formal education with experience in one or more areas of finance, such as asset management, lending, credit operations, securities investment, or insurance risk and loss control. Workers in other occupations requiring similar training and skills include accountants and auditors; budget analysts; financial analysts and personal financial advisors; insurance underwriters; loan counselors and officers; securities, commodities, and financial services sales agents; and real estate brokers and sales agents.

Sources of Additional Information

For information about careers and certification in financial management, contact:

- Financial Management Association International, College of Business Administration, University of South Florida, Tampa, FL 33620-5500. Internet: http://www.fma.org

For information about careers in financial and treasury management and the Certified Cash Manager program, contact:

- Association for Financial Professionals, 7315 Wisconsin Ave., Suite 600 West, Bethesda, MD 20814. Internet: http://www.afponline.org

For information about the Chartered Financial Analyst program, contact:

- Association for Investment Management and Research, P.O. Box 3668, 560 Ray Hunt Dr., Charlottesville, VA 22903-0668. Internet: http://www.aimr.org

For information about the Certified in Financial Management designation, contact:

- Institute of Management Accountants, 10 Paragon Drive, Montvale, NJ, 07645-1759. Internet: http://www.imanet.org/

Firefighting Occupations

(O*NET 33-1021.01, 33-1021.02, 33-2011.01, 33-2011.02, 33-2021.01, 33-2021.02, and 33-2022.00)

Significant Points

- Firefighting involves hazardous conditions and long, irregular hours.
- About 9 out of 10 firefighting workers were employed by municipal or county fire departments.
- Applicants for municipal firefighting jobs generally must pass written, physical, and medical examinations.
- Keen competition for jobs is expected.

Nature of the Work

Every year, fires and other emergencies take thousands of lives and destroy property worth billions of dollars. Firefighters help protect the public against these dangers by rapidly responding to a variety of emergencies. They are frequently the first emergency personnel at the scene of a traffic accident or medical emergency and may be called upon to put out a fire, treat injuries, or perform other vital functions.

During duty hours, firefighters must be prepared to respond immediately to a fire or any other emergency that arises. Because fighting fires is dangerous and complex, it requires organization and teamwork. At every emergency scene, firefighters perform specific duties assigned by a superior officer. At fires, they connect hose lines to hydrants, operate a pump to send water to high pressure hoses, and position ladders to enable them to deliver water to the fire. They also rescue victims and provide emergency medical attention as needed, ventilate smoke-filled areas, and attempt to salvage the contents of buildings. Their duties may change several times while the company is in action. Sometimes they remain at the site of a disaster for days at a time, rescuing trapped survivors and assisting with medical treatment.

Firefighters have assumed a range of responsibilities, including emergency medical services. In fact, most calls to which firefighters respond involve medical emergencies, and about half of all fire departments provide ambulance service for victims. Firefighters receive training in emergency medical procedures, and many fire departments require them to be certified as emergency medical technicians.

Firefighters work in a variety of settings, including urban and suburban areas, airports, chemical plants, other industrial sites, and rural areas like grasslands and forests. In addition, some firefighters work in hazardous materials units that are trained for the control, prevention, and cleanup of oil spills and other hazardous materials incidents. Workers in urban and suburban areas, airports, and industrial sites typically use conventional firefighting equipment and tactics, while forest fires and major hazardous materials spills call for different methods.

In national forests and parks, *forest fire inspectors and prevention specialists* spot fires from watchtowers and report their findings to headquarters by telephone or radio. Forest rangers patrol to ensure travelers and campers comply with fire regulations. When fires break out, crews of firefighters are brought in to suppress the blaze using heavy equipment, handtools, and water hoses. Forest firefighting, like urban firefighting, can be rigorous work. One of the most effective means of battling the blaze is by creating fire lines through cutting down trees and digging out grass and all other combustible vegetation, creating bare land in the path of the fire that deprives it of fuel. Elite firefighters, called smoke jumpers, parachute from airplanes to reach otherwise inaccessible areas. This can be extremely hazardous because the crews have no way to escape if the wind shifts and causes the fire to burn toward them.

Between alarms, firefighters clean and maintain equipment, conduct practice drills and fire inspections, and participate in physical fitness activities. They also prepare written reports on fire incidents and review fire science literature to keep abreast of technological developments and changing administrative practices and policies.

Most fire departments have a fire prevention division, usually headed by a fire marshal and staffed by *fire inspectors*. Workers in this division conduct inspections of structures to prevent fires and ensure fire code compliance. These firefighters also work with developers and planners to check and approve plans for new buildings. Fire prevention personnel often speak on these subjects in schools and before public assemblies and civic organizations.

Some firefighters become *fire investigators*, who determine the origin and causes of fires. They collect evidence, interview witnesses, and prepare reports on fires in cases where the cause may be arson or criminal negligence. They often are called upon to testify in court.

Working Conditions

Firefighters spend much of their time at fire stations, which usually have features common to a residential facility like a dormitory. When an alarm sounds, firefighters respond rapidly, regardless of the weather or hour. Firefighting involves risk of death or injury from sudden cave-ins of floors, toppling walls, traffic accidents when responding to calls, and exposure to flames and smoke. Firefighters may also come in contact with poisonous, flammable, or explosive gases and chemicals, as well as radioactive or other hazardous materials that may have immediate or long-term effects on their health. For these reasons, they must wear protective gear that can be very heavy and hot.

Work hours of firefighters are longer and vary more widely than hours of most other workers. Many work more than 50 hours a week, and sometimes they may work even longer. In some agencies, they are on duty for 24 hours, then off for 48 hours, and receive an extra day off at intervals. In others, they work a day shift of 10 hours for 3 or 4 days, a night shift of 14 hours for 3 or 4 nights, have 3 or 4 days off, and then repeat the cycle. In addition, firefighters often work extra hours at fires and other emergencies and are regularly assigned to work on holidays. Fire lieutenants and fire captains often work the same hours as the firefighters they supervise. Duty hours include time when firefighters study, train, and perform fire prevention duties.

Employment

Employment figures in this statement include only paid career firefighters—they do not cover volunteer firefighters, who perform the same duties and may comprise the majority of firefighters in a residential area. According the United States Fire Administration, nearly 70 percent of fire companies are staffed by volunteer fire fighters. Paid career firefighters held about 282,000 jobs in 2002. First-line supervisors/managers of firefighting and prevention workers held about 63,000 jobs; and fire inspectors held about 14,000.

About 9 out of 10 firefighting workers were employed by municipal or county fire departments. Some large cities have thousands of career firefighters, while many small towns have only a few. Most of the remainder worked in fire departments on federal and state installations, including airports. Private firefighting companies employ a small number of firefighters and usually operate on a subscription basis.

In response to the expanding role of firefighters, some municipalities have combined fire prevention, public fire education, safety, and emergency medical services into a single organization commonly referred to as a public safety organization. Some local and regional fire departments are being consolidated into countywide establishments in order to reduce administrative staffs and cut costs, and to establish consistent training standards and work procedures.

Training, Other Qualifications, and Advancement

Applicants for municipal firefighting jobs generally must pass a written exam; tests of strength, physical stamina, coordination, and agility; and a medical examination that includes drug screening. Workers may be monitored on a random basis for drug use after accepting employment. Examinations are generally open to persons who are at least 18 years of age and have a high school education or the equivalent. Those who receive the highest scores in all phases of testing have the best chances for appointment. The completion of community college courses in fire science may improve an applicant's chances for appointment. In recent years, an increasing proportion of entrants to this occupation have had some postsecondary education.

As a rule, entry-level workers in large fire departments are trained for several weeks at the department's training center or academy. Through classroom instruction and practical training, the recruits study firefighting techniques, fire prevention, hazardous materials control, local building codes, and emergency medical procedures, including first aid and cardiopulmonary resuscitation. They also learn how to use axes, chain saws, fire extinguishers, ladders, and other firefighting and rescue equipment. After successfully completing this training, they are assigned to a fire company, where they undergo a period of probation.

A number of fire departments have accredited apprenticeship programs lasting up to 5 years. These programs combine formal, technical instruction with on-the-job training under the supervision of experienced firefighters. Technical instruction covers subjects such as firefighting techniques and equipment, chemical hazards associated with various combustible building materials, emergency medical procedures, and fire prevention and safety. Fire departments frequently conduct training programs, and some firefighters attend training sessions sponsored by the U.S. National Fire Academy. These training sessions cover topics including executive development, anti-arson techniques, disaster preparedness, hazardous materials control, and public fire safety and education. Some states also have extensive firefighter training and certification programs. In addition, a number of colleges and universities offer courses leading to 2- or 4-year degrees in fire engineering or fire science. Many fire departments offer firefighters incentives such as tuition reimbursement or higher pay for completing advanced training.

Among the personal qualities firefighters need are mental alertness, self-discipline, courage, mechanical aptitude, endurance, strength, and a sense of public service. Initiative and good judgment are also extremely important because firefighters make quick decisions in emergencies. Because members of a crew live and work closely together under conditions of stress and danger for extended periods, they must be dependable and able to get along well with others. Leadership qualities are necessary for officers, who must establish and maintain discipline and efficiency, as well as direct the activities of firefighters in their companies.

Most experienced firefighters continue studying to improve their job performance and prepare for promotion examinations. To progress to higher level positions, they acquire expertise in advanced firefighting equipment and techniques, building construction, emergency medical technology, writing, public speaking, management and budgeting procedures, and public relations.

Opportunities for promotion depend upon written examination results, job performance, interviews, and seniority. Increasingly, fire departments use assessment centers, which simulate a variety of actual job performance tasks, to screen for the best candidates for promotion. The line of promotion usually is to engineer, lieutenant, captain, battalion chief, assistant chief, deputy chief, and finally to chief. Many fire departments now require a bachelor's degree, preferably in fire science, public administration, or a related field, for promotion to positions higher than battalion chief. A master's degree is required for executive fire officer certification from the National Fire Academy and for state chief officer certification.

Job Outlook

Prospective firefighters are expected to face keen competition for available job openings. Many people are attracted to firefighting because it is challenging and provides the opportunity to perform an essential public service, a high school education is usually sufficient for entry, and a pension is guaranteed upon retirement after 20 years. Consequently, the number of qualified applicants in most areas exceeds the number of job openings, even though the written examination and physical requirements eliminate many applicants. This situation is expected to persist in coming years.

Employment of firefighters is expected to grow about as fast as the average for all occupations through 2012 as fire departments continue to compete with other public safety providers for funding. Most job growth will occur as volunteer firefighting positions are converted to paid positions. In addition to job growth, openings are expected to result from the need to replace firefighters who retire, stop working for other reasons, or transfer to other occupations.

Layoffs of firefighters are uncommon. Fire protection is an essential service, and citizens are likely to exert considerable pressure on local officials to expand or at least preserve the level of fire protection. Even when budget cuts do occur, local fire departments usually cut expenses by postponing equipment purchases or not hiring new firefighters rather than through staff reductions.

Earnings

Median hourly earnings of firefighters were $17.42 in 2002. The middle 50 percent earned between $12.53 and $22.96. The lowest 10 percent earned less than $8.51, and the highest 10 percent earned more than $28.22. Median hourly earnings were $17.92 in local government, $15.96 in the federal government, and $13.58 in state government.

Median annual earnings of first-line supervisors/managers of firefighting and prevention workers were $55,450 in 2002. The middle 50 percent earned between $43,920 and $68,480. The lowest 10 percent earned less than $34,190, and the highest 10 percent earned more than $84,730. First-line supervisors/managers of firefighting and prevention workers employed in local government earned about $56,390 a year in 2002.

Median annual earnings of fire inspectors were $44,250 in 2002. The middle 50 percent earned between $33,880 and $56,100 a year. The lowest 10 percent earned less than $26,350, and the highest 10 percent earned more than $69,060. Fire inspectors and investigators employed in local government earned about $46,820 a year.

According to the International City-County Management Association, average salaries in 2002 for sworn full-time positions were as follows:

	Minimum annual base salary	Maximum annual base salary
Fire chief	$64,134	$82,225
Deputy chief	56,522	72,152
Assistant fire chief	55,645	69,036
Battalion chief	54,935	68,673
Fire captain	45,383	54,463
Fire lieutenant	41,800	49,404
Fire prevention/code inspector	40,387	51,531
Engineer	38,656	48,678

Firefighters who average more than a certain number of hours a week are required to be paid overtime. The hours threshold is determined by the department during the firefighter's work period, which ranges from 7 to 28 days. Firefighters often earn overtime for working extra shifts to maintain minimum staffing levels or for special emergencies.

Firefighters receive benefits that usually include medical and liability insurance, vacation and sick leave, and some paid holidays. Almost all fire departments provide protective clothing (helmets, boots, and coats) and breathing apparatus, and many also provide dress uniforms. Firefighters are generally covered by pension plans, often providing retirement at half pay after 25 years of service or if disabled in the line of duty.

Related Occupations

Like firefighters, emergency medical technicians and paramedics and police and detectives respond to emergencies and save lives.

Sources of Additional Information

Information about a career as a firefighter may be obtained from local fire departments and from:

- International Association of Firefighters, 1750 New York Ave. NW, Washington, DC 20006. Internet: http://www.iaff.org

- U.S. Fire Administration, 16825 South Seton Ave., Emmitsburg, MD 21727. Internet: http://www.usfa.fema.gov

Information about firefighter professional qualifications and a list of colleges and universities offering 2-year or 4-year degree programs in fire science or fire prevention may be obtained from:

- National Fire Academy, 16825 South Seton Ave., Emmitsburg, MD 21727. Internet: http://www.usfa.fema.gov/nfa/index.htm

Food and Beverage Serving and Related Workers

(O*NET 35-3011.00, 35-3021.00, 35-3022.00, 35-3031.00, 35-3041.00, 35-9011.00, 35-9021.00, 35-9031.00, and 35-9099.99)

Significant Points

- Most jobs are part time and many opportunities exist for young people—around one-fourth of these workers were 16 to 19 years old, about 5 times the proportion for all workers.

- Job openings are expected to be abundant through 2012, reflecting substantial replacement needs.

- Tips comprise a major portion of earnings, so keen competition is expected for jobs where potential earnings from tips are greatest—bartenders, waiters and waitresses, and other jobs in popular restaurants and fine dining establishments.

Nature of the Work

Food and beverage serving and related workers are the front line of customer service in restaurants, coffee shops, and other food service establishments. These workers greet customers, escort them to seats and hand them menus, take food and drink orders, and serve food and beverages. They also answer questions, explain menu items and specials, and keep tables and dining areas clean and set for new diners. Most work as part of a team, helping coworkers during busy times to improve workflow and customer service.

Waiters and waitresses, the largest group of these workers, take customers' orders, serve food and beverages, prepare itemized checks, and sometimes accept payment. Their specific duties vary considerably, depending on the establishment. In coffee shops serving routine, straightforward fare, such as salads, soups, and sandwiches, servers are expected to provide fast, efficient, and courteous service. In fine dining restaurants, where more complicated meals are prepared and often served over several courses, waiters and waitresses provide more formal service emphasizing personal, attentive treatment and a more leisurely pace. They may recommend certain dishes and identify ingredients or explain how various items on the menu are prepared. Some prepare salads, desserts, or other menu items tableside. Additionally, they may check the identification of patrons to ensure they meet the minimum age requirement for the purchase of alcohol and tobacco products.

Waiters and waitresses sometimes perform the duties of other food and beverage service workers. These tasks may include escorting guests to tables, serving customers seated at counters, clearing and setting up tables, or operating a cash register. However, full-service restaurants frequently hire other staff, such as hosts and hostesses cashiers, or dining room attendants, to perform these duties.

Bartenders fill drink orders either taken directly from patrons at the bar or through waiters and waitresses who place drink orders for dining room customers. Bartenders check identification of customers seated at the bar, to ensure they meet the minimum age requirement for the purchase of alcohol and tobacco products. They prepare mixed drinks, serve bottled or draught beer, and pour wine or other beverages. Bartenders must know a wide range of drink recipes and be able to mix drinks accurately, quickly, and without waste. Besides mixing and serving drinks, bartenders stock and prepare garnishes for drinks; maintain an adequate supply of ice, glasses, and other bar supplies; and keep the bar area clean for customers. They also may collect payment, operate the cash register, wash glassware and utensils, and serve food to customers seated at the bar. Bartenders usually are responsible for ordering and maintaining an inventory of liquor, mixes, and other bar supplies.

The majority of bartenders directly serve and interact with patrons. Bartenders should be friendly and enjoy mingling with customers. Bartenders at service bars, on the other hand, have less contact with customers. They work in small bars often located off the kitchen in restaurants, hotels, and clubs where only waiters and waitresses place drink orders. Some establishments, especially larger, higher volume ones, use equipment that automatically pours and mixes drinks at the push of a button. Bartenders who use this equipment, however, still must work quickly to handle a large volume of drink orders and be familiar with the ingredients for special drink requests. Much of a bartender's work still must be done by hand to fill each individual order.

Hosts and hostesses welcome guests and maintain reservation or waiting lists. They may direct patrons to coatrooms, restrooms, or to a place to wait until their table is ready.

Hosts and hostesses assign guests to tables suitable for the size of their group, escort patrons to their seats, and provide menus. They also schedule dining reservations, arrange parties, and organize any special services that are required. In some restaurants, they act as cashiers.

Dining room and cafeteria attendants and bartender helpers assist waiters, waitresses, and bartenders by cleaning tables, removing dirty dishes, and keeping serving areas stocked with supplies. Sometimes called backwaiters or runners, they bring meals out of the kitchen and assist waiters and waitresses by distributing dishes to individual diners. They also replenish the supply of clean linens, dishes, silverware, and glasses in the dining room and keep the bar stocked with glasses, liquor, ice, and drink garnishes. Dining room attendants set tables with clean tablecloths, napkins, silverware, glasses, and dishes and serve ice water, rolls, and butter. At the conclusion of meals, they remove dirty dishes and soiled linens from tables. Cafeteria attendants stock serving tables with food, trays, dishes, and silverware and may carry trays to dining tables for patrons. *Bartender helpers* keep bar equipment clean and wash glasses. *Dishwashers* clean dishes, cutlery, and kitchen utensils and equipment.

Counter attendants take orders and serve food in cafeterias, coffee shops, and carryout eateries. In cafeterias, they serve food displayed on steam tables, carve meat, dish out vegetables, ladle sauces and soups, and fill beverage glasses. In lunchrooms and coffee shops, counter attendants take orders from customers seated at the counter, transmit orders to the kitchen, and pick up and serve food. They also fill cups with coffee, soda, and other beverages and prepare fountain specialties, such as milkshakes and ice cream sundaes. Counter attendants also take carryout orders from diners and wrap or place items in containers. They clean counters, write itemized checks, and sometimes accept payment. Some counter attendants may prepare short-order items, such as sandwiches and salads.

Some food and beverage serving workers take orders from customers at counters or drive-through windows at fast-food restaurants. They assemble orders, hand them to customers, and accept payment. Many of these are *combined food preparation and serving workers* who also cook and package food, make coffee, and fill beverage cups using drink-dispensing machines.

Other workers serve food to patrons outside of a restaurant environment, such as in hotels, hospital rooms, or cars.

Working Conditions

Food and beverage service workers are on their feet most of the time and often carry heavy trays of food, dishes, and glassware. During busy dining periods, they are under pressure to serve customers quickly and efficiently. The work is relatively safe, but care must be taken to avoid slips, falls, and burns.

Part-time work is more common among food and beverage serving and related workers than among workers in almost any other occupation. In 2002, those on part-time schedules included half of all waiters and waitresses and 2 out of 5 bartenders.

Food service and drinking establishments typically maintain long dining hours and offer flexible and varied work opportunities. Many food and beverage serving and related workers work evenings, weekends, and holidays. Some work split shifts—they work for several hours during the middle of the day, take a few hours off in the afternoon, and then return to their jobs for evening hours. Many students and teenagers seek part time or seasonal work as food and beverage serving and related workers as a first job to gain work experience or to earn spending money while in school. Around one-fourth of food and beverage serving and related workers were 16 to 19 years old—about 5 times the proportion for all workers.

Employment

Food and beverage serving and related workers held 6.5 million jobs in 2002. The distribution of jobs among the various food and beverage serving workers was as follows:

Waiters and waitresses	2,097,000
Combined food preparation and serving workers, including fast food	1,990,000
Dishwashers	505,000
Counter attendants, cafeteria, food concession, and coffee	467,000
Bartenders	463,000
Dining room and cafeteria attendants and bartender helpers	409,000
Hosts and hostesses, restaurant, lounge, and coffee shop	298,000
Food servers, nonrestaurant	195,000
All other food preparation and serving related workers	117,000

The overwhelming majority of jobs for food and beverage serving and related workers were found in food services and drinking places, such as restaurants, coffee shops, and bars. Other jobs were found primarily in traveler accommodation (hotels); amusement, gambling, and recreation industries; educational services; grocery stores; nursing care facilities; civic and social organizations; and hospitals.

Jobs are located throughout the country but are typically plentiful in large cities and tourist areas. Vacation resorts offer seasonal employment, and some workers alternate between summer and winter resorts, instead of remaining in one area the entire year.

Training, Other Qualifications, and Advancement

There are no specific educational requirements for food and beverage service jobs. Many employers prefer to hire high

school graduates for waiter and waitress, bartender, and host and hostess positions, but completion of high school usually is not required for fast-food workers, counter attendants, dishwashers, and dining room attendants and bartender helpers. A job as a food and beverage service worker serves as a source of immediate income, rather than a career, for many people. Many entrants to these jobs are in their late teens or early twenties and have a high school education or less. Usually, they have little or no work experience. Many are full-time students or homemakers. Food and beverage service jobs are a major source of part-time employment for high school and college students.

Restaurants rely on good food and quality customer service to retain loyal customers and succeed in a competitive industry. Food and beverage serving and related workers who exhibit excellent personal qualities, such as a neat clean appearance, a well-spoken manner, an ability to work as a member of team, and a pleasant way with patrons, will be highly sought after.

Waiters and waitresses need a good memory to avoid confusing customers' orders and to recall faces, names, and preferences of frequent patrons. These workers also should be comfortable using computers to place orders and generate customers' bills. Some may need to be quick at arithmetic so they can total bills manually. Knowledge of a foreign language is helpful to communicate with a diverse clientele and staff. Prior experience waiting on tables is preferred by restaurants and hotels that have rigid table service standards. Jobs at these establishments often offer higher wages and have greater income potential from tips, but they may also have stiffer employment requirements, such as higher education or training standards, than other establishments.

Usually, bartenders must be at least 21 years of age, but employers prefer to hire people who are 25 or older. Bartenders should be familiar with state and local laws concerning the sale of alcoholic beverages.

Most food and beverage serving and related workers pick up their skills on the job by observing and working with more experienced workers. Some employers, particularly those in fast-food restaurants, use self-instruction programs with audiovisual presentations and instructional booklets to teach new employees food preparation and service skills. Some public and private vocational schools, restaurant associations, and large restaurant chains provide classroom training in a generalized food service curriculum.

Some bartenders acquire their skills by attending a bartending or vocational and technical school. These programs often include instruction on state and local laws and regulations, cocktail recipes, attire and conduct, and stocking a bar. Some of these schools help their graduates find jobs. Although few employers require any minimum level of educational attainment, some specialized training is usually needed in food handling and legal issues surrounding serving alcoholic beverages and tobacco. Employers are more likely to hire and promote based on people skills and personal qualities rather than education.

Due to the relatively small size of most food-serving establishments, opportunities for promotion are limited. After gaining experience, some dining room and cafeteria attendants and bartender helpers advance to waiter, waitress, or bartender jobs. For waiters, waitresses, and bartenders, advancement usually is limited to finding a job in a busier or more expensive restaurant or bar where prospects for tip earnings are better. A few bartenders open their own businesses. Some hosts and hostesses and waiters and waitresses advance to supervisory jobs, such as maitre d'hotel, dining room supervisor, or restaurant manager. In larger restaurant chains, food and beverage service workers who excel at their work often are invited to enter the company's formal management training program.

Job Outlook

Job openings are expected to be abundant for food and beverage serving and related workers. Overall employment of these workers is expected to grow about as fast as the average over the 2002-12 period, stemming from increases in population, personal incomes, and leisure time. While employment growth will account for many new jobs, the overwhelming majority of openings will arise from the need to replace the high proportion of workers who leave the occupations each year. There is substantial movement into and out of these occupations because education and training requirements are minimal, and the predominance of part-time jobs is attractive to people seeking a short-term source of income rather than a career. However, keen competition is expected for bartender, waiter and waitress, and other food and beverage service jobs in popular restaurants and fine dining establishments, where potential earnings from tips are greatest.

Projected employment growth between 2002 and 2012 varies by type of job. Employment of combined food preparation and serving workers, which includes fast-food workers, is expected to increase faster than the average in response to the continuing fast-paced lifestyle of many Americans and the addition of healthier foods at many fast-food restaurants. Increases in the number of families and the more affluent, 55-and-older population will result in more restaurants that offer table service and more varied menus—leading to average growth for waiters and waitresses and hosts and hostesses. Employment of dining room attendants and dishwashers will grow more slowly than other food and beverage serving and related workers, because diners increasingly are eating at more casual dining spots, such as coffee bars and sandwich shops, rather than at the full-service restaurants that employ more of these workers. Slower than average employment growth is expected for bartenders.

Earnings

Food and beverage serving and related workers derive their earnings from a combination of hourly wages and customer tips. Earnings vary greatly, depending on the type of job and establishment. For example, fast-food workers and hosts and hostesses usually do not receive tips, so their wage rates may be higher than those of waiters and waitresses and bartenders in full-service restaurants, who typically earn more from tips than from wages. In some restaurants, workers contribute a portion of their tips to a tip pool, which is distributed among qualifying workers. Tip pools allow workers who don't usually receive tips directly from customers, such as dining room attendants, to share in the rewards of good service.

In 2002, median hourly earnings (including tips) of waiters and waitresses were $6.80. The middle 50 percent earned between $6.13 and $8.00. The lowest 10 percent earned less than $5.70, and the highest 10 percent earned more than $11.00 an hour. For most waiters and waitresses, higher earnings are primarily the result of receiving more in tips rather than higher hourly wages. Tips usually average between 10 and 20 percent of guests' checks; waiters and waitresses working in busy, expensive restaurants earn the most.

Bartenders had median hourly earnings (including tips) of $7.21 in 2002. The middle 50 percent earned between $6.33 and $9.02. The lowest 10 percent earned less than $5.76, and the highest 10 percent earned more than $11.96 an hour. Like waiters and waitresses, bartenders employed in public bars may receive more than half of their earnings as tips. Service bartenders often are paid higher hourly wages to offset their lower tip earnings.

Median hourly earnings (including tips) of dining room and cafeteria attendants and bartender helpers were $6.99 in 2002. The middle 50 percent earned between $6.33 and $8.10. The lowest 10 percent earned less than $5.80, and the highest 10 percent earned more than $9.70 an hour. Most received over half of their earnings as wages; the rest of their income was a share of the proceeds from tip pools.

Median hourly earnings of hosts and hostesses were $7.36 in 2002. The middle 50 percent earned between $6.54 and $fs8.58. The lowest 10 percent earned less than $5.89, and the highest 10 percent earned more than $10.32 an hour. Wages comprised the majority of their earnings. In some cases, wages were supplemented by proceeds from tip pools.

Median hourly earnings of combined food preparation and serving workers, including fast food, were $6.97 in 2002. The middle 50 percent earned between $6.23 and $8.08. The lowest 10 percent earned less than $5.74, and the highest 10 percent earned more than $9.33 an hour. Although some combined food preparation and serving workers receive a part of their earnings as tips, fast-food workers usually do not.

Median hourly earnings of counter attendants in cafeterias, food concessions, and coffee shops (including tips) were $7.32 in 2002. The middle 50 percent earned between $6.52 and $8.53 an hour. The lowest 10 percent earned less than $5.87, and the highest 10 percent earned more than $10.39 an hour.

Median hourly earnings of dishwashers were $7.15 in 2002. The middle 50 percent earned between $6.40 and $8.28. The lowest 10 percent earned less than $5.82, and the highest 10 percent earned more than $9.41 an hour.

Median hourly earnings of nonrestaurant food servers were $7.52 in 2002. The middle 50 percent earned between $6.51 and $9.36. The lowest 10 percent earned less than $5.87, and the highest 10 percent earned more than $11.72 an hour.

Many beginning or inexperienced workers start earning the Federal minimum wage of $5.15 an hour. However, a few states set minimum wages higher than the federal minimum. Also, various minimum wage exceptions apply under specific circumstances to disabled workers, full-time students, youth under age 20 in their first 90 days of employment, tipped employees, and student-learners. Tipped employees are those who customarily and regularly receive more than $30 a month in tips. The employer may consider tips as part of wages, but the employer must pay at least $2.13 an hour in direct wages. Employers also are permitted to deduct from wages the cost, or fair value, of any meals or lodging provided. Many employers, however, provide free meals and furnish uniforms. Food and beverage service workers who work full time often receive typical benefits, while part-time workers usually do not.

In some large restaurants and hotels, food and beverage serving and related workers belong to unions—principally the Hotel Employees and Restaurant Employees International Union and the Service Employees International Union.

Related Occupations

Other workers whose job involves serving customers and handling money include flight attendants, gaming services workers, and retail salespersons.

Sources of Additional Information

Information about job opportunities may be obtained from local employers and local offices of state employment services agencies.

A guide to careers in restaurants plus a list of 2- and 4-year colleges offering food service programs and related scholarship information is available from:

- National Restaurant Association, 1200 17th St. NW, Washington, DC 20036-3097. Internet: http://www.restaurant.org

For general information on hospitality careers, contact:

- International Council on Hotel, Restaurant, and Institutional Education, 2613 North Parham Rd., 2nd Floor, Richmond, VA 23294. Internet: http://www.chrie.org

Gaming Services Occupations

(O*NET 39-1011.00, 39-1012.00, 39-3011.00, 39-3012.00, 39-3019.99, and 39-3099.99)

Significant Points

- These occupations have no common minimum educational requirements; each casino establishes its own requirements for education, training, and experience.

- Workers need a license issued by a regulatory agency, such as a state casino control board or commission; licensure requires proof of residency in the state in which gaming workers are employed.

- Job prospects are best for those with a degree or certification in gaming or a hospitality-related field, previous training or experience in casino gaming, and strong interpersonal and customer service skills.

Nature of the Work

Legalized gambling in the United States today includes casino gaming, state lotteries, parimutuel wagering on contests such as horse or dog racing, and charitable gaming. Gaming, the playing of games of chance, is a multibillion-dollar industry that is responsible for the creation of a number of unique service occupations.

The majority of all gaming services workers are employed in casinos. Their duties and titles may vary from one establishment to another. Despite differences in job title and task, however, workers perform many of the same basic functions in all casinos. Some positions are associated with oversight and direction—supervision, surveillance, and investigation—while others involve working with the games or patrons themselves, performing such activities as tending slot machines, handling money, writing and running tickets, and dealing cards or running games.

Like nearly every business establishment, casinos have workers who direct and oversee day-to-day operations. *Gaming supervisors* oversee the gaming operations and personnel in an assigned area. They circulate among the tables and observe the operations to ensure that all of the stations and games are covered for each shift. It is not uncommon for gaming supervisors to explain and interpret the operating rules of the house to patrons who may have difficulty understanding the rules. Gaming supervisors also may plan and organize activities to create a friendly atmosphere for the guests staying in their hotels or in casino hotels. Periodically, they address and adjust complaints about service.

Some gaming occupations demand specially acquired skills—dealing blackjack, for example—that are unique to casino work. Others require skills common to most businesses, such as the ability to conduct financial transactions. In both capacities, the workers in these jobs interact directly with patrons in attending to slot machines, making change, cashing or selling tokens and coins, writing and running for other games, and dealing cards at table games. Part of their responsibility is to make those interactions enjoyable.

Slot key persons, also called slot attendants or slot technicians, coordinate and supervise the slot department and its workers. Their duties include verifying and handling payoff winnings to patrons, resetting slot machines after completing the payoff, and refilling machines with money. Slot key persons must be familiar with a variety of slot machines and be able to make minor repairs and adjustments to the machines as needed. If major repairs are required, slot key persons determine whether the slot machine should be removed from the floor. Working the floor as frontline personnel, they enforce safety rules and report hazards.

Gaming and sportsbook writers and runners assist in the operations of games such as bingo and keno, in addition to taking bets on sporting events. They scan tickets presented by patrons and calculate and distribute winnings. Some writers and runners operate the equipment that randomly selects the numbers. Others may announce numbers selected, pick up tickets from patrons, collect bets, or receive, verify, and record patrons' cash wagers.

Gaming dealers operate table games such as craps, blackjack, and roulette. Standing or sitting behind the table, dealers provide dice, dispense cards to players, or run the equipment. Some dealers also monitor the patrons for infractions of casino rules. Gaming dealers must be skilled in customer service and in executing their game. Dealers determine winners, calculate and pay winning bets, and collect losing bets. Because of the fast-paced work environment, most gaming dealers are competent in at least two games, usually blackjack and craps.

Working Conditions

The atmosphere in casinos is generally filled with fun and often considered glamorous. However, casino work can also be physically demanding. Most occupations require that workers stand for long periods; some require the lifting of heavy items. The "glamorous" atmosphere exposes casino workers to certain hazards, such as cigarette, cigar, and pipe smoke. Noise from slot machines, gaming tables, and talking workers and patrons may be distracting to some, although workers wear protective headgear in areas where loud machinery is used to count money.

Most casinos are open 24 hours a day, seven day a week and offer three staggered shifts.

Employment

Gaming services' occupations held 192,000 jobs in 2002. Employment by occupational specialty was distributed as follows:

Gaming dealers 78,000

Gaming supervisors 39,000

Slot key persons 21,000

Gaming and sports book writers & runners 14,000

All other gaming service workers 40,000

Gaming services workers are found mainly in the traveler accommodation and gaming industries. Most are employed in commercial casinos, including land-based or riverboat casinos, in 11 states: Colorado, Illinois, Indiana, Iowa, Louisiana, Michigan, Mississippi, Missouri, Nevada, New Jersey, and South Dakota. The largest number works in land-based casinos in Nevada, and the second-largest group works in similar establishments in New Jersey. Mississippi, which boasts the greatest number of riverboat casinos in operation, employs the most workers in that venue. In addition, there are 23 states with Indian casinos. Legal lotteries are held in 40 states and the District of Columbia, and parimutuel wagering is legal in 41 states. Forty-seven states and the District of Columbia also allow charitable gaming.

For most workers, gaming licensure requires proof of residency in the state in which gaming workers are employed. But some gaming services workers do not limit themselves to one state or even one country, finding jobs on the small number of casinos located on luxury cruise liners that travel the world. These individuals live and work aboard the vessel.

Training, Other Qualifications, and Advancement

There usually are no minimum educational requirements for entry-level gaming jobs, although most employers prefer a high school diploma or GED. However, entry-level gaming services workers are required to have a license issued by a regulatory agency, such as a state casino control board or commission. Applicants for a license must provide photo identification, offer proof of residency in the state in which they anticipate working, and pay a fee. Age requirements vary by state. The licensing application process also includes a background investigation.

In addition to possessing a license, gaming services workers need superior customer service skills. Casino gaming workers provide entertainment and hospitality to patrons, and the quality of their service contributes to an establishment's success or failure. Therefore, gaming workers need good communication skills, an outgoing personality, and the ability to maintain their composure even when dealing with angry or demanding patrons. Personal integrity also is important, because workers handle large amounts of money.

Each casino establishes its own requirements for education, training, and experience. Almost all provide some in-house training in addition to requiring certification. The type and quantity of classes needed may vary.

Many institutions of higher learning give training toward certification in gaming, as well as offering an associate's, bachelor's, or master's degree in a hospitality-related field such as hospitality management, hospitality administration, or hotel management. Some schools offer training in games, gaming supervision, slot attendant and slot repair technician work, slot department management, and surveillance and security.

Gaming services workers who manage money should have some experience handling cash or using calculators or computers. For such positions, most casinos administer a math test to assess an applicant's level of competency.

Most casino supervisory staff have an associate's or bachelor's degree. Supervisors who do not have a degree usually substitute hands-on experience for formal education. Regardless of their educational background, most supervisors gain experience in other gaming occupations before moving into supervisory positions, because knowledge of games and casino operations is essential for these workers. Gaming supervisors must have leadership qualities and good communication skills to supervise employees effectively and to deal with patrons in a way that encourages return visits.

Slot key persons do not need to meet formal educational requirements to enter the occupation, but completion of slot attendant or slot technician training is helpful. As with most other gaming workers, slot key persons receive on-the-job training during the first several weeks of employment. Most slot key positions are entry level, so a desire to learn is important. Slot key persons need good communication skills and an ability to remain calm, even when dealing with angry or demanding patrons. Personal integrity also is important, because these workers handle large sums of money.

Gaming and sportsbook writers and runners must have at least a high school diploma or GED. Most of these workers receive on-the-job training. Because gaming and sportsbook writers and runners work closely with patrons, they need excellent customer service skills.

Nearly all gaming dealers are certified. Certification is available through 2- or 4-year programs in gaming or a hospitality-related field. Experienced dealers, who often are able to attract new or return business, have the best job prospects. Dealers with more experience are placed at the "high-roller" tables.

Advancement opportunities in casino gaming depend less on workers' previous casino duties and titles than on their ability and eagerness to learn new jobs. For example, an entry-level gaming worker eventually might advance to become a dealer or card room manager or to assume some other supervisory position.

Job Outlook

With demand for gaming showing no sign of waning, employment in gaming services occupations is projected to grow faster than the average for all occupations through 2012. Even during the recent downturn in the economy, profits at casinos have risen. With many states benefiting from casino gambling in the form of tax revenue or compacts with Indian tribes, additional states are rethinking their opposition to legalized gambling and will likely approve the building of more casinos and other gaming formats during the next decade. Job prospects in gaming services occupations will be best for those with a degree or certification in gaming or a hospitality-related field, previous casino gaming training or experience, and strong interpersonal and customer service skills. As a direct result of increasing demand for additional table games in gaming establishments, the most rapid growth is expected among gaming dealers. In addition to job openings arising from employment growth, opportunities will result from the need to replace workers transferring to other occupations or leaving the labor force.

The increase in gaming reflects growth in the population and in its disposable income, both of which are expected to continue. Also, more domestic and international competition for gaming patrons and higher expectations among gaming patrons for customer service should result in more jobs for gaming services workers. Job growth is expected in established gaming areas such as Las Vegas, Nevada, and Atlantic City, New Jersey, as well as in other states and areas that may legalize gaming in the coming years, including Indian tribal lands.

Earnings

Wage earnings for gaming services workers vary according to occupation, level of experience, training, location, and size of the gaming establishment. The following were median earnings for various gaming services occupations in 2002:

Gaming supervisors $39,290
Slot key persons 22,870
Gaming and sports book writers and runners 18,660
Gaming dealers 14,090

Related Occupations

Many other occupations provide hospitality and customer service. Some examples of related occupations are security guards and gaming surveillance officers, recreation and fitness workers, sales worker supervisors, cashiers, gaming change persons and booth cashiers, retail salespersons, gaming cage workers, and tellers.

Sources of Additional Information

For additional information on careers in gaming, visit your public library and your state gaming regulatory agency or casino control commission.

Information on careers in gaming also is available from:

- American Gaming Association, 555 13th St. NW, Suite 1010 East, Washington, DC 20004. Internet: http://www.americangaming.org

Grounds Maintenance Workers

(O*NET 37-1012.01, 37-1012.02, 37-3011.00, 37-3012.00, and 37-3013.00)

Significant Points

- Opportunities should be excellent, especially for workers willing to work seasonal or variable schedules, due to significant job turnover and increasing demand by landscaping services companies.

- Many beginning jobs have low earnings and are physically demanding.

- Most workers learn through short-term on-the-job training.

Nature of the Work

Attractively designed, healthy, and well-maintained lawns, gardens, and grounds create a positive first impression, establish a peaceful mood, and increase property values. Grounds maintenance workers perform the variety of tasks necessary to achieve a pleasant and functional outdoor environment. They also care for indoor gardens and plantings in commercial and public facilities, such as malls, hotels, and botanical gardens.

The duties of landscaping workers and groundskeeping workers are similar and often overlap. *Landscaping workers* physically install and maintain landscaped areas. They grade property, install lighting or sprinkler systems, and build walkways, terraces, patios, decks, and fountains. In addition to initially transporting and planting new vegetation, they transplant, mulch, fertilize, and water flowering plants, trees, and shrubs and mow and water lawns. A growing number of residential and commercial clients, such as managers of office buildings, shopping malls, multiunit residential buildings, and hotels and motels, favor full-service landscape maintenance. Landscaping workers perform a range of duties, including mowing, edging, trimming, fertilizing, dethatching, and mulching, for such clients on a regular basis during the growing season.

Groundskeeping workers, also called *groundskeepers*, maintain a variety of facilities, including athletic fields, golf courses, cemeteries, university campuses, and parks. In addition to caring for sod, plants, and trees, they rake and mulch leaves, clear snow from walkways and parking lots, and use irrigation methods to adjust the amount of water consumption and prevent waste. They see to the proper upkeep and repair of sidewalks, parking lots, groundskeeping equipment, pools, fountains, fences, planters, and benches.

Groundskeeping workers who care for athletic fields keep those with natural and those with artificial turf in top condition and mark out boundaries and paint turf with team logos and names before events. They must make sure that the underlying soil on fields with natural turf has the required composition to allow proper drainage and to support the grasses used on the field. Groundskeeping workers mow, water, fertilize, and aerate the fields regularly. They also vacuum and disinfect synthetic turf after its use, in order to prevent the growth of harmful bacteria, and they remove the turf and replace the cushioning pad periodically.

Workers who maintain golf courses are called *greenskeepers*. Greenskeepers do many of the same things that other groundskeepers do. In addition, greenskeepers periodically relocate the holes on putting greens to eliminate uneven wear of the turf and to add interest and challenge to the game. Greenskeepers also keep canopies, benches, ball washers, and tee markers repaired and freshly painted.

Some groundskeeping workers specialize in caring for cemeteries and memorial gardens. They dig graves to specified depths, generally using a backhoe. They mow grass regularly, apply fertilizers and other chemicals, prune shrubs and trees, plant flowers, and remove debris from graves.

Groundskeeping workers in parks and recreation facilities care for lawns, trees, and shrubs, maintain athletic fields and playgrounds, clean buildings, and keep parking lots, picnic areas, and other public spaces free of litter. They also may remove snow and ice from roads and walkways, erect and dismantle snow fences, and maintain swimming pools. These workers inspect buildings and equipment, make needed repairs, and keep everything freshly painted.

Supervisors of landscaping and groundskeeping workers perform various functions. They prepare cost estimates, schedule work for crews on the basis of weather conditions or the availability of equipment, perform spot checks to ensure the quality of the service, and suggest changes in work procedures. In addition, supervisors train workers in their tasks; keep employees' time records and record work performed; and even assist workers when deadlines are near.

Landscaping and groundskeeping workers use handtools such as shovels, rakes, pruning and regular saws, hedge and brush trimmers, and axes, as well as power lawnmowers, chain saws, snowblowers, and electric clippers. Some use equipment such as tractors and twin-axle vehicles. Landscaping and groundskeeping workers at parks, schools, cemeteries, and golf courses may use sod cutters to harvest sod that will be replanted elsewhere.

Pesticide handlers, sprayers, and applicators, vegetation, mix or apply pesticides, herbicides, fungicides, or insecticides through sprays, dusts, vapors, incorporation into the soil, or application of chemicals onto trees, shrubs, lawns, or botanical crops. Those working for chemical lawn service firms are more specialized, inspecting lawns for problems and applying fertilizers, herbicides, pesticides, and other chemicals to stimulate growth and prevent or control weeds, diseases, or insect infestation. Many practice integrated pest-management techniques.

Tree trimmers and pruners cut away dead or excess branches from trees or shrubs either to maintain rights-of-way for roads, sidewalks, or utilities or to improve the appearance, health, and value of trees. Tree trimmers also may fill cavities in trees to promote healing and prevent deterioration. Workers who specialize in pruning trim and shape ornamental trees and shrubs for private residences, golf courses, or other institutional grounds. Tree trimmers and pruners use handsaws, pruning hooks, shears, and clippers. When trimming near power lines, they usually use truck-mounted lifts and power pruners.

Working Conditions

Many of the jobs for grounds maintenance workers are seasonal, meaning that they are in demand mainly in the spring, summer, and fall, when most planting, mowing, trimming, and cleanup are necessary. The work, most of which is performed outdoors in all kinds of weather, can be physically demanding and repetitive, involving much bending, lifting, and shoveling. Workers in landscaping and groundskeeping may be under pressure to get the job completed, especially when they are preparing for scheduled events such as athletic competitions.

Those who work with pesticides, fertilizers, and other chemicals, as well as dangerous equipment and tools such as power lawnmowers, chain saws, and power clippers, must exercise safety precautions. Workers who use motorized equipment must take care to protect themselves against hearing damage.

Employment

Grounds maintenance workers held about 1.3 million jobs in 2002. Employment was distributed as follows:

Landscaping and groundskeeping workers 1,074,000

First-line supervisors/managers of landscaping, lawn service, and groundskeeping workers........150,000

Tree trimmers and pruners 59,000

Pesticide handlers, sprayers, and applicators, vegetation..27,000

About one-third of the workers in grounds maintenance were employed in companies providing landscaping services to buildings and dwellings. Others worked for property management and real-estate development firms, lawn and garden equipment and supply stores, and amusement and recreation facilities, such as golf courses and racetracks. Some were employed by local governments, installing and maintaining landscaping for parks, schools, hospitals, and other public facilities.

Almost 1 out of every 4 grounds maintenance workers was self-employed, providing landscape maintenance directly to customers on a contract basis. About 1 of every 6 worked part time; about a tenth were of school age.

Training, Other Qualifications, and Advancement

There usually are no minimum educational requirements for entry-level positions in grounds maintenance, although a diploma is necessary for some jobs. In 2002, most workers had a high school education or less. Short-term on-the-job training generally is sufficient to teach new hires how to operate equipment such as mowers, trimmers, leaf blowers, and small tractors and to follow correct safety procedures. Entry-level workers must be able to follow directions and learn proper planting procedures. If driving is an essential part of a job, employers look for applicants with a good driving record and some experience driving a truck. Employers also look for responsible, self-motivated individuals because grounds maintenance workers often work with little supervision. Workers who deal directly with customers must get along well with people.

Laborers who demonstrate a willingness to work hard and quickly, have good communication skills, and take an interest in the business may advance to crew leader or other supervisory positions. Advancement or entry into positions such as grounds manager and landscape contractor usually requires some formal education beyond high school and several years of progressively more responsible experience.

Most states require certification for workers who apply pesticides. Certification requirements vary, but usually include passing a test on the proper and safe use and disposal of insecticides, herbicides, and fungicides. Some states require that landscape contractors be licensed.

The Professional Grounds Management Society (PGMS) offers certification to grounds managers who have a combination of 8 years of experience and formal education beyond high school and who pass an examination covering subjects such as equipment management, personnel management, environmental issues, turf care, ornamentals, and circulatory systems. The PGMS also offers certification to groundskeepers who have a high school diploma or equivalent, plus 2 years of experience in the grounds maintenance field.

The Associated Landscape Contractors of America (ALCA) offers the designations "Certified Landscape Professional (Exterior and Interior)" and "Certified Landscape Technician (Exterior or Interior)" to those who meet established education and experience standards and who pass a specific examination. The hands-on test for technicians covers areas such as the operation of maintenance equipment and the installation of plants by reading a plan. A written safety test also is administered. The Professional Lawn Care Association of America (PLCAA) offers the designations "Certified Turfgrass Professional" (CTP) and "Certified Ornamental Landscape Professional" (COLP), which require written exams.

Some workers with groundskeeping backgrounds may start their own businesses after several years of experience.

Job Outlook

Those interested in grounds maintenance occupations should find plentiful job opportunities in the future. Demand for their services is growing, and because wages for beginners are low and the work is physically demanding, many employers have difficulty attracting enough workers to fill all openings, creating favorable job opportunities. High turnover will generate a large number of job openings to replace workers who leave the occupation.

More workers also will be needed to keep up with increasing demand by lawn care and landscaping companies.

Employment of grounds maintenance workers is expected to grow faster than the average for all occupations through the year 2012. Expected growth in the construction of all types of buildings requiring lawn care and maintenance, from office buildings to shopping malls and residential housing, plus more highways and parks, will contribute to demand for grounds maintenance workers. In addition, the upkeep and renovation of existing landscaping and grounds are continuing sources of demand for grounds maintenance workers. Owners of many buildings and facilities recognize the importance of "curb appeal" in attracting business and maintaining the value of the property and are expected to use grounds maintenance services more extensively to maintain and upgrade their properties.

Homeowners are a growing source of demand for grounds maintenance workers. Because many two-income households lack the time to take care of the lawn, they are increasingly hiring people to maintain it for them. They also know that a nice yard will increase the property's value. In addition, there is a growing interest by homeowners in their backyards, as well as a desire to make the yards more attractive for outdoor entertaining. With many newer homes having more and bigger windows overlooking the yard, it becomes more important to maintain and beautify the grounds. Also, as the population ages, more elderly homeowners will require lawn care services to help maintain their yards.

Job opportunities for nonseasonal work are more numerous in regions with temperate climates, where landscaping and lawn services are required all year. However, opportunities may vary with local economic conditions.

Earnings

Median hourly earnings in 2002 of grounds maintenance workers were as follows:

First-line supervisors/managers of landscaping, lawn service, and groundskeeping workers..........$15.89

Tree trimmers and pruners 12.07

Pesticide handlers, sprayers, and applicators, vegetation...11.94

Landscaping and groundskeeping workers 9.51

Median hourly earnings in the industries employing the largest numbers of landscaping and groundskeeping workers in 2002 were as follows:

Elementary and secondary schools $13.36

Local government 11.81

Services to buildings and dwellings...........................9.38

Other amusement and recreation industries 8.92

Lessors of real estate...8.65

Employment services 8.05

Related Occupations

Grounds maintenance workers perform most of their work outdoors and have some knowledge of plants and soils. Others whose jobs may require that they work outdoors are agricultural workers; farmers, ranchers, and agricultural managers; forest, conservation, and logging workers; landscape architects; and biological scientists.

Sources of Additional Information

For career and certification information on tree trimmers and pruners, contact:

● Tree Care Industry Association, 3 Perimeter Rd., Unit I, Manchester, NH 03103-3341. Internet: http://www.TreeCareIndustry.org

For information on work as a landscaping and groundskeeping worker, contact either of the following organizations:

● Professional Lawn Care Association of America, 1000 Johnson Ferry Rd. NE, Suite C-135, Marietta, GA, 30068-2112. Internet: http://www.plcaa.org

● Associated Landscape Contractors of America, 150 Elden St., Suite 270, Herndon, VA, 20170. Internet: http://www.alca.org

For information on becoming a licensed pesticide applicator, contact your state's Department of Agriculture or Department of Environmental Protection (or Conservation), most of which are accessible from the following Web site: http://aapco.ceris.purdue.edu/doc/statedirs/offltabl.html.

Hazardous Materials Removal Workers

(O*NET 47-4041.00)

Significant Points

● Working conditions can be hazardous, and the use of protective clothing often is required.

● Formal education beyond high school is not required, but a training program leading to a federal license is mandatory.

● Good job opportunities are expected.

Nature of the Work

Increased public awareness and federal and state regulations are resulting in the removal of hazardous materials from buildings, facilities, and the environment to prevent further contamination of natural resources and to promote public health and safety. Hazardous materials removal workers identify, remove, package, transport, and dispose of various hazardous materials, including asbestos, lead, and radioactive and nuclear materials. The removal of hazardous materials, or "hazmats," from public places and the environment also is called abatement, remediation, and decontamination.

Hazardous materials removal workers use a variety of tools and equipment, depending on the work at hand. Equipment ranges from brooms to personal protective suits that completely isolate workers from the hazardous material. The equipment required varies with the threat of contamination and can include disposable or reusable coveralls, gloves, hardhats, shoe covers, safety glasses or goggles, chemical-resistant clothing, face shields, and devices to protect one's hearing. Most workers also are required to wear respirators while working, to protect them from airborne particles. The respirators range from simple versions that cover only the mouth and nose to self-contained suits with their own air supply.

In the past, asbestos was used to fireproof roofing and flooring, for heat insulation, and for a variety of other purposes. Today, asbestos is rarely used in buildings, but there still are structures that contain the material. Embedded in materials, asbestos is fairly harmless; airborne, however, it can cause several lung diseases, including lung cancer and asbestosis. Similarly, lead was a common building component found in paint and plumbing fixtures and pipes until the late 1970s. Because lead is easily absorbed into the bloodstream, often from breathing lead dust or from eating chips of paint containing lead, it can cause serious health risks, especially in children. Due to these risks, it has become necessary to remove lead-based products and asbestos from buildings and structures.

Asbestos abatement workers and *lead abatement workers* remove asbestos, lead, and other materials from buildings scheduled to be renovated or demolished. Using a variety of hand and power tools, such as vacuums and scrapers, these workers remove the asbestos and lead from surfaces. A typical residential lead abatement project involves the use of a chemical to strip the lead-based paint from the walls of the home. Lead abatement workers apply the compound with a putty knife and allow it to dry. Then they scrape the hazardous material into an impregnable container for transport and storage. They also use sandblasters and high-pressure water sprayers to remove lead from large structures. The vacuums utilized by asbestos abatement workers have special, highly efficient filters designed to trap the asbestos, which later is disposed of or stored. During the abatement, special monitors measure the amount of asbestos and lead in the air, to protect the workers; in addition, lead abatement workers wear a personal air monitor that indicates the amount of lead to which a worker has been exposed. Workers also use monitoring devices to identify the asbestos, lead, and other materials that need to be removed from the surfaces of walls and structures.

Transportation of hazardous materials is safer today than it was in the past, but accidents still occur. *Emergency and disaster response workers* clean up hazardous materials after train derailments and trucking accidents. These workers also are

needed when an immediate cleanup is required, as would be the case after an attack by biological or chemical weapons.

Radioactive materials are classified as either high- or low-level wastes. High-level wastes are primarily nuclear-reactor fuels used to produce electricity. Low-level wastes include any radioactively contaminated protective clothing, tools, filters, medical equipment, and other items. *Decontamination technicians* perform duties similar to those of janitors and cleaners. They use brooms, mops, and other tools to clean exposed areas and remove exposed items for decontamination or disposal. With experience, these workers can advance to *radiation-protection technician* jobs and use radiation survey meters to locate and evaluate materials, operate high-pressure cleaning equipment for decontamination, and package radioactive materials for transportation or disposal.

Decommissioning and decontamination workers remove and treat radioactive materials generated by nuclear facilities and power plants. With a variety of handtools, they break down contaminated items such as "gloveboxes," which are used to process radioactive materials. At decommissioning sites, the workers clean and decontaminate the facility, as well as remove any radioactive or contaminated materials.

Treatment, storage, and disposal workers transport and prepare materials for treatment or disposal. To ensure proper treatment of the materials, laws require these workers to be able to verify shipping manifests. At incinerator facilities, treatment, storage, and disposal workers transport materials from the customer or service center to the incinerator. At landfills, they follow a strict procedure for the processing and storage of hazardous materials. They organize and track the location of items in the landfill and may help change the state of a material from liquid to solid in preparation for its storage. These workers typically operate heavy machinery, such as forklifts, earthmoving machinery, and large trucks and rigs.

Mold remediation is a new and growing part of the work of some hazardous materials removal workers. Some types of mold can cause allergic reactions, especially in people who are susceptible to them. Although mold is present in almost all structures, some mold—especially the types that cause allergic reactions—can infest a building to such a degree that extensive efforts must be taken to remove it safely. Mold typically grows in damp areas, in heating and air-conditioning ducts, within walls, and in attics and basements. Although some mold remediation work is undertaken by other construction workers, mold often must be removed by hazardous materials removal workers, who take special precautions to protect themselves and surrounding areas from being contaminated.

Hazardous materials removal workers also may be required to construct scaffolding or erect containment areas prior to abatement or decontamination. In most cases, government regulation dictates that hazardous materials removal workers be closely supervised on the worksite. The standard usually is 1 supervisor to every 10 workers. The work is highly structured, sometimes planned years in advance, and team oriented. There is a great deal of cooperation among supervisors and workers. Because of the hazard presented by the materials being removed, work areas are restricted to licensed hazardous materials removal workers, thus minimizing exposure to the public.

Working Conditions

Hazardous materials removal workers function in a highly structured environment, to minimize the danger they face. Each phase of an operation is planned in advance, and workers are trained to deal with safety breaches and hazardous situations. Crews and supervisors take every precaution to ensure that the worksite is safe. Whether they work in asbestos, mold, or lead abatement or in radioactive decontamination, hazardous materials removal workers must stand, stoop, and kneel for long periods. Some must wear fully enclosed personal protective suits for several hours at a time; these suits may be hot and uncomfortable and may cause some individuals to experience claustrophobia.

Hazardous materials removal workers face different working conditions, depending on their area of expertise. Although many work a standard 40-hour week, overtime and shift work are common, especially in asbestos and lead abatement. Asbestos abatement and lead abatement workers are found primarily in structures such as office buildings and schools. Because they are under pressure to complete their work within certain deadlines, workers may experience fatigue. Completing projects frequently requires night and weekend work, because hazardous materials removal workers often work around the schedules of others. Treatment, storage, and disposal workers are employed primarily at facilities such as landfills, incinerators, boilers, and industrial furnaces. These facilities often are located in remote areas, due to the kinds of work being done. As a result, workers employed by treatment, storage, or disposal facilities may commute long distances to their jobs.

Decommissioning and decontamination workers, decontamination technicians, and radiation protection technicians work at nuclear facilities and electric power plants. Like treatment, storage, and disposal facilities, these sites often are far from urban areas. Workers, who often perform jobs in cramped conditions, may need to use sharp tools to dismantle contaminated objects. A hazardous materials removal worker must have great self-control and a level head to cope with the daily stress associated with handling hazardous materials.

Hazardous materials removal workers may be required to travel outside their normal working areas in order to respond to emergencies, the cleanup of which sometimes take several days or weeks to complete. During the cleanup, workers may be away from home for the entire time.

Employment

Hazardous materials removal workers held about 38,000 jobs in 2002. About 7 in 10 were employed in waste management and remediation services. About 6 percent were employed by specialty trade contractors, primarily in asbestos abatement and lead abatement. A small number worked at nuclear and electric plants as decommissioning and decontamination workers and radiation safety and decontamination technicians.

Training, Other Qualifications, and Advancement

No formal education beyond a high school diploma is required for a person to become a hazardous materials removal worker. Federal regulations require an individual to have a license to work in the occupation, although, at present, there are few laws regulating mold removal. Most employers provide technical training on the job, but a formal 32- to 40-hour training program must be completed if one is to be licensed to as an asbestos abatement and lead abatement worker or a treatment, storage, and disposal worker. The program covers health hazards, personal protective equipment and clothing, site safety, recognition and identification of hazards, and decontamination. In some cases, workers discover one hazardous material while abating another. If they are not licensed to work with the newly discovered material, they cannot continue to work with it. Many experienced workers opt to take courses in additional disciplines to avoid this situation. Some employers prefer to hire workers licensed in multiple disciplines.

For decommissioning and decontamination workers employed at nuclear facilities, training is more extensive. In addition to the standard 40-hour training course in asbestos, lead, and hazardous waste, workers must take courses dealing with regulations governing nuclear materials and radiation safety. These courses add up to approximately 3 months of training, although most are not taken consecutively. Many agencies, organizations, and companies throughout the country provide training programs that are approved by the U.S. Environmental Protection Agency, the U.S. Department of Energy, and other regulatory bodies. Workers in all fields are required to take refresher courses every year in order to maintain their license.

Workers must be able to perform basic mathematical conversions and calculations, and should have good physical strength and manual dexterity. Because of the nature of the work and the time constraints sometimes involved, employers prefer people who are dependable, prompt, and detail-oriented. Because much of the work is done in buildings, a background in construction is helpful.

Job Outlook

Job opportunities are expected to be good for hazardous materials removal workers. The occupation is characterized by a relatively high rate of turnover, resulting in a number of job openings each year stemming from experienced workers leaving the occupation. In addition, many potential workers are not attracted to this occupation, because they may prefer work that is less strenuous and has safer working conditions. Experienced workers will have especially favorable opportunities, particularly in the private sector, as more state and local governments contract out hazardous materials removal work to private companies.

Employment of hazardous materials removal workers is expected to grow much faster than the average for all occupations through the year 2012, reflecting increasing concern for a safe and clean environment. Special-trade contractors will have strong demand for the largest segment of these workers, namely, asbestos abatement and lead abatement workers; lead abatement should offer particularly good opportunities. Mold remediation is an especially rapidly growing part of the occupation at the present time, but it is unclear whether its rapid growth will continue: until a few years ago, mold remediation was not considered a significant problem, and perhaps a few years from now, less attention will be paid to it again.

Employment of decontamination technicians, radiation safety technicians, and decommissioning and decontamination workers is expected to grow in response to increased pressure for safer and cleaner nuclear and electric generator facilities. In addition, the number of closed facilities that need decommissioning may continue to grow, due to federal legislation. These workers also are less affected by economic fluctuations, because the facilities in which they work must operate, regardless of the state of the economy.

Earnings

Median hourly earnings of hazardous materials removal workers were $15.61 in 2002. The middle 50 percent earned between $12.37 and $22.18 per hour. The lowest 10 percent earned less than $10.29 per hour, and the highest 10 percent earned more than $26.60 per hour. The median hourly earnings in remediation and other waste management services, the largest industry employing hazardous materials removal workers in 2002, were $14.92 in 2002.

Miscellaneous special trade contractors	$13.78
Sanitary services	13.30

According to the limited data available, treatment, storage, and disposal workers usually earn slightly more than asbestos abatement and lead abatement workers. Decontamination and decommissioning workers and radiation protection technicians, though constituting the smallest group, tend to earn the highest wages.

Related Occupations

Asbestos abatement workers and lead abatement workers share skills with other construction trades workers, including painters and paperhangers; insulation workers; and sheet metal workers. Treatment, storage, and disposal workers, decommissioning and decontamination workers, and decontamination and radiation safety technicians work closely with plant and system operators, such as power-plant operators, distributors, and dispatchers and water and liquid waste treatment plant operators.

Sources of Additional Information

For more information on hazardous materials removal workers, including information on training, contact

- Laborers-AGC Education and Training Fund, 37 Deerfield Rd., P.O. Box 37, Pomfret, CT 06259. Internet: http://www.laborerslearn.org

There are more than 500 occupations registered by the U.S. Department of Labor's National Apprenticeship system. For more information on the Labor Department's registered apprenticeship system, and links to state apprenticeship programs, check their Web site: http:// www.doleta.gov.

Heating, Air-Conditioning, and Refrigeration Mechanics and Installers

(O*NET 49-9021.01 and 49-9021.02)

Significant Points

- Job prospects for heating, air-conditioning, and refrigeration mechanics and installers are expected to be good, particularly for those with technical school or formal apprenticeship training.

- The Air-Conditioning Excellence program, offered through North American Technician Excellence, is the standard for certification of experienced technicians.

Nature of the Work

What would those living in Chicago do without heating, those in Miami do without air-conditioning, or blood banks all over the country do without refrigeration? Heating and air-conditioning systems control the temperature, humidity, and the total air quality in residential, commercial, industrial, and other buildings. Refrigeration systems make it possible to store and transport food, medicine, and other perishable items. Heating, air-conditioning, and refrigeration mechanics and installers—also called technicians—install, maintain, and repair such systems. Because heating, ventilation, air-conditioning, and refrigeration systems often are referred to as HVACR systems, these workers also may be called HVACR technicians.

Heating, air-conditioning, and refrigeration systems consist of many mechanical, electrical, and electronic components, such as motors, compressors, pumps, fans, ducts, pipes, thermostats, and switches. In central heating systems, for example, a furnace heats air that is distributed throughout the building via a system of metal or fiberglass ducts. Technicians must be able to maintain, diagnose, and correct problems throughout the entire system. To do this, they adjust system controls to recommended settings and test the performance of the entire system using special tools and test equipment.

Technicians often specialize in either installation or maintenance and repair, although they are trained to do both. Some specialize in one type of equipment—for example, oil burners, solar panels, or commercial refrigerators. Technicians may work for large or small contracting companies or directly for a manufacturer or wholesaler. Those working for smaller operations tend to do both installation and servicing, and work with heating, cooling, and refrigeration equipment. Service contracts—which involve heating, air-conditioning, and refrigeration work for particular customers on a regular basis—are becoming more common. Service agreements help to reduce the seasonal fluctuations of this work.

Heating and air-conditioning mechanics install, service, and repair heating and air-conditioning systems in both residences and commercial establishments. *Furnace installers*, also called *heating equipment technicians*, follow blueprints or other specifications to install oil, gas, electric, solid-fuel, and multiple-fuel heating systems. *Air-conditioning mechanics* install and service central air-conditioning systems. After putting the equipment in place, they install fuel and water supply lines, air ducts and vents, pumps, and other components. They may connect electrical wiring and controls and check the unit for proper operation. To ensure the proper functioning of the system, furnace installers often use combustion test equipment, such as carbon dioxide and oxygen testers.

After a furnace has been installed, heating equipment technicians often perform routine maintenance and repair work to keep the system operating efficiently. During the fall and winter, for example, when the system is used most, they service and adjust burners and blowers. If the system is not operating properly, they check the thermostat, burner nozzles, controls, or other parts to diagnose and then correct the problem.

During the summer, when the heating system is not being used, heating equipment technicians do maintenance work, such as replacing filters, ducts, and other parts of the system that may accumulate dust and impurities during the operating season. During the winter, air-conditioning mechanics inspect the systems and do required maintenance, such as overhauling compressors.

Refrigeration mechanics install, service, and repair industrial and commercial refrigerating systems and a variety of refrigeration equipment. They follow blueprints, design specifications, and manufacturers' instructions to install motors, compressors, condensing units, evaporators, piping, and other components. They connect this equipment to the ductwork, refrigerant lines, and electrical power source. After making the connections, they charge the system with refrigerant, check it for proper operation, and program control systems.

When heating, air-conditioning, and refrigeration mechanics service equipment, they must use care to conserve, recover, and recycle chlorofluorocarbon (CFC) and hydrochlorofluorocarbon (HCFC) refrigerants used in air-conditioning and refrigeration systems. The release of CFCs and HCFCs contributes to the depletion of the stratospheric ozone layer, which protects plant and animal life from ultraviolet radiation. Technicians conserve the refrigerant by making sure that there are no leaks in the system; they recover it by venting the refrigerant into proper cylinders; and they recycle it for reuse with special filter-dryers.

Heating, air-conditioning, and refrigeration mechanics and installers are adept at using a variety of tools, including hammers, wrenches, metal snips, electric drills, pipe cutters and benders, measurement gauges, and acetylene torches, to work with refrigerant lines and air ducts. They use voltmeters, thermometers, pressure gauges, manometers, and other testing devices to check airflow, refrigerant pressure, electrical circuits, burners, and other components.

Other craftworkers sometimes install or repair cooling and heating systems. For example, on a large air-conditioning installation job, especially where workers are covered by union contracts, ductwork might be done by sheet metal workers and duct installers; electrical work by electricians; and installation of piping, condensers, and other components by pipelayers, plumbers, pipefitters, and steamfitters. Home appliance repairers usually service room air-conditioners and household refrigerators.

Working Conditions

Heating, air-conditioning, and refrigeration mechanics and installers work in homes, stores of all kinds, hospitals, office buildings, and factories—anywhere there is climate-control equipment. They may be assigned to specific jobsites at the beginning of each day, or if they are making service calls, they may be dispatched to jobs by radio, telephone, or pager. Increasingly, employers are using cell phones to coordinate technicians' schedules.

Technicians may work outside in cold or hot weather or in buildings that are uncomfortable because the air-conditioning or heating equipment is broken. In addition, technicians might have to work in awkward or cramped positions and sometimes are required to work in high places. Hazards include electrical shock, burns, muscle strains, and other injuries from handling heavy equipment. Appropriate safety equipment is necessary when handling refrigerants because contact can cause skin damage, frostbite, or blindness. Inhalation of refrigerants when working in confined spaces also is a possible hazard.

The majority of mechanics and installers work at least a 40-hour week. During peak seasons they often work overtime or irregular hours. Maintenance workers, including those who provide maintenance services under contract, often work evening or weekend shifts and are on call. Most employers try to provide a full workweek year-round by scheduling both installation and maintenance work, and many manufacturers and contractors now provide or even require service contracts. In most shops that service both heating and air-conditioning equipment, employment is stable throughout the year.

Heating, air-conditioning, and refrigeration mechanics and installers held about 249,000 jobs in 2002; almost half worked for cooling and heating contractors. The remainder was employed in a variety of industries throughout the country, reflecting a widespread dependence on climate-control systems. Some worked for fuel oil dealers, refrigeration and air-conditioning service and repair shops, schools, and stores that sell heating and air-conditioning systems. Local governments, the federal government, hospitals, office buildings, and other organizations that operate large air-conditioning, refrigeration, or heating systems employed others. About 15 percent of mechanics and installers were self-employed.

Employment

Heating, air-conditioning, and refrigeration mechanics and installers held about 249,000 jobs in 2002; almost half worked for cooling and heating contractors. The remainder was employed in a variety of industries throughout the country, reflecting a widespread dependence on climate-control systems. Some worked for fuel oil dealers, refrigeration and air-conditioning service and repair shops, schools, and stores that sell heating and air-conditioning systems. Local governments, the federal government, hospitals, office buildings, and other organizations that operate large air-conditioning, refrigeration, or heating systems employed others. About 15 percent of mechanics and installers were self-employed.

Training, Other Qualifications, and Advancement

Because of the increasing sophistication of heating, air-conditioning, and refrigeration systems, employers prefer to hire those with technical school or apprenticeship training. Many mechanics and installers, however, still learn the trade informally on the job.

Many secondary and postsecondary technical and trade schools, junior and community colleges, and the U.S. Armed Forces offer 6-month to 2-year programs in heating, air-conditioning, and refrigeration. Students study theory, design, and equipment construction, as well as electronics. They also learn the basics of installation, maintenance, and repair.

Apprenticeship programs frequently are run by joint committees representing local chapters of the Air-Conditioning Contractors of America, the Mechanical Contractors Association of America, the National Association of Plumbing-Heating-Cooling Contractors, and locals of the Sheet Metal Workers' International Association or the United Association of Journeymen and Apprentices of the Plumbing and Pipefitting Industry of the United States and Canada. Other

apprenticeship programs are sponsored by local chapters of the Associated Builders and Contractors and the National Association of Home Builders. Formal apprenticeship programs normally last 3 to 5 years and combine on-the-job training with classroom instruction. Classes include subjects such as the use and care of tools, safety practices, blueprint reading, and the theory and design of heating, ventilation, air-conditioning, and refrigeration systems. Applicants for these programs must have a high school diploma or equivalent. Math and reading skills are essential.

Those who acquire their skills on the job usually begin by assisting experienced technicians. They may begin by performing simple tasks such as carrying materials, insulating refrigerant lines, or cleaning furnaces. In time, they move on to more difficult tasks, such as cutting and soldering pipes and sheet metal and checking electrical and electronic circuits.

Courses in shop math, mechanical drawing, applied physics and chemistry, electronics, blueprint reading, and computer applications provide a good background for those interested in entering this occupation. Some knowledge of plumbing or electrical work also is helpful. A basic understanding of electronics is becoming more important because of the increasing use of this technology in equipment controls. Because technicians frequently deal directly with the public, they should be courteous and tactful, especially when dealing with an aggravated customer. They also should be in good physical condition because they sometimes have to lift and move heavy equipment.

All technicians who purchase or work with refrigerants must be certified in their proper handling. To become certified to purchase and handle refrigerants, technicians must pass a written examination specific to the type of work in which they specialize. The three possible areas of certification are: Type I—servicing small appliances, Type II—high-pressure refrigerants, and Type III—low-pressure refrigerants. Exams are administered by organizations approved by the U.S. Environmental Protection Agency, such as trade schools, unions, contractor associations, or building groups.

Several organizations have begun to offer basic self-study, classroom, and Internet courses for individuals with limited experience. In addition to understanding how systems work, technicians must be knowledgeable about refrigerant products and the legislation and regulations that govern their use. The Air-Conditioning Excellence program, which is offered through North American Technician Excellence (NATE), generally has been adopted as the standard for certification of experienced technicians.

Advancement usually takes the form of higher wages. Some technicians, however, may advance to positions as supervisor or service manager. Others may move into areas such as sales and marketing. Still others may become building superintendents, cost estimators, or, with the necessary certification, teachers. Those with sufficient money and managerial skill can open their own contracting business.

Job Outlook

Job prospects for heating, air-conditioning, and refrigeration mechanics and installers are expected to be good, particularly for those with technical school or formal apprenticeship training. Employment of heating, air-conditioning, and refrigeration mechanics and installers is expected to grow faster than the average for all occupations through the year 2012. As the population and economy grow, so does the demand for new residential, commercial, and industrial climate-control systems. Technicians who specialize in installation work may experience periods of unemployment when the level of new construction activity declines, but maintenance and repair work usually remains relatively stable. People and businesses depend on their climate-control systems and must keep them in good working order, regardless of economic conditions.

Renewed concern for energy conservation should continue to prompt the development of new energy-saving heating and air-conditioning systems. An emphasis on better energy management should lead to the replacement of older systems and the installation of newer, more efficient systems in existing homes and buildings. Also, demand for maintenance and service work should increase as businesses and homeowners strive to keep systems operating at peak efficiency. Regulations prohibiting the discharge of CFC and HCFC refrigerants took effect in 1993, and regulations banning CFC production became effective in 2000. Consequently, these regulations should continue to result in demand for technicians to replace many existing systems, or modify them to use new environmentally safe refrigerants. In addition, the continuing focus on improving indoor air quality should contribute to the creation of more jobs for heating, air-conditioning, and refrigeration technicians. Also, growth of business establishments that use refrigerated equipment—such as supermarkets and convenience stores—will contribute to a growing need for technicians. In addition to job openings created by employment growth, thousands of openings will result from the need to replace workers who transfer to other occupations or leave the labor force.

Earnings

Median hourly earnings of heating, air-conditioning, and refrigeration mechanics and installers were $16.78 in 2002. The middle 50 percent earned between $12.95 and $21.37 an hour. The lowest 10 percent earned less than $10.34, and the top 10 percent earned more than $26.20. Median hourly earnings in the industries employing the largest numbers of heating, air-conditioning, and refrigeration mechanics and installers in 2002 were as follows:

Hardware, and plumbing and heating
  equipment and supplies merchant wholesalers....$18.78

Commercial and industrial machinery and
  equipment (except automotive and electronic)
  repair and maintenance..17.16

Direct selling establishments....................................17.14

Elementary and secondary schools 16.80

Building equipment contractors 16.03

Apprentices usually begin at about 50 percent of the wage rate paid to experienced workers. As they gain experience and improve their skills, they receive periodic increases until they reach the wage rate of experienced workers.

Heating, air-conditioning, and refrigeration mechanics and installers enjoy a variety of employer-sponsored benefits. In addition to typical benefits such as health insurance and pension plans, some employers pay for work-related training and provide uniforms, company vans, and tools.

About 20 percent of heating, air-conditioning, and refrigeration mechanics and installers are members of a union. The unions to which the greatest numbers of mechanics and installers belong are the Sheet Metal Workers' International Association and the United Association of Journeymen and Apprentices of the Plumbing and Pipefitting Industry of the United States and Canada.

Related Occupations

Heating, air-conditioning, and refrigeration mechanics and installers work with sheet metal and piping, and repair machinery, such as electrical motors, compressors, and burners. Other workers who have similar skills include boilermakers; home appliance repairers; electricians; sheet metal workers; and pipelayers, plumbers, pipefitters, and steamfitters.

Sources of Additional Information

For more information about opportunities for training, certification, and employment in this trade, contact local vocational and technical schools; local heating, air-conditioning, and refrigeration contractors; a local of the unions or organizations previously mentioned; a local joint union-management apprenticeship committee; or the nearest office of the state employment service or apprenticeship agency.

For information on career opportunities, training, and technician certification, contact:

- Air-Conditioning Contractors of America (ACCA), 2800 Shirlington Rd., Suite 300, Arlington, VA 22206. Internet: http://www.acca.org

- Refrigeration Service Engineers Society (RSES), 1666 Rand Rd., Des Plaines, IL 60016-3552. Internet: http://www.rses.org

- Plumbing-Heating-Cooling Contractors (PHCC), 180 S. Washington St., P.O. Box 6808, Falls Church, VA 22046. Internet: http://www.phccweb.org

- Sheet Metal and Air-Conditioning Contractors' National Association, 4201 Lafayette Center Dr., Chantilly, VA 20151-1209. Internet: http://www.smacna.org

For information on technician testing and certification, contact:

- North American Technician Excellence (NATE), 4100 North Fairfax Dr., Suite 210, Arlington, VA 22203. Internet: http://www.natex.org

For information on career opportunities and training, contact:

- Associated Builders and Contractors, Workforce Development Department, 4250 North Fairfax Dr., 9th Floor, Arlington, VA 22203.

- Home Builders Institute, 1201 15th St. NW, 6th Floor, Washington, DC 20005-2800. Internet: http://www.hbi.org

- Mechanical Contractors Association of America, 1385 Piccard Dr., Rockville, MD 20850-4329. Internet: http://www.mcaa.org

- Air-Conditioning and Refrigeration Institute, 4100 North Fairfax Dr., Suite 200, Arlington, VA 22203. Internet: http://www.ari.org

There are more than 500 occupations registered by the U.S. Department of Labor's National Apprenticeship System. For more information on the Labor Department's registered apprenticeship system and links to state apprenticeship programs, check their Web site: http://www.doleta.gov.

Hotel, Motel, and Resort Desk Clerks

(O*NET 43-4081.00)

Significant Points

- Numerous job openings should arise for hotel, motel, and resort desk clerks due to employment growth and the need to replace workers who leave these occupations.

- A high school diploma or its equivalent is the most common educational requirement.

- Because many hotel, motel, and resort desk clerks deal directly with the public, a professional appearance and a pleasant personality are imperative.

- These occupations are well suited to flexible work schedules.

Nature of the Work

Hotel, motel, and resort desk clerks perform a variety of services for guests of hotels, motels, and other lodging establishments. Regardless of the type of accommodation, most desk clerks have similar responsibilities. Primarily, they register arriving guests, assign rooms, and check out guests at the end of their stay. They also keep records of room assignments and other registration-related information on computers. When guests check out, desk clerks prepare and explain the charges, as well as process payments.

Front-desk clerks always are in the public eye and, through their attitude and behavior, greatly influence the public's impressions of the establishment. When answering questions about services, checkout times, the local community, or other matters of public interest, clerks must be courteous and helpful. Should guests report problems with their rooms, clerks contact members of the housekeeping or maintenance staff to correct the problems.

In some smaller hotels and motels, clerks may have a variety of additional responsibilities that usually are performed by specialized employees in larger establishments. In the smaller places, desk clerks often are responsible for all front-office operations, information, and services. For example, they may perform the work of a bookkeeper, advance reservation agent, cashier, laundry attendant, and telephone switchboard operator.

Working Conditions

Working conditions vary for hotel, motel, and resort desk clerks, but most work in areas that are clean, well lit, and relatively quiet. This is especially true for clerks who greet customers and visitors; they usually work in highly visible areas that are furnished to make a good impression. Because a number of clerks may share the same workspace, it may be crowded and noisy.

Although most hotel, motel, and resort desk clerks work a standard 40-hour week, about 1 out of 5 works part time. Because hotels and motels need to be staffed 24 hours a day, evening, late-night, weekend, and holiday work is common. In general, employees with the least seniority tend to be assigned the least desirable shifts. Some high school and college students work part time in these occupations, after school or during vacations.

The work performed by hotel, motel, and resort desk clerks may be repetitive and stressful, especially when these workers are trying to serve the needs of difficult or angry customers. When flights are canceled, reservations mishandled, or guests dissatisfied, these clerks must bear the brunt of the customers' anger. Hotel desk clerks and ticket agents may be on their feet most of the time. In addition, prolonged exposure to a video display terminal may lead to eyestrain for the many clerks who work with computers.

Employment

Hotel, motel, and resort desk clerks held about 178,000 jobs in 2002. The occupation is well suited to flexible work schedules, as nearly 1 in 4 hotel clerks worked part time in 2002. Because hotels and motels need to be staffed 24 hours a day, evening and weekend work is common.

Training, Other Qualifications, and Advancement

Despite the fact that hiring requirements for hotel, motel, and resort desk clerks vary, a high school diploma or its equivalent is the most common educational requirement. Increasingly, familiarity or experience with computers and good interpersonal skills are becoming equally important as the diploma to employers.

Many hotel, motel, and resort desk clerks deal directly with the public, so a professional appearance and a pleasant personality are important. A clear speaking voice and fluency in the English language also are essential because these employees frequently use the telephone or public-address systems. Good spelling and computer literacy often are needed, particularly because most work involves considerable use of the computer. In addition, speaking a foreign language fluently is becoming increasingly helpful.

Hotel, motel, and resort desk clerks generally receive orientation and training on the job. It usually includes an explanation of the job duties and information about the establishment, such as the locations of rooms and the available services. New employees learn job tasks through on-the-job training under the guidance of a supervisor or an experienced clerk. They often need additional training in how to use the computerized reservation, room assignment, and billing systems and equipment. Most clerks continue to receive instruction on new procedures and on company policies after their initial training ends.

Advancement for hotel, motel, and resort desk clerks usually comes by transfer to a position with more responsibilities or by promotion to a supervisory position. Clerks can improve their chances for advancement by taking home-study or group-study courses in lodging management, such as those sponsored by the Educational Institute of the American Hotel and Motel Association.

Job Outlook

Employment of hotel, motel, and resort desk clerks is expected to grow faster than the average for all occupations through 2012, as more hotels, motels, and other lodging establishments are built and occupancy rates rise. Job opportunities for hotel and motel desk clerks also will result from a need to replace workers, because many of these clerks either transfer to other occupations that offer better pay and advancement opportunities or simply leave the workforce altogether. Opportunities for part-time work should continue to be plentiful, with front desks often staffed 24 hours a day, 7 days a week.

Employment of hotel and motel desk clerks should benefit from an increase in business and leisure travel. Shifts in preferences away from long vacations and toward long weekends and other, more frequent, shorter trips also should boost demand for these workers, because such stays increase the number of nights spent in hotels. The expansion of budget and extended-stay hotels relative to larger, luxury establishments reflects a change in the composition of the hotel and motel industry. As employment shifts from luxury hotels to those extended-stay establishments offering larger rooms with kitchenettes and laundry services, the proportion of hotel desk clerks should increase in relation to staff such as waiters and waitresses and recreation workers. Desk clerks are able to handle more of the guest's needs in these establishments, answering the main switchboard, providing business services, and coordinating services such as dry cleaning or grocery shopping.

New technologies automating check-in and checkout procedures now allow some guests to bypass the front desk in many larger establishments, reducing staffing needs. As some of the more traditional duties are automated, however, many desk clerks are assuming a wider range of responsibilities.

Employment of desk clerks is sensitive to cyclical swings in the economy. During recessions, vacation and business travel declines, and hotels and motels need fewer clerks. Similarly, employment is affected by seasonal fluctuations in tourism and travel.

Earnings

Annual earnings in 2002 were less than $13,020 for the lowest-paid 10 percent of hotel clerks. The median annual earnings for hotel, motel, and resort desk clerks were $17,370.

Earnings of hotel, motel, and resort desk clerks also vary considerably depending on the location, size, and type of establishment in which they work. For example, clerks at large luxury hotels and at those located in metropolitan and resort areas generally are paid more than clerks at less exclusive or "budget" establishments and than those working at hotels and motels in less populated areas.

In addition to their hourly wage, full-time hotel, motel, and resort desk clerks who work evenings, nights, weekends, or holidays may receive shift differential pay. Some employers offer educational assistance to their employees.

Related Occupations

A number of other workers deal with the public, receive and provide information, or direct people to others who can assist them. Among these workers are customer service representatives, dispatchers, security guards and gaming surveillance workers, tellers, and counter and rental clerks.

Sources of Additional Information

Information on careers in the lodging industry, as well as information about professional development and training programs, may be obtained from:

- Educational Institute of the American Hotel and Lodging Association, 800 N. Magnolia Ave., Suite 1800, Orlando, FL 32803. Internet: http://www.ei-ahma.org

Human Resources Assistants, Except Payroll and Timekeeping

(O*NET 43-4161.00)

Significant Points

- Numerous job openings should arise for human resource assistants due to employment growth and the need to replace workers who leave these occupations.

- A high school diploma or its equivalent is the most common educational requirement.

- Because many human resource assistants deal directly with the public, a professional appearance and a pleasant personality are imperative.

- This occupation is well suited to flexible work schedules.

Nature of the Work

Human resources assistants maintain the personnel records of an organization's employees. These records include information such as name, address, job title, and earnings, benefits such as health and life insurance, and tax withholding. On a daily basis, these assistants record information and answer questions about employee absences and supervisory reports on employees' job performance. When an employee receives a promotion or switches health insurance plans, the human resources assistant updates the appropriate form. Human resources assistants also may prepare reports for managers elsewhere within the organization. For example, they might compile a list of employees eligible for an award.

In smaller organizations, some human resources assistants perform a variety of other clerical duties, including answering telephone or written inquiries from the public, sending out announcements of job openings or job examinations, and issuing application forms. When credit bureaus and finance companies request confirmation of a person's employment, the human resources assistant provides authorized information from the employee's personnel records. He or she may also contact payroll departments and insurance companies to verify changes to records.

Some human resources assistants are involved in hiring. They screen job applicants to obtain information such as their education and work experience; administer aptitude, personality, and interest tests; explain the organization's employment policies and refer qualified applicants to the employing official; and request references from present or past employers. Also, human resources assistants inform job applicants, by telephone or letter, of their acceptance for or denial of employment.

In some job settings, human resources assistants have specific job titles. For example, *assignment clerks* notify a firm's existing employees of upcoming vacancies, identify applicants who qualify for the vacancies, and assign those who are qualified to various positions. They also keep track of vacancies that arise throughout the organization, and they complete and distribute forms advertising vacancies. When filled-out applications are returned, these clerks review and verify the information in them, using personnel records. After a selection for a position is made, they notify all of the applicants of their acceptance or rejection.

As another example, *identification clerks* are responsible for security matters at defense installations. They compile and record personal data about vendors, contractors, and civilian and military personnel and their dependents. The identification clerk's job duties include interviewing applicants, corresponding with law enforcement authorities, and preparing badges, passes, and identification cards.

Working Conditions

Most human resource assistants work in areas that are clean, well lit, and relatively quiet, and most work a standard 40-hour week.

The work performed by human resource assistants may be repetitious and stressful. Prolonged exposure to a video display terminal may lead to eyestrain for the many human resource assistants who work with computers.

Employment

Human resources assistants held about 174,000 jobs in 2002. Although these workers are found in most industries, about 1 in every 4 is employed by a government agency. Colleges and universities, hospitals, department stores, and banks also employ large numbers of human resources assistants.

Training, Other Qualifications, and Advancement

Despite the fact that hiring requirements for human resources assistants vary, a high school diploma or its equivalent is the most common educational requirement. Increasingly, familiarity or experience with computers and good interpersonal skills are becoming equally important as the diploma to employers.

Many human resources assistants deal directly with the public, so a professional appearance and a pleasant personality are important. A clear speaking voice and fluency in the English language also are essential, because these employees frequently use the telephone. Good spelling and computer literacy often are needed, particularly because most work involves considerable use of the computer.

Human resources assistants often learn the skills they need in high schools, business schools, and community colleges.

Business education programs offered by these institutions typically include courses in typing, word processing, shorthand, business communications, records management, and office systems and procedures.

Some entry-level human resource assistants are college graduates with degrees in business, finance, or liberal arts. Workers with college degrees are likely to start at higher salaries and advance more easily than those without degrees.

Regardless of their level of educational attainment, human resources assistants usually receive on-the-job training. Under the guidance of a supervisor or other senior workers, new employees learn company procedures. Some formal classroom training also may be necessary, such as training in specific computer software.

Advancement for human resources assistants usually comes by transfer to a position with more responsibilities or by promotion to a supervisory position. Most companies fill office and administrative support supervisory and managerial positions by promoting individuals within their organization, so human resources assistants who acquire additional skills, experience, and training improve their opportunities for advancement.

Job Outlook

Employment of human resources assistants is expected to grow about as fast as the average for all occupations through the year 2012, as assistants continue to take on more responsibilities. For example, workers conduct Internet research to locate resumes, must be able to scan resumes of job candidates quickly and efficiently, and must be increasingly sensitive to confidential information such as salaries and Social Security numbers. In a favorable job market, more emphasis is placed on human resources departments, thus increasing the demand for assistants. However, even in economic downturns, there is demand, as human resources departments in all industries try to make their organizations more efficient by determining what type of employees to hire and strategically filling job openings. Human resources assistants may play an instrumental role in their organization's human resources policies. For example, they may talk to staffing firms and consulting firms, conduct other research, and then offer their ideas on issues such as whether to hire temporary contract workers or full-time staff.

As with other office and administrative support occupations, the growing use of computers in human resources departments means that much of the data entry that is done by human resources assistants can be eliminated, as employees themselves enter the data and send the electronic file to the human resources office. Such an arrangement, which is most feasible in large organizations with multiple human resources offices, could limit job growth among human resources assistants.

In addition to positions arising from job growth, replacement needs will account for many job openings for human resources assistants as they advance within the human resources department, take jobs unrelated to human resources administration, or leave the labor force.

Earnings

Annual earnings in 2002 for human resource assistants, except for those in payroll and timekeeping, were $30,410.

Related Occupations

A number of other workers deal with the public, receive and provide information, or direct people to others who can assist them. Among these workers are customer service representatives, dispatchers, security guards and gaming surveillance workers, tellers, and counter and rental clerks.

Sources of Additional Information

State employment service offices can provide information about employment opportunities.

Human Resources, Training, and Labor Relations Managers and Specialists

(O*NET 11-3040.00, 11-3041.00, 11-3042.00, 11-3049.99, 13-1071.01, 13-1071.02, 13-1072.00, 13-1073.00, and 13-1079.99)

Significant Points

- Entry-level jobs are filled by college graduates who have majored in a wide range of fields.

- For many specialized jobs, previous experience is an asset; for more advanced positions, including those of managers, arbitrators, and mediators, it is essential.

- Keen competition for jobs is expected due to the abundant supply of qualified college graduates and experienced workers.

Nature of the Work

Attracting the most qualified employees and matching them to the jobs for which they are best suited is important for the success of any organization. However, many enterprises are too large to permit close contact between top management and employees. Human resources, training, and labor relations managers and specialists provide this link. In the past, these workers have been associated with performing the administrative function of an organization, such as handling employee benefits questions or recruiting, interviewing, and hiring new personnel in accordance with policies and requirements that have been established in conjunction with top management. Today's human resources workers juggle these tasks and, increasingly, consult top executives regarding strategic planning. They have moved from behind-the-scenes staff work to leading the company in suggesting and changing policies. Senior management is recognizing the importance of the human resources department to their financial success.

In an effort to improve morale and productivity and to limit job turnover, they also help their firms effectively use employee skills, provide training opportunities to enhance those skills, and boost employees' satisfaction with their jobs and working conditions. Although some jobs in the human resources field require only limited contact with people outside the office, dealing with people is an essential part of the job.

In a small organization, a *human resources generalist* may handle all aspects of human resources work, and thus require a broad range of knowledge. The responsibilities of human resources generalists can vary widely, depending on their employer's needs. In a large corporation, the top human resources executive usually develops and coordinates personnel programs and policies. These policies usually are implemented by a director or manager of human resources and, in some cases, a director of industrial relations.

The *director of human resources* may oversee several departments, each headed by an experienced manager who most likely specializes in one personnel activity, such as employment, compensation, benefits, training and development, or employee relations.

Employment and placement managers oversee the hiring and separation of employees and supervise various workers, including equal employment opportunity specialists and recruitment specialists. *Employment, recruitment, and placement specialists* recruit and place workers.

Recruiters maintain contacts within the community and may travel extensively, often to college campuses, to search for promising job applicants. Recruiters screen, interview, and sometimes test applicants. They also may check references and extend job offers. These workers must be thoroughly familiar with the organization and its personnel policies in order to discuss wages, working conditions, and promotional opportunities with prospective employees. They also must keep informed about equal employment opportunity (EEO) and affirmative action guidelines and laws, such as the Americans with Disabilities Act.

EEO officers, representatives, or *affirmative action coordinators* handle EEO matters in large organizations. They investigate and resolve EEO grievances, examine corporate practices for possible violations, and compile and submit EEO statistical reports.

Employer relations representatives, who usually work in government agencies, maintain working relationships with local employers and promote the use of public employment programs and services. Similarly, *employment interviewers*—whose many job titles include *personnel consultants, personnel development specialists,* and *human resources coordinators*—help to match employers with qualified jobseekers.

Compensation, benefits, and job analysis specialists conduct programs for employers and may specialize in specific areas such as position classifications or pensions. *Job analysts*, sometimes called *position classifiers*, collect and examine detailed information about job duties in order to prepare job descriptions. These descriptions explain the duties, training, and skills that each job requires. Whenever a large organization introduces a new job or reviews existing jobs, it calls upon the expert knowledge of the job analyst.

Occupational analysts conduct research, usually in large firms. They are concerned with occupational classification systems and study the effects of industry and occupational trends upon worker relationships. They may serve as technical liaison between the firm and other firms, government, and labor unions.

Establishing and maintaining a firm's pay system is the principal job of the *compensation manager*. Assisted by staff specialists, compensation managers devise ways to ensure fair and equitable pay rates. They may conduct surveys to see how their firm's rates compare with others and to see that the firm's pay scale complies with changing laws and regulations. In addition, compensation managers often oversee their firm's performance evaluation system, and they may design reward systems such as pay-for-performance plans.

Employee benefits managers and specialists handle the company's employee benefits program, notably its health insurance and pension plans. Expertise in designing and administering benefits programs continues to take on importance as employer-provided benefits account for a growing proportion of overall compensation costs, and as benefit plans increase in number and complexity. For example, pension benefits might include savings and thrift, profit-sharing, and stock ownership plans; health benefits might include long-term catastrophic illness insurance and dental insurance. Familiarity with health benefits is a top priority for employee benefits managers and specialists, as more firms struggle to cope with the rising cost of healthcare for employees and retirees. In addition to health insurance and pension coverage, some firms offer employees life and accidental death and dismemberment insurance, disability insurance, and relatively new benefits designed to meet the needs of a changing workforce, such as parental leave, child and elder care, long-term nursing home care insurance, employee assistance and wellness programs, and flexible benefits plans. Benefits managers must keep abreast of changing federal and state regulations and legislation that may affect employee benefits.

Employee assistance plan managers, also called *employee welfare managers*, are responsible for a wide array of programs covering occupational safety and health standards and practices; health promotion and physical fitness, medical examinations, and minor health treatment, such as first aid; plant security; publications; food service and recreation activities;

carpooling and transportation programs, such as transit subsidies; employee suggestion systems; childcare and elder care; and counseling services. Childcare and elder care are increasingly important due to growth in the number of dual-income households and the elderly population. Counseling may help employees deal with emotional disorders, alcoholism, or marital, family, consumer, legal, and financial problems. Some employers offer career counseling as well. In large firms, certain programs, such as those dealing with security and safety, may be in separate departments headed by other managers.

Training and development managers and specialists conduct and supervise training and development programs for employees. Increasingly, management recognizes that training offers a way of developing skills, enhancing productivity and quality of work, and building worker loyalty to the firm. Training is widely accepted as a method of improving employee morale, but this is only one of the reasons for its growing importance. Other factors include the complexity of the work environment, the rapid pace of organizational and technological change, and the growing number of jobs in fields that constantly generate new knowledge. In addition, advances in learning theory have provided insights into how adults learn, and how training can be organized most effectively for them.

Training managers provide worker training either in the classroom or onsite. This includes setting up teaching materials prior to the class, involving the class, and issuing completion certificates at the end of the class.

Training specialists plan, organize, and direct a wide range of training activities. Trainers respond to corporate and worker service requests. They consult with onsite supervisors regarding available performance improvement services and conduct orientation sessions and arrange on-the-job training for new employees. They help rank-and-file workers maintain and improve their job skills, and possibly prepare for jobs requiring greater skill. They help supervisors improve their interpersonal skills in order to deal effectively with employees. They may set up individualized training plans to strengthen an employee's existing skills or teach new ones. Training specialists in some companies set up leadership or executive development programs among employees in lower level positions. These programs are designed to develop potential executives to replace those leaving the organization. Trainers also lead programs to assist employees with transitions due to mergers and acquisitions, as well as technological changes. In government-supported training programs, training specialists function as case managers. They first assess the training needs of clients, then guide them through the most appropriate training method. After training, clients may either be referred to employer relations representatives or receive job placement assistance.

Planning and program development is an important part of the training specialist's job. In order to identify and assess training needs within the firm, trainers may confer with managers and supervisors or conduct surveys. They also periodically evaluate training effectiveness.

Depending on the size, goals, and nature of the organization, trainers may differ considerably in their responsibilities and in the methods they use. Training methods include on-the-job training; operating schools that duplicate shop conditions for trainees prior to putting them on the shop floor; apprenticeship training; classroom training; and electronic learning, which may involve interactive Internet-based training, multimedia programs, distance learning, satellite training, other computer-aided instructional technologies, videos, simulators, conferences, and workshops.

An organization's *director of industrial relations* forms labor policy, oversees industrial labor relations, negotiates collective bargaining agreements, and coordinates grievance procedures to handle complaints resulting from management disputes with unionized employees. The director of industrial relations also advises and collaborates with the director of human resources, other managers, and members of their staff, because all aspects of personnel policy—such as wages, benefits, pensions, and work practices—may be involved in drawing up a new or revised union contract.

Labor relations managers and their staffs implement industrial labor relations programs. When a collective bargaining agreement is up for negotiation, labor relations specialists prepare information for management to use during negotiation, a process that requires the specialist to be familiar with economic and wage data and to have extensive knowledge of labor law and collective bargaining trends. The labor relations staff interprets and administers the contract with respect to grievances, wages and salaries, employee welfare, healthcare, pensions, union and management practices, and other contractual stipulations. As union membership continues to decline in most industries, industrial relations personnel are working more often with employees who are not members of a labor union.

Dispute resolution—attaining tacit or contractual agreements—has become increasingly important as parties to a dispute attempt to avoid costly litigation, strikes, or other disruptions. Dispute resolution also has become more complex, involving employees, management, unions, other firms, and government agencies. Specialists involved in dispute resolution must be highly knowledgeable and experienced, and often report to the director of industrial relations. *Conciliators*, or *mediators*, advise and counsel labor and management to prevent and, when necessary, resolve disputes over labor agreements or other labor relations issues. *Arbitrators*, sometimes called umpires or referees, decide disputes that bind both labor and management to specific terms and conditions of labor contracts. Labor relations specialists who work for unions perform many of the same functions on behalf of the union and its members.

Other emerging specialties include those of *international human resources managers*, who handle human resources issues related to a company's foreign operations, and *human resources information system specialists*, who develop and apply computer programs to process personnel information, match jobseekers with job openings, and handle other personnel matters.

Working Conditions

Personnel work usually takes place in clean, pleasant, and comfortable office settings. Arbitrators and mediators may work out of their homes. Many human resources, training, and labor relations managers and specialists work a standard 35- to 40-hour week. However, longer hours might be necessary for some workers—for example, labor relations managers and specialists, arbitrators, and mediators—when contract agreements are being prepared and negotiated.

Although most human resources, training, and labor relations managers and specialists work in the office, some travel extensively. For example, recruiters regularly attend professional meetings and visit college campuses to interview prospective employees; arbitrators and mediators often must travel to the site chosen for negotiations.

Employment

Human resources, training, and labor relations managers and specialists held about 677,000 jobs in 2002. The following tabulation shows the distribution of jobs by occupational specialty:

Training and development specialists 209,000

Human resources managers 202,000

Employment, recruitment, and placement
specialists 175,000

Compensation, benefits, and job analysis
specialists 91,000

Human resources, training, and labor relations managers and specialists were employed in virtually every industry. About 3,800 specialists were self-employed, working as consultants to public and private employers.

The private sector accounted for almost 8 out of 10 salaried jobs, including 11 percent in professional, scientific, and technical services and 10 percent each in manufacturing industries; health care and social assistance; finance and insurance firms; and administrative and support services.

Government employed about 18 percent of human resources managers and specialists. They handled the recruitment, interviewing, job classification, training, salary administration, benefits, employee relations, and other matters related to the nation's public employees.

Training, Other Qualifications, and Advancement

Because of the diversity of duties and levels of responsibility, the educational backgrounds of human resources, training, and labor relations managers and specialists vary considerably. In filling entry-level jobs, many employers seek college graduates who have majored in human resources, personnel administration, or industrial and labor relations. Other employers look for college graduates with a technical or business background or a well-rounded liberal arts education.

Many colleges and universities have programs leading to a degree in personnel, human resources, or labor relations. Some offer degree programs in personnel administration or human resources management, training and development, or compensation and benefits. Depending on the school, courses leading to a career in human resources management may be found in departments of business administration, education, instructional technology, organizational development, human services, communication, or public administration, or within a separate human resources institution or department.

Because an interdisciplinary background is appropriate in this field, a combination of courses in the social sciences, business, and behavioral sciences is useful. Some jobs may require a more technical or specialized background in engineering, science, finance, or law, for example. Most prospective human resources specialists should take courses in compensation, recruitment, training and development, and performance appraisal, as well as courses in principles of management, organizational structure, and industrial psychology. Other relevant courses include business administration, public administration, psychology, sociology, political science, economics, and statistics. Courses in labor law, collective bargaining, labor economics, labor history, and industrial psychology also provide a valuable background for the prospective labor relations specialist. As in many other fields, knowledge of computers and information systems also is useful.

An advanced degree is increasingly important for some jobs. Many labor relations jobs require graduate study in industrial or labor relations. A strong background in industrial relations and law is highly desirable for contract negotiators, mediators, and arbitrators; in fact, many people in these specialties are lawyers. A background in law also is desirable for employee benefits managers and others who must interpret the growing number of laws and regulations. A master's degree in human resources, labor relations, or in business administration with a concentration in human resources management is highly recommended for those seeking general and top management positions.

For many specialized jobs in the human resources field, previous experience is an asset; for more advanced positions, including those of managers as well as arbitrators and mediators, it is essential. Many employers prefer entry-level workers who have gained some experience through an internship or work-study program while in school. Personnel administration and human resources development require the ability to work with individuals as well as a commitment to organizational goals. This field also demands other skills that people may develop elsewhere—using computers, selling, teaching, supervising, and volunteering, among others. The field offers clerical workers opportunities for advancement to professional positions. Responsible positions sometimes are filled by experienced individuals from other fields, including business, government, education, social services administration, and the military.

The human resources field demands a range of personal qualities and skills. Human resources, training, and labor relations managers and specialists must speak and write effectively. The growing diversity of the workforce requires that they work with or supervise people with various cultural backgrounds, levels of education, and experience. They must be able to cope with conflicting points of view, function under pressure, and demonstrate discretion, integrity, fair-mindedness, and a persuasive, congenial personality.

The duties given to entry-level workers will vary, depending on whether the new workers have a degree in human resource management, have completed an internship, or have some other type of human resources-related experience. Entry-level employees commonly learn the profession by performing administrative duties—helping to enter data into computer systems, compiling employee handbooks, researching information for a supervisor, or answering the phone and handling routine questions. Entry-level workers often enter formal or on-the-job training programs in which they learn how to classify jobs, interview applicants, or administer employee benefits. They then are assigned to specific areas in the personnel department to gain experience. Later, they may advance to a managerial position, overseeing a major element of the personnel program—compensation or training, for example.

Exceptional human resources workers may be promoted to director of personnel or industrial relations, which can eventually lead to a top managerial or executive position. Others may join a consulting firm or open their own business. A Ph.D. is an asset for teaching, writing, or consulting work.

Most organizations specializing in human resources offer classes intended to enhance the marketable skills of their members. Some organizations offer certification programs, which are signs of competence and can enhance one's advancement opportunities. For example, the International Foundation of Employee Benefit Plans confers a designation to persons who complete a series of college-level courses and pass exams covering employee benefit plans. The Society for Human Resources Management has two levels of certification; both require experience and a passing score on a comprehensive exam.

Job Outlook

The abundant supply of qualified college graduates and experienced workers should create keen competition for jobs. Overall employment of human resources, training, and labor relations managers and specialists is expected to grow faster than the average for all occupations through 2012. In addition to openings due to growth, many job openings will arise from the need to replace workers who transfer to other occupations or leave the labor force.

Legislation and court rulings setting standards in various areas—occupational safety and health, equal employment opportunity, wages, health, pensions, and family leave, among others—will increase demand for human resources, training, and labor relations experts. Rising healthcare costs should continue to spur demand for specialists to develop creative compensation and benefits packages that firms can offer prospective employees. Employment of labor relations staff, including arbitrators and mediators, should grow as firms become more involved in labor relations, and attempt to resolve potentially costly labor-management disputes out of court. Additional job growth may stem from increasing demand for specialists in international human resources management and human resources information systems.

Demand may be particularly strong for certain specialists. For example, employers are expected to devote greater resources to job-specific training programs in response to the increasing complexity of many jobs, the aging of the workforce, and technological advances that can leave employees with obsolete skills. This should result in particularly strong demand for training and development specialists. In addition, increasing efforts throughout industry to recruit and retain quality employees should create many jobs for employment, recruitment, and placement specialists.

Among industries, firms involved in management, consulting, and employment services should offer many job opportunities, as businesses increasingly contract out personnel functions or hire personnel specialists on a temporary basis in order to deal with the increasing cost and complexity of training and development programs. Demand also should increase in firms that develop and administer complex employee benefits and compensation packages for other organizations.

Demand for human resources, training, and labor relations managers and specialists also are governed by the staffing needs of the firms for which they work. A rapidly expanding business is likely to hire additional human resources workers—either as permanent employees or consultants—while a business that has experienced a merger or a reduction in its workforce will require fewer human resources workers. Also, as human resources management becomes increasingly important to the success of an organization, some small and medium-size businesses that do not have a human resources department may assign employees various human resources duties together with other unrelated responsibilities. In any particular firm, the size and the job duties of the human resources staff are determined by the firm's organizational philosophy and goals, skills of its workforce, pace of technological change, government regulations, collective bargaining agreements, standards of professional practice, and labor market conditions.

Job growth could be limited by the widespread use of computerized human resources information systems that make workers more productive. Like that of other workers, employment of human resources, training, and labor relations managers and specialists, particularly in larger firms, may be adversely affected by corporate downsizing, restructuring, and mergers.

Earnings

Annual salary rates for human resources workers vary according to occupation, level of experience, training, location, and size of the firm, and whether they are union members. Median annual earnings of human resources managers were $64,710 in 2002. The middle 50 percent earned between $47,420 and $88,100. The lowest 10 percent earned less than $36,280, and the highest 10 percent earned more than $114,300. Median annual earnings in the industries employing the largest numbers of human resources managers in 2002 were:

Management of companies and enterprises	$77,690
Local government	65,590
General medical and surgical hospitals	61,720
Depository credit intermediation	60,030

Median annual earnings of training and development specialists were $42,800 in 2002. The middle 50 percent earned between $32,050 and $56,890. The lowest 10 percent earned less than $24,760, and the highest 10 percent earned more than $72,530. Median annual earnings in the industries employing the largest numbers of training and development specialists in 2002 were:

Management of companies and enterprises	$49,660
Insurance carriers	45,830
Local government	43,740
State government	40,960
Federal government	37,560

Median annual earnings of employment, recruitment, and placement specialists were $39,410 in 2002. The middle 50 percent earned between $30,390 and $54,130. The lowest 10 percent earned less than $24,440, and the highest 10 percent earned more than $73,940. Median annual earnings in 2002 were $34,850 in employment services, the industry employing the largest numbers of these specialists.

Median annual earnings of compensation, benefits, and job analysis specialists were $45,100 in 2002. The middle 50 percent earned between $35,000 and $57,230. The lowest 10 percent earned less than $28,160, and the highest 10 percent earned more than $72,250. Median annual earnings in 2002 were $48,870 in local government, the industry employing the largest numbers of these specialists.

According to a 2003 salary survey conducted by the National Association of Colleges and Employers, bachelor's degree candidates majoring in human resources, including labor relations, received starting offers averaging $35,400 a year.

The average salary for human resources managers employed by the federal government was $66,886 in 2003; for employee relations specialists, $63,345; for labor relations specialists, $72,915; and for employee development specialists, $68,735. Salaries were slightly higher in areas where the prevailing local pay level was higher. There are no formal entry-level requirements for managerial positions. Applicants must possess a suitable combination of educational attainment, experience, and record of accomplishment.

Related Occupations

All human resources occupations are closely related. Other workers with skills and expertise in interpersonal relations include counselors, education administrators, public relations specialists, lawyers, psychologists, social and human service assistants, and social workers.

Sources of Additional Information

For information about human resource management careers and certification, contact:

- Society for Human Resource Management, 1800 Duke St., Alexandria, VA 22314. Internet: http://www.shrm.org

For information about careers in employee training and development and certification, contact:

- American Society for Training and Development, 1640 King St., Box 1443, Alexandria, VA 22313. Internet: http://www.astd.org

For information about careers and certification in employee compensation and benefits, contact:

- International Foundation of Employee Benefit Plans, 18700 W. Bluemound Rd., P.O. Box 69, Brookfield, WI 53008-0069. Internet: http://www.ifebp.org

For information about academic programs in industrial relations, write to:

- Industrial Relations Research Association, 121 Labor and Industrial Relations, University of Illinois, 504 E. Armory, Champaign, IL 61820. Internet: http://www.irra.uiuc.edu

Information about personnel careers in the healthcare industry is available from:

- American Society for Healthcare Human Resources Administration, One North Franklin, 31st Floor, Chicago, IL 60606. Internet: http://www.ashhra.org

Information and Record Clerks

(O*NET 43-4011.00, 43-4021.00, 43-4031.01, 43-4031.02, 43-4031.03, 43-4041.01, 43-4041.02, 43-4051.01, and 43-4051.02)

Significant Points

- Numerous job openings should arise for most types of information and record clerks, due to employment growth and the need to replace workers who leave this large occupational group.

- A high school diploma or its equivalent is the most common educational requirement.

- Because many information and record clerks deal directly with the public, a professional appearance and a pleasant personality are imperative.

- These occupations are well suited to flexible work schedules.

Nature of the Work

Information and record clerks are found in nearly every industry in the nation, gathering data and providing information to the public. The specific duties of these clerks vary as widely as the job titles they hold.

Although their day-to-day duties differ considerably, many information and record clerks greet customers, guests, or other visitors. Many also answer telephones and either obtain information from, or provide information to, the public. Most clerks use multiline telephones, fax machines, and personal computers. *Hotel, motel, and resort desk clerks,* for example, are a guest's first contact for check-in, check-out, and other services within hotels, motels, and resorts. *Interviewers, except eligibility and loan,* found most often in medical facilities, research firms, and financial institutions, assist the public in completing forms, applications, or questionnaires. *Eligibility interviewers, government programs* determine the eligibility of individuals applying for assistance. *Receptionists and information clerks* often are a visitor's or caller's first contact within an organization, providing information and routing calls. *Reservation and transportation ticket agents and travel clerks* assist the public in making travel plans, reserving seats, and purchasing tickets for a variety of transportation services.

Court, municipal, and license clerks perform administrative duties in courts of law, municipalities, and governmental licensing agencies and bureaus. Court clerks prepare the docket of cases to be called, secure information for judges, and contact witnesses, attorneys, and litigants to obtain information for the court. Municipal clerks prepare draft agendas or bylaws for town or city councils, answer official correspondence, and keep fiscal records and accounts. License clerks issue licenses or permits, record data, administer tests, and collect fees.

New-account clerks interview individuals desiring to open bank accounts. Their principal tasks include handling customer inquiries, explaining the institution's products and services to people, and referring customers to the appropriate sales personnel. If a customer wants to open a checking or savings account or an individual retirement account, the new-account clerk will interview the customer and enter the required information into a computer for processing.

Other information and record clerks focus on maintaining, updating, and processing a variety of records, ranging from payrolls to information on the shipment of goods or bank statements. They ensure that other workers get paid on time, that customers' questions are answered, and that records of all transactions are kept.

Depending on their specific titles, these workers perform a wide variety of recordkeeping duties. *Brokerage clerks* prepare and maintain the records generated when stocks, bonds, and other types of investments are traded. *File clerks* store and retrieve various kinds of office information for use by staff members. *Human resources assistants, except payroll and timekeeping* maintain employee records. *Library assistants, clerical* assist library patrons. *Order clerks* process incoming orders for goods and services. *Correspondence clerks* reply to customers regarding claims of damage, delinquent accounts, incorrect billings, complaints of unsatisfactory service, and requests for exchanges or returns of merchandise. *Loan interviewers and clerks* and *credit authorizers, checkers, and clerks* review applicants' credit history and obtain the information needed to determine the creditworthiness of those who apply for credit cards.

The duties of record clerks vary with the size of the firm. In a small business, a bookkeeping clerk may handle all financial records and transactions, as well as have payroll and personnel duties. A large firm, by contrast, may employ specialized accounting, payroll, and human resources clerks. In general, however, clerical staffs in firms of all sizes increasingly are performing a broader variety of tasks than in the past. This is especially true for clerical occupations involving accounting work. As the growing use of computers enables bookkeeping, accounting, and auditing clerks to become more productive, these workers may assume billing, payroll, and timekeeping duties.

Another way in which computers affect these occupations is the growing use of financial software to enter and manipulate data. Computer programs automatically perform calculations on data that were previously calculated manually. Computers also enable clerks to access data within files more quickly than they would using the former method of reviewing stacks of paper. Nevertheless, most workers still keep backup paper records for research, auditing, and reference purposes. Despite the growing use of automation, interaction with the public and coworkers remains a basic part of the job of many record clerks.

Working Conditions

Working conditions vary for different types of information and record clerks, but most clerks work in areas that are clean, well lit, and relatively quiet. This is especially true for information clerks who greet customers and visitors and usually work in highly visible areas that are furnished to make a good impression. Reservation agents and interviewing clerks who spend much of their day talking on the telephone, however, commonly work away from the public, often in large centralized reservation or phone centers. Because a number of agents or clerks may share the same workspace, it may be crowded and noisy. Interviewing clerks may conduct surveys on the street or in shopping malls, or they may go door to door.

Although most information and record clerks work a standard 40-hour week, about 1 out of 5 works part time. Some high school and college students work part time in these occupations, after school or during vacations. Some jobs—such as those in the transportation industry, hospitals, and hotels, in particular—may require working evenings, late-night shifts, weekends, and holidays. Interviewing clerks conducting surveys or other research may work mainly evenings or weekends. In general, employees with the least seniority tend to be assigned the least desirable shifts.

The work performed by information clerks may be repetitious and stressful. For example, many receptionists spend all day answering telephones while performing additional clerical or secretarial tasks. Reservation agents and travel clerks work under stringent time constraints or have quotas on the number of calls answered or reservations made. Additional stress is caused by technology that enables management to electronically monitor employees' use of computer systems, tape-record telephone calls, or limit the time spent on each call.

The work of hotel, motel, and resort desk clerks and transportation ticket agents also can be stressful when these workers are trying to serve the needs of difficult or angry customers. When flights are canceled, reservations mishandled, or guests dissatisfied, these clerks must bear the brunt of the customers' anger. Hotel desk clerks and ticket agents may be on their feet most of the time, and ticket agents may have to lift heavy baggage. In addition, prolonged exposure to a video display terminal may lead to eyestrain for the many information clerks who work with computers.

Employment

Information and record clerks held 5.1 million jobs in 2002. The following tabulation shows employment for the individual occupations:

Customer service representatives	1,894,000
Receptionists and information clerks	1,100,000
Order clerks	330,000
File clerks	265,000
Interviewers, except eligibility and loan	193,000
Hotel, motel, and resort desk clerks	178,000
Reservation and transportation ticket agents and travel clerks	177,000
Human resource assistants, except payroll and timekeeping	174,000
Loan interviewers and clerks	170,000
Library assistants, clerical	120,000
Court, municipal, and license clerks	106,000
New account clerks	99,000
Eligibility interviewers, government programs	94,000
Credit authorizers, checkers, and clerks	80,000
Brokerage clerks	78,000
Correspondence clerks	33,000

Although information and record clerks are found in a variety of industries, employment is concentrated in health services; finance, insurance, and real estate; transportation, communications, and utilities; and business services.

Training, Other Qualifications, and Advancement

Despite the fact that hiring requirements for information and record clerk jobs vary from industry to industry, a high school diploma or its equivalent is the most common educational requirement. Increasingly, familiarity or experience with computers and good interpersonal skills are becoming equally important as the diploma to employers. Although many employers prefer to hire information and record clerks with a higher level of education, only a few of these clerical occupations require such a level of education. For example, brokerage firms usually seek college graduates for brokerage clerk jobs, and order clerks in high-technology firms often need to understand scientific and mechanical processes, which may require some college education. For new-account clerks and airline reservation and ticket agent jobs, some college education may be preferred.

Many information and record clerks deal directly with the public, so a professional appearance and a pleasant personality are important. A clear speaking voice and fluency in the English language also are essential, because these employees frequently use the telephone or public-address systems. Good spelling and computer literacy often are needed, particularly because most work involves considerable use of the computer. In addition, speaking a foreign language fluently is becoming increasingly helpful for those wishing to enter the lodging or travel industry.

With the exception of airline reservation and transportation ticket agents, information and record clerks generally receive orientation and training on the job. For example, orientation for hotel and motel desk clerks usually includes an explanation of the job duties and information about the establishment, such as the locations of rooms and the available services. New employees learn job tasks through on-the-job training under the guidance of a supervisor or an experienced clerk. They often need additional training in how to use the computerized reservation, room assignment, and billing systems and equipment. Most clerks continue to receive instruction on new procedures and on company policies after their initial training ends.

Receptionists usually receive on-the-job training that may include procedures for greeting visitors, for operating telephone and computer systems, and for distributing mail, fax, and parcel deliveries. Some employers look for applicants who already possess certain skills, such as computer and word-processing experience, or who have previous formal education. These workers must possess strong communication skills, because they are constantly interacting with customers.

Most airline reservation and ticket agents learn their skills through formal company training programs. In a classroom setting, they learn company and industry policies, computer systems, and ticketing procedures. They also learn to use the airline's computer system to obtain information on schedules, the availability of seats, and fares; to reserve space for passengers; and to plan passenger itineraries. In addition, they must become familiar with airport and airline code designations, regulations, and safety procedures, on all of which they may be tested. After completing classroom instruction, new agents work on the job with supervisors or experienced agents for a period during which the supervisors may monitor telephone conversations to improve the quality of customer service. Agents are expected to provide good service while limiting the time spent on each call, without being discourteous to customers. In contrast to the airlines, automobile clubs, bus lines, and railroads tend to train their ticket agents or travel clerks on the job through short in-house classes that last several days.

Most banks prefer to hire college graduates for new-account clerk positions. Nevertheless, many new-account clerks without college degrees start out as bank tellers and are promoted by demonstrating excellent communication skills and the motivation to learn new skills. If a new-account clerk has not been a teller before, he or she often will receive such training and work for several months as a teller. In either case, new-account clerks undergo formal training regarding the bank's procedures, products, and services.

Some information and record clerks learn the skills they need in high schools, business schools, and community colleges. Business education programs offered by these institutions typically include courses in typing, word processing, shorthand, business communications, records management, and office systems and procedures. Order clerks in specialized technical positions obtain their training from technical institutes and 2- and 4-year colleges.

Some entry-level clerks are college graduates with degrees in business, finance, or liberal arts. Although a degree rarely is required, many graduates accept entry-level clerical positions to get into a particular company or to enter a particular field. Some companies, such as brokerage and accounting firms, have a set plan of advancement that tracks college graduates from entry-level clerical jobs into managerial positions. Workers with college degrees are likely to start at higher salaries and advance more easily than those without degrees.

Regardless of their level of educational attainment, clerks usually receive on-the-job training. Under the guidance of a supervisor or other senior workers, new employees learn company procedures. Some formal classroom training also may be necessary, such as training in specific computer software.

Advancement for information and record clerks usually comes by transfer to a position with more responsibilities or by promotion to a supervisory position. Most companies fill office and administrative support supervisory and managerial positions by promoting individuals within their organization, so information and record clerks who acquire additional skills, experience, and training improve their opportunities for advancement. Receptionists, interviewers, and new-account clerks with word-processing or other clerical skills may advance to a better paying job as a secretary or administrative assistant. Within the airline industry, a ticket agent may advance to lead worker on the shift.

Additional training is helpful in preparing information clerks for promotion. In the lodging industry, clerks can improve their chances for advancement by taking home-study or group-study courses in lodging management, such as those sponsored by the Educational Institute of the American Hotel and Motel Association. In some industries—such as lodging, banking, insurance, or air transportation—workers commonly are promoted through the ranks. Information and record clerk positions offer good opportunities for qualified workers to get started in a business of their choice. In a number of industries, a college degree may be required for advancement to management ranks.

Job Outlook

Overall employment of information and record clerks is expected grow about as fast as the average for all occupations through 2012. In addition to many openings occurring as businesses and organizations expand, numerous job openings for information and record clerks will result from the need to replace experienced workers who transfer to other occupations or leave the labor force. Replacement needs are expected to be significant in this large occupational group, because many young people work as clerks for a few years before switching to other, higher paying jobs. These occupations are well suited to flexible work schedules, and many opportunities for part-time work will continue to be available, particularly as organizations attempt to cut labor costs by hiring more part-time or temporary workers.

The outlook for different types of information and record clerks is expected to vary in the coming decade. Economic growth and general business expansion are expected to stimulate faster-than-average growth among receptionists and information clerks. Positions as hotel, motel, and resort desk clerks are expected to grow faster than the average, as the occupational composition of the lodging industry changes and services provided by these workers expand. Employment of interviewers, except eligibility and loan, is expected to grow faster than average, with these workers benefiting from rapid growth in the health and social assistance sector. Library assistants are also expected to grow faster than the average as these workers take on more responsibilities.

Human resource assistants and new-account clerks are expected to grow about as fast as average; despite computer technology that increases their productivity, these workers will be needed to perform duties that are important to their organization. Average employment growth is expected for court, municipal, and license clerks as the number of court cases and demand for citizen services continues to increase. Employment of reservation and transportation ticket agents and travel clerks also is expected to grow about as fast as average, due to rising demand for travel services.

Employment of other information and record clerks is expected to experience little or no growth or decline. File clerks are expected are expected to have little or no growth; despite rising demand for file clerks to record and retrieve information, job growth will be slowed by productivity gains stemming from office automation and the consolidation of clerical jobs. As government programs, such as welfare, continue to be reformed, employment of eligibility interviewers will decline. Employment of correspondence clerks, as well as credit authorizers, checkers, and clerks is expected to decline due to automation and the consolidation of recordkeeping functions across all industries. Employment of both brokerage clerks and loan interviewers is expected to decline as online trading and other technological innovations continue to automate more of this type of work. With advances in electronic commerce continuing to increase the efficiency of transactions among businesses, consumers, and government, employment of order clerks also is expected to decline.

Earnings

Earnings vary widely by occupation and experience. Annual earnings in 2002 ranged from less than $13,020 for the lowest-paid 10 percent of hotel clerks to more than $53,410 for the top 10 percent of brokerage clerks. Salaries of human resource assistants tend to be higher than for other information and record clerks, while hotel, motel, and resort desk clerks tend to earn quite a bit less, as the following tabulation of median annual earnings shows:

Brokerage clerks	$33,210
Eligibility interviewers, government programs	31,010
Human resource assistants, except payroll and timekeeping	30,410
Loan interviewers and clerks	27,830
Court, municipal, and license clerks	27,300
Credit authorizers, checkers, and clerks	26,690
Customer service representatives	26,240
Correspondence clerks	25,960
Reservation and transportation ticket agents and travel clerks	25,350
New-account clerks	25,200
Order clerks	24,810
Interviewers, except eligibility and loan	21,690
Receptionists and information clerks	21,150
File clerks	20,020
Library assistants, clerical	19,450
Hotel, motel, and resort desk clerks	17,370

Earnings of hotel and motel desk clerks also vary considerably, depending on the location, size, and type of establishment in which they work. For example, clerks at large luxury hotels and at those located in metropolitan and resort areas generally are paid more than clerks at less exclusive or "budget" establishments and than those working at hotels and motels in less populated areas.

In 2003, the federal government typically paid salaries ranging from $19,898 to $23,555 a year to beginning receptionists with a high school diploma or 6 months of experience. The average annual salary for all receptionists employed by the federal government was about $25,704 in 2003.

In addition to their hourly wage, full-time information and record clerks who work evenings, nights, weekends, or holidays may receive shift differential pay. Some employers offer educational assistance to their employees. Reservation and transportation ticket agents and travel clerks receive free or reduced fares for travel on their company's carriers for themselves, their immediate families, and, in some companies, friends.

Related Occupations

A number of other workers deal with the public, receive and provide information, or direct people to others who can assist them. Among these workers are customer service representatives, dispatchers, security guards and gaming surveillance workers, tellers, and counter and rental clerks.

Sources of Additional Information

State employment service offices can provide information about employment opportunities.

Instructional Coordinators

(O*NET 25-9031.00)

Significant Points

- Many instructional coordinators are former teachers or principals.

- A bachelor's degree is the minimum educational requirement, but a graduate degree is preferred.

- The need to meet new educational standards will create more demand for instructional coordinators to train teachers and develop new materials.

Nature of the Work

Instructional coordinators, also known as curriculum specialists, staff development specialists, or directors of instructional material, play a large role in improving the quality of education in the classroom. They develop instructional materials, train teachers, and assess educational programs in terms of quality and adherence to regulations and standards. They also assist in implementing new technology in the classroom. Instructional coordinators often specialize in specific subjects, such as reading, language arts, mathematics, or social studies.

Instructional coordinators evaluate how well a school's curriculum, or plan of study, meets students' needs. They research teaching methods and techniques and develop procedures to determine whether program goals are being met. To aid in their evaluation, they may meet with members of educational committees and advisory groups to learn about subjects—English, history, or mathematics, for example—and to relate curriculum materials to these subjects, to students' needs, and to occupations for which these subjects are good preparation. They also may develop questionnaires and interview school staff about the curriculum. Based on their research and observations of instructional practice, they recommend instruction and curriculum improvements.

Another duty instructional coordinators have is to review textbooks, software, and other educational materials and make recommendations on purchases. They monitor materials ordered and the ways in which teachers use them in the classroom. They also supervise workers who catalogue, distribute, and maintain a school's educational materials and equipment.

Instructional coordinators develop effective ways to use technology to enhance student learning. They monitor the introduction of new technology, including the Internet, into a school's curriculum. In addition, instructional coordinators might recommend installing educational computer software, such as interactive books and exercises designed to enhance student literacy and develop math skills. Instructional coordinators may invite experts—such as computer hardware, software, and library or media specialists—into the classroom to help integrate technological materials into a school's curriculum.

Many instructional coordinators plan and provide onsite education for teachers and administrators. They may train teachers about the use of materials and equipment or help them to improve their skills. Instructional coordinators also mentor new teachers and train experienced ones in the latest instructional methods. This role becomes especially important when a school district introduces new content, program innovations, or a different organizational structure. For example, when a state or school district introduces standards or tests that must be met by students in order to pass to the next grade, instructional coordinators often must advise teachers on the content of the standards and provide instruction on implementing the standards in the classroom.

Working Conditions

Instructional coordinators, including those employed by school districts, often work year round, usually in offices or classrooms. Some spend much of their time traveling between schools meeting with teachers and administrators. The opportunity to shape and improve instructional curricula and work in an academic environment can be satisfying. However, some instructional coordinators find the work stressful because the occupation requires continual accountability to school administrators and it is not uncommon for people in this occupation to work long hours.

Employment

Instructional coordinators held about 98,000 jobs in 2002. More than 1 in 3 worked in local government education. About 1 in 5 worked in private education, and about 1 in 10 worked in state government education. The remainder worked mostly in the following industries: individual and family services; child daycare services; scientific research and development services; and management, scientific, and technical consulting services.,

Training, Other Qualifications, and Advancement

The minimum educational requirement for instructional coordinators is a bachelor's degree, usually in education. Most employers, however, prefer candidates with a master's or higher degree. Many instructional coordinators have training in curriculum development and instruction, or in a specific academic field, such as mathematics or history. Instructional coordinators must have a good understanding of how to teach specific groups of students, in addition to expertise in developing educational materials. As a result, many persons transfer into instructional coordinator jobs after working for several years as teachers. Work experience in an education administrator position, such as principal or assistant principal, also is beneficial. Specific requirements for instructional coordinator jobs vary depending on the particular position or school district. They may also vary by state.

Helpful college courses may include those in curriculum development and evaluation, instructional approaches, or research design, which teaches how to create and implement research studies to determine the effectiveness of a given method of curriculum or instruction, or to measure and improve student performance. Moreover, instructional coordinators usually are required to take continuing education courses to keep their skills current. Topics for continuing education courses may include teacher evaluation techniques, curriculum training, new teacher induction, consulting and teacher support, and observation and analysis of teaching.

Instructional coordinators must be able to make sound decisions about curriculum options and to organize and coordinate work efficiently. They should have strong interpersonal and communication skills. Familiarity with computer technology also is important for instructional coordinators, who are increasingly involved in gathering and coordinating technical information for students and teachers.

Depending on experience and educational attainment, instructional coordinators may advance to higher positions in a school system, or to management or executive positions in private industry.

Job Outlook

Employment of instructional coordinators is expected to grow faster than the average for all occupations through the year 2012. Over the next decade, instructional coordinators will be instrumental in developing new curricula to meet the demands of a changing society and in training the teacher workforce. Although budget cuts, particularly in the near term, may negatively impact employment to some extent, a continuing emphasis on improving the quality of education is expected to result in a relatively steady and increasing demand for these workers. As increasing federal, state and local standards impel more schools to focus on improving educational quality and student performance, growing numbers of coordinators will be needed to incorporate the standards into curriculums and make sure teachers and administrators are informed of the changes. Opportunities are expected to be best for those who specialize in subject areas that have been targeted for improvement by the No Child Left Behind Act—namely, reading, math, and science.

Instructional coordinators also will be needed to provide classes on using technology in the classroom, to keep teachers up-to-date on changes in their fields, and to demonstrate new teaching techniques. Additional job growth for instructional coordinators will stem from the increasing emphasis on lifelong learning and on programs for students with special needs, including those for whom English is a second language. These students often require more educational resources and consolidated planning and management within the educational system.

Earnings

Median annual earnings of instructional coordinators in 2002 were $47,350. The middle 50 percent earned between $34,450 and $62,460. The lowest 10 percent earned less than $25,880, and the highest 10 percent earned more than $76,820.

Related Occupations

Instructional coordinators are professionals involved in education and training and development, which requires organizational, administrative, teaching, research, and communication skills. Occupations with similar characteristics include preschool, kindergarten, elementary, middle, and secondary school teachers; postsecondary teachers; education administrators; counselors; and human resources, training, and labor relations managers and specialists.

Sources of Additional Information

Information on requirements and job opportunities for instructional coordinators is available from local school systems and state departments of education.

Lawyers

(O*NET 23-1011.00)

Significant Points

- Formal educational requirements for lawyers include a 4-year college degree, 3 years in law school, and the passing of a written bar examination.

Nature of the Work

The legal system affects nearly every aspect of our society, from buying a home to crossing the street. Lawyers form the backbone of this vital system, linking it to society in myriad ways. For that reason, they hold positions of great responsibility and are obligated to adhere to a strict code of ethics.

Lawyers, also called *attorneys*, act as both advocates and advisors in our society. As advocates, they represent one of the parties in criminal and civil trials by presenting evidence and arguing in court to support their client. As advisors, lawyers counsel their clients concerning their legal rights and obligations and suggest particular courses of action in business and personal matters. Whether acting as an advocate or an advisor, all attorneys research the intent of laws and judicial decisions and apply the law to the specific circumstances faced by their client.

The more detailed aspects of a lawyer's job depend upon his or her field of specialization and position. Although all lawyers are licensed to represent parties in court, some appear in court more frequently than others. Trial lawyers, who specialize in trial work, must be able to think quickly and speak with ease and authority. In addition, familiarity with courtroom rules and strategy is particularly important in trial work. Still, trial lawyers spend the majority of their time outside the courtroom, conducting research, interviewing clients and witnesses, and handling other details in preparation for trial.

Lawyers may specialize in a number of different areas, such as bankruptcy, probate, international, or elder law. Those specializing in environmental law, for example, may represent public-interest groups, waste disposal companies, or construction firms in their dealings with the U.S. Environmental Protection Agency (EPA) and other Federal and State agencies. These lawyers help clients prepare and file for licenses and applications for approval before certain activities may occur. In addition, they represent clients' interests in administrative adjudications.

Some lawyers concentrate in the growing field of intellectual property, helping to protect clients' claims to copyrights, artwork under contract, product designs, and computer programs. Still other lawyers advise insurance companies about the legality of insurance transactions, writing insurance policies to conform with the law and to protect companies from unwarranted claims. When claims are filed against insurance companies, these attorneys review the claims and represent the companies in court.

Most lawyers are found in private practice, where they concentrate on criminal or civil law. In criminal law, lawyers represent individuals who have been charged with crimes and argue their cases in courts of law. Attorneys dealing with civil law assist clients with litigation, wills, trusts, contracts, mortgages, titles, and leases. Other lawyers handle only public-interest cases—civil or criminal—which may have an impact extending well beyond the individual client.

Lawyers are sometimes employed full time by a single client. If the client is a corporation, the lawyer is known as "house counsel" and usually advises the company concerning legal issues related to its business activities. These issues might involve patents, government regulations, contracts with other companies, property interests, or collective-bargaining agreements with unions.

A significant number of attorneys are employed at the various levels of government. Lawyers who work for State attorneys general, prosecutors, public defenders, and courts play a key role in the criminal justice system. At the federal level, attorneys investigate cases for the U.S. Department of Justice and other agencies. Government lawyers also help develop programs, draft and interpret laws and legislation, establish enforcement procedures, and argue civil and criminal cases on behalf of the government.

Other lawyers work for legal-aid societies—private, nonprofit organizations established to serve disadvantaged people. These lawyers generally handle civil, rather than criminal, cases. A relatively small number of trained attorneys work in law schools. Most are faculty members who specialize in one or more subjects; however, some serve as administrators. Others work full time in nonacademic settings and teach part time.

Lawyers are increasingly using various forms of technology to perform their varied tasks more efficiently. While all lawyers continue to use law libraries to prepare cases, some supplement their search of conventional printed sources with computer sources, such as the Internet and legal databases. Software is used to search this legal literature automatically and to identify legal texts relevant to a specific case. In litigation involving many supporting documents, lawyers may use computers to organize and index material. Lawyers also utilize electronic filing, videoconferencing, and voice-recognition technology to share information more effectively with other parties involved in a case.

Working Conditions

Lawyers do most of their work in offices, law libraries, and courtrooms. They sometimes meet in clients' homes or places of business and, when necessary, in hospitals or prisons. They may travel to attend meetings; gather evidence; and appear before courts, legislative bodies, and other authorities.

Salaried lawyers usually have structured work schedules. Lawyers who are in private practice may work irregular hours while conducting research, conferring with clients, or preparing briefs during nonoffice hours. Lawyers often work long hours, and of those who regularly work full time, about half work 50 hours or more per week. They may face particularly heavy pressure, especially when a case is being tried. Preparation for court includes keeping abreast of the latest laws and judicial decisions.

Although legal work generally is not seasonal, the work of tax lawyers and other specialists may be an exception. Because lawyers in private practice often can determine their own workload and the point at which they will retire, many stay in practice well beyond the usual retirement age.

Employment

Lawyers held about 695,000 jobs in 2002. About 3 out of 4 lawyers practiced privately, either in law firms or in solo practices. Most of the remaining lawyers held positions in government and with corporations and nonprofit organizations. For those working in government, the greatest number were employed at the local level. In the federal government, lawyers work for many different agencies, but are concentrated in the Departments of Justice, Treasury, and Defense. For those working outside of government, lawyers are employed as house counsel by public utilities, banks, insurance companies, real-estate agencies, manufacturing firms, and other business firms and nonprofit organizations. Some salaried lawyers also have part-time independent practices; others work part time as lawyers and full time in another occupation.

Training, Other Qualifications, and Advancement

To practice law in the courts of any state or other jurisdiction, a person must be licensed, or admitted to its bar, under rules established by the jurisdiction's highest court. All states require that applicants for admission to the bar pass a written bar examination; most jurisdictions also require applicants to pass a separate written ethics examination. Lawyers who have been admitted to the bar in one jurisdiction occasionally may be admitted to the bar in another without taking an examination if they meet the latter jurisdiction's standards of good moral character and have a specified period of legal experience. Federal courts and agencies set their own qualifications for those practicing before or in them.

To qualify for the bar examination in most states, an applicant usually must earn a college degree and graduate from a law school accredited by the American Bar Association (ABA) or the proper state authorities. ABA accreditation signifies that the law school—particularly its library and faculty—meets certain standards developed to promote quality legal education. ABA currently accredits 188 law schools; others are approved by state authorities only. With certain exceptions, graduates of schools not approved by the ABA are restricted to taking the bar examination and practicing in the state or other jurisdiction in which the school is located; most of these schools are in California. In 2002, eight states accepted the study of law in a law office as qualification for taking the bar examination; three jurisdictions—California, the District of Columbia, and New Mexico—now accept the study of law by correspondence. Several states require registration and approval of students by the State Board of Law Examiners, either before the students enter law school or during their early years of legal study.

Although there is no nationwide bar examination, 48 states, the District of Columbia, Guam, the Northern Mariana Islands, Puerto Rico, and the Virgin Islands require the 6-hour Multistate Bar Examination (MBE) as part of the overall bar examination; the MBE is not required in Louisiana and Washington. The MBE covers issues of broad interest, and sometimes a locally prepared state bar examination is given in addition to the MBE. The 3-hour Multistate Essay Examination (MEE) is used as part of the bar examination in several states. States vary in their use of MBE and MEE scores.

Many states have begun to require Multistate Performance Testing (MPT) to test the practical skills of beginning lawyers. This program has been well received, and many more states are expected to require performance testing in the future. Requirements vary by state, although the test usually is taken at the same time as the bar exam and is a one-time requirement.

The required college and law school education usually takes 7 years of full-time study after high school—4 years of undergraduate study, followed by 3 years of law school. Law school applicants must have a bachelor's degree to qualify for admission. To meet the needs of students who can attend only part time, a number of law schools have night or part-time divisions, which usually require 4 years of study; about 1 in 10 graduates from ABA-approved schools attended part time.

Although there is no recommended "prelaw" major, prospective lawyers should develop proficiency in writing and speaking, reading, researching, analyzing, and thinking logically—skills needed to succeed both in law school and in the profession. Regardless of major, a multidisciplinary background is recommended. Courses in English, foreign languages, public speaking, government, philosophy, history, economics, mathematics, and computer science, among others, are useful. Students interested in a particular aspect of law may find related courses helpful. For example, prospective patent lawyers need a strong background in engineering or science, and future tax lawyers must have extensive knowledge of accounting.

Acceptance by most law schools depends on the applicant's ability to demonstrate an aptitude for the study of law, usually through good undergraduate grades, the Law School Admission Test (LSAT), the quality of the applicant's undergraduate school, any prior work experience, and, sometimes, a personal interview. However, law schools vary in the weight they place on each of these and other factors.

All law schools approved by the ABA, except those in Puerto Rico, require applicants to take the LSAT. Nearly all law schools require applicants to have certified transcripts sent to the Law School Data Assembly Service, which then submits applicants' LSAT scores and their standardized records of college grades to the law schools of their choice. Both this service and the LSAT are administered by the Law School Admission Council. Competition for admission to many law schools—especially the most prestigious ones—generally is intense, with the number of applicants to most law schools greatly exceeding the number that can be admitted.

During the first year or year and a half of law school, students usually study core courses, such as constitutional law, contracts, property law, torts, civil procedure, and legal writing. In the remaining time, they may elect specialized courses in fields such as tax, labor, or corporate law. Law students often acquire practical experience by participating in school-sponsored legal clinic activities; in the school's moot court competitions, in which students conduct appellate arguments; in practice trials under the supervision of experienced lawyers and judges; and through research and writing on legal issues for the school's law journal.

A number of law schools have clinical programs in which students gain legal experience through practice trials and projects under the supervision of practicing lawyers and law school faculty. Law school clinical programs might include work in legal-aid clinics, for example, or on the staff of legislative committees. Part-time or summer clerkships in law firms, government agencies, and corporate legal departments also provide valuable experience. Such training can lead directly to a job after graduation and can help students decide what kind of practice best suits them. Clerkships may also be an important source of financial aid.

In 2001, law students in 52 jurisdictions were required to pass the Multistate Professional Responsibility Examination (MPRE), which tests their knowledge of the ABA codes on professional responsibility and judicial conduct. In some states, the MPRE may be taken during law school, usually after completing a course on legal ethics.

Law school graduates receive the degree of *juris doctor* (J.D.) as the first professional degree. Advanced law degrees may be desirable for those planning to specialize, research, or teach. Some law students pursue joint degree programs, which usually require an additional semester or year of study. Joint degree programs are offered in a number of areas, including law and business administration or public administration.

After graduation, lawyers must keep informed about legal and nonlegal developments that affect their practice. Currently, 40 states and jurisdictions mandate continuing legal education (CLE). Many law schools and state and local bar associations provide continuing education courses that help lawyers stay abreast of recent developments. Some states allow CLE credits to be obtained through participation in seminars on the Internet.

The practice of law involves a great deal of responsibility. Individuals planning careers in law should like to work with people and be able to win the respect and confidence of their clients, associates, and the public. Perseverance, creativity, and reasoning ability also are essential to lawyers, who often analyze complex cases and handle new and unique legal problems.

Most beginning lawyers start in salaried positions. Newly hired salaried attorneys usually start as associates and work with more experienced lawyers or judges. After several years of gaining more responsibilities, some lawyers are admitted to partnership in their firm or go into practice for themselves. Some experienced lawyers are nominated or elected to judgeships.Others become full-time law school faculty or administrators; a growing number of these lawyers have advanced degrees in other fields as well.

Some attorneys use their legal training in administrative or managerial positions in various departments of large corporations. A transfer from a corporation's legal department to another department often is viewed as a way to gain administrative experience and rise in the ranks of management.

Job Outlook

Employment of lawyers is expected to grow about as fast as the average through 2012, primarily as a result of growth in the population and in the general level of business activities. Employment growth of lawyers also will result from growth in demand for legal services in such areas as elder, antitrust, environmental, and intellectual-property law. In addition, the wider availability and affordability of legal clinics and prepaid legal service programs should result in increased use of legal services by middle-income people.

Growth in demand will be somewhat mitigated, because, in an effort to reduce money spent on legal fees, many businesses increasingly are using large accounting firms and paralegals to perform some of the same functions that lawyers do. For example, accounting firms may provide employee-benefit counseling, process documents, or handle various other services previously performed by a law firm. Also, mediation and dispute resolution increasingly are being used as alternatives to litigation.

Competition for job openings should continue to be keen because of the large number of students graduating from law school each year. Graduates with superior academic records from well-regarded law schools will have the best job opportunities. Perhaps as a result of competition for attorney positions, lawyers are increasingly finding work in nontraditional areas for which legal training is an asset, but not normally a requirement—for example, administrative, managerial, and business positions in banks, insurance firms, real-estate companies, government agencies, and other organizations. Employment opportunities are expected to continue to arise in these organizations at a growing rate.

As in the past, some graduates may have to accept positions in areas outside of their field of interest or for which they feel overqualified. Some recent law school graduates who have been unable to find permanent positions are turning to the growing number of temporary staffing firms that place attorneys in short-term jobs until they are able to secure full-time positions. This service allows companies to hire lawyers on an "as-needed" basis and permits beginning lawyers to develop practical skills while looking for permanent positions.

Due to the competition for jobs, a law graduate's geographic mobility and work experience assume greater importance. The willingness to relocate may be an advantage in getting a job, but, to be licensed in another state, a lawyer may have to take an additional state bar examination. In addition, employers are increasingly seeking graduates who have advanced law degrees and experience in a specialty, such as tax, patent, or admiralty law.

Employment growth for lawyers will continue to be concentrated in salaried jobs, as businesses and all levels of government employ a growing number of staff attorneys and as employment in the legal services industry grows. Most salaried positions are in urban areas where government agencies, law firms, and big corporations are concentrated. The number of self-employed lawyers is expected to decrease slowly, reflecting the difficulty of establishing a profitable new practice in the face of competition from larger, established law firms. Moreover, the growing complexity of law, which encourages specialization, along with the cost of maintaining up-to-date legal research materials, favors larger firms.

For lawyers who wish to work independently, establishing a new practice will probably be easiest in small towns and expanding suburban areas. In such communities, competition from larger, established law firms is likely to be less keen than in big cities, and new lawyers may find it easier to become known to potential clients.

Some lawyers are adversely affected by cyclical swings in the economy. During recessions, demand declines for some discretionary legal services, such as planning estates, drafting wills, and handling real-estate transactions. Also, corporations are less likely to litigate cases when declining sales and profits result in budgetary restrictions. Some corporations and law firms will not hire new attorneys until business improves, and these establishments may even cut staff to contain costs. Several factors, however, mitigate the overall impact of recessions on lawyers; during recessions, for example, individuals and corporations face other legal problems, such as bankruptcies, foreclosures, and divorces requiring legal action.

Earnings

In 2002, the median annual earnings of all lawyers was $90,290. The middle half of the occupation earned between $61,060 and $136,810. The lowest paid 10 percent earned less than $44,490; at least 10 percent earned more than $145,600. Median annual earnings in the industries employing the largest numbers of lawyers in 2002 are given in the following tabulation:

Management of companies and enterprises $131,970
Federal government 98,790
Legal services 93,970
Local government 69,710
State government...67,910

Median salaries of lawyers 6 months after graduation from law school in 2001 varied by type of work, as indicated by Table 1.

TABLE 1

Median salaries of lawyers 6 months after graduation, 2001

Type of work	Salary
All graduates..	$60,000
Private practice..	90,000
Business/industry	60,000
Judicial clerkship and government	40,300
Academe	40,000

Source: National Association of Law Placement

Salaries of experienced attorneys vary widely according to the type, size, and location of their employer. Lawyers who own their own practices usually earn less than do those who are partners in law firms. Lawyers starting their own practice may need to work part time in other occupations to supplement their income until their practice is well established.

Most salaried lawyers are provided health and life insurance, and contributions are made on their behalf to retirement plans. Lawyers who practice independently are covered only if they arrange and pay for such benefits themselves.

Related Occupations

Legal training is necessary in many other occupations, including paralegal and legal assistant; law clerk; title examiner, abstractor, and searcher; arbitrator, mediator, and conciliator; judge, magistrate judge, and magistrate; and administrative law judge, adjudicator, and hearing officer.

Sources of Additional Information

Information on law schools and a career in law may be obtained from:

● American Bar Association, 750 North Lake Shore Dr., Chicago, IL 60611. Internet: http://www.abanet.org

Information on the LSAT, the Law School Data Assembly Service, the law school application process, and the financial aid available to law students may be obtained from:

● Law School Admission Council, P.O. Box 40, Newtown, PA 18940. Internet: http://www.lsac.org

Information on obtaining a job as a lawyer with the federal government is available from the Office of Personnel Management through a telephone-based system. Consult your telephone directory under "U.S. Government" for a local number, or call (703) 724-1850; Federal Relay Service: (800) 877-8339. The first number is not toll free, and charges may accrue. Information also is available from the Internet site http://www.usajobs.opm.gov.

The requirements for admission to the bar in a particular state or other jurisdiction also may be obtained at the state capital, from the clerk of the Supreme Court, or from the administrator of the State Board of Bar Examiners.

Library Assistants, Clerical

(O*NET 43-4121.00)

Significant Points

● Numerous job openings should arise for most types of library assistants due to employment growth and the need to replace workers who leave this occupational group.

● A high school diploma or its equivalent is the most common educational requirement.

● Because many library assistants deal directly with the public, a professional appearance and a pleasant personality are imperative.

● These occupations are well suited to flexible work schedules.

Nature of the Work

Library assistants assist librarians and, in some cases, library technicians in organizing library resources and making them available to users.

Library assistants, clerical—sometimes referred to as library media assistants, library aides, or circulation assistants—register patrons so that they can borrow materials from the library. They record the borrower's name and address from an application and then issue a library card. Most library assistants enter patrons' records into computer databases.

At the circulation desk, library assistants lend and collect books, periodicals, videotapes, and other materials. When an item is borrowed, assistants stamp the due date on the material and record the patron's identification from his or her library card. They inspect returned materials for damage, check due dates, and compute fines for overdue material. Library assistants review records, compile a list of overdue materials, and send out notices reminding patrons that their materials are overdue. They also answer patrons' questions and refer those they cannot answer to a librarian.

Throughout the library, assistants sort returned books, periodicals, and other items and put them on their designated shelves, in the appropriate files, or in storage areas. They locate materials to be loaned, to either a patron or another library. Many card catalogues are computerized, so library assistants must be familiar with computers. If any materials have been damaged, these workers try to repair them. For example, they use tape or paste to repair torn pages or book covers and other specialized processes to repair more valuable materials.

Some library assistants specialize in helping patrons who have vision problems. Sometimes referred to as library, talking-books, or braille-and-talking-books clerks, they review the borrower's list of desired reading materials. They locate those materials or closely related substitutes from the library collection of large-type or braille volumes, tape cassettes, and open-reel talking books, complete the requisite paperwork, and give or mail the materials to the borrower.

Working Conditions

Most library assistants work in areas that are clean, well lit, and relatively quiet.

Opportunities for flexible schedules are abundant; nearly half of these workers work part time. Some high school and college students work part time in this occupation, after school or during vacations. Some jobs may require working evenings or weekends. In general, employees with the least seniority tend to be assigned the least desirable shifts.

The work performed by library assistants may be repetitious. In addition, prolonged exposure to a video display terminal may lead to eyestrain for the many information clerks who work with computers.

Employment

Library assistants held about 120,000 jobs in 2002. More than one half of these workers were employed by local government in public libraries; most of the remaining employees worked in school libraries. Opportunities for flexible schedules are abundant; nearly half of these workers were on part-time schedules.

Training, Other Qualifications, and Advancement

Despite the fact that hiring requirements for library assistants vary, a high school diploma or its equivalent is the most common educational requirement. Increasingly, familiarity or experience with computers and good interpersonal skills are becoming equally important as the diploma to employers.

Many library assistants deal directly with the public, so a professional appearance and a pleasant personality are important. A clear speaking voice and fluency in the English language also are essential, because these employees frequently use the telephone or public-address systems. Good spelling and computer literacy often are needed, particularly because most work involves considerable use of the computer.

Regardless of their level of educational attainment, clerks usually receive on-the-job training. Under the guidance of a supervisor or other senior workers, new employees learn company procedures. Some formal classroom training also may be necessary, such as training in specific computer software. Most library assistants continue to receive instruction on new procedures and on company policies after their initial training ends.

Additional training in library science or library-related computer software is helpful in preparing library assistants for promotion.

Job Outlook

Opportunities should be good through 2012 for persons interested in jobs as library assistants. Turnover of these workers is quite high, reflecting the limited investment in training and subsequent weak attachment to this occupation. The work is attractive to retirees, students, and others who want a part-time schedule, and there is a lot of movement into and out of the occupation. Many openings will become available each year to replace workers who transfer to another occupation or who leave the labor force. Some positions become available as library assistants move within the organization. Library assistants can be promoted to library technicians and, eventually, supervisory positions in public-service or technical-service areas. Advancement opportunities are greater in larger libraries.

Employment is expected to grow faster than the average for all occupations through 2012. The vast majority of library assistants work in public or school libraries. Efforts to contain costs in local governments and academic institutions of all types may result in more hiring of library support staff than librarians. Also, due to changing roles within libraries, library assistants are taking on more responsibility. Because most are employed by public institutions, library assistants are not directly affected by the ups and downs of the business cycle. Some of these workers may lose their jobs, however, if there are cuts in government budgets.

Earnings

In 2002, median annual earnings for library assistants were $19,450.

In addition to their hourly wage, full-time library assistants who work evenings, nights, and weekends may receive shift differential pay. Some employers offer educational assistance to their employees.

Related Occupations

A number of other workers deal with the public, receive and provide information, or direct people to others who can assist them. Among these workers are customer service representatives, dispatchers, security guards and gaming surveillance workers, tellers, and counter and rental clerks.

Sources of Additional Information

Information about a career as a library assistant can be obtained from either of the following organizations:

- Council on Library/Media Technology, 100 W. Broadway, Columbia, MO 65203. Internet: http://colt.ucr.edu

- American Library Association, 50 East Huron St., Chicago, IL 60611. Internet: http://www.ala.org/hrdr

Public libraries and libraries in academic institutions also can provide information about job openings for library assistants.

Licensed Practical and Licensed Vocational Nurses

(O*NET 29-2061.00)

Significant Points

- Training lasting about 1 year is available in about 1,100 state-approved programs, mostly in vocational or technical schools.

- Nursing care facilities will offer the most new jobs.

- Applicants for jobs in hospitals may face competition as the number of hospital jobs for LPNs declines.

Nature of the Work

Licensed practical nurses (LPNs), or licensed vocational nurses (LVNs), care for the sick, injured, convalescent, and disabled under the direction of physicians and registered nurses.

Most LPNs provide basic bedside care, taking vital signs such as temperature, blood pressure, pulse, and respiration. They also prepare and give injections and enemas, monitor catheters, apply dressings, treat bedsores, and give alcohol rubs and massages. LPNs monitor their patients and report adverse reactions to medications or treatments. They collect samples for testing, perform routine laboratory tests, feed patients, and record food and fluid intake and output. To help keep patients comfortable, LPNs assist with bathing, dressing, and personal hygiene. In states where the law allows, they may administer prescribed medicines or start intravenous fluids. Some LPNs help deliver, care for, and feed infants. Experienced LPNs may supervise nursing assistants and aides.

In addition to providing routine beside care, LPNs in nursing care facilities help evaluate residents' needs, develop care plans, and supervise the care provided by nursing aides. In doctors' offices and clinics, they also may make appointments, keep records, and perform other clerical duties. LPNs who work in private homes may prepare meals and teach family members simple nursing tasks.

Working Conditions

Most licensed practical nurses in hospitals and nursing care facilities work a 40-hour week, but because patients need around-the-clock care, some work nights, weekends, and holidays. They often stand for long periods and help patients move in bed, stand, or walk.

LPNs may face hazards from caustic chemicals, radiation, and infectious diseases such as hepatitis. They are subject to back injuries when moving patients and shock from electrical equipment. They often must deal with the stress of heavy workloads. In addition, the patients they care for may be confused, irrational, agitated, or uncooperative.

Employment

Licensed practical nurses held about 702,000 jobs in 2002. About 28 percent of LPNs worked in hospitals, 26 percent in nursing care facilities, and another 12 percent in offices of physicians. Others worked for home healthcare services, employment services, community care facilities for the elderly, public and private educational services, outpatient care centers, and federal, state, and local government agencies; about 1 in 5 worked part time.

Training, Other Qualifications, and Advancement

All states and the District of Columbia require LPNs to pass a licensing examination after completing a state-approved practical nursing program. A high school diploma or its equivalent usually is required for entry, although some programs accept candidates without a diploma or are designed as part of a high school curriculum.

In 2002, approximately 1,100 state-approved programs provided training in practical nursing. Almost 6 out of 10 students were enrolled in technical or vocational schools, while 3 out of 10 were in community and junior colleges. Others were in high schools, hospitals, and colleges and universities.

Most practical nursing programs last about 1 year and include both classroom study and supervised clinical practice (patient care). Classroom study covers basic nursing concepts and patient care-related subjects, including anatomy, physiology, medical-surgical nursing, pediatrics, obstetrics, psychiatric nursing, the administration of drugs, nutrition, and first aid. Clinical practice usually is in a hospital, but sometimes includes other settings.

LPNs should have a caring, sympathetic nature. They should be emotionally stable, because work with the sick and injured can be stressful. They also should have keen observational, decisionmaking, and communication skills. As part of a healthcare team, they must be able to follow orders and work under close supervision.

Job Outlook

Employment of LPNs is expected to grow about as fast as the average for all occupations through 2012 in response to the long-term care needs of an increasing elderly population and the general growth of healthcare. Replacement needs will be a major source of job openings, as many workers leave the occupation permanently.

Applicants for jobs in hospitals may face competition as the number of hospital jobs for LPNs declines. An increasing proportion of sophisticated procedures, which once were performed only in hospitals, is being performed in physicians' offices and in outpatient care centers such as ambulatory surgical and emergency medical centers, due largely to advances in technology. Consequently, employment of LPNs is projected to grow faster than average in these sectors as healthcare expands outside the traditional hospital setting.

Employment of LPNs in nursing care facilities is expected to grow faster than the average. Such facilities will offer the most new jobs for LPNs as the number of aged and disabled persons in need of long-term care rises. In addition to caring for the aged and the disabled, LPNs in nursing care facilities will care for the increasing number of patients who will have been discharged from the hospital, but have not recovered enough to return home.

Employment of LPNs is expected to grow much faster than average in home healthcare services. This growth is in response to an increasing number of older persons with functional disabilities, consumer preference for care in the home, and technological advances that make it possible to bring increasingly complex treatments into the home.

Earnings

Median annual earnings of licensed practical nurses were $31,440 in 2002. The middle 50 percent earned between $26,430 and $37,050. The lowest 10 percent earned less than $22,860, and the highest 10 percent earned more than $44,040. Median annual earnings in the industries employing the largest numbers of licensed practical nurses in 2002 were as follows:

Employment services $40,550

Home health care services 32,850

Nursing care facilities...32,220

General medical and surgical hospitals..................30,310

Offices of physicians 28,710

Related Occupations

LPNs work closely with people while helping them. So do emergency medical technicians and paramedics, social and human service assistants, surgical technologists, and teacher assistants.

Sources of Additional Information

For information about practical nursing, contact any of the following organizations:

- National League for Nursing, 61 Broadway, New York, NY 10006. Internet: http://www.nln.org

- National Federation of Licensed Practical Nurses, Inc., 605 Poole Dr., Garner, NC 27529.

★ ★ ★ ★ ★ ★ ★ ★ ★ ★

Loan Counselors and Officers

(O*NET 13-2071.00 and 13-2072.00)

Significant Points

- Loan officer positions generally require a bachelor's degree in finance, economics, or a related field; training or experience in banking, lending, or sales is advantageous.

- Average employment growth is expected for loan officers despite rising demand for loans, because technology is making loan processing and approval simpler and faster.

- Earnings often fluctuate with the number of loans generated, rising substantially when the economy is good and interest rates are low.

Nature of the Work

For many individuals, taking out a loan may be the only way to afford a house, car, or college education. For businesses, loans likewise are essential to start many companies, purchase inventory, or invest in capital equipment. *Loan officers* facilitate this lending by finding potential clients and assisting them in applying for loans. Loan officers also gather personal information about clients and businesses to ensure that an informed decision is made regarding the creditworthiness of the borrower and the probability of repayment. *Loan counselors* provide guidance to prospective loan applicants who have problems qualifying for traditional loans. The guidance they provide may include determining the most appropriate type of loan for a particular customer, and explaining specific requirements and restrictions associated with the loan. Some of the functions of a loan counselor also may be performed by a loan officer. Within some institutions, such as credit unions, loan counselor is an alternate title for loan officer.

Loan officers usually specialize in commercial, consumer, or mortgage loans. Commercial or business loans help companies pay for new equipment or expand operations; consumer loans include home equity, automobile, and personal loans; mortgage loans are made to purchase real estate or to refinance an existing mortgage. As banks and other financial institutions begin to offer new types of loans and a growing variety of financial services, loan officers will have to keep abreast of these new product lines so that they can meet their customers' needs.

In many instances, loan officers act as salespeople. Commercial loan officers, for example, contact firms to determine their needs for loans. If a firm is seeking new funds, the loan officer will try to persuade the company to obtain the loan from his or her institution. Similarly, mortgage loan officers develop relationships with commercial and residential real estate agencies so that, when an individual or firm buys a property, the real estate agent might recommend contacting a specific loan officer for financing.

Once this initial contact has been made, loan officers guide clients through the process of applying for a loan. This process begins with a formal meeting or telephone call with a prospective client, during which the loan officer obtains basic information about the purpose of the loan and explains the different types of loans and credit terms that are available to the applicant. Loan officers answer questions about the process and sometimes assist clients in filling out the application.

After a client completes the application, the loan officer begins the process of analyzing and verifying the information on the application to determine the client's creditworthiness. Often, loan officers can quickly access the client's credit history by computer and obtain a credit "score." This score represents the creditworthiness of a person or business as assigned by a software program that makes the evaluation. In cases in which a credit history is not available or in which unusual financial circumstances are present, the loan officer may request additional financial information from the client or, in the case of commercial loans, copies of the company's financial statements. With this information, loan officers who specialize in evaluating a client's credit-worthiness—often called loan underwriters—may conduct a financial analysis or other risk assessment. Loan officers include this information and their written comments in a loan file, which is used to analyze whether the prospective loan meets the lending institution's requirements. Loan officers then decide, in consultation with their managers, whether to grant the loan. If the loan is approved, a repayment schedule is arranged with the client.

A loan may be approved that would otherwise be denied if the customer can provide the lender with appropriate collateral—property pledged as security for the repayment of a loan. For example, when lending money for a college education, a bank may insist that borrowers offer their home as collateral. If the borrowers were ever unable to repay the loan, the home would be seized under court order and sold to raise the necessary money.

Some loan officers, referred to as *loan collection officers*, contact borrowers with delinquent loan accounts to help them find a method of repayment in order to avoid their defaulting on the loan. If a repayment plan cannot be developed, the loan collection officer initiates collateral liquidation, in which the lender seizes the collateral used to secure the loan—a home or car, for example—and sells it to repay the loan.

Working Conditions

Working as a loan officer usually involves considerable travel. For example, commercial and mortgage loan officers frequently work away from their offices and rely on laptop computers, cellular telephones, and pagers to keep in contact with their offices and clients. Mortgage loan officers often work out of their home or car, visiting offices or homes of clients while completing loan applications. Commercial loan officers sometimes travel to other cities to prepare complex loan agreements. Consumer loan officers and loan counselors, however, are likely to spend most of their time in an office.

Most loan officers and counselors work a standard 40-hour week, but many work longer, depending on the number of clients and the demand for loans. Mortgage loan officers can work especially long hours because they are free to take on as many customers as they choose. Loan officers usually carry a heavy caseload and sometimes cannot accept new clients until they complete current cases. They are especially busy when interest rates are low, a condition that triggers a surge in loan applications.

Employment

Loan counselors and officers together held about 255,000 jobs in 2002. The majority of this employment consisted of loan officers—nearly 88 percent—with the remaining 31,000 jobs being held by loan counselors. Approximately 40 percent of loan officers and counselors were employed by commercial banks, savings institutions, and credit unions. Mortgage and consumer finance companies employed an additional 33 percent. Loan officers are employed throughout the nation, but most work in urban and suburban areas. At some banks, particularly in rural areas, the branch or assistant manager often handles the loan application process.

Training, Other Qualifications, and Advancement

Loan officer positions generally require a bachelor's degree in finance, economics, or a related field. Most employers prefer applicants who are familiar with computers and their applications in banking. For commercial or mortgage loan officer jobs, training or experience in sales is highly valued by potential employers. Loan officers without college degrees usually advance to these positions from other jobs in an organization after acquiring several years of work experience in various other occupations, such as teller or customer service representative.

There are currently no specific licensing requirements for loan counselors and officers working in banks or credit unions. Training and licensing requirements for loan counselors and officers who work in mortgage banks or brokerages vary by state. These criteria also may vary depending on whether workers are employed by a mortgage bank or mortgage brokerage.

Various banking-related associations and private schools offer courses and programs for students interested in lending, as well as for experienced loan officers who want to keep their skills current. Completion of these courses and programs generally enhances one's employment and advancement opportunities.

Persons planning a career as a loan officer or counselor should be capable of developing effective working relationships with others, confident in their abilities, and highly motivated. For public relations purposes, loan officers must be willing to attend community events as representatives of their employer.

Capable loan officers and counselors may advance to larger branches of the firm or to managerial positions, while less capable workers—and those having weak academic preparation—could be assigned to smaller branches and might find promotion difficult without obtaining training to upgrade their skills. Advancement beyond a loan officer position usually includes supervising other loan officers and clerical staff.

Job Outlook

Employment of loan counselors and officers is projected to grow about as fast as the average for all occupations through 2012. College graduates and those with banking, lending, or sales experience should have the best job prospects. Employment growth stemming from economic expansion and population increases—factors that generate demand for loans—will be partially offset by increased automation that speeds lending processes and by the spread of alternative methods of applying for and obtaining loans. Job opportunities for workers in these occupations are influenced by the volume of loan applications, which is determined largely by interest rates and by the overall level of economic activity. However, besides those resulting from growth, additional job openings will result from the need to replace workers who retire or otherwise leave the occupation permanently.

The use of credit scoring has made the loan evaluation process much simpler than in the past, and even unnecessary in some cases. Credit scoring allows loan officers, particularly loan underwriters, to evaluate many more loans in much less time, thus increasing loan officers' efficiency. In addition, the mortgage application process has become highly automated and standardized. This simplification has enabled online mortgage loan vendors to offer loan shopping services over the Internet. Online vendors accept loan applications from customers over the Internet and determine which lenders have the best interest rates for particular loans. With this knowledge, customers can go directly to the lending institution, thereby bypassing mortgage loan brokers. Shopping for loans on the Internet—though currently not a widespread practice—is expected to become more common over the next 10 years, particularly for mortgages, thus reducing demand for loan officers.

Although loans remain a major source of revenue for banks, demand for new loans fluctuates and affects the income and employment opportunities of loan officers. When the economy is on the upswing or when interest rates decline dramatically, there is a surge in real estate buying and mortgage refinancing that requires loan officers to work long hours processing applications and induces lenders to hire additional loan officers. Loan officers often are paid by commission on the value of the loans they place, and some have high earnings when demand for mortgages is high. When the real estate market slows, loan officers often suffer a decline in earnings and may even be subject to layoffs. The same applies to commercial loan officers, whose workloads increase during good economic times as companies seek to invest more in their businesses. In difficult economic conditions, loan collection officers are likely to see an increase in the number of delinquent loans.

Earnings

Median annual earnings of loan counselors were $32,010 in 2002. The middle 50 percent earned between $26,330 and $41,660. The lowest 10 percent earned less than $22,800, while the top 10 percent earned more than $57,400.

Median annual earnings of loan officers were $43,980 in 2002. The middle 50 percent earned between $32,360 and $62,160. The lowest 10 percent earned less than $25,790, while the top 10 percent earned more than $88,450. Median annual earnings in the industries employing the largest numbers of loan officers in 2002 were:

Activities related to credit intermediation $47,240

Management of companies and enterprises 46,420

Nondepository credit intermediation 44,770

Depository credit intermediation 41,450

The form of compensation for loan officers varies. Most loan officers are paid a commission that is based on the number of loans they originate. In this way, commissions are used to motivate loan officers to bring in more loans. Some institutions pay only salaries, while others pay their loan officers a salary plus a commission or bonus based on the number of loans originated. Banks and other lenders sometimes offer their loan officers free checking privileges and somewhat lower interest rates on personal loans.

According to a salary survey conducted by Robert Half International, a staffing services firm specializing in accounting and finance, mortgage loan officers earned between $36,000 and $45,750 in 2002; consumer loan officers with 1 to 3 years of experience earned between $42,250 and $56,750; and commercial loan officers with 1 to 3 years of experience made between $48,000 and $64,500. With over 3 years of experience, commercial loan officers made between $66,000 and $92,000, and consumer loan officers earned between $55,500 and $75,750. Earnings of loan officers with graduate degrees or professional certifications were approximately 10 to 15 percent higher than these figures. Loan officers who are paid on a commission basis usually earn more than those on salary only, and those who work for smaller banks generally earn less than those employed by larger institutions.

Related Occupations

Loan officers help the public manage financial assets and secure loans. Occupations that involve similar functions include those of securities and financial services sales representatives, personal financial advisors, real estate brokers and sales agents, and insurance sales agents.

Sources of Additional Information

Information about a career as a mortgage loan officer can be obtained from:

- Mortgage Bankers Association of America, 1919 Pennsylvania Ave., NW, Washington, DC 20006-3438. Internet: http://www.mbaa.org

State bankers' associations can furnish specific information about job opportunities in their state. Also, individual banks can supply information about job openings and the activities, responsibilities, and preferred qualifications of their loan officers.

Maintenance and Repair Workers, General

(O*NET 49-9042.00)

Significant Points

- General maintenance and repair workers are employed in almost every industry.

- Most workers are trained on the job; others learn by working as helpers to other repairers or to construction workers such as carpenters, electricians, or machinery repairers.

- Job openings should be plentiful due to significant turnover in this large occupation.

Nature of the Work

Most craft workers specialize in one kind of work, such as plumbing or carpentry. General maintenance and repair workers, however, have skills in many different crafts. They repair and maintain machines, mechanical equipment, and buildings and work on plumbing, electrical, and air-conditioning and heating systems. They build partitions, make plaster or drywall repairs, and fix or paint roofs, windows, doors, floors, woodwork, and other parts of building structures. They also maintain and repair specialized equipment and machinery found in cafeterias, laundries, hospitals, stores, offices, and factories. Typical duties include troubleshooting and fixing faulty electrical switches, repairing air-conditioning motors, and unclogging drains. New buildings sometimes have computer-controlled systems, requiring workers to acquire basic computer skills. For example, new air-conditioning systems often can be controlled from a central computer terminal. In addition, light sensors can be electronically controlled to turn off lights automatically after a set amount of time.

General maintenance and repair workers inspect and diagnose problems and determine the best way to correct them, frequently checking blueprints, repair manuals, and parts catalogs. They obtain supplies and repair parts from distributors or storerooms. Using common hand and power tools such as screwdrivers, saws, drills, wrenches, and hammers, as well as specialized equipment and electronic testing devices, these workers replace or fix worn or broken parts, where necessary, or make adjustments to correct malfunctioning equipment and machines.

General maintenance and repair workers also perform routine preventive maintenance and ensure that machines continue to run smoothly, building systems operate efficiently, and the physical condition of buildings does not deteriorate. Following a checklist, they may inspect drives, motors, and belts, check fluid levels, replace filters, and perform other maintenance actions. Maintenance and repair workers keep records of their work.

Employees in small establishments, where they are often the only maintenance worker, make all repairs, except for very large or difficult jobs. In larger establishments, their duties may be limited to the general maintenance of everything in a workshop or a particular area.

Working Conditions

General maintenance and repair workers often carry out several different tasks in a single day, at any number of locations. They may work inside of a single building or in several different buildings. They may have to stand for long periods, lift heavy objects, and work in uncomfortably hot or cold environments, in awkward and cramped positions, or on ladders. They are subject to electrical shock, burns, falls, cuts, and bruises. Most general maintenance workers work a 40-hour week. Some work evening, night, or weekend shifts or are on call for emergency repairs.

Those employed in small establishments often operate with only limited supervision. Those working in larger establishments frequently are under the direct supervision of an experienced worker.

Employment

General maintenance and repair workers held 1.3 million jobs in 2002. They were employed in almost every industry. Around 1 in 5 worked in manufacturing industries, almost evenly distributed through all sectors. About 17 percent worked for different government bodies. Others worked for wholesale and retail firms and for real-estate firms that operate office and apartment buildings.

Training, Other Qualifications, and Advancement

Many general maintenance and repair workers learn their skills informally on the job. They start as helpers, watching and learning from skilled maintenance workers. Helpers begin by doing simple jobs, such as fixing leaky faucets and replacing lightbulbs, and progress to more difficult tasks, such as overhauling machinery or building walls. Some learn their skills by working as helpers to other repair or construction workers, including carpenters, electricians, or machinery repairers.

Necessary skills also can be learned in high school shop classes and postsecondary trade or vocational schools. It generally takes from 1 to 4 years of on-the-job training or school, or a combination of both, to become fully qualified, depending on the skill level required. Because a growing number of new buildings rely on computers to control various of their systems, general maintenance and repair workers may need basic computer skills, such as how to log onto a central computer system and navigate through a series of menus. Usually, companies that install computer-controlled equipment provide on-site training for general maintenance and repair workers.

Graduation from high school is preferred for entry into this occupation. High school courses in mechanical drawing, electricity, woodworking, blueprint reading, science, mathematics, and computers are useful. Mechanical aptitude, the ability to use shop mathematics, and manual dexterity are

important. Good health is necessary because the job involves much walking, standing, reaching, and heavy lifting. Difficult jobs require problem-solving ability, and many positions require the ability to work without direct supervision.

Many general maintenance and repair workers in large organizations advance to maintenance supervisor or become a craftworker such as an electrician, a heating and air-conditioning mechanic, or a plumber. Within small organizations, promotion opportunities are limited.

Job Outlook

Job openings should be plentiful. General maintenance and repair is a large occupation with significant turnover, and many job openings should result from the need to replace workers who transfer to other occupations or stop working for other reasons.

Employment of general maintenance and repair workers is expected to grow about as fast as average for all occupations through 2012. Employment is related to the number of buildings—for example, office and apartment buildings, stores, schools, hospitals, hotels, and factories—and the amount of equipment needing maintenance and repair. However, as machinery becomes more advanced and requires less maintenance, the need for general maintenance and repair workers diminishes.

Earnings

Median hourly earnings of general maintenance and repair workers were $14.12 in 2002. The middle 50 percent earned between $10.61 and $18.48. The lowest 10 percent earned less than $8.25, and the highest 10 percent earned more than $22.78. Median hourly earnings in the industries employing the largest numbers of general maintenance and repair workers in 2002 are shown in the following tabulation:

Local government	$14.83
Elementary and secondary schools	14.01
Activities related to real estate	11.79
Lessors of real estate	11.64
Traveler accommodation	10.58

Some general maintenance and repair workers are members of unions, including the American Federation of State, County, and Municipal Employees and the United Automobile Workers.

Related Occupations

Some duties of general maintenance and repair workers are similar to those of carpenters; pipelayers, plumbers, pipefitters, and steamfitters; electricians; and heating, air-conditioning, and refrigeration mechanics. Other duties are similar to those of coin, vending, and amusement machine servicers and repairers; electrical and electronics installers and repairers; electronic home entertainment equipment installers and repairers; and radio and telecommunications equipment installers and repairers.

Sources of Additional Information

Information about job opportunities may be obtained from local employers and local offices of the State Employment Service.

Management Analysts

(O*NET 13-1111.00)

Significant Points

- Thirty percent are self-employed, about one and a half times the average for other management, business, and financial occupations.

- Most positions in private industry require a master's degree and additional years of specialized experience; a bachelor's degree is sufficient for entry-level government jobs.

- Despite projected faster-than-average employment growth, intense competition is expected for jobs.

Nature of the Work

As business becomes more complex, the nation's firms are continually faced with new challenges. Firms increasingly rely on management analysts to help them remain competitive amidst these changes. Management analysts, often referred to as *management consultants* in private industry, analyze and propose ways to improve an organization's structure, efficiency, or profits. For example, a small but rapidly growing company that needs help improving the system of control over inventories and expenses may decide to employ a consultant who is an expert in just-in-time inventory management. In another case, a large company that has recently acquired a new division may hire management analysts to help reorganize the corporate structure and eliminate duplicate or nonessential jobs. In recent years, information technology and electronic commerce have provided new opportunities for management analysts. Companies hire consultants to develop strategies for entering and remaining competitive in the new electronic marketplace.

Firms providing management analysis range in size from a single practitioner to large international organizations employing thousands of consultants. Some analysts and consultants specialize in a specific industry, such as healthcare or telecommunications, while others specialize by type of business function, such as human resources, marketing, logistics, or information systems. In government, manage-ment analysts tend to specialize by type of agency. The work of management analysts and consultants varies with each client or employer, and from project to project. Some projects require a team of consultants, each specializing in one area. In other projects, consultants work independently with the organization's managers. In all cases, analysts and consultants collect, review, and analyze information in order to make recommendations to managers.

Both public and private organizations use consultants for a variety of reasons. Some lack the internal resources needed to handle a project, while others need a consultant's expertise to determine what resources will be required and what problems may be encountered if they pursue a particular opportunity. To retain a consultant, a company first solicits proposals from a number of consulting firms specializing in the area in which it needs assistance. These proposals include the estimated cost and scope of the project, staffing requirements, references from a number of previous clients, and a completion deadline. The company then selects the proposal that best suits its needs.

After obtaining an assignment or contract, management analysts first define the nature and extent of the problem. During this phase, they analyze relevant data, which may include annual revenues, employment, or expenditures, and interview managers and employees while observing their operations. The analyst or consultant then develops solutions to the problem. In the course of preparing their recommendations, they take into account the nature of the organization, the relationship it has with others in the industry, and its internal organization and culture. Insight into the problem often is gained by building and solving mathematical models.

Once they have decided on a course of action, consultants report their findings and recommendations to the client. These suggestions usually are submitted in writing, but oral presentations regarding findings also are common. For some projects, management analysts are retained to help implement the suggestions they have made.

Management analysts in government agencies use the same skills as their private-sector colleagues to advise managers on many types of issues, most of which are similar to the problems faced by private firms. For example, if an agency is planning to purchase personal computers, it must first determine which type to buy, given its budget and data processing needs. In this case, management analysts would assess the prices and characteristics of various machines and determine which best meets the agency's needs.

Working Conditions

Management analysts usually divide their time between their offices and the client's site. In either situation, much of an analyst's time is spent indoors in clean, well-lit offices. Because they must spend a significant portion of their time with clients, analysts travel frequently.

Analysts and consultants generally work at least 40 hours a week. Uncompensated overtime is common, especially when project deadlines are approaching. Analysts may experience a great deal of stress as a result of trying to meet a client's demands, often on a tight schedule.

Self-employed consultants can set their workload and hours and work at home. On the other hand, their livelihood depends on their ability to maintain and expand their client base. Salaried consultants also must impress potential clients to get and keep clients for their company.

Employment

Management analysts held about 577,000 jobs in 2002. Thirty percent of these workers were self-employed, about one and a half times the average for other management, business, and financial occupations. Management analysts are found throughout the country, but employment is concentrated in large metropolitan areas. Most work in management, scientific, and technical consulting firms, in computer systems design and related services firms, and for federal, state, and local governments. The majority of those working for the federal government are in the U.S. Department of Defense.

Training, Other Qualifications, and Advancement

Educational requirements for entry-level jobs in this field vary widely between private industry and government. Most employers in private industry generally seek individuals with a master's degree in business administration or a related discipline. Some employers also require additional years of experience in the field in which the worker plans to consult, in addition to a master's degree. Some will hire workers with a bachelor's degree as a research analyst or associate. Research analysts usually need to pursue a master's degree in order to advance to a consulting position. Most government agencies hire people with a bachelor's degree and no pertinent work experience for entry-level management analyst positions.

Few universities or colleges offer formal programs of study in management consulting; however, many fields of study provide a suitable educational background for this occupation because of the wide range of areas addressed by management analysts. These include most academic programs in business and management, such as accounting and marketing, as well as economics, computer and information sciences, and engineering. In addition to the appropriate formal education, most entrants to this occupation have years of experience in management, human resources, information technology, or other specialties. Analysts also routinely attend conferences to keep abreast of current developments in their field.

Management analysts often work with minimal supervision, so they need to be self-motivated and disciplined. Analytical skills, the ability to get along with a wide range of people, strong oral and written communication skills, good judgment, time management skills, and creativity are other desirable qualities. The ability to work in teams also is an important attribute as consulting teams become more common.

As consultants gain experience, they often become solely responsible for a specific project, taking on more responsibility and managing their own hours. At the senior level, consultants may supervise lower level workers and become more involved in seeking out new business. Those with exceptional skills may eventually become a partner in the firm. Others with entrepreneurial ambition may open their own firm.

A high percentage of management consultants are self-employed, partly because business startup costs are low. Self-employed consultants also can share office space, administrative help, and other resources with other self-employed consultants or small consulting firms, thus reducing overhead costs. Because many small consulting firms fail each year for lack of managerial expertise and clients, persons interested in opening their own firm must have good organizational and marketing skills and several years of consulting experience.

The Institute of Management Consultants USA, Inc. (IMC USA) offers a wide range of professional development programs and resources, such as meetings and workshops, which can be helpful for management consultants. The IMC USA also offers the Certified Management Consultant (CMC) designation to those who meet minimum levels of education and experience, submit client reviews, and pass an interview and exam covering the IMC USA's Code of Ethics. Management consultants with a CMC designation must be recertified every 3 years. Certification is not mandatory for management consultants, but it may give a jobseeker a competitive advantage.

Job Outlook

Despite projected rapid employment growth, keen competition is expected for jobs as management analysts. Because analysts can come from such diverse educational backgrounds, the pool of applicants from which employers can draw is quite large. Furthermore, the independent and challenging nature of the work, combined with high earnings potential, makes this occupation attractive to many. Job opportunities are expected to be best for those with a graduate degree, industry expertise, and a talent for salesmanship and public relations.

Employment of management analysts is expected to grow faster than the average for all occupations through 2012, as industry and government increasingly rely on outside expertise to improve the performance of their organizations. Job growth is projected in very large consulting firms with international expertise and in smaller consulting firms that specialize in specific areas, such as biotechnology, healthcare, information technology, human resources, engineering, and marketing. Growth in the number of individual practitioners may be hindered, however, by increasing use of consulting teams, which permits examination of a variety of different issues and problems within an organization.

Employment growth of management analysts and consultants has been driven by a number of changes in the business environment that have forced firms to take a closer look at their operations. These changes include developments in information technology and the growth of electronic commerce. Traditional companies hire analysts to help design intranets or company Web sites, or establish online businesses. New Internet start-up companies hire analysts not only to design Web sites, but also to advise them in more traditional business practices, such as pricing strategies, marketing, and inventory and human resource management. In order to offer clients better quality and a wider variety of services, consulting firms are partnering with traditional computer software and technology firms. Also, many computer firms are developing consulting practices of their own in order to take advantage of this expanding market. Although information technology consulting should remain one of the fastest growing consulting areas, the volatility of the computer services industry necessitates that the most successful management analysts have knowledge of traditional business practices in addition to computer applications, systems integration, and Web design and management skills.

The growth of international business also has contributed to an increase in demand for management analysts. As U.S. firms expand their business abroad, many will hire management analysts to help them form the right strategy for entering the market; advise on legal matters pertaining to specific countries; or help with organizational, administrative, and other issues, especially if the U.S. company is involved in a partnership or merger with a local firm. These trends provide management analysts with more opportunities to travel or work abroad, but also require them to have a more comprehensive knowledge of international business and foreign cultures and languages.

Furthermore, as international and domestic markets have become more competitive, firms have needed to use resources more efficiently. Management analysts increasingly are sought to help reduce costs, streamline operations, and develop marketing strategies. As this process continues and businesses downsize, even more opportunities will be created for analysts to perform duties that previously were handled internally. Finally, management analysts also will be in greater demand in the public sector, as federal, state, and local government agencies seek ways to become more efficient.

Though management consultants are continually expanding their services, employment growth could be hampered by increasing competition for clients from occupations that do not traditionally perform consulting work, such as accountants, financial analysts, lawyers, and computer systems analysts. Furthermore, economic downturns also can have adverse effects on employment for some management consultants. In these times, businesses look to cut costs and consultants can be considered excess expense. On the other hand, some consultants might experience an increase in work during recessions because they advise businesses on how to cut costs and remain profitable.

Earnings

Salaries for management analysts vary widely by years of experience and education, geographic location, sector of expertise, and size of employer. Generally, management analysts employed in large firms or in metropolitan areas have the highest salaries. Median annual wage and salary earnings of management analysts in 2002 were $60,340. The middle 50 percent earned between $46,160 and $83,590. The lowest 10 percent earned less than $35,990, and the highest 10 percent earned more than $115,670. Median annual earnings in the industries employing the largest numbers of management analysts and consultants in 2002 were:

Management, scientific, and technical consulting services	$71,790
Computer systems design and related services	66,120
Federal government	65,480
Insurance carriers	51,780
State government	47,340

According to a 2002 survey by the Association of Management Consulting Firms, earnings—including bonuses and profit sharing—averaged $47,826 for research associates in member firms; $61,496 for entry-level consultants, $78,932 for management consultants, $112,716 for senior consultants, $168,998 for junior partners, and $254,817 for senior partners.

Salaried management analysts usually receive common benefits such as health and life insurance, a retirement plan, vacation, and sick leave, as well as less common benefits such as profit sharing and bonuses for outstanding work. In addition, all travel expenses usually are reimbursed by the employer. Self-employed consultants have to maintain their own office and provide their own benefits.

Related Occupations

Management analysts collect, review, and analyze data; make recommendations; and implement their ideas. Occupations with similar duties include accountants and auditors; budget analysts; cost estimators; financial analysts and personal financial advisors; operations research analysts; economists; and market and survey researchers. Some management analysts specialize in information technology and work with computers, as do computer systems analysts, database administrators, and computer scientists. Most management analysts also have managerial experience similar to that of administrative services managers; advertising, marketing, promotions, public relations, and sales managers; financial managers; human resources, training, and labor relations managers and specialists; and top executives.

Sources of Additional Information

Information about career opportunities in management consulting is available from:

- Association of Management Consulting Firms, 380 Lexington Ave., Suite 1700, New York, NY 10168. Internet: http://www.amcf.org

Information about the Certified Management Consultant designation can be obtained from:

- Institute of Management Consultants USA, Inc., 2025 M St. NW, Suite 800, Washington DC 20036. Internet: http://www.imcusa.org

Information on obtaining a management analyst position with the federal government is available from the Office of Personnel Management (OPM) through a telephone-based system. Consult your telephone directory under U.S. Government for a local number or call (703) 724-1850; Federal Relay Service: (800) 877-8339. The first number is not toll-free, and charges may result. Information also is available from the OPM Internet site: http://www.usajobs.opm.gov.

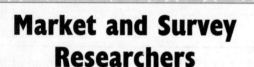

Market and Survey Researchers

(O*NET 19-3021.00 and 19-3022.00)

Significant Points

- Strong demand is expected for market and survey researchers.

- A master's degree is the minimum requirement for many private sector jobs.

- Quantitative skills are critical.

Nature of the Work

Market, or marketing research analysts are concerned with the potential sales of a product or service. They analyze statistical data on past sales to predict future sales. They gather data on competitors and analyze prices, sales, and methods of marketing and distribution. Market research analysts devise methods and procedures for obtaining the data they need. They often design telephone, mail, or Internet surveys to assess consumer preferences. Some surveys are conducted as personal interviews by going door-to-door, leading focus group discussions, or setting up booths in public places such as shopping malls. Trained interviewers, under the market research analyst's direction, usually conduct the surveys.

After compiling the data, market research analysts evaluate them and make recommendations to their client or employer based upon their findings. They provide a company's management with information needed to make decisions on the promotion, distribution, design, and pricing of products or services. The information may also be used to determine the advisability of adding new lines of merchandise, opening new branches, or otherwise diversifying the company's operations. Market research analysts might also

develop advertising brochures and commercials, sales plans, and product promotions such as rebates and giveaways.

Survey researchers design and conduct surveys for a variety of clients such as corporations, government agencies, political candidates, and service providers. They use surveys to collect information that is used for research, making fiscal or policy decisions, measuring policy effectiveness, and improving customer satisfaction. Analysts may conduct opinion research to determine public attitudes on various issues, which may help political or business leaders and others assess public support for their electoral prospects or social policies. Like market research analysts, survey researchers may use a variety of mediums to conduct surveys, such as the Internet, personal or telephone interviews, or mail questionnaires. They also may supervise interviewers who conduct surveys in person or over the telephone.

Survey researchers design surveys in many different formats, depending upon the scope of research and method of collection. Interview surveys, for example, are common because they can increase survey participation rates. Survey researchers may consult with economists, statisticians, market research analysts, or other data users in order to design surveys. They also may present survey results to clients.

Working Conditions

Market and survey researchers generally have structured work schedules. Some often work alone, writing reports, preparing statistical charts, and using computers, but they also may be an integral part of a research team. Market researchers who conduct personal interviews will have frequent contact with the public. Most work under pressure of deadlines and tight schedules, which may require overtime. Their routine may be interrupted by special requests for data, as well as by the need to attend meetings or conferences. Travel may be necessary.

Employment

Market and survey researchers held about a total of 155,000 jobs in 2002. Most of these jobs were held by market research analysts, who held 135,000 jobs. Private industry provided about 97 percent of salaried market research analyst jobs. Because of the applicability of market research to many industries, market research analysts are employed in most industries. The industries which employ the largest number of market research analysts are management, scientific, and technical consulting firms, insurance carriers, computer systems design and related firms, software publishers, securities and commodities brokers, and advertising and related firms.

Survey researchers held about 20,000 jobs in 2002. Survey researchers were mainly employed by professional, scientific, and technical services firms, including management, scientific and technical consulting firms, and scientific research and development firms; employment services, state government, and internet service providers and web search portals. A number of market and survey researchers combine a full-time job in government, academia, or business with part-time or consulting work in another setting. About 8 percent of market and survey researchers are self-employed.

Besides the jobs described above, many market and survey researchers held faculty positions in colleges and universities. Marketing faculties have flexible work schedules and may divide their time among teaching, research, consulting, and administration.

Training, Other Qualifications, and Advancement

A master's degree is the minimum requirement for many private sector market and survey research jobs, and for advancement to more responsible positions. Market and survey researchers may earn advanced degrees in business administration, marketing, statistics, communications, or some closely related discipline. Some schools help graduate students find internships or part-time employment in government agencies, consulting firms, financial institutions, or marketing research firms prior to graduation.

In addition to courses in business, marketing, and consumer behavior, prospective market and survey researchers should take other liberal arts and social science courses, including economics, psychology, English, and sociology. Because of the importance of quantitative skills to market and survey researchers, courses in mathematics, statistics, sampling theory and survey design, and computer science are extremely helpful.

Bachelor's degree holders who majored in marketing and related fields may qualify for many entry-level positions that might or might not be related to market and survey research. These positions include research assistant, administrative or management trainee, marketing interviewer, and salesperson, among others. Many businesses, research and consulting firms, and government agencies seek individuals who have strong computer and quantitative skills and can perform complex research. Many corporation and government executives have a strong background in marketing.

In addition to being required for most market and survey research jobs in business and industry, a master's degree is usually the minimum requirement for a job as an instructor in junior and community colleges. In most colleges and universities, however, a Ph.D. is necessary for appointment as an instructor. A Ph.D. and extensive publications in academic journals are required for a professorship, tenure, and promotion.

Aspiring market and survey researchers should gain experience gathering and analyzing data, conducting interviews or surveys, and writing reports on their findings while in college. This experience can prove invaluable later in obtaining a full-time position in the field, because much of the work, in the beginning, may center on these duties. With experience, market and survey researchers eventually are assigned their own research projects.

Those considering careers as market and survey researchers should be able to pay attention to details because much time is spent on precise data analysis. Patience and persistence are necessary qualities because market and survey researchers must spend long hours on independent study and problem solving. At the same time, they must work well with others, because they often oversee interviews of a wide variety of individuals. Communication skills are very important because market and survey researchers must be able to present their findings both orally and in writing, in a clear, concise manner.

Job Outlook

Employment of market and survey researchers is expected to grow faster than the average for all occupations through 2012. Many job openings are likely to result from the need to replace experienced workers who transfer to other occupations or who retire or leave the labor force for other reasons. Opportunities should be best for those with a master's or Ph.D. degree in marketing or a related field and strong quantitative skills.

Demand for market research analysts should be strong because of an increasingly competitive economy. Marketing research provides organizations valuable feedback from purchasers, allowing companies to evaluate consumer satisfaction and more effectively plan for the future. As companies seek to expand their market and as consumers become better informed, the need for marketing professionals will increase. As globalization of the marketplace continues, market researchers will also be increasingly utilized to analyze foreign markets and competition for goods and services.

Market research analysts should have opportunities in a wide range of employment settings, particularly in marketing research firms, as companies find it more profitable to contract for marketing research services rather than support their own marketing department. Increasingly, marketing research analysts are not only collecting and analyzing information, but are also helping the client implement their ideas and recommendations. Other organizations, including computer systems design companies, financial services organizations, healthcare institutions, advertising firms, manufacturing firms producing consumer goods, and insurance companies may offer job opportunities for market research analysts. Survey researchers will be needed to meet the growing demand for market and opinion research, as an increasingly competitive economy requires businesses to more effectively and efficiently allocate advertising funds.

Bachelor's degree holders may face competition for the limited number of market and survey research jobs for which they are eligible. However, they will qualify for a number of other positions, however, in which they can take advantage of their knowledge in conducting research, developing surveys, or analyzing data. Some graduates with bachelor's degrees will find jobs in industry and business as management or sales trainees or as administrative assistants.

Bachelor's degree holders with good quantitative skills, including a strong background in mathematics, statistics, survey design, and computer science, may be hired by private firms as research assistants or interviewers.

Ph.D. degree holders in marketing and related fields should have a range of opportunities in industry and consulting firms. As in many other disciplines, however, Ph.D. holders are likely to face keen competition for tenured teaching positions in colleges and universities.

Earnings

Median annual earnings of market research analysts in 2002 were $53,810. The middle 50 percent earned between $38,760and $76,310. The lowest 10 percent earned less than $29,390, and the highest 10 percent earned more than $100,160. Median annual earnings in the industries employing the largest numbers of market research analysts in 2002 were as follows:

Management of companies and enterprises	$56,750
Insurance carriers	46,700
Other professional, scientific, and technical services	46,380
Management, scientific, and technical consulting services	44,580

Median annual earnings of survey researchers in 2002 were $22,200. The middle 50 percent earned between $17,250 and $38,530. The lowest 10 percent earned less than $15,140, and the highest 10 percent earned more than $57,080. Median annual earnings of survey researchers in 2002 in other professional, scientific, and technical services were $19,610.

Related Occupations

Market and survey researchers do research to find out how well the market receives products or services. This may include planning, implementation, and analysis of surveys to determine people's needs and preferences. Other jobs using these skills include economists, psychologists, sociologists, statisticians, and urban and regional planners.

Sources of Additional Information

For information about careers and salaries in market and survey research, contact:

- Marketing Research Association, 1344 Silas Deane Hwy., Suite 306, Rocky Hill, CT 06067-0230. Internet: http://www.mra-net.org

- Council of American Survey Research Organizations, 3 Upper Devon, Port Jefferson, NY 11777. Internet: http://www.casro.org

Material Moving Occupations

(O*NET 53-1021.00, 53-7011.00, 53-7021.00, 53-7031.00, 53-7032.01, 53-7032.02, 53-7033.00, 53-7041.00, and 53-7051.00)

Significant Points

- Job openings should be numerous because the occupation is very large and turnover is relatively high.

- Most jobs require little work experience or specific training.

- Pay is low, and the seasonal nature of the work may reduce earnings.

Nature of the Work

Material moving workers are categorized into two groups—operators and laborers. Operators use machinery to move construction materials, earth, petroleum products, and other heavy materials. Generally, they move materials over short distances—around a construction site, factory, or warehouse. Some move materials onto or off of trucks and ships. Operators control equipment by moving levers or foot pedals, operating switches, or turning dials. They may also set up and inspect equipment, make adjustments, and perform minor repairs when needed. Laborers and hand material movers manually handle freight, stock, or other materials; clean vehicles, machinery, and other equipment; feed materials into or remove materials from machines or equipment; and pack or package products and materials.

Material moving occupations are classified by the type of equipment they operate or goods they handle. Each piece of equipment requires different skills to move different types of loads.

Industrial truck and tractor operators drive and control industrial trucks or tractors equipped to move materials around a warehouse, storage yard, factory, or construction site. A typical industrial truck, often called a forklift or lift truck, has a hydraulic lifting mechanism and forks. Industrial truck and tractor operators also may operate tractors that pull trailers loaded with materials, goods, or equipment within factories and warehouses, or around outdoor storage areas.

Excavating and loading machine and dragline operators operate or tend machinery equipped with scoops, shovels, or buckets, to dig and load sand, gravel, earth, or similar materials into trucks or onto conveyors. Construction and mining industries employ the majority of excavation and loading machine and dragline operators. *Dredge operators* excavate and maintain navigable channels in waterways by operating dredges to remove sand, gravel, or other materials from lakes, rivers, or streams. *Underground mining loading machine operators* operate underground loading machines to load coal, ore, or rock into shuttle or mine car or onto conveyors. Loading equipment may include power shovels, hoisting engines equipped with cable-drawn scraper or scoop, or machines equipped with gathering arms and conveyor.

Crane and tower operators operate mechanical boom and cable or tower and cable equipment to lift and move materials, machinery, or other heavy objects. They extend or retract a horizontally mounted boom to lower or raise a hook attached to the loadline. Most operators coordinate their maneuvers in response to hand signals and radioed instructions. Operators position the loads from the onboard console or from a remote console at the site. While crane and tower operators are noticeable at office building and other construction sites, the biggest group works in primary metal, metal fabrication, and transportation equipment manufacturing industries that use heavy, bulky materials. *Hoist and winch operators* control movement of cables, cages, and platforms to move workers and materials for manufacturing, logging, and other industrial operations. They work in such positions as derrick operators and hydraulic boom operators. Many hoist and winch operators are found in manufacturing or construction industries.

Pump operators and their helpers tend, control, or operate power-driven pumps and manifold systems that transfer gases, oil, or other materials to vessels or equipment. They maintain the equipment to regulate the flow of materials according to a schedule set up by petroleum engineers and production supervisors. *Gas compressor and gas pumping station operators* operate steam, gas, electric motor, or internal combustion engine-driven compressors. They transmit, compress, or recover gases, such as butane, nitrogen, hydrogen, and natural gas. *Wellhead pumpers* operate power pumps and auxiliary equipment to produce flow of oil or gas from wells in oilfields.

Tank, car, truck, and ship loaders operate ship loading and unloading equipment, conveyors, hoists, and other specialized material handling equipment such as railroad tank car unloading equipment. They may gauge or sample shipping tanks and test them for leaks. *Conveyor operators and tenders* control or tend conveyor systems that move materials to or from stockpiles, processing stations, departments, or vehicles. *Shuttle car operators* operate diesel or electric-powered shuttle car in underground mine to transport materials from working face to mine cars or conveyor.

Laborers and hand freight, stock, and material movers manually move materials or perform other unskilled general labor. These workers move freight, stock, and other materials to and from storage and production areas, loading docks, delivery vehicles, ships, and containers. Their specific duties vary by industry and work setting. Specialized workers within this group include baggage and cargo handlers, who work in transportation industries, and truck loaders and unloaders. In factories, they may move raw materials or finished goods between loading docks, storage areas, and work areas as well as sort materials and supplies and prepare them according to their work orders

Hand packers and *packagers* manually pack, package, or wrap a variety of materials. They may inspect items for defects, label cartons, stamp information on products, keep records of items packed, and stack packages on loading docks. This group also includes order fillers, who pack materials for shipment, as well as grocery store courtesy clerks. In grocery stores, they may bag groceries, carry packages to customers' cars, and return shopping carts to designated areas.

Machine feeders and *offbearers* feed materials into or remove materials from automatic equipment or machines tended by other workers. *Cleaners of vehicles and equipment* clean machinery, vehicles, storage tanks, pipelines, and similar equipment using water and other cleaning agents, vacuums, hoses, brushes, cloths, and other cleaning equipment. *Refuse* and *recyclable material collectors* gather trash, garbage, and recyclables from homes and businesses along a regularly scheduled route, and deposit the refuse in their truck for transport to a dump, landfill, or recycling center. They lift and empty garbage cans or recycling bins by hand, or operate a hydraulic lift truck that picks up and empties dumpsters.

Working Conditions

Many material moving workers work outdoors in every type of climate and weather condition. The work tends to be repetitive and physically demanding. They may lift and carry heavy objects, and stoop, kneel, crouch, or crawl in awkward positions. Some work at great heights, or outdoors in all weather conditions. Some jobs expose workers to harmful materials or chemicals, fumes, odors, loud noise, or dangerous machinery. To avoid injury, these workers wear safety clothing, such as gloves and hardhats, and devices to protect their eyes, mouth, or hearing. These jobs have become much safer as safety equipment such as overhead guards on forklift trucks has become common. As with most machinery, accidents usually can be avoided by observing proper operating procedures and safety practices.

Material movers generally work 8-hour shifts, though longer shifts also are common. In many industries that work around the clock, material movers work evening or "graveyard" shifts. Some may work at night because the establishment may not want to disturb customers during normal business hours. Refuse and recyclable material collectors often work shifts starting at 5 or 6 a.m. Some material movers work only during certain seasons, such as when the weather permits construction activity.

Employment

Material movers held 4.9 million jobs in 2002. They were distributed among the detailed occupations as follows:

Laborers and freight, stock, and material
movers, hand 2,231,000

Hand packers and packagers 920,000

Industrial truck and tractor operators 594,000

Cleaners of vehicles and equipment 344,000

Machine feeders and offbearers............................164,000

First-line supervisors/managers of helpers,
    laborers, and material movers, hand..................147,000

Refuse and recyclable material collectors 134,000

Excavating and loading machine and
    dragline operators 80,000

Conveyor operators and tenders 58,000

Crane and tower operators 50,000

Tank car, truck, and ship loaders..........................17,000

Pump operators, except wellhead pumpers 13,000

Wellhead pumpers 11,000

Hoist and winch operators 9,000

Gas compressor and gas pumping station
    operators...7,300

Loading machine operators, underground
    mining 4,000

Dredge operators 3,500

Shuttle car operators 3,200

All other material moving workers 78,000

About 29 percent of all material movers worked in the wholesale trade or retail trade industries. About 23 percent worked in manufacturing and 14 percent worked in transportation and warehousing. Significant numbers of material movers also worked in construction and mining. In addition, 13 percent of material moving workers were employed in the employment services industry where they are employed on a temporary or contract basis. For example, companies that need workers for only a few days, to move materials or to clean up a site, may contract with temporary help agencies specializing in providing suitable workers on a short-term basis. A small proportion of material movers were self-employed.

Material movers work in every part of the country. Some work in remote locations on large construction projects, such as highways and dams, or in factory or mining operations.

Training, Other Qualifications, and Advancement

Most material moving jobs require little work experience or specific training. Some employers prefer applicants with a high school diploma, but most simply require workers to be at least 18 years old and physically able to perform the work. For those jobs requiring physical exertion, employers may require that applicants pass a physical exam. Some employers also require drug testing or background checks before employment. These workers often are younger than workers in other occupations—reflecting the limited training but significant physical requirements of many of these jobs.

Material movers generally learn skills informally, on the job, from more experienced workers or supervisors. However, workers who use industrial trucks, other dangerous equipment, or handle toxic chemicals must receive specialized training in safety awareness and procedures. Many of the training requirements are standardized through the U.S. Occupational Safety and Health Administration (OSHA). This training usually is provided by the employer. Employers must also certify that each operator has received the training and evaluate each operator at least once every three years.

Material moving equipment operators need a good sense of balance, distance judgment, and eye-hand-foot coordination. For those jobs that involve dealing with the public, such as grocery store courtesy clerks, workers should be pleasant and courteous. Most jobs require reading and basic mathematics skills to read procedures manuals and billing and other documents. Mechanical aptitude and high school training in automobile or diesel mechanics are helpful because workers may perform some maintenance on their equipment. Experience operating mobile equipment, such as tractors on farms or heavy equipment in the Armed Forces, is an asset. As material moving equipment becomes more automated, many workers will need basic computer and technical knowledge to operate the equipment.

Experience in many of these jobs may allow workers to qualify or become trainees for jobs such as construction trades workers; assemblers or other production workers; motor vehicle operators; or vehicle and mobile equipment mechanics, installers, and repairers. In many workplaces, new workers often work in a material moving position before being promoted to a better paying and more highly skilled job. Some may eventually advance to become supervisors.

Job Outlook

Job openings should be numerous because the occupation is very large and turnover is relatively high—characteristic of occupations requiring little formal training. Many openings will arise from the need to replace workers who transfer to other occupations, or who retire or leave the labor force for other reasons.

Employment in material moving occupations will increase more slowly than average for all occupations through 2012. Employment growth will stem from an expanding economy and increased spending on the nation's infrastructure, such as highways and bridges. However, equipment improvements, including the growing automation of material handling in factories and warehouses, will continue to raise productivity and moderate the demand for material movers.

Job growth for material movers largely depends on growth in the industries employing them and the type of equipment the workers operate or the materials they handle. For example, employment of operators in manufacturing will decline due to increased automation and efficiency in the production process. On the other hand, employment will grow rapidly in temporary help organizations as firms contract out material moving services. Employment also will grow in warehousing and storage as more firms contract out their warehousing functions to firms that specialize in them.

Both construction and manufacturing are very sensitive to changes in economic conditions, so the number of job openings in these industries may fluctuate from year to year. Although increasing automation may eliminate some manual tasks, new jobs will be created to operate and maintain material moving equipment.

Earnings

Median hourly earnings of material moving workers in 2002 were relatively low, as indicated by the following tabulation:

Gas compressor and gas pumping station operators...$20.44

First-line supervisors/managers of helpers, laborers, and material movers, hand......................17.87

Pump operators, except wellhead pumpers 17.53

Crane and tower operators 17.47

Wellhead pumpers 16.24

Tank car, truck, and ship loaders............................15.63

Excavating and loading machine and dragline operators..15.58

Hoist and winch operators 15.09

Industrial truck and tractor operators 12.54

Conveyor operators and tenders 11.66

Refuse and recyclable material collectors 11.60

Machine feeders and offbearers..............................10.50

Laborers and freight, stock, and material movers, hand 9.48

Cleaners of vehicles and equipment 8.20

Hand packers and packagers 8.03

All other material moving workers 12.58

Pay rates vary according to experience and job responsibilities. Pay usually is higher in metropolitan areas. The seasonality of work may reduce earnings.

Related Occupations

Other workers who operate mechanical equipment include bus drivers; construction equipment operators; machine setters, operators, and tenders—metal and plastic; rail transportation workers; and truck drivers and driver/sales workers. Other entry-level workers who perform mostly physical work are agricultural workers; building cleaning workers; construction laborers; forest, conservation, and logging workers; and grounds maintenance workers.

Sources of Additional Information

For information about job opportunities and training programs, contact local state employment service offices, building or construction contractors, manufacturers, and wholesale and retail establishments.

Information on safety and training requirements is available from:

- U.S. Department of Labor, Occupational Safety and Health Administration (OSHA), 200 Constitution Ave. NW, Washington, DC 20210. Internet: http://www.osha.gov

Information on industrial truck and tractor operators is available from:

- Industrial Truck Association, 1750 K St. NW, Suite 460, Washington, DC 20006.

Medical and Health Services Managers

(O*NET 11-9111.00)

Significant Points

- Earnings of medical and health services managers are high, but long work hours are common.

- A master's degree is the standard credential for most positions, although a bachelor's degree is adequate for some entry-level positions in smaller facilities.

- Employment will grow fastest in practitioners' offices and in home healthcare services.

- Applicants with work experience in healthcare and strong business and management skills should have the best opportunities.

Nature of the Work

Healthcare is a business and, like every other business, it needs good management to keep it running smoothly. The occupation, medical and health services manager, encompasses all individuals who plan, direct, coordinate, and supervise the delivery of healthcare. medical and health services managers include specialists and generalists. Specialists are in charge of specific clinical departments or services, while generalists manage or help to manage an entire facility or system.

The structure and financing of healthcare is changing rapidly. Future medical and health services managers must be prepared to deal with evolving integrated healthcare delivery systems, technological innovations, an increasingly complex regulatory environment, restructuring of work,

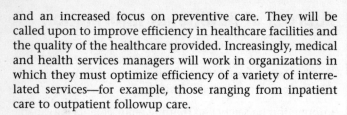

and an increased focus on preventive care. They will be called upon to improve efficiency in healthcare facilities and the quality of the healthcare provided. Increasingly, medical and health services managers will work in organizations in which they must optimize efficiency of a variety of interrelated services—for example, those ranging from inpatient care to outpatient followup care.

Large facilities usually have several assistant administrators to aid the top administrator and to handle daily decisions. Assistant administrators may direct activities in clinical areas such as nursing, surgery, therapy, medical records, or health information.

In smaller facilities, top administrators handle more of the details of daily operations. For example, many nursing home administrators manage personnel, finance, facility operations, and admissions and have a larger role in resident care.

Clinical managers have more specific responsibilities than do generalists, and they have training or experience in a specific clinical area. For example, directors of physical therapy are experienced physical therapists, and most health information and medical record administrators have a bachelor's degree in health information or medical record administration. Clinical managers establish and implement policies, objectives, and procedures for their departments; evaluate personnel and work; develop reports and budgets; and coordinate activities with other managers.

In group medical practices, managers work closely with physicians. Whereas an office manager may handle business affairs in small medical groups, leaving policy decisions to the physicians themselves, larger groups usually employ a full-time administrator to help formulate business strategies and coordinate day-to-day business.

A small group of 10 to 15 physicians might employ 1 administrator to oversee personnel matters, billing and collection, budgeting, planning, equipment outlays, and patient flow. A large practice of 40 to 50 physicians may have a chief administrator and several assistants, each responsible for different areas.

Medical and health services managers in managed care settings perform functions similar to those of their counterparts in large group practices, except that they may have larger staffs to manage. In addition, they may do more work in the areas of community outreach and preventive care than do managers of a group practice.

Some medical and health services managers oversee the activities of a number of facilities in health systems. Such systems may contain both inpatient and outpatient facilities and offer a wide range of patient services.

Working Conditions

Most medical and health services managers work long hours. Facilities such as nursing care facilities and hospitals operate around the clock, and administrators and managers may be called at all hours to deal with problems. They also may travel to attend meetings or inspect satellite facilities.

Some managers work in comfortable, private offices; others share space with other managers or staff. They may spend considerable time walking to consult with coworkers.

Employment

Medical and health services managers held about 244,000 jobs in 2002. About 37 percent worked in hospitals, and another 17 percent worked in offices of physicians or nursing care facilities. The remainder worked mostly in home healthcare services, federal government healthcare facilities, ambulatory facilities run by state and local governments, outpatient care centers, insurance carriers, and community care facilities for the elderly.

Training, Other Qualifications, and Advancement

Medical and health services managers must be familiar with management principles and practices. A master's degree in health services administration, long-term care administration, health sciences, public health, public administration, or business administration is the standard credential for most generalist positions in this field. However, a bachelor's degree is adequate for some entry-level positions in smaller facilities and at the departmental level within healthcare organizations. Physicians' offices and some other facilities may substitute on-the-job experience for formal education.

For clinical department heads, a degree in the appropriate field and work experience may be sufficient for entry. However, a master's degree in health services administration or a related field may be required to advance. For example, nursing service administrators usually are chosen from among supervisory registered nurses with administrative abilities and a graduate degree in nursing or health services administration.

Bachelor's, master's, and doctoral degree programs in health administration are offered by colleges, universities, and schools of public health, medicine, allied health, public administration, and business administration. In 2003, 67 schools had accredited programs leading to the master's degree in health services administration, according to the Accrediting Commission on Education for Health Services Administration.

Some graduate programs seek students with undergraduate degrees in business or health administration; however, many graduate programs prefer students with a liberal arts or health profession background. Candidates with previous work experience in healthcare also may have an advantage. Competition for entry to these programs is keen, and applicants need above-average grades to gain admission. Graduate programs usually last between 2 and 3 years. They may include up to 1 year of supervised administrative experience, and course work in areas such as hospital organization and management, marketing, accounting and budgeting, human resources administration, strategic planning, health economics, and health information systems. Some programs allow students to specialize in one type of facility—hospitals, nursing care facilities, mental health facilities, or medical groups. Other programs encourage a generalist approach to health administration education.

New graduates with master's degrees in health services administration may start as department managers or as staff employees. The level of the starting position varies with the experience of the applicant and the size of the organization. Hospitals and other health facilities offer postgraduate residencies and fellowships, which usually are staff positions. Graduates from master's degree programs also take jobs in large group medical practices, clinics, mental health facilities, nursing care corporations, and consulting firms.

Graduates with bachelor's degrees in health administration usually begin as administrative assistants or assistant department heads in larger hospitals. They also may begin as department heads or assistant administrators in small hospitals or nursing care facilities.

All states and the District of Columbia require nursing care facility administrators to have a bachelor's degree, pass a licensing examination, complete a state-approved training program, and pursue continuing education. A license is not required in other areas of medical and health services management.

Medical and health services managers often are responsible for millions of dollars' worth of facilities and equipment and hundreds of employees. To make effective decisions, they need to be open to different opinions and good at analyzing contradictory information. They must understand finance and information systems, and be able to interpret data. Motivating others to implement their decisions requires strong leadership abilities. Tact, diplomacy, flexibility, and communication skills are essential because medical and health services managers spend most of their time interacting with others.

Medical and health services managers advance by moving into more responsible and higher paying positions, such as assistant or associate administrator, or by moving to larger facilities.

Job Outlook

Employment of medical and health services managers is expected to grow faster than the average for all occupations through 2012, as the health services industry continues to expand and diversify. Opportunities will be especially good in offices of physicians and other health practitioners, home healthcare services, and outpatient care centers. Applicants with work experience in the healthcare field and strong business and management skills should have the best opportunities.

Hospitals will continue to employ the most medical and health services managers over the projection period. However, the number of new jobs created in hospitals is expected to increase at a slower rate than in many other industries, as

hospitals focus on controlling costs and increasing the utilization of clinics and other alternate care sites. Medical and health services managers with experience in large facilities will enjoy the best job opportunities, as hospitals become larger and more complex. Employment will grow the fastest in practitioners' offices and in home healthcare agencies. Many services previously provided in hospitals will continue to shift to these sectors, especially as medical technologies improve. Demand in medical group practice management will grow as medical group practices become larger and more complex. Medical and health services managers will need to deal with the pressures of cost containment and financial accountability, as well as with the increased focus on preventive care. They also will become more involved in trying to improve the health of their communities. Managers with specialized experience in a particular field, such as reimbursement, should have good opportunities.

Medical and health services managers also will be employed by healthcare management companies who provide management services to hospitals and other organizations, as well as to specific departments such as emergency, information management systems, managed care contract negotiations, and physician recruiting.

Earnings

Median annual earnings of medical and health services managers were $61,370 in 2002. The middle 50 percent earned between $47,910 and $80,150. The lowest 10 percent earned less than $37,460, and the highest 10 percent earned more than $109,080. Median annual earnings in the industries employing the largest numbers of medical and health services managers in 2002 were as follows:

General medical and surgical hospitals	$65,950
Home health care services	56,320
Outpatient care centers	55,650
Offices of physicians	55,600
Nursing care facilities	55,320

Earnings of medical and health services managers vary by type and size of the facility, as well as by level of responsibility. For example, the Medical Group Management Association reported that, in 2002, median salaries for administrators were $78,258 in practices with fewer than 7 physicians; $92,727 in practices with 7 to 25 physicians; and $125,988 in practices with more than 26 physicians. According to a survey by *Modern Healthcare* magazine, median annual compensation in 2003 for managers of selected clinical departments was $71,800 in respiratory care, $79,000 in physical therapy, $84,500 in home healthcare, $85,100 in laboratory services, $89,100 in rehabilitation services, $89,500 in medical imaging/diagnostic radiology, and $98,400 in nursing services. Salaries also varied according to size of facility and geographic region.

Related Occupations

Medical and health services managers have training or experience in both health and management. Other occupations requiring knowledge of both fields are insurance underwriters and social and community service managers.

Sources of Additional Information

Information about undergraduate and graduate academic programs in this field is available from:

- Association of University Programs in Health Administration, 730 11th St. NW, Washington, DC 20001-4510. Internet: http://www.aupha.org

For a list of accredited graduate programs in medical and health services administration, contact:

- Accrediting Commission on Education for Health Services Administration, 730 11th St. NW, Washington, DC 20001-4510. Internet: http://www.acehsa.org

For information about career opportunities in long-term care administration, contact:

- American College of Health Care Administrators, 300 N. Lee St., Suite 301, Alexandria, VA 22314. Internet: http://www.achca.org

For information about career opportunities in medical group practices and ambulatory care management, contact:

- Medical Group Management Association, 104 Inverness Terrace East, Englewood, CO 80112-5306.

For information about medical and healthcare office managers, contact:

- Professional Association of Health Care Office Management, 461 East Ten Mile Rd., Pensacola, FL 32534-9712.

Medical Assistants

(O*NET 31-9092.00)

Significant Points

- Some medical assistants are trained on the job, but many complete 1- or 2-year programs in vocational-technical high schools, postsecondary vocational schools, and community and junior colleges.

- Medical assistants is projected to be the fastest growing occupation over the 2002-12 period.

- Job prospects should be best for medical assistants with formal training or experience, particularly those with certification.

Nature of the Work

Medical assistants perform routine administrative and clinical tasks to keep the offices of physicians, podiatrists, chiro-practors, and other health practitioners running smoothly. They should not be confused with physician assistants, who examine, diagnose, and treat patients under the direct supervision of a physician.

The duties of medical assistants vary from office to office, depending on the location and size of the practice and the practitioner's specialty. In small practices, medical assistants usually are "generalists," handling both administrative and clinical duties and reporting directly to an office manager, physician, or other health practitioner. Those in large practices tend to specialize in a particular area, under the supervision of department administrators.

Medical assistants perform many administrative duties, including answering telephones, greeting patients, updating and filing patients' medical records, filling out insurance forms, handling correspondence, scheduling appointments, arranging for hospital admission and laboratory services, and handling billing and bookkeeping.

Clinical duties vary according to state law and include taking medical histories and recording vital signs, explaining treatment procedures to patients, preparing patients for examination, and assisting the physician during the examination. Medical assistants collect and prepare laboratory specimens or perform basic laboratory tests on the premises, dispose of contaminated supplies, and sterilize medical instruments. They instruct patients about medications and special diets, prepare and administer medications as directed by a physician, authorize drug refills as directed, telephone prescriptions to a pharmacy, draw blood, prepare patients for x rays, take electrocardiograms, remove sutures, and change dressings.

Medical assistants also may arrange examining-room instruments and equipment, purchase and maintain supplies and equipment, and keep waiting and examining rooms neat and clean.

Assistants who specialize have additional duties. *Podiatric medical assistants* make castings of feet, expose and develop x rays, and assist podiatrists in surgery. *Ophthalmic medical assistants* help ophthalmologists provide eye care. They conduct diagnostic tests, measure and record vision, and test eye muscle function. They also show patients how to insert, remove, and care for contact lenses, and they apply eye dressings. Under the direction of the physician, ophthalmic medical assistants may administer eye medications. They also maintain optical and surgical instruments and may assist the ophthalmologist in surgery.

Working Conditions

Medical assistants work in well-lighted, clean environments. They constantly interact with other people and may have to handle several responsibilities at once.

Most full-time medical assistants work a regular 40-hour week. Some work part time, evenings, or weekends.

Employment

Medical assistants held about 365,000 jobs in 2002. Almost 60 percent worked in offices of physicians; about 14 percent worked in public and private hospitals, including inpatient and outpatient facilities; and almost 10 percent worked in offices of other health practitioners, such as chiropractors and podiatrists. The rest worked mostly in outpatient care centers, public and private educational services, other ambulatory healthcare services, state and local government agencies, medical and diagnostic laboratories, nursing care facilities, and employment services.

Training, Other Qualifications, and Advancement

Most employers prefer graduates of formal programs in medical assisting. Such programs are offered in vocational-technical high schools, postsecondary vocational schools, and community and junior colleges. Postsecondary programs usually last either 1 year, resulting in a certificate or diploma, or 2 years, resulting in an associate degree. Courses cover anatomy, physiology, and medical terminology, as well as typing, transcription, recordkeeping, accounting, and insurance processing. Students learn laboratory techniques, clinical and diagnostic procedures, pharmaceutical principles, the administration of medications, and first aid. They study office practices, patient relations, medical law, and ethics. Accredited programs include an internship that provides practical experience in physicians' offices, hospitals, or other healthcare facilities.

Two agencies recognized by the U.S. Department of Education accredit programs in medical assisting: The Commission on Accreditation of Allied Health Education Programs (CAAHEP) and the Accrediting Bureau of Health Education Schools (ABHES). In 2002, there were 495 medical assisting programs accredited by CAAHEP and about 170 accredited by ABHES. The Committee on Accreditation for Ophthalmic Medical Personnel approved 14 programs in ophthalmic medical assisting.

Formal training in medical assisting, while generally preferred, is not always required. Some medical assistants are trained on the job, although this practice is less common than in the past. Applicants usually need a high school diploma or the equivalent. Recommended high school courses include mathematics, health, biology, typing, bookkeeping, computers, and office skills. Volunteer experience in the healthcare field also is helpful.

Although medical assistants are not licensed, some states require them to take a test or a course before they can perform certain tasks, such as taking x rays. Employers prefer to hire experienced workers or certified applicants who have passed a national examination, indicating that the medical assistant meets certain standards of competence. The American Association of Medical Assistants awards the Certified Medical Assistant credential; the American Medical Technologists awards the Registered Medical Assistant credential; the American Society of Podiatric Medical Assistants awards the Podiatric Medical Assistant Certified credential; and the Joint Commission on Allied Health Personnel in Ophthalmology awards credentials at three levels: Certified Ophthalmic Assistant, Certified Ophthalmic Technician, and Certified Ophthalmic Medical Technologist.

Medical assistants deal with the public; therefore, they must be neat and well groomed and have a courteous, pleasant manner. Medical assistants must be able to put patients at ease and explain physicians' instructions. They must respect the confidential nature of medical information. Clinical duties require a reasonable level of manual dexterity and visual acuity.

Medical assistants may be able to advance to office manager. They may qualify for a variety of administrative support occupations or may teach medical assisting. With additional education, some enter other health occupations, such as nursing and medical technology.

Job Outlook

Employment of medical assistants is expected to grow much faster than the average for all occupations through the year 2012 as the health services industry expands because of technological advances in medicine, and a growing and aging population. Increasing utilization of medical assistants in the rapidly-growing healthcare industries will result in fast employment growth for the occupation. In fact, medical assistants is projected to be the fastest growing occupation over the 2002–12 period.

Employment growth will be driven by the increase in the number of group practices, clinics, and other healthcare facilities that need a high proportion of support personnel, particularly the flexible medical assistant who can handle both administrative and clinical duties. Medical assistants work primarily in outpatient settings, which are expected to exhibit much faster-than-average growth.

In view of the preference of many healthcare employers for trained personnel, job prospects should be best for medical assistants with formal training or experience, and particularly for those with certification.

Earnings

The earnings of medical assistants vary, depending on their experience, skill level, and location. Median annual earnings of medical assistants were $23,940 in 2002. The middle 50 percent earned between $20,260 and $28,410. The lowest 10 percent earned less than $17,640, and the highest 10 percent earned more than $34,130. Median annual earnings in the industries employing the largest numbers of medical assistants in 2002 were as follows:

General medical and surgical hospitals................$24,460

Offices of physicians 24,260

Outpatient care centers 23,980

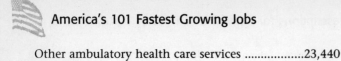

Other ambulatory health care services 23,440

Offices of other health practitioners 21,620

Related Occupations

Workers in other medical support occupations include dental assistants, medical records and health information technicians, medical secretaries, occupational therapist assistants and aides, pharmacy aides, and physical therapist assistants and aides.

Sources of Additional Information

Information about career opportunities, educational programs in medical assisting accredited by the Commission on Accreditation of Allied Health Education Programs, and the Certified Medical Assistant exam is available from:

- American Association of Medical Assistants, 20 North Wacker Dr., Suite 1575, Chicago, IL 60606. Internet: http://www.aama-ntl.org

Information about career opportunities and the Registered Medical Assistant certification exam is available from:

- Registered Medical Assistants of American Medical Technologists, 710 Higgins Rd., Park Ridge, IL 60068-5765.

For a list of ABHES-accredited educational programs in medical assisting, contact:

- Accrediting Bureau of Health Education Schools, 7777 Leesburg Pike, Suite 314 N., Falls Church, VA 22043. Internet: http://www.abhes.org

Information about career opportunities, training programs, and the Certified Ophthalmic Assistant exam is available from:

- Joint Commission on Allied Health Personnel in Ophthalmology, 2025 Woodlane Dr., St. Paul, MN 55125-2998. Internet: http://www.jcahpo.org

Information about careers for podiatric assistants is available from:

- American Society of Podiatric Medical Assistants, 2124 S. Austin Blvd., Cicero, IL 60804. Internet: http://www.aspma.org

Medical Records and Health Information Technicians

(O*NET 29-2071.00)

Significant Points

- This is one of the few health occupations in which there is little or no direct contact with patients.

- Medical records and health information technicians entering the field usually have an associate degree; courses include anatomy, physiology, medical terminology, and computer science.

- Job prospects should be very good, particularly in offices of physicians.

Nature of the Work

Every time a patient receives healthcare, a record is maintained of the observations, medical or surgical interventions, and treatment outcomes. This record includes information that the patient provides concerning his or her symptoms and medical history, the results of examinations, reports of x rays and laboratory tests, diagnoses, and treatment plans. Medical records and health information technicians organize and evaluate these records for completeness and accuracy.

Technicians begin to assemble patients' health information by first making sure their initial medical charts are complete. They ensure that all forms are completed and properly identified and signed, and that all necessary information is in the computer. They regularly communicate with physicians or other healthcare professionals to clarify diagnoses or to obtain additional information.

Medical records and health information technicians assign a code to each diagnosis and procedure. They consult classification manuals and also rely on their knowledge of disease processes. Technicians then use computer software to assign the patient to one of several hundred "diagnosis-related groups," or DRGs. The DRG determines the amount for which the hospital will be reimbursed if the patient is covered by Medicare or other insurance programs using the DRG system. Technicians who specialize in coding are called health information coders, medical record coders, coder/abstractors, or coding specialists. In addition to the DRG system, coders use other coding systems, such as those geared towards ambulatory settings or long-term care.

Technicians also use computer programs to tabulate and analyze data to help improve patient care, to control costs, for use in legal actions, in response to surveys, or for use in research studies. Cancer registrars compile, maintain, and review records of cancer patients to provide information to physicians and for use in research studies.

Medical records and health information technicians' duties vary with the size of the facility. In large to medium-sized facilities, technicians may specialize in one aspect of health information, or supervise health information clerks and transcriptionists while a medical records and health information administrator manages the department. In small facilities, a credentialed medical records and health information technician sometimes manages the department.

Working Conditions

Medical records and health information technicians usually work a 40-hour week. Some overtime may be required. In hospitals—where health information departments often are open 24 hours a day, 7 days a week—technicians may work day, evening, and night shifts.

Medical records and health information technicians work in pleasant and comfortable offices. This is one of the few health occupations in which there is little or no direct contact with patients. Because accuracy is essential in their jobs, technicians must pay close attention to detail. Technicians who work at computer monitors for prolonged periods must guard against eyestrain and muscle pain.

Employment

Medical records and health information technicians held about 147,000 jobs in 2002. Thirty-seven percent of all jobs were in hospitals. The rest were mostly in offices of physicians, nursing care facilities, outpatient care centers, and home healthcare services. Insurance firms that deal in health matters employ a small number of health information technicians to tabulate and analyze health information. Public health departments also hire technicians to supervise data collection from healthcare institutions and to assist in research.

Training, Other Qualifications, and Advancement

Medical records and health information technicians entering the field usually have an associate degree from a community or junior college. In addition to general education, coursework includes medical terminology, anatomy and physiology, legal aspects of health information, coding and abstraction of data, statistics, database management, quality improvement methods, and computer science. Applicants can improve their chances of admission into a program by taking biology, chemistry, health, and computer science courses in high school.

Hospitals sometimes advance promising health information clerks to jobs as medical records and health information technicians, although this practice may be less common in the future. Advancement usually requires 2 to 4 years of job experience and completion of a hospital's in-house training program.

Most employers prefer to hire Registered Health Information Technicians (RHIT), who must pass a written examination offered by the American Health Information Management Association (AHIMA). To take the examination, a person must graduate from a 2-year associate degree program accredited by the Commission on Accreditation of Allied Health Education Programs (CAAHEP) of the American Medical Association. Technicians trained in non-CAAHEP-accredited programs, or on the job, are not eligible to take the examination. In 2003, CAAHEP accredited 182 programs for health information technicians. Technicians who specialize in coding may obtain voluntary certification.

Experienced medical records and health information technicians usually advance in one of two ways—by specializing or managing. Many senior technicians specialize in coding, particularly Medicare coding, or in cancer registry.

In large medical records and health information departments, experienced technicians may advance to section supervisor, overseeing the work of the coding, correspondence, or discharge sections, for example. Senior technicians with RHIT credentials may become director or assistant director of a medical records and health information department in a small facility. However, in larger institutions, the director is usually an administrator, with a bachelor's degree in medical records and health information administration.

Job Outlook

Job prospects should be very good. Employment of medical records and health information technicians is expected to grow much faster than the average for all occupations through 2012, due to rapid growth in the number of medical tests, treatments, and procedures that will be increasingly scrutinized by third-party payers, regulators, courts, and consumers.

Although employment growth in hospitals will not keep pace with growth in other healthcare industries, many new jobs will nevertheless be created. The fastest employment growth and a majority of the new jobs are expected in offices of physicians, due to increasing demand for detailed records, especially in large group practices. Rapid growth also is expected in nursing care facilities, home healthcare services, and outpatient care centers. Additional job openings will result from the need to replace technicians who retire or leave the occupation permanently.

Earnings

Median annual earnings of medical records and health information technicians were $23,890 in 2002. The middle 50 percent earned between $19,550 and $30,600. The lowest 10 percent earned less than $16,460, and the highest 10 percent earned more than $38,640. Median annual earnings in the industries employing the largest numbers of medical records and health information technicians in 2002 were as follows:

Nursing care facilities	$25,160
General medical and surgical hospitals	24,910
Outpatient care centers	22,380
Offices of physicians	21,320

Related Occupations

Medical records and health information technicians need a strong clinical background to analyze the contents of medical records. Other workers who need knowledge of medical terminology, anatomy, and physiology, but have little or no direct contact with the patient, include medical secretaries and medical transcriptionists.

Sources of Additional Information

Information on careers in medical records and health information technology, including a list of programs accredited by the Commission on Accreditation of Allied Health Education Programs (CAAHEP), is available from:

- American Health Information Management Association, 233 N. Michigan Ave., Suite 2150, Chicago, IL 60601-5800. Internet: http://www.ahima.org

Medical Scientists

(O*NET 19-1041.00 and 19-1042.00)

Significant Points

- Epidemiologists typically require a master's degree in public health or, in some cases, a medical degree; other medical scientists need a Ph.D. degree in a biological science.

- Competition is expected for most positions.

- Most medical scientists work in research and development.

Nature of the Work

Medical scientists research human diseases in order to improve human health. Most medical scientists work in research and development. Some conduct basic research to advance knowledge of living organisms, including viruses, bacteria, and other infectious agents. Past research has resulted in the development of vaccines, medicines, and treatments for many diseases. Basic medical research continues to provide the building blocks necessary to develop solutions to human health problems. Medical scientists also engage in clinical investigation, technical writing, drug application review, patent examination, or related activities.

Medical scientists study biological systems to understand the causes of disease and other health problems and to develop treatments. They try to identify changes in a cell or chromosomes that signal the development of medical problems, such as different types of cancer. For example, a medical scientist involved in cancer research may formulate a combination of drugs that will lessen the effects of the disease. Medical scientists who are also physicians can administer these drugs to patients in clinical trials, monitor their reactions, and observe the results. Those who are not physicians normally collaborate with a physician who deals directly with patients. Medical scientists examine the results of clinical trials and, if necessary, adjust the dosage levels to reduce negative side effects or to try to induce even better results. In addition to developing treatments for health problems, medical scientists attempt to discover ways to prevent health problems, such as affirming the link between smoking and lung cancer, or between alcoholism and liver disease.

Many medical scientists work independently in private industry, university, or government laboratories, often exploring new areas of research or expanding on specialized research that they started in graduate school. Medical scientists working in colleges and universities, hospitals, and nonprofit medical research organizations typically submit grant proposals to obtain funding for their projects. Colleges and universities, private industry, and federal government agencies, such as the National Institutes of Health and the National Science Foundation, contribute to the support of scientists whose research proposals are determined to be financially feasible and have the potential to advance new ideas or processes.

Medical scientists who work in applied research or product development use knowledge provided by basic research to develop new drugs and medical treatments. They usually have less autonomy than basic researchers to choose the emphasis of their research, relying instead on market-driven directions based on the firm's products and goals. Medical scientists doing applied research and product development in private industry may be required to express their research plans or results to nonscientists who are in a position to veto or approve their ideas, and they must understand the impact of their work on business. Scientists increasingly work as part of teams, interacting with engineers, scientists of other disciplines, business managers, and technicians.

Medical scientists who conduct research usually work in laboratories and use electron microscopes, computers, thermal cyclers, or a wide variety of other equipment. Some may work directly with individual patients or larger groups as they administer drugs and monitor and observe the patients during clinical trials. Medical scientists who are also physicians may administer gene therapy to human patients, draw blood, excise tissue, or perform other invasive procedures.

Some medical scientists work in managerial, consulting, or administrative positions, usually after spending some time doing research and learning about the firm, agency, or project. In the 1980s, swift advances in basic medical knowledge related to genetics and molecules spurred growth in the field of biotechnology. Medical scientists using this technology manipulate the genetic material of animals, attempting to make organisms more productive or resistant to disease. Research using biotechnology techniques, such as recombining DNA, has led to the discovery of important drugs, including human insulin and growth hormone. Many other substances not previously available in large quantities are now produced by biotechnological means; some may be useful in treating diseases such as Parkinson's or Alzheimer's. Today, many medical scientists are involved in the science of genetic engineering—isolating, identifying, and sequencing human genes and then determining their functionality. This work continues to lead to the discovery of the genes associated with specific diseases and inherited traits, such as certain types of cancer or obesity. These advances in biotechnology have opened up research opportunities in almost all areas of medical science.

Some medical scientists specialize in epidemiology. This branch of medical science investigates and describes the determinants of disease, disability, and other health outcomes and develops the means for prevention and control. Epidemiologists may study many different diseases such as tuberculosis, influenza, or cholera, often focusing on epidemics.

Epidemiologists can be separated into two groups, research and clinical. Research epidemiologists conduct basic and advanced research on infectious diseases that affect the entire body, such as AIDS or typhus—attempting to eradicate or control these diseases. Others may focus only on localized infections of the brain, lungs, or digestive tract, for example. Research epidemiologists work at colleges and universities, schools of public health, medical schools, and research and development services firms. For example, government agencies such as the Department of Defense may contract with a research firm's epidemiologists to evaluate the incidence of malaria in certain parts of the world. While some perform consulting services, other research epidemiologists may work as college and university faculty.

Clinical epidemiologists work primarily in consulting roles at hospitals, informing the medical staff of infectious outbreaks and providing containment solutions. These clinical epidemiologists sometimes are referred to as infection control professionals. Consequently, many epidemiologists in this specific area often are physicians. Epidemiologists who are not physicians often collaborate with physicians to find ways to contain diseases and outbreaks. In addition to traditional duties of studying and controlling diseases, clinical epidemiologists also may be required to develop standards and guidelines for the treatment and control of communicable diseases. Some clinical epidemiologists may work in outpatient settings.

Working Conditions

Medical scientists typically work regular hours in offices or laboratories and usually are not exposed to unsafe or unhealthy conditions. Those who work with dangerous organisms or toxic substances in the laboratory must follow strict safety procedures to avoid contamination. Medical scientists also spend time working in clinics and hospitals administering drugs and treatments to patients in clinical trials. On occasion, epidemiologists may be required to work evenings and weekends to attend meetings and hearings for medical investigations.

Some medical scientists depend on grant money to support their research. They may be under pressure to meet deadlines and to conform to rigid grant-writing specifications when preparing proposals to seek new or extended funding.

Employment

Medical scientists, including epidemiologists, held about 62,000 jobs in 2002. Medical scientists accounted for 58,000 of the total; epidemiologists, 3,900. In addition, many medical scientists held faculty positions in colleges and universities, but they are classified as college or university faculty.

Almost 30 percent of medical scientists were employed in scientific research and development services firms, another 24 percent worked in government, 14 percent in pharmaceutical and medicine manufacturing, 13 percent in private hospitals, and most of the remainder worked in private educational services and ambulatory health care services. About 1,000 were self-employed.

Among epidemiologists, nearly 45 percent were employed in government, another 20 percent worked in management, scientific, and technical consulting services firms, 14 percent in private hospitals, and 12 percent in scientific research and development services firms.

Training, Other Qualifications, and Advancement

A Ph.D. degree in a biological science is the minimum education required for most prospective medical scientists, except epidemiologists, because the work of medical scientists is almost entirely research oriented. A Ph.D. degree qualifies one to do research on basic life processes or on particular medical problems or diseases, and to analyze and interpret the results of experiments on patients. Some medical scientists obtain a medical degree instead of a Ph.D., but may not be licensed physicians because they have not taken the state licensing examination or completed a residency program, typically because they prefer research to clinical practice. Medical scientists who administer drug or gene therapy to human patients, or who otherwise interact medically with patients—drawing blood, excising tissue, or performing other invasive procedures—must be licensed physicians. To be licensed, physicians must graduate from an accredited medical school, pass a licensing examination, and complete 1 to 7 years of graduate medical education. It is particularly helpful for medical scientists to earn both Ph.D. and medical degrees.

Students planning careers as medical scientists should have a bachelor's degree in a biological science. In addition to required courses in chemistry and biology, undergraduates should study allied disciplines such as mathematics, physics, and computer science, or courses in their field of interest. Once they have completed undergraduate studies, they can then select a specialty area for their advanced degree, such as cytology, genomics, or pathology. In addition to formal education, medical scientists usually spend several years in a postdoctoral position before they apply for permanent jobs. Postdoctoral work provides valuable laboratory experience, including experience in specific processes and techniques such as gene splicing, which is transferable to other research projects. In some institutions, the postdoctoral position can lead to a permanent job.

Medical scientists should be able to work independently or as part of a team and be able to communicate clearly and concisely, both orally and in writing. Those in private industry, especially those who aspire to consulting and administrative positions, should possess strong communication skills so they can provide instruction and advice to physicians and other healthcare professionals.

The minimum educational requirement for epidemiology is a master's degree from a school of public health. Some jobs require a Ph.D. or medical degree, depending on the work performed. Epidemiologists who work in hospitals and healthcare centers often must have a medical degree with specific training in infectious diseases. Currently, 134 infectious disease training programs exist in 42 states. Some employees in research epidemiology positions are required to be licensed physicians, as they are required to administer drugs in clinical trials.

Epidemiologists who perform laboratory tests often require the knowledge and expertise of a licensed physician in order to administer drugs to patients in clinical trials. Epidemiologists who are not physicians frequently work closely with one.

Very few students select epidemiology for undergraduate study. Undergraduates, nonetheless, should study biological sciences and should have a solid background in chemistry, mathematics, and computer science. Once a student is prepared for graduate studies, he or she can choose a specialty within epidemiology. For example, those interested in studying environmental epidemiology should focus on environmental coursework, such as water pollution, air pollution, or pesticide use. The core work of environmental studies includes toxicology and molecular biology, and students may continue with advanced coursework in environmental or occupational epidemiology. Some epidemiologists are registered nurses and medical technologists seeking advancement.

Job Outlook

Employment of medical scientists is expected to grow faster than the average for all occupations through 2012. Despite projected rapid job growth for medical scientists, doctoral degree holders can expect to face considerable competition for basic research positions. The federal government funds much basic research and development, including many areas of medical research. Recent budget increases at the National Institutes of Health have led to large increases in federal basic research and development expenditures, with the number of grants awarded to researchers growing in number and dollar amount. At the same time, the number of newly trained medical scientists has continued to increase at least as fast as employment opportunities, so both new and established scientists have experienced greater difficulty winning and renewing research grants. If the number of advanced degrees awarded continues to grow unabated, as expected, this competitive situation is likely to persist.

Medical scientists enjoyed rapid gains in employment between the mid-1980s and mid-1990s, in part reflecting increased staffing requirements in new biotechnology companies. Employment growth should slow somewhat as increases in the number of new biotechnology firms slow and existing firms merge or are absorbed into larger ones. However, much of the basic medical research done in recent years has resulted in new knowledge, including the isolation and identification of new genes. Medical scientists will be needed to take this knowledge to the next stage, which is understanding how certain genes function within an entire organism, so that gene therapies can be developed to treat diseases. Even pharmaceutical and other firms not solely engaged in biotechnology are expected to increasingly use biotechnology techniques, thus creating employment for medical scientists.

Expected expansion in research related to health issues such as AIDS, cancer, and Alzheimer's disease also should result in employment growth. Although medical scientists greatly contributed to developing many vaccines and antibiotics, more medical research will be required to better understand these and other epidemics and to improve human health.

Opportunities in epidemiology also should be highly competitive, as the number of available positions remains limited. However, an increasing focus on monitoring patients at hospitals and healthcare centers to ensure positive patient outcomes will contribute to job growth. In addition, a heightened awareness of bioterrorism and infectious diseases such as West Nile Virus or SARS should also spur demand for these workers. As hospitals enhance their infection control programs, many will seek to boost the quality and quantity of their staff. Besides job openings due to employment growth, additional openings will result as workers leave the labor force or transfer to other occupations. Because employment of epidemiologists is somewhat tied to the healthcare industry, industry conditions will influence occupational demand.

Medical scientists and some epidemiologists are less likely to lose their jobs during recessions than are those in many other occupations because they are employed on long-term research projects. However, a recession could influence the amount of money allocated to new research and development efforts, particularly in areas of risky or innovative medical research. A recession also could limit the possibility of extension or renewal of existing projects.

Earnings

Median annual earnings of medical scientists, except epidemiologists, were $56,980 in 2002. The middle 50 percent earned between $40,180 and $82,720. The lowest 10 percent earned less than $29,980, and the highest 10 percent earned more than $114,640. Median annual earnings in the industries employing the largest numbers of medical scientists in 2002 were:

Pharmaceutical and medicine manufacturing $72,330

Scientific research and development services 61,470

General medical and surgical hospitals.................50,660

Colleges, universities, and professional schools 35,520

Median annual earnings of epidemiologists were $53,840 in 2002. The middle 50 percent earned between $44,900 and $66,510. The lowest 10 percent earned less than $35,910, and the highest 10 percent earned more than $85,930.

Related Occupations

Many other occupations deal with living organisms and require a level of training similar to that of medical scientists. These include biological scientists, agricultural and food scientists, and health occupations such as physicians and surgeons, dentists, and veterinarians.

Sources of Additional Information

For a brochure entitled *Is a Career in the Pharmaceutical Sciences Right for Me*, contact:

- American Association of Pharmaceutical Scientists (AAPS), 2107 Wilson Blvd., Suite #700, Arlington, VA 22201.

For a career brochure entitled *A Million and One*, contact:

- American Society for Microbiology, Education Department, 1752 N St. NW, Washington, D.C. 20036-2804. Internet: http://www.asmusa.org

For information on infectious diseases training programs, contact:

- Infectious Diseases Society of America, Guide to Training Programs, 66 Canal Center Plaza, Suite #600, Alexandria, VA 22314. Internet: http://www.idsociety.org

Information on obtaining a medical scientist position with the federal government is available from the Office of Personnel Management (OPM) through a telephone-based system. Consult your telephone directory under U.S. Government for a local number or call (703) 724-1850; Federal Relay Service: (800) 877-8339. The first number is not tollfree, and charges may result. Information also is available from the OPM Internet site: http://www.usajobs.opm.gov.

Medical Transcriptionists

(O*NET 31-9094.00)

Significant Points

- Job opportunities will be good.

- Employers prefer medical transcriptionists who have completed a postsecondary training program at a vocational school or community college.

- Many medical transcriptionists telecommute from home-based offices as employees or subcontractors for hospitals and transcription services or as self-employed, independent contractors.

- About 4 out of 10 worked in hospitals, and another 3 out of 10 worked in offices of physicians.

Nature of the Work

Medical transcriptionists listen to dictated recordings made by physicians and other healthcare professionals and transcribe them into medical reports, correspondence, and other administrative material. They generally listen to recordings on a headset, using a foot pedal to pause the recording when necessary, and key the text into a personal computer or word processor, editing as necessary for grammar and clarity. The documents they produce include discharge summaries, history and physical examination reports, operative reports, consultation reports, autopsy reports, diagnostic imaging studies, progress notes, and referral letters. Medical transcriptionists return transcribed documents to the physicians or other healthcare professionals who dictated them for review and signature or correction. These documents eventually become part of patients' permanent files.

To understand and accurately transcribe dictated reports into a format that is clear and comprehensible for the reader, medical transcriptionists must understand medical terminology, anatomy and physiology, diagnostic procedures, pharmacology, and treatment assessments. They also must be able to translate medical jargon and abbreviations into their expanded forms. To help identify terms appropriately, transcriptionists refer to standard medical reference materials—both printed and electronic; some of these are available over the Internet. Medical transcriptionists must comply with specific standards that apply to the style of medical records, in addition to the legal and ethical requirements involved with keeping patient information confidential.

Experienced transcriptionists spot mistakes or inconsistencies in a medical report and check to correct the information. Their ability to understand and correctly transcribe patient assessments and treatments reduces the chance of patients receiving ineffective or even harmful treatments and ensures high quality patient care.

Currently, most healthcare providers transmit dictation to medical transcriptionists using either digital or analog dictating equipment. The Internet has grown to be a popular mode for transmitting documentation. Many transcriptionists receive dictation over the Internet and are able to quickly return transcribed documents to clients for approval. Another emerging trend is the implementation of speech recognition technology, which electronically translates sound into text and creates drafts of reports. Reports are then formatted; edited for mistakes in translation, punctuation, or grammar; and checked for consistency and possible medical errors. Transcriptionists working in areas with standardized terminology, such as radiology or pathology, are more likely to encounter speech recognition technology. However, use of speech recognition technology will become more widespread as the technology becomes more sophisticated.

Medical transcriptionists who work in physicians' offices and clinics may have other office duties, such as receiving patients, scheduling appointments, answering the telephone, and handling incoming and outgoing mail. Medical secretaries may also transcribe as part of their jobs. Court reporters have similar duties, but with a different focus. They take verbatim reports of speeches, conversations, legal proceedings, meetings, and other events when written accounts of spoken words are necessary for correspondence, records, or legal proof.

Working Conditions

The majority of these workers are employed in comfortable settings, such as hospitals, physicians' offices, transcription service offices, clinics, laboratories, medical libraries, government medical facilities, or at home. Many medical transcriptionists telecommute from home-based offices as employees or subcontractors for hospitals and transcription services or as self-employed, independent contractors.

Work in this occupation presents hazards from sitting in the same position for long periods, and workers can suffer wrist, back, neck, or eye problems due to strain and risk repetitive motion injuries such as carpal tunnel syndrome. The pressure to be accurate and productive also can be stressful.

Many medical transcriptionists work a standard 40-hour week. Self-employed medical transcriptionists are more likely to work irregular hours—including part time, evenings, weekends, or on-call at any time.

Employment

Medical transcriptionists held about 101,000 jobs in 2002. About 4 out of 10 worked in hospitals, and another 3 out of 10 worked in offices of physicians. Others worked for business support services, offices of other health practitioners, medical and diagnostic laboratories, outpatient care centers, and home healthcare services.

Training, Other Qualifications, and Advancement

Employers prefer to hire transcriptionists who have completed postsecondary training in medical transcription, offered by many vocational schools, community colleges, and distance-learning programs. Completion of a 2-year associate degree or 1-year certificate program—including coursework in anatomy, medical terminology, legal issues relating to healthcare documentation, and English grammar and punctuation—is highly recommended, but not always required. Many of these programs include supervised on-the-job experience. Some transcriptionists, especially those already familiar with medical terminology due to previous experience as a nurse or medical secretary, become proficient through on-the-job training.

The American Association for Medical Transcription (AAMT) awards the voluntary designation Certified Medical Tran-

scriptionist (CMT) to those who earn passing scores on written and practical examinations. As in many other fields, certification is recognized as a sign of competence. Because medical terminology is constantly evolving, medical transcriptionists are encouraged to regularly update their skills. Every 3 years, CMTs must earn continuing education credits to be recertified.

In addition to understanding medical terminology, transcriptionists must have good English grammar and punctuation skills, as well as proficiency with personal computers and word processing software. Normal hearing acuity and good listening skills also are necessary. Employers often require applicants to take pre-employment tests.

With experience, medical transcriptionists can advance to supervisory positions, home-based work, editing, consulting, or teaching. With additional education or training, some become medical records and health information technicians, medical coders, or medical records and health information administrators.

Job Outlook

Job opportunities will be good. Employment of medical transcriptionists is projected to grow faster than the average for all occupations through 2012. Demand for medical transcription services will be spurred by a growing and aging population. Older age groups receive proportionately greater numbers of medical tests, treatments, and procedures that require documentation. A high level of demand for transcription services also will be sustained by the continued need for electronic documentation that can be easily shared among providers, third-party payers, regulators, and consumers. Growing numbers of medical transcriptionists will be needed to amend patients' records, edit for grammar, and identify discrepancies in medical records.

Contracting out transcription work overseas and advancements in speech recognition technology are not expected to significantly reduce the need for well-trained medical transcriptionists domestically. Contracting out transcription work abroad—to countries such as India—has grown more popular as transmitting confidential health information over the Internet has become more secure; however, the demand for overseas transcription services is expected to supplement the demand for well-trained domestic medical transcriptionists. Speech-recognition technology allows physicians and other health professionals to dictate medical reports to a computer that immediately creates an electronic document. In spite of the advances in this technology, it has been difficult for the software to grasp and analyze the human voice and the English language with all its diversity. As a result, there will continue to be a need for skilled medical transcriptionists to identify and appropriately edit the inevitable errors created by speech recognition systems, and create a final document.

Hospitals will continue to employ a large percentage of medical transcriptionists, but job growth there will not be as fast as in other industries. Increasing demand for standardized records should result in rapid employment growth in offices of physicians or other health practitioners, especially in large group practices.

Earnings

Medical transcriptionists had median hourly earnings of $13.05 in 2002. The middle 50 percent earned between $10.87 and $15.63. The lowest 10 percent earned less than $9.27, and the highest 10 percent earned more than $17.97. Median hourly earnings in the industries employing the largest numbers of medical transcriptionists in 2002 were as follows:

General medical and surgical hospitals	$13.20
Offices of physicians	13.00
Business support services	12.42

Compensation methods for medical transcriptionists vary. Some are paid based on the number of hours they work or on the number of lines they transcribe. Others receive a base pay per hour with incentives for extra production. Employees of transcription services and independent contractors almost always receive production-based pay. Independent contractors earn more than transcriptionists who work for others but have higher expenses than their corporate counterparts, receive no benefits, and may face higher risk of termination than employed transcriptionists.

Related Occupations

A number of other workers type, record information, and process paperwork. Among these are Court reporters; human resources assistants, except payroll and timekeeping; receptionists and information clerks; and secretaries and administrative assistants. Other workers who provide medical support include medical assistants and medical records and health information technicians.

Sources of Additional Information

For information on a career as a medical transcriptionist, send a self-addressed, stamped envelope to:

● American Association for Medical Transcription, 100 Sycamore Ave., Modesto, CA 95354-0550. Internet: http://www.aamt.org

State employment service offices can provide information about job openings for medical transcriptionists.

Nursing, Psychiatric, and Home Health Aides

(O*NET 31-1011.00, 31-1012.00, and 31-1013.00)

Significant Points

● Most jobs are in nursing and residential care facilities, hospitals, and home healthcare services.

● Modest entry requirements, low pay, high physical and emotional demands, and lack of advancement opportunities characterize this occupation.

● Numerous job openings and excellent job opportunities are expected.

Nature of the Work

Nursing and psychiatric aides help care for physically or mentally ill, injured, disabled, or infirm individuals confined to hospitals, nursing care facilities, and mental health settings. Home health aides' duties are similar, but they work in patients' homes or residential care facilities.

Nursing aides, also known as nursing assistants, geriatric aides, unlicensed assistive personnel, or hospital attendants, perform routine tasks under the supervision of nursing and medical staff. They answer patients' call lights, deliver messages, serve meals, make beds, and help patients eat, dress, and bathe. Aides also may provide skin care to patients; take their temperatures, pulse rate, respiration rate, and blood pressure; and help patients get in and out of bed and walk. They also may escort patients to operating and examining rooms, keep patients' rooms neat, set up equipment, store and move supplies, or assist with some procedures. Aides observe patients' physical, mental, and emotional conditions and report any change to the nursing or medical staff.

Nursing aides employed in nursing care facilities often are the principal caregivers, having far more contact with residents than other members of the staff. Because some residents may stay in a nursing care facility for months or even years, aides develop ongoing relationships with them and interact with them in a positive, caring way.

Home health aides help elderly, convalescent, or disabled persons live in their own homes instead of in a health facility. Under the direction of nursing or medical staff, they provide health-related services, such as administering oral medications. Like nursing aides, home health aides may check patients' pulse rates, temperatures, and respiration rates; help with simple prescribed exercises; keep patients' rooms neat; and help patients move from bed, bathe, dress, and groom. Occasionally, they change nonsterile dressings, give massages and alcohol rubs, or assist with braces and artificial limbs. Experienced home health aides also may assist with medical equipment such as ventilators, which help patients breathe.

Most home health aides work with elderly or disabled persons who need more extensive care than family or friends can provide. Some help discharged hospital patients who have relatively short-term needs.

In home health agencies, a registered nurse, physical therapist, or social worker usually assigns specific duties and supervises home health aides, who keep records of the services they perform and record patients' condition and progress. They report changes in patients' conditions to the supervisor or case manager.

Psychiatric aides, also known as mental health assistants or psychiatric nursing assistants, care for mentally impaired or emotionally disturbed individuals. They work under a team that may include psychiatrists, psychologists, psychiatric nurses, social workers, and therapists. In addition to helping patients dress, bathe, groom, and eat, psychiatric aides socialize with them and lead them in educational and recreational activities. Psychiatric aides may play games such as cards with the patients, watch television with them, or participate in group activities, such as sports or field trips. They observe patients and report any physical or behavioral signs that might be important for the professional staff to know. They accompany patients to and from examinations and treatment. Because they have such close contact with patients, psychiatric aides can have a great deal of influence on their patients' outlook and treatment.

Working Conditions

Most full-time aides work about 40 hours a week, but because patients need care 24 hours a day, some aides work evenings, nights, weekends, and holidays. Many work part time. Aides spend many hours standing and walking, and they often face heavy workloads. Because they may have to move patients in and out of bed or help them stand or walk, aides must guard against back injury. Aides also may face hazards from minor infections and major diseases, such as hepatitis, but can avoid infections by following proper procedures.

Aides often have unpleasant duties, such as emptying bedpans and changing soiled bed linens. The patients they care for may be disoriented, irritable, or uncooperative. Psychiatric aides must be prepared to care for patients whose illness may cause violent behavior. While their work can be emotionally demanding, many aides gain satisfaction from assisting those in need.

Home health aides may go to the same patient's home for months or even years. However, most aides work with a number of different patients, each job lasting a few hours, days, or weeks. Home health aides often visit multiple patients on the same day.

Home health aides generally work alone, with periodic visits by their supervisor. They receive detailed instructions explaining when to visit patients and what services to perform. Aides are individually responsible for getting to patients' homes, and they may spend a good portion of the working day traveling from one patient to another. Because mechanical lifting devices available in institutional settings are seldom available in patients' homes, home health aides are particularly susceptible to injuries resulting from overexertion when they assist patients.

Employment

Nursing, psychiatric, and home health aides held about 2.0 million jobs in 2002. Nursing aides held the most jobs—approximately 1.4 million. Home health aides held roughly 580,000 jobs and psychiatric aides held about 59,000 jobs. Around 2 in 5 nursing aides worked in nursing care facilities, and about one-fourth worked in hospitals. Most home health aides (about one-third) were employed by home healthcare services. Others were employed in social assistance agencies, nursing and residential care facilities, and employment services. More than half of all psychiatric aides worked in hospitals, primarily in psychiatric and substance abuse hospitals—although some also worked in the psychiatric units of general medical and surgical hospitals. Others were employed in state government agencies; residential mental retardation, mental health, and substance abuse facilities; individual and family services; and outpatient care centers.

Training, Other Qualifications, and Advancement

In many cases, neither a high school diploma nor previous work experience is necessary for a job as a nursing, psychiatric, or home health aide. A few employers, however, require some training or experience. Hospitals may require experience as a nursing aide or home health aide. Nursing care facilities often hire inexperienced workers who must complete a minimum of 75 hours of mandatory training and pass a competency evaluation program within 4 months of their employment. Aides who complete the program are certified and placed on the state registry of nursing aides. Some states require psychiatric aides to complete a formal training program.

The federal government has guidelines for home health aides whose employers receive reimbursement from Medicare. Federal law requires home health aides to pass a competency test covering 12 areas: Communication skills; documentation of patient status and care provided; reading and recording vital signs; basic infection control procedures; basic body functions; maintenance of a healthy environment; emergency procedures; physical, emotional, and developmental characteristics of patients; personal hygiene and grooming; safe transfer techniques; normal range of motion and positioning; and basic nutrition.

A home health aide may receive training before taking the competency test. Federal law suggests at least 75 hours of classroom and practical training, supervised by a registered nurse. Training and testing programs may be offered by the employing agency, but must meet the standards of the Center for Medicare and Medicaid Services. Training programs vary with state regulations.

The National Association for Home Care offers national certification for home health aides. The certification is a voluntary demonstration that the individual has met industry standards.

Nursing aide training is offered in high schools, vocational-technical centers, some nursing care facilities, and some community colleges. Courses cover body mechanics, nutrition, anatomy and physiology, infection control, communication skills, and resident rights. Personal care skills, such as how to help patients bathe, eat, and groom, also are taught.

Some employers other than nursing care facilities provide classroom instruction for newly hired aides, while others rely exclusively on informal on-the-job instruction from a licensed nurse or an experienced aide. Such training may last several days to a few months. From time to time, aides also may attend lectures, workshops, and inservice training.

These occupations can offer individuals an entry into the world of work. The flexibility of night and weekend hours also provides high school and college students a chance to work during the school year.

Applicants should be tactful, patient, understanding, emotionally stable, and dependable and should have a desire to help people. They also should be able to work as part of a team, have good communication skills, and be willing to perform repetitive, routine tasks. Home health aides should be honest and discreet, because they work in private homes.

Aides must be in good health. A physical examination, including state-regulated tests such as those for tuberculosis, may be required.

Opportunities for advancement within these occupations are limited. To enter other health occupations, aides generally need additional formal training. Some employers and unions provide opportunities by simplifying the educational paths to advancement. Experience as an aide also can help individuals decide whether to pursue a career in the health-care field.

Job Outlook

Numerous job openings for nursing, psychiatric, and home health aides will arise from a combination of fast employment growth and high replacement needs. High replacement needs in this large occupation reflect modest entry requirements, low pay, high physical and emotional demands, and lack of opportunities for advancement. For these same reasons, many people are unwilling to perform the kind of work required by the occupation. Therefore, persons who are interested in, and suited for, this work should have excellent job opportunities.

Overall employment of nursing, psychiatric, and home health aides is projected to grow faster than the average for all occupations through the year 2012, although individual occupational growth rates will vary. Employment of home health aides is expected to grow the fastest, as a result of both growing demand for home healthcare services from an aging population and efforts to contain healthcare costs by moving patients out of hospitals and nursing care facilities as quickly as possible. Consumer preference for care in the home and improvements in medical technologies for in-home treatment also will contribute to faster-than-average employment growth for home health aides.

Nursing aide employment will not grow as fast as home health aide employment, largely because nursing aides are concentrated in slower growing nursing care facilities. Nevertheless, employment of nursing aides is expected to grow faster than the average for all occupations in response to an increasing emphasis on rehabilitation and the long-term care needs of an increasing elderly population. Financial pressures on hospitals to discharge patients as soon as possible should produce more admissions to nursing care facilities. Modern medical technology also will increase the employment of nursing aides, because, as the technology saves and extends more lives, it increases the need for long-term care provided by aides.

Employment of psychiatric aides—the smallest of the three occupations—is expected to grow about as fast as the average for all occupations. The number of jobs for psychiatric aides in hospitals, where half of those in the occupation work, will grow slower than the average due to attempts to contain costs by limiting inpatient psychiatric treatment. Employment in other sectors will rise in response to growth in the number of older persons—many of whom will require mental health services, increasing public acceptance of formal treatment for substance abuse, and a lessening of the stigma attached to those receiving mental health care.

Earnings

Median hourly earnings of nursing aides, orderlies, and attendants were $9.59 in 2002. The middle 50 percent earned between $8.06 and $11.39 an hour. The lowest 10 percent earned less than $6.98, and the highest 10 percent earned more than $13.54 an hour. Median hourly earnings in the industries employing the largest numbers of nursing aides, orderlies, and attendants in 2002 were as follows:

Employment services	$11.38
Local government	10.33
General medical and surgical hospitals	10.09
Nursing care facilities	9.27
Community care facilities for the elderly	8.98

Nursing and psychiatric aides in hospitals generally receive at least 1 week's paid vacation after 1 year of service. Paid holidays and sick leave, hospital and medical benefits, extra pay for late-shift work, and pension plans also are available to many hospital, and some nursing care facility, employees.

Median hourly earnings of home health aides were $8.70 in 2002. The middle 50 percent earned between $7.54 and $10.37 an hour. The lowest 10 percent earned less than $6.56, and the highest 10 percent earned more than $12.34 an hour. Median hourly earnings in the industries employing the largest numbers of home health aides in 2002 were as follows:

Employment services	$9.21
Residential mental retardation, mental health, and substance abuse facilities	8.91

Home health aides receive slight pay increases with experience and added responsibility. Usually, they are paid only for the time worked in the home; normally, they are not paid for travel time between jobs. Most employers hire only on-call hourly workers and provide no benefits.

Median hourly earnings of psychiatric aides were $11.04 in 2002. The middle 50 percent earned between $8.97 and $13.74 an hour. The lowest 10 percent earned less than $7.52, and the highest 10 percent earned more than $16.16 an hour. Median hourly earnings in the industries employing the largest numbers of psychiatric aides in 2002 were as follows:

State government..$13.14

Psychiatric and substance abuse hospitals 11.32

General medical and surgical hospitals....................11.04

Related Occupations

Nursing, psychiatric, and home health aides help people who need routine care or treatment. So do childcare workers, medical assistants, occupational therapist assistants and aides, personal and home care aides, and physical therapist assistants and aides.

Sources of Additional Information

Information about employment opportunities may be obtained from local hospitals, nursing care facilities, home health-care agencies, psychiatric facilities, state boards of nursing, and local offices of the state employment service.

General information about training, referrals to state and local agencies about job opportunities, a list of relevant publications, and information on certification of home health aides are available from:

- National Association for Home Care, 228 7th St. SE, Washington, DC 20003. Internet: http://www.nahc.org

Occupational Therapist Assistants and Aides

(O*NET 31-2011.00 and 31-2012.00)

Significant Points

- Occupational therapist assistants generally must complete an associate degree or a certificate program; in contrast, occupational therapist aides usually receive most of their training on the job.

- Occupational therapists are expected to delegate more hands-on therapy work to occupational therapist assistants and aides.

- Employment is projected to increase much faster than the average, reflecting growth in the number of individuals with disabilities or limited function who require therapeutic services.

Nature of the Work

Occupational therapist assistants and aides work under the direction of occupational therapists to provide rehabilitative services to persons with mental, physical, emotional, or developmental impairments. The ultimate goal is to improve clients' quality of life and ability to perform daily activities. For example, occupational therapist assistants help injured workers re-enter the labor force by teaching them how to compensate for lost motor skills or help individuals with learning disabilities increase their independence.

Occupational therapist assistants help clients with rehabilitative activities and exercises outlined in a treatment plan developed in collaboration with an occupational therapist. Activities range from teaching the proper method of moving from a bed into a wheelchair to the best way to stretch and limber the muscles of the hand. Assistants monitor an individual's activities to make sure that they are performed correctly and to provide encouragement. They also record their client's progress for the occupational therapist. If the treatment is not having the intended effect, or the client is not improving as expected, the therapist may alter the treatment program in hopes of obtaining better results. In addition, occupational therapist assistants document the billing of the client's health insurance provider.

Occupational therapist aides typically prepare materials and assemble equipment used during treatment. They are responsible for a range of clerical tasks, including scheduling appointments, answering the telephone, restocking or ordering depleted supplies, and filling out insurance forms or other paperwork. Aides are not licensed, so the law does not allow them to perform as wide a range of tasks as occupational therapist assistants.

Working Conditions

The hours and days that occupational therapist assistants and aides work vary with the facility and with whether they are full- or part-time employees. Many outpatient therapy offices and clinics have evening and weekend hours to help coincide with patients' personal schedules.

Occupational therapist assistants and aides need to have a moderate degree of strength, due to the physical exertion required in assisting patients with their treatment. For example, assistants and aides may need to lift patients. Constant kneeling, stooping, and standing for long periods also are part of the job.

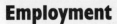

Employment

Occupational therapist assistants and aides held about 27,000 jobs in 2002. Occupational therapist assistants held about 18,000 jobs, and occupational therapist aides held approximately 8,300. Over 30 percent of jobs for assistants and aides were in hospitals, 23 percent were in offices of other health practitioners (which includes offices of occupational therapists), and 18 percent were in nursing care facilities. The rest were primarily in community care facilities for the elderly, home healthcare services, individual and family services, and State government agencies.

Training, Other Qualifications, and Advancement

An associate degree or a certificate from an accredited community college or technical school is generally required to qualify for occupational therapist assistant jobs. In contrast, occupational therapist aides usually receive most of their training on the job.

There were 161 accredited occupational therapist assistant programs in 2003. The first year of study typically involves an introduction to healthcare, basic medical terminology, anatomy, and physiology. In the second year, courses are more rigorous and usually include occupational therapist courses in areas such as mental health, adult physical disabilities, gerontology, and pediatrics. Students also must complete 16 weeks of supervised fieldwork in a clinic or community setting. Applicants to occupational therapist assistant programs can improve their chances of admission by taking high school courses in biology and health and by performing volunteer work in nursing care facilities, occupational or physical therapists' offices, or other healthcare settings.

Occupational therapist assistants are regulated in most states and must pass a national certification examination after they graduate. Those who pass the test are awarded the title "Certified Occupational Therapist Assistant."

Occupational therapist aides usually receive most of their training on the job. Qualified applicants must have a high school diploma, strong interpersonal skills, and a desire to help people in need. Applicants may increase their chances of getting a job by volunteering their services, thus displaying initiative and aptitude to the employer.

Assistants and aides must be responsible, patient, and willing to take directions and work as part of a team. Furthermore, they should be caring and want to help people who are not able to help themselves.

Job Outlook

Employment of occupational therapist assistants and aides is expected to grow much faster than the average for all occupations through 2012. The impact of proposed Federal legislation imposing limits on reimbursement for therapy services may adversely affect the job market for occupational therapist assistants and aides in the near term. However, over the long run, demand for occupational therapist assistants and aides will continue to rise, due to growth in the number of individuals with disabilities or limited function. Job growth will result from an aging population, including the baby-boom generation, which will need more occupational therapy services. Increasing demand also will result from advances in medicine that allow more people with critical problems to survive and then need rehabilitative therapy. Third-party payers, concerned with rising healthcare costs, are expected to encourage occupational therapists to delegate more hands-on therapy work to occupational therapist assistants and aides. By having assistants and aides work more closely with clients under the guidance of a therapist, the cost of therapy should decline.

Earnings

Median annual earnings of occupational therapist assistants were $36,660 in 2002. The middle 50 percent earned between $31,090 and $43,030. The lowest 10 percent earned less than $25,600, and the highest 10 percent earned more than $48,480.

Median annual earnings of occupational therapist aides were $22,040 in 2002. The middle 50 percent earned between $18,040 and $29,130. The lowest 10 percent earned less than $15,400, and the highest 10 percent earned more than $38,170.

Related Occupations

Occupational therapist assistants and aides work under the supervision and direction of occupational therapists. Other workers in the healthcare field who work under similar supervision include dental assistants, medical assistants, phar+macy aides, pharmacy technicians, and physical therapist assistants and aides.

Sources of Additional Information

For information on a career as an occupational therapist assistant or aide, and a list of accredited programs, contact:

● American Occupational Therapy Association, 4720 Montgomery Lane, Bethesda, MD 20824-1220. Internet: http://www.aota.org

Occupational Therapists

(O*NET 29-1122.00)

Significant Points

● Employment is projected to increase faster than the average, as rapid growth in the number of middle-aged and elderly individuals increases the demand for therapeutic services.

- A bachelor's degree in occupational therapy is the minimum educational requirement; beginning in 2007, however, a master's degree or higher will be required.

- Occupational therapists are increasingly taking on supervisory roles.

- More than a quarter of occupational therapists work part time.

Nature of the Work

Occupational therapists (OTs) help people improve their ability to perform tasks in their daily living and working environments. They work with individuals who have conditions that are mentally, physically, developmentally, or emotionally disabling. They also help them to develop, recover, or maintain daily living and work skills. Occupational therapists help clients not only to improve their basic motor functions and reasoning abilities, but also to compensate for permanent loss of function. Their goal is to help clients have independent, productive, and satisfying lives.

Occupational therapists assist clients in performing activities of all types, ranging from using a computer to caring for daily needs such as dressing, cooking, and eating. Physical exercises may be used to increase strength and dexterity, while other activities may be chosen to improve visual acuity and the ability to discern patterns. For example, a client with short-term memory loss might be encouraged to make lists to aid recall, and a person with coordination problems might be assigned exercises to improve hand-eye coordination. Occupational therapists also use computer programs to help clients improve decisionmaking, abstract-reasoning, problem-solving, and perceptual skills, as well as memory, sequencing, and coordination—all of which are important for independent living.

Therapists instruct those with permanent disabilities, such as spinal cord injuries, cerebral palsy, or muscular dystrophy, in the use of adaptive equipment, including wheelchairs, splints, and aids for eating and dressing. They also design or make special equipment needed at home or at work. Therapists develop computer-aided adaptive equipment and teach clients with severe limitations how to use that equipment in order to communicate better and control various aspects of their environment.

Some occupational therapists treat individuals whose ability to function in a work environment has been impaired. These practitioners arrange employment, evaluate the work environment, plan work activities, and assess the client's progress. Therapists also may collaborate with the client and the employer to modify the work environment so that the work can be successfully completed.

Occupational therapists may work exclusively with individuals in a particular age group or with particular disabilities. In schools, for example, they evaluate children's abilities, recommend and provide therapy, modify classroom equipment, and help children participate as fully as possible in school programs and activities. Occupational therapy also is beneficial to the elderly population. Therapists help the elderly lead more productive, active, and independent lives through a variety of methods, including the use of adaptive equipment.

Occupational therapists in mental-health settings treat individuals who are mentally ill, mentally retarded, or emotionally disturbed. To treat these problems, therapists choose activities that help people learn to engage in and cope with daily life. Activities include time management skills, budgeting, shopping, homemaking, and the use of public transportation. Occupational therapists also may work with individuals who are dealing with alcoholism, drug abuse, depression, eating disorders, or stress-related disorders.

Assessing and recording a client's activities and progress is an important part of an occupational therapist's job. Accurate records are essential for evaluating clients, for billing, and for reporting to physicians and other healthcare providers.

Working Conditions

Occupational therapists in hospitals and other healthcare and community settings usually worked a 40-hour week. Those in schools may participate in meetings and other activities during and after the school day. In 2002, more than a quarter of occupational therapists worked part time.

In large rehabilitation centers, therapists may work in spacious rooms equipped with machines, tools, and other devices generating noise. The work can be tiring, because therapists are on their feet much of the time. Those providing home healthcare services may spend time driving from appointment to appointment. Therapists also face hazards such as back strain from lifting and moving clients and equipment.

Therapists increasingly are taking on supervisory roles. Due to rising healthcare costs, third-party payers are beginning to encourage occupational therapist assistants and aides to take more hands-on responsibility. By having assistants and aides work more closely with clients under the guidance of a therapist, the cost of therapy should decline.

Employment

Occupational therapists held about 82,000 jobs in 2002. About 1 in 10 occupational therapists held more than one job. The largest number of jobs was in hospitals. Other major employers were offices of other health practitioners (which includes offices of occupational therapists), public and private educational services, and nursing care facilities. Some occupational therapists were employed by home healthcare services, outpatient care centers, offices of physicians, individual and family services, community care facilities for the elderly, and government agencies.

A small number of occupational therapists were self-employed in private practice. These practitioners saw clients referred by physicians or other health professionals or provided contract or consulting services to nursing care facilities, schools, adult daycare programs, and home healthcare agencies.

Training, Other Qualifications, and Advancement

Currently, a bachelor's degree in occupational therapy is the minimum requirement for entry into this field. Beginning in 2007, however, a master's degree or higher will be the minimum educational requirement. As a result, students in bachelor's-level programs should complete their coursework and fieldwork before 2007. All states, Puerto Rico, and the District of Columbia regulate the practice of occupational therapy. To obtain a license, applicants must graduate from an accredited educational program and pass a national certification examination. Those who pass the exam are awarded the title "Occupational Therapist Registered (OTR)."

In 2003, entry-level education was offered in 38 bachelor's degree programs, 3 postbaccalaureate certificate programs for students with a degree other than occupational therapy, and 86 entry-level master's degree programs. There were 48 programs that offered a combined bachelor's and master's degree and 5 offered an entry-level doctoral degree. Most schools have full-time programs, although a growing number also offer weekend or part-time programs.

Occupational therapy coursework includes physical, biological, and behavioral sciences and the application of occupational therapy theory and skills. Completion of 6 months of supervised fieldwork also is required.

Persons considering this profession should take high school courses in biology, chemistry, physics, health, art, and the social sciences. College admissions offices also look favorably at paid or volunteer experience in the healthcare field.

Occupational therapists need patience and strong interpersonal skills to inspire trust and respect in their clients. Ingenuity and imagination in adapting activities to individual needs are assets. Those working in home healthcare services must be able to adapt to a variety of settings.

Job Outlook

Employment of occupational therapists is expected to increase faster than the average for all occupations through 2012. The impact of proposed federal legislation imposing limits on reimbursement for therapy services may adversely affect the job market for occupational therapists in the near term. However, over the long run, the demand for occupational therapists should continue to rise as a result of growth in the number of individuals with disabilities or limited function who require therapy services. The baby-boom generation's movement into middle age, a period when the incidence of heart attack and stroke increases, will spur the demand for therapeutic services. Growth in the population 75 years and older—an age group that suffers from high incidences of disabling conditions—also will increase the demand for therapeutic services. In addition, medical advances now enable more patients with critical problems to survive—patients who ultimately may need extensive therapy.

Hospitals will continue to employ a large number of occupational therapists to provide therapy services to acutely ill inpatients. Hospitals also will need occupational therapists to staff their outpatient rehabilitation programs.

Employment growth in schools will result from the expansion of the school-age population and extended services for disabled students. Therapists will be needed to help children with disabilities prepare to enter special education programs.

Earnings

Median annual earnings of occupational therapists were $51,990 in 2002. The middle 50 percent earned between $42,910 and $61,620. The lowest 10 percent earned less than $35,130, and the highest 10 percent earned more than $74,390. Median annual earnings in the industries employing the largest numbers of occupational therapists in 2002 were as follows:

Offices of other health practitioners $53,660
Nursing care facilities..53,930
General medical and surgical hospitals..................53,210
Elementary and secondary schools 45,740

Related Occupations

Occupational therapists use specialized knowledge to help individuals perform daily living skills and achieve maximum independence. Other workers performing similar duties include audiologists, chiropractors, physical therapists, recreational therapists, rehabilitation counselors, respiratory therapists, and speech-language pathologists.

Sources of Additional Information

For more information on occupational therapy as a career, contact:

● American Occupational Therapy Association, 4720 Montgomery Lane, Bethesda, MD 20824-1220. Internet: http://www.aota.org

Office Clerks, General

(O*NET 43-9061.00)

Significant Points

● Although most jobs are entry level, applicants with previous office experience, computer skills, and sound communication abilities may have an advantage.

● Part-time and temporary positions are common.

● Plentiful job opportunities will stem from employment growth, the large size of the occupation, and high replacement needs.

Nature of the Work

Rather than performing a single specialized task, general office clerks often have daily responsibilities that change with the needs of the specific job and the employer. Whereas some clerks spend their days filing or typing, others enter data at a computer terminal. They also can be called upon to operate photocopiers, fax machines, and other office equipment; prepare mailings; proofread copies; and answer telephones and deliver messages.

The specific duties assigned to a clerk vary significantly, depending upon the type of office in which he or she works. An office clerk in a doctor's office, for example, would not perform the same tasks that a clerk in a large financial institution or in the office of an auto-parts wholesaler would perform. Although they may sort checks, keep payroll records, take inventory, and access information, clerks also perform duties unique to their employer, such as organizing medications, making transparencies for a presentation, or filling orders received by fax machine.

The specific duties assigned to a clerk also vary by level of experience. Whereas inexperienced employees make photocopies, stuff envelopes, or record inquiries, experienced clerks usually are given additional responsibilities. For example, they may maintain financial or other records, set up spreadsheets, verify statistical reports for accuracy and completeness, handle and adjust customer complaints, work with vendors, make travel arrangements, take inventory of equipment and supplies, answer questions on departmental services and functions, or help prepare invoices or budgetary requests. Senior office clerks may be expected to monitor and direct the work of lower level clerks.

Working Conditions

For the most part, general office clerks work in comfortable office settings. Those on full-time schedules usually work a standard 40-hour week; however, some work shifts or overtime during busy periods. About 1 in 4 clerks works part time.

Employment

General office clerks held about 3 million jobs in 2002. Most are employed in relatively small businesses. Although they work in every sector of the economy, almost half worked in local government; health care and social assistance; administrative and support services; finance and insurance; or professional, scientific, and technical services industries.

Training, Other Qualifications, and Advancement

Although most office clerk jobs are entry-level administrative support positions, employers may prefer or require previous office or business experience. Employers usually require a high school diploma, and some require typing, basic computer skills, and other general office skills. Familiarity with computer word-processing software and applications is becoming increasingly important.

Training for this occupation is available through business education programs offered in high schools, community and junior colleges, and postsecondary vocational schools. Courses in office practices, word processing, and other computer applications are particularly helpful.

Because general office clerks usually work with other office staff, they should be cooperative and able to work as part of a team. Employers prefer individuals who are able to perform a variety of tasks and satisfy the needs of the many departments within a company. In addition, applicants should have good communication skills, be detail-oriented, and be adaptable.

General office clerks who exhibit strong communication, interpersonal, and analytical skills may be promoted to supervisory positions. Others may move into different, more senior clerical or administrative jobs, such as receptionist, secretary, or administrative assistant. After gaining some work experience or specialized skills, many workers transfer to jobs with higher pay or greater advancement potential. Advancement to professional occupations within an establishment normally requires additional formal education, such as a college degree.

Job Outlook

Employment growth, the large size of the occupation, and high replacement needs should result in plentiful job opportunities for general office clerks. In addition to those for full-time jobs, many job openings are expected for part-time and temporary general office clerks. Prospects should be brightest for those who have knowledge of basic computer applications and office machinery, such as fax machines and scanners, and good writing and communication skills. As general clerical duties continue to be consolidated, employers will increasingly seek well-rounded individuals with highly developed communication skills and the ability to perform multiple tasks.

Employment of general office clerks is expected to grow about as fast as average for all occupations through the year 2012. The employment outlook for these workers will be affected by the increasing use of computers, expanding office automation, and the consolidation of clerical tasks. Automation has led to productivity gains, allowing a wide variety of duties to be performed by fewer office workers. However, automation also has led to a consolidation of clerical staffs and a diversification of job responsibilities. This consolidation increases the demand for general office clerks, because they perform a variety of clerical tasks. It will become increasingly common within small businesses to find a single general office clerk in charge of all clerical work.

Job opportunities may vary from year to year, because the strength of the economy affects demand for general office clerks. Companies tend to hire more workers when the economy is strong. Industries least likely to be affected by economic fluctuation tend to be the most stable places for employment.

Earnings

Median annual earnings of general office clerks were $22,280 in 2002; the middle 50 percent earned between $17,630 and $28,190 annually. The lowest 10 percent earned less than $14,260, and the highest 10 percent earned more than $34,890. Median annual salaries in the industries employing the largest numbers of general office clerks in 2002 are shown below:

Local government $25,020

Elementary and secondary schools 23,310

General medical and surgical hospitals..................23,250

Colleges, universities, and professional schools 22,540

Employment services 20,630

Related Occupations

The duties of general office clerks can include a combination of bookkeeping, typing, office machine operation, and filing. Other office and administrative support workers who perform similar duties include financial clerks, information and records clerks, secretaries and administrative assistants, and data entry and information processing workers. Nonclerical entry-level workers include cashiers, counter and rental clerks, and food and beverage serving and related workers.

Sources of Additional Information

State employment service offices and agencies can provide information about job openings for general office clerks.

Paralegals and Legal Assistants

(O*NET 23-2011.00)

Significant Points

- While some paralegals train on the job, employers increasingly prefer graduates of postsecondary paralegal education programs; college graduates who have taken some paralegal courses are especially in demand in some markets.

- Paralegals are projected to grow faster than average, as law offices try to reduce costs by assigning them tasks formerly carried out by lawyers.

- Paralegals are employed by law firms, corporate legal departments, and various government offices and they may specialize in many different areas of the law.

Nature of the Work

While lawyers assume ultimate responsibility for legal work, they often delegate many of their tasks to paralegals. In fact, paralegals—also called legal assistants—continue to assume a growing range of tasks in the nation's legal offices and perform many of the same tasks as lawyers. Nevertheless, they are still explicitly prohibited from carrying out duties which are considered to be the practice of law, such as setting legal fees, giving legal advice, and presenting cases in court.

One of a paralegal's most important tasks is helping lawyers prepare for closings, hearings, trials, and corporate meetings. Paralegals investigate the facts of cases and ensure that all relevant information is considered. They also identify appropriate laws, judicial decisions, legal articles, and other materials that are relevant to assigned cases. After they analyze and organize the information, paralegals may prepare written reports that attorneys use in determining how cases should be handled. Should attorneys decide to file lawsuits on behalf of clients, paralegals may help prepare the legal arguments, draft pleadings and motions to be filed with the court, obtain affidavits, and assist attorneys during trials. Paralegals also organize and track files of all important case documents and make them available and easily accessible to attorneys.

In addition to this preparatory work, paralegals also perform a number of other vital functions. For example, they help draft contracts, mortgages, separation agreements, and trust instruments. They also may assist in preparing tax returns and planning estates. Some paralegals coordinate the activities of other law office employees and maintain financial office records. Various additional tasks may differ, depending on the employer.

Paralegals are found in all types of organizations, but most are employed by law firms, corporate legal departments, and various government offices. In these organizations, they can work in many different areas of the law, including litigation, personal injury, corporate law, criminal law, employee benefits, intellectual property, labor law, bankruptcy, immigration, family law, and real estate. As the law has become more complex, paralegals have responded by becoming more specialized. Within specialties, functions often are broken down further so that paralegals may deal with a specific area. For example, paralegals specializing in labor law may deal exclusively with employee benefits.

The duties of paralegals also differ widely based on the type of organization in which they are employed. Paralegals who work for corporations often assist attorneys with employee contracts, shareholder agreements, stock-option plans, and employee benefit plans. They also may help prepare and file annual financial reports, maintain corporate minute books and record resolutions, and prepare forms to secure loans for the corporation. Paralegals often monitor and review government regulations to ensure that the corporation is aware of new requirements and it operates within the law.

The duties of paralegals who work in the public sector usually vary within each agency. In general, they analyze legal material for internal use, maintain reference files, conduct research for attorneys, and collect and analyze evidence for agency hearings. They may then prepare informative or explanatory material on laws, agency regulations, and agency policy for general use by the agency and the public. Paralegals employed in community legal-service projects help the poor, the aged, and others in need of legal assistance. They file forms, conduct research, prepare documents, and when authorized by law, may represent clients at administrative hearings.

Paralegals in small and medium-sized law firms usually perform a variety of duties that require a general knowledge of the law. For example, they may research judicial decisions on improper police arrests or help prepare a mortgage contract. Paralegals employed by large law firms, government agencies, and corporations, however, are more likely to specialize in one aspect of the law.

Computer use and technical knowledge has become essential to paralegal work. Computer software packages and the Internet are increasingly used to search legal literature stored in computer databases and on CD-ROM. In litigation involving many supporting documents, paralegals may use computer databases to retrieve, organize, and index various materials. Imaging software allows paralegals to scan documents directly into a database, while billing programs help them to track hours billed to clients. Computer software packages also may be used to perform tax computations and explore the consequences of possible tax strategies for clients.

Working Conditions

Paralegals employed by corporations and government usually work a standard 40-hour week. Although most paralegals work year round, some are temporarily employed during busy times of the year, then released when the workload diminishes. Paralegals who work for law firms sometimes work very long hours when they are under pressure to meet deadlines. Some law firms reward such loyalty with bonuses and additional time off.

These workers handle many routine assignments, particularly when they are inexperienced. As they gain experience, paralegals usually assume more varied tasks with additional responsibility. Paralegals do most of their work at desks in offices and law libraries. Occasionally, they travel to gather information and perform other duties.

Employment

Paralegals and legal assistants held about 200,000 jobs in 2002. Private law firms employed 7 out of 10 paralegals and legal assistants; most of the remainder worked for corporate legal departments and various levels of government. Within

the federal government, the U.S. Department of Justice is the largest employer, followed by the Social Security Administration and the U.S. Department of Treasury. A small number of paralegals own their own businesses and work as freelance legal assistants, contracting their services to attorneys or corporate legal departments.

Training, Other Qualifications, and Advancement

There are several ways to become a paralegal. The most common is through a community college paralegal program that leads to an associate's degree. The other common method of entry, mainly for those who have a college degree, is through a certification program that leads to a certification in paralegal studies. A small number of schools also offer bachelor's and master's degrees in paralegal studies. Some employers train paralegals on the job, hiring college graduates with no legal experience or promoting experienced legal secretaries. Other entrants have experience in a technical field that is useful to law firms, such as a background in tax preparation for tax and estate practice, criminal justice, or nursing or health administration for personal injury practice.

Formal paralegal training programs are offered by an estimated 600 colleges and universities, law schools, and proprietary schools. Approximately 250 paralegal programs are approved by the American Bar Association (ABA). Although this approval is neither required nor sought by many programs, graduation from an ABA-approved program can enhance one's employment opportunities. The requirements for admission to these programs vary. Some require certain college courses or a bachelor's degree; others accept high school graduates or those with legal experience; and a few schools require standardized tests and personal interviews.

Paralegal programs include 2-year associate's degree programs, 4-year bachelor's degree programs, and certificate programs that can take only a few months to complete. Most certificate programs provide intensive paralegal training for individuals who already hold college degrees, while associate's and bachelor's degree programs usually combine paralegal training with courses in other academic subjects. The quality of paralegal training programs varies; the better programs usually include job placement. Programs increasingly include courses introducing students to the legal applications of computers, including how to perform legal research using the Internet. Many paralegal training programs include an internship in which students gain practical experience by working for several months in a private law firm, office of a public defender or attorney general, bank, corporate legal department, legal-aid organization, or government agency. Experience gained in internships is an asset when seeking a job after graduation. Prospective students should examine the experiences of recent graduates before enrolling in those programs.

Although most employers do not require certification, earning a voluntary certificate from a professional society may offer advantages in the labor market. The National

Association of Legal Assistants, for example, has established standards for certification requiring various combinations of education and experience. Paralegals who meet these standards are eligible to take a 2-day examination, given three times each year at several regional testing centers. Those who pass this examination may use the designation Certified Legal Assistant (CLA). In addition, the Paralegal Advanced Competency Exam, established in 1996 and administered through the National Federation of Paralegal Associations, offers professional recognition to paralegals with a bachelor's degree and at least 2 years of experience. Those who pass this examination may use the designation Registered Paralegal (RP).

Paralegals must be able to document and present their findings and opinions to their supervising attorney. They need to understand legal terminology and have good research and investigative skills. Familiarity with the operation and applications of computers in legal research and litigation support also is increasingly important. Paralegals should stay informed of new developments in the laws that affect their area of practice. Participation in continuing legal education seminars allows paralegals to maintain and expand their legal knowledge.

Because paralegals frequently deal with the public, they should be courteous and uphold the ethical standards of the legal profession. The National Association of Legal Assistants, the National Federation of Paralegal Associations, and a few states have established ethical guidelines for paralegals to follow.

Paralegals usually are given more responsibilities and less supervision as they gain work experience. Experienced paralegals who work in large law firms, corporate legal departments, and government agencies may supervise and delegate assignments to other paralegals and clerical staff. Advancement opportunities also include promotion to managerial and other law-related positions within the firm or corporate legal department. However, some paralegals find it easier to move to another law firm when seeking increased responsibility or advancement.

Job Outlook

Paralegals and legal assistants are projected to grow faster than the average for all occupations through 2012. Some employment growth stems from law firms and other employers with legal staffs increasingly hiring paralegals to lower the cost and increase the availability and efficiency of legal services. The majority of job openings for paralegals in the future will be new jobs created by employment growth, but additional job openings will arise as people leave the occupation. Despite projections of fast employment growth, competition for jobs should continue as many people seek to go into this profession; however, highly skilled, formally trained paralegals have excellent employment potential.

Private law firms will continue to be the largest employers of paralegals, but a growing array of other organizations, such as corporate legal departments, insurance companies, real estate and title insurance firms, and banks hire paralegals. Corporations, in particular, are boosting their in-house legal departments to cut costs. Demand for paralegals also is expected to grow as an increasing population requires legal services, especially in areas such as intellectual property, healthcare, international, elder issues, criminal, and environmental law. The growth of prepaid legal plans also should contribute to the demand for legal services. Paralegal employment is expected to increase as organizations presently employing paralegals assign them a growing range of tasks, and as paralegals are increasingly employed in small and medium-sized establishments. A growing number of experienced paralegals are expected to establish their own businesses.

Job opportunities for paralegals will expand in the public sector as well. Community legal-service programs, which provide assistance to the poor, aged, minorities, and middle-income families, will employ additional paralegals to minimize expenses and serve the most people. Federal, state, and local government agencies, consumer organizations, and the courts also should continue to hire paralegals in increasing numbers.

To a limited extent, paralegal jobs are affected by the business cycle. During recessions, demand declines for some discretionary legal services, such as planning estates, drafting wills, and handling real estate transactions. Corporations are less inclined to initiate certain types of litigation when falling sales and profits lead to fiscal belt tightening. As a result, full-time paralegals employed in offices adversely affected by a recession may be laid off or have their work hours reduced. On the other hand, during recessions, corporations and individuals are more likely to face other problems that require legal assistance, such as bankruptcies, foreclosures, and divorces. Paralegals, who provide many of the same legal services as lawyers at a lower cost, tend to fare relatively better in difficult economic conditions.

Earnings

Earnings of paralegals and legal assistants vary greatly. Salaries depend on education, training, experience, type and size of employer, and geographic location of the job. In general, paralegals who work for large law firms or in large metropolitan areas earn more than those who work for smaller firms or in less populated regions. In addition to a salary, many paralegals receive bonuses. In 2002, full-time, wage and salary paralegals and legal assistants had median annual earnings, including bonuses, of $37,950. The middle 50 percent earned between $30,020 and $48,760. The top 10 percent earned more than $61,150, while the bottom 10 percent earned less than $24,470. Median annual earnings in the industries employing the largest numbers of paralegals in 2002 were as follows:

Federal government	$53,770
Legal services	36,780
Local government	36,030
State government	34,750

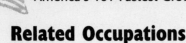

Related Occupations

Several other occupations call for a specialized understanding of the law and the legal system, but do not require the extensive training of a lawyer. These include law clerks; title examiners, abstractors, and searchers; claims adjusters, appraisers, examiners, and investigators; and occupational health and safety specialists and technicians.

Sources of Additional Information

General information on a career as a paralegal can be obtained from:

- Standing Committee on Legal Assistants, American Bar Association, 541 N. Fairbanks Ct., Chicago, IL 60611. Internet: http://www.abanet.org

For information on the Certified Legal Assistant exam, schools that offer training programs in a specific state, and standards and guidelines for paralegals, contact:

- National Association of Legal Assistants, Inc., 1516 South Boston St., Suite 200, Tulsa, OK 74119. Internet: http://www.nala.org

Information on a career as a paralegal, schools that offer training programs, job postings for paralegals, the Paralegal Advanced Competency Exam, and local paralegal associations can be obtained from:

- National Federation of Paralegal Associations, P.O. Box 33108, Kansas City, MO 64114. Internet: http://www.paralegals.org

Information on paralegal training programs, including the pamphlet "How to Choose a Paralegal Education Program," may be obtained from:

- American Association for Paralegal Education, 407 Wekiva Springs Road, Suite 241, Longwood, FL 32779. Internet: http://www.aafpe.org

Information on obtaining a position as a paralegal specialist with the federal government is available from the Office of Personnel Management (OPM) through a telephone-based system. Consult your telephone directory under U.S. Government for a local number or call (703) 724-1850; Federal Relay Service: (800) 877-8339. The first number is not toll-free, and charges may result. Information also is available from the OPM Internet site: http://www.usajobs.opm.gov.

Personal and Home Care Aides

(O*NET 39-9021.00)

Significant Points

- Excellent job opportunities are expected, due to rapid employment growth and high replacement needs. Almost a third of personal and home care aides work part time; most aides work with a number of different clients, each job lasting a few hours, days, or weeks.

- Occupational characteristics include low skill requirements, low pay, and high emotional demands.

Nature of the Work

Personal and home care aides help elderly, disabled, and ill persons live in their own homes or in residential care facilities instead of in a health facility. Most personal and home care aides work with elderly or disabled clients who need more extensive personal and home care than family or friends can provide. Some aides work with families in which a parent is incapacitated and small children need care. Others help discharged hospital patients who have relatively short-term needs. (Home health aides—who provide health-related services, rather than mainly housekeeping and routine personal care—are discussed in the statement on nursing, psychiatric, and home health aides, elsewhere in this book.)

Personal and home care aides—also called homemakers, caregivers, companions, and personal attendants—provide housekeeping and routine personal care services. They clean clients' houses, do laundry, and change bed linens. Aides may plan meals (including special diets), shop for food, and cook. Aides also may help clients move from bed, bathe, dress, and groom. Some accompany clients outside the home, serving as a guide and companion.

Personal and home care aides provide instruction and psychological support to their patients. They may advise families and patients on such things as nutrition, cleanliness, and household tasks. Aides also may assist in toilet training a severely mentally handicapped child, or they may just listen to clients talk about their problems.

In home healthcare agencies, a registered nurse, physical therapist, or social worker assigns specific duties and supervises personal and home care aides. Aides keep records of services performed and of clients' condition and progress. They report changes in the client's condition to the supervisor or case manager. In carrying out their work, aides cooperate with other healthcare professionals, including registered nurses, therapists, and other medical staff.

Working Conditions

The personal and home care aide's daily routine may vary. Aides may go to the same home every day for months or even years. However, most aides work with a number of different clients, each job lasting a few hours, days, or weeks. Aides often visit four or five clients on the same day.

Surroundings differ from case to case. Some homes are neat and pleasant, whereas others are untidy or depressing. Some clients are pleasant and cooperative; others are angry, abusive, depressed, or otherwise difficult.

Personal and home care aides generally work on their own, with periodic visits by their supervisor. They receive detailed instructions explaining when to visit clients and what services to perform for them. Almost a third of aides work part time, and some work weekends or evenings to suit the needs of their clients.

Aides are individually responsible for getting to the client's home. They may spend a good portion of the working day traveling from one client to another. Because mechanical lifting devices that are available in institutional settings are seldom available in patients' homes, aides must be careful to avoid overexertion or injury when they assist clients.

Employment

Personal and home care aides held about 608,000 jobs in 2002. The majority of jobs were in home healthcare services, individual and family services, private households, and residential mental retardation, mental health, and substance abuse facilities. Self-employed aides have no agency affiliation or supervision and accept clients, set fees, and arrange work schedules on their own.

Training, Other Qualifications, and Advancement

In some states, this occupation is open to individuals who have no formal training. On-the-job training is then generally provided. Other states may require formal training. The National Association for Home Care offers national certification for personal and home care aides. Certification is a voluntary demonstration that the individual has met industry standards.

Successful personal and home care aides like to help people and do not mind hard work. They should be responsible, compassionate, emotionally stable, and cheerful. In addition, aides should be tactful, honest, and discreet, because they work in private homes. Aides also must be in good health. A physical examination, including state-mandated tests, such as those for tuberculosis, may be required.

Advancement for personal and home care aides is limited. In some agencies, workers start out performing homemaker duties, such as cleaning. With experience and training, they may take on personal care duties.

Job Outlook

Excellent job opportunities are expected for this occupation, as rapid employment growth and high replacement needs produce a large number of job openings.

Employment of personal and home care aides is projected to grow much faster than the average for all occupations through the year 2012. The number of elderly people, an age group characterized by mounting health problems and requiring some assistance, is projected to rise substantially. In addition to the elderly, however, patients in other age groups will increasingly rely on home care, a trend that reflects several developments, including efforts to contain costs by moving patients out of hospitals and nursing care facilities as quickly as possible, the realization that treat-

ment can be more effective in familiar rather than clinical surroundings, and the development and improvement of medical technologies for in-home treatment.

In addition to job openings created by the increase in demand for these workers, replacement needs are expected to produce numerous openings. The relatively low skill requirements, low pay, and high emotional demands of the work result in high replacement needs. For these same reasons, many people are reluctant to seek jobs in the occupation. Therefore, persons who are interested in and suited for this work—particularly those with experience or training as personal care, home health, or nursing aides—should have excellent job opportunities.

Earnings

Median hourly earnings of personal and home care aides were $7.81 in 2002. The middle 50 percent earned between $6.65 and $9.06 an hour. The lowest 10 percent earned less than $5.90, and the highest 10 percent earned more than $10.67 an hour. Median hourly earnings in the industries employing the largest numbers of personal and home care aides in 2002 were as follows:

Residential mental retardation, mental health
and substance abuse facilities $8.63
Vocational rehabilitation services 8.40
Community care facilities for the elderly 8.14
Individual and family services...................................8.12
Home health care services 6.72

Most employers give slight pay increases with experience and added responsibility. Aides usually are paid only for the time they work in the home and normally are not paid for travel time between jobs. Employers often hire on-call hourly workers and provide no benefits.

Related Occupations

Personal and home care aide is a service occupation combining the duties of caregivers and social service workers. Workers in related occupations that involve personal contact to help others include childcare workers; nursing, psychiatric, and home health aides; occupational therapist assistants and aides; and physical therapist assistants and aides.

Sources of Additional Information

General information about training, referrals to state and local agencies about job opportunities, a list of relevant publications, and information on certification for personal and home care aides are available from:

● National Association for Home Care, 228 7th St. SE, Washington, DC 20003. Internet: http://www.nahc.org

Pharmacists

(O*NET 29-1051.00)

Significant Points

- Pharmacists are becoming more involved in drug therapy decisionmaking and patient counseling.

- A license is required; one must graduate from an accredited college of pharmacy and pass a state examination.

- Very good employment opportunities are expected.

- Earnings are very high, but some pharmacists work long hours, nights, weekends, and holidays.

Nature of the Work

Pharmacists dispense drugs prescribed by physicians and other health practitioners and provide information to patients about medications and their use. They advise physicians and other health practitioners on the selection, dosages, interactions, and side effects of medications. Pharmacists also monitor the health and progress of patients in response to drug therapy to ensure safe and effective use of medication. Pharmacists must understand the use, clinical effects, and composition of drugs, including their chemical, biological, and physical properties. Compounding—the actual mixing of ingredients to form powders, tablets, capsules, ointments, and solutions—is a small part of a pharmacist's practice, because most medicines are produced by pharmaceutical companies in a standard dosage and drug delivery form. Traditionally, most pharmacists work in a community setting, such as a retail drugstore, or in a healthcare facility, such as a hospital, nursing home, mental health institution, or neighborhood health clinic.

Pharmacists in community and retail pharmacies counsel patients and answer questions about prescription drugs, including questions regarding possible side effects or interactions among various drugs. They provide information about over-the-counter drugs and make recommendations after talking with the patient. They also may give advice about diet, exercise, or stress management, or about durable medical equipment and home healthcare supplies. They also may complete third-party insurance forms and other paperwork. Those who own or manage community pharmacies may sell non-health-related merchandise, hire and supervise personnel, and oversee the general operation of the pharmacy. Some community pharmacists provide specialized services to help patients manage conditions such as diabetes, asthma, smoking cessation, or high blood pressure. Some community pharmacists are also certified to administer vaccinations.

Pharmacists in healthcare facilities dispense medications and advise the medical staff on the selection and effects of drugs. They may make sterile solutions and buy medical supplies. They also assess, plan, and monitor drug programs or regimens. They counsel patients on the use of drugs while in the hospital, and on their use at home when the patients are discharged. Pharmacists also may evaluate drug use patterns and outcomes for patients in hospitals or managed care organizations.

Pharmacists who work in home healthcare monitor drug therapy and prepare infusions—solutions that are injected into patients—and other medications for use in the home.

Some pharmacists specialize in specific drug therapy areas, such as intravenous nutrition support, oncology (cancer), nuclear pharmacy (used for chemotherapy), geriatric pharmacy, and psychopharmacotherapy (the treatment of mental disorders with drugs).

Most pharmacists keep confidential computerized records of patients' drug therapies to ensure that harmful drug interactions do not occur. Pharmacists are responsible for the accuracy of every prescription that is filled, but they often rely upon pharmacy technicians and pharmacy aides to assist them in the dispensing process. Thus, the pharmacist may delegate prescription-filling and administrative tasks and supervise their completion. They also frequently oversee pharmacy students serving as interns in preparation for graduation and licensure.

Increasingly, pharmacists pursue nontraditional pharmacy work. Some are involved in research for pharmaceutical manufacturers, developing new drugs and therapies and testing their effects on people. Others work in marketing or sales, providing expertise to clients on a drug's use, effectiveness, and possible side effects. Some pharmacists also work for health insurance companies, developing pharmacy benefit packages and carrying out cost-benefit analyses on certain drugs. Other pharmacists work for the government and pharmacy associations. Finally, some pharmacists are employed full time or part time as college faculty, teaching classes and performing research in a wide range of areas.

Working Conditions

Pharmacists work in clean, well-lighted, and well-ventilated areas. Many pharmacists spend most of their workday on their feet. When working with sterile or potentially dangerous pharmaceutical products, pharmacists wear gloves and masks and work with other special protective equipment. Many community and hospital pharmacies are open for extended hours or around the clock, so pharmacists may work evenings, nights, weekends, and holidays. Consultant pharmacists may travel to nursing homes or other facilities to monitor patients' drug therapy.

About 19 percent of pharmacists worked part time in 2002. Most full-time salaried pharmacists worked about 40 hours a week. Some, including many self-employed pharmacists, worked more than 50 hours a week.

Employment

Pharmacists held about 230,000 jobs in 2002. About 62 percent work in community pharmacies that are either independently owned or part of a drugstore chain, grocery store, department store, or mass merchandiser. Most community pharmacists are salaried employees, but some are self-employed owners. About 22 percent of salaried pharmacists work in hospitals, and others work in clinics, mail-order pharmacies, pharmaceutical wholesalers, home healthcare agencies, or the federal government.

Training, Other Qualifications, and Advancement

A license to practice pharmacy is required in all states, the District of Columbia, and U.S. territories. To obtain a license, one must graduate from a college of pharmacy accredited by the American Council on Pharmaceutical Education (ACPE) and pass an examination. All states except California require the North American Pharmacist Licensure Exam (NAPLEX) and the Multistate Pharmacy Jurisprudence Exam (MPJE), both administered by the National Association of Boards of Pharmacy. California has its own pharmacist licensure exam. In addition to the NAPLEX and MPJE, some states require additional exams unique to their state. All states except California currently grant a license without extensive re-examination to qualified pharmacists already licensed by another state. In Florida, reexamination is not required if a pharmacist passed the NAPLEX and MPJE within 12 years of his or her application for license transfer. Many pharmacists are licensed to practice in more than one state. States may require continuing education for license renewal. Persons interested in a career as a pharmacist should check with state boards of pharmacy for details on examination requirements and license transfer procedures.

In 2002, 85 colleges of pharmacy were accredited to confer degrees by the American Council on Pharmaceutical Education. Pharmacy programs grant the degree of Doctor of Pharmacy (Pharm.D.), which requires at least 6 years of postsecondary study and the passing of the licensure examination of a state board of pharmacy. Courses offered at colleges of pharmacy are designed to teach students how to dispense prescriptions and communicate with patients and other health care providers about drug information and patient care. Students also learn professional ethics.. In addition to classroom study, students in the Pharm.D. program are provided in-depth exposure to and active participation in a variety of pharmacy practice settings under the supervision of licensed pharmacists. The Pharm.D. degree has replaced the Bachelor of Pharmacy (B.Pharm.) degree, which is no longer offered to new students and will cease to be awarded after 2005.

The Pharm.D. is a 4-year program that requires at least 2 years of college study prior to admittance, although most applicants have 3 years prior to entering the program. Entry requirements usually include courses in mathematics and natural sciences, such as chemistry, biology, and physics, as well as courses in the humanities and social sciences. Approximately half of all colleges require the applicant to take the Pharmacy College Admissions Test (PCAT).

In 2003, the American Association of Colleges of Pharmacy (AACP) launched the Pharmacy College Application Service, known as PharmCAS, for students interested in applying to schools and colleges of pharmacy. This centralized service allows applicants to use a single Web-based application and one set of transcripts to apply to multiple Pharm.D. degree programs. A total of 43 pharmacy programs participated in 2003.

In the 2002-03 academic year, 66 colleges of pharmacy awarded the master of science degree or the Ph.D. degree. Both the master's and Ph.D. degrees are awarded after completion of a Pharm.D. degree. These degrees are designed for those who want more laboratory and research experience. Many master's and Ph.D. degree holders do research for a drug company or teach at a university. Other options for pharmacy graduates who are interested in further training include 1- or 2-year residency programs or fellowships. Pharmacy residencies are postgraduate training programs in pharmacy practice, and usually require the completion of a research study. Pharmacy fellowships are highly individualized programs designed to prepare participants to work in research laboratories. Some pharmacists who run their own pharmacy obtain a master's degree in business administration (MBA).

Areas of graduate study include pharmaceutics and pharmaceutical chemistry (physical and chemical properties of drugs and dosage forms), pharmacology (effects of drugs on the body), and pharmacy administration.

Prospective pharmacists should have scientific aptitude, good communication skills, and a desire to help others. They also must be conscientious and pay close attention to detail, because the decisions they make affect human lives.

In community pharmacies, pharmacists usually begin at the staff level. In independent pharmacies, after they gain experience and secure the necessary capital, some become owners or part owners of pharmacies. Pharmacists in chain drugstores may be promoted to pharmacy supervisor or manager at the store level, then to manager at the district or regional level, and later to an executive position within the chain's headquarters.

Hospital pharmacists may advance to supervisory or administrative positions. Pharmacists in the pharmaceutical industry may advance in marketing, sales, research, quality control, production, packaging, or other areas.

Job Outlook

Very good employment opportunities are expected for pharmacists over the 2002-12 period because the number of degrees granted in pharmacy is expected to be less than the number of job openings created by employment growth and the need to replace pharmacists who retire or otherwise leave the occupation. Recently, enrollments in pharmacy programs are rising as more students are attracted by high salaries and good job prospects. Despite this increase in enrollments, pharmacist jobs should still be more numerous than those seeking employment.

Employment of pharmacists is expected to grow faster than the average for all occupations through the year 2012, due to the increased pharmaceutical needs of a growing elderly population and increased use of medications. The growing numbers of middle-aged and elderly people—who, on average, use more prescription drugs than do younger people—will continue to spur demand for pharmacists in all employment settings. Other factors likely to increase the demand for pharmacists include scientific advances that will make more drug products available, new developments in genome research and medication distribution systems, increasingly sophisticated consumers seeking more information about drugs, and coverage of prescription drugs by a greater number of health insurance plans and by Medicare.

Community pharmacies are taking steps to manage increasing prescription volume. Automation of drug dispensing and greater employment of pharmacy technicians and pharmacy aides will help these establishments to dispense more prescriptions.

With its emphasis on cost control, managed care encourages the use of lower cost prescription drug distributors, such as mail-order firms and online pharmacies, for purchases of certain medications. Prescriptions ordered through the mail via the Internet are filled in a central location and shipped to the patient at a lower cost. Mail-order and online pharmacies typically use automated technology to dispense medication and employ fewer pharmacists. If the utilization of mail-order pharmacies increases rapidly, job growth among pharmacists could be limited.

Employment of pharmacists will not grow as fast in hospitals as in other industries, as hospitals reduce inpatient stays, downsize, and consolidate departments. The increase in outpatient surgeries means more patients are discharged and purchase medications through retail, supermarket, or mail-order pharmacies, rather than through the hospital. An aging population means more pharmacy services are required in nursing homes, assisted living facilities, and home care settings, where the most rapid job growth among pharmacists is expected.

New opportunities are emerging for pharmacists in managed-care organizations, where they may analyze trends and patterns in medication use for their populations of patients, and for pharmacists trained in research, disease management, and pharmacoeconomics—determining the costs and benefits of different drug therapies. Pharmacists also will have opportunities to work in research and development as well as sales and marketing for pharmaceutical manufacturing firms. New breakthroughs in biotechnology will increase the potential for drugs to treat diseases and expand the opportunities for pharmacists to conduct research and sell medications.

Job opportunities for pharmacists in patient care will arise as cost-conscious insurers and health systems continue to emphasize the role of pharmacists in primary and preventive health services. Health insurance companies realize that the expense of using medication to treat diseases and various health conditions often is considerably less than the potential costs for patients whose conditions go untreated. Pharmacists also can reduce the expenses resulting from unexpected complications due to allergic reactions or medication interactions.

Earnings

Median annual wage and salary earnings of pharmacists in 2002 were $77,050. The middle 50 percent earned between $66,210 and $87,250 a year. The lowest 10 percent earned less than $54,110, and the highest 10 percent earned more than $94,570 a year. Median annual earnings in the industries employing the largest numbers of pharmacists in 2002 were as follows:

Grocery stores $78,270

Health and personal care stores............................76,800

General medical and surgical hospitals.................76,620

Related Occupations

Pharmacy technicians and pharmacy aides also work in pharmacies. Persons in other professions who may work with pharmaceutical compounds include biological scientists, medical scientists, and chemists and materials scientists. Increasingly, pharmacists are involved in patient care and therapy, work that they have in common with physicians and surgeons.

Sources of Additional Information

For information on pharmacy as a career, preprofessional and professional requirements, programs offered by colleges of pharmacy, and student financial aid, contact:

● American Association of Colleges of Pharmacy, 1426 Prince St., Alexandria, VA 22314. Internet: http://www.aacp.org

General information on careers in pharmacy is available from:

● American Society of Health-System Pharmacists, 7272 Wisconsin Ave., Bethesda, MD 20814. Internet: http://www.ashp.org

● National Association of Chain Drug Stores, 413 N. Lee St., P.O. Box 1417-D49, Alexandria, VA 22313-1480. Internet: http://www.nacds.org

Information on the North American Pharmacist Licensure Exam (NAPLEX) and the Multistate Pharmacy Jurisprudence Exam (MPJE) is available from:

● National Association of Boards of Pharmacy, 700 Busse Hwy., Park Ridge, IL 60068. Internet: http://www.nabp.net

State licensure requirements are available from each state's Board of Pharmacy. Information on specific college entrance requirements, curriculums, and financial aid is available from any college of pharmacy.

Pharmacy Technicians

(O*NET 29-2052.00)

Significant Points

- Job opportunities are expected to be good, especially for those with certification or previous work experience.

- Many technicians work evenings, weekends, and holidays.

- Two-thirds of all jobs are in retail pharmacies.

Nature of the Work

Pharmacy technicians help licensed pharmacists provide medication and other healthcare products to patients. Technicians usually perform routine tasks to help prepare prescribed medication for patients, such as counting tablets and labeling bottles. Technicians refer any questions regarding prescriptions, drug information, or health matters to a *pharmacist*.

Pharmacy aides work closely with pharmacy technicians. They are often clerks or cashiers who primarily answer telephones, handle money, stock shelves, and perform other clerical duties. Pharmacy technicians usually perform more complex tasks than do pharmacy aides, although, in some states, their duties and job titles overlap.

Pharmacy technicians who work in retail or mail-order pharmacies have varying responsibilities, depending on state rules and regulations. Technicians receive written prescriptions or requests for prescription refills from patients. They also may receive prescriptions sent electronically from the doctor's office. They must verify that the information on the prescription is complete and accurate. To prepare the prescription, technicians must retrieve, count, pour, weigh, measure, and sometimes mix the medication. Then, they prepare the prescription labels, select the type of prescription container, and affix the prescription and auxiliary labels to the container. Once the prescription is filled, technicians price and file the prescription, which must be checked by a pharmacist before it is given to a patient. Technicians may establish and maintain patient profiles, prepare insurance claim forms, and stock and take inventory of prescription and over-the-counter medications.

In hospitals, nursing homes, and assisted-living facilities, technicians have added responsibilities. They read patient charts and prepare and deliver the medicine to patients. The pharmacist must check the order before it is delivered to the patient. The technician then copies the information about the prescribed medication onto the patient's profile. Technicians also may assemble a 24-hour supply of medicine for every patient. They package and label each dose separately. The package is then placed in the medicine cabinet of each patient until the supervising pharmacist checks it for accuracy. It is then given to the patient.

Working Conditions

Pharmacy technicians work in clean, organized, well-lighted, and well-ventilated areas. Most of their workday is spent on their feet. They may be required to lift heavy boxes or to use stepladders to retrieve supplies from high shelves.

Technicians work the same hours that pharmacists work. These may include evenings, nights, weekends, and holidays. Because some hospital and retail pharmacies are open 24 hours a day, technicians may work varying shifts. As their seniority increases, technicians often have increased control over the hours they work. There are many opportunities for part-time work in both retail and hospital settings.

Employment

Pharmacy technicians held about 211,000 jobs in 2002. Two-thirds of all jobs were in retail pharmacies, either independently owned or part of a drugstore chain, grocery store, department store, or mass retailer. About 22 percent of jobs were in hospitals and a small proportion was in mail-order and Internet pharmacies, clinics, pharmaceutical wholesalers, and the federal government.

Training, Other Qualifications, and Advancement

Although most pharmacy technicians receive informal on-the-job training, employers favor those who have completed formal training and certification. However, there are currently few state and no federal requirements for formal training or certification of pharmacy technicians. Employers who have neither the time nor money to give on-the-job training often seek formally educated pharmacy technicians. Formal education programs and certification emphasize the technician's interest in and dedication to the work. In addition to the military, some hospitals, proprietary schools, vocational or technical colleges, and community colleges offer formal education programs.

Formal pharmacy technician education programs require classroom and laboratory work in a variety of areas, including medical and pharmaceutical terminology, pharmaceutical calculations, pharmacy recordkeeping, pharmaceutical techniques, and pharmacy law and ethics. Technicians also are required to learn medication names, actions, uses, and doses. Many training programs include internships, in which students gain hands-on experience in actual pharmacies. Students receive a diploma, a certificate, or an associate degree, depending on the program.

Prospective pharmacy technicians with experience working as an aide in a community pharmacy or volunteering in a hospital may have an advantage. Employers also prefer applicants with strong customer service and communication skills and with experience managing inventories, counting, measuring, and using computers. Technicians entering the field need strong mathematics, spelling, and reading skills. A background in chemistry, English, and health education also may be beneficial. Some technicians are hired without formal training, but under the condition that they obtain certification within a specified period to retain employment.

The Pharmacy Technician Certification Board administers the National Pharmacy Technician Certification Examination. This exam is voluntary in most states and displays the competency of the individual to act as a pharmacy technician. However, more states and employers are requiring certification as reliance on pharmacy technicians grows. Eligible candidates must have a high school diploma or GED and no felony convictions, and those who pass the exam earn the title of Certified Pharmacy Technician (CPhT). The exam is offered several times per year at various locations nationally. Employers, often pharmacists, know that individuals who pass the exam have a standardized body of knowledge and skills. Many employers will also reimburse the costs of the exam as an incentive for certification.

Certified technicians must be recertified every 2 years. Technicians must complete 20 contact hours of pharmacy-related topics within the 2-year certification period to become eligible for recertification. Contact hours are awarded for on-the-job training, attending lectures, and college coursework. At least 1 contact hour must be in pharmacy law. Contact hours can be earned from several different sources, including pharmacy associations, pharmacy colleges, and pharmacy technician training programs. Up to 10 contact hours can be earned when the technician is employed under the direct supervision and instruction of a pharmacist.

Successful pharmacy technicians are alert, observant, organized, dedicated, and responsible. They should be willing and able to take directions. They must enjoy precise work—details are sometimes a matter of life and death. Although a pharmacist must check and approve all their work, they should be able to work on their own without constant instruction from the pharmacist. Candidates interested in becoming pharmacy technicians cannot have prior records of drug or substance abuse.

Strong interpersonal and communication skills are needed because there is a lot of interaction with patients, coworkers, and healthcare professionals. Teamwork is very important because technicians are often required to work with pharmacists, aides, and other technicians.

Job Outlook

Good job opportunities are expected for full-time and part-time work, especially for technicians with formal training or previous experience. Job openings for pharmacy technicians will result from the expansion of retail pharmacies and other employment settings, and from the need to replace workers who transfer to other occupations or leave the labor force.

Employment of pharmacy technicians is expected to grow faster than the average for all occupations through 2012 due to the increased pharmaceutical needs of a larger and older population, and to the greater use of medication. The increased number of middle-aged and elderly people—who, on average, use more prescription drugs than do younger people—will spur demand for technicians in all practice settings. With advances in science, more medications are becoming available to treat more conditions.

Cost-conscious insurers, pharmacies, and health systems will continue to emphasize the role of technicians. As a result, pharmacy technicians will assume responsibility for more routine tasks previously performed by pharmacists. Pharmacy technicians also will need to learn and master new pharmacy technology as it surfaces. For example, robotic machines are used to dispense medicine into containers; technicians must oversee the machines, stock the bins, and label the containers. Thus, while automation is increasingly incorporated into the job, it will not necessarily reduce the need for technicians.

Almost all states have legislated the maximum number of technicians who can safely work under a pharmacist at one time. In some states, technicians have assumed more medication dispensing duties as pharmacists have become more involved in patient care, resulting in more technicians per pharmacist. Changes in these laws could directly affect employment.

Earnings

Median hourly earnings of wage and salary pharmacy technicians in 2002 were $10.70. The middle 50 percent earned between $8.74 and $13.19; the lowest 10 percent earned less than $7.44, and the highest 10 percent earned more than $15.82. Median hourly earnings in the industries employing the largest numbers of pharmacy technicians in 2002 were as follows:

General medical and surgical hospitals..................$12.32

Grocery stores 11.34

Drugs and druggists' sundries merchant
    wholesalers 10.60

Health and personal care stores..................................9.70

Department stores 9.69

Certified technicians may earn more. Shift differentials for working evenings or weekends also can increase earnings. Some technicians belong to unions representing hospital or grocery store workers.

Related Occupations

This occupation is most closely related to pharmacists and pharmacy aides. Workers in other medical support occupations include dental assistants, licensed practical and licensed vocational nurses, medical transcriptionists, medical records and health information technicians, occupational therapist assistants and aides, physical therapist assistants and aides, and surgical technologists.

Sources of Additional Information

For information on the Certified Pharmacy Technician designation, contact:

- Pharmacy Technician Certification Board, 2215 Constitution Ave. NW, Washington DC 20037. Internet: http://www.ptcb.org

For a list of accredited pharmacy technician training programs, contact:

- American Society of Health-System Pharmacists, 7272 Wisconsin Ave., Bethesda, MD 20814. Internet: http://www.ashp.org

Physical Therapist Assistants and Aides

(O*NET 31-2021.00 and 31-2022.00)

Significant Points

- Employment in the occupation is projected to increase much faster than the average, reflecting the growing number of individuals with disabilities or limited function and the increasing use of physical therapist assistants to reduce the cost of therapeutic services.

- Physical therapist assistants generally have an associate degree, but physical therapist aides usually learn skills on the job.

- Almost three-fourths of all jobs were in hospitals or offices of physical therapists.

Nature of the Work

Physical therapist assistants and aides perform components of physical therapy procedures and related tasks selected by a supervising physical therapist. These workers assist physical therapists in providing services that help improve mobility, relieve pain, and prevent or limit permanent physical disabilities of patients suffering from injuries or disease. Patients include accident victims and individuals with disabling conditions such as low-back pain, arthritis, heart disease, fractures, head injuries, and cerebral palsy.

Physical therapist assistants perform a variety of tasks. Components of treatment procedures performed by these workers, under the direction and supervision of physical therapists, involve exercises, massages, electrical stimulation, paraffin baths, hot and cold packs, traction, and ultrasound. Physical therapist assistants record the patient's responses to treatment and report the outcome of each treatment to the physical therapist.

Physical therapist aides help make therapy sessions productive, under the direct supervision of a physical therapist or physical therapist assistant. They usually are responsible for keeping the treatment area clean and organized and for preparing for each patient's therapy. When patients need assistance moving to or from a treatment area, aides push them in a wheelchair or provide them with a shoulder to lean on. Because they are not licensed, aides do not perform the clinical tasks of a physical therapist assistant.

The duties of aides include some clerical tasks, such as ordering depleted supplies, answering the phone, and filling out insurance forms and other paperwork. The extent to which an aide or an assistant performs clerical tasks depends on the size and location of the facility.

Working Conditions

The hours and days that physical therapist assistants and aides work vary with the facility and with whether they are full- or part-time employees. Many outpatient physical therapy offices and clinics have evening and weekend hours, to help coincide with patients' personal schedules.

Physical therapist assistants and aides need a moderate degree of strength because of the physical exertion required in assisting patients with their treatment. In some cases, assistants and aides need to lift patients. Constant kneeling, stooping, and standing for long periods also are part of the job.

Employment

Physical therapist assistants and aides held about 87,000 jobs in 2002. Physical therapist assistants held about 50,000 jobs, physical therapist aides approximately 37,000. Both work alongside physical therapists in a variety of settings. Almost three-fourths of all jobs were in hospitals or in offices of other health practitioners (which includes offices of physical therapists). Others worked primarily in nursing care facilities, offices of physicians, home healthcare services, and outpatient care centers.

Training, Other Qualifications, and Advancement

Physical therapist aides are trained on the job, but physical therapist assistants typically earn an associate degree from an accredited physical therapist assistant program. Not all states require licensure or registration in order for the physical therapist assistant to practice. The states that require licensure stipulate specific educational and examination criteria. Complete information on practice acts and regulations can be obtained from the state licensing boards. Additional requirements may include certification in cardiopulmonary resuscitation (CPR) and other first aid and a minimum number of hours of clinical experience.

According to the American Physical Therapy Association, there were 245 accredited physical therapist assistant programs in the United States as of 2003. Accredited physical therapist assistant programs are designed to last 2 years, or 4 semesters, and culminate in an associate degree. Programs are divided into academic study and hands-on clinical experience. Academic course work includes algebra, anatomy and physiology, biology, chemistry, and psychology. Many programs require that students complete a semester of anatomy and physiology and have certifications in CPR and other first aid even before they begin their clinical field experience. Both educators and prospective employers view clinical experience as integral to ensuring that students understand the responsibilities of a physical therapist assistant.

Employers typically require physical therapist aides to have a high school diploma, strong interpersonal skills, and a desire to assist people in need. Most employers provide clinical on-the-job training.

Job Outlook

Employment of physical therapist assistants and aides is expected to grow much faster than the average through the year 2012. The impact of proposed federal legislation imposing limits on reimbursement for therapy services may adversely affect the short-term job outlook for physical therapist assistants and aides. However, over the long run, demand for physical therapist assistants and aides will continue to rise, in accordance with growth in the number of individuals with disabilities or limited function. The growing elderly population is particularly vulnerable to chronic and debilitating conditions that require therapeutic services. These patients often need additional assistance in their treatment, making the roles of assistants and aides vital. The large baby-boom generation is entering the prime age for heart attacks and strokes, further increasing the demand for cardiac and physical rehabilitation. In addition, future medical developments should permit an increased percentage of trauma victims to survive, creating added demand for therapy services.

Physical therapists are expected to increasingly utilize assistants to reduce the cost of physical therapy services. Once a patient is evaluated and a treatment plan is designed by the physical therapist, the physical therapist assistant can provide many aspects of treatment, as prescribed by the therapist.

Earnings

Median annual earnings of physical therapist assistants were $36,080 in 2002. The middle 50 percent earned between $30,260 and $42,780. The lowest 10 percent earned less than $23,530, and the highest 10 percent earned more than $48,910. Median annual earnings of physical therapist assistants in 2002 were $35,870 in general medical and surgical hospitals and $35,750 in offices of other health practitioners.

Median annual earnings of physical therapist aides were $20,670 in 2002. The middle 50 percent earned between $17,430 and $24,560. The lowest 10 percent earned less than $15,290, and the highest 10 percent earned more than $29,990. Median annual earnings of physical therapist aides in 2002 were $20,690 in general medical and surgical hospitals and $19,840 in offices of other health practitioners.

Related Occupations

Physical therapist assistants and aides work under the supervision of physical therapists. Other workers in the health-care field who work under similar supervision include dental assistants, medical assistants, occupational therapist assistants and aides, pharmacy aides, and pharmacy technicians.

Sources of Additional Information

Career information on physical therapist assistants and a list of schools offering accredited programs can be obtained from:

- The American Physical Therapy Association, 1111 North Fairfax St., Alexandria, VA 22314-1488. Internet: http://www.apta.org

Physical Therapists

(O*NET 29-1123.00)

Significant Points

- Employment is expected to increase faster than the average, as growth in the number of individuals with disabilities or limited function spurs demand for therapy services.

- After graduating from an accredited physical therapist educational program, therapists must pass a licensure exam before they can practice.

- About two-thirds of physical therapists work either in hospitals or in offices of physical therapists.

Nature of the Work

Physical therapists (PTs) provide services that help restore function, improve mobility, relieve pain, and prevent or limit permanent physical disabilities of patients suffering from injuries or disease. They restore, maintain, and promote overall fitness and health. Their patients include accident victims and individuals with disabling conditions such as low-back pain, arthritis, heart disease, fractures, head injuries, and cerebral palsy.

Therapists examine patients' medical histories and then test and measure the patients' strength, range of motion, balance and coordination, posture, muscle performance, respiration, and motor function. They also determine patients' ability to be independent and reintegrate into the community or workplace after injury or illness. Next, physical therapists develop treatment plans describing a treatment strategy, its purpose, and its anticipated outcome. Physical therapist assistants, under the direction and supervision of a physical therapist, may be involved in implementing treatment plans with patients. Physical therapist aides perform routine support tasks, as directed by the therapist.

Treatment often includes exercise for patients who have been immobilized and lack flexibility, strength, or endurance. Physical therapists encourage patients to use their own muscles to increase their flexibility and range of motion before finally advancing to other exercises that improve strength, balance, coordination, and endurance. The goal is to improve how an individual functions at work and at home.

Physical therapists also use electrical stimulation, hot packs or cold compresses, and ultrasound to relieve pain and reduce swelling. They may use traction or deep-tissue massage to relieve pain. Therapists also teach patients to use assistive and adaptive devices, such as crutches, prostheses, and wheelchairs. They also may show patients exercises to do at home to expedite their recovery.

As treatment continues, physical therapists document the patient's progress, conduct periodic examinations, and modify treatments when necessary. Besides tracking the patient's progress, such documentation identifies areas requiring more or less attention.

Physical therapists often consult and practice with a variety of other professionals, such as physicians, dentists, nurses, educators, social workers, occupational therapists, speech-language pathologists, and audiologists.

Some physical therapists treat a wide range of ailments; others specialize in areas such as pediatrics, geriatrics, orthopedics, sports medicine, neurology, and cardiopulmonary physical therapy.

Working Conditions

Physical therapists practice in hospitals, clinics, and private offices that have specially equipped facilities, or they treat patients in hospital rooms, homes, or schools.

In 2002, most full-time physical therapists worked a 40-hour week; some worked evenings and weekends to fit their patients' schedules. More than 1 in 5 physical therapists worked part time. The job can be physically demanding because therapists often have to stoop, kneel, crouch, lift, and stand for long periods. In addition, physical therapists move heavy equipment and lift patients or help them turn, stand, or walk.

Employment

Physical therapists held about 137,000 jobs in 2002. The number of jobs is greater than the number of practicing physical therapists, because some physical therapists hold two or more jobs. For example, some may work in a private practice, but also work part time in another healthcare facility.

About two-thirds of jobs for physical therapists were either in hospitals or in offices of other health practitioners (which includes offices of physical therapists). Other jobs were in home healthcare services, nursing care facilities, outpatient care centers, and offices of physicians.

Some physical therapists were self-employed in private practices, seeing individual patients and contracting to provide services in hospitals, rehabilitation centers, nursing care facilities, home healthcare agencies, adult daycare programs, and schools. Physical therapists also teach in academic institutions and conduct research.

Training, Other Qualifications, and Advancement

All states require physical therapists to pass a licensure exam before they can practice, after graduating from an accredited physical therapist educational program.

According to the American Physical Therapy Association, there were 203 accredited physical therapist programs in 2003. Of the accredited programs, 113 offered master's degrees, and 90 offered doctoral degrees. All physical therapist programs seeking accreditation are required to offer degrees at the master's degree level and above, in accordance with the Commission on Accreditation in Physical Therapy Education.

Physical therapist programs start with basic science courses such as biology, chemistry, and physics and then introduce specialized courses, including biomechanics, neuroanatomy, human growth and development, manifestations of disease, examination techniques, and therapeutic procedures. Besides getting classroom and laboratory instruction, students receive supervised clinical experience. Among the courses that are useful when one applies to a physical therapist educational program are anatomy, biology, chemistry, social science, mathematics, and physics. Before granting admission, many professional education programs require experience as a volunteer in a physical therapy department of a hospital or clinic.

Physical therapists should have strong interpersonal skills in order to be able to educate patients about their physical therapy treatments. PTs also should be compassionate and possess a desire to help patients. Similar traits are needed to interact with the patient's family.

Physical therapists are expected to continue their professional development by participating in continuing education courses and workshops. In fact, a number of states require continuing education as a condition of maintaining one's licensure.

Job Outlook

Employment of physical therapists is expected to grow faster than the average for all occupations through 2012. The impact of proposed federal legislation imposing limits on reimbursement for therapy services may adversely affect the short-term job outlook for physical therapists. However, over the long run, the demand for physical therapists should continue to rise as growth in the number of individuals with disabilities or limited function spurs demand for therapy services. The growing elderly population is particularly vulnerable to chronic and debilitating conditions that require therapeutic services. Also, the baby-boom generation is entering the prime age for heart attacks and strokes, increasing the demand for cardiac and physical rehabilitation. Further, young people will need physical therapy as technological advances save the lives of a larger proportion of newborns with severe birth defects.

Future medical developments also should permit a higher percentage of trauma victims to survive, creating additional demand for rehabilitative care. In addition, growth may result from advances in medical technology that could permit the treatment of more disabling conditions.

Widespread interest in health promotion also should increase demand for physical therapy services. A growing number of employers are using physical therapists to evaluate worksites, develop exercise programs, and teach safe work habits to employees in the hope of reducing injuries.

Earnings

Median annual earnings of physical therapists were $57,330 in 2002. The middle 50 percent earned between $48,480 and $70.050. The lowest 10 percent earned less than $40,200, and the highest 10 percent earned more than $86,260. Median annual earnings in the industries employing the largest numbers of physical therapists in 2002 were as follows:

Home health care services $62,480

Offices of other health practitioners 58,510

Offices of physicians 57,640

Nursing care facilities..57,570

General medical and surgical hospitals..................57,200

Related Occupations

Physical therapists rehabilitate persons with physical disabilities. Others who work in the rehabilitation field include audiologists, chiropractors, occupational therapists, recreational therapists, rehabilitation counselors, respiratory therapists, and speech-language pathologists.

Sources of Additional Information

Additional career information and a list of accredited educational programs in physical therapy are available from:

● American Physical Therapy Association, 1111 North Fairfax St., Alexandria, VA 22314-1488. Internet: http://www.apta.org

Physician Assistants

(O*NET 29-1071.00)

Significant Points

● The typical physician assistant program lasts about 2 years and requires at least 2 years of college and some healthcare experience for admission.

● Most applicants to physician assistant programs hold a bachelor's or master's degree.

● Job opportunities should be good, particularly in rural and inner city clinics.

● Earnings are high.

Nature of the Work

Physician assistants (PAs) provide healthcare services under the supervision of physicians. They should not be confused with medical assistants, who perform routine clinical and clerical tasks. PAs are formally trained to provide diagnostic, therapeutic, and preventive healthcare services, as delegated by a physician. Working as members of the healthcare team, they take medical histories, examine and treat patients, order and interpret laboratory tests and x rays, make diagnoses, and prescribe medications. They also treat minor injuries, by suturing, splinting, and casting. PAs record progress notes, instruct and counsel patients, and order or carry out therapy. In 47 states and the District of Columbia, physician assistants may prescribe medications. PAs also may have managerial duties. Some order medical and laboratory supplies and equipment and may supervise technicians and assistants.

Physician assistants work under the supervision of a physician. However, PAs may be the principal care providers in rural or inner-city clinics, where a physician is present for only 1 or 2 days each week. In such cases, the PA confers with the supervising physician and other medical professionals as needed or as required by law. PAs also may make house calls or go to hospitals and nursing care facilities to check on patients, after which they report back to the physician.

The duties of physician assistants are determined by the supervising physician and by state law. Aspiring PAs should investigate the laws and regulations in the states in which they wish to practice.

Many PAs work in primary care specialties, such as general internal medicine, pediatrics, and family medicine. Others specialty areas include general and thoracic surgery, emergency medicine, orthopedics, and geriatrics. PAs specializing in surgery provide preoperative and postoperative care and may work as first or second assistants during major surgery.

Working Conditions

Although PAs usually work in a comfortable, well-lighted environment, those in surgery often stand for long periods, and others do considerable walking. Schedules vary according to the practice setting, and often depend on the hours of the supervising physician. The workweek of hospital-based PAs may include weekends, nights, or early morning hospital rounds to visit patients. These workers also may be on call. PAs in clinics usually work a 40-hour week.

Employment

Physician assistants held about 63,000 jobs in 2002. The number of jobs is greater than the number of practicing PAs because some hold two or more jobs. For example, some PAs work with a supervising physician, but also work in another practice, clinic, or hospital. According to the American Academy of Physician Assistants, almost 90 percent of certified PAs were in clinical practice in 2003.

More than half of jobs for PAs were in the offices of physicians or other health practitioners. About a quarter were in hospitals. The rest were mostly in outpatient care centers, the federal government, educational services, and employment services.

Training, Other Qualifications, and Advancement

All states require that new PAs complete an accredited, formal education program. In 2002 there were about 133 accredited or provisionally accredited education programs for physician assistants. Sixty-eight of these programs offered a master's degree, and the rest offered either a bachelor's degree or an associate degree. Most PA graduates have at least a bachelor's degree.

Admission requirements vary, but many programs require 2 years of college and some work experience in the healthcare field. Students should take courses in biology, English, chemistry, mathematics, psychology, and the social sciences. Most applicants to PA programs hold a bachelor's or master's degree. Many PAs have backgrounds as registered nurses, while others come from varied backgrounds, including military corpsman/medics and allied health occupations such as respiratory therapists, physical therapists, and emergency medical technicians and paramedics.

PA programs usually last at least 2 years and are full time. Most programs are in schools of allied health, academic health centers, medical schools, or 4-year colleges; a few are in community colleges, the military, or hospitals. Many accredited PA programs have clinical teaching affiliations with medical schools.

PA education includes classroom instruction in biochemistry, pathology, human anatomy, physiology, microbiology, clinical pharmacology, clinical medicine, geriatric and home healthcare, disease prevention, and medical ethics. Students obtain supervised clinical training in several areas, including primary care medicine, inpatient medicine, surgery, obstetrics and gynecology, geriatrics, emergency medicine, psychiatry, and pediatrics. Sometimes, PA students serve one or more of these "rotations" under the supervision of a physician who is seeking to hire a PA. The rotations often lead to permanent employment.

All states and the District of Columbia have legislation governing the qualifications or practice of physician assistants. All jurisdictions require physician assistants to pass the Physician Assistants National Certifying Examination, administered by the National Commission on Certification of Physician Assistants (NCCPA) and open to graduates of accredited PA education programs. Only those successfully completing the examination may use the credential "Physician Assistant-Certified." In order to remain certified, PAs must complete 100 hours of continuing medical education every 2 years. Every 6 years, they must pass a recertification examination or complete an alternative program combining learning experiences and a take-home examination.

Some PAs pursue additional education in a specialty such as surgery, neonatology, or emergency medicine. PA postgraduate residency training programs are available in areas such as internal medicine, rural primary care, emergency medicine, surgery, pediatrics, neonatology, and occupational medicine. Candidates must be graduates of an accredited program and be certified by the NCCPA.

Physician assistants need leadership skills, self-confidence, and emotional stability. They must be willing to continue studying throughout their career to keep up with medical advances.

As they attain greater clinical knowledge and experience, PAs can advance to added responsibilities and higher earnings. However, by the very nature of the profession, clinically practicing PAs always are supervised by physicians.

Job Outlook

Employment of PAs is expected to grow much faster than the average for all occupations through the year 2012, due to anticipated expansion of the health services industry and an emphasis on cost containment, resulting in increasing utilization of PAs by physicians and healthcare institutions.

Physicians and institutions are expected to employ more PAs to provide primary care and to assist with medical and surgical procedures because PAs are cost-effective and productive members of the healthcare team. Physician assistants can relieve physicians of routine duties and procedures. Telemedicine—using technology to facilitate interactive consultations between physicians and physician assistants—also will expand the use of physician assistants. Job opportunities for PAs should be good, particularly in rural and inner-city clinics, because those settings have difficulty attracting physicians.

Besides the traditional office-based setting, PAs should find a growing number of jobs in institutional settings such as hospitals, academic medical centers, public clinics, and prisons. Additional PAs may be needed to augment medical staffing in inpatient teaching hospital settings as the number of hours physician residents are permitted to work is reduced, encouraging hospitals to use PAs to supply some physician resident services. Opportunities will be best in states that allow PAs a wider scope of practice.

Earnings

Median annual earnings of physician assistants were $64,670 in 2002. The middle 50 percent earned between $49,640 and $77,280. The lowest 10 percent earned less than $35,410, and the highest 10 percent earned more than $90,350. Median annual earnings of physician assistants in 2002 were $65,910 in general medical and surgical hospitals and $64,170 in offices of physicians.

According to the American Academy of Physician Assistants, median income for physician assistants in full-time clinical practice in 2003 was about $72,457; median income for first-year graduates was about $63,437. Income varies by specialty, practice setting, geographical location, and years of experience.

Related Occupations

Other health workers who provide direct patient care that requires a similar level of skill and training include audiologists, occupational therapists, physical therapists, and speech-language pathologists.

Sources of Additional Information

For information on a career as a physician assistant, contact:

- American Academy of Physician Assistants Information Center, 950 North Washington St., Alexandria, VA 22314-1552. Internet: http://www.aapa.org

For a list of accredited programs and a catalog of individual PA training programs, contact:

- Association of Physician Assistant Programs, 950 North Washington St., Alexandria, VA 22314-1552. Internet: http://www.apap.org

For eligibility requirements and a description of the Physician Assistant National Certifying Examination, contact:

- National Commission on Certification of Physician Assistants, Inc., 6849–B Peachtree Dunwoody Rd., Atlanta, GA 30328. Internet: http://www.nccpa.net

Physicians and Surgeons

(O*NET 29-1061.00, 29-1062.00, 29-1063.00, 29-1064.00, 29-1065.00, 29-1066.00, 29-1067.00, and 29-1069.99)

Significant Points

- Many physicians and surgeons work long, irregular hours; almost one-third of physicians worked 60 or more hours a week in 2002.

- New physicians are much less likely to enter solo practice and more likely to work as salaried employees of group medical practices, clinics, hospitals, or health networks.

- Formal education and training requirements are among the most demanding of any occupation, but earnings are among the highest.

Nature of the Work

Physicians and surgeons serve a fundamental role in our society and have an effect upon all our lives. They diagnose illnesses and prescribe and administer treatment for people suffering from injury or disease. Physicians examine patients, obtain medical histories, and order, perform, and interpret diagnostic tests. They counsel patients on diet, hygiene, and preventive healthcare.

There are two types of physicians: M.D.—Doctor of Medicine—and D.O.—Doctor of Osteopathic Medicine. M.D.s also are known as allopathic physicians. While both M.D.s and D.O.s may use all accepted methods of treatment, including drugs and surgery, D.O.s place special emphasis on the body's musculoskeletal system, preventive medicine, and holistic patient care. D.O.s are more likely than M.D.s to be primary care specialists, although they can be found in all specialties. About half of D.O.s practice general or family medicine, general internal medicine, or general pediatrics.

Physicians work in one or more of several specialties, including, but not limited to, anesthesiology, family and general medicine, general internal medicine, general pediatrics, obstetrics and gynecology, psychiatry, and surgery.

Anesthesiologists. Anesthesiologists focus on the care of surgical patients and pain relief. Like other physicians, they evaluate and treat patients and direct the efforts of those on their staffs. Anesthesiologists confer with other physicians and surgeons about appropriate treatments and procedures before, during, and after operations. These critical specialists are responsible for maintenance of the patient's vital life functions—heart rate, body temperature, blood pressure, breathing—through continual monitoring and assessment during surgery.

Family and general practitioners. Family and general practitioners are often the first point of contact for people seeking health care, acting as the traditional family doctor. They assess and treat a wide range of conditions, ailments, and injuries, from sinus and respiratory infections to broken bones and scrapes. Family and general practitioners typically have a patient base of regular, long-term visitors. Patients with more serious conditions are referred to specialists or other healthcare facilities for more intensive care.

General internists. General internists diagnose and provide nonsurgical treatment for diseases and injuries of internal organ systems. They provide care mainly for adults who have a wide range of problems associated with the internal organs, such as the stomach, kidneys, liver, and digestive tract. Internists use a variety of diagnostic techniques to treat patients through medication or hospitalization. Like general practitioners, general internists are commonly looked upon as primary care specialists. They have patients referred to them by other specialists, in turn referring patients to those and yet other specialists when more complex care is required.

General pediatricians. Providing care from birth to early adulthood, pediatricians are concerned with the health of infants, children, and teenagers. They specialize in the diagnosis and treatment of a variety of ailments specific to young people and track their patients' growth to adulthood. Like most physicians, pediatricians work with different healthcare workers, such as nurses and other physicians, to assess and treat children with various ailments, such as muscular dystrophy. Most of the work of pediatricians, however, involves treating day-to-day illnesses that are common to children—minor injuries, infectious diseases, and immunizations—much as a general practitioner treats adults. Some pediatricians specialize in serious medical conditions and pediatric surgery, treating autoimmune disorders or serious chronic ailments.

Obstetricians and gynecologists. Obstetricians and gynecologists (ob/gyns) are specialists whose focus is women's health. They are responsible for general medical care for women, but also provide care related to pregnancy and the reproductive system. Like general practitioners, ob/gyns are concerned with the prevention, diagnosis, and treatment of general health problems, but they focus on ailments specific to the female anatomy, such as breast and cervical cancer, urinary tract and pelvic disorders, and hormonal disorders. Ob/gyns also specialize in childbirth, treating and counseling women throughout their pregnancy, from giving prenatal diagnoses to delivery and postpartum care. Ob/gyns track the health of, and treat, both mother and fetus as the pregnancy progresses.

Psychiatrists. Psychiatrists are the primary caregivers in the area of mental health. They assess and treat mental illnesses through a combination of psychotherapy, psychoanalysis, hospitalization, and medication. Psychotherapy involves regular discussions with patients about their problems; the psychiatrist helps them find solutions through changes in their behavioral patterns, the exploration of their past experiences, and group and family therapy sessions. Psychoanalysis involves long-term psychotherapy and counseling for patients. In many cases, medications are administered to correct chemical imbalances that may be causing emotional problems. Psychiatrists may also administer electroconvulsive therapy to those of their patients who do not respond to, or who cannot take, medications.

Surgeons. Surgeons are physicians who specialize in the treatment of injury, disease, and deformity through operations. Using a variety of instruments, and with patients under general or local anesthesia, a surgeon corrects physical deformities, repairs bone and tissue after injuries, or performs preventive surgeries on patients with debilitating diseases or disorders. Although a large number perform general surgery, many surgeons choose to specialize in a specific area. One of the most prevalent specialties is orthopedic surgery: the treatment of the skeletal system and associated organs. Others include neurological surgery (treatment of the brain and nervous system), ophthalmology (treatment of the eye), orthopedic surgery, otolaryngology (treatment of the ear, nose, and throat), and plastic or reconstructive surgery. Like primary care and other specialist physicians, surgeons also examine patients, perform and interpret diagnostic tests, and counsel patients on preventive health care.

A number of other medical specialists, including allergists, cardiologists, dermatologists, emergency physicians, gastroenterologists, pathologists, and radiologists, also work in clinics, hospitals, and private offices.

Working Conditions

Many physicians—primarily general and family practitioners, general internists, pediatricians, ob/gyns, and psychiatrists—work in small private offices or clinics, often assisted by a small staff of nurses and other administrative personnel. Increasingly, physicians are practicing in groups or healthcare organizations that provide backup coverage and allow for more time off. These physicians often work as part of a team coordinating care for a population of patients; they are less independent than solo practitioners of the past.

Surgeons and anesthesiologists typically work in well-lighted, sterile environments while performing surgery and often stand for long periods. Most work in hospitals or in surgical outpatient centers. Many physicians and surgeons work long, irregular hours. Almost one-third of physicians worked 60 hours or more a week in 2002. Physicians and surgeons must travel frequently between office and hospital to care for their patients. Those who are on call deal with many patients' concerns over the phone and may make emergency visits to hospitals or nursing homes.

Employment

Physicians and surgeons held about 583,000 jobs in 2002; approximately 1 out of 6 was self-employed. About half of salaried physicians and surgeons were in office-based practice, and almost a quarter were employed by hospitals. Others practiced in federal, state, and local government; educational services; and outpatient care centers.

A growing number of physicians are partners or salaried employees of group practices. Organized as clinics or as associations of physicians, medical groups can afford expensive medical equipment and realize other business advantages.

The New England and Middle Atlantic states have the highest ratio of physicians to population; the South Central states have the lowest. D.O.s are more likely than M.D.s to practice in small cities and towns and in rural areas. M.D.s tend to locate in urban areas, close to hospital and education centers.

Training, Other Qualifications, and Advancement

It takes many years of education and training to become a physician: 4 years of undergraduate school, 4 years of medical school, and 3 to 8 years of internship and residency, depending on the specialty selected. A few medical schools offer a combined undergraduate and medical school programs that last 6 rather than the customary 8 years.

Premedical students must complete undergraduate work in physics, biology, mathematics, English, and inorganic and organic chemistry. Students also take courses in the humanities and the social sciences. Some students volunteer at local hospitals or clinics to gain practical experience in the health professions.

The minimum educational requirement for entry into a medical school is 3 years of college; most applicants, however, have at least a bachelor's degree, and many have advanced degrees. There are 146 medical schools in the United States—126 teach allopathic medicine and award a Doctor of Medicine (M.D.) degree; 20 teach osteopathic medicine and award the Doctor of Osteopathic Medicine (D.O.) degree. Acceptance to medical school is highly competitive. Applicants must submit transcripts, scores from the Medical College Admission Test, and letters of recommendation. Schools also consider applicants' character, personality, leadership qualities, and participation in extracurricular activities. Most schools require an interview with members of the admissions committee.

Students spend most of the first 2 years of medical school in laboratories and classrooms, taking courses such as anatomy, biochemistry, physiology, pharmacology, psychology, microbiology, pathology, medical ethics, and laws governing medicine. They also learn to take medical histories, examine patients, and diagnose illnesses. During their last 2 years, students work with patients under the supervision of experienced physicians in hospitals and clinics, learning acute, chronic, preventive, and rehabilitative care. Through rotations in internal medicine, family practice, obstetrics and gynecology, pediatrics, psychiatry, and surgery, they gain experience in the diagnosis and treatment of illness.

Following medical school, almost all M.D.s enter a residency—graduate medical education in a specialty that takes the form of paid on-the-job training, usually in a hospital. Most D.O.s serve a 12-month rotating internship after graduation and before entering a residency, which may last 2 to 6 years.

All states, the District of Columbia, and U.S. territories license physicians. To be licensed, physicians must graduate from an accredited medical school, pass a licensing examination, and complete 1 to 7 years of graduate medical education. Although physicians licensed in one state usually can get a license to practice in another without further examination, some states limit reciprocity. Graduates of foreign medical schools generally can qualify for licensure after passing an examination and completing a U.S. residency.

M.D.s and D.O.s seeking board certification in a specialty may spend up to 7 years in residency training, depending on the specialty. A final examination immediately after residency or after 1 or 2 years of practice also is necessary for certification by the American Board of Medical Specialists or the American Osteopathic Association. There are 24 specialty boards, ranging from allergy and immunology to urology. For certification in a subspecialty, physicians usually need another 1 to 2 years of residency.

A physician's training is costly. More than 80 percent of medical students borrow money to cover their expenses.

People who wish to become physicians must have a desire to serve patients, be self-motivated, and be able to survive the pressures and long hours of medical education and practice. Physicians also must have a good bedside manner, emotional stability, and the ability to make decisions in emergencies. Prospective physicians must be willing to study throughout their career in order to keep up with medical advances.

Job Outlook

Employment of physicians and surgeons will grow about as fast as the average for all occupations through the year 2012 due to continued expansion of the health services industries. The growing and aging population will drive overall growth in the demand for physician services, as consumers continue to demand high levels of care using the latest technologies, diagnostic tests, and therapies.

Demand for physicians' services is highly sensitive to changes in consumer preferences, healthcare reimbursement policies, and legislation. For example, if changes to health coverage result in consumers facing higher out-of-pocket costs, they may demand fewer physician services. Demand for physician services may also be tempered by patients relying more on other healthcare providers—such as physician assistants, nurse practitioners, optometrists, and nurse anesthetists—for some healthcare services. In addition, new technologies will increase physician productivity. Telemedicine will allow physicians to treat patients or consult with other providers remotely. Increasing use of electronic medical records, test and prescription orders, billing, and scheduling will also improve physician productivity.

Opportunities for individuals interested in becoming physicians and surgeons are expected to be favorable. Reports of shortages in some specialties or geographic areas should attract new entrants, encouraging schools to expand programs and hospitals to expand available residency slots. However, because physician training is so lengthy, employment change happens gradually. In the short term, to meet increased demand, experienced physicians may work longer hours, delay retirement, or take measures to increase productivity, such as using more support staff to provide services. Opportunities should be particularly good in rural and low-income areas, because some physicians find these areas unattractive due to lower earnings potential, isolation from medical colleagues, or other reasons.

Unlike their predecessors, newly trained physicians face radically different choices of where and how to practice. New physicians are much less likely to enter solo practice and more likely to take salaried jobs in group medical practices, clinics, and health networks.

Earnings

Physicians have among the highest earnings of any occupation. According to the Medical Group Management Association's Physician Compensation and Production Survey, median total compensation for physicians in 2002 varied by specialty, as shown in Table 1. Total compensation for physicians reflects the amount reported as direct compensation for tax purposes, plus all voluntary salary reductions. Salary, bonus and/or incentive payments, research stipends, honoraria, and distribution of profits were included in total compensation.

TABLE 1

Total compensation of physicians by specialty, 2002

Anesthesiology	$306,964
Surgery, general	255,438
Obstetrics/gynecology	233,061
Psychiatry	163,144
Internal medicine	155,530
Pediatrics/adolescent medicine	152,690
Family practice (without obstetrics)	150,267

Source: Medical Group Management Association, Physician Compensation and Production Report, 2003.

Self-employed physicians—those who own or are part owners of their medical practice—generally have higher median incomes than salaried physicians. Earnings vary according to number of years in practice, geographic region, hours worked, and skill, personality, and professional reputation. Self-employed physicians and surgeons must provide for their own health insurance and retirement.

Related Occupations

Physicians work to prevent, diagnose, and treat diseases, disorders, and injuries. Professionals in other occupations requiring similar skills and critical judgment include chiropractors, dentists, optometrists, physician assistants, podiatrists, registered nurses, and veterinarians.

Sources of Additional Information

For a list of medical schools and residency programs, as well as general information on premedical education, financial aid, and medicine as a career, contact:

- Association of American Medical Colleges, Section for Student Services, 2450 N St. NW, Washington, DC 20037-1126. Internet: http://www.aamc.org
- American Association of Colleges of Osteopathic Medicine, 5550 Friendship Blvd., Suite 310, Chevy Chase, MD 20815-7231. Internet: http://www.aacom.org

For general information on physicians, contact:

- American Medical Association, Department of Communications and Public Relations, 515 N. State St., Chicago, IL 60610. Internet: http://www.ama-assn.org
- American Osteopathic Association, Division of Public Relations, 142 East Ontario St., Chicago, IL 60611. Internet: http://www.aoa-net.org

For information about various medical specialties, contact:

- American Society of Anesthesiologists, 520 N. Northwest Hwy., Park Ridge, IL 60068-2573. Internet: http://www.asahq.org
- American Board of Anesthesiology, 4101 Lake Boone Trail, Suite 510, Raleigh, NC 27607-7506. Internet: http://www.abanes.org
- Society of General Internal Medicine, 2501 M St. NW, Suite 575, Washington, DC 20037. Internet: http://www.sgim.org
- American Academy of Pediatrics, 141 Northwest Point Blvd., Elk Grove Village, IL 60007-1098. Internet: http://www.aap.org
- American Board of Obstetrics and Gynecology, 2915 Vine St., Dallas, TX 75204. Internet: http://www.abog.org
- American College of Obstetrics and Gynecologists, 409 12th St. SW, P.O. Box 96920, Washington, DC 20090-6920. Internet: http://www.acog.org
- American Psychiatric Association, 1000 Wilson Blvd., Suite 1825, Arlington, VA 22209-3901. Internet: http://www.psych.org
- American College of Surgeons, 633 North Saint Clair St., Chicago, IL 60611-3211. Internet: http://www.facs.org

Information on federal scholarships and loans is available from the directors of student financial aid at schools of medicine.

Information on licensing is available from state boards of examiners.

Pipelayers, Plumbers, Pipefitters, and Steamfitters

(O*NET 47-2151.00, 47-2152.01, 47-2152.02, and 47-2152.03)

Significant Points

- Job opportunities should be excellent because not enough people are seeking training.

- Most workers learn the trade through 4 or 5 years of formal apprenticeship training.

- Pipelayers, plumbers, pipefitters, and steamfitters make up one of the largest and highest paid construction occupations.

Nature of the Work

Most people are familiar with plumbers, who come to their home to unclog a drain or install an appliance. In addition to these activities, however, pipelayers, plumbers, pipefitters, and steamfitters install, maintain, and repair many different types of pipe systems. For example, some systems move water to a municipal water treatment plant and then to residential, commercial, and public buildings. Other systems dispose of waste, provide gas to stoves and furnaces, or supply air-conditioning. Pipe systems in powerplants carry the steam that powers huge turbines. Pipes also are used in manufacturing plants to move material through the production process. Specialized piping systems are very important in both pharmaceutical and computer-chip manufacturing.

Although pipelaying, plumbing, pipefitting, and steamfitting sometimes are considered a single trade, workers generally specialize in one of the four areas. *Pipelayers* lay clay, concrete, plastic, or cast-iron pipe for drains, sewers, water mains, and oil or gas lines. Before laying the pipe, pipelayers prepare and grade the trenches either manually or with machines. *Plumbers* install and repair the water, waste disposal, drainage, and gas systems in homes and commercial and industrial buildings. Plumbers also install plumbing fixtures—bathtubs, showers, sinks, and toilets—and appliances such as dishwashers and water heaters. *Pipefitters* install and repair both high- and low-pressure pipe systems used in manufacturing, in the generation of electricity, and in heating and cooling buildings. They also install automatic controls that are increasingly being used to regulate these systems. Some pipefitters specialize in only one type of system. *Steamfitters*, for example, install pipe systems that move

liquids or gases under high pressure. *Sprinklerfitters* install automatic fire sprinkler systems in buildings.

Pipelayers, plumbers, pipefitters, and steamfitters use many different materials and construction techniques, depending on the type of project. Residential water systems, for example, incorporate copper, steel, and plastic pipe that can be handled and installed by one or two workers. Municipal sewerage systems, on the other hand, are made of large cast-iron pipes; installation normally requires crews of pipefitters. Despite these differences, all pipelayers, plumbers, pipefitters, and steamfitters must be able to follow building plans or blueprints and instructions from supervisors, lay out the job, and work efficiently with the materials and tools of the trade. Computers often are used to create blueprints and plan layouts.

When construction plumbers install piping in a house, for example, they work from blueprints or drawings that show the planned location of pipes, plumbing fixtures, and appliances. Recently, plumbers have become more involved in the design process. Their knowledge of codes and the operation of plumbing systems can cut costs. They first lay out the job to fit the piping into the structure of the house with the least waste of material. Then they measure and mark areas in which pipes will be installed and connected. Construction plumbers also check for obstructions such as electrical wiring and, if necessary, plan the pipe installation around the problem.

Sometimes, plumbers have to cut holes in walls, ceilings, and floors of a house. For some systems, they may hang steel supports from ceiling joists to hold the pipe in place. To assemble a system, plumbers—using saws, pipe cutters, and pipe-bending machines—cut and bend lengths of pipe. They connect lengths of pipe with fittings, using methods that depend on the type of pipe used. For plastic pipe, plumbers connect the sections and fittings with adhesives. For copper pipe, they slide a fitting over the end of the pipe and solder it in place with a torch.

After the piping is in place in the house, plumbers install the fixtures and appliances and connect the system to the outside water or sewer lines. Finally, using pressure gauges, they check the system to ensure that the plumbing works properly.

Working Conditions

Because pipelayers, plumbers, pipefitters, and steamfitters frequently must lift heavy pipes, stand for long periods, and sometimes work in uncomfortable or cramped positions, they need physical strength as well as stamina. They also may have to work outdoors in inclement weather. In addition, they are subject to possible falls from ladders, cuts from sharp tools, and burns from hot pipes or soldering equipment.

Pipelayers, plumbers, pipefitters, and steamfitters engaged in construction generally work a standard 40-hour week; those involved in maintaining pipe systems, including those who provide maintenance services under contract, may have to work evening or weekend shifts, as well as be on call. These maintenance workers may spend quite a bit of time traveling to and from worksites.

Employment

Pipelayers, plumbers, pipefitters, and steamfitters constitute one of the largest construction occupations, holding about 550,000 jobs in 2002. About 7 in 10 worked for plumbing, heating, and air-conditioning contractors engaged in new construction, repair, modernization, or maintenance work. Others did maintenance work for a variety of industrial, commercial, and government employers. For example, pipefitters were employed as maintenance personnel in the petroleum and chemical industries, in which manufacturing operations require the moving of liquids and gases through pipes. About 1 of every 10 pipelayers, plumbers, pipefitters, and steamfitters was self-employed. One in three pipelayers, plumbers, pipefitters, and steamfitters belong to a union.

Jobs for pipelayers, plumbers, pipefitters, and steamfitters are distributed across the country in about the same proportion as the general population.

Training, Other Qualifications, and Advancement

Virtually all pipelayers, plumbers, pipefitters, and steamfitters undergo some type of apprenticeship training. Many apprenticeship programs are administered by local union-management committees made up of members of the United Association of Journeymen and Apprentices of the Plumbing and Pipefitting Industry of the United States and Canada, and local employers who are members of either the Mechanical Contractors Association of America, the National Association of Plumbing-Heating-Cooling Contractors, or the National Fire Sprinkler Association.

Nonunion training and apprenticeship programs are administered by local chapters of the Associated Builders and Contractors, the National Association of Plumbing-Heating-Cooling Contractors, the American Fire Sprinkler Association, or the Home Builders Institute of the National Association of Home Builders.

Apprenticeships—both union and nonunion—consist of 4 or 5 years of on-the-job training, in addition to at least 144 hours per year of related classroom instruction. Classroom subjects include drafting and blueprint reading, mathematics, applied physics and chemistry, safety, and local plumbing codes and regulations. On the job, apprentices first learn basic skills, such as identifying grades and types of pipe, using the tools of the trade, and safely unloading materials. As apprentices gain experience, they learn how to work with various types of pipe and how to install different piping systems and plumbing fixtures. Apprenticeship gives trainees a thorough knowledge of all aspects of the trade. Although most pipelayers, plumbers, pipefitters, and steamfitters are trained through apprenticeship, some still learn their skills informally on the job.

Applicants for union or nonunion apprentice jobs must be at least 18 years old and in good physical condition. Apprenticeship committees may require applicants to have a high school diploma or its equivalent. Armed Forces training in pipelaying, plumbing, and pipefitting is considered very good preparation. In fact, persons with this background may be given credit for previous experience when entering a civilian apprenticeship program. Secondary or postsecondary courses in shop, plumbing, general mathematics, drafting, blueprint reading, computers, and physics also are good preparation.

Although there are no uniform national licensing requirements, most communities require plumbers to be licensed. Licensing requirements vary from area to area, but most localities require workers to pass an examination that tests their knowledge of the trade and of local plumbing codes.

With additional training, some pipelayers, plumbers, pipefitters, and steamfitters become supervisors for mechanical and plumbing contractors. Others, especially plumbers, go into business for themselves, often starting as a self-employed plumber working from home. Some eventually become owners of businesses employing many workers and may spend most of their time as managers rather than as plumbers. Others move into closely related areas such as construction management or building inspection.

Job Outlook

Job opportunities are expected to be excellent, as demand for skilled pipelayers, plumbers, pipefitters, and steamfitters is expected to outpace the supply of workers trained in this craft. Many potential workers may prefer work that is less strenuous and has more comfortable working conditions.

Employment of pipelayers, plumbers, pipefitters, and steamfitters is expected to grow about as fast as the average for all occupations through the year 2012. Demand for plumbers will stem from building renovation, including the increasing installation of sprinkler systems; repair and maintenance of existing residential systems; and maintenance activities for places having extensive systems of pipes, such as powerplants, water and wastewater treatment plants, pipelines, office buildings, and factories. The enforcement of laws pertaining to the certification requirements of workers on jobsites will create additional opportunities and demand for skilled workers. However, the number of new jobs will be limited by the growing use of plastic pipe and fittings, which are much easier to install and repair than other types, and by increasingly efficient sprinkler systems. In addition to new positions resulting from employment growth, many jobs will become available each year because of the need to replace experienced workers who retire or leave the occupation for other reasons.

Traditionally, many organizations with extensive pipe systems have employed their own plumbers or pipefitters to maintain equipment and keep systems running smoothly. But, to reduce labor costs, many of these firms no longer employ a full-time, in-house plumber or pipefitter. Instead, when they need a plumber, they rely on workers provided under service contracts by plumbing and pipefitting contractors.

Construction projects provide only temporary employment. So, when a project ends, pipelayers, plumbers, pipefitters, and steamfitters working on the project may experience bouts of unemployment. Because construction activity varies from area to area, job openings, as well as apprenticeship opportunities, fluctuate with local economic conditions. However, employment of pipelayers, plumbers, pipefitters, and steamfitters generally is less sensitive to changes in economic conditions than is employment of some other construction trades. Even when construction activity declines, maintenance, rehabilitation, and replacement of existing piping systems, as well as the increasing installation of fire sprinkler systems, provide many jobs for pipelayers, plumbers, pipefitters, and steamfitters.

Earnings

Pipelayers, plumbers, pipefitters, and steamfitters are among the highest paid construction occupations. In 2002, median hourly earnings of pipelayers were $13.70. The middle 50 percent earned between $10.96 and $18.43. The lowest 10 percent earned less than $9.20, and the highest 10 percent earned more than $24.31. Also in 2002, median hourly earnings of plumbers, pipefitters, and steamfitters were $19.31. The middle 50 percent earned between $14.68 and $25.87. The lowest 10 percent earned less than $11.23, and the highest 10 percent earned more than $32.27. Median hourly earnings in the industries employing the largest numbers of plumbers, pipefitters, and steamfitters in 2002 are shown below.

Nonresidential building construction $19.65
Building equipment contractors 19.52
Utility system construction 17.81
Ship and boat building 16.62
Local government 16.21

Apprentices usually begin at about 50 percent of the wage rate paid to experienced pipelayers, plumbers, pipefitters, and steamfitters. Wages increase periodically as skills improve. After an initial waiting period, apprentices receive the same benefits as experienced pipelayers, plumbers, pipefitters, and steamfitters.

Many pipelayers, plumbers, pipefitters, and steamfitters are members of the United Association of Journeymen and Apprentices of the Plumbing and Pipefitting Industry of the United States and Canada.

Related Occupations

Other occupations in which workers install and repair mechanical systems in buildings are boilermakers; electri-

cians; elevator installers and repairers; heating, air-conditioning, and refrigeration mechanics and installers; industrial machinery installation, repair, and maintenance workers, except millwrights; millwrights; sheet metal workers; and stationary engineers and boiler operators. Other related occupations include construction managers and construction and building inspectors.

Sources of Additional Information

For information about apprenticeships or work opportunities in pipelaying, plumbing, pipefitting, and steamfitting, contact local plumbing, heating, and air-conditioning contractors; a local or state chapter of the National Association of Plumbing, Heating, and Cooling Contractors; a local chapter of the Mechanical Contractors Association; a local chapter of the United Association of Journeymen and Apprentices of the Plumbing and Pipefitting Industry of the United States and Canada; or the nearest office of your state employment service or apprenticeship agency.

For information about apprenticeship opportunities for pipelayers, plumbers, pipefitters, and steamfitters, contact:

- United Association of Journeymen and Apprentices of the Plumbing and Pipefitting Industry, 901 Massachusetts Ave. NW, Washington, DC 20001. Internet: http://www.ua.org

For more information about training programs for pipelayers, plumbers, pipefitters, and steamfitters, contact:

- Associated Builders and Contractors, Workforce Development Department, 4250 North Fairfax Dr., 9th Floor, Arlington, VA 22203.
- National Association of Home Builders, 1201 15th St. NW, Washington, DC 20005. Internet: http://www.nahb.org
- Home Builders Institute, 1201 15th St. NW, Washington, DC 20005. Internet: http://www.hbi.org

For general information about the work of pipelayers, plumbers, and pipefitters, contact:

- Mechanical Contractors Association of America, 1385 Piccard Dr., Rockville, MD 20850. Internet: http://www.mcaa.org
- National Association of Plumbing-Heating-Cooling Contractors, 180 S. Washington St, Falls Church, VA 22040. Internet: http://www.phccweb.org

For general information about the work of sprinklerfitters, contact:

- American Fire Sprinkler Association, Inc., 9696 Skillman St. Suite 300, Dallas, TX 75243-8264. Internet: http://www.firesprinkler.org
- National Fire Sprinkler Association, P.O. Box 1000, Patterson, NY 12563. Internet: http://www.nfsa.org

There are more than 500 occupations registered by the U.S. Department of Labor's National Apprenticeship system. For more information on the Labor Department's registered apprenticeship system and links to state apprenticeship programs, check their Web site: http://www.doleta.gov.

Police and Detectives

(O*NET 33-1012.00, 33-3021.01, 33-3021.02, 33-3021.03, 33-3021.04, 33-3021.05, 33-3031.00, 33-3051.01, and 33-3051.02)

Significant Points

- Police work can be dangerous and stressful.

- Civil service regulations govern the appointment of police and detectives.

- Competition should remain keen for higher-paying jobs with state and federal agencies and police departments in affluent areas; opportunities will be better in local and special police departments that offer relatively low salaries or in urban communities where the crime rate is relatively high.

- Applicants with college training in police science or military police experience should have the best opportunities.

Nature of the Work

People depend on police officers and detectives to protect their lives and property. Law enforcement officers, some of whom are state or federal special agents or inspectors, perform these duties in a variety of ways, depending on the size and type of their organization. In most jurisdictions, they are expected to exercise authority when necessary, whether on or off duty.

Uniformed police officers who work in municipal police departments of various sizes, small communities, and rural areas have general law enforcement duties including maintaining regular patrols and responding to calls for service. They may direct traffic at the scene of a fire, investigate a burglary, or give first aid to an accident victim. In large police departments, officers usually are assigned to a specific type of duty. Many urban police agencies are becoming more involved in community policing—a practice in which an officer builds relationships with the citizens of local neighborhoods and mobilizes the public to help fight crime.

Police agencies are usually organized into geographic districts, with uniformed officers assigned to patrol a specific area, such as part of the business district or outlying residential neighborhoods. Officers may work alone, but in large agencies they often patrol with a partner. While on patrol, officers attempt to become thoroughly familiar with their patrol area and remain alert for anything unusual. Suspicious circumstances and hazards to public safety are investigated or noted, and officers are dispatched to individual calls for assistance within their district. During their shift, they may identify, pursue, and arrest suspected criminals, resolve problems within the community, and enforce traffic laws.

Public college and university police forces, public school district police, and agencies serving transportation systems and facilities are examples of special police agencies. These agencies have special geographic jurisdictions or enforcement responsibilities in the United states. Most sworn personnel in special agencies are uniformed officers, a smaller number are investigators.

Some police officers specialize in such diverse fields as chemical and microscopic analysis, training and firearms instruction, or handwriting and fingerprint identification. Others work with special units such as horseback, bicycle, motorcycle or harbor patrol, canine corps, or special weapons and tactics (SWAT) or emergency response teams. A few local and special law enforcement officers primarily perform jail-related duties or work in courts. Regardless of job duties or location, police officers and detectives at all levels must write reports and maintain meticulous records that will be needed if they testify in court.

Sheriffs and deputy sheriffs enforce the law on the county level. Sheriffs are usually elected to their posts and perform duties similar to those of a local or county police chief. Sheriffs' departments tend to be relatively small, most having fewer than 25 sworn officers. A deputy sheriff in a large agency will have law enforcement duties similar to those of officers in urban police departments. Police and sheriffs' deputies who provide security in city and county courts are sometimes called bailiffs.

State police officers (sometimes called *state troopers or highway patrol officers*) arrest criminals statewide and patrol highways to enforce motor vehicle laws and regulations. Uniformed officers are best known for issuing traffic citations to motorists who violate the law. At the scene of accidents, they may direct traffic, give first aid, and call for emergency equipment. They also write reports used to determine the cause of the accident. State police officers are frequently called upon to render assistance to other law enforcement agencies, especially those in rural areas or small towns.

State law enforcement agencies operate in every state except Hawaii. Most full-time sworn personnel are uniformed officers who regularly patrol and respond to calls for service. Others are investigators, perform court-related duties, or work in administrative or other assignments.

Detectives are plainclothes investigators who gather facts and collect evidence for criminal cases. Some are assigned to interagency task forces to combat specific types of crime. They conduct interviews, examine records, observe the activities of suspects, and participate in raids or arrests. Detectives and state and federal agents and inspectors usually specialize in one of a wide variety of violations such as homicide or fraud. They are assigned cases on a rotating basis and work on them until an arrest and conviction occurs or the case is dropped.

The federal government maintains a high profile in many areas of law enforcement. *Federal Bureau of Investigation (FBI) agents* are the government's principal investigators, responsible for investigating violations of more than 260 statutes and conducting sensitive national security investigations. Agents may conduct surveillance, monitor court-authorized wiretaps, examine business records, investigate white-collar crime, track the interstate movement of stolen property, collect evidence of espionage activities, or participate in sensitive undercover assignments. The FBI investigates organized crime, public corruption, financial crime, fraud against the government, bribery, copyright infringement, civil rights violations, bank robbery, extortion, kidnapping, air piracy, terrorism, espionage, interstate criminal activity, drug trafficking, and other violations of federal statutes.

U.S. Drug Enforcement Administration (DEA) agents enforce laws and regulations relating to illegal drugs. Not only is the DEA the lead agency for domestic enforcement of federal drug laws, it also has sole responsibility for coordinating and pursuing U.S. drug investigations abroad. Agents may conduct complex criminal investigations, carry out surveillance of criminals, and infiltrate illicit drug organizations using undercover techniques.

U.S. marshals and deputy marshals protect the federal courts and ensure the effective operation of the judicial system. They provide protection for the federal judiciary, transport federal prisoners, protect federal witnesses, and manage assets seized from criminal enterprises. They enjoy the widest jurisdiction of any federal law enforcement agency and are involved to some degree in nearly all federal law enforcement efforts. In addition, U.S. marshals pursue and arrest federal fugitives.

U.S. Immigration and Naturalization Service (INS) agents and inspectors facilitate the entry of legal visitors and immigrants to the U.S. and detain and deport those arriving illegally. They consist of border patrol agents, immigration inspectors, criminal investigators and immigration agents, and detention and deportation officers. *U.S. Border Patrol agents* protect more than 8,000 miles of international land and water boundaries. Their missions are to detect and prevent the smuggling and unlawful entry of undocumented foreign nationals into the U.S., apprehend those persons found in violation of the immigration laws, and interdict contraband, such as narcotics. *Immigration inspectors* interview and examine people seeking entrance to the U.S. and its territories. They inspect passports to determine whether people are legally eligible to enter the United States. Immigration inspectors also prepare reports, maintain records, and process applications and petitions for immigration or temporary residence in the United States.

Bureau of Alcohol, Tobacco, and Firearms (ATF) agents regulate and investigate violations of federal firearms and explosives laws, as well as federal alcohol and tobacco tax regulations. *Customs agents* investigate violations of narcotics smuggling, money laundering, child pornography, customs fraud, and enforcement of the Arms Export Control Act. Domestic and foreign investigations involve the development and use of informants, physical and electronic surveillance, and examination of records from importers/exporters, banks, couriers, and manufacturers. They conduct interviews, serve on joint task forces with other agencies, and get and execute search warrants.

Customs inspectors inspect cargo, baggage, and articles worn or carried by people and carriers including vessels, vehicles, trains and aircraft entering or leaving the U.S. to enforce laws governing imports and exports. These inspectors examine, count, weigh, gauge, measure, and sample commercial and noncommercial cargoes entering and leaving the United States. Customs inspectors seize prohibited or smuggled articles, intercept contraband, and apprehend, search, detain, and arrest violators of U.S. laws.

U.S. Secret Service special agents protect the President, Vice President, and their immediate families; Presidential candidates; former Presidents; and foreign dignitaries visiting the United States. Secret Service agents also investigate counterfeiting, forgery of government checks or bonds, and fraudulent use of credit cards.

The U.S. Department of State *Bureau of Diplomatic Security special agents* are engaged in the battle against terrorism. Overseas, they advise ambassadors on all security matters and manage a complex range of security programs designed to protect personnel, facilities, and information. In the U.S., they investigate passport and visa fraud, conduct personnel security investigations, issue security clearances, and protect the Secretary of State and a number of foreign dignitaries. They also train foreign civilian police and administer a counter-terrorism reward program.

Other federal agencies employ police and special agents with sworn arrest powers and the authority to carry firearms. These agencies include the Postal Service, the Bureau of Indian Affairs Office of Law Enforcement, the Forest Service, the National Park Service, and the Federal Air Marshals.

Working Conditions

Police work can be very dangerous and stressful. In addition to the obvious dangers of confrontations with criminals, officers need to be constantly alert and ready to deal appropriately with a number of other threatening situations. Many law enforcement officers witness death and suffering resulting from accidents and criminal behavior. A career in law enforcement may take a toll on officers' private lives.

Uniformed officers, detectives, agents, and inspectors are usually scheduled to work 40-hour weeks, but paid overtime is common. Shift work is necessary because protection must be provided around the clock. Junior officers frequently work weekends, holidays, and nights. Police officers and detectives are required to work at any time their services are needed and may work long hours during investigations. In most jurisdictions, whether on or off duty, officers are expected to be armed and to exercise their arrest authority whenever necessary.

The jobs of some federal agents such as U.S. Secret Service and DEA special agents require extensive travel, often on very short notice. They may relocate a number of times over the course of their careers. Some special agents in agencies such as the U.S. Border Patrol work outdoors in rugged terrain for long periods and in all kinds of weather.

Employment

Police and detectives held about 840,000 jobs in 2002. About 81 percent were employed by local governments. State police agencies employed about 11 percent and various federal agencies employed about 6 percent. A small proportion worked for educational services, rail transportation, and contract investigation and security services.

According to the U.S. Bureau of Justice Statistics, police and detectives employed by local governments primarily worked in cities with more than 25,000 inhabitants. Some cities have very large police forces, while thousands of small communities employ fewer than 25 officers each.

Training, Other Qualifications, and Advancement

Civil service regulations govern the appointment of police and detectives in practically all states, large municipalities, and special police agencies, as well as in many smaller ones. Candidates must be U.S. citizens, usually at least 20 years of age, and must meet rigorous physical and personal qualifications. In the federal government, candidates must be at least 21 years of age but less than 37 years of age at the time of appointment. Physical examinations for entrance into law enforcement often include tests of vision, hearing, strength, and agility. Eligibility for appointment usually depends on performance in competitive written examinations and previous education and experience. In larger departments, where the majority of law enforcement jobs are found, applicants usually must have at least a high school education. Federal and state agencies typically require a college degree. Candidates should enjoy working with people and meeting the public.

Because personal characteristics such as honesty, sound judgment, integrity, and a sense of responsibility are especially important in law enforcement, candidates are interviewed by senior officers, and their character traits and backgrounds are investigated. In some agencies, candidates are interviewed by a psychiatrist or a psychologist, or given a personality test. Most applicants are subjected to lie detector examinations or drug testing. Some agencies subject sworn personnel to random drug testing as a condition of continuing employment.

Before their first assignments, officers usually go through a period of training. In state and large local departments, recruits get training in their agency's police academy, often for 12 to 14 weeks. In small agencies, recruits often attend a regional or state academy. Training includes classroom instruction in constitutional law and civil rights, state laws and local ordinances, and accident investigation. Recruits also receive training and supervised experience in patrol, traffic control, use of firearms, self-defense, first aid, and emergency response. Police departments in some large cities hire high school graduates who are still in their teens as police cadets or trainees. They do clerical work and attend classes, usually for 1 to 2 years, at which point they reach the minimum age requirement and may be appointed to the regular force.

Police officers usually become eligible for promotion after a probationary period ranging from 6 months to 3 years. In a large department, promotion may enable an officer to become a detective or specialize in one type of police work, such as working with juveniles. Promotions to corporal, sergeant, lieutenant, and captain usually are made according to a candidate's position on a promotion list, as determined by scores on a written examination and on-the-job performance.

To be considered for appointment as an FBI agent, an applicant either must be a graduate of an accredited law school or a college graduate with a major in accounting, fluency in a foreign language, or 3 years of related full-time work experience. All new agents undergo 16 weeks of training at the FBI academy on the U.S. Marine Corps base in Quantico, Virginia.

Applicants for special agent jobs with the U.S. Secret Service and the Bureau of Alcohol, Tobacco, and Firearms must have a bachelor's degree or a minimum of 3 years' related work experience. Prospective special agents undergo 10 weeks of initial criminal investigation training at the Federal Law Enforcement Training Center in Glynco, Georgia, and another 17 weeks of specialized training with their particular agencies.

Applicants for special agent jobs with the U.S. Drug Enforcement Administration (DEA) must have a college degree and either 1 year of experience conducting criminal investigations, 1 year of graduate school, or have achieved at least a 2.95 grade point average while in college. DEA special agents undergo 14 weeks of specialized training at the FBI Academy in Quantico, Virginia.

U.S. Border Patrol agents must be U.S. citizens, be younger than 37 years of age at the time of appointment, possess a valid driver's license, and pass a three-part examination on reasoning and language skills. A bachelor's degree or previous work experience that demonstrates the ability to handle stressful situations, make decisions, and take charge is required for a position as a Border Patrol agent. Applicants may qualify through a combination of education and work experience.

Postal inspectors must have a bachelor's degree and 1 year of related work experience. It is desirable that they have one of several professional certifications, such as that of certified public accountant. They also must pass a background suitability investigation, meet certain health requirements, undergo a drug screening test, possess a valid state driver's license, and be a U.S. citizen between 21 and 36 years of age when hired.

Law enforcement agencies are encouraging applicants to take postsecondary school training in law enforcement-related subjects. Many entry-level applicants for police jobs have completed some formal postsecondary education and a significant number are college graduates. Many junior colleges, colleges, and universities offer programs in law enforcement or administration of justice. Other courses helpful in preparing for a career in law enforcement include accounting, finance, electrical engineering, computer science, and foreign languages. Physical education and sports are helpful in developing the competitiveness, stamina, and agility needed for many law enforcement positions. Knowledge of a foreign language is an asset in many Federal agencies and urban departments.

Continuing training helps police officers, detectives, and special agents improve their job performance. Through police department academies, regional centers for public safety employees established by the states, and federal agency training centers, instructors provide annual training in self-defense tactics, firearms, use-of-force policies, sensitivity and communications skills, crowd-control techniques, relevant legal developments, and advances in law enforcement equipment. Many agencies pay all or part of the tuition for officers to work toward degrees in criminal justice, police science, administration of justice, or public administration, and pay higher salaries to those who earn such a degree.

Job Outlook

The opportunity for public service through law enforcement work is attractive to many because the job is challenging and involves much personal responsibility. Furthermore, law enforcement officers in many agencies may retire with a pension after 20 or 25 years of service, allowing them to pursue a second career while still in their 40s. Because of relatively attractive salaries and benefits, the number of qualified candidates exceeds the number of job openings in Federal law enforcement agencies and in most state police departments—resulting in increased hiring standards and selectivity by employers. Competition should remain keen for higher paying jobs with state and federal agencies and police departments in more affluent areas. Opportunities will be better in local and special police departments, especially in departments that offer relatively low salaries, or in urban communities where the crime rate is relatively high. Applicants with college training in police science, military police experience, or both should have the best opportunities.

Employment of police and detectives is expected to grow faster than the average for all occupations through 2012. A more security-conscious society and concern about drug-related crimes should contribute to the increasing demand for police services.

The level of government spending determines the level of employment for police and detectives. The number of job opportunities, therefore, can vary from year to year and from place to place. Layoffs, on the other hand, are rare because retirements enable most staffing cuts to be handled through attrition. Trained law enforcement officers who lose their jobs because of budget cuts usually have little difficulty finding jobs with other agencies. The need to replace workers who retire, transfer to other occupations, or stop working for other reasons will be the source of many job openings.

Earnings

Police and sheriff's patrol officers had median annual earnings of $42,270 in 2002. The middle 50 percent earned between $32,300 and $53,500. The lowest 10 percent earned less than $25,270, and the highest 10 percent earned more than $65,330. Median annual earnings were $47,090 in state government, $42,020 in local government, and $41,600 in federal government.

In 2002, median annual earnings of police and detective supervisors were $61,010. The middle 50 percent earned between $47,210 and $74,610. The lowest 10 percent earned less than $36,340, and the highest 10 percent earned more than $90,070. Median annual earnings were $78,230 in federal government, $64,410 in state government, and $59,830 in local government.

In 2002, median annual earnings of detectives and criminal investigators were $51,410. The middle 50 percent earned between $39,010 and $65,980. The lowest 10 percent earned less than $31,010, and the highest 10 percent earned more than $80,380. Median annual earnings were $66,500 in federal government, $47,700 in local government, and $46,600 in state government.

Federal law provides special salary rates to federal employees who serve in law enforcement. Additionally, federal special agents and inspectors receive law enforcement availability pay (LEAP)—equal to 25 percent of the agent's grade and step—awarded because of the large amount of overtime that these agents are expected to work. For example, in 2003 FBI agents enter federal service as GS-10 employees on the pay scale at a base salary of $39,115, yet earned about $48,890 a year with availability pay. They can advance to the GS-13 grade level in field nonsupervisory assignments at a base salary of $61,251, which is worth $76,560 with availability pay. FBI supervisory, management, and executive positions in grades GS-14 and GS-15 pay a base salary of about $72,381 or $85,140 a year, respectively, and equaled $90,480 or $106,430 per year including availability pay. Salaries were slightly higher in selected areas where the prevailing local pay level was higher. Because federal agents may be eligible for a special law enforcement benefits package, applicants should ask their recruiter for more information.

According to the International City-County Management Association's annual Police and Fire Personnel, Salaries, and Expenditures Survey, average salaries for sworn full-time positions in 2002 were as follows:

	Minimum annual base salary	Maximum annual base salary
Police chief	$68,337	$87,037
Deputy chief	59,790	75,266

Police captain	56,499	70,177
Police lieutenant	52,446	63,059
Police sergeant	46,805	55,661
Police corporal	39,899	49,299

Total earnings for local, state, and special police and detectives frequently exceed the stated salary because of payments for overtime, which can be significant. In addition to the common benefits—paid vacation, sick leave, and medical and life insurance—most police and sheriffs' departments provide officers with special allowances for uniforms. Because police officers usually are covered by liberal pension plans, many retire at half pay after 20 or 25 years of service.

Related Occupations

Police and detectives maintain law and order, collect evidence and information, and conduct investigations and surveillance. Workers in related occupations include correctional officers, private detectives and investigators, and security guards and gaming surveillance officers.

Sources of Additional Information

Information about entrance requirements may be obtained from federal, state, and local law enforcement agencies.

Further information about qualifications for employment as a FBI Special Agent is available from the nearest state FBI office. The address and phone number are listed in the local telephone directory. Internet: http://www.fbi.gov.

Information on career opportunities, qualifications, and training for U.S. Secret Service Special Agents is available from the Secret Service Personnel Division at (202) 406-5800, (888) 813-8777 or (888) 813-USSS. Internet: http://www.treas.gov/usss.

Information about qualifications for employment as a DEA Special Agent is available from the nearest DEA office, or call (800) DEA-4288. Internet: http://www.usdoj.gov/dea

Information about career opportunities, qualifications, and training to become a deputy marshal is available from:

- U.S. Marshals Service, Human Resources Division—Law Enforcement Recruiting, Washington, DC 20530-1000. Internet: http://www.usdoj.gov/marshals

For information on operations and career opportunities in the U.S. Bureau of Alcohol, Tobacco and Firearms operations, contact:

- U.S. Bureau of Alcohol, Tobacco and Firearms, Personnel Division, 650 Massachusetts Ave. NW, Room 4100, Washington, DC 20226. Internet: http://www.atf.treas.gov

Information about careers in U.S. Customs and Border Protection is available from:

- U.S. Customs and Border Protection, 1300 Pennsylvania Ave., NW, Washington, DC 20229. Internet: http://www.cbp.gov

Psychologists

(O*NET 19-3031.01, 19-3031.02, 19-3031.03, and 19-3032.00)

Significant Points

- More than 1 out of 4 psychologists are self-employed, nearly four times the average for professional workers.

- Most specialists, including clinical and counseling psychologists, need a doctoral degree; school and industrial-organizational psychologists need a master's degree.

- Opportunities in psychology are limited for those with only a bachelor's degree.

Nature of the Work

Psychologists study the human mind and human behavior. Research psychologists investigate the physical, cognitive, emotional, or social aspects of human behavior. Psychologists in health service provider fields provide mental health care in hospitals, clinics, schools, or private settings. Psychologists employed in applied settings such as business, industry, government or non-profits provide training, conduct research, design systems, and act as advocates for psychology.

Like other social scientists, psychologists formulate hypotheses and collect data to test their validity. Research methods vary depending on the topic under study. Psychologists sometimes gather information through controlled laboratory experiments or by administering personality, performance, aptitude, and intelligence tests. Other methods include observation, interviews, questionnaires, clinical studies, and surveys.

Psychologists apply their knowledge to a wide range of endeavors, including health and human services, management, education, law, and sports. In addition to working in a variety of settings, psychologists usually specialize in one of a number of different areas.

Clinical psychologists—who constitute the largest specialty—most often work in counseling centers, independent or group practices, hospitals, or clinics. They help mentally and emotionally disturbed clients adjust to life and may help medical and surgical patients deal with illnesses or injuries. Some clinical psychologists work in physical rehabilitation settings, treating patients with spinal cord injuries, chronic pain or illness, stroke, arthritis, and neurological conditions. Others help people deal with times of personal crisis, such as divorce or the death of a loved one.

Clinical psychologists often interview patients and give diagnostic tests. They may provide individual, family, or group psychotherapy, and design and implement behavior modification programs. Some clinical psychologists collaborate with physicians and other specialists to develop and implement treatment and intervention programs that patients can understand and comply with. Other clinical psychologists work in universities and medical schools, where they train graduate students in the delivery of mental health and behavioral medicine services. Some administer community mental health programs.

Areas of specialization within clinical psychology include health psychology, neuropsychology, and geropsychology. *Health psychologists* promote good health through health maintenance counseling programs designed to help people achieve goals, such as to stop smoking or lose weight. *Neuropsychologists* study the relation between the brain and behavior. They often work in stroke and head injury programs. *Geropsychologists* deal with the special problems faced by the elderly. The emergence and growth of these specialties reflects the increasing participation of psychologists in providing direct services to special patient populations.

Often, clinical psychologists will consult with other medical personnel regarding the best treatment for patients, especially treatment that includes medications. Clinical psychologists generally are not permitted to prescribe medications to treat patients; only psychiatrists and other medical doctors may prescribe medications. However, one state, New Mexico, has passed legislation allowing clinical psychologists who undergo additional training to prescribe medication, and similar proposals have been made in additional states.

Counseling psychologists use various techniques, including interviewing and testing, to advise people on how to deal with problems of everyday living. They work in settings such as university counseling centers, hospitals, and individual or group practices.

School psychologists work in elementary and secondary schools or school district offices to resolve students' learning and behavior problems. They collaborate with teachers, parents, and school personnel to improve classroom management strategies or parenting skills, counter substance abuse, work with students with disabilities or gifted and talented students, and improve teaching and learning strategies. They may evaluate the effectiveness of academic programs, behavior management procedures, and other services provided in the school setting.

Industrial-organizational psychologists apply psychological principles and research methods to the workplace in the interest of improving productivity and the quality of work-life. They also are involved in research on management and marketing problems. They conduct applicant screening, training and development, counseling, and organizational development and analysis. An industrial psychologist might work with management to reorganize the work setting to improve productivity or quality of life in the workplace. They frequently act as consultants, brought in by management in order to solve a particular problem.

Developmental psychologists study the physiological, cognitive, and social development that takes place throughout life. Some specialize in behavior during infancy, childhood, and adolescence, or changes that occur during maturity or old age. They also may study developmental disabilities and their effects. Increasingly, research is developing ways to help elderly people remain independent as long as possible.

Social psychologists examine people's interactions with others and with the social environment. They work in organizational consultation, marketing research, systems design, or other applied psychology fields. Prominent areas of study include group behavior, leadership, attitudes, and perception.

Experimental or *research psychologists* work in university and private research centers and in business, nonprofit, and governmental organizations. They study behavior processes using human beings and animals, such as rats, monkeys, and pigeons. Prominent areas of study in experimental research include motivation, thought, attention, learning and memory, sensory and perceptual processes, effects of substance abuse, and genetic and neurological factors affecting behavior.

Working Conditions

A psychologist's subfield and place of employment determine working conditions. Clinical, school, and counseling psychologists in private practice have their own offices and set their own hours. However, they often offer evening and weekend hours to accommodate their clients. Those employed in hospitals, nursing homes, and other health facilities may work shifts including evenings and weekends, while those who work in schools and clinics generally work regular hours.

Psychologists employed as faculty by colleges and universities divide their time between teaching and research and also may have administrative responsibilities. Many have part-time consulting practices. Most psychologists in government and industry have structured schedules.

Increasingly, many psychologists work as part of a team and consult with other psychologists and professionals. Many experience pressures due to deadlines, tight schedules, and overtime work. Their routine may be interrupted frequently. Travel usually is required, in order to attend conferences or conduct research.

Employment

Psychologists held about 139,000 jobs in 2002. Educational institutions employed about 3 out of 10 salaried psychologists in positions other than teaching, such as counseling, testing, research, and administration. Three out of 10 were employed in health care, primarily in offices of mental health practitioners and in outpatient care facilities, private hospitals, nursing and residential care facilities, and individual and family service organizations. Government agencies at the state and local levels employed 1 in 10 psychologists, primarily in public hospitals, clinics, correctional facilities, and other settings. Some psychologists work in, research organizations, management consulting firms, marketing research firms, religious organizations, and other businesses.

After several years of experience, some psychologists—usually those with doctoral degrees—enter private practice or set up private research or consulting firms. More than 1 out of 4 psychologists were self-employed.

In addition to the jobs described above, many psychologists held faculty positions at colleges and universities, and as high school psychology teachers.

Training, Other Qualifications, and Advancement

A doctoral degree usually is required for employment as an independent licensed clinical or counseling psychologist. Psychologists with a Ph.D. qualify for a wide range of teaching, research, clinical, and counseling positions in universities, healthcare services, elementary and secondary schools, private industry, and government. Psychologists with a Doctor of Psychology (Psy.D.) degree usually work in clinical positions or in private practices.

A doctoral degree usually requires 5 to 7 years of graduate study. The Ph.D. degree culminates in a dissertation based on original research. Courses in quantitative research methods, which include the use of computer-based analysis, are an integral part of graduate study and are necessary to complete the dissertation. The Psy.D. may be based on practical work and examinations rather than a dissertation. In clinical or counseling psychology, the requirements for the doctoral degree usually include at least a 1-year internship.

Persons with a master's degree in psychology may work as industrial-organizational psychologists or school psychologists. They also may work as psychological assistants, under the supervision of doctoral-level psychologists, and conduct research or psychological evaluations. A master's degree in psychology requires at least 2 years of full-time graduate study. Requirements usually include practical experience in an applied setting and a master's thesis based on an original research project. Competition for admission to graduate programs is keen. Some universities require applicants to have an undergraduate major in psychology. Others prefer only coursework in basic psychology with courses in the biological, physical, and social sciences; and statistics and mathematics.

A bachelor's degree in psychology qualifies a person to assist psychologists and other professionals in community mental health centers, vocational rehabilitation offices, and correctional programs. They may work as research or administrative assistants or become sales or management trainees in business. Some work as technicians in related fields, such as marketing research.

In the federal government, candidates having at least 24 semester hours in psychology and one course in statistics qualify for entry-level positions. However, competition for these jobs is keen because this is one of the few areas in which one can work as a psychologist without an advanced degree.

The American Psychological Association (APA) presently accredits doctoral training programs in clinical, counseling, and school psychology. The National Council for Accreditation of Teacher Education, with the assistance of the National Association of School Psychologists, also is involved in the accreditation of advanced degree programs in school psychology. The APA also accredits institutions that provide internships for doctoral students in school, clinical, and counseling psychology.

Psychologists in independent practice or those who offer any type of patient care—including clinical, counseling, and school psychologists—must meet certification or licensing requirements in all states and the District of Columbia. Licensing laws vary by state and by type of position and require licensed or certified psychologists to limit their practice to areas in which they have developed professional competence through training and experience. Clinical and counseling psychologists usually require a doctorate in psychology, completion of an approved internship, and 1 to 2 years of professional experience. In addition, all states require that applicants pass an examination. Most state licensing boards administer a standardized test, and many supplement that with additional oral or essay questions. Most states certify those with a master's degree as school psychologists after completion of an internship. Some states require continuing education for license renewal.

The National Association of School Psychologists (NASP) awards the Nationally Certified School Psychologist (NCSP) designation, which recognizes professional competency in school psychology at a national level, rather than at a state level. Currently, 22 states recognize the NCSP and allow those with the certification to transfer credentials from one state to another without taking a new state certification exam. In those states that recognize the NCSP, the requirements for state licensure and the NCSP often are the same or similar. Requirements for the NCSP include completion of 60 graduate semester hours in school psychology; a 1,200-hour internship, 600 hours of which must be completed in a school setting; and a passing score on the National School Psychology Examination.

The American Board of Professional Psychology (ABPP) recognizes professional achievement by awarding specialty certification, primarily in clinical psychology, clinical neuropsychology, and counseling, forensic, industrial-organizational, and school psychology. Candidates for ABPP certification need a doctorate in psychology, postdoctoral training in their specialty, 5 years of experience, professional endorsements, and a passing grade on an examination.

Aspiring psychologists who are interested in direct patient care must be emotionally stable, mature, and able to deal effectively with people. Sensitivity, compassion, good communication skills, and the ability to lead and inspire others are particularly important qualities for persons wishing to do clinical work and counseling. Research psychologists should be able to do detailed work independently and as part of a team. Patience and perseverance are vital qualities because achieving results from psychological treatment of patients or from research usually takes a long time.

Job Outlook

Overall employment of psychologists is expected to grow faster than the average for all occupations through 2012, due to increased demand for psychological services in schools, hospitals, social service agencies, mental health centers, substance abuse treatment clinics, consulting firms, and private companies. Clinical, counseling, and school psychologists will grow faster than the average, while industrial-organizational psychologists will have average growth.

Among the specialties in this field, school psychologists may enjoy the best job opportunities. Growing awareness of how students' mental health and behavioral problems, such as bullying, affect learning is increasing demand for school psychologists to offer student counseling and mental health services. Clinical and counseling psychologists will be needed to help people deal with depression and other mental disorders, marriage and family problems, job stress, and addiction. The rise in healthcare costs associated with unhealthy lifestyles, such as smoking, alcoholism, and obesity, has made prevention and treatment more critical. The increase in the number of employee assistance programs, which help workers deal with personal problems, also should spur job growth in clinical and counseling specialties. Industrial-organizational psychologists will be in demand to help to boost worker productivity and retention rates in a wide range of businesses. Industrial-organizational psychologists will help companies deal with issues such as workplace diversity and antidiscrimination policies. Companies also will use psychologists' expertise in survey design, analysis, and research to develop tools for marketing evaluation and statistical analysis.

Demand should be particularly strong for persons holding doctorates from leading universities in applied specialties, such as counseling, health, and school psychology. Psychologists with extensive training in quantitative research methods and computer science may have a competitive edge over applicants without this background.

Master's degree holders in fields other than school or industrial-organizational psychology will face keen competition for jobs, because of the limited number of positions that require only a master's degree. Master's degree holders may find jobs as psychological assistants or counselors, providing mental health services under the direct supervision of a licensed psychologist. Still others may find jobs involving research and data collection and analysis in universities, government, or private companies.

Opportunities directly related to psychology will be limited for bachelor's degree holders. Some may find jobs as assistants in rehabilitation centers or in other jobs involving data collection and analysis. Those who meet state certification requirements may become high school psychology teachers.

Earnings

Median annual earnings of wage and salary clinical, counseling, and school psychologists in 2002 were $51,170. The middle 50 percent earned between $38,560 and $66,970. The lowest 10 percent earned less than $30,090, and the highest 10 percent earned more than $87,060. Median annual earnings in the industries employing the largest numbers of clinical, counseling, and school psychologists in 2002 were as follows:

Offices of other health practitioners $59,600

Elementary and secondary schools 54,480

Offices of physicians 51,140

Outpatient care centers 44,010

Individual and family services................................37,490

Median annual earnings of wage and salary industrial-organizational psychologists in 2002 were $63,710. The middle 50 percent earned between $48,540 and $81,880. The lowest 10 percent earned less than $36,620, and the highest 10 percent earned more than $112,660.

Related Occupations

Psychologists are trained to conduct research and teach, evaluate, counsel, and advise individuals and groups with special needs. Others who do this kind of work include: clergy, counselors, physicians and surgeons, social workers, sociologists, and special education teachers.

Sources of Additional Information

For information on careers, educational requirements, financial assistance, and licensing in all fields of psychology, contact:

- American Psychological Association, 750 1st St. NE, Washington, DC 20002. Internet: http://www.apa.org

For information on careers, educational requirements, certification, and licensing of school psychologists, contact:

- National Association of School Psychologists, 4340 East West Hwy., Suite 402, Bethesda, MD 20814. Internet: http://www.nasponline.org

Information about state licensing requirements is available from:

- Association of State and Provincial Psychology Boards, P.O. Box 241245, Montgomery, AL 36124-1245. Internet: http://www.asppb.org

Information about psychology specialty certifications is available from:

- American Board of Professional Psychology, Inc., 514 East Capitol Ave., Jefferson City, MO 65101. Internet: http://www.abpp.org

Public Relations Specialists

(O*NET 27-3031.00)

Significant Points

- Although employment is projected to increase faster than average, keen competition is expected for entry-level jobs.

- Opportunities should be best for college graduates who combine a degree in public relations, journalism, or another communications-related field with a public relations internship or other related work experience.

- The ability to communicate effectively is essential.

Nature of the Work

An organization's reputation, profitability, and even its continued existence can depend on the degree to which its targeted "publics" support its goals and policies. Public relations specialists—also referred to as communications specialists and media specialists, among other titles—serve as advocates for businesses, nonprofit associations, universities, hospitals, and other organizations, and build and maintain positive relationships with the public. As managers recognize the growing importance of good public relations to the success of their organizations, they increasingly rely on public relations specialists for advice on the strategy and policy of such programs.

Public relations specialists handle organizational functions such as media, community, consumer, industry, and governmental relations; political campaigns; interest-group representation; conflict mediation; or employee and investor relations. They help an organization and its public adapt mutually to each other. However, public relations are not only about "telling the organization's story." Understanding the attitudes and concerns of consumers, employees, and various other groups also is a vital part of the job. To improve communication, public relations specialists establish and maintain cooperative relationships with representatives of community, consumer, employee, and public interest groups, and with representatives from print and broadcast journalism.

Informing the general public, interest groups, and stockholders of an organization's policies, activities, and accomplishments is an important part of a public relations specialist's job. The work also involves keeping management aware of public attitudes and the concerns of the many groups and organizations with which they must deal.

Media specialists draft press releases and contact people in the media who might print or broadcast their material. Many radio or television special reports, newspaper stories, and magazine articles start at the desks of public relations specialists. Sometimes, the subject is an organization and its policies towards its employees or its role in the community. Often, the subject is a public issue, such as health, energy, or the environment.

Public affairs specialists also arrange and conduct programs to keep up contact between organization representatives and the public. For example, they set up speaking engagements and often prepare speeches for company officials. These media specialists represent employers at community projects; make film, slide, or other visual presentations at meetings and school assemblies; and plan conventions. In addition, they are responsible for preparing annual reports and writing proposals for various projects.

In government, public relations specialists—who may be called press secretaries, information officers, public affairs specialists, or communication specialists—keep the public informed about the activities of government agencies and officials. For example, public affairs specialists in the U.S. Department of State keep the public informed of travel advisories and of U.S. positions on foreign issues. A press secretary for a member of Congress keeps constituents aware of the representative's accomplishments.

In large organizations, the key public relations executive, who often is a vice president, may develop overall plans and policies with other executives. In addition, public relations departments employ public relations specialists to write, research, prepare materials, maintain contacts, and respond to inquiries.

People who handle publicity for an individual or who direct public relations for a small organization may deal with all aspects of the job. They contact people, plan and research, and prepare materials for distribution. They also may handle advertising or sales promotion work to support marketing.

Working Conditions

Some public relations specialists work a standard 35- to 40-hour week, but unpaid overtime is common. Occasionally, they must be at the job or on call around the clock, especially if there is an emergency or crisis. Public relations offices are busy places; work schedules can be irregular and frequently interrupted. Schedules often have to be rearranged so that workers can meet deadlines, deliver speeches, attend meetings and community activities, or travel.

Employment

Public relations specialists held about 158,000 jobs in 2002. Public relations specialists are concentrated in service-providing industries such as advertising and related services; health care and social assistance; educational services; and government. Others worked for communications firms, financial institutions, and government agencies. About 11,000 public relations specialists were self-employed.

Public relations specialists are concentrated in large cities, where press services and other communications facilities are readily available and many businesses and trade associations have their headquarters. Many public relations consulting firms, for example, are in New York, Los Angeles, San Francisco, Chicago, and Washington, DC. There is a trend, however, for public relations jobs to be dispersed throughout the nation, closer to clients.

Training, Other Qualifications, and Advancement

There are no defined standards for entry into a public relations career. A college degree combined with public relations experience, usually gained through an internship, is considered excellent preparation for public relations work; in fact, internships are becoming vital to obtaining employment. The ability to communicate effectively is essential. Many entry-level public relations specialists have a college major in public relations, journalism, advertising, or communication. Some firms seek college graduates who have worked in electronic or print journalism. Other employers seek applicants with demonstrated communication skills and training or experience in a field related to the firm's business—information technology, health, science, engineering, sales, or finance, for example.

Many colleges and universities offer bachelor's and postsecondary degrees in public relations, usually in a journalism or communications department. In addition, many other colleges offer at least one course in this field. A common public relations sequence includes courses in public relations principles and techniques; public relations management and administration, including organizational development; writing, emphasizing news releases, proposals, annual reports, scripts, speeches, and related items; visual communications, including desktop publishing and computer graphics; and research, emphasizing social science research and survey design and implementation. Courses in advertising, journalism, business administration, finance, political science, psychology, sociology, and creative writing also are helpful. Specialties are offered in public relations for business, government, and nonprofit organizations.

Many colleges help students gain part-time internships in public relations that provide valuable experience and training. The U.S. Armed Forces also can be an excellent place to gain training and experience. Membership in local chapters of the Public Relations Student Society of America (affiliated with the Public Relations Society of America) or the International Association of Business Communicators provides an opportunity for students to exchange views with public relations specialists and to make professional contacts that may help them find a job in the field. A portfolio of published articles, television or radio programs, slide presentations, and other work is an asset in finding a job. Writing for a school publication or television or radio station provides valuable experience and material for one's portfolio.

Creativity, initiative, good judgment, and the ability to express thoughts clearly and simply are essential. Decision making, problem-solving, and research skills also are impor-

tant. People who choose public relations as a career need an outgoing personality, self-confidence, an understanding of human psychology, and an enthusiasm for motivating people. They should be competitive, yet able to function as part of a team and open to new ideas.

Some organizations, particularly those with large public relations staffs, have formal training programs for new employees. In smaller organizations, new employees work under the guidance of experienced staff members. Beginners often maintain files of material about company activities, scan newspapers and magazines for appropriate articles to clip, and assemble information for speeches and pamphlets. They also may answer calls from the press and public, work on invitation lists and details for press conferences, or escort visitors and clients. After gaining experience, they write news releases, speeches, and articles for publication or design and carry out public relations programs. Public relations specialists in smaller firms usually get all-around experience, whereas those in larger firms tend to be more specialized.

The Public Relations Society of America accredits public relations specialists who have at least 5 years of experience in the field and have passed a comprehensive 6-hour examination (5 hours written, 1 hour oral). The International Association of Business Communicators also has an accreditation program for professionals in the communication field, including public relations specialists. Those who meet all the requirements of the program earn the Accredited Business Communicator (ABC) designation. Candidates must have at least 5 years of experience in a communication field and pass a written and oral examination. They also must submit a portfolio of work samples demonstrating involvement in a range of communication projects and a thorough understanding of communication planning. Employers may consider professional recognition through accreditation a sign of competence in this field, which could be especially helpful in a competitive job market.

Promotion to supervisory jobs may come as public relations specialists show that they can handle more demanding assignments. In public relations firms, a beginner might be hired as a research assistant or account coordinator and be promoted to account executive, senior account executive, account manager, and, eventually, vice president. A similar career path is followed in corporate public relations, although the titles may differ. Some experienced public relations specialists start their own consulting firms.

Job Outlook

Keen competition will likely continue for entry-level public relations jobs, as the number of qualified applicants is expected to exceed the number of job openings. Many people are attracted to this profession due to the high-profile nature of the work. Opportunities should be best for college graduates who combine a degree in journalism, public relations, advertising, or another communications-related field with a public relations internship or other related work experience. Applicants without the appropriate educational background or work experience will face the toughest obstacles.

Employment of public relations specialists is expected to increase faster than the average for all occupations through 2012. The need for good public relations in an increasingly competitive business environment should spur demand for public relations specialists in organizations of all types and sizes. The value of a company is measured not just by its balance sheet, but also by the strength of its relationships with those upon whom it depends for its success. And, in the wake of corporate scandals, more emphasis will be placed on improving the image of the client, as well as building public confidence.

Employment in public relations firms should grow as firms hire contractors to provide public relations services rather than support full-time staff. In addition to those arising from employment growth, job opportunities should result from the need to replace public relations specialists who take other jobs or who leave the occupation altogether.

Earnings

Median annual earnings for salaried public relations specialists were $41,710 in 2002. The middle 50 percent earned between $31,300 and $56,180; the lowest 10 percent earned less than $24,240, and the top 10 percent earned more than $75,100. Median annual earnings in the industries employing the largest numbers of public relations specialists in 2002 were:

Advertising and related services $48,070

Local government 42,000

Business, professional, labor, political, and
similar organizations 39,330

Colleges, universities, and professional schools 36,820

According to a joint survey conducted by the International Association of Business Communicators and the Public Relations Society of America, the median annual income for a public relations specialist was $66,800 in 2002.

Related Occupations

Public relations specialists create favorable attitudes among various organizations, special interest groups, and the public through effective communication. Other workers with similar jobs include advertising, marketing, promotions, public relations, and sales managers; demonstrators, product promoters, and models; news analysts, reporters, and correspondents; lawyers; market and survey researchers; sales representatives, wholesale and manufacturing; and police and detectives involved in community relations.

Sources of Additional Information

A comprehensive directory of schools offering degree programs, a sequence of study in public relations, a brochure on careers in public relations, and a $5 brochure entitled *Where Shall I Go to Study Advertising and Public Relations* are available from:

- Public Relations Society of America, Inc., 33 Irving Place, New York, NY 10003-2376. Internet: http://www.prsa.org

For information on accreditation for public relations professionals, contact:

- International Association of Business Communicators, One Hallidie Plaza, Suite 600, San Francisco, CA 94102.

Radiologic Technologists and Technicians

(O*NET 29-2034.01)

Significant Points

- Formal training programs in radiography range in length from 1 to 4 years and lead to a certificate, associate degree, or bachelor's degree.

- Although hospitals will remain the primary employer, a greater number of new jobs will be found in physicians' offices and diagnostic imaging centers.

- Job opportunities are expected to be favorable; some employers report difficulty hiring sufficient numbers of radiologic technologists and technicians.

Nature of the Work

Radiologic technologists and technicians take x rays and administer nonradioactive materials into patients' bloodstreams for diagnostic purposes. Some specialize in diagnostic imaging technologies, such as computerized tomography (CT) and magnetic resonance imaging (MRI).

In addition to radiologic technologists and technicians, others who conduct diagnostic imaging procedures include cardiovascular technologists and technicians, diagnostic medical sonographers, and nuclear medicine technologists.

Radiologic technologists and technicians, also referred to as *radiographers*, produce x ray films (radiographs) of parts of the human body for use in diagnosing medical problems. They prepare patients for radiologic examinations by explaining the procedure, removing articles such as jewelry, through which x rays cannot pass, and positioning patients so that the parts of the body can be appropriately radiographed. To prevent unnecessary radiation exposure, these workers surround the exposed area with radiation protection devices, such as lead shields, or limit the size of the x ray beam. Radiographers position radiographic equipment at the correct angle and height over the appropriate area of a patient's body. Using instruments similar to a measuring tape, they may measure the thickness of the section to be radiographed and set controls on the x ray machine to produce radiographs of the appropriate density, detail, and contrast. They place the x ray film under the part of the patient's body to be examined and make the exposure. They then remove the film and develop it.

Experienced radiographers may perform more complex imaging procedures. For fluoroscopies, radiographers prepare a solution of contrast medium for the patient to drink, allowing the radiologist (a physician who interprets radiographs) to see soft tissues in the body. Some radiographers, called *CT technologists*, operate CT scanners to produce cross-sectional images of patients. Radiographers who operate machines that use strong magnets and radio waves, rather than radiation, to create an image are called *MRI technologists*.

Radiologic technologists and technicians must follow physicians' orders precisely and conform to regulations concerning the use of radiation to protect themselves, their patients, and their coworkers from unnecessary exposure.

In addition to preparing patients and operating equipment, radiologic technologists and technicians keep patient records and adjust and maintain equipment. They also may prepare work schedules, evaluate equipment purchases, or manage a radiology department.

Working Conditions

Most full-time radiologic technologists and technicians work about 40 hours a week; they may have evening, weekend, or on-call hours. Opportunities for part-time and shift work also are available.

Because technologists and technicians are on their feet for long periods and may lift or turn disabled patients, physical stamina is important. Technologists and technicians work at diagnostic machines, but may also perform some procedures at patients' bedsides. Some travel to patients in large vans equipped with sophisticated diagnostic equipment.

Although radiation hazards exist in this occupation, they are minimized by the use of lead aprons, gloves, and other shielding devices, as well as by instruments monitoring radiation exposure. Technologists and technicians wear badges measuring radiation levels in the radiation area, and detailed records are kept on their cumulative lifetime dose.

Employment

Radiologic technologists and technicians held about 174,100 jobs in 2002. Almost 1 in 5 worked part time. About half of all jobs were in hospitals. Most of the rest were in offices of physicians; medical and diagnostic laboratories, including diagnostic imaging centers; and outpatient care centers.

Training, Other Qualifications, and Advancement

Preparation for this profession is offered in hospitals, colleges and universities, vocational-technical institutes, and the U.S. Armed Forces. Hospitals, which employ most radio-logic technologists and technicians, prefer to hire those with formal training.

Formal training programs in radiography range in length from 1 to 4 years and lead to a certificate, associate degree, or bachelor's degree. Two-year associate degree programs are most prevalent.

Some 1-year certificate programs are available for experienced radiographers or individuals from other health occupations, such as medical technologists and registered nurses, who want to change fields or specialize in CT or MRI. A bachelor's or master's degree in one of the radiologic technologies is desirable for supervisory, administrative, or teaching positions.

The Joint Review Committee on Education in Radiologic Technology accredits most formal training programs for the field. The committee accredited 587 radiography programs in 2003. Radiography programs require, at a minimum, a high school diploma or the equivalent. High school courses in mathematics, physics, chemistry, and biology are helpful. The programs provide both classroom and clinical instruction in anatomy and physiology, patient care procedures, radiation physics, radiation protection, principles of imaging, medical terminology, positioning of patients, medical ethics, radiobiology, and pathology.

Federal legislation protects the public from the hazards of unnecessary exposure to medical and dental radiation by ensuring operators of radiologic equipment are properly trained. Under this legislation, the federal government sets voluntary standards that the states, in turn, may use for accrediting training programs and certifying individuals who engage in medical or dental radiography.

In 2003, about 38 states licensed radiologic technologists and technicians. Voluntary registration is offered by the American Registry of Radiologic Technologists. To be eligible for registration, technologists generally must have graduated from an accredited program and pass an examination. Many employers prefer to hire registered radiographers. To be recertified, radiographers must complete 24 hours of continuing education every other year.

Radiologic technologists and technicians should be sensitive to patients' physical and psychological needs. They must pay attention to detail, follow instructions, and work as part of a team. In addition, operating complicated equipment requires mechanical ability and manual dexterity.

With experience and additional training, staff technologists may become specialists, performing CT scanning, angiography, and magnetic resonance imaging. Experienced technologists also may be promoted to supervisor, chief radiologic technologist, and, ultimately, department administrator or director. Depending on the institution, courses or a master's degree in business or health administration may be necessary for the director's position. Some technologists progress by leaving the occupation to become instructors or directors in radiologic technology programs; others take jobs as sales representatives or instructors with equipment manufacturers.

Job Outlook

Job opportunities are expected to be favorable. Some employers report difficulty hiring sufficient numbers of radiologic technologists and technicians. Imbalances between the demand for, and supply of, qualified workers should spur efforts to attract and retain qualified radiologic technologists and technicians. As an example of such efforts, employers may provide more flexible training programs or improve compensation and working conditions.

Radiologic technologists who also are experienced in more complex diagnostic imaging procedures, such as CT or MRI, will have better employment opportunities as employers seek to control costs by using multiskilled employees.

Employment of radiologic technologists and technicians is expected to grow faster than the average for all occupations through 2012, as the population grows and ages, increasing the demand for diagnostic imaging. Although healthcare providers are enthusiastic about the clinical benefits of new technologies, the extent to which they are adopted depends largely on cost and reimbursement considerations. For example, digital imaging technology can improve quality and efficiency, but remains expensive. Some promising new technologies may not come into widespread use because they are too expensive and third-party payers may not be willing to pay for their use.

Hospitals will remain the principal employer of radiologic technologists and technicians. However, a greater number of new jobs will be found in offices of physicians and diagnostic imaging centers. Health facilities such as these are expected to grow rapidly through 2012, due to the strong shift toward outpatient care, encouraged by third-party payers and made possible by technological advances that permit more procedures to be performed outside the hospital. Some job openings also will arise from the need to replace technologists and technicians who leave the occupation.

Earnings

Median annual earnings of radiologic technologists and technicians were $38,970 in 2002. The middle 50 percent earned between $32,370 and $46,510. The lowest 10 percent earned less than $27,190, and the highest 10 percent earned more than $55,430. Median annual earnings in the industries employing the largest numbers of radiologic technologists and technicians in 2002 were as follows:

Medical and diagnostic laboratories $42,470

General medical and surgical hospitals..................39,580

Offices of physicians 36,490

Related Occupations

Radiologic technologists and technicians operate sophisticated equipment to help physicians, dentists, and other health practitioners diagnose and treat patients. Workers in related occupations include cardiovascular technologists and technicians, clinical laboratory technologists and technicians, diagnostic medical sonographers, nuclear medicine technologists, radiation therapists, and respiratory therapists.

Sources of Additional Information

For career information, send a stamped, self-addressed business-size envelope with your request to:

- American Society of Radiologic Technologists, 15000 Central Ave. SE, Albuquerque, NM 87123-3917. Telephone (tollfree): 800-444-2778. Internet: http://www.asrt.org

For the current list of accredited education programs in radiography, write to:

- Joint Review Committee on Education in Radiologic Technology, 20 N. Wacker Dr., Suite 900, Chicago, IL 60606-2901. Internet: http://www.jrcert.org

For information on certification, contact:

- American Registry of Radiologic Technologists, 1255 Northland Dr., St. Paul, MN 55120-1155. Internet: http://www.arrt.org

Receptionists and Information Clerks

(O*NET 43-4171.00)

Significant Points

- Numerous job openings should arise for receptionists and information clerks due to employment growth and the need to replace workers who leave these occupations.

- A high school diploma or its equivalent is the most common educational requirement.

- Because receptionists and information clerks deal directly with the public, a professional appearance and a pleasant personality are imperative.

- These occupations are well suited to flexible work schedules.

Nature of the Work

Receptionists and information clerks are charged with a responsibility that may have a lasting impact on the success of an organization: making a good first impression. These workers often are the first representatives of an organization a visitor encounters, so they need to be courteous, professional, and helpful. Receptionists answer telephones, route calls, greet visitors, respond to inquiries from the public, and provide information about the organization. Some receptionists are responsible for the coordination of all mail into and out of the office. In addition, receptionists contribute to the security of an organization by helping to monitor the access of visitors—a function that has become increasingly important in recent years.

Whereas some tasks are common to most receptionists and information clerks, the specific responsibilities of receptionists vary with the type of establishment in which they work. For example, receptionists in hospitals and in doctors' offices may gather patients' personal and financial information and direct them to the proper waiting rooms. In beauty or hair salons, by contrast, receptionists arrange appointments, direct customers to the hairstylist, and may serve as cashiers. In factories, large corporations, and government offices, they may provide identification cards and arrange for escorts to take visitors to the proper office. Those working for bus and train companies respond to inquiries about departures, arrivals, stops, and other related matters.

Increasingly, receptionists are using multiline telephone systems, personal computers, and fax machines. Despite the widespread use of automated answering systems or voice mail, many receptionists still take messages and inform other employees of visitors' arrivals or cancellation of an appointment. When they are not busy with callers, most receptionists are expected to perform a variety of office duties, including opening and sorting mail, collecting and distributing parcels, transmitting and delivering facsimiles, updating appointment calendars, preparing travel vouchers, and performing basic bookkeeping, word processing, and filing.

Working Conditions

Most receptionists and information clerks work in areas that are clean, well lit, and relatively quiet. This is especially true for receptionists who greet customers and visitors; they usually work in highly visible areas that are furnished to make a good impression.

Although most receptionists and information clerks work a standard 40-hour week, about 3 out of 10 work part time.

The work performed by receptionists and information clerks may be repetitious and stressful. For example, many receptionists spend all day answering telephones while performing additional clerical or secretarial tasks. Additional stress is caused by technology that enables management to electronically monitor employees' use of computer systems, tape-record telephone calls, or limit the time spent on each call. Prolonged exposure to a video display terminal may lead to eyestrain for the many information clerks who work with computers.

Employment

Receptionists and information clerks held about 1.1 million jobs in 2002. Almost 90 percent worked in service-providing industries. Among service-providing industries, health care and social assistance industries—including doctors' and dentists' offices, hospitals, nursing homes, urgent-care centers, surgical centers, and clinics—employed one-third of all receptionists and information clerks. Manufacturing, wholesale and retail trade, government, and real-estate industries also employed large numbers of receptionists and information clerks. About 3 of every 10 receptionists and information clerks worked part time.

Training, Other Qualifications, and Advancement

Despite the fact that hiring requirements for receptionists and information clerks vary, a high school diploma or its equivalent is the most common educational requirement. Increasingly, familiarity or experience with computers and good interpersonal skills are becoming equally important as the diploma to employers.

Many receptionists and information clerks deal directly with the public, so a professional appearance and a pleasant personality are important. A clear speaking voice and fluency in the English language also are essential because these employees frequently use the telephone or public-address systems. Good spelling and computer literacy often are needed, particularly because most work involves considerable use of the computer.

Receptionists and information clerks often learn the skills they need in high schools, business schools, and community colleges. Business education programs offered by these institutions typically include courses in typing, word processing, shorthand, business communications, records management, and office systems and procedures.

Receptionists usually receive on-the-job training that may include procedures for greeting visitors, for operating telephone and computer systems, and for distributing mail, fax, and parcel deliveries. Some employers look for applicants who already possess certain skills, such as computer and word-processing experience, or those who have previous formal education.

Receptionists and information clerks with word-processing or other clerical skills may advance to a better-paying job as a secretary or administrative assistant.

Job Outlook

Employment of receptionists and information clerks is expected to grow faster than the average for all occupations through 2012. This increase will result from rapid growth in services industries—including physicians' offices, law firms, temporary-help agencies, and consulting firms—where most are employed. In addition, turnover in this large occupation will create numerous openings as receptionists and information clerks transfer to other occupations or leave the labor force altogether. Opportunities should be best for persons with a wide range of clerical and technical skills, particularly those with related work experience.

Technology should have conflicting effects on the demand for receptionists and information clerks. The increasing use of voice mail and other telephone automation reduces the need for receptionists by allowing one receptionist to perform work that formerly required several. However, the increasing use of other technology has caused a consolidation of clerical responsibilities and growing demand for workers with diverse clerical and technical skills. Because receptionists and information clerks may perform a wide variety of clerical tasks, they should continue to be in demand. Further, they perform many tasks that are interpersonal in nature and are not easily automated, ensuring continued demand for their services in a variety of establishments.

Earnings

In 2002, median annual earnings for all receptionists and information clerks were $21,150.

In 2003, the federal government typically paid salaries ranging from $19,898 to $23,555 a year to beginning receptionists with a high school diploma or 6 months of experience. The average annual salary for all receptionists employed by the federal government was about $25,704 in 2003.

Related Occupations

A number of other workers deal with the public, receive and provide information, or direct people to others who can assist them. Among these workers are customer service representatives, dispatchers, security guards and gaming surveillance workers, tellers, and counter and rental clerks.

Sources of Additional Information

State employment offices can provide information on job openings for receptionists.

Recreation and Fitness Workers

(O*NET 39-9031.00 and 39-9032.00)

Significant Points

- Educational requirements for recreation workers range from a high school diploma to a graduate degree, whereas fitness workers usually need certification.

- Competition will remain keen for full-time career positions in recreation; however, job prospects for fitness workers will be more favorable.

- The recreation field offers many part-time and seasonal job opportunities.

Nature of the Work

People spend much of their leisure time participating in a wide variety of organized recreational activities, such as aerobics, arts and crafts, the performing arts, camping, and sports. Recreation and fitness workers plan, organize, and direct these activities in local playgrounds and recreation areas, parks, community centers, health clubs, fitness centers, religious organizations, camps, theme parks, and tourist attractions. Increasingly, recreational and fitness workers also are found in workplaces, where they organize and direct leisure activities and athletic programs for employees of all ages.

Recreation workers hold a variety of positions at different levels of responsibility. *Recreation leaders*, who are responsible for a recreation program's daily operation, primarily organize and direct participants. They may lead and give instruction in dance, drama, crafts, games, and sports; schedule use of facilities; keep records of equipment use; and ensure that recreation facilities and equipment are used properly. Workers who provide instruction and coach groups in specialties such as art, music, drama, swimming, or tennis may be called *activity specialists*. *Recreation supervisors* oversee recreation leaders and plan, organize, and manage recreational activities to meet the needs of a variety of populations. These workers often serve as liaisons between the director of the park or recreation center and the recreation leaders. Recreation supervisors with more specialized responsibilities also may direct special activities or events or oversee a major activity, such as aquatics, gymnastics, or performing arts. *Directors of recreation and parks* develop and manage comprehensive recreation programs in parks, playgrounds, and other settings. Directors usually serve as technical advisors to state and local recreation and park commissions and may be responsible for recreation and park budgets.

Camp counselors lead and instruct children and teenagers in outdoor-oriented forms of recreation, such as swimming, hiking, horseback riding, and camping. In addition, counselors provide campers with specialized instruction in subjects such as archery, boating, music, drama, gymnastics, tennis, and computers. In resident camps, counselors also provide guidance and supervise daily living and general socialization. Camp directors typically supervise camp counselors, plan camp activities or programs, and perform the various administrative functions of a camp.

Fitness workers instruct or coach groups or individuals in various exercise activities. Because gyms and health clubs offer a variety of exercise activities such as weightlifting, yoga, aerobics, and karate, fitness workers typically specialize in only a few areas. *Fitness trainers* help clients to assess their level of physical fitness and help them to set and reach fitness goals. They also demonstrate various exercises and help clients to improve their exercise techniques. They may keep records of their clients' exercise sessions in order to assess their progress towards physical fitness. *Personal trainers* work with clients on a one-on-one basis in either a gym or the client's home. *Aerobics instructors* conduct group exercise sessions that involve aerobic exercise, stretching, and muscle conditioning. Some fitness workers may perform the duties of both aerobics instructors and fitness trainers. *Fitness directors* oversee the operations of a health club or fitness center. Their work involves creating and maintaining programs that meet the needs of the club's members.

Working Conditions

Recreation and fitness workers may work in a variety of settings—for example, a health club, cruise ship, woodland recreational park, or playground in the center of a large urban community. Regardless of setting, most recreation workers spend much of their time outdoors and may work in a variety of weather conditions, whereas most fitness workers spend their time indoors at fitness centers and health clubs. Recreation and fitness directors and supervisors, however, typically spend most of their time in an office, planning programs and special events. Directors and supervisors generally engage in less physical activity than do lower level recreation and fitness workers. Nevertheless, recreation and fitness workers at all levels risk suffering injuries during physical activities.

Many recreation and fitness workers work about 40 hours a week. People entering this field, especially camp counselors, should expect some night and weekend work and irregular hours. About 36 percent work part time and many recreation jobs are seasonal.

Employment

Recreation and fitness workers held about 485,000 jobs in 2002, and many additional workers held summer jobs in this occupation. About 62 percent were recreation workers; the rest were fitness trainers and aerobics instructors. Of those with year-round jobs as recreation workers, almost 40 percent worked for local governments, primarily in the park and recreation departments. Around 14 percent of recreation workers were employed in civic and social organizations, such as the Boy or Girl Scouts or Red Cross. Another 12 percent of recreation workers were employed by nursing and other personal care facilities.

Almost all fitness trainers and aerobics instructors worked in physical fitness facilities, health clubs, and fitness centers, mainly within the amusement and recreation services industry or civic and social organizations. About 5 percent of fitness workers were self-employed; many of these were personal trainers.

The recreation field has an unusually large number of part-time, seasonal, and volunteer jobs. These jobs include summer camp counselors, craft specialists, and afterschool and weekend recreation program leaders. In addition, many teachers and college students accept jobs as recreation and fitness workers when school is not in session. The vast majority of volunteers serve as activity leaders at local day-camp programs, or in youth organizations, camps, nursing homes, hospitals, senior centers, and other settings.

Training, Other Qualifications, and Advancement

Educational requirements for recreation workers range from a high school diploma—or sometimes less for many summer jobs—to graduate degrees for some administrative positions in large public recreation systems. Full-time career professional positions usually require a college degree with a major in parks and recreation or leisure studies, but a bachelor's degree in any liberal arts field may be sufficient for some jobs in the private sector. In industrial recreation, or "employee services" as it is more commonly called, companies prefer to hire those with a bachelor's degree in recreation or leisure studies and a background in business administration.

Specialized training or experience in a particular field, such as art, music, drama, or athletics, is an asset for many jobs. Some jobs also require certification. For example, a lifesaving certificate is a prerequisite for teaching or coaching water-related activities. Graduates of associate degree programs in parks and recreation, social work, and other human services disciplines also enter some career recreation positions. High school graduates occasionally enter career positions, but this is not common. Some college students work part time as recreation workers while earning degrees.

A bachelor's degree and experience are preferred for most recreation supervisor jobs and required for higher level administrative jobs. However, an increasing number of recreation workers who aspire to administrative positions obtain master's degrees in parks and recreation or related disciplines. Certification in the recreation field may be helpful for advancement. Also, many persons in other disciplines, including social work, forestry, and resource management, pursue graduate degrees in recreation.

Programs leading to an associate or bachelor's degree in parks and recreation, leisure studies, or related fields are offered at several hundred colleges and universities. Many also offer master's or doctoral degrees in the field. In 2002, 100 bachelor's degree programs in parks and recreation were accredited by the National Recreation and Park Association (NRPA). Accredited programs provide broad exposure to the history, theory, and practice of park and recreation management. Courses offered include community organization; supervision and administration; recreational needs of special populations, such as the elderly or disabled; and supervised fieldwork. Students may specialize in areas such as therapeutic recreation, park management, outdoor recreation, industrial or commercial recreation, or camp management. Certification in the recreation field is offered by the NRPA National Certification Board. Continuing education is necessary to remain certified.

Generally, fitness trainers and aerobics instructors must obtain a certification in the fitness field to obtain employment. Certification may be offered in various areas of exercise such as personal training, weight training, and aerobics. There are many organizations that offer certification testing in the fitness field, some of which are listed in the Sources of Additional Information section of this statement. Certification generally is good for 2 years, after which workers must become recertified. Recertification is accomplished by attending continuing education classes. Most fitness workers are required to maintain a cardiopulmonary resuscitation (CPR) certification. Some employers also require workers to be certified in first aid.

An increasing number of employers require fitness workers to have a bachelor's degree in a field related to health or fitness, such as exercise science or physical education. Some employers allow workers to substitute a college degree for certification, while others require both a degree and certification. A bachelor's degree and, in some cases, a master's degree in exercise science, physical education, or a related area, along with experience, usually is required to advance to management positions in a health club or fitness center. Many fitness workers become personal trainers, in addition to their main job in a fitness center, or as a full-time job. Some workers go into business for themselves and open up their own fitness centers.

Persons planning recreation and fitness careers should be outgoing, good at motivating people, and sensitive to the needs of others. Excellent health and physical fitness are required due to the physical nature of the job. Volunteer experience, part-time work during school, or a summer job can lead to a full-time career as a recreation worker. As in many fields, managerial skills are needed to advance to supervisory or managerial positions. College courses in management, business administration, accounting, and personnel management are helpful for advancement to supervisory or managerial jobs.

Job Outlook

Competition will be keen for career positions as recreation workers because the field attracts many applicants and because the number of career positions is limited compared with the number of lower level seasonal jobs. Opportunities for staff positions should be best for persons with formal training and experience gained in part-time or seasonal recreation jobs. Those with graduate degrees should have the best opportunities for supervisory or administrative positions. Opportunities are expected to be better for fitness trainers and aerobics instructors because of relatively rapid growth in employment. Job openings for both recreation and fitness workers also will stem from the need to replace the large numbers of workers who leave these occupations each year.

Overall employment of recreation and fitness workers is expected to grow faster than the average for all occupations through 2012, as an increasing number of people spend more time and money on recreation, fitness, and leisure services and as more businesses recognize the benefits of recreation and fitness programs and other services such as wellness programs. Average employment growth is projected for recreation workers—reflecting growth in local government and civic and social organizations, industries that employ just over half of all recreation workers. Employment growth among recreation workers may be inhibited, however, by budget constraints that some local governments may face over the 2002-12 projection period. Employment of fitness workers—who are concentrated in the rapidly growing arts, entertainment and recreation industry—is expected to increase much faster than average due to rising interest in personal training, aerobics instruction, and other fitness activities.

The recreation field provides a large number of temporary, seasonal jobs. These positions, which typically are filled by high school or college students, generally do not have formal education requirements and are open to anyone with the desired personal qualities. Employers compete for a share of the vacationing student labor force and, although salaries in recreation often are lower than those in other fields, the nature of the work and the opportunity to work outdoors are attractive to many.

Earnings

Median hourly earnings of recreation workers who worked full time in 2002 were $8.69. The middle 50 percent earned between about $7.09 and $11.36, while the top 10 percent earned $15.72 or more. However, earnings of recreation directors and others in supervisory or managerial positions can be substantially higher. Most public and private recreation agencies provide full-time recreation workers with typical benefits; part-time workers receive few, if any, benefits. Median hourly earnings in the industries employing the largest numbers of recreation workers in 2002 were:

Nursing care facilities..$9.30
Local government 8.98
Individual and family services...................................8.71
Civic and social organizations..................................7.73
Other amusement and recreation industries..............7.53

Median hourly earnings of fitness trainers and aerobics instructors in 2002 were $11.51. The middle 50 percent earned between $8.06 and $18.18, while the top 10 percent earned $26.22 or more. Earnings of successful self-employed personal trainers can be much higher. Median hourly earnings in the industries employing the largest numbers of recreation workers in 2002 were:

Other amusement and recreation industries $13.81
Civic and social organizations...................................9.24
Other schools and instruction..................................8.93

Related Occupations

Recreation workers must exhibit leadership and sensitivity when dealing with people. Other occupations that require similar personal qualities include: counselors, probation officers and correctional treatment specialists, psychologists, recreational therapists, and social workers. Occupations that focus on physical fitness, as do fitness workers, include athletes, coaches, umpires, and related workers.

Sources of Additional Information

For information on jobs in recreation, contact employers such as local government departments of parks and recreation, nursing and personal care facilities, the Boy or Girl Scouts, or local social or religious organizations.

For information on careers, certification, and academic programs in parks and recreation, contact:

- National Recreation and Park Association, Division of Professional Services, 22377 Belmont Ridge Rd., Ashburn, VA 20148-4501. Internet: http://www.nrpa.org

For career information about camp counselors, contact:

- American Camping Association, 5000 State Road 67 North, Martinsville, IN 46151-7902. Internet: http://www.acacamps.org

For information on careers and certification in the fitness field, contact:

- American Council on Exercise, 4851 Paramount Dr., San Diego, CA 92123. Internet: http://www.acefitness.org

- National Strength and Conditioning Association, 4575 Galley Rd., Suite 400B, Colorado Springs, CO 80915. Internet: http://www.nsca-lift.org

- American College of Sports Medicine, PO Box 1440, Indianapolis, IN 46206-1440. Internet: http://www.acsm.org\

Registered Nurses

(O*NET 29-1111.00)

Significant Points

- Registered nurses constitute the largest healthcare occupation, with 2.3 million jobs.

- More new jobs are expected to be created for registered nurses than for any other occupation.

- Job opportunities are expected to be very good.

- The three major educational paths to registered nursing are a bachelor's degree, an associate degree, and a diploma.

Nature of the Work

Registered nurses (RNs) work to promote health, prevent disease, and help patients cope with illness. They are advocates and health educators for patients, families, and communities. When providing direct patient care, they observe, assess, and record symptoms, reactions, and progress in patients; assist physicians during surgeries, treatments, and examinations; administer medications; and assist in convalescence and rehabilitation. RNs also develop and manage nursing care plans, instruct patients and their families in proper care, and help individuals and groups take steps to improve or maintain their health. While state laws govern the tasks that RNs may perform, it is usually the work setting that determines their daily job duties.

Hospital nurses form the largest group of nurses. Most are staff nurses, who provide bedside nursing care and carry out medical regimens. They also may supervise licensed practical nurses and nursing aides. Hospital nurses usually are assigned to one department, such as surgery, maternity, pediatrics, the emergency room, intensive care, or the treatment of cancer patients. Some may rotate among departments.

Office nurses care for outpatients in physicians' offices, clinics, ambulatory surgical centers, and emergency medical centers. They prepare patients for, and assist with, examinations; administer injections and medications; dress wounds and incisions; assist with minor surgery; and maintain records. Some also perform routine laboratory and office work.

Nursing care facility nurses manage care for residents with conditions ranging from a fracture to Alzheimer's disease. Although they often spend much of their time on administrative and supervisory tasks, RNs also assess residents' health, develop treatment plans, supervise licensed practical nurses and nursing aides, and perform invasive procedures, such as starting intravenous fluids. They also work in specialty-care departments, such as long-term rehabilitation units for patients with strokes and head injuries.

Home health nurses provide nursing services to patients at home. RNs assess patients' home environments and instruct patients and their families. Home health nurses care for a broad range of patients, such as those recovering from illnesses and accidents, cancer, and childbirth. They must be able to work independently and may supervise home health aides.

Public health nurses work in government and private agencies, including clinics, schools, retirement communities, and other community settings. They focus on populations, working with individuals, groups, and families to improve the overall health of communities. They also work with communities to help plan and implement programs. Public health nurses instruct individuals, families, and other groups regarding health issues such as preventive care, nutrition, and childcare. They arrange for immunizations, blood pressure testing, and other health screening. These nurses also work with community leaders, teachers, parents, and physicians in community health education.

Occupational health nurses, also called *industrial nurses*, provide nursing care at worksites to employees, customers, and others with injuries and illnesses. They give emergency care, prepare accident reports, and arrange for further care if necessary. They also offer health counseling, conduct health examinations and inoculations, and assess work environments to identify potential or actual health problems.

Head nurses or *nurse supervisors* direct nursing activities, primarily in hospitals. They plan work schedules and assign duties to nurses and aides, provide or arrange for training, and visit patients to observe nurses and to ensure that the patients receive proper care. They also may ensure that records are maintained and equipment and supplies are ordered.

At the advanced level, *nurse practitioners* provide basic, primary healthcare. They diagnose and treat common acute illnesses and injuries. Nurse practitioners also can prescribe medications—but certification and licensing requirements vary by state. Other advanced practice nurses include *clinical nurse specialists, certified registered nurse anesthetists,* and *certified nurse midwives.* Advanced practice nurses must meet educational and clinical practice requirements beyond the basic nursing education and licensing required of all RNs.

Working Conditions

Most nurses work in well-lighted, comfortable healthcare facilities. Home health and public health nurses travel to patients' homes, schools, community centers, and other sites. Nurses may spend considerable time walking and standing. Patients in hospitals and nursing care facilities require 24-hour care; consequently, nurses in these institutions may work nights, weekends, and holidays. RNs also may be on call—available to work on short notice. Office, occupational health, and public health nurses are more likely to work regular business hours. More than 1 in 5 RNs worked part time in 2002 and nearly 1 in 10 held more than one job.

Nursing has its hazards, especially in hospitals, nursing care facilities, and clinics, in all three of which nurses may care for individuals with infectious diseases. Nurses must observe rigid standardized guidelines to guard against disease and other dangers, such as those posed by radiation, accidental needle sticks, chemicals used to sterilize instruments, and anesthetics. In addition, they are vulnerable to back injury when moving patients, shocks from electrical equipment, and hazards posed by compressed gases.

Employment

As the largest healthcare occupation, registered nurses held about 2.3 million jobs in 2002. Almost 3 out of 5 jobs were in hospitals, in inpatient and outpatient departments. Others worked in offices of physicians, nursing care facilities, home healthcare services, employment services, government agencies, and outpatient care centers. The remainder worked mostly in social assistance agencies and educational services, public and private. About 1 in 5 RNs worked part time.

Training, Other Qualifications, and Advancement

In all states and the District of Columbia, students must graduate from an approved nursing program and pass a national licensing examination in order to obtain a nursing license. Nurses may be licensed in more than one state, either by examination, by the endorsement of a license issued by another state, or through a multi-state licensing agreement. All states require periodic renewal of licenses, which may involve continuing education.

There are three major educational paths to registered nursing: a bachelor's of science degree in nursing (BSN), an associate degree in nursing (ADN), and a diploma. BSN programs, offered by colleges and universities, take about 4 years to complete. In 2002, 678 nursing programs offered degrees at the bachelor's level. ADN programs, offered by community and junior colleges, take about 2 to 3 years to complete. About 700 RN programs in 2002 were at the ADN level. Diploma programs, administered in hospitals, last about 3 years. Only a small and declining number of programs offer diplomas. Generally, licensed graduates of any of the three types of educational programs qualify for entry-level positions as staff nurses.

Many ADN- and diploma-educated nurses later enter bachelor's programs to prepare for a broader scope of nursing practice. Often, they can find a staff nurse position and then take advantage of tuition reimbursement benefits to work toward a BSN by completing one of many RN-to-BSN programs.

Accelerated BSN programs also are available for individuals who have a bachelor's or higher degree in another field and who are interested in moving into nursing. In 2002, more than 110 of these programs were available. Accelerated BSN programs last 12 to 18 months and provide the fastest route to a BSN for individuals who already hold a degree. Accelerated master's degree programs in nursing also are available and take about 3 years to complete.

Individuals considering nursing should carefully weigh the advantages and disadvantages of enrolling in a BSN program, because, if they do, their advancement opportunities usually are broader. In fact, some career paths are open only to nurses with bachelor's or advanced degrees. A bachelor's degree often is necessary for administrative positions and is a prerequisite for admission to graduate nursing programs in research, consulting, teaching, or a clinical specialization.

Nursing education includes classroom instruction and supervised clinical experience in hospitals and other healthcare facilities. Students take courses in anatomy, physiology, microbiology, chemistry, nutrition, psychology and other behavioral sciences, and nursing. Course work also includes the liberal arts.

Supervised clinical experience is provided in hospital departments such as pediatrics, psychiatry, maternity, and surgery. A growing number of programs include clinical experience in nursing care facilities, public health departments, home health agencies, and ambulatory clinics.

Nurses should be caring, sympathetic, responsible, and detail oriented. They must be able to direct or supervise others, correctly assess patients' conditions, and determine when consultation is required. They need emotional stability to cope with human suffering, emergencies, and other stresses.

Experience and good performance can lead to promotion to more responsible positions. In management, nurses can advance to assistant head nurse or head nurse and, from there, to assistant director, director, and vice president. Increasingly, management-level nursing positions require a graduate or an advanced degree in nursing or health services administration. They also require leadership, negotiation skills, and good judgment. Graduate programs preparing executive-level nurses usually last about 2 years.

Within patient care, nurses can move into a nursing specialty such as clinical nurse specialist, nurse practitioner, certified nurse midwife, or certified registered nurse anesthetist. These positions require about 2 years of graduate education leading to a master's degree.

Some nurses move into the business side of health care. Their nursing expertise and experience on a healthcare team equip them with the ability to manage ambulatory, acute, home health, and chronic care services. Employers—including hospitals, insurance companies, pharmaceutical manufacturers, and managed care organizations, among others—need RNs for health planning and development, marketing, consulting, policy development, and quality assurance. Other nurses work as college and university faculty or conduct research.

Job Outlook

Job opportunities for RNs are expected to be very good. Employment of registered nurses is expected to grow faster than the average for all occupations through 2012, and because the occupation is very large, many new jobs will result. In fact, more new jobs are expected be created for RNs than for any other occupation. Thousands of job openings also will result from the need to replace experienced nurses who leave the occupation, especially as the median age of the registered nurse population continues to rise.

Faster-than-average growth will be driven by technological advances in patient care, which permit a greater number of medical problems to be treated, and an increasing emphasis on preventive care. In addition, the number of older people, who are much more likely than younger people to need nursing care, is projected to grow rapidly.

Employers in some parts of the country are reporting difficulty in attracting and retaining an adequate number of RNs, due primarily to an aging RN workforce and insufficient nursing school enrollments. Imbalances between the supply of, and demand for, qualified workers should spur efforts to attract and retain qualified RNs. For example, employers may restructure workloads, improve compensation and working conditions, and subsidize training or continuing education.

Employment in hospitals, the largest sector, is expected to grow more slowly than in most other healthcare sectors. While the intensity of nursing care is likely to increase, requiring more nurses per patient, the number of inpatients (those who remain in the hospital for more than 24 hours) is not likely to increase much. Patients are being discharged earlier and more procedures are being done on an outpatient basis, both inside and outside hospitals. Rapid growth is expected in hospital outpatient facilities, such as those providing same-day surgery, rehabilitation, and chemotherapy.

An increasing proportion of sophisticated procedures, which once were performed only in hospitals, are being performed in physicians' offices and in outpatient care centers, such as freestanding ambulatory surgical and emergency centers. Accordingly, employment is expected to grow faster than average in these places as healthcare in general expands.

Employment in nursing care facilities is expected to grow faster than average due to increases in the number of elderly, many of whom require long-term care. In addition, the financial pressure on hospitals to discharge patients as soon as possible should produce more admissions to nursing care facilities. Job growth also is expected in units that provide specialized long-term rehabilitation for stroke and head injury patients, as well as units that treat Alzheimer's victims.

Employment in home healthcare is expected to increase rapidly in response to the growing number of older persons with functional disabilities, consumer preference for care in the home, and technological advances that make it possible to bring increasingly complex treatments into the home. The type of care demanded will require nurses who are able to perform complex procedures.

In evolving integrated healthcare networks, nurses may rotate among various employment settings. Because jobs in traditional hospital nursing positions are no longer the only option, RNs will need to be flexible. Opportunities should be excellent, particularly for nurses with advanced education and training.

Earnings

Median annual earnings of registered nurses were $48,090 in 2002. The middle 50 percent earned between $40,140 and $57,490. The lowest 10 percent earned less than $33,970, and the highest 10 percent earned more than $69,670. Median annual earnings in the industries employing the largest numbers of registered nurses in 2002 were as follows:

Employment services $55,980
General medical and surgical hospitals..................49,190
Home health care services 45,890
Offices of physicians 44,870
Nursing care facilities...43,850

Many employers offer flexible work schedules, childcare, educational benefits, and bonuses.

Related Occupations

Workers in other healthcare occupations with responsibilities and duties related to those of registered nurses are emergency medical technicians and paramedics, occupational therapists, physical therapists, physician assistants, respiratory therapists, and social workers.

Sources of Additional Information

For information on a career as a registered nurse and nursing education, contact:

- National League for Nursing, 61 Broadway, New York, NY 10006. Internet: http://www.nln.org

For a list of BSN, graduate, and accelerated nursing programs, contact:

- American Association of Colleges of Nursing, 1 Dupont Circle NW, Suite 530, Washington, DC 20036. Internet: http://www.aacn.nche.edu

Information on registered nurses also is available from:

- American Nurses Association, 600 Maryland Ave. SW, Washington, DC 20024-2571. Internet: http://www.nursingworld.org

Respiratory Therapists

(O*NET 29-1126.00 and 29-2054.00)

Significant Points

- An associate degree has become the general requirement for entry into this field.

- Hospitals will continue to employ the vast majority of respiratory therapists, but a growing number of therapists will work in other settings.

- Job opportunities will be very good, especially for therapists with cardiopulmonary care skills or experience working with newborns and infants.

Nature of the Work

Respiratory therapists and *respiratory therapy technicians*—also known as respiratory care practitioners—evaluate, treat, and care for patients with breathing or other cardiopulmonary disorders. Respiratory therapists, practicing under physician direction, assume primary responsibility for all respiratory care therapeutic treatments and diagnostic procedures, including the supervision of respiratory therapy technicians. Respiratory therapy technicians follow specific, well-defined respiratory care procedures, under the direction of respiratory therapists and physicians. In clinical practice, many of the daily duties of therapists and technicians overlap, although therapists generally have greater responsibility than technicians. For example, respiratory therapists will primarily consult with physicians and other healthcare staff to help develop and modify individual patient care plans. Respiratory therapists are also more likely to provide complex therapy requiring considerable independent judgment, such as caring for patients on life support in hospital inten-

sive care units. In this statement, the term *respiratory therapists* includes both respiratory therapists and respiratory therapy technicians.

To evaluate patients, respiratory therapists interview them, perform limited physical examinations, and conduct diagnostic tests. For example, respiratory therapists test patients' breathing capacity and determine the concentration of oxygen and other gases in patients' blood. They also measure patients' pH, which indicates the acidity or alkalinity level of the blood. To evaluate a patient's lung capacity, respiratory therapists have the patient breathe into an instrument that measures the volume and flow of oxygen during inhalation and exhalation. By comparing the reading with the norm for the patient's age, height, weight, and sex, respiratory therapists can provide information that helps determine whether the patient has any lung deficiencies. To analyze oxygen, carbon dioxide, and pH levels, therapists draw an arterial blood sample, place it in a blood gas analyzer, and relay the results to a physician. Physicians rely on data provided by respiratory therapists to make treatment decisions.

Respiratory therapists treat all types of patients, ranging from premature infants whose lungs are not fully developed to elderly people whose lungs are diseased. Respiratory therapists provide temporary relief to patients with chronic asthma or emphysema, as well as emergency care to patients who are victims of a heart attack, stroke, drowning, or shock.

To treat patients, respiratory therapists use oxygen or oxygen mixtures, chest physiotherapy, and aerosol medications. When a patient has difficulty getting enough oxygen into their blood, therapists increase the patient's concentration of oxygen by placing an oxygen mask or nasal cannula on a patient and set the oxygen flow at the level prescribed by a physician. Therapists also connect patients who cannot breathe on their own to ventilators that deliver pressurized oxygen into the lungs. The therapists insert a tube into the patient's trachea, or windpipe; connect the tube to the ventilator; and set the rate, volume, and oxygen concentration of the oxygen mixture entering the patient's lungs.

Therapists perform regular checks on patients and equipment. If the patient appears to be having difficulty, or if the oxygen, carbon dioxide, or pH level of the blood is abnormal, therapists change the ventilator setting according to the doctor's orders or check the equipment for mechanical problems. In home care, therapists teach patients and their families to use ventilators and other life-support systems. In addition, therapists visit patients several times a month to inspect and clean equipment and to ensure its proper use. Therapists also make emergency visits if equipment problems arise.

Respiratory therapists perform chest physiotherapy on patients to remove mucus from their lungs and make it easier for them to breathe. For example, during surgery, anesthesia depresses respiration, so chest physiotherapy may be prescribed to help get the patient's lungs back to normal and to prevent congestion. Chest physiotherapy also helps patients suffering from lung diseases, such as cystic fibrosis, that cause mucus to collect in the lungs. Therapists place patients in positions that help drain mucus, and then they thump and vibrate the patients' rib cages and instruct the patients to cough.

Respiratory therapists also administer aerosols—liquid medications suspended in a gas that forms a mist which is inhaled—and teach patients how to inhale the aerosol properly to ensure its effectiveness.

In some hospitals, therapists perform tasks that fall outside their traditional role. Therapists' tasks are expanding into cardiopulmonary procedures such as taking electrocardiograms and administering stress tests, as well as other areas—for example, drawing blood samples from patients. Therapists also keep records of materials used and charges to patients.

Working Conditions

Respiratory therapists generally work between 35 and 40 hours a week. Because hospitals operate around the clock, therapists may work evenings, nights, or weekends. They spend long periods standing and walking between patients' rooms. In an emergency, therapists work under a great deal of stress. Respiratory therapists employed in home healthcare must travel frequently to the homes of patients.

Respiratory therapists are trained to work with gases stored under pressure that can be hazardous. Adherence to safety precautions and regular maintenance and testing of equipment minimize the risk of injury. As in many other health occupations, respiratory therapists run a risk of catching an infectious disease, but carefully following proper procedures minimizes this risk.

Employment

Respiratory therapists held about 112,000 jobs in 2002. More than 4 out of 5 jobs were in hospital departments of respiratory care, anesthesiology, or pulmonary medicine. Most of the remaining jobs were found in offices of physicians or other health practitioners, consumer goods rental firms that supply respiratory equipment for home use, nursing care facilities, and home healthcare services. Holding a second job is relatively common for respiratory therapists. About 17 percent held another job, compared with 5 percent of workers in all occupations.

Training, Other Qualifications, and Advancement

Formal training is necessary for entry into this field. Training is offered at the postsecondary level by colleges and universities, medical schools, vocational-technical institutes, and the Armed Forces. An associate degree has become the general requirement for entry into this field. Most programs award associate or bachelor's degrees and prepare graduates for jobs as advanced respiratory therapists. Other programs award associate degrees or certificates and lead to jobs as entry-level respiratory therapists. According to the Commis-

sion on Accreditation of Allied Health Education Programs (CAAHEP), 59 entry-level and 319 advanced respiratory therapy programs are presently accredited in the United States, including Puerto Rico.

Areas of study in respiratory therapy programs include human anatomy and physiology, pathophysiology, chemistry, physics, microbiology, pharmacology, and mathematics. Other courses deal with therapeutic and diagnostic procedures and tests, equipment, patient assessment, cardiopulmonary resuscitation, application of clinical practice guidelines, patient care outside of hospitals, cardiac and pulmonary rehabilitation, respiratory health promotion and disease prevention, and medical recordkeeping and reimbursement.

More than 40 states license respiratory care personnel. Aspiring respiratory care practitioners should check on licensure requirements with the board of respiratory care examiners for the state in which they plan to work. Also, most employers require respiratory therapists to maintain a cardiopulmonary resuscitation (CPR) certification.

The National Board for Respiratory Care (NBRC) offers voluntary certification and registration to graduates of programs accredited by CAAHEP or the Committee on Accreditation for Respiratory Care (CoARC). Two credentials are awarded to respiratory therapists who satisfy the requirements: Registered Respiratory Therapist (RRT) and Certified Respiratory Therapist (CRT). Graduates from accredited programs in respiratory therapy may take the CRT examination. CRTs who meet education and experience requirements can take two separate examinations leading to the award of the RRT credential. The CRT examination is the standard in the states requiring licensure.

Most employers require applicants for entry-level or generalist positions to hold the CRT or at least be eligible to take the certification examination. Supervisory positions and intensive-care specialties usually require the RRT or RRT eligibility.

Therapists should be sensitive to patients' physical and psychological needs. Respiratory care practitioners must pay attention to detail, follow instructions, and work as part of a team. In addition, operating advanced equipment requires proficiency with computers.

High school students interested in a career in respiratory care should take courses in health, biology, mathematics, chemistry, and physics. Respiratory care involves basic mathematical problem solving and an understanding of chemical and physical principles. For example, respiratory care workers must be able to compute dosages of medication and calculate gas concentrations.

Respiratory therapists advance in clinical practice by moving from general care to care of critical patients who have significant problems in other organ systems, such as the heart or kidneys. Respiratory therapists, especially those with 4-year degrees, may also advance to supervisory or managerial positions in a respiratory therapy department.

Respiratory therapists in home healthcare and equipment rental firms may become branch managers. Some respiratory therapists advance by moving into teaching positions.

Job Outlook

Job opportunities are expected to be very good, especially for respiratory therapists with cardiopulmonary care skills or experience working with infants. Employment of respiratory therapists is expected to increase faster than the average for all occupations through the year 2012, because of substantial growth in numbers of the middle-aged and elderly population—a development that will heighten the incidence of cardiopulmonary disease.

Older Americans suffer most from respiratory ailments and cardiopulmonary diseases such as pneumonia, chronic bronchitis, emphysema, and heart disease. As their numbers increase, the need for respiratory therapists will increase as well. In addition, advances in treating victims of heart attacks, accident victims, and premature infants (many of whom are dependent on a ventilator during part of their treatment) will increase the demand for the services of respiratory care practitioners.

Although hospitals will continue to employ the vast majority of therapists, a growing number can expect to work outside of hospitals in home healthcare services, offices of physicians or other health practitioners, or consumer goods rental firms.

Earnings

Median annual earnings of respiratory therapists were $40,220 in 2002. The middle 50 percent earned between $34,430 and $46,130. The lowest 10 percent earned less than $30,270, and the highest 10 percent earned more than $54,030. In general medical and surgical hospitals, median annual earnings of respiratory therapists were $40,390 in 2002.

Median annual earnings of respiratory therapy technicians were $34,130 in 2002. The middle 50 percent earned between $28,460 and $41,140. The lowest 10 percent earned less than $23,230, and the highest 10 percent earned more than $47,800. Median annual earnings of respiratory therapy technicians employed in general medical and surgical hospitals were $34,210 in 2002.

Related Occupations

Under the supervision of a physician, respiratory therapists administer respiratory care and life support to patients with heart and lung difficulties. Other workers who care for, treat, or train people to improve their physical condition include registered nurses, occupational therapists, physical therapists, and radiation therapists.

Sources of Additional Information

Information concerning a career in respiratory care is available from:

- American Association for Respiratory Care, 11030 Ables Ln., Dallas, TX 75229-4593. Internet: http://www.aarc.org

For a list of accredited educational programs for respiratory care practitioners, contact:

- Commission on Accreditation for Allied Health Education Programs, 39 East Wacker Dr., Chicago, IL 60601. Internet: http://www.caahep.org

- Committee on Accreditation for Respiratory Care, 1248 Harwood Rd., Bedford, TX 76021-4244.

Information on gaining credentials in respiratory care and a list of state licensing agencies can be obtained from:

- National Board for Respiratory Care, Inc., 8310 Nieman Rd., Lenexa, KS 66214-1579. Internet: http://www.nbrc.org

Retail Salespersons

(O*NET 41-2031.00)

Significant Points

- Good employment opportunities are expected because of the need to replace the large number of workers who leave the occupation each year.

- Many salespersons work evenings, weekends, and long hours from Thanksgiving through the beginning of January, during sales, and in other peak retail periods.

- Opportunities for part-time and temporary work are plentiful, attracting people looking to supplement their income; however, most of those selling high-priced items work full time and have substantial experience.

- There are no formal education requirements, although a high school diploma is preferred; employers look for people who enjoy working with others and who have tact, patience, an interest in sales work, a neat appearance, and the ability to communicate clearly.

Nature of the Work

Whether selling shoes, computer equipment, or automobiles, retail salespersons assist customers in finding what they are looking for and try to interest them in buying the merchandise. They describe a product's features, demonstrate its use, or show various models and colors. For some sales jobs, particularly those involving expensive and complex items, retail salespersons need special knowledge or skills. For example, salespersons who sell automobiles must be able to explain the features of various models, information about warranties, the meaning of manufacturers' specifications, and the types of options and financing available.

Consumers spend millions of dollars every day on merchandise and often form their impression of a store by evaluating its sales force. Therefore, retailers stress the importance of providing courteous and efficient service in order to remain competitive. When, for example, a customer wants an item that is not on the sales floor, the salesperson may check the stock room, place a special order, or call another store to locate the item.

In addition to selling, most retail salespersons—especially those who work in department and apparel stores—make out sales checks; receive cash, checks, and charge payments; bag or package purchases; and give out change and receipts. Depending on the hours they work, retail salespersons may have to open or close cash registers. This work may include counting the money in the register; separating charge slips, coupons, and exchange vouchers; and making deposits at the cash office. Salespersons often are held responsible for the contents of their registers, and repeated shortages are cause for dismissal in many organizations.

Salespersons also may handle returns and exchanges of merchandise, wrap gifts, and keep their work areas neat. In addition, they may help stock shelves or racks, arrange for mailing or delivery of purchases, mark price tags, take inventory, and prepare displays.

Frequently, salespersons must be aware of special sales and promotions. They also must recognize security risks and thefts and know how to handle or prevent such situations.

Working Conditions

Most salespersons in retail trade work in clean, comfortable, well-lighted stores. However, they often stand for long periods and may need supervisory approval to leave the sales floor.

The Monday-through-Friday, 9-to-5 workweek is the exception rather than the rule in retail trade. Most salespersons work evenings and weekends, particularly during sales and other peak retail periods. Because the holiday season is the busiest time for most retailers, many employers restrict the use of vacation time to some period other than Thanksgiving through the beginning of January.

The job can be rewarding for those who enjoy working with people. Patience and courtesy are required, especially when the work is repetitive and the customers are demanding.

Employment

Retail salespersons held about 4.1 million wage and salary jobs in 2002. They worked in stores ranging from small specialty shops employing a few workers to giant department stores with hundreds of salespersons. In addition, some were self-employed representatives of direct-sales companies and mail-order houses. The largest employers of retail salespersons are department stores, clothing and accessories stores,

building material and garden equipment and supplies dealers, and motor vehicle dealers.

This occupation offers many opportunities for part-time work and is especially appealing to students, retirees, and others seeking to supplement their income. However, most of those selling "big-ticket" items, such as cars, jewelry, furniture, and electronic equipment, work full time and have substantial experience.

Because retail stores are found in every city and town, employment is distributed geographically in much the same way as the population.

Training, Other Qualifications, and Advancement

There usually are no formal education requirements for this type of work, although a high school diploma or equivalent is preferred. Employers look for people who enjoy working with others and who have the tact and patience to deal with difficult customers. Among other desirable characteristics are an interest in sales work, a neat appearance, and the ability to communicate clearly and effectively. The ability to speak more than one language may be helpful for employment in communities where people from various cultures tend to live and shop. Before hiring a salesperson, some employers may conduct a background check, especially for a job selling high-priced items.

In most small stores, an experienced employee or the proprietor instructs newly hired sales personnel in making out sales checks and operating cash registers. In large stores, training programs are more formal and are usually conducted over several days. Topics generally discussed are customer service, security, the store's policies and procedures, and how to work a cash register. Depending on the type of product they are selling, employees may be given additional specialized training by manufacturers' representatives. For example, those working in cosmetics receive instruction on the types of products the store has available and for whom the cosmetics would be most beneficial. Likewise, salespersons employed by motor vehicle dealers may be required to participate in training programs designed to provide information on the technical details of standard and optional equipment available on new models. Because providing the best service to customers is a high priority for many employers, employees often are given periodic training to update and refine their skills.

As salespersons gain experience and seniority, they usually move to positions of greater responsibility and may be given their choice of departments in which to work. This often means moving to areas with potentially higher earnings and commissions. The highest earnings potential usually is found in selling big-ticket items, although such a position often requires the most knowledge of the product and the greatest talent for persuasion.

Opportunities for advancement vary in small stores. In some establishments, advancement is limited because one person—often the owner—does most of the managerial work. In others, some salespersons are promoted to assistant managers.

Traditionally, capable salespersons without college degrees could advance to management positions. Today, however, large retail businesses usually prefer to hire college graduates as management trainees, making a college education increasingly important. Despite this trend, motivated and capable employees without college degrees still may advance to administrative or supervisory positions in large establishments.

Retail selling experience may be an asset when one is applying for sales positions with larger retailers or in other industries, such as financial services, wholesale trade, or manufacturing.

Job Outlook

As in the past, employment opportunities for retail salespersons are expected to be good because of the need to replace the large number of workers who transfer to other occupations or leave the labor force each year. In addition, many new jobs will be created for retail salespersons. Employment is expected to grow about as fast as the average for all occupations through the year 2012, reflecting rising retail sales stemming from a growing population. Opportunities for part-time work should be abundant, and demand will be strong for temporary workers during peak selling periods, such as the end-of-year holiday season. The availability of part-time and temporary work attracts many people seeking to supplement their income.

During economic downturns, sales volumes and the resulting demand for sales workers usually decline. Purchases of costly items, such as cars, appliances, and furniture, tend to be postponed during difficult economic times. In areas of high unemployment, sales of many types of goods decline. However, because turnover among retail salespersons is high, employers often can adjust employment levels simply by not replacing all those who leave.

Despite the growing popularity of electronic commerce, Internet sales have not decreased the need for retail salespersons. Retail stores commonly use an online presence just to complement their in-store sales—there are very few Internet-only apparel and specialty stores. Retail salespersons will remain important in assuring customers that they will receive specialized service and in improving customer satisfaction, something Internet services cannot do. Therefore, the impact of electronic commerce on employment of retail salespersons will be minimal.

Earnings

The starting wage for many retail sales positions is the federal minimum wage, which was $5.15 an hour in 2002. In areas where employers have difficulty attracting and retaining workers, wages tend to be higher than the legislated minimum.

Median hourly earnings of retail salespersons, including commission, were $8.51 in 2002. The middle 50 percent earned between $7.08 and $11.30 an hour. The lowest 10 percent earned less than $6.18, and the highest 10 percent earned more than $16.96 an hour. Median hourly earnings in the industries employing the largest numbers of retail salespersons in 2002 were as follows:

Automobile dealers $18.25
Building material and supplies dealers 10.41
Department stores 8.12
Other general merchandise stores 7.84
Clothing stores..7.77

Compensation systems vary by type of establishment and merchandise sold. Salespersons receive hourly wages, commissions, or a combination of wages and commissions. Under a commission system, salespersons receive a percentage of the sales that they make. This system offers sales workers the opportunity to increase their earnings considerably, but they may find that their earnings strongly depend on their ability to sell their product and on the ups and downs of the economy. Employers may use incentive programs such as awards, banquets, bonuses, and profit-sharing plans to promote teamwork among the sales staff.

Benefits may be limited in smaller stores, but benefits in large establishments usually are comparable to those offered by other employers. In addition, nearly all salespersons are able to buy their store's merchandise at a discount, with the savings depending upon the type of merchandise.

Related Occupations

Salespersons use sales techniques, coupled with their knowledge of merchandise, to assist customers and encourage purchases. Workers in a number of other occupations who use these same skills include sales representatives, wholesale and manufacturing; securities, commodities, and financial services sales agents; counter and rental clerks; real estate brokers and sales agents; purchasing managers, buyers, and purchasing agents; insurance sales agents; sales engineers; and cashiers.

Sources of Additional Information

Information on careers in retail sales may be obtained from the personnel offices of local stores or from state merchants' associations.

General information about retailing is available from:

- National Retail Federation, 325 7th St. NW, Suite 1100, Washington, DC 20004.

Information about retail sales employment opportunities is available from:

- Retail, Wholesale, and Department Store Union, 30 East 29th St., 4th Floor, New York, NY 10016. Internet: http://www.rwdsu.org

Information about training for a career in automobile sales is available from:

- National Automobile Dealers Association, Public Relations Department, 8400 Westpark Dr., McLean, VA 22102-3591. Internet: http://www.nada.org

Roofers

(O*NET 47-2181.00)

Significant Points

- Most roofers acquire their skills informally on the job; some roofers train through 3-year apprenticeship programs.

- Jobs for roofers should be plentiful because the work is hot, strenuous, and dirty, resulting in higher job turnover than in most construction trades.

- Demand for roofers is less susceptible to downturns in the economy than demand for other construction trades because most roofing work consists of repair and reroofing.

Nature of the Work

A leaky roof can damage ceilings, walls, and furnishings. To protect buildings and their contents from water damage, roofers repair and install roofs made of tar or asphalt and gravel; rubber or thermoplastic; metal; or shingles made of asphalt, slate, fiberglass, wood, tile, or other material. Repair and reroofing—replacing old roofs on existing buildings—provide many job opportunities for these workers. Roofers also may waterproof foundation walls and floors.

There are two types of roofs—flat and pitched (sloped). Most commercial, industrial, and apartment buildings have flat or slightly sloping roofs. Most houses have pitched roofs. Some roofers work on both types; others specialize.

Most flat roofs are covered with several layers of materials. Roofers first put a layer of insulation on the roof deck. Over the insulation, they then spread a coat of molten bitumen, a tarlike substance. Next, they install partially overlapping layers of roofing felt—a fabric saturated in bitumen—over the surface. Roofers use a mop to spread hot bitumen over the surface and under the next layer. This seals the seams and makes the surface watertight. Roofers repeat these steps to build up the desired number of layers, called "plies." The top layer either is glazed to make a smooth finish or has gravel embedded in the hot bitumen to create a rough surface.

An increasing number of flat roofs are covered with a single-ply membrane of waterproof rubber or thermoplastic compounds. Roofers roll these sheets over the roof's insulation and seal the seams. Adhesive, mechanical fasteners, or stone ballast hold the sheets in place. The building must be of sufficient strength to hold the ballast.

Most residential roofs are covered with shingles. To apply shingles, roofers first lay, cut, and tack 3-foot strips of roofing felt lengthwise over the entire roof. Then, starting from the bottom edge, they staple or nail overlapping rows of shingles to the roof. Workers measure and cut the felt and shingles to fit intersecting roof surfaces and to fit around vent pipes and chimneys. Wherever two roof surfaces intersect, or shingles reach a vent pipe or chimney, roofers cement or nail flashing-strips of metal or shingle over the joints to make them watertight. Finally, roofers cover exposed nailheads with roofing cement or caulking to prevent water leakage. Roofers who use tile, metal shingles, or shakes follow a similar process.

Some roofers also waterproof and dampproof masonry and concrete walls and floors. To prepare surfaces for waterproofing, they hammer and chisel away rough spots, or remove them with a rubbing brick, before applying a coat of liquid waterproofing compound. They also may paint or spray surfaces with a waterproofing material, or attach waterproofing membrane to surfaces. When dampproofing, they usually spray a bitumen-based coating on interior or exterior surfaces.

Working Conditions

Roofing work is strenuous. It involves heavy lifting, as well as climbing, bending, and kneeling. Roofers work outdoors in all types of weather, particularly when making repairs. These workers risk slips or falls from scaffolds, ladders, or roofs, or burns from hot bitumen. In addition, roofs become extremely hot during the summer.

Employment

Roofers held about 166,000 jobs in 2002. Almost all wage and salary roofers worked for roofing contractors. About 1 out of every 3 roofers was self-employed. Many self-employed roofers specialized in residential work.

Training, Other Qualifications, and Advancement

Most roofers acquire their skills informally by working as helpers for experienced roofers. Safety training is increasing to reduce the number of accidents on the job and is one of the first classes that a worker takes. Trainees start by carrying equipment and material and erecting scaffolds and hoists. Within 2 or 3 months, trainees are taught to measure, cut, and fit roofing materials and, later, to lay asphalt or fiberglass shingles. Because some roofing materials are used infrequently, it can take several years to get experience working on all the various types of roofing applications.

Some roofers train through 3-year apprenticeship programs administered by local union-management committees representing roofing contractors and locals of the United Union of Roofers, Waterproofers, and Allied Workers. The apprenticeship program generally consists of a minimum of 2,000 hours of on-the-job training annually, plus a minimum of 144 hours of classroom instruction a year in subjects such as tools and their use, arithmetic, and safety. On-the-job training for apprentices is similar to that for helpers, except that the apprenticeship program is more structured. Apprentices also learn to dampproof and waterproof walls.

Good physical condition and good balance are essential for roofers. A high school education, or its equivalent, is helpful, as are courses in mechanical drawing and basic mathematics. Most apprentices are at least 18 years old. Experience with metal-working is helpful for workers who install metal roofing.

Roofers may advance to supervisor or estimator for a roofing contractor, or become contractors themselves.

Job Outlook

Jobs for roofers should be plentiful through the year 2012, primarily because of the need to replace workers who transfer to other occupations or leave the labor force. Turnover is higher than in most construction trades—roofing work is hot, strenuous, and dirty, and a significant number of workers treat roofing as a temporary job until something better comes along. Some roofers leave the occupation to go into other construction trades.

Employment of roofers is expected to grow about as fast as the average for all occupations through the year 2012. Roofs deteriorate faster and are more susceptible to weather damage than most other parts of buildings and periodically need to be repaired or replaced. Roofing has a much higher proportion of repair and replacement work than most other construction occupations. As a result, demand for roofers is less susceptible to downturns in the economy than demand for other construction trades. In addition to repair and reroofing work on the growing stock of buildings, new construction of industrial, commercial, and residential buildings will add to the demand for roofers. Jobs should be easiest to find during spring and summer when most roofing is done.

Earnings

In 2002, median hourly earnings of roofers were $14.51. The middle 50 percent earned between $11.23 and $19.56. The lowest 10 percent earned less than $9.15, and the highest 10 percent earned more than $25.35. The median hourly earnings of roofers in the foundation, structure, and building exterior contractors industry were $14.57 in 2002.

Apprentices usually start at about 40 percent to 50 percent of the rate paid to experienced roofers and receive periodic raises as they acquire the skills of the trade. Earnings for roofers are reduced on occasion because poor weather often limits the time they can work.

Some roofers are members of the United Union of Roofers, Waterproofers, and Allied Workers.

Related Occupations

Roofers use shingles, bitumen and gravel, single-ply plastic or rubber sheets, or other materials to waterproof building surfaces. Workers in other occupations who cover surfaces with special materials for protection and decoration include carpenters; carpet, floor, and tile installers and finishers; cement masons, concrete finishers, segmental pavers, and terrazzo workers; drywall installers, ceiling tile installers, and tapers; and plasterers and stucco masons.

Sources of Additional Information

For information about apprenticeships or job opportunities in roofing, contact local roofing contractors, a local chapter of the roofers union, a local joint union-management apprenticeship committee, or the nearest office of your State employment service or apprenticeship agency.

For information about the work of roofers, contact:

- National Roofing Contractors Association, 10255 W. Higgins Rd., Suite 600, Rosemont, IL 60018-5607. Internet: http://www.nrca.net

- United Union of Roofers, Waterproofers, and Allied Workers, 1660 L St. NW, Suite 800, Washington, DC 20036. Internet: http://www.unionroofers.org

There are more than 500 occupations registered by the U.S. Department of Labor's National Apprenticeship system. For more information on the Labor Department's registered apprenticeship system and links to state apprenticeship programs, check their Web site: http://www.doleta.gov.

Sales Representatives, Wholesale and Manufacturing

(O*NET 41-4011.01, 41-4011.02, 41-4011.03, 41-4011.04, 41-4011.05, 41-4011.06, and 41-4012.00)

Significant Points

- Earnings of sales representatives usually are based on a combination of salary and commission.

- Many individuals with previous sales experience enter the occupation without a college degree; however, a bachelor's degree increasingly is required.

- Prospects will be best for those with the appropriate knowledge or technical expertise, and the personal traits necessary for successful selling.

Nature of the Work

Sales representatives are an important part of manufacturers' and wholesalers' success. Regardless of the type of product they sell, their primary duties are to interest wholesale and retail buyers and purchasing agents in their merchandise, and to address any of the client's questions or concerns. Sales representatives represent one or several manufacturers or wholesale distributors by selling one product or a complimentary line of products. Sales representatives also advise clients on methods to reduce costs, use their products, and increase sales. They market their company's products to manufacturers, wholesale and retail establishments, construction contractors, government agencies, and other institutions.

Depending on where they work, sales representatives have different job titles. Those employed directly by a manufacturer or wholesaler often are called *sales representatives*. *Manufacturers' agents* or *manufacturers' representatives* are self-employed sales workers or independent firms who contract their services to all types of manufacturing companies. However, many of these titles are used interchangeably.

Sales representatives spend much of their time traveling to and visiting with prospective buyers and current clients. During a sales call, they discuss the client's needs and suggest how their merchandise or services can meet those needs. They may show samples or catalogs that describe items their company stocks and inform customers about prices, availability, and ways in which their products can save money and improve productivity. Because a vast number of manufacturers and wholesalers sell similar products, sales representatives must emphasize any unique qualities of their products and services. Manufacturers' agents or manufacturers' representatives might sell several complimentary products made by different manufacturers and, thus, take a broad approach to their customers' business. Sales representatives may help install new equipment and train employees. They also take orders and resolve any problems with or complaints about the merchandise.

Obtaining new accounts is an important part of the job. Sales representatives follow leads from other clients, track advertisements in trade journals, participate in trade shows and conferences, and may visit potential clients unannounced. In addition, they may spend time meeting with and entertaining prospective clients during evenings and weekends.

In a process that can take several months, sales representatives present their product and negotiate the sale. Aided by a laptop computer connected to the Internet, they often can answer technical and nontechnical questions immediately.

Frequently, sales representatives who lack technical expertise work as a team with a technical expert. In this arrangement, the technical expert—sometimes a sales engineer—will attend the sales presentation to explain the product and answer questions or concerns. The sales representative makes the preliminary contact with customers, introduces the company's product, and closes the sale. The representative is then able to spend more time maintaining and soliciting accounts and less time acquiring technical knowledge. After the sale, representatives may make followup visits to ensure that the equipment is functioning properly and may even help train customers' employees to operate and maintain new equipment. Those selling consumer goods often suggest how and where merchandise should be displayed. Working with retailers, they may help arrange promotional programs, store displays, and advertising.

Sales representatives have several duties beyond selling products. They also analyze sales statistics; prepare reports; and handle administrative duties, such as filing their expense account reports, scheduling appointments, and making travel plans. They study literature about new and existing products and monitor the sales, prices, and products of their competitors.

Manufacturers' agents who operate a sales agency must also manage their business. This requires organizational and general business skills, as well as knowledge of accounting, marketing, and administration.

Working Conditions

Some sales representatives have large territories and travel considerably. A sales region may cover several states, so they may be away from home for several days or weeks at a time. Others work near their "home base" and travel mostly by automobile. Due to the nature of the work and the amount of travel, sales representatives may work more than 40 hours per week.

Although the hours are long and often irregular, most sales representatives have the freedom to determine their own schedule. Sales representatives often are on their feet for long periods and may carry heavy sample products, which necessitates some physical stamina.

Dealing with different types of people can be stimulating but demanding. Sales representatives often face competition from representatives of other companies. Companies usually set goals or quotas that representatives are expected to meet. Because their earnings depend on commissions, manufacturers' agents are also under the added pressure to maintain and expand their clientele.

Employment

Manufacturers' and wholesale sales representatives held about 1.9 million jobs in 2002. About half of all salaried representatives worked in wholesale trade. Others were employed in manufacturing and mining. Due to the diversity of products and services sold, employment opportunities are available in every part of the country in a wide range of industries.

In addition to those working directly for a firm, many sales representatives are self-employed manufacturers' agents. They often form small sales firms and work for a straight commission based on the value of their own sales. However, manufacturers' agents usually gain experience and recognition with a manufacturer or wholesaler before becoming self-employed.

Training, Other Qualifications, and Advancement

The background needed for sales jobs varies by product line and market. Many employers hire individuals with previous sales experience who do not have a college degree, but often prefer those with some college education. Increasingly employers prefer or require a bachelor's degree as the job requirements have become more technical and analytical. Nevertheless, for some consumer products, factors such as sales ability, personality, and familiarity with brands are more important than educational background. On the other hand, firms selling complex, technical products may require a technical degree in addition to some sales experience. Many sales representatives attend seminars in sales techniques or take courses in marketing, economics, communication, or even a foreign language to provide the extra edge needed to make sales. In general, companies are looking for the best and brightest individuals who have the personality and desire to sell. Sales representatives need to be familiar with computer technology as computers are increasingly used in the workplace to place and track orders and to monitor inventory levels.

Many companies have formal training programs for beginning sales representatives lasting up to 2 years. However, most businesses are accelerating these programs to reduce costs and expedite the returns from training. In some programs, trainees rotate among jobs in plants and offices to learn all phases of production, installation, and distribution of the product. In others, trainees take formal classroom instruction at the plant, followed by on-the-job training under the supervision of a field sales manager.

New workers may get training by accompanying experienced workers on their sales calls. As they gain familiarity with the firm's products and clients, these workers are given increasing responsibility until they are eventually assigned their own territory. As businesses experience greater competition, increased pressure is placed upon sales representatives to produce sales.

Sales representatives stay abreast of new products and the changing needs of their customers in a variety of ways. They attend trade shows at which new products and technologies are showcased. They also attend conferences and conventions to meet other sales representatives and clients and discuss new product developments. In addition, the entire sales force may participate in company-sponsored meetings to review sales performance, product development, sales goals, and profitability.

Those who want to become sales representatives should be goal-oriented and persuasive, and work well both independently and as part of a team. A pleasant personality and appearance, the ability to communicate well with people, and problem-solving skills are highly valued. Furthermore, completing a sale can take several months and thus requires patience and perseverance.

Frequently, promotion takes the form of an assignment to a larger account or territory where commissions are likely to be greater. Experienced sales representatives may move into jobs as sales trainers, who instruct new employees on selling techniques and company policies and procedures. Those who have good sales records and leadership ability may advance to higher-level positions such as sales supervisor, district manager, or vice president of sales. In addition to advancement opportunities within a firm, some manufacturers' agents go into business for themselves. Others find opportunities in purchasing, advertising, or marketing research.

Job Outlook

Employment of sales representatives, wholesale and manufacturing, is expected to grow about as fast as the average for all occupations through the year 2012 due to continued growth in the variety and number of goods to be sold. Also, many job openings will result from the need to replace workers who transfer to other occupations or leave the labor force.

Prospective customers will still require sales workers to demonstrate or illustrate the particulars of a good or service. However, computer technology makes sales representatives more effective and productive, for example, by allowing them to provide accurate and current information to customers during sales presentations.

Job prospects for wholesale sales representatives will be better than those for manufacturing sales representatives because manufacturers are expected to continue contracting out sales duties to independent agents rather than using in-house or direct selling personnel. Agents are paid only if they sell, which reduces the overhead cost to their clients. Also, by using an agent who usually contracts his or her services to more than one company, companies can share costs with the other companies involved with that agent. As their customers and manufacturers continue to merge with other companies, independent agents and other wholesale trade firms will, in response, also merge with each other to better serve their clients. Although the demand for independent sales agents will increase over the 2002-12 projection period, the supply is expected to remain stable or decline because of the difficulties associated with self-employment. This factor could lead to many opportunities for sales representatives to start their own independent sales agencies.

Those interested in this occupation should keep in mind that direct selling opportunities in manufacturing are likely to be best for products for which there is strong demand. Furthermore, jobs will be most plentiful in small wholesale and manufacturing firms because a growing number of these companies will rely on agents to market their products as a way to control their costs and expand their customer base.

Employment opportunities and earnings may fluctuate from year to year because sales are affected by changing economic conditions, legislative issues, and consumer preferences. Job prospects will be best for persons with the appropriate knowledge or technical expertise as well as the personal traits necessary for successful selling.

Earnings

Compensation methods vary significantly by the type of firm and product sold. Most employers use a combination of salary and commission or salary plus bonus. Commissions usually are based on the amount of sales, whereas bonuses may depend on individual performance, on the performance of all sales workers in the group or district, or on the company's performance.

Median annual earnings of sales representatives, wholesale and manufacturing, technical and scientific products, were $55,740, including commission, in 2002. The middle 50 percent earned between $39,480 and $79,380 a year. The lowest 10 percent earned less than $28,770, and the highest 10 percent earned more than $108,010 a year. Median annual earnings in the industries employing the largest numbers of sales representatives, technical and scientific products, in 2002 were as follows:

Wholesale electronic markets and agents and brokers	$64,070
Professional and commercial equipment and supplies merchant wholesalers	60,890
Drugs and druggists' sundries merchant wholesalers	57,890
Machinery, equipment, and supplies merchant wholesalers	53,140
Electrical and electronic goods merchant wholesalers	50,550

Median annual earnings of sales representatives, wholesale and manufacturing, except technical and scientific products, were $42,730, including commission, in 2002. The middle 50 percent earned between $30,660 and $60,970 a year. The lowest 10 percent earned less than $22,610, and the highest 10 percent earned more than $88,990 a year. Median annual earnings in the industries employing the largest numbers of sales representatives, except technical and scientific products, in 2002 were as follows:

Wholesale electronic markets and agents and brokers	$48,320
Machinery, equipment, and supplies merchant wholesalers	44,030
Professional and commercial equipment and supplies merchant wholesalers	43,880
Grocery and related product wholesalers	41,840
Miscellaneous nondurable goods merchant wholesalers	37,940

In addition to their earnings, sales representatives usually are reimbursed for expenses such as transportation costs, meals, hotels, and entertaining customers. They often receive benefits such as health and life insurance, pension plan, vacation and sick leave, personal use of a company car, and frequent flyer mileage. Some companies offer incentives such as free vacation trips or gifts for outstanding sales workers.

Unlike those working directly for a manufacturer or wholesaler, manufacturers' agents are paid strictly on commission and usually are not reimbursed for expenses. Depending on the type of product or products they are selling, their experience in the field, and the number of clients, their earnings can be significantly higher or lower than those working in direct sales.

Related Occupations

Sales representatives, wholesale and manufacturing, must have sales ability and knowledge of the products they sell. Other occupations that require similar skills include advertising, marketing, promotions, and public relations, and sales managers; insurance sales agents; purchasing managers, buyers, and purchasing agents; real estate brokers and sales agents; retail salespersons; sales engineers; and securities, commodities, and financial services sales agents.

Sources of Additional Information

Information on careers for manufacturers' representatives and agents is available from:

- Manufacturers' Agents National Association, P.O. Box 3467, Laguna Hills, CA 92654-3467. Internet: http://www.manaonline.org

- Manufacturers' Representatives Educational Research Foundation, P.O. Box 247, Geneva, IL 60134. Internet: http://www.mrerf.org

Security Guards and Gaming Surveillance Officers

(O*NET 33-9031.00 and 33-9032.00)

Significant Points

- Opportunities for most jobs should be favorable, but competition is expected for higher paying positions at facilities requiring longer periods of training and a high level of security, such as nuclear power plants and weapons installations.

- Because of limited formal training requirements and flexible hours, this occupation attracts many individuals seeking a second or part-time job.

- Some positions, such as those of armored car guards, are hazardous.

Nature of the Work

Guards, who are also called *security officers*, patrol and inspect property to protect against fire, theft, vandalism, terrorism, and illegal activity. These workers protect their employer's investment, enforce laws on the property, and deter criminal activity or other problems. They use radio and telephone communications to call for assistance from police, fire, or emergency medical services as the situation dictates. Security guards write comprehensive reports outlining their observations and activities during their assigned shift. They may also interview witnesses or victims, prepare case reports, and testify in court.

Although all security guards perform many of the same duties, specific duties vary based on whether the guard works in a "static" security position or on a mobile patrol. Guards assigned to static security positions usually serve the client at one location for a specific length of time. These guards must become closely acquainted with the property and people associated with it and often monitor alarms and closed-circuit TV cameras. In contrast, guards assigned to mobile patrol duty drive or walk from location to location and conduct security checks within an assigned geographical zone. They may detain or arrest criminal violators, answer service calls concerning criminal activity or problems, and issue traffic violation warnings.

Specific job responsibilities also vary with the size, type, and location of the employer. In department stores, guards protect people, records, merchandise, money, and equipment. They often work with undercover store detectives to prevent theft by customers or store employees and help in the apprehension of shoplifting suspects prior to arrival by police. Some shopping centers and theaters have officers mounted on horses or bicycles who patrol their parking lots to deter car theft and robberies. In office buildings, banks, and hospitals, guards maintain order and protect the institutions' property, staff, and customers. At air, sea, and rail terminals and other transportation facilities, guards protect people, freight, property, and equipment. They may screen passengers and visitors for weapons and explosives using metal detectors and high-tech equipment, ensure nothing is stolen while being loaded or unloaded, and watch for fires and criminals.

Guards who work in public buildings such as museums or art galleries protect paintings and exhibits by inspecting people and packages entering and leaving the building. In factories, laboratories, government buildings, data processing centers, and military bases, security officers protect information, products, computer codes, and defense secrets and check the credentials of people and vehicles entering and leaving the premises. Guards working at universities, parks, and sports stadiums perform crowd control, supervise parking and seating, and direct traffic. Security guards stationed at the entrance to bars and places of adult entertainment, such as nightclubs, prevent access by minors, collect cover charges at the door, maintain order among customers, and protect property and patrons.

Armored car guards protect money and valuables during transit. In addition, they protect individuals responsible for making commercial bank deposits from theft or bodily injury. When the armored car arrives at the door of a business, an armed guard enters, signs for the money, and returns to the truck with the valuables in hand. Carrying money between the truck and the business can be extremely hazardous for guards. Because of this risk, armored car guards usually wear bullet-proof vests.

All security officers must show good judgment and common sense, follow directions and directives from supervisors, accurately testify in court, and follow company policy and guidelines. Guards should have a professional appearance and attitude and be able to interact with the public. They also must be able to take charge and direct others in emergencies or other dangerous incidents. In a large organization, the security manager is often in charge of a trained guard force divided into shifts; whereas in a small organization, a single worker may be responsible for all security.

Gaming surveillance officers and gaming investigators act as security agents for casino managers and patrons. They observe casino operations for irregular activities, such as cheating or theft, by either employees or patrons. To do this, surveillance officers and investigators often monitor activities from a catwalk over one-way mirrors located above the casino floor. Many casinos use audio and video equipment, allowing surveillance officers and investigators to observe these same areas via monitors. Recordings are kept as a record and are sometimes used as evidence against alleged criminals in police investigations.

Working Conditions

Most security guards and gaming surveillance officers spend considerable time on their feet, either assigned to a specific post or patrolling buildings and grounds. Guards may be stationed at a guard desk inside a building to monitor electronic security and surveillance devices or to check the credentials of persons entering or leaving the premises. They also may be stationed at a guardhouse outside the entrance to a gated facility or community and use a portable radio or cellular telephone that allows them to be in constant contact with a central station. The work usually is routine, but guards must be constantly alert for threats to themselves and the property they are protecting. Guards who work during the day may have a great deal of contact with other employees and members of the public. Gaming surveillance often takes place behind a bank of monitors controlling several cameras in a casino, which can cause eyestrain.

Guards usually work at least 8-hour shifts for 40 hours per week and often are on call in case an emergency arises. Some employers have three shifts, and guards rotate to equally divide daytime, weekend, and holiday work. Guards usually eat on the job instead of taking a regular break away from the site. More than 1 in 7 guards worked part time, and many individuals held a second job as a guard to supplement their primary earnings.

Employment

Security guards and gaming surveillance officers held more than 1.0 million jobs in 2002. More than half of jobs for security guards were in investigation and security services, including guard and armored car services. These organizations provide security services on a contract basis, assigning their guards to buildings and other sites as needed. Most other security officers were employed directly by educational services, hospitals, food services and drinking places, traveler accommodation (hotels), department stores, manufacturing firms, lessors of real estate (residential and nonresidential buildings), and governments. Guard jobs are found throughout the country, most commonly in metropolitan areas. Gaming surveillance officers worked primarily in gambling industries; traveler accommodation, which includes casino hotels; and local government. Gaming surveillance officers were employed only in those states and Indian reservations where gambling has been legalized.

A significant number of law enforcement officers work as security guards when off-duty to supplement their incomes. Often working in uniform and with the official cars assigned to them, they add a high profile security presence to the establishment with which they have contracted. At construction sites and apartment complexes, for example, their presence often prevents trouble before it starts.

Training, Other Qualifications, and Advancement

Most states require that guards be licensed. To be licensed as a guard, individuals must usually be at least 18 years old, pass a background check, and complete classroom training in such subjects as property rights, emergency procedures, and detention of suspected criminals. Drug testing often is required, and may be random and ongoing.

Many employers of unarmed guards do not have any specific educational requirements. For armed guards, employers usually prefer individuals who are high school graduates or hold an equivalent certification. Many jobs require a driver's license. For positions as armed guards, employers often seek people who have had responsible experience in other occupations.

Guards who carry weapons must be licensed by the appropriate government authority, and some receive further certification as special police officers, which allows them to make limited types of arrests while on duty. Armed guard positions have more stringent background checks and entry require-

ments than those of unarmed guards because of greater insurance liability risks. Compared to unarmed security guards, armed guards and special police typically enjoy higher earnings and benefits, greater job security, more advancement potential, and usually are given more training and responsibility.

Rigorous hiring and screening programs consisting of background, criminal record, and fingerprint checks are becoming the norm in the occupation. Applicants are expected to have good character references, no serious police record, and good health. They should be mentally alert, emotionally stable, and physically fit in order to cope with emergencies. Guards who have frequent contact with the public should communicate well.

The amount of training guards receive varies. Training requirements are higher for armed guards because their employers are legally responsible for any use of force. Armed guards receive formal training in areas such as weapons retention and laws covering the use of force.

Many employers give newly hired guards instruction before they start the job and also provide on-the-job training. An increasing number of states are making ongoing training a legal requirement for retention of certification. Guards may receive training in protection, public relations, report writing, crisis deterrence, and first aid, as well as specialized training relevant to their particular assignment.

Guards employed at establishments placing a heavy emphasis on security usually receive extensive formal training. For example, guards at nuclear power plants undergo several months of training before being placed on duty under close supervision. They are taught to use firearms, administer first aid, operate alarm systems and electronic security equipment, and spot and deal with security problems. Guards authorized to carry firearms may be periodically tested in their use.

Although guards in small companies may receive periodic salary increases, advancement opportunities are limited. Most large organizations use a military type of ranking that offers the possibility of advancement in position and salary. Some guards may advance to supervisor or security manager positions. Guards with management skills may open their own contract security guard agencies.

In addition to the keen observation skills required to perform their jobs, gaming surveillance officers and gaming investigators must have excellent verbal and writing abilities to document violations or suspicious behavior. They also need to be physically fit and have quick reflexes because they sometimes must detain individuals until local law enforcement officials arrive.

Surveillance officers and investigators usually do not need a bachelor's degree, but some training beyond high school is required; previous security experience is a plus. Several educational institutes offer certification programs. Training classes usually are conducted in a casino-like atmosphere using surveillance camera equipment.

Job Outlook

Opportunities for security guards and gaming surveillance officers should be favorable. Numerous job openings will stem from employment growth attributable to the desire for increased security, and from the need to replace those who leave this large occupation each year. In addition to full-time job opportunities, the limited training requirements and flexible hours attract many persons seeking part-time or second jobs. However, competition is expected for higher paying positions that require longer periods of training; these positions usually are found at facilities that require a high level of security, such as nuclear power plants or weapons installations.

Employment of security guards and gaming surveillance officers is expected to grow faster than the average for all occupations through 2012 as concern about crime, vandalism, and terrorism continue to increase the need for security. Demand for guards also will grow as private security firms increasingly perform duties—such as monitoring crowds at airports and providing security in courts—which were formerly handled by government police officers and marshals. Because enlisting the services of a security guard firm is easier and less costly than assuming direct responsibility for hiring, training, and managing a security guard force, job growth is expected to be concentrated among contract security guard agencies. Casinos will continue to hire more surveillance officers as more states legalize gambling and as the number of casinos increases in states where gambling is already legal. Additionally, casino security forces will employ more technically trained personnel as technology becomes increasingly important in thwarting casino cheating and theft.

Earnings

Median annual earnings of security guards were $19,140 in 2002. The middle 50 percent earned between $15,910 and $23,920. The lowest 10 percent earned less than $13,740, and the highest 10 percent earned more than $31,540. Median annual earnings in the industries employing the largest numbers of security guards in 2002 were as follows:

Elementary and secondary schools	$24,470
General medical and surgical hospitals	24,050
Local government	22,120
Traveler accommodation	21,390
Investigation and security services	17,910

Gaming surveillance officers and gaming investigators had median annual earnings of $23,110 in 2002. The middle 50 percent earned between $19,620 and $28,420. The lowest 10 percent earned less than $15,930, and the highest 10 percent earned more than $35,170.

Related Occupations

Guards protect property, maintain security, and enforce regulations and standards of conduct in the establishments at which they work. Related security and protective service occupations include correctional officers, police and detectives, and private detectives and investigators.

Sources of Additional Information

Further information about work opportunities for guards is available from local security and guard firms and state employment service offices. Information about licensing requirements for guards may be obtained from the state licensing commission or the state police department. In states where local jurisdictions establish licensing requirements, contact a local government authority such as the sheriff, county executive, or city manager.

Sheet Metal Workers

(O*NET 47-2211.00)

Significant Points

- Nearly two-thirds of the jobs are found in the construction industry; about one quarter are in manufacturing.

- Apprenticeship programs lasting 4 or 5 years are considered the best training.

- Job opportunities in construction should be good.

Nature of the Work

Sheet metal workers make, install, and maintain heating, ventilation, and air-conditioning duct systems; roofs; siding; rain gutters; downspouts; skylights; restaurant equipment; outdoor signs; railroad cars; tailgates; customized precision equipment; and many other products made from metal sheets. They also may work with fiberglass and plastic materials. Although some workers specialize in fabrication, installation, or maintenance, most do all three jobs. Sheet metal workers do both construction-related sheet metal work and mass production of sheet metal products in manufacturing.

Sheet metal workers first study plans and specifications to determine the kind and quantity of materials they will need. They then measure, cut, bend, shape, and fasten pieces of sheet metal to make ductwork, countertops, and other custom products. In an increasing number of shops, sheet metal workers use computerized metalworking equipment. This enables them to perform their tasks more quickly and to experiment with different layouts to find the one that results in the least waste of material. They cut, drill, and form parts with computer-controlled saws, lasers, shears, and presses.

In shops without computerized equipment, and for products that cannot be made on such equipment, sheet metal workers use hand calculators to make the required calculations and use tapes, rulers, and other measuring devices for layout work. They then cut or stamp the parts on machine tools.

Before assembling pieces, sheet metal workers check each part for accuracy using measuring instruments such as calipers and micrometers and, if necessary, finish it by using hand, rotary, or squaring shears and hacksaws. After the parts have been inspected, workers fasten seams and joints together with welds, bolts, cement, rivets, solder, specially formed sheet metal drive clips, or other connecting devices. They then take the parts to the construction site, where they further assemble the pieces as they install them. These workers install ducts, pipes, and tubes by joining them end to end and hanging them with metal hangers secured to a ceiling or a wall. They also use shears, hammers, punches, and drills to make parts at the worksite or to alter parts made in the shop.

Some jobs are done completely at the jobsite. When installing a metal roof, for example, sheet metal workers measure and cut the roofing panels that are needed to complete the job. They secure the first panel in place and interlock and fasten the grooved edge of the next panel into the grooved edge of the first. Then, they nail or weld the free edge of the panel to the structure. This two-step process is repeated for each additional panel. Finally, the workers fasten machine-made molding at joints, along corners, and around windows and doors for a neat, finished effect.

In addition to installation, some sheet metal workers specialize in testing, balancing, adjusting, and servicing existing air-conditioning and ventilation systems to make sure they are functioning properly and to improve their energy efficiency. Properly installed duct systems are a key component to heating, ventilation, and air-conditioning (HVAC) systems, which causes duct installers to sometimes be referred to as *HVAC technicians*. A duct system allows for even air distribution while minimizing leaks and temperature differentiation that can cause other problems, such as mold.

Sheet metal workers in manufacturing plants make sheet metal parts for products such as aircraft or industrial equipment. Although some of the fabrication techniques used in large-scale manufacturing are similar to those used in smaller shops, the work may be highly automated and repetitive. Sheet metal workers doing such work may be responsible for reprogramming the computer control systems of the equipment they operate.

Working Conditions

Sheet metal workers usually work a 40-hour week. Those who fabricate sheet metal products work in shops that are well-lighted and well-ventilated. However, they stand for long periods and lift heavy materials and finished pieces. Sheet metal workers must follow safety practices because working around high-speed machines can be dangerous. They also are subject to cuts from sharp metal, burns from soldering and welding, and falls from ladders and scaffolds. They usually wear safety glasses but must not wear jewelry or loose-fitting clothing that could easily be caught in a machine. They may work at a variety of different production stations to reduce the repetitiveness of the work.

Those performing installation work do considerable bending, lifting, standing, climbing, and squatting, sometimes in close quarters or in awkward positions. Although duct systems and kitchen equipment are installed indoors, the installation of siding, roofs, and gutters involves much outdoor work, requiring sheet metal workers to be exposed to various kinds of weather.

Employment

Sheet metal workers held about 205,000 jobs in 2002. Nearly two-thirds of all sheet metal workers were found in the construction industry. Of those employed in construction, almost half worked for plumbing, heating, and air-conditioning contractors; most of the rest worked for roofing and sheet metal contractors. Some worked for other special trade contractors and for general contractors engaged in residential and commercial building. One-quarter of all sheet metal workers work outside of construction and are found in manufacturing industries, such as the fabricated metal products, machinery, and aerospace products and parts industries. Some work for the federal government.

Compared with workers in most construction craft occupations, relatively few sheet metal workers are self-employed.

Training, Other Qualifications, and Advancement

Apprenticeship generally is considered to be the best way to learn this trade. The apprenticeship program consists of 4 or 5 years of on-the-job training and an average of 200 hours per year of classroom instruction. Apprenticeship programs provide comprehensive instruction in both sheet metal fabrication and installation. They may be administered by local joint committees composed of the Sheet Metal Workers' International Association and local chapters of the Sheet Metal and Air-Conditioning Contractors National Association.

On the job, apprentices learn the basics of pattern layout and how to cut, bend, fabricate, and install sheet metal. They begin by learning to install and maintain basic ductwork and gradually advance to more difficult jobs, such as making more complex ducts, commercial kitchens, and decorative pieces. They also use materials such as fiberglass, plastics, and other nonmetallic materials. Some workers may focus on exterior or architectural sheet metal installation.

In the classroom, apprentices learn drafting, plan and specification reading, trigonometry and geometry applicable to layout work, the use of computerized equipment, welding, and the principles of heating, air-conditioning, and ventilating systems. Safety is stressed throughout the program. In addition, apprentices learn the relationship between sheet metal work and other construction work.

Some persons pick up the trade informally, usually by working as helpers to experienced sheet metal workers. Most begin by carrying metal and cleaning up debris in a metal shop while they learn about materials and tools and their uses. Later, they learn to operate machines that bend or cut metal. In time, helpers go out on the jobsite to learn installation. Those who acquire their skills this way often take vocational school courses in mathematics or sheet metal fabrication to supplement their work experience. To be promoted to the journey level, helpers usually must pass the same written examination as apprentices. Most sheet metal workers in large-scale manufacturing receive on-the-job training, with additional classwork or in-house training when necessary.

Applicants for jobs as apprentices or helpers should be in good physical condition and have mechanical and mathematical aptitude as well as good reading skills. Good eye-hand coordination, spatial and form perception, and manual dexterity also are important. Local apprenticeship committees require a high school education or its equivalent. Courses in algebra, trigonometry, geometry, mechanical drawing, and shop provide a helpful background for learning the trade, as does related work experience obtained in the Armed Services.

It is important for experienced sheet metal workers to keep abreast of new technological developments, such as the growing use of computerized layout and laser-cutting machines. Workers often take additional training, provided by the union or by their employer, to improve existing skills or to acquire new ones.

Sheet metal workers in construction may advance to supervisory jobs. Some of these workers take additional training in welding and do more specialized work. Others go into the contracting business for themselves. Because a sheet metal contractor must have a shop with equipment to fabricate products, this type of contracting business is more expensive to start than other types of construction contracting. Sheet metal workers in manufacturing may advance to positions as supervisors or quality inspectors. Some of these workers may move into other management positions.

Job Outlook

Job opportunities are expected to be good for sheet metal workers in the construction industry and in construction-related sheet metal fabrication, reflecting both employment growth and openings arising each year as experienced sheet metal workers leave the occupation. In addition, many potential workers may prefer work that is less strenuous and that has more comfortable working conditions, thus limiting the number of applicants for sheet metal jobs. Opportunities should be particularly good for individuals who acquire apprenticeship training. Job prospects in manufac-

turing will not be as good because construction is expected to grow faster than the manufacturing industries that employ sheet metal workers. Because some sheet metal manufacturing is labor-intensive, manufacturers sometimes move production to lower wage areas or countries.

Employment of sheet metal workers in construction is expected to grow about as fast as the average for all occupations through 2012, reflecting growth in the demand for sheet metal installations as more industrial, commercial, and residential structures are built. The need to install energy-efficient air-conditioning, heating, and ventilation systems in the increasing stock of old buildings and to perform other types of renovation and maintenance work also should boost employment. In addition, the popularity of decorative sheet metal products and increased architectural restoration are expected to add to the demand for sheet metal workers. On the other hand, slower-than-average job growth is projected for sheet metal workers in manufacturing.

Sheet metal workers in construction may experience periods of unemployment, particularly when construction projects end and economic conditions dampen construction activity. Nevertheless, employment of sheet metal workers is less sensitive to declines in new construction than is the employment of some other construction workers, such as carpenters. Maintenance of existing equipment—which is less affected by economic fluctuations than is new construction—makes up a large part of the work done by sheet metal workers. Installation of new air-conditioning and heating systems in existing buildings continues during construction slumps, as individuals and businesses adopt more energy-efficient equipment to cut utility bills. In addition, a large proportion of sheet metal installation and maintenance is done indoors, so sheet metal workers usually lose less work-time due to bad weather than other construction workers do.

Earnings

In 2002, median hourly earnings of sheet metal workers were $16.62. The middle 50 percent earned between $12.15 and $23.03. The lowest 10 percent of all sheet metal workers earned less than $9.50, and the highest 10 percent earned more than $29.53. The median hourly earnings of the largest industries employing sheet metal workers in 2002 are shown below.

Federal government $19.73

Building equipment contractors 17.47

Building finishing contractors.................................16.77

Foundation, structure, and building exterior
   contractors 15.48

Architectural and structural metals
   manufacturing 14.60

Apprentices normally start at about 40 to 50 percent of the rate paid to experienced workers. As apprentices acquire more skills throughout the course of their training, they receive periodic increases until their pay approaches that of experienced workers. In addition, union workers in some areas receive supplemental wages from the union when they are on layoff or shortened workweeks.

Related Occupations

To fabricate and install sheet metal products, sheet metal workers combine metalworking skills and knowledge of construction materials and techniques. Other occupations in which workers lay out and fabricate metal products include assemblers and fabricators; machinists; machine setters, operators, and tenders—metal and plastic; and tool and die makers. Construction occupations requiring similar skills and knowledge include glaziers and heating, air-conditioning, and refrigeration mechanics and installers.

Sources of Additional Information

For more information about apprenticeships or other work opportunities, contact local sheet metal contractors or heating, refrigeration, and air-conditioning contractors; a local of the Sheet Metal Workers International Association; a local of the Sheet Metal and Air-Conditioning Contractors National Association; a local joint union-management apprenticeship committee; or the nearest office of your state employment service or apprenticeship agency.

For general and training information about sheet metal workers, contact:

- International Training Institute for the Sheet Metal and Air-Conditioning Industry, 601 N. Fairfax St., Suite 240, Alexandria, VA 22314. Internet: http://www.sheetmetal-iti.org

- Sheet Metal and Air-Conditioning Contractors National Association, 4201 Lafayette Center Dr., Chantilly, VA 20151-1209. Internet: http://www.smacna.org

- Sheet Metal Workers International Association, 1750 New York Ave. NW, Washington, DC 20006. Internet: http://www.smwia.org

There are more than 500 occupations registered by the U.S. Department of Labor's National Apprenticeship system. For more information on the Labor Department's registered apprenticeship system and links to state apprenticeship programs, check their Web site: http://www.doleta.gov.

Social and Human Service Assistants

(O*NET 21-1093.00)

Significant Points

- While a bachelor's degree usually is not required, employers increasingly seek individuals with relevant work experience or education beyond high school.

- Employment is projected to grow much faster than average.

- Job opportunities should be excellent, particularly for applicants with appropriate postsecondary education, but pay is low.

Nature of the Work

Social and human service assistant is a generic term for people with a wide array of job titles, including human service worker, case management aide, social work assistant, community support worker, mental health aide, community outreach worker, life skill counselor, or gerontology aide. They usually work under the direction of professionals from a variety of fields, such as nursing, psychiatry, psychology, rehabilitative or physical therapy, or social work. The amount of responsibility and supervision they are given varies a great deal. Some have little direct supervision; others work under close direction.

Social and human service assistants provide direct and indirect client services to ensure that individuals in their care reach their maximum level of functioning. They assess clients' needs, establish their eligibility for benefits and services such as food stamps, Medicaid, or welfare, and help to obtain them. They also arrange for transportation and escorts, if necessary, and provide emotional support. Social and human service assistants monitor and keep case records on clients and report progress to supervisors and case managers.

Social and human service assistants play a variety of roles in a community. They may organize and lead group activities, assist clients in need of counseling or crisis intervention, or administer a food bank or emergency fuel program. In halfway houses, group homes, and government-supported housing programs, they assist adults who need supervision with personal hygiene and daily living skills. They review clients' records, ensure that they take correct doses of medication, talk with family members, and confer with medical personnel and other caregivers to gain better insight into clients' backgrounds and needs. Social and human service assistants also provide emotional support and help clients become involved in their own well-being, in community recreation programs, and in other activities.

In psychiatric hospitals, rehabilitation programs, and outpatient clinics, social and human service assistants work with professional care providers, such as psychiatrists, psychologists, and social workers, to help clients master everyday living skills, communicate more effectively, and get along better with others. They support the client's participation in a treatment plan, such as individual or group counseling or occupational therapy.

Working Conditions

Working conditions of social and human service assistants vary. Some work in offices, clinics, and hospitals, while others work in group homes, shelters, sheltered workshops, and day programs. Many spend their time in the field visiting clients. Most work a 40-hour week, although some work in the evening and on weekends.

The work, while satisfying, can be emotionally draining. Understaffing and relatively low pay may add to the pressure. Turnover is reported to be high, especially among workers without academic preparation for this field.

Employment

Social and human service assistants held about 305,000 jobs in 2002. More than half worked in the health care and social assistance industries. Almost one third were employed by state and local governments, primarily in public welfare agencies and facilities for mentally disabled and developmentally challenged individuals.

Training, Other Qualifications, and Advancement

While a bachelor's degree usually is not required for entry into this occupation, employers increasingly seek individuals with relevant work experience or education beyond high school. Certificates or associate degrees in subjects such as social work, human services, gerontology, or one of the social or behavioral sciences meet most employers' requirements. Some jobs may require a bachelor's or master's degree in human services or a related field such as counseling, rehabilitation, or social work.

Human services degree programs have a core curriculum that trains students to observe patients and record information, conduct patient interviews, implement treatment plans, employ problem-solving techniques, handle crisis intervention matters, and use proper case management and referral procedures. General education courses in liberal arts, sciences, and the humanities also are part of the curriculum. Many degree programs require completion of a supervised internship.

Educational attainment often influences the kind of work employees may be assigned and the degree of responsibility that may be entrusted to them. For example, workers with no more than a high school education are likely to receive extensive on-the-job training to work in direct-care services, while employees with a college degree might be assigned to do supportive counseling, coordinate program activities, or manage a group home. Social and human service assistants with proven leadership ability, either from previous experience or as a volunteer in the field, often have greater autonomy in their work. Regardless of the academic or work background of employees, most employers provide some form of inservice training, such as seminars and workshops, to their employees.

There may be additional hiring requirements in group homes. For example, employers may require employees to have a valid driver's license or to submit to a criminal background investigation.

Employers try to select applicants who have effective communication skills, a strong sense of responsibility, and the ability to manage time effectively. Many human services jobs involve direct contact with people who are vulnerable to exploitation or mistreatment; therefore, patience, understanding, and a strong desire to help others are highly valued characteristics.

Formal education almost always is necessary for advancement. In general, advancement requires a bachelor's or master's degree in human services, counseling, rehabilitation, social work, or a related field.

Job Outlook

Job opportunities for social and human service assistants are expected to be excellent, particularly for applicants with appropriate postsecondary education. The number of social and human service assistants is projected to grow much faster than the average for all occupations between 2002 and 2012—ranking the occupation among the most rapidly growing. Many additional job opportunities will arise from the need to replace workers who advance into new positions, retire, or leave the workforce for other reasons. There will be more competition for jobs in urban areas than in rural areas, but qualified applicants should have little difficulty finding employment. Faced with rapid growth in the demand for social and human services many employers increasingly rely on social and human service assistants to undertake greater responsibility for delivering services to clients.

Opportunities are expected to be good in private social service agencies, which provide such services as adult daycare and meal delivery programs. Employment in private agencies will grow as state and local governments continue to contract out services to the private sector in an effort to cut costs. Demand for social services will expand with the growing elderly population, who are more likely to need these services. In addition, more social and human service assistants will be needed to provide services to pregnant teenagers, the homeless, the mentally disabled and developmentally challenged, and substance abusers. Some private agencies have been employing more social and human service assistants in place of social workers, who are more educated and, thus, more highly paid.

Job training programs also are expected to require additional social and human service assistants. As social welfare policies shift focus from benefit-based programs to work-based initiatives, there will be more demand for people to teach job skills to the people who are new to, or returning to, the workforce.

Residential care establishments should face increased pressures to respond to the needs of the mentally and physically disabled. Many of these patients have been deinstitutionalized and lack the knowledge or the ability to care for themselves. Also, more community-based programs, supported independent-living sites, and group residences are expected to be established to house and assist the homeless and the mentally and physically disabled. As substance abusers are increasingly being sent to treatment programs instead of prison, employment of social and human service assistants in substance abuse treatment programs also will grow.

The number of jobs for social and human service assistants in state and local governments will grow but not as fast as employment for social and human service assistants in other industries. Employment in the public sector may fluctuate with the level of funding provided by state and local governments. Also, some state and local governments are contracting out selected social services to private agencies in order to save money.

Earnings

Median annual earnings of social and human service assistants were $23,370 in 2002. The middle 50 percent earned between $18,670 and $29,520. The top 10 percent earned more than $37,550, while the lowest 10 percent earned less than $15,420.

Median annual earnings in the industries employing the largest numbers of social and human service assistants in 2002 were:

State government	$31,280
Local government	26,570
Individual and family services	22,210
Community food and housing, and emergency and other relief services	21,840
Residential mental retardation, mental health and substance abuse facilities	20,010

Related Occupations

Workers in other occupations that require skills similar to those of social and human service assistants include social workers; clergy; counselors; childcare workers; occupational therapist assistants and aides; physical therapist assistants and aides; and nursing, psychiatric, and home health aides.

Sources of Additional Information

Information on academic programs in human services may be found in most directories of 2- and 4-year colleges, available at libraries or career counseling centers.

For information on programs and careers in human services, contact:

- National Organization for Human Service Education, 375 Myrtle Ave., Brooklyn, NY 11205. Internet: http://www.nohse.org

- Council for Standards in Human Services Education, Harrisburg Area Community College, Human Services Program, One HACC Dr., Harrisburg, PA 17110-2999. Internet: http://www.cshse.org

Information on job openings may be available from state employment service offices or directly from city, county, or state departments of health, mental health and mental retardation, and human resources.

Social Workers

(O*NET 21-1021.00, 21-1022.00, and 21-1023.00)

Significant Points

- While a bachelor's degree is the minimum requirement, a master's degree in social work or a related field has become the standard for many positions.

- Employment is projected to grow faster than average.

- Competition for jobs is expected in cities, but opportunities should be good in rural areas.

Nature of the Work

Social work is a profession for those with a strong desire to help improve people's lives. Social workers help people function the best way they can in their environment, deal with their relationships, and solve personal and family problems. Social workers often see clients who face a life-threatening disease or a social problem. These problems may include inadequate housing, unemployment, serious illness, disability, or substance abuse. Social workers also assist families that have serious domestic conflicts, including those involving child or spousal abuse.

Social workers often provide social services in health-related settings that now are governed by managed care organizations. To contain costs, these organizations are emphasizing short-term intervention, ambulatory and community-based care, and greater decentralization of services.

Most social workers specialize. Although some conduct research or are involved in planning or policy development, most social workers prefer an area of practice in which they interact with clients.

Child, family, and school social workers provide social services and assistance to improve the social and psychological functioning of children and their families and to maximize the family well-being and academic functioning of children. Some social workers assist single parents; arrange adoptions; and help find foster homes for neglected, abandoned, or abused children. In schools, they address such problems as teenage pregnancy, misbehavior, and truancy. They also advise teachers on how to cope with problem students. Some social workers may specialize in services for senior citizens. They run support groups for family caregivers or for the adult children of aging parents. Some advise elderly people or family members about choices in areas such as housing, transportation, and long-term care; they also coordinate and monitor services. Through employee assistance programs, they may help workers cope with job-related pressures or with personal problems that affect the quality of their work. Child, family, and school social workers typically work in individual and family services agencies, schools, or state or local governments. These social workers may be known as child welfare social workers, family services social workers, child protective services social workers, occupational social workers, or gerontology social workers.

Medical and public health social workers provide persons, families, or vulnerable populations with the psychosocial support needed to cope with chronic, acute, or terminal illnesses, such as Alzheimer's disease, cancer, or AIDS. They also advise family caregivers, counsel patients, and help plan for patients' needs after discharge by arranging for at-home services—from meals-on-wheels to oxygen equipment. Some work on interdisciplinary teams that evaluate certain kinds of patients—geriatric or organ transplant patients, for example. Medical and public health social workers may work for hospitals, nursing and personal care facilities, individual and family services agencies, or local governments.

Mental health and substance abuse social workers assess and treat individuals with mental illness, or substance abuse problems, including abuse of alcohol, tobacco, or other drugs. Such services include individual and group therapy, outreach, crisis intervention, social rehabilitation, and training in skills of everyday living. They may also help plan for supportive services to ease patients' return to the community. Mental health and substance abuse social workers are likely to work in hospitals, substance abuse treatment centers, individual and family services agencies, or local governments. These social workers may be known as clinical social workers.

Other types of social workers include social work planners and policymakers, who develop programs to address such issues as child abuse, homelessness, substance abuse, poverty, and violence. These workers research and analyze policies, programs, and regulations. They identify social problems and suggest legislative and other solutions. They may help raise funds or write grants to support these programs.

Working Conditions

Full-time social workers usually work a standard 40-hour week; however, some occasionally work evenings and weekends to meet with clients, attend community meetings, and handle emergencies. Some, particularly in voluntary non-profit agencies, work part time. Social workers usually spend most of their time in an office or residential facility, but also may travel locally to visit clients, meet with service providers, or attend meetings. Some may use one of several offices within a local area in which to meet with clients. The work, while satisfying, can be emotionally draining. Understaffing and large caseloads add to the pressure in some agencies. To tend to patient care or client needs, many hospitals and long-term care facilities are employing social workers on teams with a broad mix of occupations— including clinical specialists, registered nurses, and health aides.

Employment

Social workers held about 477,000 jobs in 2002. About 4 out of 10 jobs were in state or local government agencies, primarily in departments of health and human services. Most private sector jobs were in the health care and social assistance industry. Although most social workers are employed in cities or suburbs, some work in rural areas. The following tabulation shows 2002 employment by type of social worker.

Child, family, and school social workers 274,000

Medical and public health social workers............107,000

Mental health and substance abuse
  social workers 95,000

Training, Other Qualifications, and Advancement

A bachelor's degree in social work (BSW) degree is the most common minimum requirement to qualify for a job as a social worker; however, majors in psychology, sociology, and related fields may be adequate to qualify for some entry-level jobs, especially in small community agencies. Although a bachelor's degree is sufficient for entry into the field, an advanced degree has become the standard for many positions. A master's degree in social work (MSW) is typically required for positions in health settings and is required for clinical work. Some jobs in public and private agencies also may require an advanced degree, such as a master's degree in social services policy or administration. Supervisory, administrative, and staff training positions usually require an advanced degree. College and university teaching positions and most research appointments normally require a doctorate in social work (DSW or Ph.D.).

As of 2002, the Council on Social Work Education (CSWE) accredited 436 BSW programs and 149 MSW programs. The Group for the Advancement of Doctoral Education (GADE) listed 78 doctoral programs in social work (DSW or Ph.D.). BSW programs prepare graduates for direct service positions such as caseworker. They include courses in social work values and ethics, dealing with a culturally diverse clientele, at-risk-populations, promotion of social and economic justice, human behavior and the social environment, social welfare policy and services, social work practice, social research methods, and field education. Accredited BSW programs require a minimum of 400 hours of supervised field experience.

Master's degree programs prepare graduates for work in their chosen field of concentration and continue to develop the skills required to perform clinical assessments, manage large caseloads, and explore new ways of drawing upon social services to meet the needs of clients. Master's programs last 2 years and include a minimum of 900 hours of supervised field instruction, or internship. A part-time program may take 4 years. Entry into a master's program does not require a bachelor's in social work, but courses in psychology, biology, sociology, economics, political science, and social work are recommended. In addition, a second language can be very helpful. Most master's programs offer advanced standing for those with a bachelor's degree from an accredited social work program.

All states and the District of Columbia have licensing, certification, or registration requirements regarding social work practice and the use of professional titles. Although standards for licensing vary by state, a growing number of states are placing greater emphasis on communications skills, professional ethics, and sensitivity to cultural diversity issues. Additionally, the National Association of Social Workers (NASW) offers voluntary credentials. Social workers with an MSW may be eligible for the Academy of Certified Social Workers (ACSW), the Qualified Clinical Social Worker (QCSW), or the Diplomate in Clinical Social Work (DCSW) credential based on their professional experience. Credentials are particularly important for those in private practice; some health insurance providers require social workers to have them in order to be reimbursed for services.

Social workers should be emotionally mature, objective, and sensitive to people and their problems. They must be able to handle responsibility, work independently, and maintain good working relationships with clients and coworkers. Volunteer or paid jobs as a social work aide offer ways of testing one's interest in this field.

Advancement to supervisor, program manager, assistant director, or executive director of a social service agency or department is possible, but usually requires an advanced degree and related work experience. Other career options for social workers include teaching, research, and consulting. Some of these workers also help formulate government policies by analyzing and advocating policy positions in government agencies, in research institutions, and on legislators' staffs.

Some social workers go into private practice. Most private practitioners are clinical social workers who provide psychotherapy, usually paid for through health insurance or by the client themselves. Private practitioners must have at least a master's degree and a period of supervised work experience. A network of contacts for referrals also is essential. Many private practitioners work part time while they work full time elsewhere.

Job Outlook

Competition for social worker jobs is stronger in cities, where demand for services often is highest and training programs for social workers are prevalent. However, opportunities should be good in rural areas, which often find it difficult to attract and retain qualified staff. By specialty, job prospects may be best for those social workers with a background in gerontology and substance abuse treatment.

Employment of social workers is expected to grow faster than the average for all occupations through 2012. The rapidly growing elderly population and the aging baby boom generation will create greater demand for health and social services, resulting in particularly rapid job growth among gerontology social workers. Many job openings also will stem from the need to replace social workers who leave the occupation.

As hospitals continue to limit the length of patient stays, the demand for social workers in hospitals will grow more slowly than in other areas. Because hospitals are releasing patients earlier than in the past, social worker employment in home healthcare services is growing. However, the expanding senior population is an even larger factor. Employment opportunities for social workers with backgrounds in gerontology should be good in the growing numbers of assisted-living and senior-living communities. The expanding senior population will also spur demand for social workers in nursing homes, long-term care facilities, and hospices.

Employment of substance abuse social workers will grow rapidly over the 2002-12 projection period. Substance abusers are increasingly being placed into treatment programs instead of being sentenced to prison. As this trend grows, demand will increase for treatment programs and social workers to assist abusers on the road to recovery.

Employment of social workers in private social service agencies will increase. However, agencies increasingly will restructure services and hire more lower-paid social and human service assistants instead of social workers. Employment in state and local government agencies may grow somewhat in response to increasing needs for public welfare, family services, and child protection services; however, many of these services will be contracted out to private agencies. Employment levels in public and private social services agencies may fluctuate, depending on need and government funding levels.

Employment of school social workers also is expected to steadily grow. Expanded efforts to respond to rising student enrollments and continued emphasis on integrating disabled children into the general school population may lead to more jobs. Availability of state and local funding will be a major factor in determining the actual job growth in schools.

Opportunities for social workers in private practice will expand but growth may be somewhat hindered by restrictions that managed care organizations put on mental health services. The growing popularity of employee assistance programs is expected to spur some demand for private practitioners, some of whom provide social work services to corporations on a contractual basis. However, the popularity of employee assistance programs will fluctuate with the business cycle, as businesses are not likely to offer these services during recessions.

Earnings

Median annual earnings of child, family, and school social workers were $33,150 in 2002. The middle 50 percent earned between $26,310 and $42,940. The lowest 10 percent earned less than $21,270, and the top 10 percent earned more than $54,250. Median annual earnings in the industries employing the largest numbers of child, family, and school social workers in 2002 were:

Elementary and secondary schools	$44,100
Local government	38,140
State government	34,000
Individual and family services	29,150
Other residential care facilities	28,470

Median annual earnings of medical and public health social workers were $37,380 in 2002. The middle 50 percent earned between $29,700 and $46,540. The lowest 10 percent earned less than $23,840, and the top 10 percent earned more than $56,320. Median annual earnings in the industries employing the largest numbers of medical and public health social workers in 2002 were:

General medical and surgical hospitals	$42,730
Local government	37,620
State government	35,250
Nursing care facilities	33,330
Individual and family services	31,000

Median annual earnings of mental health and substance abuse social workers were $32,850 in 2002. The middle 50 percent earned between $25,940 and $42,160. The lowest 10 percent earned less than $21,050, and the top 10 percent earned more than $52,240. Median annual earnings in the industries employing the largest numbers of mental health and substance abuse social workers in 2002 were:

State government	$38,430
Local government	35,700
Psychiatric and substance abuse hospitals	34,610
Outpatient care centers	31,370
Individual and family services	31,300

Related Occupations

Through direct counseling or referral to other services, social workers help people solve a range of personal problems. Workers in occupations with similar duties include the clergy, counselors, probation officers and correctional treatment specialists, psychologists, and social and human services assistants.

Sources of Additional Information

For information about career opportunities in social work and voluntary credentials for social workers, contact:

● National Association of Social Workers, 750 First St. NE, Suite 700, Washington, DC 20002-4241. Internet: http://www.socialworkers.org

For a listing of accredited social work programs, contact:

● Council on Social Work Education, 1725 Duke St., Suite 500, Alexandria, VA 22314-3457. Internet: http://www.cswe.org

Information on licensing requirements and testing procedures for each state may be obtained from state licensing authorities, or from:

● Association of Social Work Boards, 400 South Ridge Pkwy., Suite B, Culpeper, VA 22701. Internet: http://www.aswb.org

Speech-Language Pathologists

(O*NET 29-1127.00)

Significant Points

● Employment of speech-language pathologists is expected to grow rapidly because the expanding population in older age groups is prone to medical conditions that result in speech, language, and swallowing problems.

● About half worked in educational services, and most others were employed by healthcare and social assistance facilities.

● A master's degree in speech-language pathology is the standard credential.

Nature of the Work

Speech-language pathologists, sometimes called *speech therapists*, assess, diagnose, treat, and help to prevent speech, language, cognitive, communication, voice, swallowing, fluency, and other related disorders.

Speech-language pathologists work with people who cannot make speech sounds, or cannot make them clearly; those with speech rhythm and fluency problems, such as stuttering; people with voice quality problems, such as inappropriate pitch or harsh voice; those with problems understanding and producing language; those who wish to improve their communication skills by modifying an accent; those with cognitive communication impairments, such as attention, memory, and problem solving disorders; and those with hearing loss who use hearing aids or cochlear implants in order to develop auditory skills and improve communication. They also work with people who have swallowing difficulties.

Speech and language difficulties can result from a variety of causes including stroke, brain injury or deterioration, developmental delays, cerebral palsy, cleft palate, voice pathology, mental retardation, hearing impairment, or emotional problems. Problems can be congenital, developmental, or acquired. Speech-language pathologists use written and oral tests, as well as special instruments, to diagnose the nature and extent of impairment and to record and analyze speech, language, and swallowing irregularities. Speech-language pathologists develop an individualized plan of care, tailored to each patient's needs. For individuals with little or no speech capability, speech-language pathologists may select augmentative or alternative communication methods, including automated devices and sign language, and teach their use. They teach these individuals how to make sounds, improve their voices, or increase their language skills to communicate more effectively. Speech-language pathologists help patients develop, or recover, reliable communication skills so patients can fulfill their educational, vocational, and social roles.

Most speech-language pathologists provide direct clinical services to individuals with communication or swallowing disorders. In speech and language clinics, they may independently develop and carry out treatment programs. In medical facilities, they may work with physicians, social workers, psychologists, and other therapists. Speech-language pathologists in schools develop individual or group programs, counsel parents, and may assist teachers with classroom activities.

Speech-language pathologists keep records on the initial evaluation, progress, and discharge of clients. This helps pinpoint problems, tracks client progress, and justifies the cost of treatment when applying for reimbursement. They counsel individuals and their families concerning communication disorders and how to cope with the stress and misunderstanding that often accompany them. They also work with family members to recognize and change behavior patterns that impede communication and treatment and show them communication-enhancing techniques to use at home.

Some speech-language pathologists conduct research on how people communicate. Others design and develop equipment or techniques for diagnosing and treating speech problems.

Working Conditions

Speech-language pathologists usually work at a desk or table in clean comfortable surroundings. In medical settings, they may work at the patient's bedside and assist in positioning the patient. In school settings they may participate in classroom activities. While the job is not physically demanding, it requires attention to detail and intense concentration. The emotional needs of clients and their families may be demanding. Most full-time speech-language pathologists work between 35 and 40 hours per week; some work part time. Those who work on a contract basis may spend a substantial amount of time traveling between facilities.

Employment

Speech-language pathologists held about 94,000 jobs in 2002. About half of jobs were in educational services, including preschools, elementary and secondary schools, and colleges and universities. Others were in hospitals;

offices of other health practitioners, including speech-language pathologists; nursing care facilities; home healthcare services; individual and family services; outpatient care centers; child day care services; or other facilities.

A few speech-language pathologists are self-employed in private practice. They contract to provide services in schools, offices of physicians, hospitals, or nursing care facilities, or work as consultants to industry.

Training, Other Qualifications, and Advancement

Of the 46 states that regulate licensing, almost all require a master's degree or equivalent. A passing score on a national examination on speech-language pathology offered through the Praxis Series of the Educational Testing Service is needed, as well. Other requirements are 300 to 375 hours of supervised clinical experience and 9 months of postgraduate professional clinical experience. Thirty-eight states have continuing education requirements for licensure renewal. Medicaid, Medicare, and private health insurers generally require a practitioner to be licensed to qualify for reimbursement.

About 233 colleges and universities offer graduate programs in speech-language pathology. Courses cover anatomy and physiology of the areas of the body involved in speech, language, swallowing, and hearing; the development of normal speech, language, swallowing, and hearing; the nature of disorders; acoustics; and psychological aspects of communication. Graduate students also learn to evaluate and treat speech, language, swallowing, and hearing disorders and receive supervised clinical training in communication disorders.

Speech-language pathologists can acquire the Certificate of Clinical Competence in Speech-Language Pathology (CCC-SLP) offered by the American Speech-Language-Hearing Association. To earn a CCC, a person must have a graduate degree and 375 hours of supervised clinical experience, complete a 36-week postgraduate clinical fellowship, and pass the Praxis Series examination in speech-language pathology administered by the Educational Testing Service (ETS).

Speech-language pathologists should be able to effectively communicate diagnostic test results, diagnoses, and proposed treatment in a manner easily understood by their clients. They must be able to approach problems objectively and provide support to clients and their families. Because a client's progress may be slow, patience, compassion, and good listening skills are necessary.

Job Outlook

Employment of speech-language pathologists is expected to grow faster than the average for all occupations through the year 2012. Members of the baby boom generation are now entering middle age, when the possibility of neurological disorders and associated speech, language, swallowing, and

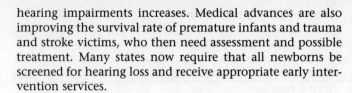

hearing impairments increases. Medical advances are also improving the survival rate of premature infants and trauma and stroke victims, who then need assessment and possible treatment. Many states now require that all newborns be screened for hearing loss and receive appropriate early intervention services.

In health services facilities, the impact of proposed federal legislation imposing limits on reimbursement for therapy services may adversely affect the short-term job outlook for therapy providers. However, over the long run, the demand for therapists should continue to rise as growth in the number of individuals with disabilities or limited function spurs demand for therapy services.

Employment in educational services will increase along with growth in elementary and secondary school enrollments, including enrollment of special education students. Federal law guarantees special education and related services to all eligible children with disabilities. Greater awareness of the importance of early identification and diagnosis of speech, language, swallowing, and hearing disorders will also increase employment.

The number of speech-language pathologists in private practice will rise due to the increasing use of contract services by hospitals, schools, and nursing care facilities. In addition to job openings stemming from employment growth, a number of openings for speech-language pathologists will arise from the need to replace those who leave the occupation.

Earnings

Median annual earnings of speech-language pathologists were $49,450 in 2002. The middle 50 percent earned between $39,930 and $60,190. The lowest 10 percent earned less than $32,580, and the highest 10 percent earned more than $74,010. Median annual earnings in the industries employing the largest numbers of speech-language pathologists in 2002 were as follows:

Offices of other health practitioners $53,090

General medical and surgical hospitals..................52,940

Elementary and secondary schools 46,060

According to a 2003 survey by the American Speech-Language-Hearing Association, the median annual salary for full-time certified speech-language pathologists who worked on a calendar-year basis, generally 11 or 12 months annually, was $48,000. For those who worked on an academic-year basis, usually 9 or 10 months annually, the median annual salary was $44,800. Certified speech-language pathologists who worked 25 or fewer hours per week had a median hourly salary of $40.00. Starting salaries for certified speech-language pathologists with one to three years experience were $42,000 for those who worked on a calendar-year basis and $37,000 for those who worked on an academic-year basis.

Related Occupations

Speech-language pathologists specialize in the prevention, diagnosis, and treatment of speech and language problems. Workers in related occupations include audiologists, occupational therapists, optometrists, physical therapists, psychologists, recreational therapists, and rehabilitation counselors.

Sources of Additional Information

State licensing boards can provide information on licensure requirements. State departments of education can supply information on certification requirements for those who wish to work in public schools.

General information on careers in speech-language pathology is available from:

● American Speech-Language-Hearing Association, 10801 Rockville Pike, Rockville, MD 20852. Internet: http://www.asha.org

Surgical Technologists

(O*NET 29-2055.00)

Significant Points

● Training programs last 9 to 24 months and lead to a certificate, diploma, or associate degree.

● Job opportunities are expected to be favorable.

● Hospitals will continue to be the primary employer, although much faster employment growth is expected in offices of physicians and in outpatient care centers, including ambulatory surgical centers.

Nature of the Work

Surgical technologists, also called scrubs and surgical or operating room technicians, assist in surgical operations under the supervision of surgeons, registered nurses, or other surgical personnel. Surgical technologists are members of operating room teams, which most commonly include surgeons, anesthesiologists, and circulating nurses. Before an operation, surgical technologists help prepare the operating room by setting up surgical instruments and equipment, sterile drapes, and sterile solutions. They assemble both sterile and nonsterile equipment, as well as adjust and check it to ensure it is working properly. Technologists also get patients ready for surgery by washing, shaving, and disinfecting incision sites. They transport patients to the operating room, help position them on the operating table, and cover them with sterile surgical "drapes." Technologists also observe patients' vital signs, check charts, and assist the surgical team with putting on sterile gowns and gloves.

During surgery, technologists pass instruments and other sterile supplies to surgeons and surgeon assistants. They may hold retractors, cut sutures, and help count sponges, needles, supplies, and instruments. Surgical technologists help prepare, care for, and dispose of specimens taken for laboratory analysis and help apply dressings. Some operate sterilizers, lights, or suction machines, and help operate diagnostic equipment.

After an operation, surgical technologists may help transfer patients to the recovery room and clean and restock the operating room.

Working Conditions

Surgical technologists work in clean, well-lighted, cool environments. They must stand for long periods and remain alert during operations. At times they may be exposed to communicable diseases and unpleasant sights, odors, and materials.

Most surgical technologists work a regular 40-hour week, although they may be on call or work nights, weekends and holidays on a rotating basis.

Employment

Surgical technologists held about 72,000 jobs in 2002. About three-quarters of jobs for surgical technologists were in hospitals, mainly in operating and delivery rooms. Other jobs were in offices of physicians or dentists who perform outpatient surgery and in outpatient care centers, including ambulatory surgical centers. A few, known as private scrubs, are employed directly by surgeons who have special surgical teams, like those for liver transplants.

Training, Other Qualifications, and Advancement

Surgical technologists receive their training in formal programs offered by community and junior colleges, vocational schools, universities, hospitals, and the military. In 2002, the Commission on Accreditation of Allied Health Education Programs (CAAHEP) recognized 361 accredited programs. High school graduation normally is required for admission. Programs last 9 to 24 months and lead to a certificate, diploma, or associate degree.

Programs provide classroom education and supervised clinical experience. Students take courses in anatomy, physiology, microbiology, pharmacology, professional ethics, and medical terminology. Other studies cover the care and safety of patients during surgery, sterile techniques, and surgical procedures. Students also learn to sterilize instruments; prevent and control infection; and handle special drugs, solutions, supplies, and equipment.

Most employers prefer to hire certified technologists. Technologists may obtain voluntary professional certification from the Liaison Council on Certification for the Surgical

Technologist by graduating from a CAAHEP-accredited program and passing a national certification examination. They may then use the Certified Surgical Technologist (CST) designation. Continuing education or reexamination is required to maintain certification, which must be renewed every 4 years.

Certification may also be obtained from the National Center for Competency Testing. To qualify to take the exam, candidates follow one of three paths: complete an accredited training program, undergo a 2-year hospital on-the-job training program, or acquire seven years of experience working in the field. After passing the exam, individuals may use the designation Tech in Surgery-Certified, TS-C (NCCT). This certification may be renewed every 5 years through either continuing education or reexamination.

Surgical technologists need manual dexterity to handle instruments quickly. They also must be conscientious, orderly, and emotionally stable to handle the demands of the operating room environment. Technologists must respond quickly and know procedures well to have instruments ready for surgeons without having to be told. They are expected to keep abreast of new developments in the field. Recommended high school courses include health, biology, chemistry, and mathematics.

Technologists advance by specializing in a particular area of surgery, such as neurosurgery or open heart surgery. They also may work as circulating technologists. A circulating technologist is the "unsterile" member of the surgical team who prepares patients; helps with anesthesia; obtains and opens packages for the "sterile" persons to remove the sterile contents during the procedure; interviews the patient before surgery; keeps a written account of the surgical procedure; and answers the surgeon's questions about the patient during the surgery. With additional training, some technologists advance to first assistants, who help with retracting, sponging, suturing, cauterizing bleeders, and closing and treating wounds. Some surgical technologists manage central supply departments in hospitals, or take positions with insurance companies, sterile supply services, and operating equipment firms.

Job Outlook

Job opportunities are expected to be favorable. Employment of surgical technologists is expected to grow faster than the average for all occupations through the year 2012 as the volume of surgery increases. The number of surgical procedures is expected to rise as the population grows and ages. As members of the baby boom generation approach retirement age, the over-50 population, who generally require more surgical procedures, will account for a larger portion of the general population. Technological advances, such as fiber optics and laser technology, will also permit new surgical procedures to be performed.

Hospitals will continue to be the primary employer of surgical technologists, although much faster employment growth is expected in offices of physicians and in outpatient care centers, including ambulatory surgical centers.

Earnings

Median annual earnings of surgical technologists were $31,210 in 2002. The middle 50 percent earned between $26,000 and $36,740. The lowest 10 percent earned less than $21,920, and the highest 10 percent earned more than $43,470. Median annual earnings of surgical technologists in 2002 were $33,790 in offices of physicians and $30,590 in general medical and surgical hospitals.

Related Occupations

Other health occupations requiring approximately 1 year of training after high school include dental assistants, licensed practical and licensed vocational nurses, clinical laboratory technicians, and medical assistants.

Sources of Additional Information

For additional information on a career as a surgical technologist and a list of CAAHEP-accredited programs, contact:

- Association of Surgical Technologists, 7108-C South Alton Way, Centennial, CO 80112. Internet: http://www.ast.org

For information on becoming a Certified Surgical Technologist, contact:

- Liaison Council on Certification for the Surgical Technologist, 128 S. Tejon St., Suite 301, Colorado Springs, CO 80903. Internet: http://www.lcc-st.org

For information on becoming a Tech in Surgery-Certified, contact:

- National Center for Competency Testing, 7007 College Blvd., Suite 250, Overland Park, KS 66211.

Taxi Drivers and Chauffeurs

(O*NET 53-3041.00)

Significant Points

- Taxi drivers and chauffeurs may work any schedule, including full-time, part-time, night, evening, and weekend work.

- Many taxi drivers and chauffeurs like the independent, unsupervised work of driving their automobile.

- Local governments set license standards that include minimum qualifications for driving experience and training; many taxi and limousine companies set higher standards.

- Job opportunities will be good because of the need to replace the many people who work in this occupation for short periods and then leave.

Nature of the Work

Anyone who has been in a large city knows the importance of taxi and limousine service. *Taxi drivers*, also known as *cab drivers*, help passengers get to and from their homes, workplaces, and recreational pursuits such as dining, entertainment, and shopping. They also help out-of-town business people and tourists get around in unfamiliar surroundings.

At the start of their driving shift, taxi drivers usually report to a taxicab service or garage where they are assigned a vehicle, most frequently a large, conventional automobile modified for commercial passenger transport. They record their name, work date, and cab identification number on a trip sheet. Drivers check the cab's fuel and oil levels and make sure that the lights, brakes, and windshield wipers are in good working order. Drivers adjust rear and side mirrors and their seat for comfort. Any equipment or part not in good working order is reported to the dispatcher or company mechanic.

Taxi drivers pick up passengers in 1 of 3 ways: "cruising" the streets to pick up random passengers; prearranging pickups; and picking up passengers from taxistands established in highly trafficked areas. In urban areas, the majority of passengers "wave down" drivers cruising the streets. Customers may also prearrange a pickup by calling a cab company and giving a location, approximate pickup time, and destination. The cab company dispatcher then relays the information to a driver by two-way radio, cellular telephone, or onboard computer. Outside of urban areas, the majority of trips are dispatched in this manner. Drivers also pick up passengers waiting at cabstands or in taxi lines at airports, train stations, hotels, restaurants, and other places where people frequently seek taxis.

Some drivers transport individuals with special needs, such as those with disabilities and the elderly. These drivers, also known as *paratransit drivers*, operate specially equipped vehicles designed to accommodate a variety of needs in non-emergency situations. Although special certification is not necessary, some additional training on the equipment and passenger needs may be required.

Drivers should be familiar with streets in the areas they serve so they can use the most efficient route to destinations. They should know the locations of frequently requested destinations, such as airports, bus and railroad terminals, convention centers, hotels, and other points of interest. In case of emergency, the driver should also know the location of fire and police stations and hospitals.

Upon reaching the destination, drivers determine the fare and announce it to the rider. Fares often consist of many parts. In many cabs, a taximeter measures the fare based on the length of the trip and the amount of time the trip took. Drivers turn the taximeter on when passengers enter the cab and turn it off when they reach the final destination. The fare also may include a surcharge for additional passengers, a fee for handling luggage, or a drop charge—an additional flat fee added for use of the cab. In some cases, fares are determined by a system of zones through which the taxi passes during a trip. Each jurisdiction determines the rate and structure of the fare system covering licensed taxis. Passengers generally add a tip or gratuity to the fare. The amount of the gratuity depends on the passengers' satisfaction with the quality and efficiency of the ride and courtesy of the driver. Drivers issue receipts upon request by the passenger. They enter onto the trip sheet all information regarding the trip, including the place and time of pickup and dropoff and the total fee. These logs help taxi company management check the driver's activity and efficiency. Drivers also must fill out accident reports when necessary.

Chauffeurs operate limousines, vans, and private cars for limousine companies, private businesses, government agencies, and wealthy individuals. Chauffeur service differs from taxi service in that all trips are prearranged. Many chauffeurs transport customers in large vans between hotels and airports, bus, or train terminals. Others drive luxury automobiles, such as limousines, to business events, entertainment venues, and social events. Still others provide full-time personal transportation for wealthy families and private companies.

At the start of the workday, chauffeurs prepare their automobiles or vans for use. They inspect the vehicle for cleanliness and, when needed, vacuum the interior and wash the exterior body, windows, and mirrors. They check fuel and oil levels and make sure the lights, tires, brakes, and windshield wipers work. Chauffeurs may perform routine maintenance and make minor repairs, such as changing tires or adding oil and other fluids when needed. If a vehicle requires more complicated repair, they take it to a professional mechanic.

Chauffeurs cater to passengers with attentive customer service and a special regard for detail. They help riders into the car by holding open doors, holding umbrellas when it is raining, and loading packages and luggage into the trunk of the car. They may perform errands for their employers such as delivering packages or picking up clients arriving at airports. Many chauffeurs offer conveniences and luxuries in their limousines to ensure a pleasurable ride, such as newspapers, magazines, music, drinks, televisions, and telephones. A growing number of chauffeurs work as full-service *executive assistants*, simultaneously acting as driver, secretary, and itinerary planner.

Working Conditions

Taxi drivers and chauffeurs occasionally have to load and unload heavy luggage and packages. Driving for long periods can be tiring and uncomfortable, especially in densely populated urban areas. Drivers must be alert to conditions on the road, especially in heavy and congested traffic or in bad weather. They must take precautions to prevent accidents and avoid sudden stops, turns, and other driving maneuvers that would jar passengers. Taxi drivers also risk robbery because they work alone and often carry large amounts of cash.

Work hours of taxi drivers and chauffeurs vary greatly. Some jobs offer full-time or part-time employment with work hours that can change from day to day or remain the same every day. It is often necessary for drivers to report to work on short notice. Chauffeurs who work for a single employer may be on call much of the time. Evening and weekend work are common for limousine and taxicab services.

The needs of the client or employer dictate the work schedule for chauffeurs. The work of taxi drivers is much less structured. Working free of supervision, they may break for a meal or a rest whenever their vehicle is unoccupied. Many taxi drivers and chauffeurs like the independent, unsupervised work of driving their automobile.

This occupation is attractive to individuals seeking flexible work schedules, such as college and postgraduate students, and to anyone seeking a second source of income. For example, other service workers, such as ambulance drivers and police officers, often consider moonlighting as taxi drivers and chauffeurs.

Full-time taxi drivers usually work one shift a day, which may last from 8 to 12 hours. Part-time drivers may work half a shift each day or work a full shift once or twice a week. Drivers may work shifts at all times of the day and night, because most taxi companies offer services 24 hours a day. Early morning and late night shifts are common. Drivers work long hours during holidays, weekends, and other special times during which demand for their services may be heavier. Independent drivers, however, often set their own hours and schedules.

Design improvements in newer cabs have reduced the stress and increased the comfort and efficiency of drivers. Many regulatory bodies overseeing taxi and chauffeur services require standard amenities such as air-conditioning and general upkeep of the vehicles. Modern taxicabs also are sometimes equipped with sophisticated tracking devices, fare meters, and dispatching equipment. Satellites and tracking systems link many of these state-of-the-art vehicles with company headquarters. In a matter of seconds, dispatchers can deliver directions, traffic advisories, weather reports, and other important communications to drivers anywhere in the transporting area. The satellite link also allows dispatchers to track vehicle location, fuel consumption, and engine performance. Drivers can easily communicate with dispatchers to discuss delivery schedules and courses of action should there be mechanical problems. For instance, automated dispatch systems help dispatchers locate the closest driver to a customer in order to maximize efficiency and quality of service. When threatened with crime or violence, drivers may have special "trouble lights" to alert authorities of emergencies and guarantee that help arrives quickly.

Taxi drivers and chauffeurs meet many different types of people. Dealing with rude customers and waiting for passengers requires patience. Many municipalities and taxicab and chauffeur companies require taxi drivers to wear clean and neat clothes. Many chauffeurs wear formal attire such as a tuxedo, a coat and tie, a dress, or a uniform and cap.

Employment

Taxi drivers and chauffeurs held about 132,000 jobs in 2002. Over one quarter worked for taxi and limousine service companies. Many taxi drivers and chauffeurs were self-employed.

Training, Other Qualifications, and Advancement

Local governments set license standards and requirements for taxi drivers and chauffeurs that include minimum qualifications for driving experience and training. Many taxi and limousine companies set higher standards than required by law. It is common for companies to review applicants' medical, credit, criminal, and driving records. In addition, many companies require a higher minimum age than that which is legally required and prefer that drivers be high school graduates.

Persons interested in driving a limousine or taxicab must first have a regular automobile driver's license. They also must acquire a chauffeur or taxi driver's license, commonly called a "hack" license. Local authorities generally require applicants for a hack license to pass a written exam or complete a training program that may include up to 80 hours of classroom instruction. To qualify through either an exam or a training program, applicants must know local geography, motor vehicle laws, safe driving practices, regulations governing taxicabs, and display some aptitude for customer service. Many training programs include a test on English proficiency, usually in the form of listening comprehension; applicants who do not pass the English exam must take an English course along with the formal driving program. In addition, some classroom instruction includes route management, mapreading, and service for passengers with disabilities. Many taxicab or limousine companies sponsor applicants and give them a temporary permit that allows them to drive, although the applicant may not yet have finished the training program or passed the test. However, some jurisdictions, such as New York City, have discontinued this practice and now require driver applicants to complete the licensing process before operating a taxi or limousine.

Some taxi and limousine companies give new drivers on-the-job training. They show drivers how to operate the taximeter and communications equipment, and how to complete paperwork. Other topics covered may include driver safety and popular sightseeing and entertainment destinations. Many companies have contracts with social service agencies and transportation services to transport elderly and disabled citizens in nonemergency situations. To support these services, new drivers may get special training on how to handle wheelchair lifts and other mechanical devices.

Taxi drivers and chauffeurs should be able to get along with many different types of people. They must be patient when waiting for passengers or when dealing with rude customers. It is also helpful for drivers to be tolerant and have even tempers when driving in heavy and congested traffic. Drivers should be dependable because passengers expect to be picked up at a prearranged time and taken to the correct destination. To be successful, drivers must be responsible and self-motivated because they work with little supervision. Increasingly, companies encourage drivers to develop their own loyal customer base to improve their businesses.

Many taxi drivers and chauffeurs are called *lease drivers*. These drivers pay a daily, weekly, or monthly fee to the company allowing them to lease their vehicle. In the case of limousines, leasing also permits the driver access to the company's dispatch system. The fee also may include a charge for vehicle maintenance, insurance, and a deposit on the vehicle. Lease drivers may take their cars home with them when they are not on duty.

Opportunities for advancement are limited for taxi drivers and chauffeurs. Experienced drivers may obtain preferred routes or shifts. Some advance to dispatcher or manager jobs; others may start their own limousine company.

In small and medium-sized communities, drivers are sometimes able to buy their taxi, limousine, or other type of automobile and go into business for themselves. These independent owner-drivers require an additional permit allowing them to operate their vehicle as a company. Some big cities limit the number of operating permits. In these cities, drivers become owner-drivers by buying permits from owner-drivers who leave the business. Although many owner-drivers are successful, some fail to cover expenses and eventually lose their permit and automobile. Good business sense and courses in accounting, business, and business arithmetic can help an owner-driver to become successful. Knowledge of mechanics enables owner-drivers to perform their own routine maintenance and minor repairs to cut expenses.

Job Outlook

Persons seeking jobs as taxi drivers and chauffeurs should encounter good opportunities, because of the need to replace the many people who work in this occupation for short periods and then transfer to other occupations or leave the labor force. However, opportunities for drivers vary greatly in terms of earnings, work hours, and working conditions, depending on economic and regulatory conditions. Opportunities should be best for persons with good driving records and the ability to work flexible schedules.

Employment of taxi drivers and chauffeurs is expected to grow faster than the average for all occupations through the year 2012, as local and suburban travel increases with population growth. Employment growth also will stem from federal legislation requiring services for persons with disabilities. Rapidly growing metropolitan areas should offer the best job opportunities.

The number of job openings can fluctuate with the cycle of the overall economy because the demand for taxi and limousine transportation depends on travel and tourism. During economic slowdowns, drivers are seldom laid off, but they may have to increase their work hours and earnings may decline. In economic upturns, job openings are numerous as many drivers transfer to other occupations. Extra drivers may be hired during holiday seasons and peak travel and tourist times.

Earnings

Earnings of taxi drivers and chauffeurs vary greatly, depending on factors such as the number of hours worked, customers' tips, and geographic location. Median hourly earnings of salaried taxi drivers and chauffeurs, including tips, were $8.91 in 2002. The middle 50 percent earned between $7.31 and $11.45 an hour. The lowest 10 percent earned less than $6.31, and the highest 10 percent earned more than $15.18 an hour. Median hourly earnings in the industries employing the largest numbers of taxi drivers and chauffeurs in 2002 were as follows:

Taxi and limousine service	$9.71
Other transit and ground passenger transportation	8.70
Individual and family services	8.14
Automotive equipment rental and leasing	7.99
Traveler accommodation	7.96

Related Occupations

Other workers who have similar jobs include bus drivers and truck drivers and driver/sales workers.

Sources of Additional Information

Information on licensing and registration of taxi drivers and chauffeurs is available from local government agencies that regulate taxicabs. For information about work opportunities as a taxi driver or chauffeur, contact local taxi or limousine companies or state employment service offices.

For general information about the work of limousine drivers, contact:

- National Limousine Association, 49 South Maple Ave., Marlton, NJ 08053. Internet: http://www.limo.org

Teacher Assistants

(O*NET 25-9041.00)

Significant Points

- About 4 in 10 teacher assistants work part time.

- Educational requirements range from a high school diploma to some college training.

- Workers with experience in special education, or who can speak a foreign language, will be especially in demand.

Nature of the Work

Teacher assistants provide instructional and clerical support for classroom teachers, allowing teachers more time for lesson planning and teaching. Teacher assistants tutor and assist children in learning class material using the teacher's lesson plans, providing students with individualized attention. Teacher assistants also supervise students in the cafeteria, schoolyard, and hallways or on field trips. They record grades, set up equipment, and help prepare materials for instruction. Teacher assistants also are called teacher aides or instructional aides. Some assistants refer to themselves as paraeducators or paraprofessionals.

Some teacher assistants perform exclusively noninstructional or clerical tasks, such as monitoring nonacademic settings. Playground and lunchroom attendants are examples of such assistants. Most teacher assistants, however, perform a combination of instructional and clerical duties. They generally provide instructional reinforcement to children under the direction and guidance of teachers. They work with students individually or in small groups—listening while students read, reviewing or reinforcing class lessons, or helping them find information for reports. At the secondary school level, teacher assistants often specialize in a certain subject, such as math or science. Teacher assistants often take charge of special projects and prepare equipment or exhibits, such as for a science demonstration. Some assistants work in computer laboratories, helping students using computers and educational software programs.

In addition to instructing, assisting, and supervising students, teacher assistants grade tests and papers, check homework, keep health and attendance records, do typing and filing, and duplicate materials. They also stock supplies, operate audiovisual equipment, and keep classroom equipment in order.

Many teacher assistants work extensively with special education students. As schools become more inclusive, integrating special education students into general education classrooms, teacher assistants in general education and special education classrooms increasingly assist students with disabilities. Teacher assistants attend to a disabled student's physical needs, including feeding, teaching good grooming habits, or assisting students riding the schoolbus. They also provide personal attention to students with other special needs, such as those from disadvantaged families, those who speak English as a second language, or those who need remedial education. Teacher assistants help assess a student's progress by observing performance and recording relevant data.

Teacher assistants also work with infants and toddlers who have developmental delays or other disabilities. Under the guidance of a teacher or therapist, teacher assistants perform exercises or play games to help the child develop physically and behaviorally. Some teacher assistants work with young adults to help them obtain a job or to apply for community services for the disabled.

Working Conditions

Approximately 4 in 10 teacher assistants work part time. However, even among full-time workers, nearly 40 percent work less than 8 hours per day. Most assistants who provide educational instruction work the traditional 9- to 10-month school year. Teacher assistants work in a variety of settings—including private homes and preschools, and local government offices, where they would deal with young adults—but most work in classrooms in elementary, middle, and secondary schools. They also work outdoors supervising recess when weather allows, and they spend much of their time standing, walking, or kneeling.

Seeing students develop and gain appreciation of the joy of learning can be very rewarding. However, working closely with students can be both physically and emotionally tiring. Teacher assistants who work with special education students often perform more strenuous tasks, including lifting, as they help students with their daily routine. Those who perform clerical work may tire of administrative duties, such as copying materials or typing.

Employment

Teacher assistants held almost 1.3 million jobs in 2002. Nearly 3 in 4 work for state and local government education institutions; mostly at the preschool and elementary school level. Private schools, daycare centers, and religious organizations hire most of the rest.

Training, Other Qualifications, and Advancement

Educational requirements for teacher assistants vary by state or school district and range from a high school diploma to some college training, although employers increasingly prefer applicants with some college training. Teacher assistants with instructional responsibilities usually require more training than do those who do not perform teaching tasks. In addition, as a result of the No Child Left Behind Act of 2001, teacher assistants in Title 1 schools—those with a large proportion of students from low-income households—will be required to meet one of three requirements: have a minimum of 2 years of college, hold a 2-year or higher degree, or pass a rigorous state and local assessment. Many schools also require previous experience in working with children and a valid driver's license. Some schools may require the applicant to pass a background check.

A number of 2-year and community colleges offer associate degree programs that prepare graduates to work as teacher assistants. However, most teacher assistants receive on-the-job training. Those who tutor and review lessons with students must have a thorough understanding of class materials and instructional methods and should be familiar with the organization and operation of a school. Teacher assistants also must know how to operate audiovisual equipment, keep records, and prepare instructional materials, as well as have adequate computer skills.

Teacher assistants should enjoy working with children from a wide range of cultural backgrounds and be able to handle classroom situations with fairness and patience. Teacher assistants also must demonstrate initiative and a willingness to follow a teacher's directions. They must have good writing skills and be able to communicate effectively with students and teachers. Teacher assistants who speak a second language, especially Spanish, are in great demand for communicating with growing numbers of students and parents whose primary language is not English.

Advancement for teacher assistants—usually in the form of higher earnings or increased responsibility—comes primarily with experience or additional education. Some school districts provide time away from the job or tuition reimbursement so that teacher assistants can earn their bachelor's degrees and pursue licensed teaching positions. In return for tuition reimbursement, assistants are often required to teach a certain length of time for the school district.

Job Outlook

Employment of teacher assistants is expected to grow somewhat faster than the average for all occupations through 2012. Although school enrollments are projected to increase only slowly over the next decade, the student population for which teacher assistants are most needed—special education students and students for whom English is not their first language—is expected to increase more rapidly than the general school-age population. Legislation that requires students with disabilities and non-native English speakers to receive an education "equal" to that of other students, will generate jobs for teacher assistants to accommodate these students' special needs. Children with special needs require much personal attention, and special education teachers, as well as general education teachers with special education students, rely heavily on teacher assistants.

Additionally, a greater focus on educational quality and accountability, as required by the No Child Left Behind Act, is likely to lead to an increased demand for teacher assistants. Growing numbers of teacher assistants will be needed to help teachers prepare students for standardized testing and to provide extra assistance to students who perform poorly on standardized tests. An increasing number of after-school programs and summer programs also will create new opportunities for teacher assistants. In addition to those stemming from employment growth, numerous job openings will arise as assistants transfer to other occupations or leave the labor force to assume family responsibilities, to return to school, or for other reasons characteristic of occupations that require limited formal education and offer relatively low pay.

Opportunities for teacher assistant jobs are expected to be best for persons with at least 2 years of formal education after high school. Persons who can speak a foreign language should be in particular demand in school systems with large numbers of students whose families do not speak English at home. Demand is expected to vary by region of the country. Areas in which the population and school enrollments are expanding rapidly, such as many communities in the South and West, should have rapid growth in the demand for teacher assistants.

Earnings

Median annual earnings of teacher assistants in 2002 were $18,660. The middle 50 percent earned between $14,880 and $23,600. The lowest 10 percent earned less than $12,900, and the highest 10 percent earned more than $29,050.

Teacher assistants who work part time ordinarily do not receive benefits. Full-time workers usually receive health coverage and other benefits.

In 2002, about 3 out of 10 teacher assistants belonged to unions—mainly the American Federation of Teachers and the National Education Association—which bargain with school systems over wages, hours, and the terms and conditions of employment.

Related Occupations

Teacher assistants who instruct children have duties similar to those of preschool, kindergarten, elementary, middle, and secondary school teachers, special education teachers, and school librarians. However, teacher assistants do not have the same level of responsibility or training. The support activities of teacher assistants and their educational backgrounds are similar to those of childcare workers, library technicians, and library assistants. Teacher assistants who work with children with disabilities perform many of the same functions as occupational therapy assistants and aides.

Sources of Additional Information

For information on teacher assistants, including training and certification, contact:

- American Federation of Teachers, Paraprofessional and School Related Personnel Division, 555 New Jersey Ave. NW, Washington, DC 20001.

- National Education Association, Educational Support Personnel division, 1201 16th Street, NW | Washington, DC 20036.

For information on a career as a teacher assistant, contact:

- National Resource Center for Paraprofessionals, 6526 Old Main Hill, Utah State University, Logan, UT 84322. Internet: http://www.nrcpara.org

Human resource departments of school systems, school administrators, and state departments of education also can provide details about employment opportunities and required qualifications for teacher assistant jobs.

Teachers—Adult Literacy and Remedial and Self-Enrichment Education

(O*NET 25-3011.00 and 25-3021.00)

Significant Points

- Many adult literacy and remedial and self-enrichment teachers work part time and receive no benefits; unpaid volunteers also teach these subjects.

- Opportunities for teachers of English as a second language are expected to be very good, due to the expected increase in the number of residents with limited English skills who seek classes.

- Demand for self-enrichment courses is expected to rise with growing numbers of people who embrace lifelong learning and of retirees who have more free time to take classes.

Nature of the Work

Self-enrichment teachers teach courses that students take for pleasure or personal enrichment; these classes are not usually intended to lead to a particular degree or vocation. Self-enrichment teachers may instruct children or adults in a wide variety of areas, such as cooking, dancing, creative writing, photography, or personal finance. In contrast, *adult literacy and remedial education teachers* provide adults and out-of-school youths with the education they need to read, write, and speak English and to perform elementary mathematical calculations—basic skills that equip them to solve problems well enough to become active participants in our society, to hold a job, and to further their education. The instruction provided by these teachers can be divided into three principle categories: *remedial or adult basic education (ABE)*, which is geared toward adults whose skills are either at or below an eighth-grade level; *adult secondary education (ASE)*, which is geared towards students who wish to obtain their General Educational Development (GED) certificate or other high school equivalency credential; and *English literacy*, which provides instruction for adults with limited proficiency in English. Traditionally, the students in adult literacy and remedial (basic) education classes were made up primarily of those who did not graduate high school or who passed through school without the knowledge needed to meet their educational goals or to participate fully in today's high-skill society. Increasingly, however, students in these classes are immigrants or other people whose native language is not English. Educators who work with adult English-language learners are usually called *teachers of English as a second language* (ESL) or *teachers of English to speakers of other languages* (ESOL).

Self-enrichment teachers, due to the wide range of classes and subjects they teach, may have styles and methods of instruction that differ greatly. The majority of self-enrichment classes are relatively informal and nonintensive in terms of instructional demands. Some classes, such as pottery or sewing, may be largely hands-on, requiring students to practice doing things themselves in order to learn. In that case, teachers may demonstrate methods or techniques for their class and subsequently supervise students' progress as they attempt to carry out the same or similar tasks or actions. Other classes, such as those involving financial planning or religion and spirituality, may be somewhat more academic in nature. Teachers of these classes are likely to rely more heavily on lectures and group discussions as methods of instruction. Classes offered through religious institutions, such as marriage preparation or classes in religion for children, may also be taught by self-enrichment teachers.

Many of the classes that self-enrichment educators teach are shorter in duration than classes taken for academic credit; some finish in 1 or 2 days to several weeks. These brief classes tend to be introductory in nature and generally focus on only one topic—for example, a cooking class that teaches students how to make bread. Some self-enrichment classes introduce children and youths to activities such as piano or drama, and may be designed to last anywhere from 1 week to several months. These and other self-enrichment classes may be scheduled to occur after school or during school vacations.

Remedial education teachers, more commonly called adult basic education teachers, teach basic academic courses in mathematics, languages, history, reading, writing, science, and other areas, using instructional methods geared toward adult learning. They teach these subjects to students 16 years of age and older who demonstrate the need to increase their skills in one or more of the subject areas mentioned. Classes are taught to appeal to a variety of learning styles and usually include large-group, small-group, and one-on-one instruction. Because the students often are at different proficiency levels for different subjects, adult basic education teachers must make individual assessments of each student's abilities beforehand. In many programs, the assessment is used to develop an individualized education plan for each student. Teachers are required to evaluate students periodically to determine their progress and potential for advancement to the next level.

Teachers in remedial or adult basic education may have to assist students in acquiring effective study skills and the self-confidence they need to reenter an academic environment. Teachers also may encounter students with a learning or physical disability that requires additional expertise. Teachers should possess an understanding of how to help these students achieve their goals, but they also may need to have the knowledge to detect challenges their students may have and provide them with access to a broader system of additional services that are required to address their challenges.

For students who wish to get a GED credential in order to get a job or qualify for postsecondary education, adult secondary education or GED teachers provide help in acquiring the necessary knowledge and skills to pass the test. The GED tests students in subject areas such as reading, writing, mathematics, science, and social studies, while at the same time measuring students' communication, information-processing, problem-solving, and critical-thinking skills. The emphasis in class is on acquiring the knowledge needed to pass the GED test, as well as preparing students for success in further educational endeavors.

ESOL teachers help adults to speak, listen, read, and write in English, often in the context of real-life situations to promote learning. More advanced students may concentrate on writing and conversational skills or focus on learning more academic or job-related communication skills. ESOL teachers teach adults who possess a wide range of cultures and abilities and who speak a variety of languages. Some of their students have a college degree and many advance quickly through the program owing to a variety of factors, such as their age, previous language experience, educational background, and native language. Others may need additional time due to these same factors. Because the teacher and students often do not share a common language, creativity is an important part of fostering communication in the classroom and achieving learning goals.

All adult literacy, remedial, and self-enrichment teachers must prepare lessons beforehand, do any related paperwork, and stay current in their fields. Attendance for students is mostly voluntary and course work is rarely graded. Many teachers also must learn the latest uses for computers in the classroom, as computers are increasingly being used to supplement instruction in basic skills and in teaching ESOL.

Working Conditions

A large number of adult literacy and remedial and self-enrichment education teachers work part time. Some have several part-time teaching assignments or work full time in addition to their part-time teaching job. Classes for adults are held on days and at times that best accommodate students who may have a job or family responsibilities. Similarly, self-enrichment classes for children are usually held after school or during school vacation periods.

Because many of these teachers work with adult students, they do not encounter some of the behavioral or social problems sometimes found with younger students. Adults attend by choice, are highly motivated, and bring years of experience to the classroom—attributes that can make teaching these students rewarding and satisfying. Self-enrichment teachers must have a great deal of patience, particularly when working with young children.

Employment

Teachers of adult literacy, remedial, and self-enrichment education held about 280,000 jobs in 2002. About 1 in 5 was self-employed. Many additional teachers worked as unpaid volunteers.

Nearly three-quarters, or 200,000, of the jobs were held by self-enrichment teachers. The largest numbers of these workers were employed by public and private educational institutions, religious organizations, and providers of social assistance and amusement and recreation services.

Adult literacy, basic education, and GED teachers and instructors held about 80,000 jobs. Many of the jobs are federally funded, with additional funds coming from state and local governments. The education industry employs the majority of these teachers, who work in adult learning centers, libraries, or community colleges. Others work for social service organizations such as job-training or residential care facilities. Still others work for state and local governments, providing basic education at juvenile detention and corrections institutions, among other places.

Training, Other Qualifications, and Advancement

The main qualification for self-enrichment teachers is expertise in their subject area; however, requirements may vary greatly with both the type of class taught and the place of employment. In some cases, a portfolio of one's work may be required. For example, to secure a job teaching a photography course, an applicant would need to show examples of previous work. Special certification may be required to teach some subjects, such as a Red Cross water safety instructor certificate to teach swimming. Some self-enrichment teachers are trained educators or other professionals who teach enrichment classes in their spare time. In some disciplines, such as art or music, specific teacher training programs are available. Prospective dance teachers, for example, may complete programs that prepare them to instruct any number of types of dance—from ballroom dancing to ballet. Self-enrichment teachers also should have good speaking skills and a talent for making the subject interesting. Patience and the ability to explain and instruct students at a basic level are important as well, particularly when one is working with children.

Requirements for teaching adult literacy and basic and secondary education vary by state and by program. Federally funded programs run by state and local governments require high accountability and student achievement standards. Those programs run by religious, community, or volunteer organizations, rather than state-run, federally funded programs, generally develop standards based on their own needs and organizational goals. Most state and local governments and educational institutions require that adult teachers have at least a bachelor's degree and, preferably, a master's degree. Some—especially school districts that hire adult education teachers—require an elementary or secondary school teaching certificate. A few have begun requiring a special certificate in ESOL or adult education. Teaching experience, especially with adults, also is preferred or required. Volunteers usually do not need a bachelor's degree, but often must attend a training program before they are allowed to work with students.

Most programs recommend that adult literacy and basic and secondary education teachers take classes or workshops on teaching adults, using technology to teach, working with learners from a variety of cultures, and teaching adults with learning disabilities. ESOL teachers also should have courses or training in second-language acquisition theory and linguistics. In addition, knowledge of the citizenship and naturalization process may be useful. Knowledge of a second language is not necessary to teach ESOL students, but can be helpful in understanding the students' perspectives. GED teachers should know what is required to pass the GED and be able to instruct students in the subject matter. Training for literacy volunteers usually consists of instruction on effective teaching practices, needs assessment, lesson planning, the selection of appropriate instructional materials, characteristics of adult learners, and cross-cultural awareness.

Adult education and literacy teachers must have the ability to work with a variety of cultures, languages, and educational and economic backgrounds. They must be understanding and respectful of their students' circumstances and be familiar with their concerns. All teachers, both paid and volunteer, should be able to communicate well and motivate their students.

Professional development among adult education and literacy teachers varies widely. Both part-time and full-time teachers are expected to participate in ongoing professional development activities in order to keep current on new developments in the field and to enhance skills already acquired. Each state's professional development system reflects the unique needs and organizational structure of that state. Attendance by teachers at professional development workshops and other activities is often outlined in state or local policy. Some teachers are able to access professional development activities through alternative delivery systems such as the Internet or distance learning.

Opportunities for advancement in these professions, particularly for adult education and literacy teachers, again vary from state to state and program to program. Some part-time teachers are able to move into full-time teaching positions or program administrator positions, such as coordinator or director, when such vacancies occur. Others may decide to use their classroom experience to move into policy work at a nonprofit organization or with the local, state, or federal government or to perform research. Self-enrichment teachers also may advance to administrative positions or may even go on to start their own school or program. Experienced self-enrichment teachers may mentor new instructors and volunteers.

Job Outlook

Opportunities for jobs as adult literacy, remedial, and self-enrichment education teachers are expected to be favorable. Employment is expected to grow faster than the average for all occupations through 2012, and a large number of job openings is expected, due to the need to replace people who leave the occupation or retire.

Self-enrichment education teachers account for the largest proportion of jobs in these occupations. The need for self-enrichment teachers is expected to grow as more people embrace lifelong learning and as the baby boomers begin to retire and have more time to take classes. Subjects that are not easily researched on the Internet and those that provide hands-on experiences, such as cooking, crafts, and the arts, will be in greater demand. Also, classes on spirituality and self-improvement are expected to be popular.

As employers increasingly require a more literate workforce, workers' demand for adult literacy, basic education, and secondary education classes is expected to grow. Significant employment growth is anticipated especially for ESOL teachers, who will be needed by the increasing number of immigrants and other residents living in this country who need to learn, or enhance their skills in, English. In addition, a greater proportion of these groups is expected to take ESOL classes. Demand for ESOL teachers will be greatest in states such as California, Florida, Texas, and New York, due to their large populations of residents who have limited English skills. However, parts of the Midwest and Plains states have begun to attract large numbers of immigrants, making for especially good opportunities in those areas as well.

The demand for adult literacy and basic and secondary education often fluctuates with the economy. When the economy is good and workers are hard to find, employers relax their standards and hire workers without a degree or GED or those with limited proficiency in English. As the economy softens, more students find that they need additional education to get a job. However, adult education classes often are subject to changes in funding levels, which can cause the number of teaching jobs to fluctuate from year to year. In addition, factors such as immigration policies and the relative prosperity of the United States compared with other countries may have an impact on the number of immigrants entering this country and, consequently, on the demand for ESOL teachers.

Earnings

Median hourly earnings of self-enrichment teachers were $14.09 in 2002. The middle 50 percent earned between $9.86 and $19.69. The lowest 10 percent earned less than $7.37, and the highest 10 percent earned more than $26.49. Self-enrichment teachers are generally paid by the hour or for each class that they teach.

Median hourly earnings of adult literacy, remedial education, and GED teachers and instructors were $17.50 in 2002. The middle 50 percent earned between $13.21 and $24.00. The lowest 10 percent earned less than $10.08, and the highest 10 percent earned more than $34.30. Part-time adult literacy and remedial education and GED instructors are usually paid by the hour or for each class that they teach, and receive few benefits or none at all. Full-time teachers are generally paid a salary and receive health insurance and other benefits if they work for a school system or government.

Related Occupations

The work of adult literacy, remedial, and self-enrichment teachers is closely related to that of other types of teachers, especially preschool, kindergarten, elementary school, middle school, and secondary school teachers. In addition, adult literacy and basic and secondary education teachers require a wide variety of skills and aptitudes. Not only must they be able to teach and motivate students (including, at times, those with learning disabilities), but they also must often take on roles as advisers and mentors. Workers in other occupations that require these aptitudes include special-education teachers, counselors, and social workers. Self-enrichment teachers teach a wide variety of subjects that may be related to the work done by those in many other occupations, such as dancers and choreographers; artists and related workers; musicians, singers, and related workers; recreation and fitness workers; and athletes, coaches, umpires, and related workers.

Sources of Additional Information

Information on adult literacy, basic and secondary education programs, and teacher certification requirements is available from state departments of education, local school districts, and literacy resource centers. Information also may be obtained through local religious and charitable organizations.

For information on adult education and family literacy programs, contact

- The U.S. Department of Education, Office of Vocational and Adult Education, 4090 MES, 400 Maryland Ave. SW, Washington, DC 20202. Internet: http://www.ed.gov/offices/OVAE

For information on teaching English as a second language, contact

- The National Center for ESL Literacy Education, 4646 40th St. NW, Washington, DC 20016. Internet: http://www.cal.org/ncle

Teachers—Postsecondary

(O*NET 25-1011.00, 25-1021.00, 25-1022.00, 25-1031.00, 25-1032.00, 25-1041.00, 25-1042.00, 25-1043.00, 25-1051.00, 25-1052.00, 25-1053.00, 25-1054.00, 25-1061.00, 25-1062.00, 25-1063.00, 25-1064.00, 25-1065.00, 25-1066.00, 25-1067.00, 25-1069.99, 25-1071.00, 25-1072.00, 25-1081.00, 25-1082.00, 25-1111.00, 25-1112.00, 25-1113.00, 25-1121.00, 25-1122.00, 25-1123.00, 25-1124.00, 25-1125.00, 25-1126.00, 25-1191.00, 25-1192.00, 25-1193.00, 25-1194.00, and 25-1199.99)

Significant Points

- Opportunities for college and university teaching jobs are expected to improve, but many new openings will be for part-time or non-tenure-track positions.

- Prospects for teaching jobs will continue to be better in academic fields that offer attractive alternative nonacademic job opportunities—health specialties, business, and computer science, for example—which attract fewer applicants for academic positions.

- Educational qualifications for postsecondary teacher jobs range from expertise in a particular field to a Ph.D., depending on the subject being taught and the type of educational institution.

- One out of eight postsecondary teachers is a graduate teaching assistant—and one out of ten is a vocational or career and technical education teacher.

Nature of the Work

Postsecondary teachers instruct students in a wide variety of academic and vocational subjects beyond the high school level that may lead to a degree or simply to improvement in one's knowledge or skills. These teachers include college and university faculty, postsecondary career and technical education teachers, and graduate teaching assistants.

College and university faculty make up the majority of postsecondary teachers. They teach and advise more than 15 million full- and part-time college students and perform a significant part of our nation's research. Faculty also keep up with new developments in their field and may consult with government, business, nonprofit, and community organizations.

Faculty usually are organized into departments or divisions, based on academic subject or field. They usually teach several different related courses in their subject—algebra, calculus, and statistics, for example. They may instruct undergraduate or graduate students or both. College and university faculty may give lectures to several hundred students in large halls, lead small seminars, or supervise students in laboratories. They prepare lectures, exercises, and laboratory experiments; grade exams and papers; and advise and work with students individually. In universities, they also supervise graduate students' teaching and research. College faculty work with an increasingly varied student population made up of growing shares of part-time, older, and culturally and racially diverse students.

Faculty keep abreast of developments in their field by reading current literature, talking with colleagues, and participating in professional conferences. They may also do their own research to expand knowledge in their field. They may perform experiments; collect and analyze data; and examine original documents, literature, and other source material. From this process, they arrive at conclusions, and publish their findings in scholarly journals, books, and electronic media.

Most college and university faculty extensively use computer technology, including the Internet; electronic mail; software programs, such as statistical packages; and CD-ROMs. They may use computers in the classroom as teaching aids and may post course content, class notes, class schedules, and other information on the Internet. Some faculty are increasingly using sophisticated telecommunications and videoconferencing equipment and the Internet to teach courses to students at remote sites. The use of e-mail, chat rooms, and other techniques has greatly improved communications between students and teachers and among students.

Most faculty members serve on academic or administrative committees that deal with the policies of their institution, departmental matters, academic issues, curricula, budgets, equipment purchases, and hiring. Some work with student and community organizations. Department chairpersons are faculty members who usually teach some courses but have heavier administrative responsibilities.

The proportion of time spent on research, teaching, administrative, and other duties varies by individual circumstance and type of institution. Faculty members at universities normally spend a significant part of their time doing research; those in 4-year colleges, somewhat less; and those in 2-year colleges, relatively little. The teaching load, however, often is heavier in 2-year colleges and somewhat lighter at 4-year institutions. Full professors at all types of institutions usually spend a larger portion of their time conducting research than do assistant professors, instructors, and lecturers.

Postsecondary vocational education teachers, also known as *postsecondary career and technical education teachers*, provide instruction for occupations that require specialized training, but may not require a 4-year degree, such as welder, dental hygienist, x-ray technician, auto mechanic, and cosmetologist. Classes often are taught in an industrial or laboratory setting where students are provided hands-on experience. For example, welding instructors show students various welding techniques and essential safety practices, watch them use tools and equipment, and have them repeat procedures until they meet the specific standards required by the trade. Increasingly, career and technical education teachers are integrating academic and vocational curriculums so that students obtain a variety of skills that can be applied to the "real world."

Career and technical education teachers have many of the same responsibilities that other college and university faculty have. They must prepare lessons, grade papers, attend faculty meetings, and keep abreast of developments in their field. Career and technical education teachers at community colleges and career and technical schools also often play a key role in students' transition from school to work by helping to establish internship programs for students and by providing information about prospective employers.

Graduate teaching assistants, often referred to as *graduate TAs*, assist faculty, department chairs, or other professional staff at colleges and universities by performing teaching or teaching-related duties. In addition to their work responsibilities, assistants have their own school commitments, as they are also students who are working towards earning a graduate degree, such as a Ph.D. Some teaching assistants have full responsibility for teaching a course—usually one that is introductory in nature—which can include preparation of lectures and exams, and assigning final grades to students. Others provide assistance to faculty members, which may consist of a variety of tasks such as grading papers, monitoring exams, holding office hours or help-sessions for students, conducting laboratory sessions, or administering quizzes to the class. Teaching assistants generally meet initially with the faculty member whom they are going to assist in order to determine exactly what is expected of them, as each faculty member may have his or her own needs. For example, some faculty members prefer assistants to sit in on classes, while others assign them other tasks to do during class time. Graduate teaching assistants may work one-on-one with a faculty member or, for large classes, they may be one of several assistants.

Working Conditions

Postsecondary teachers usually have flexible schedules. They must be present for classes, usually 12 to 16 hours per week, and for faculty and committee meetings. Most establish regular office hours for student consultations, usually 3 to 6 hours per week. Otherwise, teachers are free to decide when and where they will work and how much time to devote to course preparation, grading, study, research, graduate student supervision, and other activities.

Some teach night and weekend classes. This is particularly true for teachers at 2-year community colleges or institutions with large enrollments of older students who have full-time jobs or family responsibilities. Most colleges and universities require teachers to work 9 months of the year, which allows them the time to teach additional courses, do research, travel, or pursue nonacademic interests during the summer and school holidays. Colleges and universities usually have funds to support research or other professional development needs, including travel to conferences and research sites.

About 3 out of 10 college and university faculty worked part time in 2002. Some part-timers, known as "adjunct faculty," have primary jobs outside of academia—in government, private industry, or nonprofit research—and teach "on the side." Others prefer to work part-time hours or seek full-time jobs but are unable to obtain them due to intense competition for available openings. Some work part time in more than one institution. Many adjunct faculty are not qualified for tenure-track positions because they lack a doctoral degree.

University faculty may experience a conflict between their responsibilities to teach students and the pressure to do research and publish their findings. This may be a particular problem for young faculty seeking advancement in 4-year research universities. Also, recent cutbacks and the hiring of more part-time faculty have put a greater administrative burden on full-time faculty. Requirements to teach online classes also have added greatly to the workloads of postsecondary teachers. Many find that developing the courses to put online, plus learning how to operate the technology and answering large amounts of e-mail, is very time-consuming.

Like college and university faculty, there is usually a great deal of flexibility in graduate TAs' work schedules, which allows them the time to pursue their own academic coursework and studies. The number of hours that TAs work varies depending on their assignments. Work may be stressful, particularly when assistants are given full responsibility for teaching a class; however, these types of positions allow graduate students the opportunity to gain valuable teaching experience. This experience is especially helpful for those graduate teaching assistants who seek to become faculty members at colleges and universities after completing their degree.

Employment

Postsecondary teachers held nearly 1.6 million jobs in 2002. Most were employed in public and private 4-year colleges and universities and in 2-year community colleges. Postsecondary career and technical education teachers also are employed by schools and institutes that specialize in training people in a specific field, such as technology centers or culinary schools. Some career and technical education teachers work for state and local governments and job training facilities. The following tabulation shows postsecondary teaching jobs in specialties having 20,000 or more jobs in 2002:

Graduate teaching assistants	128,000
Vocational education teachers	119,000
Health specialties teachers	86,000
Business teachers	67,000
Art, drama, and music teachers	58,000
English language and literature teachers	55,000
Education teachers	42,000
Biological science teachers	47,000
Mathematical science teachers	41,000
Nursing instructors and teachers	37,000
Computer science teachers	33,000
Engineering teachers	29,000
Psychology teachers	26,000

Training, Other Qualifications, and Advancement

The education and training required of postsecondary teachers varies widely, depending on the subject taught and educational institution employing them. Educational requirements for teachers are generally the highest at 4-year research universities but, at career and technical institutes, experience and expertise in a related occupation is the most valuable qualification.

Postsecondary teachers should communicate and relate well with students, enjoy working with them, and be able to motivate them. They should have inquiring and analytical minds, and a strong desire to pursue and disseminate knowledge. Additionally, they must be self-motivated and able to work in an environment in which they receive little direct supervision.

Training requirements for postsecondary career and technical education teachers vary by state and by subject. In general, teachers need a bachelor's or higher degree, plus work or other experience in their field. In some fields, a license or certificate that demonstrates one's qualifications may be all that is required. Teachers update their skills through continuing education, in order to maintain certification. They must also maintain ongoing dialogue with businesses to determine the most current skills needed in the workplace.

Four-year colleges and universities usually consider doctoral degree holders for full-time, tenure-track positions, but may hire master's degree holders or doctoral candidates for certain disciplines, such as the arts, or for part-time and temporary jobs. Most college and university faculty are in four academic ranks—professor, associate professor, assistant professor, and instructor. These positions usually are considered to be tenure-track positions. Most faculty members are hired as instructors or assistant professors. A smaller number of additional faculty members, called lecturers, are usually employed on contracts for a single academic term and are not on the tenure track.

In 2-year colleges, master's degree holders fill most full-time positions. However, with increasing competition for available jobs, institutions can be more selective in their hiring practices. Many 2-year institutions increasingly prefer job applicants to have some teaching experience or experience with distance learning. Preference also may be given to those holding dual master's degrees, because they can teach more subjects. In addition, with greater competition for jobs, master's degree holders may find it increasingly difficult to obtain employment as they are passed over in favor of candidates holding a Ph.D.

Doctoral programs take an average of 6 to 8 years of full-time study beyond the bachelor's degree, including time spent completing a master's degree and a dissertation. Some programs, such as those in the humanities, take longer to complete; others, such as those in engineering, usually are shorter. Candidates specialize in a subfield of a discipline—for example, organic chemistry, counseling psychology, or European history—but also take courses covering the entire discipline. Programs include 20 or more increasingly specialized courses and seminars plus comprehensive examinations on all major areas of the field. Candidates also must complete a dissertation—a written report on original research in the candidate's major field of study. The dissertation sets forth an original hypothesis or proposes a model and tests it. Students in the natural sciences and engineering usually do laboratory work; in the humanities, they study original documents and other published material. The dissertation is done under the guidance of one or more faculty advisors and usually takes 1 or 2 years of full-time work.

In some fields, particularly the natural sciences, some students spend an additional 2 years on postdoctoral research and study before taking a faculty position. Some Ph.D.s extend postdoctoral appointments, or take new ones, if they are unable to find a faculty job. Most of these appointments offer a nominal salary.

Obtaining a position as a graduate teaching assistant is a good way to gain college teaching experience. To qualify, candidates must be enrolled in a graduate school program. In addition, some colleges and universities require teaching assistants to attend classes or take some training prior to being given responsibility for a course.

Although graduate teaching assistants usually work at the institution and in the department where they are earning their degree, teaching or internship positions for graduate students at institutions that do not grant a graduate degree have become more common in recent years. For example, a program called Preparing Future Faculty, administered by the Association of American Colleges and Universities and the Council of Graduate Schools, has led to the creation of many now-independent programs that offer graduate students at research universities the opportunity to work as teaching assistants at other types of institutions, such as liberal arts or community colleges. Working with a mentor, the graduate students teach classes and learn how to improve their teaching techniques. They may attend faculty and committee meetings, develop a curriculum, and learn how to balance the teaching, research, and administrative roles that faculty play. These programs provide valuable learning opportunities for graduate students interested in teaching at the postsecondary level, and also help to make these students aware of the differences among the various types of institutions at which they may someday work.

For faculty, a major step in the traditional academic career is attaining tenure. New tenure-track faculty usually are hired as instructors or assistant professors, and must serve a period—usually 7 years—under term contracts. At the end of the period, their record of teaching, research, and overall contribution to the institution is reviewed; tenure is granted if the review is favorable. Those denied tenure usually must leave the institution. Tenured professors cannot be fired without just cause and due process. Tenure protects the faculty's academic freedom—the ability to teach and conduct research without fear of being fired for advocating unpopular ideas. It also gives both faculty and institutions the stability needed for effective research and teaching and provides financial security for faculty. Some institutions have adopted post-tenure review policies to encourage ongoing evaluation of tenured faculty.

The number of tenure-track positions is expected to decline as institutions seek flexibility in dealing with financial matters and changing student interests. Institutions will rely more heavily on limited term contracts and part-time, or adjunct, faculty, thus shrinking the total pool of tenured faculty. In a trend that is expected to continue, some institutions now offer limited-term contracts to prospective faculty—typically 2-, 3-, or 5-year full-time contracts. These contracts may be terminated or extended when they expire. Institutions are not obligated to grant tenure to the contract holders. In addition, some institutions have limited the percentage of faculty who can be tenured.

For most postsecondary teachers, advancement involves a move into administrative and managerial positions, such as departmental chairperson, dean, and president. At 4-year institutions, such advancement requires a doctoral degree. At 2-year colleges, a doctorate is helpful but not usually required, except for advancement to some top administrative positions.

Job Outlook

Overall, employment of postsecondary teachers is expected to grow much faster than the average for all occupations through 2012. A significant proportion of these new jobs will be part-time positions. Good job opportunities are expected as retirements of current postsecondary teachers and continued increases in student enrollments create numerous openings for teachers at all types of postsecondary institutions.

Projected growth in college and university enrollment over the next decade stems largely from the expected increase in the population of 18- to 24-year-olds. Adults returning to college and an increase in foreign-born students also will add to the number of students, particularly in the fastest growing states of California, Texas, Florida, New York, and Arizona. In addition, workers' growing need to regularly update their skills will continue to create new opportunities for postsecondary teachers, particularly at community colleges and for-profit institutions that cater to working adults. However, many postsecondary educational institutions receive a significant portion of their funding from state and local governments, and, over the early years of the projection period, tight state and local budgets will limit the ability of many schools to expand. Nevertheless, a significant number of openings also is expected to arise due to the need to replace the large numbers of postsecondary teachers who are likely to retire over the next decade. Many postsecondary teachers were hired in the late 1960s and 1970s to teach the baby boomers, and they are expected to retire in growing numbers in the years ahead.

Postsecondary institutions are a major employer of workers holding doctoral degrees, and opportunities for Ph.D. recipients seeking jobs as postsecondary teachers are expected to be somewhat better than in previous decades. The number of earned doctorate degrees is projected to rise by only 4 percent over the 2002-12 period, sharply lower than the 10-percent increase over the previous decade. In spite of this positive trend, competition will remain tight for those seeking tenure-track positions at 4-year colleges and universities, as many of the job openings are expected to be either part-time or renewable term appointments.

Opportunities for graduate teaching assistants are expected to be very good. Graduate enrollments over the 2002-12 period are projected to increase at a rate that is somewhat slower than that of the previous decade, while total undergraduate enrollments in degree-granting institutions are expected to increase at nearly twice the rate of the preceding decade, creating many teaching opportunities. Constituting more than 12 percent of all postsecondary teachers, graduate teaching assistants play an integral role in the postsecondary education system, and they are expected to continue to do so in the future.

Because one of the main reasons why students attend postsecondary institutions is to obtain a job, the best job prospects for postsecondary teachers are likely to be in fields where job growth is expected to be strong over the next decade. These will include fields such as business, health specialties, nursing, and computer and biological sciences. Community colleges and other institutions offering career and technical education have been among the most rapidly growing, and these institutions are expected to offer some of the best opportunities for postsecondary teachers.

Earnings

Median annual earnings of all postsecondary teachers in 2002 were $49,040. The middle 50 percent earned between $34,310 and $69,580. The lowest 10 percent earned less than $23,080, and the highest 10 percent earned more than $92,430.

Earnings for college faculty vary according to rank and type of institution, geographic area, and field. According to a 2002-03 survey by the American Association of University Professors, salaries for full-time faculty averaged $64,455. By rank, the average was $86,437 for professors, $61,732 for associate professors, $51,545 for assistant professors, $37,737 for instructors, and $43,914 for lecturers. Faculty in 4-year institutions earn higher salaries, on average, than do those in 2-year schools. In 2002-03, average faculty salaries in public institutions—$63,974—were lower than those in private independent institutions—$74,359—but higher than those in religiously affiliated private colleges and universities—$57,564. In fields with high-paying nonacademic alternatives—medicine, law, engineering, and business, among others—earnings exceed these averages. In others—such as the humanities and education—they are lower.

Many faculty members have significant earnings, in addition to their base salary, from consulting, teaching additional courses, research, writing for publication, or other employment. In addition, many college and university faculty enjoy some unique benefits, including access to campus facilities, tuition waivers for dependents, housing and travel allowances, and paid sabbatical leaves. Part-time faculty usually have fewer benefits than do full-time faculty.

Earnings for postsecondary career and technical education teachers vary widely by subject, academic credentials, experience, and region of the country. Part-time instructors usually receive few benefits.

Related Occupations

Postsecondary teaching requires the ability to communicate ideas well, motivate students, and be creative. Workers in other occupations that require these skills are a teachers—preschool, kindergarten, elementary, middle, and secondary; education administrators; librarians; counselors; writers and editors; public relations specialists; and management analysts. Faculty research activities often are similar to those of scientists, as well as to those of managers and administrators in industry, government, and nonprofit research organizations.

Sources of Additional Information

Professional societies related to a field of study often provide information on academic and nonacademic employment opportunities.

Special publications on higher education, such as *The Chronicle of Higher Education*, list specific employment opportunities for faculty. These publications are available in libraries.

For information on the Preparing Future Faculty program, contact:

- Association of American Colleges and Universities, 1818 R St. NW, Washington, DC 20009. Internet: http://www.aacu-edu.org

For information on postsecondary career and technical education teaching positions, contact state departments of career and technical education.

General information on adult and career and technical education is available from:

- Association for Career and Technical Education, 1410 King St., Alexandria, VA 22314. Internet: http://www.acteonline.org

Teachers—Preschool, Kindergarten, Elementary, Middle, and Secondary

(O*NET 25-2011.00, 25-2012.00, 25-2021.00, 25-2022.00, 25-2023.00, 25-2031.00, and 25-2032.00)

Significant Points

- Public school teachers must have at least a bachelor's degree, complete an approved teacher education program, and be licensed.

- Many states offer alternative licensing programs to attract people into teaching, especially for hard-to-fill positions.

- Excellent job opportunities are expected as a large number of teachers retire over the next 10 years, particularly at the secondary school level; opportunities will vary somewhat by geographic area and subject taught.

Nature of the Work

Teachers act as facilitators or coaches, using interactive discussions and "hands-on" approaches to help students learn and apply concepts in subjects such as science, mathematics, or English. They utilize "props" or "manipulatives" to help children understand abstract concepts, solve problems, and develop critical thought processes. For example, they teach the concepts of numbers or of addition and subtraction by playing board games. As the children get older, the teachers use more sophisticated materials, such as science apparatus, cameras, or computers.

To encourage collaboration in solving problems, students are increasingly working in groups to discuss and solve problems together. Preparing students for the future workforce is the major stimulus generating the changes in education. To be prepared, students must be able to interact with others, adapt to new technology, and think through problems logically. Teachers provide the tools and the environment for their students to develop these skills.

Preschool, kindergarten, and elementary school teachers play a vital role in the development of children. What children learn and experience during their early years can shape their views of themselves and the world and can affect their later success or failure in school, work, and their personal lives. Preschool, kindergarten, and elementary school teachers introduce children to mathematics, language, science, and social studies. They use games, music, artwork, films, books, computers, and other tools to teach basic skills.

Preschool children learn mainly through play and interactive activities. *Preschool teachers* capitalize on children's play to further language and vocabulary development (using storytelling, rhyming games, and acting games), improve social skills (having the children work together to build a neighborhood in a sandbox), and introduce scientific and mathematical concepts (showing the children how to balance and count blocks when building a bridge or how to mix colors when painting). Thus, a less structured approach, including small-group lessons, one-on-one instruction, and learning through creative activities such as art, dance, and music, is adopted to teach preschool children,. Play and hands-on teaching also are used in kindergarten classrooms, but there academics begin to take priority. Letter recognition, phonics, numbers, and awareness of nature and science, introduced at the preschool level, are taught primarily by *kindergarten teachers*.

Most *elementary school teachers* instruct one class of children in several subjects. In some schools, two or more teachers work as a team and are jointly responsible for a group of students in at least one subject. In other schools, a teacher may teach one special subject—usually music, art, reading, science, arithmetic, or physical education—to a number of classes. A small but growing number of teachers instruct multilevel classrooms, with students at several different learning levels.

Middle school teachers and *secondary school teachers* help students delve more deeply into subjects introduced in elementary school and expose them to more information about the world. Middle and secondary school teachers specialize in a specific subject, such as English, Spanish, mathematics, history, or biology. They also can teach subjects that are career oriented. *Vocational education teachers*, also referred to as career and technical or career-technology teachers, instruct and train students to work in a wide variety of fields, such as healthcare, business, auto repair, communications, and, increasingly, technology. They often teach courses that are in high demand by area employers, who may provide input into the curriculum and offer internships to students. Many vocational teachers play an active role in building and overseeing these partnerships. Additional responsibilities of middle and secondary school teachers may include career guidance and job placement, as well as follow-ups with students after graduation.

Teachers may use films, slides, overhead projectors, and the latest technology in teaching, including computers, telecommunication systems, and video discs. The use of computer resources, such as educational software and the Internet, exposes students to a vast range of experiences and promotes interactive learning. Through the Internet, students can communicate with students in other countries. Students also use the Internet for individual research projects and to gather information. Computers are used in other classroom activities as well, from solving math problems to learning English as a second language. Teachers also may use computers to record grades and perform other administrative and clerical duties. They must continually update their skills so that they can instruct and use the latest technology in the classroom.

Teachers often work with students from varied ethnic, racial, and religious backgrounds. With growing minority populations in most parts of the country, it is important for teachers to work effectively with a diverse student population. Accordingly, some schools offer training to help teachers enhance their awareness and understanding of different cultures. Teachers may also include multicultural programming in their lesson plans, to address the needs of all students, regardless of their cultural background.

Teachers design classroom presentations to meet students' needs and abilities. They also work with students individually. Teachers plan, evaluate, and assign lessons; prepare, administer, and grade tests; listen to oral presentations; and maintain classroom discipline. They observe and evaluate a student's performance and potential and increasingly are asked to use new assessment methods. For example, teachers may examine a portfolio of a student's artwork or writing in order to judge the student's overall progress. They then can provide additional assistance in areas in which a student needs help. Teachers also grade papers, prepare report cards, and meet with parents and school staff to discuss a student's academic progress or personal problems.

In addition to conducting classroom activities, teachers oversee study halls and homerooms, supervise extracurricular activities, and accompany students on field trips. They may identify students with physical or mental problems and refer the students to the proper authorities. Secondary school teachers occasionally assist students in choosing courses, colleges, and careers. Teachers also participate in education conferences and workshops.

In recent years, site-based management, which allows teachers and parents to participate actively in management decisions regarding school operations, has gained popularity. In many schools, teachers are increasingly involved in making decisions regarding the budget, personnel, textbooks, curriculum design, and teaching methods.

Working Conditions

Seeing students develop new skills and gain an appreciation of knowledge and learning can be very rewarding. However, teaching may be frustrating when one is dealing with unmotivated or disrespectful students. Occasionally, teachers must cope with unruly behavior and violence in the schools. Teachers may experience stress in dealing with large classes, students from disadvantaged or multicultural backgrounds, or heavy workloads. Inner-city schools in particular, may be run down and lack the amenities of schools in wealthier communities. Accountability standards also may increase stress levels, with teachers expected to produce students who are able to exhibit satisfactory performance on standardized tests in core subjects.

Teachers are sometimes isolated from their colleagues because they work alone in a classroom of students. However, some schools allow teachers to work in teams and with mentors to enhance their professional development.

Including school duties performed outside the classroom, many teachers work more than 40 hours a week. Part-time schedules are more common among preschool and kindergarten teachers. Although some school districts have gone to all-day kindergartens, most kindergarten teachers still teach two kindergarten classes a day. Most teachers work the traditional 10-month school year with a 2-month vacation during the summer. During the vacation break, those on the 10-month schedule may teach in summer sessions, take other jobs, travel, or pursue personal interests. Many enroll in college courses or workshops to continue their education. Teachers in districts with a year-round schedule typically work 8 weeks, are on vacation for 1 week, and have a 5-week midwinter break. Preschool teachers working in daycare settings often work year round.

Most states have tenure laws that prevent teachers from being fired without just cause and due process. Teachers may obtain tenure after they have satisfactorily completed a probationary period of teaching, normally 3 years. Tenure does not absolutely guarantee a job, but it does provide some security.

Employment

Preschool, kindergarten, elementary school, middle school, and secondary school teachers, except special education, held about 3.8 million jobs in 2002. Of the teachers in those jobs, about 1.5 million were elementary school teachers, 1.1 million were secondary school teachers, 602,000 were middle school teachers, 424,000 were preschool teachers, and 168,000 were kindergarten teachers. The majority of kindergarten, elementary school, middle school, and secondary school teachers, except special education worked in local government educational services. About 10 percent worked for private schools. Preschool teachers, except special education were most often employed in child daycare services (63 percent), religious organizations (9 percent), local government educational services (9 percent), and private educational services (7 percent). Employment of teachers is geographically distributed much the same as the population is.

Training, Other Qualifications, and Advancement

All 50 states and the District of Columbia require public school teachers to be licensed. Licensure is not required for teachers in private schools. Usually licensure is granted by the State Board of Education or a licensure advisory committee. Teachers may be licensed to teach the early childhood grades (usually preschool through grade 3); the elementary grades (grades 1 through 6 or 8); the middle grades (grades 5 through 8); a secondary-education subject area (usually grades 7 through 12); or a special subject, such as reading or music (usually grades kindergarten through 12).

Requirements for regular licenses to teach kindergarten through grade 12 vary by state. However, all states require general education teachers to have a bachelor's degree and to have completed an approved teacher training program with a prescribed number of subject and education credits, as well as supervised practice teaching. Some states also require technology training and the attainment of a minimum grade point average. A number of states require that teachers obtain a master's degree in education within a specified period after they begin teaching.

Almost all states require applicants for a teacher's license to be tested for competency in basic skills, such as reading and writing, and in teaching. Almost all also require the teacher to exhibit proficiency in his or her subject. Nowadays, school systems are moving toward implementing performance-based systems for licensure, which usually require the teacher to demonstrate satisfactory teaching performance over an extended period in order to obtain a provisional license, in addition to passing an examination in one's subject. Most states require continuing education for renewal of the teacher's license. Many states have reciprocity agreements that make it easier for teachers licensed in one state to become licensed in another.

Many states offer alternative licensure programs for teachers who have bachelor's degrees in the subject they will teach, but who lack the necessary education courses required for a regular license. Alternative licensure programs originally were designed to ease shortages of teachers of certain subjects, such as mathematics and science. The programs have expanded to attract other people into teaching, including recent college graduates and those changing from another career to teaching. In some programs, individuals begin teaching quickly under provisional licensure. After working under the close supervision of experienced educators for 1 or 2 years while taking education courses outside school hours, they receive regular licensure if they have progressed satisfactorily. In other programs, college graduates who do not meet licensure requirements take only those courses that they lack and then become licensed. This approach may take 1 or 2 semesters of full-time study. States may issue emergency licenses to individuals who do not meet the requirements for a regular license when schools cannot attract enough qualified teachers to fill positions. Teachers who need to be licensed may enter programs that grant a master's degree in education, as well as a license.

In many states, vocational teachers have many of the same requirements for teaching as their academic counterparts. However, because knowledge and experience in a particular field are an important criteria for the job, some states will license vocational education teachers without a bachelor's degree, provided they can demonstrate expertise in their field. A minimum number of hours in education courses may also be required.

Licensing requirements for preschool teachers also vary by state. Requirements for public preschool teachers are generally higher than those for private preschool teachers. Some states require a bachelor's degree in early childhood education, others require an associate's degree, and still others require certification by a nationally recognized authority. The Child Development Associate (CDA) credential, the most common type of certification, requires a mix of classroom training and experience working with children, along with an independent assessment of an individual's competence.

In some cases, teachers of kindergarten through high school may attain professional certification in order to demonstrate competency beyond that required for a license. The National Board for Professional Teaching Standards offers a voluntary national certification. To become nationally accredited, experienced teachers must prove their aptitude by compiling a portfolio showing their work in the classroom and by passing a written assessment and evaluation of their teaching knowledge. Currently, teachers may become certified in a variety of areas, on the basis of the age of the students and, in some cases, the subject taught. For example, teachers may obtain a certificate for teaching English language arts to early adolescents (aged 11 to 15), or they may become certified as early childhood generalists. All states recognize national certification, and many states and school districts provide special benefits to teachers holding such certification. Benefits typically include higher salaries and reimbursement for continuing education and certification fees. In addition, many states allow nationally certified teachers to carry a license from one state to another.

The National Council for Accreditation of Teacher Education currently accredits more than 550 teacher education programs across the United States. Generally, 4-year colleges require students to wait until their sophomore year before applying for admission to teacher education programs. Traditional education programs for kindergarten and elementary school teachers include courses—designed specifically for those preparing to teach—in mathematics, physical science, social science, music, art, and literature, as well as prescribed professional education courses, such as philosophy of education, psychology of learning, and teaching methods. Aspiring secondary school teachers most often major in the subject they plan to teach while also taking a program of study in teacher preparation. Teacher education programs are now required to include classes in the use of computers and other technologies in order to maintain their accreditation. Most programs require students to perform a student-teaching internship.

Many states now offer professional development schools—partnerships between universities and elementary or secondary schools. Students enter these 1-year programs after completion of their bachelor's degree. Professional development schools merge theory with practice and allow the student to experience a year of teaching firsthand, under professional guidance.

In addition to being knowledgeable in their subject, teachers must have the ability to communicate, inspire trust and confidence, and motivate students, as well as understand the students' educational and emotional needs. Teachers must be able to recognize and respond to individual and cultural differences in students and employ different teaching methods that will result in higher student achievement. They should be organized, dependable, patient, and creative. Teachers also must be able to work cooperatively and communicate effectively with other teachers, support staff, parents, and members of the community.

With additional preparation, teachers may move into positions as school librarians, reading specialists, curriculum specialists, or guidance counselors. Teachers may become administrators or supervisors, although the number of these positions is limited and competition can be intense. In some systems, highly qualified, experienced teachers can become senior or mentor teachers, with higher pay and additional responsibilities. They guide and assist less experienced teachers while keeping most of their own teaching responsibilities. Preschool teachers usually work their way up from assistant teacher, to teacher, to lead teacher—who may be responsible for the instruction of several classes—and, finally, to director of the center. Preschool teachers with a bachelor's degree frequently are qualified to teach kindergarten through grade 3 as well. Teaching at these higher grades often results in higher pay.

Job Outlook

Job opportunities for teachers over the next 10 years will vary from good to excellent, depending on the locality, grade level, and subject taught. Most job openings will be attributable to the expected retirement of a large number of teachers. In addition, relatively high rates of turnover, especially among beginning teachers employed in poor, urban schools, also will lead to numerous job openings for teachers. Competition for qualified teachers among some localities will likely continue, with schools luring teachers from other states and districts with bonuses and higher pay.

Through 2012, overall student enrollments, a key factor in the demand for teachers, are expected to rise more slowly than in the past. As the children of the baby-boom generation get older, smaller numbers of young children will enter school behind them, resulting in average employment growth for all teachers, from preschool through secondary grades. Projected enrollments will vary by region. Fast-growing states in the South and West—particularly California, Texas, Georgia, Idaho, Hawaii, Alaska, and New Mexico—will experience the largest enrollment increases. Enrollments in the Northeast and Midwest are expected to hold relatively steady or decline. The job market for teachers also continues to vary by school location and by subject taught. Many inner cities—often characterized by overcrowded, ill-equipped schools and higher-than-average poverty rates—and rural areas—characterized by their remote location and relatively low salaries—have difficulty attracting and retaining enough teachers, so job prospects should be better in these areas than in suburban districts. Currently, many school districts have difficulty hiring qualified teachers in some subject areas—mathematics, science (especially chemistry and physics), bilingual education, and foreign languages. Qualified vocational teachers, at both the middle school and secondary school levels, also are currently in demand in a variety of fields. Specialties that have an adequate number of qualified teachers include general elementary education, physical education, and social studies. Teachers who are geographically mobile and who obtain licensure in more than one subject should have a distinct advantage in finding a job. Increasing enrollments of minorities, coupled with a shortage of minority teachers, should cause efforts to recruit minority teachers to intensify. Also, the number of non-English-speaking students has grown dramatically, creating demand for bilingual teachers and for those who teach English as a second language. The number of teachers employed is dependent as well on state and local expenditures for education and on the enactment of legislation to increase the quality of education. A number of initiatives, such as reduced class size (primarily in the early elementary grades), mandatory preschool for 4-year-olds, and all-day kindergarten, have been implemented in a few states, but not nationwide. Additional teachers—particularly preschool and early elementary school teachers—will be needed if states or localities implement any of these measures. At the federal level, legislation that is likely to affect teachers recently was put into place with the enactment of the No Child Left Behind Act. Although the full impact of this act is not yet known, its emphasis on ensuring that all schools hire and retain only qualified teachers may lead to an increase in funding for schools that currently lack such teachers.

The supply of teachers is expected to increase in response to reports of improved job prospects, better pay, more teacher involvement in school policy, and greater public interest in education. In recent years, the total number of bachelor's and master's degrees granted in education has increased steadily. Because of a shortage of teachers in certain locations, and in anticipation of the loss of a number of teachers to retirement, many states have implemented policies that will encourage more students to become teachers. In addition, more teachers may be drawn from a reserve pool of career changers, substitute teachers, and teachers completing alternative certification programs.

Earnings

Median annual earnings of kindergarten, elementary, middle, and secondary school teachers ranged from $39,810 to $44,340 in 2002; the lowest 10 percent earned $24,960 to $29,850; the top 10 percent earned $62,890 to $68,530. Median earnings for preschool teachers were $19,270.

According to the American Federation of Teachers, beginning teachers with a bachelor's degree earned an average of $30,719 in the 2001–02 school year. The estimated average salary of all public elementary and secondary school teachers in the 2001–02 school year was $44,367. Private school teachers generally earn less than public school teachers.

In 2002, more than half of all elementary, middle, and secondary school teachers belonged to unions—mainly the American Federation of Teachers and the National Education Association—that bargain with school systems over wages, hours, and other terms and conditions of employment. Fewer preschool and kindergarten teachers were union members—about 15 percent in 2002.

Teachers can boost their salary in a number of ways. In some schools, teachers receive extra pay for coaching sports and working with students in extracurricular activities. Getting a master's degree or national certification often results in a raise in pay, as does acting as a mentor. Some teachers earn extra income during the summer by teaching summer school or performing other jobs in the school system.

Related Occupations

Preschool, kindergarten, elementary school, middle school, and secondary school teaching requires a variety of skills and aptitudes, including a talent for working with children; organizational, administrative, and recordkeeping abilities; research and communication skills; the power to influence, motivate, and train others; patience; and creativity. Workers in other occupations requiring some of these aptitudes include teachers—postsecondary; counselors; teacher assistants; education administrators; librarians; child care workers; public relations specialists; social workers; and athletes, coaches, umpires, and related workers.

Sources of Additional Information

Information on licensure or certification requirements and approved teacher training institutions is available from local school systems and state departments of education.

Information on the teaching profession and on how to become a teacher can be obtained from:

- Recruiting New Teachers, Inc., 385 Concord Ave., Suite 103, Belmont, MA 02478. Internet: http://www.rnt.org

This organization also sponsors another Internet site that provides helpful information on becoming a teacher:

- http://www.recruitingteachers.org

Information on teachers' unions and education-related issues may be obtained from any of the following sources:

- American Federation of Teachers, 555 New Jersey Ave. NW, Washington, DC 20001.

- National Education Association, 1201 16th St. NW, Washington, DC 20036.

A list of institutions with accredited teacher education programs can be obtained from:

- National Council for Accreditation of Teacher Education, 2010 Massachusetts Ave. NW, Suite 500, Washington, DC 20036-1023. Internet: http://www.ncate.org

For information on vocational education and vocational education teachers, contact:

- Association for Career and Technical Education, 1410 King St., Alexandria, VA 22314. Internet: http://www.acteonline.org

For information on careers in educating children and issues affecting preschool teachers, contact either of the following organizations:

- National Association for the Education of Young Children, 1509 16th St. NW, Washington, DC 20036. Internet: http://www.naeyc.org

- Council for Professional Recognition, 2460 16th St. NW, Washington, DC 20009-3575. Internet: http://www.cdacouncil.org

For information on teachers and the No Child Left Behind Act, contact: U.S. Department of Education, 400 Maryland Avenue, SW, Washington, DC, 20202. Internet: http://www.ed.gov.

Teachers—Special Education

(O*NET 25-2041.00, 25-2042.00, and 25-2043.00)

Significant Points

- Excellent job prospects are expected due to rising enrollments of special education students and reported shortages of qualified teachers.

- A bachelor's degree, completion of an approved teacher preparation program, and a license are required to qualify; many states require a master's degree.

- Many states offer alternative licensure programs to attract people into these jobs.

Nature of the Work

Special education teachers work with children and youths who have a variety of disabilities. A small number of special education teachers work with students with mental retardation or autism, primarily teaching them life skills and basic literacy. However, the majority of special education teachers work with children with mild to moderate disabilities, using the general education curriculum, or modifying it, to meet the child's individual needs. Most special education teachers instruct students at the elementary, middle, and secondary school level, although some teachers work with infants and toddlers.

The various types of disabilities that qualify individuals for special education programs include specific learning disabilities, speech or language impairments, mental retardation, emotional disturbance, multiple disabilities, hearing impairments, orthopedic impairments, visual impairments, autism, combined deafness and blindness, traumatic brain injury, and other health impairments. Students are classified under one of the categories, and special education teachers are prepared to work with specific groups. Early identification of a child with special needs is an important part of a special education teacher's job. Early intervention is essential in educating children with disabilities.

Special education teachers use various techniques to promote learning. Depending on the disability, teaching methods can include individualized instruction, problem-solving assignments, and small-group work. When students need special accommodations in order to take a test, special education teachers see that appropriate ones are provided, such as having the questions read orally or lengthening the time allowed to take the test.

Special education teachers help to develop an Individualized Education Program (IEP) for each special education student. The IEP sets personalized goals for each student and is tailored to the student's individual learning style and ability. The program includes a transition plan outlining specific steps to prepare special education students for middle school or high school or, in the case of older students, a job or postsecondary study. Teachers review the IEP with the student's parents, school administrators, and, often, the student's general education teacher. Teachers work closely with parents to inform them of their child's progress and suggest techniques to promote learning at home.

Special education teachers design and teach appropriate curricula, assign work geared toward each student's ability, and grade papers and homework assignments. They are involved in the students' behavioral and academic development, helping the students develop emotionally, feel comfortable in social situations, and be aware of socially acceptable behavior. Preparing special education students for daily life after graduation also is an important aspect of the job. Teachers provide students with career counseling or help them learn routine skills, such as balancing a checkbook.

As schools become more inclusive, special education teachers and general education teachers are increasingly working together in general education classrooms. Special education teachers help general educators adapt curriculum materials and teaching techniques to meet the needs of students with disabilities. They coordinate the work of teachers, teacher assistants, and related personnel, such as therapists and social workers, to meet the requirements of inclusive special education programs. A large part of a special education teacher's job involves interacting with others. Special education teachers communicate frequently with parents, social workers, school psychologists, occupational and physical therapists, school administrators, and other teachers.

Special education teachers work in a variety of settings. Some have their own classrooms and teach only special education students; others work as special education resource teachers and offer individualized help to students in general education classrooms; still others teach together with general education teachers in classes composed of both general and special education students. Some teachers work with special education students for several hours a day in a resource room, separate from their general education classroom. Considerably fewer special education teachers work in residential facilities or tutor students in homebound or hospital environments.

Special education teachers who work with infants usually travel to the child's home to work with the child and his or her parents. Many of these infants have medical problems that slow or preclude normal development. Special education teachers show parents techniques and activities designed to stimulate the infant and encourage the growth of the child's skills. Toddlers usually receive their services at a preschool where special education teachers help them develop social, self-help, motor, language, and cognitive skills, often through the use of play.

Technology is playing an increasingly important role in special education. Teachers use specialized equipment such as computers with synthesized speech, interactive educational software programs, and audiotapes to assist children.

Working Conditions

Special education teachers enjoy the challenge of working with students with disabilities and the opportunity to establish meaningful relationships with them. Although helping these students can be highly rewarding, the work also can be emotionally and physically draining. Many special education teachers are under considerable stress due to heavy workloads and administrative tasks. They must produce a substantial amount of paperwork documenting each student's progress, and they work under the threat of litigation by students' parents if correct procedures are not followed or if the parents feel that their child is not receiving an adequate education. The physical and emotional demands of the job cause some special education teachers to leave the occupation.

Some schools offer year-round education for special education students, but most special education teachers work only the traditional 10-month school year.

Employment

Special education teachers held a total of about 433,000 jobs in 2002. A great majority, almost 90 percent, work in public schools. Another 7 percent work at private schools. About half work in elementary schools. A few worked for individual and social assistance agencies or residential facilities, or in homebound or hospital environments.

Training, Other Qualifications, and Advancement

All 50 states and the District of Columbia require special education teachers to be licensed. The state board of education or a licensure advisory committee usually grants licenses, and licensure varies by state. In many states, special education teachers receive a general education credential to teach kindergarten through grade 12. These teachers then train in a specialty, such as learning disabilities or behavioral disorders. Some states offer general special education licenses, while others license several different specialties within special education, and still others require teachers to obtain a general education license first and an additional license in special education afterwards.

All states require a bachelor's degree and the completion of an approved teacher preparation program with a prescribed number of subject and education credits and supervised practice teaching. Many states require a master's degree in special education, involving at least 1 year of additional course work, including a specialization, beyond the bachelor's degree.

Some states have reciprocity agreements allowing special education teachers to transfer their licenses from one state to another, but many still require that the teacher pass licensing requirements for the state in which they work. In the future, employers may recognize certification or standards offered by a national organization.

Many colleges and universities across the United States offer programs in special education, at the undergraduate, master's, and doctoral degree levels. Special education teachers usually undergo longer periods of training than do general education teachers. Most bachelor's degree programs are 4-year programs that include general and specialized courses in special education. However, an increasing number of institutions are requiring a 5th year or other postbaccalaureate preparation. Among the courses offered are educational psychology, legal issues of special education, and child growth and development; courses imparting knowledge and skills needed for teaching students with disabilities also are given. Some programs require specialization, while others offer generalized special education degrees or a course of study in several specialized areas. The last year of the program usually is spent student teaching in a classroom supervised by a certified teacher.

Alternative and emergency licenses are available in many states, due to the need to fill special education teaching positions. Alternative licenses are designed to bring college grad-uates and those changing careers into teaching more quickly. Requirements for an alternative license may be less stringent than for a regular license. Requirements vary by state. In some programs, individuals begin teaching quickly under a provisional license and can obtain a regular license by teaching under the supervision of licensed teachers for a period of 1 to 2 years while taking education courses. Emergency licenses are granted when states have difficulty finding licensed special education teachers to fill positions.

Special education teachers must be patient, able to motivate students, understanding of their students' special needs, and accepting of differences in others. Teachers must be creative and apply different types of teaching methods to reach students who are having difficulty learning. Communication and cooperation are essential traits, because special education teachers spend a great deal of time interacting with others, including students, parents, and school faculty and administrators.

Special education teachers can advance to become supervisors or administrators. They may also earn advanced degrees and become instructors in colleges that prepare others to teach special education. In some school systems, highly experienced teachers can become mentors to less experienced ones, providing guidance to those teachers while maintaining a light teaching load.

Job Outlook

Employment of special education teachers is expected to increase faster than the average for all occupations through 2012. Although slowdowns in student enrollments may constrain employment growth somewhat, additional positions for these workers will be created by continued increases in the number of special education students needing services, by legislation emphasizing training and employment for individuals with disabilities, and by educational reforms requiring higher standards for graduation. The need to replace special education teachers who switch to general education, change careers altogether, or retire will lead to additional job openings. At the same time, many school districts report shortages of qualified teachers. As a result, special education teachers should have excellent job prospects.

The job outlook varies by geographic area and specialty. Although many areas of the country report difficulty finding qualified applicants, positions in inner cities and rural areas usually are more plentiful than job openings in suburban or wealthy urban areas. Student populations, in general, also are expected to increase significantly in several states in the West and South, resulting in increased demand for special education teachers in those regions. In addition, job opportunities may be better in certain specialties—such as speech or language impairments and learning disabilities—because of large increases in the enrollment of special education students classified under those categories. Legislation encouraging early intervention and special education for infants, toddlers, and preschoolers has created a need for early childhood special education teachers. Bilingual special education teachers and those with multicultural experience also are needed to work with an increasingly diverse student population.

The number of students requiring special education services has grown steadily in recent years, a trend that is expected to continue. Learning disabilities will continue to be identified and diagnosed at earlier ages. In addition, medical advances have resulted in more children surviving serious accidents or illnesses, but with impairments that require special accommodations. The percentage of foreign-born special education students also is expected to grow, as teachers begin to recognize learning disabilities in that population. Finally, more parents are expected to seek special services for those of their children who have difficulty meeting the new, higher standards required of students.

Earnings

Median annual earnings in 2002 of special education teachers who worked primarily in preschools, kindergartens, and elementary schools were $42,690. The middle 50 percent earned between $34,160 and $54,340. The lowest 10 percent earned less than $28,680, and the highest 10 percent earned more than $67,810.

Median annual earnings in 2002 of middle school special education teachers were $41,350. The middle 50 percent earned between $33,460 and $52,370. The lowest 10 percent earned less than $28,560, and the highest 10 percent earned more than $65,070.

Median annual earnings in 2002 of special education teachers who worked primarily in secondary schools were $44,130. The middle 50 percent earned between $35,320 and $56,850. The lowest 10 percent earned less than $29,630, and the highest 10 percent earned more than $71,020.

In 2002, about 62 percent of special education teachers belonged to unions—mainly the American Federation of Teachers and the National Education Association—that bargain with school systems over wages, hours, and the terms and conditions of employment.

In most schools, teachers receive extra pay for coaching sports and working with students in extracurricular activities. Some teachers earn extra income during the summer, working in the school system or in other jobs.

Related Occupations

Special education teachers work with students who have disabilities and special needs. Other occupations involved with the identification, evaluation, and development of students with disabilities include: psychologists, social workers, speech-language pathologists and audiologists, counselors, teacher assistants, occupational therapists, recreational therapists, and teachers—preschool, kindergarten, elementary, middle, and secondary.

Sources of Additional Information

For information on professions related to early intervention and education for children with disabilities, a list of accredited schools, information on teacher certification and financial aid, and general information on related personnel issues—including recruitment, retention, and the supply of, and demand for, special education professionals—contact:

- National Clearinghouse for Professions in Special Education, Council for Exceptional Children, 1110 N. Glebe Rd., Suite 300, Arlington, VA 22201. Internet: http://www.special-ed-careers.org

To learn more about the special education teacher certification and licensing requirements in your state, contact your state's department of education.

Top Executives

(O*NET 11-1011.01, 11-1011.02, 11-1021.00, and 11-1031.00)

Significant Points

- Top executives are among the highest paid workers; however, long hours, considerable travel, and intense pressure to succeed are common.

- The formal education and experience of top executives varies as widely as the nature of their responsibilities.

- Keen competition is expected because the prestige and high pay attract a large number of qualified applicants.

- Most government chief executives and legislators are elected; local government managers are appointed.

Nature of the Work

All organizations have specific goals and objectives that they strive to meet. Top executives devise strategies and formulate policies to ensure that these objectives are met. Although they have a wide range of titles—such as chief executive officer, chief operating officer, board chair, president, vice president, school superintendent, county administrator, or tax commissioner—all formulate policies and direct the operations of businesses and corporations, nonprofit institutions, governments, and other organizations.

A corporation's goals and policies are established by the *chief executive officer* in collaboration with other top executives, who are overseen by a board of directors. In a large corporation, the chief executive officer meets frequently with subordinate executives to ensure that operations are conducted in accordance with these policies. The chief executive officer of a corporation retains overall accountability; however, a chief operating officer may be delegated several responsibilities, including the authority to oversee executives who direct the activities of various departments and implement the organization's policies on a day-to-day basis. In publicly held and nonprofit corporations, the board of directors ultimately is accountable for the success or failure of the enterprise, and the chief executive officer reports to the board.

The nature of other high-level executives' responsibilities depends upon the size of the organization. In large organizations, the duties of such executives are highly specialized. Some managers, for instance, are responsible for the overall performance of one aspect of the organization, such as manufacturing, marketing, sales, purchasing, finance, personnel, training, administrative services, computer and information systems, property management, transportation, or the legal services department.

In smaller organizations, such as independent retail stores or small manufacturers, a partner, owner, or general manager often is responsible for purchasing, hiring, training, quality control, and day-to-day supervisory duties.

Chief financial officers direct the organization's financial goals, objectives, and budgets. They oversee the investment of funds and manage associated risks, supervise cash management activities, execute capital-raising strategies to support a firm's expansion, and deal with mergers and acquisitions.

Chief information officers are responsible for the overall technological direction of their organizations. They are increasingly involved in the strategic business plan of a firm as part of the executive team. To perform effectively, they also need knowledge of administrative procedures, such as budgeting, hiring, and supervision. These managers propose budgets for projects and programs, and make decisions on staff training and equipment purchases. They hire and assign computer specialists, information technology workers, and support personnel to carry out specific parts of the projects. They supervise the work of these employees, review their output, and establish administrative procedures and policies. Chief information officers also provide organizations with the vision to master information technology as a competitive tool.

Chief executives and legislators at the federal, state, and local levels direct government activities and pass laws that affect us daily. These officials consist of the President and Vice President of the United States; members of Congress; state governors and lieutenant governors; members of the state legislators; county chief executives and commissioners; city, town, and township council members; mayors; and city, county, town, and township managers.

Most chief executives are elected by their constituents, but many managers are hired by a local government executive, council, or commission, to whom they are directly responsible. These officials formulate and establish government policy and develop federal, state, or local laws and regulations.

Chief executives, government—like their counterparts in the private sector—have overall responsibility for the operation of their organizations. Working with legislators, they set goals and arrange programs to attain them. These executives also appoint department heads, who oversee the civil servants who carry out programs enacted by legislative bodies. As in the private sector, government chief executives oversee budgets and ensure that resources are used properly and that programs are carried out as planned.

Chief executive officers carry out a number of other important functions, such as meeting with legislators and constituents to determine the level of support for proposed programs. In addition, they often nominate citizens to boards and commissions, encourage business investment, and promote economic development in their communities. To do all of these varied tasks effectively, chief executives of large governments rely on a staff of highly skilled aides to research issues that concern the public. Executives who control small governmental bodies, however, often do this work by themselves.

Legislators are elected officials who develop, enact, or amend laws. They include U.S. Senators and Representatives, state senators and representatives, and county, city, and town commissioners and council members. Legislators introduce, examine, and vote on bills to pass official legislation. In preparing such legislation, they study staff reports and hear testimony from constituents, representatives of interest groups, board and commission members, and others with an interest in the issue under consideration. They usually must approve budgets and the appointments of nominees for leadership posts whose names are submitted by the chief executive. In some bodies, the legislative council appoints the city, town, or county manager.

General and operations managers plan, direct, or coordinate the operations of companies or public and private sector organizations. Their duties include formulating policies, managing daily operations, and planning the use of materials and human resources, but are too diverse and general in nature to be classified in any one area of management or administration, such as personnel, purchasing, or administrative services. In some organizations, the duties of general and operations managers may overlap the duties of chief executive officers.

Working Conditions

Top executives typically have spacious offices and numerous support staff. General managers in large firms or nonprofit organizations usually have comfortable offices close to those of the top executives to whom they report. Long hours, including evenings and weekends, are standard for most top executives and general managers, although their schedules may be flexible.

Substantial travel between international, national, regional, and local offices to monitor operations and meet with customers, staff, and other executives often is required of managers and executives. Many managers and executives also attend meetings and conferences sponsored by various associations. The conferences provide an opportunity to meet with prospective donors, customers, contractors, or government officials and allow managers and executives to keep abreast of technological and managerial innovations.

In large organizations, job transfers between local offices or subsidiaries are common for persons on the executive career track. Top executives are under intense pressure to succeed; depending on the organization, this may mean earning higher profits, providing better service, or attaining fundraising and charitable goals. Executives in charge of poorly performing organizations or departments usually find their jobs in jeopardy.

The working conditions of legislators and government chief executives vary with the size and budget of the governmental unit. Time spent at work ranges from a few hours a week for some local leaders to stressful weeks of 60 or more hours for members of the U.S. Congress. Similarly, some jobs require only occasional out-of-town travel, while others involve long periods away from home, such as when attending sessions of the legislature.

U.S. Senators and Representatives, governors and lieutenant governors, and chief executives and legislators in municipalities work full time, year-round, as do most county and city managers. Many state legislators work full time on government business while the legislature is in session (usually for 2 to 6 months a year or every other year) and work only part time when the legislature is not in session. Some local elected officials work a schedule that is officially designated as part time, but actually is the equivalent of a full-time schedule when unpaid duties are taken into account. In addition to their regular schedules, most chief executives are on call to handle emergencies.

Employment

Top executives held about 2.7 million jobs in 2002. Employment by detailed occupation was distributed as follows:

General and operations managers	2,049,000
Chief executives	553,000
Legislators	67,000

Top executives are found in every industry, but service-providing industries, including government, employ almost 8 out of 10.

Chief executives and legislators in the federal government consist of the 100 senators, 435 representatives, and the President and Vice President. State governors, lieutenant governors, legislators, chief executives, professional managers, and council and commission members of local governments make up the remainder.

Government chief executives and legislators who do not hold full-time, year-round positions often continue to work in the occupation that they held before being elected.

Training, Other Qualifications, and Advancement

The formal education and experience of top executives varies as widely as the nature of their responsibilities. Many top executives have a bachelor's or higher degree in business administration or liberal arts. College presidents typically have a doctorate in the field in which they originally taught, and school superintendents often have a master's degree in education administration.A brokerage office manager needs a strong background in securities and finance, and department store executives generally have extensive experience in retail trade.

Some top executives in the public sector have a background in public administration or liberal arts. Others might have a background related to their jobs. For example, a health commissioner might have a graduate degree in health services administration or business administration.

Because many top executive positions are filled by promoting experienced lower-level managers when an opening occurs, many top managers have been promoted from within the organization. In industries such as retail trade or transportation, for instance, it is possible for individuals without a college degree to work their way up within the company and become managers. However, many companies prefer that their top executives have specialized backgrounds and, therefore, hire individuals who have been managers in other organizations.

Top executives must have highly developed personal skills. An analytical mind able to quickly assess large amounts of information and data is very important, as is the ability to consider and evaluate the interrelationships of numerous factors. Top executives also must be able to communicate clearly and persuasively. Other qualities critical for managerial success include leadership, self-confidence, motivation, decisiveness, flexibility, sound business judgment, and determination.

Advancement may be accelerated by participation in company training programs that impart a broader knowledge of company policy and operations. Managers also can help their careers by becoming familiar with the latest developments in management techniques at national or local training programs sponsored by various industry and trade associations. Managers who have experience in a particular field, such as accounting or engineering, may attend executive development programs to facilitate their promotion to an even higher level. Participation in conferences and seminars can expand knowledge of national and international issues influencing the organization and can help the participants to develop a network of useful contacts.

General managers may advance to top executive positions, such as executive vice president, in their own firm or they may take a corresponding position in another firm. They may even advance to peak corporate positions such as chief operating officer or chief executive officer. Chief executive officers often become members of the board of directors of one or more firms, typically as a director of their own firm and often as chair of its board of directors. Some top executives establish their own firms or become independent consultants.

Apart from meeting minimum age, residency, and citizenship requirements, candidates for a legislative position have no established training or qualifications. Candidates come from a wide variety of occupations—such as lawyer, private sector manager or executive, or business owner—but many do have some political experience as staffers or members of government bureaus, boards, or commissions. Successful candidates usually become well known through their political campaigns and some have built voter name recognition through their work with community religious, fraternal, or social organizations.

Increasingly, candidates target information to voters through advertising paid for by their respective campaigns, so fundraising skills are essential for candidates. Management-level work experience and public service help to develop the fundraising, budgeting, public speaking, and problem-solving skills that are needed to run an effective political campaign. Candidates must make decisions quickly, sometimes on the basis of limited or contradictory information. They also should be able to inspire and motivate their constituents and staff. Additionally, they must know how to reach compromises and satisfy conflicting demands of constituents. National, state, and some local campaigns require massive amounts of energy and stamina, traits vital to successful candidates.

Virtually all town, city, and county managers have at least a bachelor's degree, and many hold a higher degree. A master's degree in public administration is recommended, including courses in public financial management and legal issues in public administration. Working in management support positions in government is a prime source of the experience and personal contacts required to eventually secure a manager position. For example, applicants often gain experience as management analysts or assistants in government departments, working for committees, councils, or chief executives. In this capacity, they learn about planning, budgeting, civil engineering, and other aspects of running a government. With sufficient experience, they may be hired to manage a small government.

Generally, a town, city, or county manager is first hired by a smaller community. Advancement often takes the form of securing positions with progressively larger towns, cities, or counties. A broad knowledge of local issues, combined with communication skills and the ability to compromise, are essential for advancement in this field.

Advancement opportunities for elected officials are not clearly defined. Because elected positions normally require a period of residency and because local public support is critical, officials usually advance to other offices only in the jurisdictions where they live. For example, council members may run for mayor or for a position in the state government, and state legislators may run for governor or for the U.S. Congress. Many officials are not politically ambitious, however, and do not seek advancement. Others lose their bids for reelection or voluntarily leave the occupation. A lifetime career as a government chief executive or legislator is rare.

Job Outlook

Keen competition is expected for top executive positions, with the prestige and high pay attracting a large number of qualified applicants. Because this is a large occupation, numerous openings will occur each year as executives transfer to other positions, start their own businesses, or retire. However, many executives who leave their jobs transfer to other executive positions, which tend to limit the number of job openings for new entrants.

Experienced managers whose accomplishments reflect strong leadership qualities and the ability to improve the efficiency or competitive position of an organization will have the best opportunities. In an increasingly global economy, experience in international economics, marketing, information systems, and knowledge of several languages also may be beneficial.

Employment of top executives—including chief executives, general and operations managers, and legislators—is expected to grow about as fast as the average for all occupations through 2012. Because top managers are essential to the success of any organization, they should be more immune to automation and corporate restructuring—factors that are expected to adversely affect employment of lower level managers. Projected employment growth of top executives varies by industry, reflecting the projected change in industry employment over the 2002-12 period. For example, employment growth is expected to be faster than average in professional, scientific, and technical services and administrative and support services. However, employment is projected to decline in some manufacturing industries.

Few new governments at any level are likely to be formed, and the number of chief executives and legislators in existing governments rarely changes. However, some increase will occur at the local level as counties, cities, and towns take on professional managers or move from volunteer to paid career executives to deal with population growth, federal regulations, and long-range planning.

Elections give newcomers the chance to unseat incumbents or to fill vacated positions. The level of competition in elections varies from place to place. There tends to be less competition in small communities that offer part-time positions with low or no salaries and little or no staff, compared with large municipalities with prestigious full-time positions offering high salaries, staff, and greater exposure.

Earnings

Top executives are among the highest paid workers in the U.S. economy. However, salary levels vary substantially depending upon the level of managerial responsibility, length of service, and type, size, and location of the firm. For example, a top manager in a very large corporation can earn significantly more than a counterpart in a small firm.

Median annual earnings of general and operations managers in 2002 were $68,210. The middle 50 percent earned between $45,720 and $104,970. Because the specific responsibilities of general and operations managers vary significantly within industries, earnings also tend to vary considerably. Median annual earnings in the industries employing the largest numbers of general and operations managers in 2002 were:

Management of companies and enterprises	$94,600
Building equipment contractors	74,550
Depository credit intermediation	68,110
Local government	60,470
Grocery stores	44,980

Median annual earnings of chief executives in 2002 were $126,260. Median annual earnings in the industries employing the largest numbers of chief executives in 2002 were:

Management of companies and enterprises	$145,600
Architectural, engineering, and related services	133,880
Depository credit intermediation	123,220
Colleges, universities, and professional schools	103,120
Local government	73,990

Salaries vary substantially by type and level of responsibilities and by industry. According to a survey by Abbott, Langer & Associates, the median income of chief executive officers in the nonprofit sector was $81,000 in 2003, but some of the highest paid made $600,000.

In addition to salaries, total compensation often includes stock options, dividends, and other performance bonuses. The use of executive dining rooms and company aircraft and cars, expense allowances, and company-paid insurance premiums and physical examinations also are among benefits commonly enjoyed by top executives in private industry. A number of chief executive officers also are provided with company-paid club memberships, a limousine with chauffeur, and other amenities.

Median annual earnings of legislators were $15,220 in 2002. The middle 50 percent earned between $13,180 and $38,540. The lowest 10 percent earned less than $12,130, and the highest 10 percent earned more than $69,380.

Earnings of public administrators vary widely, depending on the size of the governmental unit and on whether the job is part time, full time and year round, or full time for only a few months a year. Salaries range from little or nothing for a small-town council member to $400,000 a year for the President of the United States.

The National Conference of State Legislatures reports that the annual salary for rank-and-file legislators in the 40 states that paid an annual salary ranged from $10,000 to more than $99,000 in 2003. In eight states, legislators received a daily salary plus an additional allowance for living expenses while legislatures were in session.

The Council of State Governments reports in its *Book of the States, 2002-2003* that gubernatorial annual salaries ranged from $50,000 in American Samoa to $179,000 in New York. In addition to a salary, most governors received benefits such as transportation and an official residence. In 2003, U.S. Senators and Representatives earned $154,700, the Senate and House Majority and Minority leaders earned $171,900, and the Vice President was paid $198,600.

Related Occupations

Top executives plan, organize, direct, control, and coordinate the operations of an organization and its major departments or programs. The members of the board of directors and lower-level managers also are involved in these activities. Many other management occupations have similar responsibilities; however, they are concentrated in specific industries or are responsible for a specific department within an organization. A few examples are administrative services managers, education administrators, financial managers, food service managers, and advertising, marketing, promotions, public relations, and sales managers.

Sources of Additional Information

For a variety of information on top executives, including educational programs and job listings, contact:

- American Management Association, 1601 Broadway, 6th Floor, New York, NY 10019. Internet: http://www.amanet.org

- Institute of Certified Professional Managers, James Madison University, MSC 5504, Harrisonburg, VA 22807. Internet: http://cob.jmu.edu/icpm/

- International Public Management Association for Human Resources, 1617 Duke St., Alexandria, VA 22314. Internet: http://www.ipma-hr.org

- National Management Association, 2210 Arbor Blvd., Dayton, OH 45439. Internet: http://www.nma1.org

Information on appointed officials in local government can be obtained from:

- Council of State Governments, P.O. Box 11910, 2760 Research Park Dr., Lexington, KY 40578-1910. Internet: http://www.statesnews.org

- National Association of Counties, 440 First St. NW, 8th Floor, Washington, DC 20001. Internet: http://www.naco.org

- National Conference of State Legislatures, 7700 East First Place, Denver, CO 80230. Internet: http://www.ncsl.org

- National League of Cities, 1301 Pennsylvania Ave. NW, Washington, DC 20004. Internet: http://www.nlc.org

For information on executive financial management careers and certification, contact:

- Financial Executives International, 200 Campus Dr., P.O. Box 674, Florham Park, NJ 07932-0674. Internet: http://www.fei.org

- Financial Management Association International, College of Business Administration, University of South Florida, 4202 East Fowler Ave., BSN 3331, Tampa, FL 33620-5500. Internet: http://www.fma.org

Truck Drivers and Driver/Sales Workers

(O*NET 53-3031.00, 53-3032.01, 53-3032.02, and 53-3033.00)

Significant Points

- Job opportunities should be favorable.

- Competition is expected for jobs offering the highest earnings or most favorable work schedules.

- A commercial driver's license is required to operate most larger trucks.

Nature of the Work

Truck drivers are a constant presence on the nation's highways and interstates, delivering everything from automobiles to canned foods. Firms of all kinds rely on trucks for pickup and delivery of goods because no other form of transportation can deliver goods door to door. Even if goods travel in part by ship, train, or airplane, trucks carry nearly all goods at some point in their journey from producer to consumer.

Before leaving the terminal or warehouse, truck drivers check the fuel level and oil in their trucks. They also inspect the trucks to make sure the brakes, windshield wipers, and lights are working and that a fire extinguisher, flares, and other safety equipment are aboard and in working order. Drivers make sure their cargo is secure and adjust their mirrors so that both sides of the truck are visible from the driver's seat. Drivers report equipment that is inoperable, missing, or loaded improperly to the dispatcher.

Once under way, drivers must be alert to prevent accidents. Drivers can see farther down the road, because large trucks sit higher than most other vehicles. This allows drivers to seek traffic lanes that allow for a steady speed, while keeping sight of varying road conditions.

Delivery time varies according to the type of merchandise and its final destination. Local drivers may provide daily service for a specific route, while other drivers make intercity and interstate deliveries that take longer and may vary from job to job. The driver's responsibilities and assignments change according to the time spent on the road, the type of payloads transported, and vehicle size.

New technologies are changing the way truck drivers work, especially long-distance truck drivers. Satellites and Global Positioning Systems (GPS) link many trucks with company headquarters. Troubleshooting information, directions, weather reports, and other important communications can be delivered to the truck, anywhere, within seconds. Drivers can easily communicate with the dispatcher to discuss delivery schedules and courses of action in the event of mechan-ical problems. The satellite linkup also allows the dispatcher to track the truck's location, fuel consumption, and engine performance. Many drivers also work with computerized inventory tracking equipment. It is important for the producer, warehouse, and customer to know the product's location at all times in order to keep costs low and the quality of service high.

Heavy truck and tractor-trailer drivers drive trucks or vans with a capacity of at least 26,000 pounds Gross Vehicle Weight (GVW). They transport goods including cars, livestock, and other materials in liquid, loose, or packaged form. Many routes are from city to city and cover long distances. Some companies use two drivers on very long runs—one drives while the other sleeps in a berth behind the cab. "Sleeper" runs may last for days, or even weeks, usually with the truck stopping only for fuel, food, loading, and unloading.

Some heavy truck and tractor-trailer drivers who have regular runs transport freight to the same city on a regular basis. Other drivers perform unscheduled runs because shippers request varying service to different cities every day.

After these truck drivers reach their destination or complete their operating shift, the U.S. Department of Transportation requires that they complete reports detailing the trip, the condition of the truck, and the circumstances of any accidents. In addition, federal regulations require employers to subject drivers to random alcohol and drug tests while they are on duty.

Long-distance heavy truck and tractor-trailer drivers spend most of their working time behind the wheel, but may load or unload their cargo after arriving at the final destination. This is especially common when drivers haul specialty cargo, because they may be the only one at the destination familiar with procedures or certified to handle the materials. Auto-transport drivers, for example, position cars on the trailers at the manufacturing plant and remove them at the dealerships. When picking up or delivering furniture, drivers of long-distance moving vans hire local workers to help them load or unload.

Light or delivery services truck drivers drive trucks or vans with a capacity under 26,000 pounds GVW. They deliver or pick up merchandise and packages within a specific area. This may include short "turnarounds" to deliver a shipment to a nearby city, pick up another loaded truck or van, and drive it back to their home base the same day. These services may require use of electronic delivery tracking systems to track the whereabouts of the merchandise or packages. Light or delivery services truck drivers usually load or unload the merchandise at the customer's place of business. They may have helpers if there are many deliveries to make during the day, or if the load requires heavy moving. Typically, before the driver arrives for work, material handlers load the trucks and arrange items to improve delivery efficiency. Customers must sign receipts for goods and pay drivers the balance due on the merchandise if there is a cash-on-delivery arrangement. At the end of the day, drivers turn in receipts, money, records of deliveries made, and any reports on mechanical problems with their trucks.

Some local truck drivers have sales and customer service responsibilities. The primary responsibility of *driver/sales workers*, or *route drivers*, is to deliver and sell their firm's products over established routes or within an established territory. They sell goods such as food products, including restaurant takeout items, or pick up and deliver items such as laundry. Their response to customer complaints and requests can make the difference between a large order and a lost customer. Route drivers may also take orders and collect payments.

The duties of driver/sales workers vary according to their industry, the policies of their particular company, and the emphasis placed on their sales responsibility. Most have wholesale routes that deliver to businesses and stores, rather than to homes. For example, wholesale bakery driver/sales workers deliver and arrange bread, cakes, rolls, and other baked goods on display racks in grocery stores. They estimate how many of each item to stock by paying close attention to what is selling. They may recommend changes in a store's order or encourage the manager to stock new bakery products. Laundries that rent linens, towels, work clothes, and other items employ driver/sales workers to visit businesses regularly to replace soiled laundry. From time to time, they solicit new orders from businesses along their route.

After completing their route, driver/sales workers order items for the next delivery based on product sales trends, weather, and customer requests.

Working Conditions

Truck driving has become less physically demanding because most trucks now have more comfortable seats, better ventilation, and improved, ergonomically-designed cabs. Although these changes make the work environment more attractive, driving for many hours at a stretch, unloading cargo, and making many deliveries can be tiring. Local truck drivers, unlike long-distance drivers, usually return home in the evening. Some self-employed long-distance truck drivers who own and operate their trucks spend most of the year away from home.

Design improvements in newer trucks reduce stress and increase the efficiency of long-distance drivers. Many of the newer trucks are virtual mini-apartments on wheels, equipped with refrigerators, televisions, and bunks.

The U.S. Department of Transportation governs work hours and other working conditions of truck drivers engaged in interstate commerce. A long-distance driver cannot work more than 60 hours in any 7-day period. Federal regulations also require that truckers rest 10 hours for every 11 hours of driving. Many drivers, particularly on long runs, work close to the maximum time permitted because they typically are compensated according to the number of miles or hours they drive. Drivers on long runs may face boredom, loneliness, and fatigue. Drivers frequently travel at night, and on holidays and weekends, to avoid traffic delays and deliver cargo on time.

Local truck drivers frequently work 50 or more hours a week. Drivers who handle food for chain grocery stores, produce markets, or bakeries typically work long hours, starting late at night or early in the morning. Although most drivers have regular routes, some have different routes each day. Many local truck drivers, particularly driver/sales workers, load and unload their own trucks. This requires considerable lifting, carrying, and walking each day.

Employment

Truck drivers and driver/sales workers held about 3.2 million jobs in 2002. Of these workers, 431,000 were driver/sales workers and 2.8 million were truck drivers. Most truck drivers find employment in large metropolitan areas along major interstate roadways where major trucking, retail, and wholesale companies have distribution outlets. Some drivers work in rural areas, providing specialized services such as delivering newspapers to customers or coal to a railroad.

The truck transportation industry employed almost one-quarter of all truck drivers and driver/sales workers in the United States. Another quarter worked for companies engaged in wholesale or retail trade. The remaining truck drivers and driver/sales workers were distributed across many industries, including construction and manufacturing.

Over 10 percent of all truck drivers and driver/sales workers were self-employed. Of these, a significant number were owner-operators who either served a variety of businesses independently or leased their services and trucks to a trucking company.

Training, Other Qualifications, and Advancement

State and federal regulations govern the qualifications and standards for truck drivers. All drivers must comply with federal regulations and any state regulations that are stricter than federal requirements. Truck drivers must have a driver's license issued by the state in which they live, and most employers require a clean driving record. Drivers of trucks designed to carry 26,000 pounds or more—including most tractor-trailers, as well as bigger straight trucks—must obtain a commercial driver's license (CDL) from the state in which they live. All truck drivers who operate trucks transporting hazardous materials must obtain a CDL, regardless of truck size. Federal regulations governing the CDL exempt certain groups, including farmers, emergency medical technicians, firefighters, some military drivers, and snow and ice removers. In many states, a regular driver's license is sufficient for driving light trucks and vans.

To qualify for a commercial driver's license, applicants must pass a written test on rules and regulations and then demonstrate that they can operate a commercial truck safely. A national database permanently records all driving violations incurred by persons who hold commercial licenses. A state will check these records and deny a commercial driver's license to a driver who already has a license suspended or revoked in another state. Licensed drivers must accompany trainees until the trainees get their own CDL. Information on how to apply for a commercial driver's license may be obtained from state motor vehicle administrations.

While many states allow those who are at least 18 years old to drive trucks within their borders, the U.S. Department of Transportation establishes minimum qualifications for truck drivers engaged in interstate commerce. Federal Motor Carrier Safety Regulations require drivers to be at least 21 years old and to pass a physical examination once every 2 years. The main physical requirements include good hearing, at least 20/40 vision with glasses or corrective lenses, and a 70-degree field of vision in each eye. Drivers cannot be color-blind. Drivers must be able to hear a forced whisper in one ear at not less than 5 feet, with a hearing aide if needed. Drivers must have normal use of arms and legs and normal blood pressure. Drivers cannot use any controlled substances, unless prescribed by a licensed physician. Persons with epilepsy or diabetes controlled by insulin are not permitted to be interstate truck drivers. Federal regulations also require employers to test their drivers for alcohol and drug use as a condition of employment, and require periodic random tests of the drivers while they are on duty. In addition, drivers must have no criminal records such as felonies involving the use of a motor vehicle; any crime involving drugs, including driving under the influence of drugs or alcohol; and any hit-and-run accident that resulted in injury or death. All drivers must be able to read and speak English well enough to read road signs, prepare reports, and communicate with law enforcement officers and the public. Also, drivers must take a written examination on the Motor Carrier Safety Regulations of the U.S. Department of Transportation.

Many trucking operations have higher standards than those described. Many firms require that drivers be at least 22 years old, be able to lift heavy objects, and have driven trucks for 3 to 5 years. Many prefer to hire high school graduates and require annual physical examinations. Companies have an economic incentive to hire less risky drivers. Good drivers drive more efficiently, using less fuel and costing less to insure.

Taking driver-training courses is a desirable method of preparing for truck driving jobs and for obtaining a commercial driver's license. High school courses in driver training and automotive mechanics also may be helpful. Many private and public vocational-technical schools offer tractor-trailer driver training programs. Students learn to maneuver large vehicles on crowded streets and in highway traffic. They also learn to inspect trucks and freight for compliance with regulations. Some programs provide only a limited amount of actual driving experience, and completion of a program does not guarantee a job. Persons interested in attending a driving school should check with local trucking companies to make sure the school's training is acceptable. Some states require prospective drivers to complete a training course in basic truck driving before being issued their CDL. The Professional Truck Driver Institute (PTDI), a non-profit organization established by the trucking industry, manufacturers, and others, certifies driver training programs at truck driver training schools that meet industry standards and Federal Highway Administration guidelines for training tractor-trailer drivers.

Drivers must get along well with people because they often deal directly with customers. Employers seek driver/sales workers who speak well and have self-confidence, initiative, tact, and a neat appearance. Employers also look for responsible, self-motivated individuals able to work with little supervision.

Training given to new drivers by employers is usually informal, and may consist of only a few hours of instruction from an experienced driver, sometimes on the new employee's own time. New drivers may also ride with and observe experienced drivers before assignment of their own runs. Drivers receive additional training to drive special types of trucks or handle hazardous materials. Some companies give 1 to 2 days of classroom instruction covering general duties, the operation and loading of a truck, company policies, and the preparation of delivery forms and company records. Driver/sales workers also receive training on the various types of products the company carries, so that they will be effective sales workers.

Although most new truck drivers are assigned immediately to regular driving jobs, some start as extra drivers, substituting for regular drivers who are ill or on vacation. They receive a regular assignment when an opening occurs.

New drivers sometimes start on panel trucks or other small straight trucks. As they gain experience and show competent driving skills, they may advance to larger and heavier trucks and finally to tractor-trailers.

Advancement of truck drivers generally is limited to driving runs that provide increased earnings or preferred schedules and working conditions. For the most part, a local truck driver may advance to driving heavy or special types of trucks or transfer to long-distance truck driving. Working for companies that also employ long-distance drivers is the best way to advance to these positions. A few truck drivers may advance to dispatcher, manager, or traffic work—for example, planning delivery schedules.

Some long-distance truck drivers purchase a truck and go into business for themselves. Although many of these owner-operators are successful, some fail to cover expenses and eventually go out of business. Owner-operators should have good business sense as well as truck driving experience. Courses in accounting, business, and business mathematics are helpful, and knowledge of truck mechanics can enable owner-operators to perform their own routine maintenance and minor repairs.

Job Outlook

Job opportunities should be favorable for truck drivers. In addition to growth in demand for truck drivers, numerous job openings will occur as experienced drivers leave this large occupation to transfer to other fields of work, retire, or leave the labor force for other reasons. Jobs vary greatly in terms of earnings, weekly work hours, number of nights spent on the road, and quality of equipment operated. Because this occupation does not require education beyond high school, competition is expected for jobs with the most attractive earnings and working conditions.

Overall employment of truck drivers and driver/sales workers is expected to grow about as fast as the average for all occupations through the year 2012, due to growth in the economy and in the amount of freight carried by truck. The increased use of rail, air, and ship transportation requires truck drivers to pick up and deliver shipments. Demand for long-distance drivers will remain strong because these drivers transport perishable and time-sensitive goods more efficiently than do alternative modes of transportation, such as railroads. Job opportunities for truck drivers with less-than-truckload carriers will be more competitive than those with truckload carriers because of the more desirable working conditions for less-than-truckload carriers.

Faster than average growth of light and heavy truck driver employment will outweigh relatively slow growth in driver/sales worker jobs. The number of truck drivers with sales responsibilities is expected to increase more slowly than the average for all other occupations as companies increasingly shift sales, ordering, and customer service tasks to sales and office staffs, and use regular truck drivers to make deliveries to customers.

Job opportunities may vary from year to year, because the strength of the economy dictates the amount of freight moved by trucks. Companies tend to hire more drivers when the economy is strong and deliveries are in high demand. Consequently, when the economy slows, employers hire fewer drivers or even lay off drivers. Independent owner-operators are particularly vulnerable to slowdowns. Industries least likely to be affected by economic fluctuation, such as grocery stores, tend to be the most stable places for employment.

Earnings

Median hourly earnings of heavy truck and tractor-trailer drivers were $15.97 in 2002. The middle 50 percent earned between $12.51 and $20.01 an hour. The lowest 10 percent earned less than $10.01, and the highest 10 percent earned more than $23.75 an hour. Median hourly earnings in the industries employing the largest numbers of heavy truck and tractor-trailer drivers in 2002 were as follows:

General freight trucking $17.56
Grocery and related product wholesalers 16.90
Specialized freight trucking 15.79
Other specialty trade contractors 14.25
Cement and concrete product manufacturing 14.14

Median hourly earnings of light or delivery services truck drivers were $11.48 in 2002. The middle 50 percent earned between $8.75 and $15.57 an hour. The lowest 10 percent earned less than $7.03, and the highest 10 percent earned more than $20.68 an hour. Median hourly earnings in the industries employing the largest numbers of light or delivery services truck drivers in 2002 were as follows:

Couriers $17.48
General freight trucking 14.92
Grocery and related product wholesalers 12.26
Building material and supplies dealers 10.83
Automotive parts, accessories, and tire stores...........7.82

Median hourly earnings of driver/sales workers, including commission, were $9.92 in 2002. The middle 50 percent earned between $6.98 and $14.70 an hour. The lowest 10 percent earned less than $6.07, and the highest 10 percent earned more than $19.60 an hour. Median hourly earnings in the industries employing the largest numbers of driver/sales workers in 2002 were as follows:

Specialty food stores $14.98
Drycleaning and laundry services 14.74
Grocery and related product wholesalers 12.66
Limited-service eating places 6.78
Full-service restaurants...6.47

As a general rule, local truck drivers receive an hourly wage and extra pay for working overtime, usually after 40 hours. Employers pay long-distance drivers primarily by the mile. Their rate per mile can vary greatly from employer to employer and may even depend on the type of cargo. Typically, earnings increase with mileage driven, seniority, and the size and type of truck driven. Most driver/sales workers receive a commission based on their sales in addition to an hourly wage.

Most self-employed truck drivers are primarily engaged in long-distance hauling. Many truck drivers are members of the International Brotherhood of Teamsters. Some truck drivers employed by companies outside the trucking industry are members of unions representing the plant workers of the companies for which they work.

Related Occupations

Other driving occupations include ambulance drivers and attendants, except emergency medical technicians; bus drivers; and taxi drivers and chauffeurs.

Sources of Additional Information

Information on truck driver employment opportunities is available from local trucking companies and local offices of the state employment service.

Information on career opportunities in truck driving may be obtained from:

● American Trucking Associations, Inc., 2200 Mill Rd., Alexandria, VA 22314. Internet: http://www.trucking.org

A list of certified tractor-trailer driver training courses may be obtained from:

● Professional Truck Driver Institute, 2200 Mill Rd., Alexandria, VA 22314. Internet: http://www.ptdi.org

Veterinary Technologists and Technicians

(O*NET 29-2056.00)

Significant Points

● Animal lovers get satisfaction in this occupation, but aspects of the work can sometimes be unpleasant and physically and emotionally demanding.

● Entrants generally complete a 2-year or 4-year veterinary technology program, and must pass a state examination.

● Employment is expected to grow much faster than average.

Nature of the Work

Owners of pets and other animals today expect state-of-the-art veterinary care. To provide this service, veterinarians use the skills of veterinary technologists and technicians, who perform many of the same duties for a veterinarian that a nurse would for a physician, including routine laboratory and clinical procedures. Although specific job duties vary by employer, there often is little difference between the tasks done by technicians and by technologists, despite some differences in formal education and training. As a result, most workers in this occupation are called technicians.

Veterinary technologists and technicians typically conduct clinical work in a private practice under the supervision of a veterinarian—often performing various medical tests along with treating and diagnosing medical conditions and diseases in animals. For example, they may perform laboratory tests such as urinalysis and blood counts, assist with dental prophylaxis, prepare tissue samples, take blood samples, or assist veterinarians in a variety of tests and analyses in which they often utilize various items of medical equipment, such as test tubes and diagnostic equipment. While most of these duties are performed in a laboratory setting, many tasks are not. For example, some veterinary technicians obtain and record patient case histories, expose and develop x-rays, and provide specialized nursing care. Addi-

tionally, experienced veterinary technicians may discuss a pet's condition with its owners and train new clinic personnel. Veterinary technologists and technicians assisting small-animal practitioners usually care for companion animals, such as cats and dogs, but can perform a variety of duties with mice, rats, sheep, pigs, cattle, monkeys, birds, fish, and frogs. Very few veterinary technologists work in mixed animal practices where they care for both small companion animals and larger, nondomestic animals.

In addition to working in private clinics and animal hospitals, veterinary technologists and technicians also may work in research facilities. There, they may administer medications orally or topically, prepare samples for laboratory examinations, and record information on genealogy, diet, weight, medications, food intake, and clinical signs of pain and distress. Some may be required to sterilize laboratory and surgical equipment and provide routine postoperative care. At research facilities, veterinary technologists typically work under the guidance of veterinarians, physicians, and other laboratory technicians. Some veterinary technologists vaccinate newly admitted animals and occasionally are required to euthanize seriously ill, severely injured, or unwanted animals.

While the goal of most veterinary technologists and technicians goal is to promote animal health, some contribute to human health as well. Veterinary technologists occasionally assist veterinarians as they work with other scientists in medical-related fields such as gene therapy and cloning. Some find opportunities in biomedical research, wildlife medicine, the military, livestock management, or pharmaceutical sales.

Working Conditions

People who love animals get satisfaction from working with and helping them. However, some of the work may be unpleasant, physically and emotionally demanding, and sometimes dangerous. Veterinary technicians sometimes must clean cages and lift, hold, or restrain animals, risking exposure to bites or scratches. These workers must take precautions when treating animals with germicides or insecticides. The work setting can be noisy.

Veterinary technologists and technicians who witness abused animals or who euthanize unwanted, aged, or hopelessly injured animals may experience emotional stress. Those working for humane societies and animal shelters often deal with the public, some of whom might react with hostility to any implication that the owners are neglecting or abusing their pets. Such workers must maintain a calm and professional demeanor while they enforce the laws regarding animal care. In some animal hospitals, research facilities, and animal shelters, a veterinary technician is on duty 24 hours a day, which means some may work night shifts. Most full-time veterinary technologists and technicians work about 40 hours a week, while some work 50 or more hours a week.

Employment

Veterinary technologists and technicians held about 53,000 jobs in 2002. Most worked in veterinary services. The remainder worked in boarding kennels, animal shelters, stables, grooming shops, zoos, and local, state, and federal agencies.

Training, Other Qualifications, and Advancement

There are primarily two levels of education and training for entry to this occupation—a 2-year program for veterinary technicians and a 4-year program for veterinary technologists. Most entry-level veterinary technicians have a 2-year degree, usually an associate degree, from an accredited community college program in veterinary technology, in which courses are taught in clinical and laboratory settings using live animals. A few colleges offer veterinary technology programs that are longer and that may culminate in a 4-year bachelor's degree in veterinary technology. These 4-year colleges, in addition to some vocational schools, also offer 2-year programs in laboratory animal science.

In 2003, more than 80 veterinary technology programs in 41 states were accredited by the American Veterinary Medical Association (AVMA). Graduation from an AVMA-accredited veterinary technology program allows students to take the credentialing exam in any state in the country. Each state regulates veterinary technicians and technologists differently; however, all states require them to pass a credentialing exam following coursework. Passing the state exam assures the public that the technician or technologist has sufficient knowledge to work in a veterinary clinic or hospital. Candidates are tested for competency through an examination that includes oral, written, and practical portions. This process is regulated by the State Board of Veterinary Examiners, or the appropriate state agency. Depending on the state, candidates may become registered, licensed, or certified. Most states, however, use the National Veterinary Technician (NVT) exam. Prospects usually can have their passing scores transferred from one state to another, so long as both states utilize the same exam.

Employers recommend American Association for Laboratory Animal Science (AALAS) certification for those seeking employment in a research facility. AALAS offers certification for three levels of technician competence, with a focus on three principle areas—animal husbandry and welfare, facility administration and management, and animal health. Those who wish to become certified must satisfy a combination of education and experience requirements prior to taking an exam. Work experience must be directly related to the maintenance, health, and well-being of laboratory animals and must be gained in a laboratory animal facility as defined by AALAS. Candidates who meet the necessary criteria can begin pursuing the desired certification, based on their qualifications. The lowest level of certification is Animal Laboratory Assistant Technician (ALAT); the second level is Laboratory Animal Technician (LAT); and the highest level of certification is Laboratory Animal Technologist (LATG). The examination consists of multiple-choice questions and is longer and more difficult for higher levels of certification.

Persons interested in careers as veterinary technologists and technicians should take as many high school science, biology, and math courses as possible. Science courses taken beyond high school, in an associate or bachelor's degree program, should emphasize practical skills in a clinical or laboratory setting. Because veterinary technologists and technicians often deal with pet owners, communication skills are very important. Additionally, technologists and technicians should be able to work well with others, because teamwork with veterinarians is common. Organizational ability and the ability to pay attention to detail also are important.

Technologists and technicians usually begin work as trainees in routine positions under the direct supervision of a veterinarian. Entry-level workers whose training or educational background encompasses extensive hands-on experience with a variety of laboratory equipment, including diagnostic and medical equipment, usually require a shorter period of on-the-job training. As they gain experience, technologists and technicians take on more responsibility and carry out more assignments under only general veterinary supervision, and some eventually may become supervisors.

Job Outlook

Employment of veterinary technologists and technicians is expected to grow much faster than the average for all occupations through the year 2012. Job openings also will stem from the need to replace veterinary technologists and technicians who leave the occupation over the 2002-12 period. Keen competition is expected for veterinary technologist and technician jobs in zoos, due to expected slow growth in zoo capacity, low turnover among workers, the limited number of positions, and the fact that the occupation attracts many candidates.

Pet owners are becoming more affluent and more willing to pay for advanced care because many of them consider their pet to be part of the family, spurring employment growth for veterinary technologists and technicians. The number of dogs as pets, which also drives employment growth, is expected to increase more slowly during the projection period than in the previous decade. However, the rapidly growing number of cats as pets is expected to boost the demand for feline medicine, offsetting any reduced demand for veterinary care for dogs. The availability of advanced veterinary services, such as preventive dental care and surgical procedures, may provide opportunities for workers specializing in those areas. Biomedical facilities, diagnostic laboratories, wildlife facilities, humane societies, animal control facilities, drug or food manufacturing companies, and food safety inspection facilities will provide more jobs for veterinary technologists and technicians. Furthermore, demand for these workers will stem from the desire to replace veterinary assistants with more highly skilled technicians and technologists in animal clinics and hospitals, shelters, kennels, and humane societies.

Employment of veterinary technicians and technologists is relatively stable during periods of economic recession. Lay-offs are less likely to occur among veterinary technologists and technicians than in some other occupations because animals will continue to require medical care.

Earnings

Median annual earnings of veterinary technologists and technicians were $22,950 in 2002. The middle 50 percent earned between $19,210 and $27,890. The bottom 10 percent earned less than $16,170, and the top 10 percent earned more than $33,750.

Related Occupations

Others who work extensively with animals include animal care and service workers. Like veterinary technologists and technicians, they must have patience and feel comfortable with animals. However, the level of training required for these occupations is less than that needed by veterinary technologists and technicians. Veterinarians also work extensively with animals. They prevent, diagnose, and treat diseases, disorders, and injuries in animals.

Sources of Additional Information

For information on certification as a laboratory animal technician or technologist, contact:

- American Association for Laboratory Animal Science, 9190 Crestwyn Hills Dr., Memphis, TN 38125. Internet: http://www.aalas.org

For information on careers in veterinary medicine and a listing of AVMA-accredited veterinary technology programs, contact:

- American Veterinary Medical Association, 1931 N. Meacham Rd., Suite 100, Schaumburg, IL 60173-4360. Internet: http://www.avma.org

For information on veterinary technology programs, contact:

- Association of American Veterinary Medical Colleges, 1101 Vermont Ave. NW, Suite 710, Washington DC 20005. Internet: http://www.aavmc.org

For information on becoming a veterinary technician, contact:

- National Association of Veterinary Technicians in America, P.O. Box 224, Battle Ground, IN 47920. Internet: http://www.navta.net

Welding, Soldering, and Brazing Workers

(O*NET 51-4121.01, 51-4121.02, 51-4121.03, 51-4121.04, 51-4121.05, 51-4122.01, 51-4122.02, and 51-4122.03)

Significant Points

- Job prospects should be excellent.

- Training ranges from a few weeks of school or on-the-job training for low-skilled positions to several years of combined school and on-the-job training for highly skilled jobs.

Nature of the Work

Welding is the most common way of permanently joining metal parts. In this process, heat is applied to metal pieces, melting and fusing them to form a permanent bond. Because of its strength, welding is used in shipbuilding, automobile manufacturing and repair, aerospace applications, and thousands of other manufacturing activities. Welding also is used to join beams when constructing buildings, bridges, and other structures, and to join pipes in pipelines, power plants, and refineries.

Welders use many types of welding equipment set up in a variety of positions, such as flat, vertical, horizontal, and overhead. They may perform manual welding, in which the work is entirely controlled by the welder, or semiautomatic welding, in which the welder uses machinery, such as a wire feeder, to perform welding tasks.

Arc welding is the most common type of welding. Standard arc welding involves two large metal alligator clips that carry a strong electrical current. One clip is attached to any part of the workpiece being welded. The second clip is connected to a thin welding rod. When the rod touches the workpiece, a powerful electrical circuit is created. The massive heat created by the electrical current causes both the workpiece and the steel core of the rod to melt together, cooling quickly to form a solid bond. During welding, the flux that surrounds the rod's core vaporizes, forming an inert gas that serves to protect the weld from atmospheric elements that might weaken it. Welding speed is important. Variations in speed can change the amount of flux applied, weakening the weld, or weakening the surrounding metal by increasing heat exposure.

Two common but advanced types of welding are Gas Tungsten Arc (TIG) and Gas Metal Arc (MIG) welding. TIG welding often is used with stainless steel or aluminum. While TIG uses welding rods, MIG uses a spool of continuously fed wire, which allows the welder to join longer stretches of metal without stopping to replace the rod. In TIG welding, the welder holds the welding rod in one hand and an electric torch in the other hand. The torch is used to simultaneously melt the rod and the workpiece. In MIG welding, the welder holds the wire feeder, which functions like the alligator clip in arc welding. Instead of using gas flux surrounding the rod, TIG and MIG protect the initial weld from the environment by blowing inert gas onto the weld.

Like arc welding, soldering and brazing use molten metal to join two pieces of metal. However, the metal added during the process has a melting point lower than that of the workpiece, so only the added metal is melted, not the workpiece.

Soldering uses metals with a melting point below 800 degrees Fahrenheit; brazing uses metals with a higher melting point. Because soldering and brazing do not melt the workpiece, these processes normally do not create the distortions or weaknesses in the workpiece that can occur with welding. Soldering commonly is used to join electrical, electronic, and other small metal parts. Brazing produces a stronger joint than does soldering, and often is used to join metals other than steel, such as brass. Brazing can also be used to apply coatings to parts to reduce wear and protect against corrosion.

Skilled welding, soldering, and brazing workers generally plan work from drawings or specifications or use their knowledge of fluxes and base metals to analyze the parts to be joined. These workers then select and set up welding equipment, execute the planned welds, and examine welds to ensure that they meet standards or specifications. Highly skilled welders often are trained to work with a wide variety of materials in addition to steel, such as titanium, aluminum, or plastics. Some welders have more limited duties, however. They perform routine jobs that already have been planned and laid out and do not require extensive knowledge of welding techniques.

Automated welding is used in an increasing number of production processes. In these instances, a machine or robot performs the welding tasks while monitored by a welding machine operator. Welding, soldering, and brazing machine setters, operators, and tenders follow specified layouts, work orders, or blueprints. Operators must load parts correctly and constantly monitor the machine to ensure that it produces the desired bond.

The work of arc, plasma, and oxy-gas cutters is closely related to that of welders. However, instead of joining metals, cutters use the heat from an electric arc, a stream of ionized gas (plasma), or burning gases to cut and trim metal objects to specific dimensions. Cutters also dismantle large objects, such as ships, railroad cars, automobiles, buildings, or aircraft. Some operate and monitor cutting machines similar to those used by welding machine operators. Plasma cutting has been increasing in popularity because, unlike other methods, it can cut a wide variety of metals, including stainless steel, aluminum, and titanium.

Working Conditions

Welding, soldering, and brazing workers often are exposed to a number of hazards, including the intense light created by the arc, poisonous fumes, and very hot materials. They wear safety shoes, goggles, hoods with protective lenses, and other devices designed to prevent burns and eye injuries and to protect them from falling objects. They normally work in well-ventilated areas to limit their exposure to fumes. Automated welding, soldering, and brazing machine operators are not exposed to as many dangers, however, and a face shield or goggles usually provide adequate protection for these workers.

Welders and cutters may work outdoors, often in inclement weather, or indoors, sometimes in a confined area designed to contain sparks and glare. Outdoors, they may work on a scaffold or platform high off the ground. In addition, they may be required to lift heavy objects and work in a variety of awkward positions, while bending, stooping, or standing to perform work overhead.

Although about 55 percent of welders, solderers, and brazers work a 40-hour week, overtime is common, and some welders work up to 70 hours per week. Welders also may work in shifts as long as 12 hours. Some welders, solderers, brazers, and machine operators work in factories that operate around the clock, necessitating shift work.

Employment

Welding, soldering, and brazing workers held about 452,000 jobs in 2002. Of these jobs, about 2 of every 3 were found in manufacturing. Jobs were concentrated in transportation equipment manufacturing (motor vehicle body and parts and ship and boat building), machinery manufacturing (agriculture, construction, and mining machinery), and architectural and structural metals manufacturing. Most jobs for welding, soldering, and brazing machine setters, operators, and tenders were found in the same manufacturing industries as skilled welding, soldering, and brazing workers.

Training, Other Qualifications, and Advancement

Training for welding, soldering, and brazing workers can range from a few weeks of school or on-the-job training for low-skilled positions to several years of combined school and on-the-job training for highly skilled jobs. Formal training is available in high schools, vocational schools, and postsecondary institutions, such as vocational-technical institutes, community colleges, and private welding schools. The Armed Forces operate welding schools as well. Some employers provide training. Courses in blueprint reading, shop mathematics, mechanical drawing, physics, chemistry, and metallurgy are helpful. Knowledge of computers is gaining importance, especially for welding, soldering, and brazing machine operators, who are becoming responsible for the programming of computer-controlled machines, including robots.

Some welders become certified, a process whereby the employer sends a worker to an institution, such as an independent testing lab or technical school, to weld a test specimen according to specific codes and standards required by the employer. Testing procedures are based on the standards and codes set by one of several industry associations with which the employer may be affiliated. If the welding inspector at the examining institution determines that the worker has performed according to the employer's guidelines, the inspector will then certify the welder being tested as able to work with a particular welding procedure.

Welding, soldering, and brazing workers need good eyesight, hand-eye coordination, and manual dexterity. They should be able to concentrate on detailed work for long periods and be able to bend, stoop, and work in awkward positions. In addition, welders increasingly need to be willing to receive training and perform tasks in other production jobs.

Welders can advance to more skilled welding jobs with additional training and experience. For example, they may become welding technicians, supervisors, inspectors, or instructors. Some experienced welders open their own repair shops.

Job Outlook

Job prospects should be excellent, as many potential entrants who could be welders may prefer to attend college or may prefer work that has more comfortable working conditions. Employment of welding, soldering, and brazing workers is expected to grow about as fast as the average for all occupations over the 2002-12 period. In addition, many openings will arise as workers retire or leave the occupation for other reasons.

The major factor affecting employment of welders is the health of the industries in which they work. Because almost every manufacturing industry uses welding at some stage of manufacturing or in the repair and maintenance of equipment, a strong economy will keep demand for welders high. A downturn affecting industries such as auto manufacturing, construction, or petroleum, however, would have a negative impact on the employment of welders in those areas, and could cause some layoffs. Levels of government funding for shipbuilding as well as for infrastructure repairs and improvements are expected to be another important determinant of the future number of welding jobs.

Regardless of the state of the economy, the pressures to improve productivity and hold down labor costs are leading many companies to invest more in automation, especially computer-controlled and robotically-controlled welding machinery. This will reduce the demand for some low-skilled welders, solderers, and brazers because these simple, repetitive jobs are being automated. The growing use of automation, however, should increase demand for welding, soldering, and brazing machine setters, operators, and tenders. Welders working on construction projects or in equipment repair will not be affected by technology change to the same extent, because their jobs are not as easily automated.

Technology is helping to improve welding, creating more uses for welding in the workplace and expanding employment opportunities. For example, new ways are being developed to bond dissimilar materials and nonmetallic materials, such as plastics, composites, and new alloys. Also, laser beam and electron beam welding, new fluxes, and other new technologies and techniques are improving the results of welding, making it useful in a wider assortment of applications. Improvements in technology have also boosted welding productivity, making welding more competitive with other methods of joining materials.

Earnings

Median hourly earnings of welders, cutters, solderers, and brazers were $14.02 in 2002. The middle 50 percent earned between $11.41 and $17.34. The lowest 10 percent had earnings of less than $9.41, while the top 10 percent earned over $21.79. The range of earnings of welders reflects the wide range of skill levels. Median hourly earnings in the industries employing the largest numbers of welders, cutters, solderers, and brazers in 2002 were:

Motor vehicle parts manufacturing.........................$16.02

Agriculture, construction, and mining machinery manufacturing 13.74

Architectural and structural metals manufacturing 13.34

Commercial and industrial machinery and equipment (except automotive and electronic) repair and maintenance...13.06

Motor vehicle body and trailer manufacturing........12.83

Median hourly earnings of welding, soldering, and brazing machine setters, operators, and tenders were $13.90 in 2002. The middle 50 percent earned between $11.22 and $17.77. The lowest 10 percent had earnings of less than $9.36, while the top 10 percent earned over $24.60. Median hourly earnings in motor vehicle parts manufacturing, the industry employing the largest numbers of welding machine operators in 2002 were $18.29.

Many welders belong to unions. Among these are the International Association of Machinists and Aerospace Workers; the International Brotherhood of Boilermakers, Iron Ship Builders, Blacksmiths, Forgers and Helpers; the International Union, United Automobile, Aerospace and Agricultural Implement Workers of America; the United Association of Journeymen and Apprentices of the Plumbing, Pipefitting, Sprinkler Fitting Industry of the United States and Canada; and the United Electrical, Radio, and Machine Workers of America.

Related Occupations

Welding, soldering, and brazing workers are skilled metal workers. Other metal workers include Machinists; machine setters, operators, and tenders—metal and plastic; computer-control programmers and operators; tool and die makers; sheet metal workers; and Boilermakers. Assemblers and fabricators of electrical and electronic equipment often assemble parts using soldering.

Sources of Additional Information

For information on training opportunities and jobs for welding, soldering, and brazing workers, contact local employers, the local office of the state employment service, or schools providing welding, soldering, or brazing training.

Information on careers and educational opportunities in welding is available from:

- American Welding Society, 550 N.W. Lejeune Rd., Miami, FL 33126-5699. Internet: http://www.aws.org

Writers and Editors

(O*NET 27-3041.00, 27-3042.00, 27-3043.01, 27-3043.02, 27-3043.03, and 27-3043.04)

Significant Points

- Most jobs in this occupation require a college degree in communications, journalism, or English, although a degree in a technical subject may be useful for technical-writing positions.

- The outlook for most writing and editing jobs is expected to be competitive, because many people with writing or journalism training are attracted to the occupation.

- Online publications and services are growing in number and sophistication, spurring the demand for writers and editors, especially those with Web experience.

Nature of the Work

Communicating through the written word, writers and editors generally fall into one of three categories. *Writers and authors* develop original fiction and nonfiction for books, magazines, trade journals, online publications, company newsletters, radio and television broadcasts, motion pictures, and advertisements. *Editors* examine proposals and select material for publication or broadcast. They review and revise a writer's work for publication or dissemination. *Technical writers* develop technical materials, such as equipment manuals, appendices, or operating and maintenance instructions. They also may assist in layout work.

Most writers and editors have at least a basic familiarity with technology, regularly using personal computers, desktop or electronic publishing systems, scanners, and other electronic communications equipment. Many writers prepare material directly for the Internet. For example, they may write for electronic newspapers or magazines, create short fiction or poetry, or produce technical documentation that is available only online. Also, they may write text for Web sites. These writers should be knowledgeable about graphic design, page layout, and desktop publishing software. In addition, they should be familiar with interactive technologies of the Web so that they can blend text, graphics, and sound together.

Writers—especially of nonfiction—are expected to establish their credibility with editors and readers through strong research and the use of appropriate sources and citations. Sustaining high ethical standards and meeting publication deadlines are essential.

Creative writers, poets, and lyricists, including novelists, playwrights, and screenwriters, create original works—such as prose, poems, plays, and song lyrics—for publication or performance. Some works may be commissioned (at the request of a sponsor); others may be written for hire (on the basis of the completion of a draft or an outline).

Nonfiction writers either propose a topic or are assigned one, often by an editor or publisher. They gather information about the topic through personal observation, library and Internet research, and interviews. Writers then select the material they want to use, organize it, and use the written word to express ideas and convey information. Writers also revise or rewrite sections, searching for the best organization or the right phrasing. *Copy writers* prepare advertising copy for use by publication or broadcast media or to promote the sale of goods and services. *Newsletter writers* produce information for distribution to association memberships, corporate employees, organizational clients, or the public.

Freelance writers sell their work to publishers, publication enterprises, manufacturing firms, public-relations departments, or advertising agencies. Sometimes, they contract with publishers to write a book or an article. Others may be hired to complete specific assignments, such as writing about a new product or technique.

Editors review, rewrite, and edit the work of writers. They may also do original writing. An editor's responsibilities vary with the employer and type and level of editorial position held. Editorial duties may include planning the content of books, technical journals, trade magazines, and other general-interest publications. Editors also decide what material will appeal to readers, review and edit drafts of books and articles, offer comments to improve the work, and suggest possible titles. In addition, they may oversee the production of the publications. In the book-publishing industry, an editor's primary responsibility is to review proposals for books and decide whether to buy the publication rights from the author.

Major newspapers and newsmagazines usually employ several types of editors. The *executive editor* oversees *assistant editors* who have responsibility for particular subjects, such as local news, international news, feature stories, or sports. Executive editors generally have the final say about what stories are published and how they are covered. The *managing editor* usually is responsible for the daily operation of the news department. *Assignment editors* determine which reporters will cover a given story. *Copy editors* mostly review and edit a reporter's copy for accuracy, content, grammar, and style.

In smaller organizations, such as small daily or weekly newspapers or membership or publications departments of nonprofit or similar organizations, a single editor may do everything or share responsibility with only a few other people. Executive and managing editors typically hire writers, reporters, and other employees. They also plan budgets and negotiate contracts with freelance writers, sometimes called "stringers" in the news industry. In broadcasting companies, *program directors* have similar responsibilities.

Editors and program directors often have assistants, many of whom hold entry-level jobs. These assistants, such as copy editors and *production assistants*, review copy for errors in grammar, punctuation, and spelling and check the copy for readability, style, and agreement with editorial policy. They suggest revisions, such as changing words and rearranging sentences, to improve clarity or accuracy. They also carry out research for writers and verify facts, dates, and statistics. Production assistants arrange page layouts of articles, photographs, and advertising; compose headlines; and prepare copy for printing. *Publication assistants* who work for publishing houses may read and evaluate manuscripts submitted by freelance writers, proofread printers' galleys, or answer letters about published material. Production assistants on small newspapers or in radio stations compile articles available from wire services or the Internet, answer phones, and make photocopies.

Technical writers put technical information into easily understandable language. They prepare operating and maintenance manuals, catalogs, parts lists, assembly instructions, sales promotion materials, and project proposals. Many technical writers work with engineers on technical subject matters to prepare written interpretations of engineering and design specifications and other information for a general readership. They plan and edit technical materials and oversee the preparation of illustrations, photographs, diagrams, and charts.

Science and medical writers prepare a range of formal documents presenting detailed information on the physical or medical sciences. They convey research findings for scientific or medical professions and organize information for advertising or public-relations needs. Many writers work with researchers on technical subjects to prepare written interpretations of data and other information for a general readership.

Working Conditions

Some writers and editors work in comfortable, private offices; others work in noisy rooms filled with the sound of keyboards and computer printers, as well as the voices of other writers tracking down information over the telephone. The search for information sometimes requires that the writer travel to diverse workplaces, such as factories, offices, or laboratories, but many find their material through telephone interviews, the library, and the Internet.

For some writers, the typical workweek runs 35 to 40 hours. However, writers occasionally work overtime to meet publication deadlines. Those who prepare morning or weekend publications and broadcasts work some nights and weekends. Freelance writers generally work more flexible hours, but their schedules must conform to the needs of the client. Deadlines and erratic work hours, often part of the daily routine in these jobs, may cause stress, fatigue, or burnout.

Changes in technology and electronic communications also affect a writer's work environment. For example, laptops allow writers to work from home or on the road. Writers and editors who use computers for extended periods may experience back pain, eyestrain, or fatigue.

Employment

Writers and editors held about 319,000 jobs in 2002. More than one-third were self-employed. Writers and authors held about 139,000 jobs; editors, about 130,000 jobs; and technical writers, about 50,000 jobs. More than one-half of jobs for writers and editors were salaried positions in the information sector, which includes newspaper, periodical, book, and directory publishers; radio and television broadcasting; software publishers; motion picture and sound recording industries; Internet service providers, web search portals, and data processing services; and Internet publishing and broadcasting. Substantial numbers also worked in advertising and related services, computer systems design and related services, and public and private educational services. Other salaried writers and editors worked in computer and electronic product manufacturing, government agencies, religious organizations, and business, professional, labor, political, and similar organizations.

Jobs with major book publishers, magazines, broadcasting companies, advertising agencies, and public-relations firms are concentrated in New York, Chicago, Los Angeles, Boston, Philadelphia, and San Francisco. Jobs with newspapers, business and professional journals, and technical and trade magazines are more widely dispersed throughout the country.

Thousands of other individuals work as freelance writers, earning some income from their articles, books, and, less commonly, television and movie scripts. Most support themselves with income derived from other sources.

Training, Other Qualifications, and Advancement

A college degree generally is required for a position as a writer or editor. Although some employers look for a broad liberal arts background, most prefer to hire people with degrees in communications, journalism, or English. For those who specialize in a particular area, such as fashion, business, or legal issues, additional background in the chosen field is expected. Knowledge of a second language is helpful for some positions.

Increasingly, technical writing requires a degree in, or some knowledge about, a specialized field—engineering, business, or one of the sciences, for example. In many cases, people with good writing skills can learn specialized knowledge on the job. Some transfer from jobs as technicians, scientists, or engineers. Others begin as research assistants or as trainees in a technical information department, develop technical communication skills, and then assume writing duties.

Writers and editors must be able to express ideas clearly and logically and should love to write. Creativity, curiosity, a broad range of knowledge, self-motivation, and perseverance also are valuable. Writers and editors must demonstrate good judgment and a strong sense of ethics in deciding what material to publish. Editors also need tact and the ability to guide and encourage others in their work.

For some jobs, the ability to concentrate amid confusion and to work under pressure is essential. Familiarity with electronic publishing, graphics, and video production equipment increasingly is needed. Online newspapers and magazines require knowledge of computer software used to combine online text with graphics, audio, video, and animation.

High school and college newspapers, literary magazines, community newspapers, and radio and television stations all provide valuable, but sometimes unpaid, practical writing experience. Many magazines, newspapers, and broadcast stations have internships for students. Interns write short pieces, conduct research and interviews, and learn about the publishing or broadcasting business.

In small firms, beginning writers and editors hired as assistants may actually begin writing or editing material right away. Opportunities for advancement can be limited, however. Many writers look for work on a short-term, project-by-project basis. Many small or not-for-profit organizations either do not have enough regular work or cannot afford to employ writers on a full-time basis. However, they routinely contract out work to freelance writers as needed.

In larger businesses, jobs usually are more formally structured. Beginners generally do research, fact checking, or copy editing. Advancement to full-scale writing or editing assignments may occur more slowly for newer writers and editors in larger organizations than for employees of smaller companies. Advancement often is more predictable, though, coming with the assignment of more important articles.

Job Outlook

Employment of writers and editors is expected to grow about as fast as the average for all occupations through the year 2012. The outlook for most writing and editing jobs is expected to be competitive, because many people with writing or journalism training are attracted to the occupation.

Employment of salaried writers and editors for newspapers, periodicals, book publishers, and nonprofit organizations is expected to increase as demand grows for these publications. Magazines and other periodicals increasingly are developing market niches, appealing to readers with special interests. Businesses and organizations are developing newsletters and Web sites, and more companies are experimenting with publishing materials directly for the Internet. Online publications and services are growing in number and sophistication, spurring the demand for writers and editors, especially those with Web experience. Advertising and public-relations agencies, which also are growing, should be another source of new jobs.

Opportunities should be best for technical writers and those with training in a specialized field. Demand for technical writers and writers with expertise in specialty areas, such as law, medicine, or economics, is expected to increase because of the continuing expansion of scientific and technical information and the need to communicate it to others. Developments and discoveries in the law, science, and technology generate demand for people to interpret technical information for a more general audience. Rapid growth and change in the high-technology and electronics industries result in a greater need for people to write users' guides, instruction manuals, and training materials. This work requires people who are not only technically skilled as writers, but also familiar with the subject area.

In addition to job openings created by employment growth, some openings will arise as experienced workers retire, transfer to other occupations, or leave the labor force. Replacement needs are relatively high in this occupation; many freelancers leave because they cannot earn enough money.

Earnings

Median annual earnings for salaried writers and authors were $42,790 in 2002. The middle 50 percent earned between $29,150 and $58,930. The lowest 10 percent earned less than $21,320, and the highest 10 percent earned more than $85,140. Median annual earnings were $54,520 in advertising and related services and $33,550 in newspaper, periodical, book, and directory publishers.

Median annual earnings for salaried editors were $41,170 in 2002. The middle 50 percent earned between $30,770 and $56,360. The lowest 10 percent earned less than $24,010, and the highest 10 percent earned more than $76,620. Median annual earnings in newspaper, periodical, book, and directory publishers were $40,280.

Median annual earnings for salaried technical writers were $50,580 in 2002. The middle 50 percent earned between $39,100 and $64,750. The lowest 10 percent earned less than $30,270, and the highest 10 percent earned more than $80,900. Median annual earnings in computer systems design and related services were $51,730.

According to the Society for Technical Communication, the median annual salary for entry level technical writers was $41,000 in 2002. The median annual salary for mid-level non-supervisory technical writers was $49,900 and for senior-level non-supervisory technical writers, $66,000.

Related Occupations

Writers and editors communicate ideas and information. Other communications occupations include announcers; interpreters and translators; news analysts, reporters, and correspondents; and public relations specialists.

Sources of Additional Information

For information on careers in technical writing, contact:

● Society for Technical Communication, Inc., 901 N. Stuart St., Suite 904, Arlington, VA 22203. Internet: http://www.stc.org

THE QUICK JOB SEARCH

Seven Steps to Getting a Good Job in Less Time

The Complete Text of a Results-Oriented Booklet by Michael Farr

Millions of job seekers have found better jobs faster using the techniques in The Quick Job Search. So can you! The Quick Job Search covers the essential steps proven to cut job search time in half and is used widely by job search programs throughout North America. Topics include how to identify your key skills, define and research your ideal job, write a great resume quickly, use the most effective job search methods, get more interviews, answer tough interview questions in three steps, and much more.

While it is a section in this book, The Quick Job Search is available as a separate booklet and in an expanded form as Seven Steps to Getting a Job Fast.

◆

The Quick Job Search Is Short, But It May Be All You Need

While *The Quick Job Search* is short, it covers the basics on how to explore career options and conduct an effective job search. While these topics can seem complex, I have found some simple truths about job searches:

★ If you are going to work, you might as well define what you really want to do and are good at.

★ If you are looking for a job, you might as well use techniques that will reduce the time it takes to find one—and that help you get a better job than you might otherwise.

That's what I emphasize in this little book.

Trust Me—Do the Worksheets. I know you will resist completing the worksheets. But trust me, they are worth your time. Doing them will give you a better sense of what you are good at, what you want to do, and how to go about getting it. You will also most likely get more interviews and present yourself better. Is this worth giving up a night of TV? Yes, I think so.

Once you finish this minibook and its activities, you will have spent more time planning your career than most people do. And you will know more than the average job seeker about finding a job.

Why Such a Short Book? I've taught job seeking skills for many years, and I've written longer and more detailed books than this one. Yet I have often been asked to tell someone, in a few minutes or hours, the most important things they should do in their career planning or job search. Instructors and counselors also ask the same question because they have only a short time to spend with folks they're trying to help. I've given this a lot of thought, and the seven topics in this minibook are the ones I think are most important to know.

This minibook is short enough to scan in a morning and conduct a more effective job search that afternoon. Doing all the activities would take more time but would prepare you far better. Of course, you can learn more about all of the topics it covers, but this little book may be all you need.

You can't just read about getting a job. The best way to get a job is to go out and get interviews! And the best way to get interviews is to make a job out of getting a job.

After many years of experience, I have identified just seven basic things you need to do that make a big difference in your job search. Each will be covered and expanded on in this minibook.

1. Identify your key skills.

2. Define your ideal job.

3. Learn the two most effective job search methods.

4. Write a superior resume.

5. Organize your time to get two interviews a day.

6. Dramatically improve your interviewing skills.

7. Follow up on all leads.

Step 1 Identify Your Key Skills and Develop a "Skills Language" to Describe Yourself

> ### Quip
>
> *We all have thousands of skills. Consider the many skills required to do even a simple thing like ride a bike or bake a cake. But, of all the skills you have, employers want to know those key skills you have for the job they need done. You must clearly identify these key skills, and then emphasize them in interviews.*

One employer survey found that about 90 percent of the people interviewed by the employers did not present the skills they had to do the job they sought. They could not answer the basic question "Why should I hire you?"

Knowing and describing your skills are essential to doing well in interviews. This same knowledge is important in deciding what type of job you will enjoy and do well. For these reasons, I consider identifying your skills a necessary part of a successful career plan or job search.

The Three Types of Skills

Most people think of their "skills" as job-related skills, such as using a computer. But we all have other types of skills that are important for success on a job—and that are important to employers. The triangle at right presents skills in three groups, and I think that this is a very useful way to consider skills for our purposes.

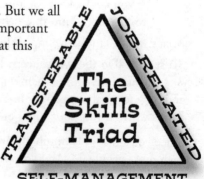

The Skills Triad

Let's review these three types of skills—self-management, transferable, and job-related—and identify those that are most important to you.

Self-Management Skills

Write down three things about yourself that you think make you a good worker.

YOUR "GOOD WORKER" TRAITS

1. _____

2. _____

3. _____

You just wrote down the most important things for an employer to know about you! They describe your basic personality and your ability to adapt to new environments. They are some of the most important skills to emphasize in interviews, yet most job seekers don't realize their importance—and don't mention them.

Review the Self-Management Skills Checklist that follows and put a check mark beside any skills you have. The key self-management skills listed first cover abilities that employers find particularly important. If one or more of the key self-management skills apply to you, mentioning them in interviews can help you greatly.

SELF-MANAGEMENT SKILLS CHECKLIST

Check Your Key Self-Management Skills—Employers Value These Highly

_____ accept supervision	_____ good attendance	_____ productive
_____ get along with coworkers	_____ hard worker	_____ punctual
_____ get things done on time	_____ honest	

Check Your Other Self-Management Skills

_____ able to coordinate	_____ enthusiastic	_____ learn quickly
_____ ambitious	_____ expressive	_____ loyal
_____ assertive	_____ flexible	_____ mature
_____ capable	_____ formal	_____ methodical
_____ cheerful	_____ friendly	_____ modest
_____ competent	_____ good-natured	_____ motivated
_____ complete assignments	_____ helpful	_____ natural
_____ conscientious	_____ humble	_____ open-minded
_____ creative	_____ imaginative	_____ optimistic
_____ dependable	_____ independent	_____ original
_____ discreet	_____ industrious	_____ patient
_____ eager	_____ informal	_____ persistent
_____ efficient	_____ intelligent	_____ physically strong
_____ energetic	_____ intuitive	_____ practice new skills

(continued)

_____ reliable	_____ solve problems	_____ thrifty
_____ resourceful	_____ spontaneous	_____ trustworthy
_____ responsible	_____ steady	_____ versatile
_____ self-confident	_____ tactful	_____ well-organized
_____ sense of humor	_____ take pride in work	
_____ sincere	_____ tenacious	

List Your Other Self-Management Skills

_____

_____

After you are done with the list, circle the five skills you feel are most important and list them in the box that follows.

YOUR TOP FIVE SELF-MANAGEMENT SKILLS

1. _____
2. _____
3. _____
4. _____
5. _____

When thinking about their skills, some people find it helpful to complete the Essential Job Search Data Worksheet that starts on page 356. It organizes skills and accomplishments from previous jobs and other life experiences. Take a look at it and decide whether to complete it now or later.

Transferable Skills

We all have skills that can transfer from one job or career to another. For example, the ability to organize events could be used in a variety of jobs and may be essential for success in certain occupations. Your mission is to find a job that requires the skills you have and enjoy using.

In the following list, put a check mark beside the skills you have. You may have used them in a previous job or in some non-work setting.

Quip

It's not bragging if it's true. Using your new skills language may be uncomfortable at first, but employers need to learn about your skills. So practice saying positive things about the skills you have for the job. If you don't, who will?

TRANSFERABLE SKILLS CHECKLIST

Check Your Key Transferable Skills—Employers Value These Highly

_____ computer skills	_____ manage people	_____ organize/manage projects
_____ negotiate	_____ meet deadlines	_____ public speaking
_____ manage money, budgets	_____ meet the public	_____ written communication

Check Your Skills for Working with Things

_____ assemble things	_____ good with hands	_____ use complex equipment
_____ build things	_____ observe/inspect things	_____ use computers
_____ construct/repair things	_____ operate tools, machines	
_____ drive, operate vehicles	_____ repair things	

Check Your Skills for Working with Data

_____ analyze data	_____ compile	_____ manage money
_____ audit records	_____ count	_____ observe/inspect
_____ budget	_____ detail-oriented	_____ record facts
_____ calculate/compute	_____ evaluate	_____ research
_____ check for accuracy	_____ investigate	_____ synthesize
_____ classify things	_____ keep financial records	_____ take inventory
_____ compare	_____ locate information	

Check Your Skills for Working with People

_____ administer	_____ instruct others	_____ pleasant
_____ advise	_____ interview people	_____ sensitive
_____ care for	_____ kind	_____ sociable
_____ coach	_____ listen	_____ supervise
_____ confront others	_____ negotiate	_____ tactful
_____ counsel people	_____ outgoing	_____ tolerant
_____ demonstrate	_____ patient	_____ tough
_____ diplomatic	_____ perceptive	_____ trusting
_____ help others	_____ persuade	_____ understanding

(continued)

(continued)

Check Your Skills for Working with Words/Ideas

_____ articulate	_____ edit	_____ logical
_____ communicate verbally	_____ ingenious	_____ public speaking
_____ correspond with others	_____ inventive	_____ remember information
_____ create new ideas	_____ library or Internet research	_____ write clearly
_____ design		

Check Your Leadership Skills

_____ arrange social functions	_____ initiate new tasks	_____ results-oriented
_____ competitive	_____ make decisions	_____ risk-taker
_____ decisive	_____ manage or direct others	_____ run meetings
_____ delegate	_____ mediate problems	_____ self-confident
_____ direct others	_____ motivate people	_____ self-motivate
_____ explain things to others	_____ negotiate agreements	_____ solve problems
_____ influence others	_____ plan events	

Check Your Creative/Artistic Skills

_____ artistic	_____ drawing, art	_____ perform, act
_____ dance, body movement	_____ expressive	_____ present artistic ideas

List Your Other Transferable Skills

_____

_____

When you are finished, circle the five transferable skills you feel are most important for you to use in your next job and list them in the box below.

YOUR TOP FIVE TRANSFERABLE SKILLS

1. _____

2. _____

3. _____

4. _____

5. _____

Job-Related Skills

Job content or job-related skills are those you need to do a particular occupation. A carpenter, for example, needs to know how to use various tools. Before you select job-related skills to emphasize, you must first have a clear idea of the jobs you want. So let's put off developing your job-related skills list until you have defined the job you want. That topic is covered next.

Note

Complete the worksheet that follows after you have read "Step 2: Define Your Ideal Job."

Quip

It's a hassle, but... Completing the Essential Job Search Data Worksheet that starts on page 356 will help you define what you are good at—and remember examples of when you did things well. This information will help you define your ideal job and will be of great value in interviews. Look at the worksheet now, and promise to do it tonight.

YOUR TOP FIVE JOB-RELATED SKILLS

1. _____
2. _____
3. _____
4. _____
5. _____

Step 2

Define Your Ideal Job (You Can Compromise on It Later If Needed)

Too many people look for a job without clearly knowing what they are looking for. Before you go out seeking *a* job, I suggest that you first define exactly what you want—*the* job.

Most people think that a job objective is the same as a job title, but it isn't. You need to consider other elements of what makes a job satisfying for you. Then, later, you can decide what that job is called and what industry it might be in.

EIGHT FACTORS TO CONSIDER IN DEFINING YOUR IDEAL JOB

As you try to define your ideal job, consider the following eight important questions. Once you know what you want, your task then becomes finding a position that is as close to your ideal job as possible.

1. **What skills do you want to use?** From the skills lists in Step 1, select the top five skills that you enjoy using and most want to use in your next job. _____

_____

_____

(continued)

(continued)

2. **What type of special knowledge do you have?** Perhaps you know how to fix radios, keep accounting records, or cook food. Write down the things you know from schooling, training, hobbies, family experiences, and other sources. One or more of these knowledges could make you a very special applicant in the right setting. _____

_____

_____

3. **With what types of people do you prefer to work?** Do you like to work in competition with others, or do you prefer hardworking folks, creative personalities, or some other types? _____

_____

_____

4. **What type of work environment do you prefer?** Do you want to work inside, outside, in a quiet place, a busy place, a clean place, or have a window with a nice view? List the types of things that are most important to you. _____

_____

_____

5. **Where do you want your next job to be located—in what city or region?** Near a bus line? Close to a childcare center? If you are open to living and working anywhere, what would your ideal community be like? _____

_____

_____

6. **How much money do you hope to make in your next job?** Many people will take less money if they like a job in other ways—or if they quickly need a job to survive. Think about the minimum you would take as well as what you would eventually like to earn. Your next job will probably pay somewhere in between. _____

_____

_____

7. **How much responsibility are you willing to accept?** Usually, the more money you want to make, the more responsibility you must accept. Do you want to work by yourself, be part of a group, or be in charge? If so, at what level? _____

_____

_____

8. **What things are important or have meaning to you?** Do you have important values you would prefer to include as a basis of the work you do? For example, some people want to work to help others, clean up our environment, build things, make machines work, gain power or prestige, or care for animals or plants. Think about what is important to you and how you might include this in your next job.

_____

_____

Is It Possible to Find Your Ideal Job?

Can you find a job that meets all the criteria you just defined? Perhaps. Some people do. The harder you look, the more likely you are to find it. But you will likely need to compromise, so it is useful to know what is *most* important to include in your next job. Go back over your responses to the eight factors and mark those few things that you would most like to have or include in your ideal job. Then write a brief outline of this ideal job below. Don't worry about a job title, or whether you have the experience, or other practical matters yet.

MY IDEAL JOB WOULD BE

_____

_____

_____

_____

Explore Specific Job Titles and Industries

You might find your ideal job in an occupation you haven't considered yet. And, even if you are sure of the occupation you want, it may be in an industry that's not familiar to you. This combination of occupation and industry forms the basis for your job search, and you should consider a variety of options.

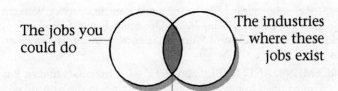

The jobs you could do   The industries where these jobs exist

Your ideal job exists in the overlap of those jobs that interest you most *and* of those industries that best meet your needs and interests!

REVIEW THE TOP JOBS IN THE WORKFORCE

There are thousands of job titles, and many jobs are highly specialized, employing just a few people. While one of these more specialized jobs may be just what you want, most work falls within more general job titles that employ large numbers of people.

The list of job titles that follows was developed by the U.S. Department of Labor. It contains approximately 270 major jobs that employ about 88 percent of the U.S. workforce.

The job titles are organized within 14 major groupings called interest areas, presented in all capital letters and bold type. These groupings will help you quickly identify fields most likely to interest you. Job titles are presented in regular type within these groupings.

(continued)

Begin with the interest areas that appeal to you most, and underline any job title that interests you. (Don't worry for now about whether you have the experience or credentials to do these jobs.) Then quickly review the remaining interest areas, underlining any job titles there that interest you. Note that some job titles are listed more than once because they fit into more than one interest area. When you have gone through all 14 interest areas, go back and circle the 5 to 10 job titles that interest you most. These are the ones you will want to research in more detail.

1. **ARTS, ENTERTAINMENT, AND MEDIA**—Actors, Producers, and Directors; Announcers; Artists and Related Workers; Athletes, Coaches, Umpires, and Related Workers; Barbers, Cosmetologists, and Other Personal Appearance Workers; Broadcast and Sound Engineering Technicians and Radio Operators; Dancers and Choreographers; Demonstrators, Product Promoters, and Models; Designers; Desktop Publishers; Interpreters and Translators; Musicians, Singers, and Related Workers; News Analysts, Reporters, and Correspondents; Photographers; Prepress Technicians and Workers; Public Relations Specialists; Recreation and Fitness Workers; Television, Video, and Motion Picture Camera Operators and Editors; Writers and Editors

2. **SCIENCE, MATH, AND ENGINEERING**—Actuaries; Aerospace Engineers; Agricultural and Food Scientists; Agricultural Engineers; Architects, Except Landscape and Naval; Atmospheric Scientists; Biological Scientists; Biomedical Engineers; Chemical Engineers; Chemists and Materials Scientists; Civil Engineers; Computer and Information Systems Managers; Computer Hardware Engineers; Computer Programmers; Computer Software Engineers; Computer Support Specialists and Systems Administrators; Computer Systems Analysts, Database Administrators, and Computer Scientists; Computer-Control Programmers and Operators; Conservation Scientists and Foresters; Construction and Building Inspectors; Drafters; Economists; Electrical and Electronics Engineers, Except Computer; Engineering and Natural Sciences Managers; Engineering Technicians; Engineers; Environmental Engineers; Environmental Scientists and Geoscientists; Industrial Engineers, Including Health and Safety; Landscape Architects; Market and Survey Researchers; Materials Engineers; Mathematicians; Mechanical Engineers; Medical Scientists; Mining and Geological Engineers, Including Mining Safety Engineers; Nuclear Engineers; Operations Research Analysts; Petroleum Engineers; Photographers; Physicists and Astronomers; Psychologists; Sales Engineers; Science Technicians; Social Scientists, Other; Surveyors, Cartographers, Photogrammetrists, and Surveying Technicians; Urban and Regional Planners

3. **PLANTS AND ANIMALS**—Agricultural Workers; Animal Care and Service Workers; Farmers, Ranchers, and Agricultural Managers; Fishers and Fishing Vessel Operators; Forest, Conservation, and Logging Workers; Grounds Maintenance Workers; Pest Control Workers; Science Technicians; Veterinarians; Veterinary Technologists and Technicians

4. **LAW, LAW ENFORCEMENT, AND PUBLIC SAFETY**—Correctional Officers; Emergency Medical Technicians and Paramedics; Firefighting Occupations; Job Opportunities in the Armed Forces; Judges, Magistrates, and Other Judicial Workers; Lawyers; Occupational Health and Safety Specialists and Technicians; Paralegals and Legal Assistants; Police and Detectives; Private Detectives and Investigators; Science Technicians; Security Guards and Gaming Surveillance Officers

5. **MECHANICS, INSTALLERS, AND REPAIRERS**—Aircraft and Avionics Equipment Mechanics and Service Technicians; Automotive Body and Related Repairers; Automotive Service Technicians and Mechanics; Coin, Vending, and Amusement Machine Servicers and Repairers; Computer, Automated Teller, and Office Machine Repairers; Diesel Service Technicians and Mechanics; Electrical and Electronics Installers and Repairers; Electronic Home Entertainment Equipment Installers and Repairers; Elevator Installers and Repairers; Heating, Air-Conditioning, and Refrigeration Mechanics and Installers; Heavy Vehicle and Mobile Equipment Service Technicians and Mechanics; Home Appliance Repairers; Industrial Machinery Installation, Repair, and Maintenance Workers, Except Millwrights; Line Installers and Repairers; Maintenance and Repair Workers, General; Millwrights; Ophthalmic Laboratory Technicians; Painting and Coating Workers, Except Construction and Maintenance; Precision Instrument and Equipment Repairers; Radio and Telecommunications Equipment Installers and Repairers; Small Engine Mechanics

6. **CONSTRUCTION, MINING, AND DRILLING**—Boilermakers; Brickmasons, Blockmasons, and Stonemasons; Carpenters; Carpet, Floor, and Tile Installers and Finishers; Cement Masons, Concrete Finishers, Segmental Pavers, and Terrazzo Workers; Construction Equipment Operators; Construction Laborers; Construction Managers; Drywall Installers, Ceiling Tile Installers, and Tapers; Electricians; Glaziers; Hazardous Materials Removal Workers; Insulation Workers; Material Moving Occupations; Painters and Paperhangers; Pipelayers,

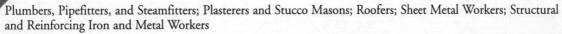

Plumbers, Pipefitters, and Steamfitters; Plasterers and Stucco Masons; Roofers; Sheet Metal Workers; Structural and Reinforcing Iron and Metal Workers

7. **TRANSPORTATION**—Air Traffic Controllers; Aircraft Pilots and Flight Engineers; Bus Drivers; Material Moving Occupations; Rail Transportation Occupations; Taxi Drivers and Chauffeurs; Truck Drivers and Driver/Sales Workers; Water Transportation Occupations

8. **INDUSTRIAL PRODUCTION**—Assemblers and Fabricators; Bookbinders and Bindery Workers; Computer-Control Programmers and Operators; Dental Laboratory Technicians; Food-Processing Occupations; Forest, Conservation, and Logging Workers; Industrial Production Managers; Inspectors, Testers, Sorters, Samplers, and Weighers; Jewelers and Precious Stone and Metal Workers; Machine Setters, Operators, and Tenders—Metal and Plastic; Machinists; Material Moving Occupations; Ophthalmic Laboratory Technicians; Painting and Coating Workers, Except Construction and Maintenance; Photographic Process Workers and Processing Machine Operators; Power Plant Operators, Distributors, and Dispatchers; Prepress Technicians and Workers; Printing Machine Operators; Semiconductor Processors; Stationary Engineers and Boiler Operators; Textile, Apparel, and Furnishings Occupations; Tool and Die Makers; Water and Liquid Waste Treatment Plant and System Operators; Water Transportation Occupations; Welding, Soldering, and Brazing Workers; Woodworkers

9. **BUSINESS DETAIL**—Administrative Services Managers; Bill and Account Collectors; Billing and Posting Clerks and Machine Operators; Bookkeeping, Accounting, and Auditing Clerks; Brokerage Clerks; Cargo and Freight Agents; Cashiers; Communications Equipment Operators; Computer Operators; Computer, Automated Teller, and Office Machine Repairers; Counter and Rental Clerks; Couriers and Messengers; Court Reporters; Credit Authorizers, Checkers, and Clerks; Customer Service Representatives; Data Entry and Information Processing Workers; Dispatchers; File Clerks; Financial Clerks; Gaming Cage Workers; Human Resources Assistants, Except Payroll and Timekeeping; Information and Record Clerks; Interviewers; Material Recording, Scheduling, Dispatching, and Distributing Occupations; Medical Records and Health Information Technicians; Medical Transcriptionists; Meter Readers, Utilities; Office and Administrative Support Worker Supervisors and Managers; Office Clerks, General; Order Clerks; Payroll and Timekeeping Clerks; Postal Service Workers; Prepress Technicians and Workers; Procurement Clerks; Production, Planning, and Expediting Clerks; Receptionists and Information Clerks; Reservation and Transportation Ticket Agents and Travel Clerks; Secretaries and Administrative Assistants; Shipping, Receiving, and Traffic Clerks; Stock Clerks and Order Fillers; Tellers; Weighers, Measurers, Checkers, and Samplers, Recordkeeping

10. **SALES AND MARKETING**—Advertising, Marketing, Promotions, Public Relations, and Sales Managers; Demonstrators, Product Promoters, and Models; Insurance Sales Agents; Material Recording, Scheduling, Dispatching, and Distributing Occupations; Real Estate Brokers and Sales Agents; Retail Salespersons; Sales Representatives, Wholesale and Manufacturing; Sales Worker Supervisors; Securities, Commodities, and Financial Services Sales Agents; Stock Clerks and Order Fillers; Travel Agents

11. **RECREATION, TRAVEL, AND OTHER PERSONAL SERVICES**—Barbers, Cosmetologists, and Other Personal Appearance Workers; Building Cleaning Workers; Chefs, Cooks, and Food Preparation Workers; Flight Attendants; Food and Beverage Serving and Related Workers; Food Service Managers; Food-Processing Occupations; Gaming Services Occupations; Hotel, Motel, and Resort Desk Clerks; Information and Record Clerks; Lodging Managers; Material Moving Occupations; Personal and Home Care Aides; Recreation and Fitness Workers; Reservation and Transportation Ticket Agents and Travel Clerks; Textile, Apparel, and Furnishings Occupations

12. **EDUCATION AND SOCIAL SERVICE**—Archivists, Curators, and Museum Technicians; Childcare Workers; Clergy; Conservation Scientists and Foresters; Counselors; Education Administrators; Financial Analysts and Personal Financial Advisors; Information and Record Clerks; Instructional Coordinators; Librarians; Library Assistants, Clerical; Library Technicians; Probation Officers and Correctional Treatment Specialists; Protestant Ministers; Psychologists; Rabbis; Roman Catholic Priests; Social and Human Service Assistants; Social Workers; Teacher Assistants

13. **GENERAL MANAGEMENT AND SUPPORT**—Accountants and Auditors; Advertising, Marketing, Promotions, Public Relations, and Sales Managers; Budget Analysts; Claims Adjusters, Appraisers, Examiners and Investigators; Cost Estimators; Financial Analysts and Personal Financial Advisors; Financial Managers; Funeral Directors; Human Resources, Training, and Labor Relations Managers and Specialists; Insurance Underwriters;

(continued)

(continued)

Loan Counselors and Officers; Management Analysts; Market and Survey Researchers; Property, Real Estate, and Community Association Managers; Purchasing Managers, Buyers, and Purchasing Agents; Tax Examiners, Collectors, and Revenue Agents; Top Executives

14. **MEDICAL AND HEALTH SERVICES**—Audiologists; Cardiovascular Technologists and Technicians; Chiropractors; Clinical Laboratory Technologists and Technicians; Dental Assistants; Dental Hygienists; Dentists; Diagnostic Medical Sonographers; Dietitians and Nutritionists; Licensed Practical and Licensed Vocational Nurses; Medical and Health Services Managers; Medical Assistants; Nuclear Medicine Technologists; Nursing, Psychiatric, and Home Health Aides; Occupational Therapist Assistants and Aides; Occupational Therapists; Opticians, Dispensing; Optometrists; Pharmacists; Pharmacy Aides; Pharmacy Technicians; Physical Therapist Assistants and Aides; Physical Therapists; Physician Assistants; Physicians and Surgeons; Podiatrists; Radiologic Technologists and Technicians; Recreational Therapists; Registered Nurses; Respiratory Therapists; Speech-Language Pathologists; Surgical Technologists

---

Thorough descriptions for the job titles in the preceding list can be found in this book. You can also find these job descriptions on the Internet at http://www.bls.gov/oco/.

The Guide for Occupational Exploration, Third Edition, provides more information on the interest areas used in the list. This book is published by JIST Works and also describes about 1,000 major jobs, arranged within groupings of related jobs.

Finally, "A Short List of Additional Resources" at the end of this minibook will give you resources for more job information.

CONSIDER MAJOR INDUSTRIES

The *Career Guide to Industries,* another book by the U.S. Department of Labor, gives very helpful reviews for the major industries mentioned in the list below. Organized in groups of related industries, this list covers about 75 percent of the nation's workforce. Many libraries and bookstores carry the *Career Guide to Industries,* or you can find the information on the Internet at http://www.bls.gov/oco/cg/.

Underline industries that interest you, and then learn more about the opportunities they present. Note that some industries pay more than others, often for the same skills or jobs, so you should explore a variety of industry options.

Agriculture, Mining, and Construction: agriculture, forestry, and fishing; construction; mining; oil and gas extraction.

Manufacturing: aerospace product and parts manufacturing; apparel manufacturing; chemical manufacturing, except pharmaceutical and medicine manufacturing; computer and electronic product manufacturing; food manufacturing; motor vehicle and parts manufacturing; pharmaceutical and medicine manufacturing; printing; steel manufacturing; textile mills and products.

Trade: automobile dealers; clothing, accessory, and general merchandise stores; grocery stores; wholesale trade.

Transportation and Utilities: air transportation; truck transportation and warehousing; utilities.

Information: broadcasting; motion picture and video industries; publishing, except software; software publishers; telecommunications.

Financial Activities: banking; insurance; securities, commodities, and other investments.

Professional and Business Services: advertising and public relations services; computer systems design and related services; employment services; management, scientific, and technical consulting services.

Education and Health Services: child daycare services; educational services; health services; social assistance, except child day care.

Leisure and Hospitality: arts, entertainment, and recreation; food services and drinking places; hotels and other accommodations.

Government: federal government, excluding the postal service; state and local government, except education and health.

YOUR TOP JOBS AND INDUSTRIES WORKSHEET

Go back over the lists of job titles and industries. For items 1 and 2 below, list the jobs that interest you most. Then select the industries that interest you most, and list them below in item 3. These are the jobs and industries you should research most carefully. Your ideal job is likely to be found in some combination of these jobs and industries, or in more specialized but related jobs and industries.

1. The 5 job titles that interest you most _____

   _____

   _____

   _____

   _____

2. The 5 next most interesting job titles _____

   _____

   _____

   _____

   _____

3. The industries that interest you most _____

   _____

   _____

   _____

   _____

And, Now, We Return to Job-Related Skills

Back on page 325, I suggested that you should first define the job you want and then identify key job-related skills you have that support your ability to do it. These are the job-related skills to emphasize in interviews.

So, now that you have determined your ideal job, you can pinpoint the job-related skills it requires. If you haven't done so, complete the Essential Job Search Data Worksheet on pages 356–360. It will give you specific skills and accomplishments to highlight.

Yes, completing that worksheet requires time, but doing so will help you clearly define key skills to emphasize in interviews, when what you say matters so much. People who complete that worksheet will do better in their interviews than those who don't.

After you complete the Essential Job Search Data Worksheet, go back to page 325 and write in Your Top Five Job-Related Skills. Include there the job-related skills you have that you would most like to use in your next job.

Use the Most Effective Methods to Reduce Your Job Search Time

Employer surveys found that most employers don't advertise their job openings. They hire people they know, people who find out about the jobs through word of mouth, and people who happen to be in the right place at the right time. While luck plays a part, you can increase your "luck" in finding job openings.

Let's look at the job search methods that people use. The U.S. Department of Labor conducts a regular survey of unemployed people actively looking for work. The survey results are presented below.

Percentage of Unemployed Using Various Job Search Methods

- Contacted employer directly: 64.5%
- Sent out resumes/filled out applications: 48.3%
- Contacted public employment agency: 20.4%
- Placed or answered help wanted ads: 14.5%
- Contacted friends or relatives: 13.5%
- Contacted private employment agency: 6.6%
- Used other active search methods: 4.4%
- Contacted school employment center: 2.3%
- Checked union or professional registers: 1.5%

Source: U.S. Department of Labor, Current Population Survey

Note

This section covers a number of job search methods. Most of the material is presented as information, with a few interactive activities. While each topic is short and reasonably interesting, taking a break now and then will help you absorb it all.

What Job Search Methods Work Best?

The survey shows that most people use more than one job search technique. For example, one person might read want ads, fill out applications, and ask friends for job leads. Others might send out resumes, contact everyone they know from professional contacts, and sign up at employment agencies.

But the survey covered only nine job search methods and, on those, asked only whether the job seeker did or did not use each method. The survey did not cover the Internet, nor did it ask whether a method worked in getting job offers.

Unfortunately, there hasn't been much recent research on the effectiveness of various job search methods. Most of what we know is based on older research and the observations of people who work with job seekers. I'll share what we do know about the effectiveness of job search methods in the content that follows.

Getting the Most Out of Less-Effective Job Search Methods

The truth is that every job search method works for some people. But experience and research show that some methods are more effective than others are. Your task in the job search is to spend more of your time using more effective methods—and increase the effectiveness of all the methods you use.

Quip

Your job search objective. Almost everyone finds a job eventually, so your objective should be to find a good job in less time. The job search methods I emphasize in this minibook will help you do just that.

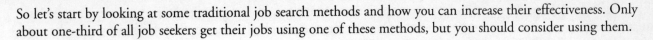

So let's start by looking at some traditional job search methods and how you can increase their effectiveness. Only about one-third of all job seekers get their jobs using one of these methods, but you should consider using them.

Help Wanted Ads

Most jobs are never advertised, and only about 15 percent of all people get their jobs through the want ads. Everyone who reads the paper knows about these openings, so competition is fierce. The Internet also lists many job openings. But, as with want ads, enormous numbers of people view these postings. Some people do get jobs this way, so go ahead and apply. Just be sure to spend most of your time using more effective methods.

Filling Out Applications

Most employers require job seekers to complete an application form. But applications are designed to collect negative information—and employers use applications to screen people out. If, for example, your training or work history is not the best, you will often never get an interview, even if you can do the job.

Completing applications is a more effective approach for young job seekers than for adults. The reason is that there is a shortage of workers for the relatively low-paying and entry-level jobs youth typically seek. As a result, employers are more willing to accept a lack of experience or lack of job skills in youth. Even so, you will get better results by filling out the application if asked to do so and then requesting an interview with the person in charge.

When you complete an application, make it neat and error-free, and do not include anything that could get you screened out. If necessary, leave a problem section blank. It can always be explained after you get an interview.

Employment Agencies

There are three types of employment agencies. One is operated by the government and is free. The others are run as for-profit businesses and charge a fee to either you or an employer. There are advantages and disadvantages to using each.

The government employment service and one-stop centers. Each state has a network of local offices to pay unemployment compensation, provide job leads, and offer other services—at no charge to you or to employers. The service's name varies by state, and it may be called "Job Service," "Department of Labor," "Unemployment Office," "Workforce Development," or another name. Many states have "One-Stop Centers" that provide employment counseling, reference books, computerized career information, job listings, and other resources.

An Internet site at www.careeronestop.org uses will give you information on the programs provided by the government employment service, plus links to other useful sites. Another Internet site called America's Job Bank, at www.ajb.dni.us, allows visitors to see all jobs listed with the government employment service and to search for jobs by region and other criteria.

The government employment service lists only 5 to 10 percent of the available openings nationally, and only about 6 percent of all job seekers get their jobs there. Even so, visit your local office early in your job search. Find out if you qualify for unemployment compensation and learn more about its services. Look into it—the price is right.

Private employment agencies. Private employment agencies are businesses that charge a fee either to you or to the employer who hires you. You will often see their ads in the help wanted section of the newspaper, and many have Web sites. Fees can be from less than one month's pay to 15 percent or more of your annual salary.

Be careful about using fee-based employment agencies. Recent research indicates that more people use and benefit from fee-based agencies than in the past. But realize that relatively few people who register with private agencies get a job through them.

If you use them, ask for interviews where the employer pays the fee. Do not sign an exclusive agreement or be pressured into accepting a job, and continue to actively look for your own leads. You can find these agencies in the phone book's yellow pages, and a government-run Web site at www.ajb.dni.us lists many of them as well.

Temporary agencies. Temporary agencies offer jobs lasting from several days to many months. They charge the employer a bit more than your salary, and then pay you and keep the difference. You pay no direct fee to the agency. Many private employment agencies now provide temporary jobs as well.

Temp agencies have grown rapidly for good reason. They provide employers with short-term help, and employers often use them to find people they may want to hire later. Temp agencies can help you survive between jobs and get experience in different work settings; working for a temp agency may lead to a regular job. They provide a very good option while you look for long-term work, and you may get a job offer while working in a temp job.

School and Employment Services

Contacting a school employment center is one of the job search methods included in the survey presented earlier. Only a small percentage of respondents said they used this option. This is probably because few had the service available.

If you are a student or graduate, find out about these services. Some schools provide free career counseling, resume-writing help, referrals to job openings, career interest tests, reference materials, and other services. Special career programs work with veterans, people with disabilities, welfare recipients, union members, professional groups, and many others. So check out these services and consider using them.

Mailing Resumes and Posting Them on the Internet

Many job search "experts" used to suggest that sending out lots of resumes was a great technique. That advice probably helped sell their resume books, but mailing resumes to people you do not know was never an effective approach. Every so often this would work, but a 95-percent failure rate and few interviews were the more common outcomes, and still are.

While mailing your resume to strangers doesn't make much sense, posting it on the Internet might because

1. It doesn't take much time.

2. Many employers have the potential of finding your resume.

But job searching on the Internet also has its limitations, just like other methods. I'll cover resumes in more detail later and provide tips on using the Internet throughout this minibook.

The Two Job Search Methods That Work Best

The fact is that most jobs are not advertised, so how do *you* find them? The same way that about two-thirds of all job seekers do: networking with people you know (which I call warm contacts) and making direct contacts with an employer (which I call cold contacts). Both of these methods are based on the most important job search rule of all:

THE MOST IMPORTANT JOB SEARCH RULE
Don't wait until the job opens before contacting the employer!

Employers fill most jobs with people they have met before jobs formally "open." So the trick is to meet people who can hire you before a job is available! Instead of saying, "Do you have any jobs open?" say, "I realize you may not have any openings now, but I would still like to talk to you about the possibility of future openings."

Method 1: Develop a Network of Contacts in Five Easy Stages

One study found that 40 percent of all people located their jobs through a lead provided by a friend, a relative, or an acquaintance. That makes people you know the number one source of job leads—more effective than all the traditional methods combined!

Developing and using your contacts is called "networking," and here's how it works:

1. **Make lists of people you know.** Make a thorough list of anyone you are friendly with. Then make a separate list of all your relatives. These two lists alone often add up to 25 to 100 people or more. Next, think of other groups of people that you have something in common with, such as former coworkers or classmates, members of your social or sports groups, members of your professional association, former employers, and members of your religious group. You may not know many of these people personally or well, but most will help you if you ask them.

2. **Contact them in a systematic way.** Next, contact each of these people. Obviously, some people will be more helpful than others, but any one of them might help you find a job lead.

3. **Present yourself well.** Begin with your friends and relatives. Call and tell them you are looking for a job and need their help. Be as clear as possible about the type of employment you want and the skills and qualifications you have. Look at the sample JIST Card and phone script later in this minibook for good presentation ideas.

4. **Ask them for leads.** It is possible that your contacts will know of a job opening that might interest you. If so, get the details and get right on it! More likely, however, they will not, so you should ask each person these three questions:

The Three Magic Networking Questions

♦ *Do you know of any openings for a person with my skills?* If the answer is no (which it usually is), then ask...

♦ *Do you know of someone else who might know of such an opening?* If your contact does, get that name and ask for another one. If he or she doesn't, ask...

♦ *Do you know of anyone who might know of someone else who might know?* Another good way to ask this is "Do you know someone who knows lots of people?" If all else fails, this will usually get you a name.

---

5. **Contact these referrals and ask them the same questions.** With each original contact, you can extend your network of acquaintances by hundreds of people. Eventually, one of these people will hire you or refer you to someone who will!

If you are persistent in following these five steps, networking may be the only job search method you need. It works.

Method 2: Contact Employers Directly

It takes more courage, but making direct contact with employers is a very effective job search technique. I call these "cold contacts" because people you don't know in advance will need to "warm up" to your inquiries. Two basic techniques for making cold contacts follow.

Use the yellow pages to find potential employers. Begin by looking at the index in your phone book's yellow pages. For each entry, ask yourself, "Would an organization of this kind need a person with my skills?" If you answer yes, then that organization or business type is a possible target. You can also rate "yes" entries based on your interest, writing an A next to those that seem very interesting, a B next to those that you are not sure of, and a C next to those that aren't interesting at all.

Next, select a type of organization that got a "yes" response, such as "hotels," and turn to that section of the yellow pages. Call each hotel listed and ask to speak to the person who is most likely to hire or supervise you. A sample telephone script is included later in this section to give you ideas about what to say.

You can easily adapt this approach to the Internet by using sites like www. yellowpages.com to get contacts anywhere in the world.

Drop in without an appointment. You can also walk into a business or organization that interests you and ask to speak to the person in charge. Particularly effective in small businesses, dropping in also works surprisingly well in larger ones. Remember to ask for an interview even if there are no openings now. If your timing is inconvenient, ask for a better time to come back for an interview.

The phone book is the most complete, up-to-date source of job search targets. The index for the yellow pages organizes potential employers into categories that are ideal for job seekers. Find a listing that interests you, and then contact employers listed there. All it takes is a 30-second phone call to get the name of the hiring authority!

Most Jobs Are with Small Employers

Businesses and organizations with 250 or fewer employees employ about 70 percent of all U.S. workers. They are also the source for as much as 80 percent of the new jobs created each year. They are simply too important to overlook in your job search! Many of them don't have personnel departments, making direct contacts even easier and more effective.

JIST Cards®—An Effective Mini Resume

Look at the sample cards that follow—they are JIST Cards, and they get results. Computer printed or even neatly written on a 3-by-5–inch card, JIST Cards include the essential information employers want to know.

JIST Cards have been used by thousands of job search programs and millions of people. Employers like their direct and timesaving format, and they have been proven as an effective tool to get job leads. Attach one to your resume. Give them to friends, relatives, and other contacts and ask them to pass them along to others who might know of an opening. Enclose them in thank-you notes after an interview. Leave one with employers as a business card. However you get them in circulation, you may be surprised at how well they work.

Sandra Zaremba

Home phone: (219) 232-7608
E-mail: SKZ1128@aol.com

Position: General Office/Clerical

Over two years' work experience, plus one year of training in office practices. Familiar with a variety of computer programs, including word processing, spreadsheets, accounting, and some database and graphic design programs. Am Internet literate and word-process 70 wpm accurately. Can post general ledger and handle payables, receivables, and most accounting tasks. Responsible for daily deposits averaging more than $200,000 monthly. Good interpersonal skills. Can meet strict deadlines and handle pressure well.

Willing to work any hours.

Organized, honest, reliable, and hard working.

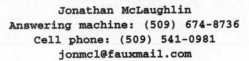

Jonathan McLaughlin
Answering machine: (509) 674-8736
Cell phone: (509) 541-0981
jonmcl@fauxmail.com

Objective: Electronics-installation, maintenance, and sales

Skills: Four years of work experience, plus two years advanced
training in electronics. AS degree in Electronics Engineering
Technology. Managed a $500,000/year business while going to school
full time, with grades in the top 25%. Familiar with all major
electronics diagnostic and repair equipment. Hands-on experience
with medical, consumer,communications, business, and industrial
electronics equipment and applications. Good problem-solving and
communication skills. Customer service oriented.

Willing to do what it takes to get the job done.

Self-motivated, dependable, learn quickly.

You can easily create JIST Cards on a computer and print them on card stock you can buy at any office supply store. Or have a few hundred printed cheaply by a local quick print shop. While they are often done as 3-by-5 cards, they can be printed in any size or format.

Use the Phone to Get Job Leads

Once you have created your JIST Card, you can use it as the basis for a phone "script" to make warm or cold calls. Revise your JIST Card content so that it sounds natural when spoken, and then edit it until you can read it out loud in about 30 seconds. Use the sample phone script that follows to help you write your own.

"Hello, my name is Pam Nykanen. I am interested in a position in hotel management. I have four years' experience in sales, catering, and accounting with a 300-room hotel. I also have an associate degree in hotel management, plus one year of experience with the Bradey Culinary Institute. During my employment, I helped double revenues from meetings and conferences and increased bar revenues by 46 percent. I have good problem-solving skills and am good with people. I am also well-organized, hard working, and detail-oriented. When may I come in for an interview?"

Once you have your script, make some practice calls to warm or cold contacts. If making cold calls, contact the person most likely to supervise you. Then present your script just as you practiced it, without stopping.

While it doesn't work every time, most people, with practice, can get one or more interviews in an hour by making such calls.

While the sample script assumes you are calling someone you don't know, it can be changed for warm contacts and referrals. Making cold calls takes courage—but works very well for many who are willing to do it.

> **Quip**
>
> *Dialing for dollars.* The phone can get you more interviews per hour than any other job search tool. But it won't work unless you use it actively.

> **Quip**
>
> *Overcome phone phobia!* Making cold calls takes guts, but job search programs find that most people can get one or more interviews an hour using cold calls. Start by calling people you know and people they refer you to. Then try calls to businesses that don't sound very interesting. As you get better, call more desirable targets.

Using the Internet in Your Job Search

I provide Internet-related tips throughout this minibook, but the Internet deserves a separate section, so here it is.

The Internet has limitations as a job search tool. While many have used it to get job leads, it has not worked well for far more. Too many assume they can simply add their resume to resume databases, and employers will line up to hire them. Just like the older approach of sending out lots of resumes, good things sometimes happen, but not often.

I recommend two points that apply to all job search methods, including using the Internet:

◆ It is unwise to rely on just one or two methods in conducting your job search.

◆ It is essential that you use an active rather than a passive approach in your job search.

Tips to Increase Your Internet Effectiveness

I encourage you to use the Internet in your job search but suggest you use it along with other techniques, including direct contacts with employers. The following suggestions can increase the effectiveness of using the Internet in your job search.

Be as specific as possible in the job you seek. This is important in using any job search method and even more so in using the Internet. The Internet is enormous, so it is essential to be as focused as possible in what you are looking for. Narrow your job title or titles to be as specific as possible. Limit your search to specific industries or areas of specialization.

Have reasonable expectations. Success on the Internet is more likely if you understand its limitations. For example, employers trying to find someone with skills in high demand, such as network engineers or nurses, are more likely to use the Internet to recruit job candidates.

> **Quip**
>
> *If the Internet is new to you, I recommend a book titled* Cyberspace Job Search Kit *by Mary Nemnich and Fred Jandt. It covers the basics plus lots of advice on using the Internet for career planning and job seeking.*

Limit your geographic options. If you don't want to move, or would move but only to certain areas, state this preference on your resume and restrict your search to those areas. Many Internet sites allow you to view only those jobs that meet your location criteria.

Create an electronic resume. With few exceptions, resumes submitted on the Internet end up as simple text files with no graphic elements. Employers search databases of many resumes for those that include key words or meet other searchable criteria. So create a simple text resume for Internet use and include on it words likely to be used by employers searching for someone with your abilities. See the resume on page 348 for an example.

Get your resume into the major resume databases. Most Internet employment sites let you add your resume for free, and then charge employers to advertise openings or to search for candidates. These easy-to-use sites often provide all sorts of useful information for job seekers.

Make direct contacts. Visit Web sites of organizations that interest you and learn more about them. Some will post openings, allow you to apply online, or even provide access to staff who can answer your questions. Even if they don't, you can always e-mail a request for the name of the person in charge of the area that interests you and then communicate with that person directly.

Network. You can network online, too, to get names and e-mail addresses of potential employer contacts or other people who might know of someone with a job opening. Look at interest groups, professional association sites, alumni sites, chat rooms, and employer sites—just some of the many creative ways to network with and to interact with people via the Internet.

Useful Internet Sites

Thousands of Internet sites provide information on careers or education. Many have links to other sites that they recommend. Service providers such as America Online (www.aol.com) and the Microsoft Network (www.msn.com) have career information and job listings plus links to other sites. Larger portal sites offer links to recommended career-related sites—Lycos (www.lycos.com) and Yahoo (www.yahoo.com) are just a couple of these portals. These major career-specific sites can get you started:

- The Riley Guide at www.rileyguide.com
- Monster.com at www.monster.com
- America's Job Bank at www.ajb.dni.us
- The JIST site at www.jist.com
- careerbuilder.com at www.careerbuilder.com

Step 4

Write a Simple Resume Now and a Better One Later

Sending out resumes and waiting for responses is not an effective job-seeking technique. But, many employers *will* ask you for one, and a resume can be a useful tool in your job search. I suggest that you begin with a simple resume you can complete quickly. I've seen too many people spend weeks working on their resume when they could have been out getting interviews instead. If you want a "better" resume, you can work on it on weekends and evenings. So let's begin with the basics.

Tips for Creating a Superior Resume

The following tips make sense for any resume format:

Write it yourself. It's okay to look at other resumes for ideas, but write yours yourself. It will force you to organize your thoughts and background.

Make it error-free. One spelling or grammar error will create a negative impressionist (see what I mean?). Get someone else to review your final draft for any errors. Then review it again because these rascals have a way of slipping in.

Make it look good. Poor copy quality, cheap paper, bad type quality, or anything else that creates a poor appearance will turn off employers to even the best resume content. Get professional help with design and printing if necessary. Many professional resume writers and even print shops offer writing and desktop design services if you need help.

Be brief, be relevant. Many good resumes fit on one page, and few justify more than two. Include only the most important points. Use short sentences and action words. If it doesn't relate to and support the job objective, cut it!

> ## Quip
>
>
> *Most jobs are never advertised because employers don't need to advertise or don't want to. Employers trust people referred to them by someone they know far more than they trust strangers. And most jobs are filled by referrals and people that the employer knows, eliminating the need to advertise. So, your job search must involve more than looking at ads.*

Be honest. Don't overstate your qualifications. If you end up getting a job you can't handle, who does it help? And a lie can result in your being fired later.

Be positive. Emphasize your accomplishments and results. A resume is no place to be too humble or to display your faults.

Be specific. Instead of saying, "I am good with people," say, "I supervised four people in the warehouse and increased productivity by 30 percent." Use numbers whenever possible, such as the number of people served, percent sales increase, or dollars saved.

You should also know that everyone feels that he or she is a resume expert. Whatever you do, someone will tell you that it's wrong. Remember that a resume is simply a job search tool. You should never delay or slow down your job search because your resume is not "good enough." The best approach is to create a simple and acceptable resume as quickly as possible and then use it. As time permits, create a better one if you feel you must.

> ### Quip
>
> *Avoid the resume pile. Resume experts often suggest that a "dynamite" resume will jump out of the pile. This is old-fashioned advice. It assumes that you are applying to large organizations and for advertised jobs. Today, most jobs are with small employers and are not advertised. My advice is to avoid joining that stack of resumes in the first place by looking for openings that others overlook.*

Chronological Resumes

Most resumes use a chronological format where the most recent experience is listed first, followed by each previous job. This arrangement works fine for someone with work experience in several similar jobs, but not as well for those with limited experience or for career changers.

Look at the two resumes for Judith Jones that follow. Both use the chronological approach. The first resume would work fine for most job search needs—and it could be completed in about an hour. Notice that the second one includes some improvements. The first resume is good, but most employers would like the additional positive information in the improved resume.

Basic Chronological Resume Example

Judith J. Jones

115 South Hawthorne Avenue
Chicago, Illinois 66204
(312) 653-9217 (home)
email: jj@earthlink.com

Leaves lots of options open by not using one job title.

JOB OBJECTIVE

Desire a position in the office management, accounting, or administrative assistant area. Prefer a position requiring responsibility and a variety of tasks.

EDUCATION AND TRAINING

Acme Business College, Lincoln, Illinois
Graduate of a one-year business program.

U.S. Army
Financial procedures, accounting functions.

John Adams High School, South Bend, Indiana
Diploma, business education.

Other: Continuing education classes and workshops in business communication, computer spreadsheet and database programs, scheduling systems, and customer relations.

Emphasis on all __related__ education is important, because it helps overcome her lack of "work" experience.

EXPERIENCE

2001-present—Claims Processor, Blue Spear Insurance Co., Wilmette, Illinois. Handle customer medical claims, develop management reports based on spreadsheets I created, exceed productivity goals.

2000-2001—Returned to school to upgrade my business and computer skills. Took courses in advanced accounting, spreadsheet and database programs, office management, human relations, and new office techniques.

1998-2000—E4, U.S. Army. Assigned to various stations as a specialist in finance operations. Promoted prior to honorable discharge.

1996-1998—Sandy's Boutique, Wilmette, Illinois. Responsible for counter sales, display design, cash register and other tasks.

1994-1996—Held part-time and summer jobs throughout high school.

Uses her education in this section to add credentials

PERSONAL

I am reliable, hard working, and good with people.

Everything supports her job objective

Improved Chronological Resume Example

Judith J. Jones

115 South Hawthorne Avenue • Chicago, Illinois 66204
(312) 653-9217 (home)
email: jj@earthlink.com

Adds lots of details to reinforce skills throughout.

More details here.

JOB OBJECTIVE

Seeking position requiring excellent business management skills in an office environment. Position should require a variety of tasks, including office management, word processing, and spreadsheet and database program use.

EDUCATION AND TRAINING

Acme Business College, Lincoln, Illinois.
Completed one-year program in Professional Office Management. Grades in top 30 percent of my class. Courses included word processing, accounting theory and systems, advanced spreadsheet and database programs, time management, and basic supervision.

John Adams High School, South Bend, Indiana.
Graduated with emphasis on business courses. Excellent grades in all business topics and won top award for word-processing speed and accuracy.

Other: Continuing education programs at my own expense, including business communications, customer relations, computer applications, sales techniques, and others.

Uses numbers to reinforce results.

EXPERIENCE

2001-present—Claims Processor, Blue Spear Insurance Company, Wilmette, Illinois. Handle 50 complex medical insurance claims per day, almost 20 percent above department average. Created a spreadsheet report process that decreased department labor costs by over $30,000 a year (one position). Received two merit raises for performance.

2000-2001—Returned to business school to gain advanced skills in accounting, office management, sales and human resources. Computer courses included word processing and graphics design, accounting and spreadsheet software, and database and networking applications. Grades in top 30 percent of class.

1998-2000—Finance Specialist (E4), U.S. Army. Responsible for the systematic processing of over 200 invoices per day from commercial vendors. Trained and supervised eight employees. Devised internal system allowing 15 percent increase in invoices processed with a decrease in personnel. Managed department with a budget equivalent of over $350,000 a year. Honorable discharge.

1996-1998—Sales Associate promoted to Assistant Manager, Sandy's Boutique, Wilmette, Illinois. Made direct sales and supervised four employees. Managed daily cash balances and deposits, made purchasing and inventory decisions, and handled all management functions during owner's absence. Sales increased 26 percent and profits doubled during my tenure.

1994-1996—Held various part-time and summer jobs through high school while maintaining good grades. Earned enough to pay all personal expenses, including car and car insurance. Learned to deal with customers, meet deadlines, work hard, handle multiple priorities, and develop other skills.

SPECIAL SKILLS AND ABILITIES

Quickly learn new computer applications and am experienced with a number of business software applications. Have excellent interpersonal, written, and oral communication and math skills. Accept supervision well, am able to supervise others, and work well as a team member. Like to get things done and have an excellent attendance record.

Tips for Writing a Simple Chronological Resume

Follow these tips for writing a basic chronological resume.

Name. Use your formal name rather than a nickname if it sounds more professional.

Address and contact information. Avoid abbreviations in your address and include your ZIP code. If you may move, use a friend's address or include a forwarding address. Most employers will not write to you, so you must provide reliable phone numbers and other contact options. Always include your area code in your phone number because you never know where your resume might travel. If you don't have an answering machine, get one—and leave it on whenever you leave home. Make sure your voice message presents you in a professional way. Include alternative ways to reach you, like a cell phone, beeper, and e-mail address.

Job objective. You should almost always have one, even if it is general. In the sample resumes, notice how Judy keeps her options open with her broad job objective. Writing "secretary" or "clerical" might limit her from being considered for jobs she might take.

Education and training. Include any training or education you've had that supports your job objective. If you did not finish a formal degree or program, list what you did complete and emphasize accomplishments. If your experience is not strong, add details here like related courses and extracurricular activities. In the two examples, Judy puts her business schooling in both the education and experience sections. Doing this fills a job gap and allows her to present her training as equal to work experience.

Previous experience. Include the basics like employer name, job title, dates employed, and responsibilities—but emphasize things like specific skills, results, accomplishments, and superior performance.

Personal data. Do not include irrelevant details like height, weight, and marital status—doing so is considered very old-fashioned. But you can include information like hobbies or leisure activities in a special section that directly supports your job objective. The first sample includes a "Personal" section in which Judy lists some of her strengths, which are often not included in a resume.

References. You do not need to list references since employers will ask for them if they want them. If your references are particularly good, you can mention this somewhere—the last section is often a good place. List your references on a separate page and give it to employers who ask. Ask your references what they will say about you and, if positive, if they would write you a letter of recommendation to give to employers.

Tips for an Improved Chronological Resume

Once you have a simple, errorless, and eye-pleasing resume, get on with your job search. There is no reason to delay! If you want to create a better resume in your spare time (evenings or weekends), try these additional tips.

Job objective. A poorly written job objective can limit the jobs an employer might consider you for. Think of the skills you have and the types of jobs you want to do; describe them in general terms. Instead of using a narrow job title like "restaurant manager," you might write "manage a small to mid-sized business."

> **Quip**
>
> *Skip the negatives.* Remember that a resume can get you screened out, but it is up to you to get the interview and the job. So, cut out anything negative in your resume!

Education and training. New graduates should emphasize their recent training and education more than those with a few years of related work experience would. A more detailed education and training section might include specific courses you took, and activities or accomplishments that support your job objective or reinforce your key skills. Include other details that reflect how hard you work, such as working your way through school or handling family responsibilities.

Skills and accomplishments. Include things that support your ability to do well in the job you seek now. Even small things count. Maybe your attendance was perfect, you met a tight deadline, or you did the work of others during vacations. Be specific and include numbers—even if you have to estimate them. The improved chronological resume example features a "Special Skills and Abilities" section and more accomplishments and skills. Notice the impact of the numbers to reinforce results.

Job titles. Past job titles may not accurately reflect what you did. For example, your job title may have been "cashier," but you also opened the store, trained new staff, and covered for the boss on vacations. Perhaps "head cashier and assistant manager" would be more accurate. Check with your previous employer if you are not sure.

Promotions. If you were promoted or got good evaluations, say so—"cashier, promoted to assistant manager," for example. A promotion to a more responsible job can be handled as a separate job if doing so results in a stronger resume.

Gaps in employment and other problem areas. Employee turnover is expensive, so few employers want to hire people who won't stay or who won't work out. Gaps in employment, jobs held for short periods, or a lack of direction in the jobs you've held are all things that concern employers. So consider your situation and try to give an explanation of a problem area. Here are a few examples:

2001—Continued my education at…

2004—Traveled extensively throughout the United States.

2000 to present—Self-employed barn painter and widget maker.

2003—Had first child, took year off before returning to work.

Use entire years to avoid displaying an employment gap you can't explain easily. For example "2002 to 2003" can cover a few months of unemployment at the beginning of 2002.

Skills and Combination Resumes

The functional or "skills" resume emphasizes your most important skills, supported by specific examples of how you have used them. This approach allows you to use any part of your life history to support your ability to do the job you want.

While a skills resume can be very effective, it requires more work to create one. And some employers don't like them because they can hide a job seeker's faults (such as job gaps, lack of formal education, or little related work experience) better than a chronological resume. Still, a skills resume may make sense for you.

Look over the sample resumes that follow for ideas. Notice that one resume includes elements of a skills *and* a chronological resume. This so-called "combination" resume makes sense if your previous job history or education and training are positive.

More Resume Examples

Find resume layout and presentation ideas in the four samples that follow.

The chronological resume sample on page 345 focuses on accomplishments through the use of numbers. While Maria's resume does not say so, it is obvious that she works hard and that she gets results.

The skills resume on page 346 is for a recent high school graduate whose only paid work experience was at a fast-food place!

The combination resume on page 347 emphasizes Mary Beth's relevant education and transferable skills because she has no work experience in the field. The resume was submitted by professional resume writer Janet L. Beckstrom of Flint, Michigan (e-mail wordcrafter@voyager.net).

The electronic resume on page 348 is appropriate for scanning or e-mail submission. It has a plain format that is easily read by scanners. It also has lots of key words that increase its chances of being selected when an employer searches a database. The resume is based on one from *Cyberspace Resume Kit* by Mary Nemnich and Fred Jandt and published by JIST Works.

> ## Quip
>
> *A resume is not the most effective tool for getting interviews. A better approach is to make direct contact with those who hire or supervise people with your skills and ask them for an interview, even if no openings exist now. Then send a resume.*

Chronological Resume Emphasizes Results

A simple chronological format with few but carefully chosen words. It has an effective summary at the beginning, and every word supports her job objective.

She emphasizes results!

Maria Marquez

4141 Beachway Road
Redondo Beach, California 90277

Messages: (213) 432-2279
E-mail: mmarq@msn.net

Objective: Management Position in a Major Hotel

Summary of Experience: Four years' experience in sales, catering, banquet services, and guest relations in 300-room hotel. Doubled sales revenues from conferences and meetings. Increased dining room and bar revenues by 44%. Won prestigious national and local awards for increased productivity and services.

Experience: Park Regency Hotel, Los Angeles, California
Assistant Manager
1999 to Present

Notice her use of numbers to increase impact of statements.

- Oversee a staff of 36 including dining room and bar, housekeeping, and public relations operations.
- Introduced new menus and increased dining room revenues by 44% Gourmet America awarded us their first place Hotel Haute Cuisine award as a result of my efforts.
- Attracted 28% more diners with the first revival of Big Band Cocktail Dances in the Los Angeles area.

Kingsmont Hotel, Redondo Beach, California
Sales and Public Relations
1997 to 1999

Bullets here and above increase readability and emphasis.

- Doubled revenues per month from conferences and meetings.
- Redecorated meeting rooms and updated sound and visual media equipment. Careful scheduling resulted in no lost revenue during this time.
- Instituted staff reward program, which resulted in an upgrade from B- to AAA+ in the *Car and Travel Handbook.*

Education: Associate Degree in Hotel Management from Henfield College of San Francisco. One-year certification program with the Boileau Culinary Institute, where I won the Grand Prize Scholarship.

While Maria had only a few years of related work experience, she used this resume to help her land a very responsible job in a large resort hotel.

Skills Resume for Someone with Limited Work Experience

A skills resume where each skill directly supports the job objective of this recent high school graduate with very limited work experience.

Lisa M. Rhodes
813 Lava Court • Denver, Colorado 81613
Home: (413) 643-2173 (leave message)
Cell phone: (413) 442-1659
Email: lrhodes@netcom.net

Position Desired
Sales-oriented position in a retail sales or distribution business.

Support for the skills comes from all life activities: school, clubs, part-time jobs.

Skills and Abilities

key skills

Communications	Good written and verbal presentation skills. Use proper grammar and have a good speaking voice.
Interpersonal	Able to get along well with coworkers and accept supervision. Received positive evaluations from previous supervisors.
Flexible	Willing to try new things and am interested in improving efficiency on assigned tasks.
Attention to Detail	Concerned with quality. My work is typically orderly and attractive. Like to see things completed correctly and on time.
Hard Working	Throughout high school, worked long hours in strenuous activities while attending school full-time. Often handled as many as 65 hours a week in school and other structured activities, while maintaining above-average grades.
Customer Contacts	Routinely handled as many as 500 customer contacts a day (10,000 per month) in a busy retail outlet. Averaged lower than a .001% complaint rate and was given the "Employee of the Month" award in my second month of employment. Received two merit increases. Never absent or late.
Cash Sales	Handled over $2,000 a day ($40,000 a month) in cash sales. Balanced register and prepared daily sales summary and deposits.
Reliable	Excellent attendance record, trusted to deliver daily cash deposits totaling over $40,000 a month.

← Good emphasis on adaptive skills.

very strong statement.

Good use of numbers

Education
Franklin High School. Took advanced English and other classes. Member of award-winning band. Excellent attendance record. Superior communication skills. Graduated in top 30% of class.

Other
Active gymnastics competitor for four years. This taught me discipline, teamwork, how to follow instructions, and hard work. I am ambitious, outgoing, reliable, and willing to work.

Lisa's resume makes it clear that she is talented and hard working.

Combination Resume for a Career Changer

Writer's comments: This client was finishing computer programming school and had no work experience in the field. After listing the topics covered in the course, I summarized her employment experience, specifying that she earned promotions quickly. This **Mary Beth Kurzak** *would be attractive to any employer.*

2188 Huron River Drive • Ann Arbor, MI 48104 • 734-555-4912 • e-mail: mbkurzak@fauxmail.com

Profile

➤ Strong educational preparation with practical applications in computer/internet programming.
➤ Highly motivated to excel in new career.
➤ A fast learner, as evidenced by success in accelerated training program.
➤ Self-directed, independent worker with proven ability to meet deadlines and work under pressure.
➤ Maintain team perspective with ability to build positive working relationships and foster open communication.

Education/Training

ADVANCED TECHNOLOGY CENTER • Dearborn, MI   xxxx-Present
Pursuing Certification in **Internet/Information Technology**   *Anticipated completion: Aug. xxxx*
An accelerated program focusing on computer and internet programming.
Highlights of Training:

Important to include specific things learned

- Networking Concepts	- Client Server	- UNIX
- Programming Concepts	- Visual Basic	- IIS
- Programming in Java/Java Script	- C/C++	- VB/ASP
- Web Authoring Using HTML	- Oracle	- CGI
- Photoshop	- DHTML, XML	- Perl

Highlights of Experience and Abilities

Experiences selected to support job objective

Customer Service
➤ Determined member eligibility and verified policy benefits.
➤ Responded to customer questions; interpreted and explained complex insurance concepts.
➤ Collaborated with health care providers regarding billing and claim procedures.

Leadership
➤ Creatively supervised 30 employees, many of whom were significantly older.
➤ Motivated employees and improved working conditions, resulting in greater camaraderie.
➤ Trained coworkers in various technical and nontechnical processes.

Analytical/Troubleshooting
➤ Investigated and resolved computer system errors.
➤ Researched discrepancies in claims and identified appropriate actions.
➤ Compiled and analyzed claims statistics.

Administrative Support and Accounting
➤ Managed and processed medical, mental health and substance abuse claims.
➤ Oversaw accounts receivable; reconciled receipts and prepared bank deposits.
➤ Coordinated 50+ line switchboard; routed calls as appropriate.

Employment History

MEDICAL SERVICES PLUS [Contracted by Health Solutions - Southfield, MI]   xxxx-xxxx
Promoted within eight months of hire.
Claims Supervisor / Claims Adjudicator

HANSEN AGENCY OF MICHIGAN • Ann Arbor, MI   xxxx-xxxx
Earned two promotions in one year.
Claims Adjudicator / Accounting Clerk / Receptionist

FORD WILLOW RUN TRANSMISSION PLANT • Ypsilanti, MI   Summer xxxx
Temporary Production Worker

PEARL HARBOR MEMORIAL MUSEUM • Pearl Harbor, HI   xxxx-xxxx
Assistant Crew Manager

References available on request

Submitted by Janet L. Beckstrom

Electronic Resume

RICHARD JONES

3456 Generic Street

Potomac MD 11721

Phone messages: (301) 927-1189

E-mail: richj@riverview.com

Format to be scanned or e-mailed. No bold, bullets, or italics.

SUMMARY OF SKILLS

Lots of key words to help get selected by computer searches by employers.

Rigger, maintenance mechanic (carpentry, electrical, plumbing, painting), work leader. Read schematic diagrams. Flooring (wood, linoleum, carpet, ceramic and vinyl tile). Plumbing (pipes, fixtures, fire systems). Certified crane and forklift operator, work planner, inspector.

+++

EXPERIENCE *Includes results statements and numbers below.*

Total of nine years in the trades—apprentice to work leader.

* MAINTENANCE MECHANIC LEADER, Smithsonian Institution, Washington, DC, April 2001 to present: Promoted to supervise nine staff in all trades, including plumbing, painting, electrical, carpentry, drywall, flooring. Prioritize and schedule work, inspect and approve completed jobs. Responsible for annual budget of $750,000 and assuring that all work done to museum standards and building codes.

* RIGGER / MAINTENANCE MECHANIC, Smithsonian Institution, February 1998 to April 2001: Built and set up exhibits. Operated cranes, rollers, forklifts, and rigged mechanical and hydraulic systems to safely move huge, priceless museum exhibits. Worked with other trades in carpentry, plumbing, painting, electrical and flooring to construct exhibits.

* RIGGER APPRENTICE, Portsmouth Naval Shipyard, Portsmouth, NH, August 1996 to January 1998: Qualified signalman for cranes. Moved and positioned heavy machines and structural parts for shipbuilding. Responsible for safe operation of over $2,000,000 of equipment on a daily basis, with no injury or accidents Used cranes, skids, rollers, jacks, forklifts and other equipment.

+++

TRAINING AND EDUCATION

HS graduate, top 50% of class.

Additional training in residential electricity, drywall, HV/AC, and refrigeration systems. Certified in heavy crane operation, forklift, regulated waste disposal, industrial blueprints.

Note

◆

Use the information from your completed Essential Job Search Data Worksheet to write your resume.

◆

Step 5

Redefine What Counts As an Interview, Then Get 2 a Day

The average job seeker gets about 5 interviews a month—fewer than 2 a week. Yet many job seekers use the methods in this minibook to get 2 interviews a day. Getting 2 interviews a day equals 10 a week and 40 a month. That's 800 percent more interviews than the average job seeker gets. Who do you think will get a job offer quicker?

But getting 2 interviews a day is nearly impossible unless you redefine what counts as an interview. If you define an interview in a different way, getting 2 a day is quite possible.

THE NEW DEFINITION OF AN INTERVIEW
*AN INTERVIEW IS ANY FACE-TO-FACE CONTACT WITH SOMEONE
WHO HAS THE AUTHORITY TO HIRE OR SUPERVISE A PERSON WITH
YOUR SKILLS—EVEN IF NO OPENING EXISTS AT THE TIME YOU INTERVIEW.*

If you use this new definition, it becomes *much* easier to get interviews. You can now interview with all sorts of potential employers, not just those who have job openings now. While most other job seekers look for advertised or actual openings, you can get interviews before a job opens up or before it is advertised and widely known. You will be considered for jobs that may soon be created but that others will not know about. And, of course, you can also interview for existing openings like everyone else does.

Spending as much time as possible on your job search and setting a job search schedule are important parts of this step.

Make Your Search a Full-Time Job

Job seekers average fewer than 15 hours a week looking for work. On average, unemployment lasts three or more months, with some people out of work far longer (older workers and higher earners, for example). My many years of experience with job seekers indicate that the more time you spend on your job search each week, the less time you will likely remain unemployed.

Of course, using the more effective job search methods presented in this minibook also helps. Many job search programs that teach job seekers my basic approach of using more effective methods and spending more time looking have proven to cut in half the average time needed to find a job. More importantly, many job seekers also find better jobs using these methods.

So, if you are unemployed and looking for a full-time job, you should plan to look on a full-time basis. It just makes sense to do so, although many do not, or they start out well but quickly get discouraged. Most job seekers simply don't have a structured plan—they have no idea what they are going to do next Thursday. The plan that follows will show you how to structure your job search like a job.

Decide How Much Time You Will Spend Looking for Work Each Week and Day

First and most importantly, decide how many hours you are willing to spend each week on your job search. You should spend a minimum of 25 hours a week on hard-core job search activities with no goofing around. Let me walk you through a simple but effective process to set a job search schedule for each week.

PLAN YOUR JOB SEARCH WEEK

1. How many hours are you willing to spend each week looking for a job? _____

2. Which days of the week will you spend looking for a job? _____

   _____

3. How many hours will you look each day? _____

4. At what times will you begin and end your job search on each of these days? _____

   _____

Create a Specific Daily Job Search Schedule

Having a specific daily schedule is essential because most job seekers find it hard to stay productive each day. The sample daily schedule that follows is the result of years of research into what schedule gets the best results. I tested many schedules in job search programs I ran, and this particular schedule worked best. So use the sample daily schedule for ideas on creating your own, but I urge you to consider using one like this. Why? Because it works.

◆

A Sample Daily Schedule That Works

Time	Activity
7 a.m.	Get up, shower, dress, eat breakfast.
8–8:15 a.m.	Organize work space, review schedule for today's interviews and promised follow-ups, check e-mail, update schedule as needed.
8:15–9 a.m.	Review old leads for follow-up needed today; develop new leads from want ads, yellow pages, the Internet, warm contact lists, and other sources; complete daily contact list.
9–10 a.m.	Make phone calls and set up interviews.
10–10:15 a.m.	Take a break.
10:15–11 a.m.	Make more phone calls, set up more interviews.
11 a.m.–Noon	Send follow-up notes and do other "office" activities as needed.
Noon–1 p.m.	Lunch break, relax.
1–3 p.m.	Go on interviews, make cold contacts in the field.
Evening	Read job search books, make calls to warm contacts not reachable during the day, work on a "better" resume, spend time with friends and family, exercise, relax.

◆

Do It Now: Get a Daily Planner and Write Down Your Job Search Schedule

This is important: If you are not accustomed to using a daily schedule book or electronic planner, promise yourself to get a good one tomorrow. Choose one that allows plenty of space for each day's plan on an hourly basis, plus room for daily to-do listings. Write in your daily schedule in advance; then add interviews as they come. Get used to carrying it with you and use it!

Dramatically Improve Your Interviewing Skills

Interviews are where the job search action is. You have to get them; then you have to do well in them. According to surveys of employers, most job seekers do not effectively present the skills they have to do the job. Even worse, most job seekers can't answer one or more problem questions.

This lack of performance in interviews is one reason why employers will often hire a job seeker who does well in the interview over someone with better credentials. The good news is that you can do simple things to dramatically improve your interviewing skills. This section will emphasize interviewing tips and techniques that make the most difference.

Your First Impression May Be the Only One You Make

Some research suggests that if the interviewer forms a negative impression in the first five minutes of an interview, your chances of getting a job offer approach zero. But I know from experience that many job seekers can create a lasting negative impression in seconds. Since a positive first impression is so important, here are some suggestions to help you get off to a good start.

Dress and groom like the interviewer is likely to be dressed—but cleaner! Employer surveys find that almost half of all people's dress or grooming creates an initial negative impression. So this is a big problem. If necessary, get advice on your interviewing outfits from someone who dresses well. Pay close attention to your grooming too—little things do count.

Be early. Leave in plenty of time to be a few minutes early to an interview.

Be friendly and respectful with the receptionist. Doing otherwise will often get back to the interviewer and result in a quick rejection.

Follow the interviewer's lead in the first few minutes. It's often informal small talk but very important for that person to see how you interact. This is a good time to make a positive comment on the organization or even something you see in the office.

Do some homework on the organization before you go. You can often get information on a business and on industry trends from the Internet or a library.

Make a good impression before you arrive. Your resume, e-mails, applications, and other written correspondence create an impression before the interview, so make them professional and error-free.

A Traditional Interview Is Not a Friendly Exchange

In a traditional interview situation, there is a job opening, and you will be one of several applicants for it. In this setting, the employer's task is to eliminate all applicants but one. The interviewer's questions are designed to elicit information that can be used to screen you out. And your objective is to avoid getting screened out. It's hardly an open and honest interaction, is it?

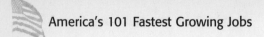

This illustrates yet another advantage of setting up interviews before an opening exists. This eliminates the stress of a traditional interview. Employers are not trying to screen you out, and you are not trying to keep them from finding out stuff about you.

Having said that, knowing how to answer questions that might be asked in a traditional interview is good preparation for any interview you face.

How to Answer Tough Interview Questions

Your answers to a few key problem questions may determine if you get a job offer. There are simply too many possible interview questions to cover one by one. Instead, the 10 basic questions below cover variations of most other interview questions. So, if you can learn to answer these 10 questions well, you will know how to answer most others.

◆

Top 10 Problem Interview Questions

1. Why should I hire you?

2. Why don't you tell me about yourself?

3. What are your major strengths?

4. What are your major weaknesses?

5. What sort of pay do you expect to receive?

6. How does your previous experience relate to the jobs we have here?

7. What are your plans for the future?

8. What will your former employer (or references) say about you?

9. Why are you looking for this type of position, and why here?

10. Why don't you tell me about your personal situation?

◆

The Three-Step Process for Answering Interview Questions

I know this might seem too simple, but the three-step process is easy to remember and can help you create a good answer to most interview questions. The technique has worked for thousands of people, so consider trying it. The three steps are

1. Understand what is really being asked.

2. Answer the question briefly.

3. Answer the real concern.

Step 1. Understand what is really being asked. Most questions are designed to find out about your self-management skills and personality, but interviewers are rarely this blunt. The employer's *real* question is often one or more of the following:

◆ Can I depend on you?

◆ Are you easy to get along with?

◆ Are you a good worker?

◆ Do you have the experience and training to do the job if we hire you?

◆ Are you likely to stay on the job for a reasonable period of time and be productive?

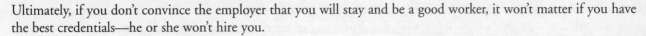

Ultimately, if you don't convince the employer that you will stay and be a good worker, it won't matter if you have the best credentials—he or she won't hire you.

Step 2. Answer the question briefly. Present the facts of your particular work experience, but...

◆ Present them as advantages, not disadvantages.

Many interview questions encourage you to provide negative information. One classic question I included in my list of Top 10 Problem Interview Questions was "What are your major weaknesses?" This is obviously a trick question, and many people are just not prepared for it.

A good response is to mention something that is not very damaging, such as *"I have been told that I am a perfectionist, sometimes not delegating as effectively as I might."* But your answer is not complete until you continue with Step 3.

Step 3. Answer the real concern by presenting your related skills.

◆ Base your answer on the key skills you have that support the job, and give examples to support these skills.

For example, an employer might say to a recent graduate, "We were looking for someone with more experience in this field. Why should we consider you?" Here is one possible answer:

"I'm sure there are people who have more experience, but I do have more than six years of work experience, including three years of advanced training and hands-on experience using the latest methods and techniques. Because my training is recent, I am open to new ideas and am used to working hard and learning quickly."

In the previous example (about your need to delegate), a good skills statement might be

"I've been working on this problem and have learned to let my staff do more, making sure that they have good training and supervision. I've found that their performance improves, and it frees me up to do other things."

Whatever your situation, learn to answer questions that present you well. It's essential to communicate your skills during an interview, and the three-step process can help you answer problem questions and dramatically improve your responses. It works!

The Most Important Interview Question of All: "Why Should I Hire You?"

This is the most important question of all to answer well. Do you have a convincing argument why someone should hire you over someone else? If you don't, you probably won't get that job you really want. So think carefully about why someone *should* hire you and practice your response. Then, make sure you communicate this in the interview, even if the interviewer never asks the question in a clear way.

Tips on Negotiating Pay—How to Earn a Thousand Dollars a Minute

Remember these few essential ideas when it comes time to negotiate your pay.

THE ONLY TIME TO NEGOTIATE IS AFTER YOU HAVE BEEN OFFERED THE JOB.

Employers want to know how much you want to be paid so that they can eliminate you from consideration. They figure if you want too much, you won't be happy with their job and won't stay. And if you will take too little, they may think you don't have enough experience. So *never* discuss your salary expectations until an employer offers you the job.

IF PRESSED, SPEAK IN TERMS OF WIDE PAY RANGES.

If you are pushed to reveal your pay expectations early in an interview, ask the interviewer what the normal pay range is for this job. Interviewers will often tell you, and you can say that you would consider offers in this range.

If you are forced to be more specific, speak in terms of a wide pay range. For example, if you figure that the company will likely pay from $20,000 to $25,000 a year, say that you would consider "any fair offer in the low to mid-twenties." This statement covers the employer's range *and goes a bit higher*. If all else fails, tell the interviewer that you would consider any reasonable offer.

For this to work, you must know in advance what the job is likely to pay. You can get this information by asking people who do similar work, or from a variety of books and Internet sources of career information.

SALARY NEGOTIATION RULE
THE ONE WHO NAMES A SPECIFIC NUMBER FIRST, LOSES.

Don't Say "No" Too Quickly

Never, ever turn down a job offer during an interview! Instead, thank the interviewer for the offer and ask to consider the offer overnight. You can turn it down tomorrow, saying how much you appreciate the offer and asking to be considered for other jobs that pay better or whatever.

But this is no time to be playing games. If you want the job, you should say so. And it is okay to ask for additional pay or other concessions. But if you simply can't accept the offer, say why and ask the interviewer to keep you in mind for future opportunities. You just never know.

Follow Up on All Contacts

It's a fact: People who follow up with potential employers and with others in their network get jobs faster than those who do not. Here are a few rules to guide you in your job search.

Rules for Effective Follow-Up

- ◆ Send a thank-you note or e-mail to every person who helps you in your job search.
- ◆ Send the note within 24 hours after speaking with the person.
- ◆ Enclose JIST Cards with thank-you notes and all other correspondence.
- ◆ Develop a system to keep following up with good contacts.

Thank-You Notes Make a Difference

While thank-you notes can be e-mailed, most people appreciate and are more impressed by a mailed note. Here are some tips about mailed thank-you notes that you can easily adapt to e-mail use.

Thank-you notes can be handwritten or typed on quality paper and matching envelopes. Keep them simple, neat, and error-free. And make sure to include a few copies of your JIST Cards. Here is an example of a simple thank-you note.

2244 Riverwood Avenue
Philadelphia, PA 17963
April 16, XXXX

Ms. Helen A. Colcord
Henderson & Associates, Inc.
1801 Washington Blvd., Suite 1201
Philadelphia, PA 17993

Dear Ms. Colcord:

Thank you for sharing your time with me so generously today. I really appreciated seeing your state-of-the-art computer equipment.

Your advice has already proved helpful. I have an appointment to meet with Mr. Robert Hopper on Friday. As you anticipated, he does intend to add more computer operators in the next few months.

In case you think of someone else who might need a person like me, I'm enclosing another JIST Card. I will let you know how the interview with Mr. Hopper goes.

Sincerely,

William Henderson

William Henderson

Use Job Lead Cards to Help Organize Follow-Ups

If you use contact management software, use it to schedule follow-up activities. But the simple paper system I describe here can work very well or can be adapted for setting up your contact management software.

Use a simple 3-by-5–inch card to record essential information about each person in your network. Buy a 3-by-5–inch card file box and tabs for each day of the month. File the cards under the date you want to contact the person, and the rest is easy.

I've found that staying in touch with a good contact every other week can pay off big. Here's a sample card to give you ideas about creating your own.

Organization: **Mutual Health Insurance**
Contact person: **Anna Tomey**
Phone number: **(555) 555-2211**
Source of lead: **Aunt Ruth**
Notes: **4/10 called. Anna on vacation. Call back 4/15. 4/15 Interview set 4/20 at 1:30. 4/20 Anna showed me around. They use the same computers we used in school. Sent thank-you note and JIST Card. Call back 5/1. 5/1 Second interview 5/8 at 9 a.m.**

In Closing

You won't get a job offer because someone knocks on your door and offers one. Job seeking does involve luck, but you are more likely to get lucky if you are out getting interviews.

I'll close this minibook with a few final tips:

- Approach your job search as if it were a job itself. Create and stick to a daily schedule, and spend at least 25 hours a week looking.

- Follow up on each lead you generate and ask each one for referrals.

- Set out each day to schedule at least two interviews, and use the new definition of an interview, which includes talking to businesses that don't have an opening now.

- Send out lots of thank-you notes and JIST Cards.

- When you want the job, tell the employer that you want it and why the company should hire you over someone else.

Don't get discouraged. There are lots of jobs out there, and someone needs an employee with your skills—your job is to find that someone.

I wish you luck in your job search and your life.

ESSENTIAL JOB SEARCH DATA WORKSHEET

Take some time to complete this worksheet carefully. It will help you write your resume and answer interview questions. You can also photocopy it and take it with you to help complete applications and as a reference throughout your job search. Use an erasable pen or pencil to allow for corrections. Whenever possible, emphasize skills and accomplishments that support your ability to do the job you want. Use extra sheets as needed.

Your name _____

Date completed _____

Job objective _____

Key Accomplishments

List three accomplishments that best prove your ability to do the kind of job you want.

1. _____

2. _____

3. _____

Education and Training

Name of high school(s); years attended _____
_____

Subjects related to job objective _____
_____

Related extracurricular activities/hobbies/leisure activities_____
_____

Accomplishments/things you did well _____
_____

Specific things you can do as a result _____
_____

Schools you attended after high school; years attended; degrees/certificates earned _____
_____

Courses related to job objective _____
_____

Related extracurricular activities/hobbies/leisure activities_____
_____

Accomplishments/things you did well _____
_____

Specific things you can do as a result _____
_____

Other Training

Include formal or informal learning, workshops, military training, things you learned on the job or from hobbies—anything that will help support your job objective. Include specific dates, certificates earned, or other details as needed. _____
_____
_____
_____

Work and Volunteer History

List your most recent job first, followed by each previous job. Military experience, unpaid or volunteer work, and work in a family business should be included here, too. If needed, use additional sheets to cover *all* significant paid or unpaid work experiences. Emphasize details that will help support your new job objective! Include numbers to support what you did: the number of people served over one or more years,

(continued)

the number of transactions processed, percentage of sales increased, total inventory value you were responsible for, payroll of the staff you supervised, total budget responsible for, and so on. Emphasize results you achieved, using numbers to support them whenever possible. Mentioning these things on your resume and in an interview will help you get the job you want!

Job 1

Dates employed _____

Name of organization _____

Supervisor's name and job title _____

Address _____

_____

Phone number/e-mail address/Web site _____

_____

What did you accomplish and do well? _____

_____

Things you learned, skills you developed or used _____

_____

Raises, promotions, positive evaluations, awards _____

_____

Computer software, hardware, and other equipment you used _____

_____

Other details that might support your job objective _____

_____

Job 2

Dates employed _____

Name of organization _____

Supervisor's name and job title _____

Address _____

_____

Phone number/e-mail address/Web site _____

_____

What did you accomplish and do well? _____

_____

Things you learned, skills you developed or used _____

_____

Raises, promotions, positive evaluations, awards _____

_____

Computer software, hardware, and other equipment you used _____

_____

Other details that might support your job objective _____

_____

Job 3

Dates employed _____

Name of organization _____

Supervisor's name and job title _____

Address _____

_____

Phone number/e-mail address/Web site _____

_____

What did you accomplish and do well? _____

_____

Things you learned, skills you developed or used _____

_____

Raises, promotions, positive evaluations, awards _____

_____

Computer software, hardware, and other equipment you used _____

_____

Other details that might support your job objective _____

_____

References

Think of people who know your work well and will say positive things about your work and character. Past supervisors are best. Contact them and tell them what type of job you want and your qualifications, and ask what they will say about you if contacted by a potential employer. Some employers will not provide references by phone, so ask them for a letter of reference for you in advance. If a past employer may say negative things, negotiate what they will say or get written references from others you worked with there.

(continued)

Reference name _____

Position or title _____

Relationship to you _____

Contact information (complete address, phone number, e-mail address) _____

_____

Reference name _____

Position or title _____

Relationship to you _____

Contact information (complete address, phone number, e-mail address) _____

_____

_____

Reference name _____

Position or title _____

Relationship to you _____

Contact information (complete address, phone number, e-mail address) _____

_____

_____

A Short List of Additional Resources

Thousands of books and uncounted Internet sites provide information on career subjects. Space limitations do not permit me to describe the many good resources available, so I list here some of the most useful ones. Because this is my list, I've included books I've written or that JIST publishes. You should be able to find these and many other resources at libraries, bookstores, and Web book-selling sites, such as www.jist.com and www.amazon.com.

Resumes and Cover Letter Books

My books. I'm told that *The Quick Resume & Cover Letter Book* is now one of the top-selling resume books at various large bookstore chains. It is very simple to follow, is inexpensive, has good design, and has good sample resumes written by professional resume writers. *America's Top Resumes for America's Top Jobs* includes a wonderfully diverse collection of resumes covering most major jobs and life situations, plus brief but helpful resume-writing advice. With its helpful worksheets and expert samples, *Same-Day Resume* can help you write a great resume quickly so you can get on with your job search.

Other books published by JIST. The following titles include many sample resumes written by professional resume writers, as well as good advice: *Cover Letter Magic,* by Enelow and Kursmark; *Cyberspace Resume Kit,* Nemnich and Jandt; *The Edge Resume & Job Search Strategy,* Corbin and Wright; *Federal Resume Guidebook,* Troutman; *Expert Resumes for Computer and Web Jobs,* Enelow and Kursmark; *Expert Resumes for Teachers and Educators,* Enelow and Kursmark; *Gallery of Best Cover Letters,* Noble; *Gallery of Best Resumes,* Noble; and *Resume Magic,* Whitcomb.

Job Search Books

My books. *The Very Quick Job Search—Get a Better Job in Half the Time* is a thorough book with detailed advice and a "quick" section of key tips you can finish in a few hours. *The Quick Interview & Salary Negotiation Book* also has a section of quick tips likely to make the biggest difference in your job search, as well as sections with more detailed information on problem questions and other topics. *Getting the Job You Really Want* includes many in-the-book activities and good career decision-making and job search advice.

Other books published by JIST. Titles include *Career Success Is Color-Blind*, Stevenson; *Cyberspace Job Search Kit*, Nemnich and Jandt; *Inside Secrets of Finding a Teaching Job*, Warner and Bryan; and *Job Search Handbook for People with Disabilities*, Ryan.

Books with Information on Jobs

Primary references. The *Occupational Outlook Handbook* is the source of job titles listed in this minibook. Published by the U.S. Department of Labor and updated every other year, the *OOH* covers about 88 percent of the workforce. A book titled the *O*NET Dictionary of Occupational Titles* has descriptions for over 1,100 jobs based on the O*NET (for Occupational Information Network) database developed by the Department of Labor. The *Enhanced Occupational Outlook Handbook* includes the *OOH* descriptions plus more than 7,000 additional descriptions of related jobs from the O*NET and other sources. The *Guide for Occupational Exploration,* Third Edition, allows you to explore major jobs based on your interests. All of these books are available from JIST.

Other books published by JIST. Here are a few good books that include job descriptions and helpful details on career options: *America's 101 Fastest Growing Jobs; America's Top 101 Jobs for College Graduates; America's Top 101 Jobs for People Without a Four-Year Degree; America's Top 101 Computer and Technical Jobs; America's Top Medical, Education & Human Services Jobs; America's Top White-Collar Jobs; Best Jobs for the 21st Century* (plus versions for people with and without degrees); *Career Guide to America's Top Industries;* and *Guide to America's Federal Jobs.*

Internet Resources

If the Internet is new to you, I recommend a book titled *Cyberspace Job Search Kit* by Mary Nemnich and Fred Jandt. It covers the basics plus offers advice on using the Internet for career planning and job seeking. *Best Career and Education Web Sites* by Rachel Singer Gordon and Anne Wolfinger gives excellent reviews of the most helpful sites and ideas on how to use them. The *Occupational Outlook Handbook*'s job descriptions also include Internet addresses. And www.jist.com lists recommended sites for career, education, and related topics, along with comments on each.

Be aware that some sites provide poor advice, so ask your librarian, instructor, or counselor for suggestions on those best for your needs.

Other Resources

Libraries. Most libraries have the books mentioned here, as well as many other resources. Many also provide Internet access so that you can research online information. Ask the librarian for help finding what you need.

People. People who hold the jobs that interest you are one of the best career information sources. Ask them what they like and don't like about their work, how they got started, and the education or training needed. Most people are helpful and will give advice you can't get any other way.

Career counseling. A good vocational counselor can help you explore career options. Take advantage of this service if it is available to you! Also consider a career-planning course or program, which will encourage you to be more thorough in your thinking.

Sample Resumes for Some of America's Fastest Growing Jobs

If you read the previous information in this section, you know that I believe that resumes are an overrated job search tool. Even so, you will probably need one, and you should have a good one.

Unlike some career authors, I do not preach that there is only one right way to do a resume. I encourage you to be an individual and to do what you think will work well for you. But I also know that some resumes are clearly better than others. The following pages contain several resumes that you can use as examples when preparing your own resume.

The resumes have these points in common:

- ◆ Each is for an occupation described in this book. The resumes are arranged in alphabetical order by job title.

- ◆ Each resume is particularly good in some way.

- ◆ Each resume was written by a professional resume writer who is a member of one or more professional associations, including the Professional Association of Resume Writers (www.parw.com) or the National Resume Writers' Association (www.nrwa.com). These writers are highly qualified and hold various credentials. Most are willing to provide help (for a fee) and welcome your contacting them (although this is not a personal endorsement).

The resumes are from the following six books, all available from JIST Publishing:

- ◆ *America's Top Resumes for America's Top Jobs,* Second Edition, by Michael Farr with Louise M. Kursmark
- ◆ *Best Resumes for College Students and New Grads,* by Louise M. Kursmark
- ◆ *Expert Resumes for Computer and Web Jobs,* by Wendy S. Enelow and Louise M. Kursmark
- ◆ *Expert Resumes for Health Care Careers,* by Wendy S. Enelow and Louise M. Kursmark
- ◆ *Expert Resumes for Managers and Executives,* by Wendy S. Enelow and Louise M. Kursmark
- ◆ *Expert Resumes for Teachers and Educators,* by Wendy S. Enelow and Louise M. Kursmark

Contact Information for Resume Contributors

The following professional resume writers contributed resumes to this section. Their names are listed in alphabetical order. Each entry indicates which resume that person contributed.

Diane Burns, CPRW, IJCTC, CCM, CEIP
President, Career Marketing Techniques
5219 Thunder Hill Rd.
Columbia, MD 21045
Phone/Fax: (410) 884-0213
E-mail: dianecprw@aol.com
Web site: www.polishedresumes.com
Resume on page 369

Art Frank
Resumes "R" Us
Palm Harbor, FL
(727) 787-6885
E-mail: AF1134@aol.com
Resume on page 365

Alice Hanson, CPRW
President, Aim Resumes
P.O. Box 75054
Seattle, WA 98125
Phone: (206) 527-3100
Fax: (206) 527-3101
E-mail: alice@aimresume.com
Web site: www.aimresume.com
Resume on page 366

Andrea J. Howard, MS Ed.
Employment Counselor, NYS Department of Labor—Division of
Employment Services
175 Central Ave.
Albany, NY 12054
Phone: (518) 462-7600, ext. 124
E-mail: USAAH3@labor.state.ny.us
Web site: www.labor.state.ny.us
Resumes on pages 367 and 370

William Kinser, CPRW, JCTC, CEIP
President, To The Point Resumes
4117 Kentmere Square
Fairfax, VA 22030-6062
Phone: (703) 352-8969
Fax: (703) 352-8969
E-mail: resumes@tothepointresumes.com
Web site: www.tothepointresumes.com
Resume on page 372

Jan Melnik, CPRW, CCM
President, Absolute Advantage
P.O. Box 718
Durham, CT 06422
Phone: (860) 349-0256
Fax: (860) 349-1343
E-mail: CompSPJan@aol.com
Web site: www.janmelnik.com
Resume on page 368

Meg Montford, CCM, CPRW
President, Abilities Enhanced
P.O. Box 9667
Kansas City, MO 64134
Phone: (816) 767-1196
Fax: (801) 650-8529
E-mail: meg@abilitiesenhanced.com
Web site: www.abilitiesenhanced.com
Resume on page 364

Vivian Van Lier, CPRW, JCTC, CEIP
President, Advantage Resume & Career Services
6701 Murietta Ave.
Valley Glen (Los Angeles), CA 91405
Phone: (818) 994-6655
Fax: (818) 994-6620
E-mail: vvanlier@aol.com
Web site: www.CuttingEdgeResumes.com
Resume on page 371

Barbers, Cosmetologists, and Other Personal Appearance Workers

LaTonya Jefferson
500 Maple Street, Apt.103
Kansas City, Missouri 64134
(816) 555-1212
LaTonyaJefferson@email.com

Hair Stylist / Cosmetologist

Accomplished professional dedicated to enhancing client appearance in areas of universal hair care. Proven skills in execution of perfect hair-coloring techniques. Builder of "totally satisfied" customer relationships. Peer mentor and public educator in all facets of cosmetology. Licensed in Kansas and Missouri. PC-competent in MS Word, Excel and the Internet. World traveler fluent in Spanish and French.

Experience

HAIR COLOR SPECIALIST, Spectacular Salon and Day Spa, Mission, KS (6/99 to Present)
Serve 18 clients per day from diverse cultural backgrounds. Participate in hair-show demonstrations.
➤ Acknowledged for highest level of salon retail sales among 10 stylists.
➤ Achieved rank of Head Colorist after only two-year employment period.

ASSISTANT MAKEUP ARTIST, Monique's Boutique Fashion Show, Kansas City, MO (9/99)
➤ Performed makeup and color services for 30 models in this annual event.

Education

INSTRUCTOR TRAINING, Superior School of Hair Styling, Leawood, KS (1999 to 2000)
➤ Completed 300 of the 350 hours required for certification.

CERTIFICATE OF COMPLETION, Midwest College of Cosmetology, Blue Springs, MO (7/98)
➤ Pivot Point Curriculum
➤ Sales Woman of the Month — awarded seven times
➤ Perfect Attendance
➤ Selected courses: Hair Chemistry; Advanced Color; Production Makeup Artist

PROFESSIONAL TRAINING, Heartland College of Beauty Arts, Kansas City, MO (1995 to 1996)
➤ Outstanding Work Award — received three times
➤ Selected courses: Ethnic Hair Care; Hair Weaving and Extensions; Hair Color

Computer Systems Analysts, Database Administrators, and Computer Scientists

Ahmed Malouf

2772 Wesleyan Road, Pinellas Park, FL 34877 — (727) 786-1258 — Mobile (727) 885-1132

OBJECTIVE

Employment with a progressive organization as a **Database Administrator** or **Computer Network Technician.**

EDUCATION

➢ Bachelor of Science, Mechanical Engineering ~ University of Central Florida, 1992
➢ Currently completing course work for Microsoft Certified Systems Engineer (**M.C.S.E.**)
 • **Network Essentials**
 • **Core**
 • **Enterprise**
 • **TCP / IP**

BUSINESS BACKGROUND

11/97-Present   Quick Cash Title Loans, Clearwater, FL   **Database Administrator**
➢ Prior to my employment, company was utilizing a spreadsheet in lieu of a database program. Using Access, I proceeded to create, test, and implement a database.
➢ Creating order out of chaos led to better control and allowed for expansion to 2 other locations, both of which were under my supervision.
➢ Database efficiency allowed for managing $35,000 per month in collections.

01/94-08/94   Integra Medical, Clearwater, FL   **Database Administrator**
➢ Designed, tested, and implemented a database system to record patient histories and track invoice payments, medical tests performed, and records of patient deductibles.
➢ System required extensive interface with various insurance companies such as AIB, AIG, and Fortune Insurance.
➢ Testing was normally performed in Miami, requiring field visits and liaison with software developers. This included downloading programs, making changes to the database management system, testing fixes, and generally bringing software up to speed.

8/94-3/96   Reconditioning Unlimited, Largo, FL   **Design Engineer**
➢ Designed and built automated pneumatic machines.
➢ Machined parts using drill press, lathe, welder, and various other machine shop apparatus.

01/93-08/94   AL&S, Houston, TX   **Assistant Engineer**
This company was a provider of digitized maps and wished to create software packages to market to tourists, car rental agencies, and hotels.
➢ Tested and designed software packages and worked with software designers to establish a user-friendly environment.
➢ Conducted ongoing training and supervision of 5 to 6 entry-level computer operators.

PERSONAL INTERESTS

Fitness, fishing, skiing, scuba diving

John Carpenter

40 Watertown Street
Binghamton, New York 13747

(607) 666-9999
hammertime@aol.com

Chief Estimator/Project Manager

Qualifications

- **Five years of experience as Chief Estimator and Project Manager.**

- **Fifteen-plus years of local engineering, design and construction expertise** in the upstate New York building industry, preparing bid estimates and managing $300,000 to $3 million construction projects.

- **Senior construction generalist with a diverse skills.** Excel within small construction companies that require "wearing many hats." Proven expertise in business development; project management for both fieldwork and administrative projects; estimating via computer applications; drafting and architectural drawing; and management of shop, carpentry and millworking operations.

- **Innovative information manager.** Repeatedly automated bidding and construction processes for past employers, increasing production and decreasing overhead. Advanced user:

  AutoCAD version 10, Generic CAD version 6, Construction Management Systems estimating software, Super Project, Varco Pruden, VP Command building design and drafting program, Novell Networking, Access, Excel, Lotus 1-2-3, Microsoft Office, GTCO digitizer tablets and HP Draft Pro Plotter.

Education and Credentials

A.A.S. Degree, Construction Technology: State University of New York, Canton College, 1984
Certified Engineer Technician: A.S.C.E.T. Professional Engineering Society.

Estimating Experience

Estimator and Project Manager   1999 — present
JAMES SMITH AND SONS CONTRACTING COMPANY, Vestal, New York
Utilize in-depth knowledge of project costs, purchasing, construction techniques and technology, and local construction services market to estimate and manage large construction projects.

- Bid and supported 4 major contract wins in FY2001, cumulatively valued at $6 million.
- Manage estimating projects that generated over $10,000 per month in gross sales FY2001.
- As chief estimator, identify upcoming opportunities and generate 3–4 project estimates a month.
- Win 1 of every 3 estimates the company decides to submit.
- Manage a millwork shop generating $400,000 in annual gross sales with 30% net profits.

Chief Estimator and Project Manager   1994 — 1999
ARCHER AND SONS, Binghamton, New York
Prepared estimates, assisted proposal and business development team, and managed major construction projects throughout New York State.

- Projects included: The Marriott Hotel, Cornell University; The Law School Renovation Project, Cornell University; various Taco Time Restaurants; and school building upgrades in upstate New York.
- All projects came in on time, within 10% of originally prepared cost estimates.

Estimator/AutoCAD Drafter
WAY-LAN CONSTRUCTION COMPANY, INC., Binghamton, New York   1985 — 1993

Physical Therapists

JILLIAN G. SLATTERY

7 Hill Crest Drive
Selkirk, NY 12158

518.653.2748
JillS@hotmail.com

QUALIFICATIONS SUMMARY

Professional **Physical Therapist** with 11 years of rehabilitative care experience in hospitals, geriatric facilities, and private agencies. ❖ Skilled in effective communication with physicians, patients, family members, Medicare, and insurance companies. ❖ Maximized the number of patients served by effectively meeting scheduling and facility limitation challenges. ❖ Recognized by management for thoroughness, efficiency, and sensitivity to patient needs on numerous occasions.

PHYSICAL THERAPY EMPLOYMENT

PHYSICAL THERAPIST, 1993–2003

Albany Veterans Hospital	Albany, NY	1999–2003
Albany Memorial Hospital	Albany, NY	1995–1999
County Nursing Facility	Schenectady, NY	1994–1995
Independent Living Associates	Rochester, NY	1992–1994

❖ Highly effective in diagnosing and preparing treatment plans for patients living with neurological and geriatric orthopedic conditions, resulting in increased independence. Heavily involved with designing discharge plans and follow-up instructions.

❖ Performed prosthetic training with amputee patients. Knowledgeable in E-STEM for wound healing and pain management, and with knee and hip replacement. Experience with technologies and techniques required for effective treatment of cardiac rehabilitation, sports injuries, and cervical and pelvic traction. Used ultrasound, gait belt training equipment, thera-bands, swimming pools, stretching exercises, and hot and cold packs.

❖ Trained PTAs, CNAs, and family members in infection control, injury prevention, and proper rehabilitative care, including wheelchair positioning, proper use of exercise equipment, and how to assist the patient without affecting independence or self-confidence.

EDUCATION & TRAINING

BS — PHYSICAL THERAPY, 1992
Russell Sage College, Troy, NY

❖ Clinical fieldwork conducted in rehabilitation centers and long-term-care facilities operated by the New York State Department of Health.

❖ GPA: 3.47

Extensive list of Certifications and Trainings available for review.

Andrea J. Ruiz

4793 Hopewell Avenue
Meriden, CT 06450
(203) 555-1010 • ajruiz@aol.com

Qualifications Summary

Accomplished and motivated **Senior Retail Sales Associate** with 5+ years' exemplary experience and performance track record characterized by continued advancement into positions of increased visibility.
- Expert organizational skills, highly effective assessment and analytical skills, and key strategic planning ability.
- Broad range of operational experience includes sales, marketing, merchandising, sales analysis, public/vendor relations, markdowns, inventory control, and shrinkage.
- Strong leadership skills and ability to train new staff.
- PC skills include Windows, Excel, and Microsoft Word; bilingual (fluent in English and Spanish).

Core Competencies
- Dynamic Assortment-Building and Planning
- Quick Problem-Solving
- Accomplishment, Goal-Oriented Approach
- Merchandising Presentation Expertise
- Expert Negotiation Ability
- Key Decision-Making Skills
- Vendor Relation Skills
- Savvy Assessment Skills

Professional Experience

1999–Present   J.C. PENNEY • Trumbull, CT
Senior Sales Associate *(promotion, 3/2000–Present)*
- Handle retail sales of Men's Sportswear; coordinate wardrobes and provide professional advice.
- Achieved "Selling Star for the Month" award, three consecutive months.
- Recipient of customer commendation letter and award pins recognizing exemplary customer service.
- Consistently exceed monthly goal for opening new customer charge accounts.
- Collaborate with Merchandising Manager in revamping department, coordinating fashion shows, and increasing traffic/exposure.

Sales Associate *(5/1999–3/2000)*
- Top producer in both American Woman and Ladies' Accessories departments.

1996–1999   LORD & TAYLOR • West Hartford, CT
Sales Associate *(part-time during academic year; full-time summers/vacations)*
- Ranked top floater among part-time staff; adept in quickly learning new departments.
- Named among top 3 sales associates in each department (Girls' Sportswear, Children's, Men's, Ladies', Home Boutique).

Education   TRINITY COLLEGE • Hartford, CT
Bachelor of Art Degree, History *(1999)* — Concentrations: Design and Photography
- Recipient of Parson's award for outstanding leadership.

Continuing Professional Education includes successful completion of corporate training programs in such topical areas as leadership/supervision, communication skills, mentoring, merchandising, motivational skills, and teamwork.

Security Guards and Gaming Surveillance Officers

Allen Michaels

1290 River Walk Dr. ◆ Ocean City, MD 21045
(410) 884.5555 ◆ Email: allen@hotmail.com

SECURITY GUARD

Physical ◆ Industrial ◆ Facility ◆ Personal

EDUCATION

AA Degree in Business, Howard Community College, Maryland
February 2002

Self-defense Courses, Ocean City PD
1994 to Present

EXPERIENCE

University of Maryland Physics Laboratory, Baltimore, Maryland   1998 to Present
Security Officer (DoD Contractor, SECRET Clearance)

- ◆ Manage two large security databases for 20,000 personnel (input and access information).
- ◆ Control the movement of property and personnel into and out of the facility. Verify government clearances and determine entry rights.
- ◆ Observe facilities for security violations.
- ◆ Respond to and investigate incidents and accidents; draft detailed reports.
- ◆ Escort visitors.
- ◆ Manage emergency calls and dispatch fire, police, or medical assistance as required.

Independent Contractor   1994 to Present
Personal Protective Services & Trainer

- ◆ Accept independent contracts to protect individuals. Drive personal vehicles and monitor the activities of clients. Ensure that clients are not disturbed, harassed, or otherwise bothered in public locations.
- ◆ Install personal home security systems.
- ◆ Conduct one-to-one classes in self-defense techniques including the use of deadly force and such weapons/aids as pepper spray.

U.S. Army, Italy and Macedonia   1994 to 1998
Security Guard

- ◆ Managed security requirements for a base: Controlled entry to and exit from restricted-access areas. Searched individuals, vehicles, and materials. Escorted authorized personnel.
- ◆ Effectively moved an arms room to the field. Inventoried, moved, and re-set up hundreds of line items of weapons worth over $5M. Operated and maintained 2.5-ton vehicles.
- ◆ Received recognition for superior performance of guard duty during the salvaging of Secretary Don White's plane in Macedonia.

Mary F. Esposito

17 TOWNSAND RD. ★ ALBANY, NY 12208
518-447-3746 / 518-456-2365
MESPOSITO@YAHOO.COM

SUMMARY

Recent **Social Work/Communications** graduate with excellent academic and counseling skills seeks a professional position allowing for continued opportunity to support and assist adolescents. Extensive exposure with prevention, intervention, and emergency-response programs has provided a solid foundation of experience and strength.

ACADEMIC ACCOMPLISHMENTS

Social Work/Communications ~ BA ~ SUNY Albany, Albany, NY ~ May 2002

★ Dean's List ~ GPA 3.43, National Honor Society, *Who's Who Among American College Students.*

YOUTH RELATED EMPLOYMENT

Director of Teen Programs ~ The Albany YMCA ~ Albany, NY ~ 1998–present.

★ Provide guidance and support to pre-teen and teen members by listening and advising. Issues involve peer concerns, questioning of values, parental conflict, and academic frustrations.
★ For the Teen Summer Camp, arranged activities that included canoeing, indoor rock climbing, rollerblading, visits to museums, and a weekend trip to Boston.

Youth Tennis Instructor ~ City of Albany Tennis Camp ~ SUNY Albany ~ Albany, NY ~ 1996–1998

★ Instructed children ages 8 through 18 with differing levels of tennis skill. Teaching methods included individual instruction as well as drills, games, and matches designed to improve the participants' tennis skills.

COUNSELING FIELD WORK

Watervliet Junior High School ~ Watervliet, NY ~ 2001

★ Tutored, mentored, and counseled students assigned by the **Guidance Department.**
★ Worked with the Mentoring and Adventure Programs in an effort to teach communication and team building.

Albany Police Department ~ **Domestic Violence Services Unit** ~ Albany, NY ~ 2000

★ Interviewed crime victims and complainants, took statements, spoke with witnesses, made victim referrals to support and assistance programs, and otherwise assisted officers assigned to the unit.

COMMUNITY INVOLVEMENT

ACT ~ **AIDS Communicating to Teens ~ Troy, NY ~** 1998–present

★ Perform in improvised skits designed to educate audience members about AIDS and how it is transmitted. Stress tolerance and compassion towards those afflicted with HIV and AIDS.

ADDEM ~ **Albany Diocesan Drug Education Ministry ~** Albany, NY ~ 1997–1999

★ Counseled and mentored elementary students to encourage good choices regarding substance abuse.

Voorheesville Fire/EMS Department ~ Voorheesville, NY ~ 1997–present

★ **Firefighter and EMT (NYS certified).** Responded to over 100 fire and EMS calls 5 straight years.

Teachers—Preschool, Kindergarten, Elementary, Middle, and Secondary

DIANNE H. CLARK

15555 Greenbranch Avenue
Valley Glen, California 91403
(818) 555-8724

TEACHER – GRADES K–1

✎ Talented teacher of grades K–1, committed to maintaining high standards of education with emphasis on developing reading skills in pupils.

✎ Thoroughly enjoys working with children and encourages creative expression.

✎ Introduces concepts into curriculum related to life and social skills.

✎ Experienced in assisting student teachers as a mentor.

✎ Received Certificate of Recognition from Los Angeles Unified School District, 1997.

"She has had a wonderful impact on our son's life... We are deeply grateful for her care and concern that children should be not just good readers, but great ones."

Parents of 1ˢᵗ Grader

CREDENTIALS

California Clear Multiple Subjects
CLADD

PROFESSIONAL EXPERIENCE

LOS ANGELES UNIFIED SCHOOL DISTRICT   1993 to Present
Teacher – K–1
MURIETTA ELEMENTARY SCHOOL, Valley Glen, CA
- Provides a warm, supportive environment for developing emotional and social growth.
- Develops lesson plans and implements curriculum featuring age-appropriate activities and geared toward stimulating interest.
- Participates in staff meetings and meets with parents, encouraging a cooperative atmosphere.
- *Student Teachers:* Assigned and trained four.
- *Committees* served on: Library, Roving and Facilities Committees.
- *Grants Received:* The Riordan Foundation Grant for books.

EDUCATION

CALIFORNIA STATE UNIVERSITY, Northridge, CA
B. A. Degree in Liberal Studies, 1992
Teaching Credential, 1993

Continuing Education and Professional Development:

Pre LAS – *Language Assessment Scale*
CLR – *California Learning Record*
EISS – *Early Intervention for Student Success*
Storyline

Literacy
Success in Reading & Writing
Standard Based Instruction
REACH

Top Executives

BUFFY A. CARLTON

1037 Grand Vista Drive • Irving, TX 75039

Home: (972) 831-2435 • Cell: (972) 820-4243 • E-mail: buffycarlton@mailbox.com

EXECUTIVE DIRECTOR

Senior non-profit and educational development specialist with a unique education-industry background, having served effectively in senior management, supervisory, and foundation-administration positions. Demonstrated history of success in creating and implementing comprehensive non-profit funding programs. Adept at developing multimillion-dollar partnerships with corporations and in securing foundation grants.

PROFESSIONAL EXPERIENCE

EDUCATION INNOVATIONS, Dallas, TX   2001–Present
Executive Director for Strategic Alliances

Develop partnerships with non-profit and for-profit organizations that deliver technology-based instruction for this Internet-based, customized network of online learning communities.
Key Achievements:
- Developed a three-year, $2 million financial-literacy program for students through corporate sponsorship.
- Secured a three-year, $1.5 million online homework-assistance program with Mega Corporation.
- Fostered successful partnerships with national newspapers, the Smithsonian Institution, major book publishers, and the U.S. Department of Education.

TEXAS ART GROUP, Dallas, TX   1999–2001
Executive Director

Developed and directed a philanthropic donation program and created innovative national sales events for this internationally renowned, culturally diverse group of more than 100 U.S. and European artists and craftspeople.
Key Achievements:
- Collaborated with non-profit organizations on revenue-producing promotional events at national venues.
- Penetrated new markets through creative approaches in reaching non-traditional markets for art sales.
- Coordinated special gallery events, including a four-day international art sale extravaganza.

NATIONAL ORGANIZATION OF SCHOOL PRINCIPALS (NOSP), Washington, DC   1989–1999
Associate Executive Director

Managed a $15 million annual budget and supervised a staff of 40, among five departments, for this 46,000-member school leadership organization that provides professional development programs to assist students and administrators in the U.S. and abroad.
Key Achievements:
- Generated more than $14 million in corporate contributions within six years.
- Reengineered the $3.3 million travel budget, reducing annual costs by $150,000.
- Launched an NOSP foundation that generated more than $110,000 within six months.
- Recruited corporate partners and jointly designed programs with international organizations.

DISTRICT OF COLUMBIA PUBLIC SCHOOLS, Washington, DC   1970–1989
Principal, Presidential High School (1985–1989)

Promoted through increasingly responsible positions with one of the largest high-school districts in the U.S., serving more than 35,000 students. (Prior positions include the following: Assistant Principal, Guidance Counselor, Vocational Design/Development Specialist, and Teacher.)

EDUCATION

M.Ed., Administration • **B.S., Vocational Education,** Georgetown University, Washington, DC

Section Three

Important Trends in Jobs and Industries

In putting this section together, my objective was to give you a quick review of major labor market trends. To accomplish that, I included two excellent articles and two informative charts that originally appeared in U.S. Department of Labor publications.

The first article is "Tomorrow's Jobs." It provides a superb—and short—review of the major trends that *will* affect your career in the years to come. Read it for ideas on selecting a career path for the long term.

The second article is "Employment Trends in Major Industries." While you may not have thought much about it, the industry you work in is just as important as your occupational choice. This great article will help you learn about the major trends affecting various industries.

The first chart, "High-Paying Occupations with Many Openings, Projected 2002–12," shows median earnings for high-paying occupations that also have a large number of openings, many of which are listed in this book.

The second chart, "Large Metropolitan Areas That Had the Fastest Employment Growth, 1998–2003," lists eleven areas of the United States that experienced a high rate of growth during a period when many areas experienced little employment growth or lost jobs.

Tomorrow's Jobs

Comments

This article, with minor changes, comes from the *Occupational Outlook Handbook* and was written by the U.S. Department of Labor staff. The material provides a good review of major labor market trends, including trends for broad types of occupations and industries.

Much of this article uses 2002 data, the most recent available at press time. By the time it is carefully collected and analyzed, the data used by the Department of Labor is typically several years old. Since labor market trends tend to be gradual, this delay does not affect the material's usefulness.

You may notice that some job titles in this article differ from those used elsewhere in *America's 101 Fastest Growing Jobs*. This is not an error. The material that follows uses a different set of occupations than I used in choosing the jobs this book describes.

Making informed career decisions requires reliable information about opportunities in the future. Opportunities result from the relationships between the population, labor force, and the demand for goods and services.

Population ultimately limits the size of the labor force—individuals working or looking for work—which constrains how much can be produced. Demand for various goods and services determines employment in the industries providing them. Occupational employment opportunities, in turn, result from demand for skills needed within specific industries. Opportunities for medical assistants and other health-care occupations, for example, have surged in response to rapid growth in demand for health services.

Examining the past and projecting changes in these relationships is the foundation of the Occupational Outlook Program. This chapter presents highlights of Bureau of Labor Statistics projections of the labor force and occupational and industry employment that can help guide your career plans.

Population

Population trends affect employment opportunities in a number of ways. Changes in population influence the demand for goods and services. For example, a growing and aging population has increased the demand for health services. Equally important, population changes produce corresponding changes in the size and demographic composition of the labor force.

The U.S. population is expected to increase by 24 million over the 2002–12 period, at a slower rate of growth than during both the 1992–2002 and 1982–92 periods (Chart 1). Continued growth will mean more consumers of goods and services, spurring demand for workers in a wide range of occupations and industries. The effects of population growth on various occupations will differ. The differences are partially accounted for by the age distribution of the future population.

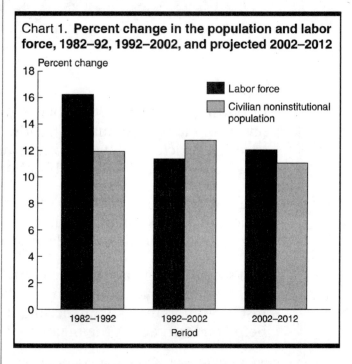

Chart 1. **Percent change in the population and labor force, 1982–92, 1992–2002, and projected 2002–2012**

The youth population, aged 16 to 24, will grow 7 percent over the 2002–12 period. As the baby boomers continue to age, the group aged 55 to 64 will increase by 43.6 percent or 11.5 million persons, more than any other group. Those aged 35 to 44 will decrease in size, reflecting the birth dearth following the baby boom generation.

Minorities and immigrants will constitute a larger share of the U.S. population in 2012. The number of Hispanics is projected to continue to grow much faster than those of all other racial and ethnic groups.

Labor Force

Population is the single most important factor in determining the size and composition of the labor force—that is, people who are either working or looking for work. The civilian labor force is projected to increase by 17.4 million, or 12 percent, to 162.3 million over the 2002–12 period.

The U.S. workforce will become more diverse by 2012. White, non-Hispanic persons will continue to make up a decreasing share of the labor force, falling from 71.3 percent in 2002 to 65.5 percent in 2012 (Chart 2). However, despite relatively slow growth, white, non-Hispanics will remain the largest group in the labor force in 2012. Hispanics are projected to account for an increasing share of the labor force by 2012, growing from 12.4 to 14.7 percent. By 2012, Hispanics will constitute a larger proportion of the labor force than will blacks, whose share will grow from 11.4 percent to 12.2 percent. Asians will continue to be the fastest growing of the four labor force groups.

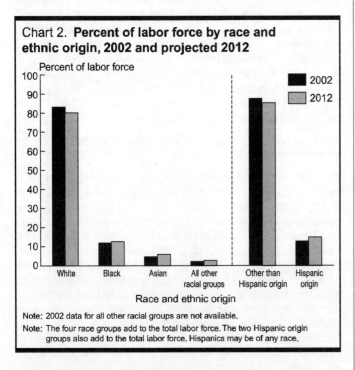

Chart 2. **Percent of labor force by race and ethnic origin, 2002 and projected 2012**

Note: 2002 data for all other racial groups are not available.
Note: The four race groups add to the total labor force. The two Hispanic origin groups also add to the total labor force. Hispanics may be of any race.

The numbers of men and women in the labor force will grow, but the number of women will grow at a faster rate than the number of men. The male labor force is projected to grow by 10 percent from 2002 to 2012, compared with 14.3 percent for women. As a result, men's share of the labor force is expected to decrease from 53.5 to 52.5 percent, while women's share is expected to increase from 46.5 to 47.5 percent.

The youth labor force, aged 16 to 24, is expected to slightly decrease its share of the labor force to 15 percent by 2012. The primary working age group, between 25 and 54 years

old, is projected to decline from 70.2 percent of the labor force in 2002 to 65.9 percent by 2012. Workers 55 and older, on the other hand, are projected to increase from 14.3 percent to 19.1 percent of the labor force between 2002 and 2012, due to the aging of the baby-boom generation (Chart 3).

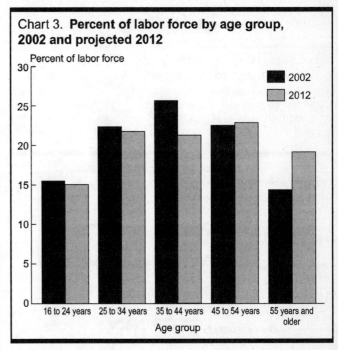

Chart 3. **Percent of labor force by age group, 2002 and projected 2012**

Employment

Total employment is expected to increase from 144 million in 2002 to 165 million in 2012, or by 14.8 percent. The 21 million jobs that will be added by 2012 will not be evenly distributed across major industrial and occupational groups. Changes in consumer demand, technology, and many other factors will contribute to the continually changing employment structure in the U.S. economy.

The following two sections examine projected employment change from both industrial and occupational perspectives. The industrial profile is discussed in terms of primary wage and salary employment. Primary employment excludes secondary jobs for those who hold multiple jobs. The exception is employment in agriculture, which includes self-employed and unpaid family workers in addition to wage and salary workers.

The occupational profile is viewed in terms of total employment—including primary and secondary jobs for wage and salary, self-employed, and unpaid family workers. Of the nearly 144 million jobs in the U.S. economy in 2002, wage and salary workers accounted for 132 million; self-employed workers accounted for 11.5 million; and unpaid family workers accounted for about 140,000. Secondary employment accounted for 1.7 million jobs. Self-employed workers held 9 out of 10 secondary jobs; wage and salary workers held most of the remainder.

Industry

Service-providing industries. The long-term shift from goods-producing to service-providing employment is expected to continue. Service-providing industries are expected to account for approximately 20.8 million of the 21.6 million new wage and salary jobs generated over the 2002–12 period (Chart 4).

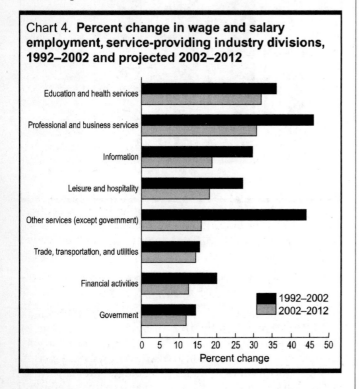

Chart 4. **Percent change in wage and salary employment, service-providing industry divisions, 1992–2002 and projected 2002–2012**

Education and health services. This industry supersector is projected to grow faster—31.8 percent—and add more jobs than any other industry supersector. About 1 out of every 4 new jobs created in the U.S. economy will be in either the healthcare and social assistance or private educational services sectors.

Healthcare and social assistance—including private hospitals, nursing and residential care facilities, and individual and family services—will grow by 32.4 percent and add 4.4 million new jobs. Employment growth will be driven by increasing demand for healthcare and social assistance because of an aging population and longer life expectancies. Also, as more women enter the labor force, demand for childcare services is expected to grow.

Private educational services will grow by 28.7 percent and add 759,000 new jobs through 2012. Rising student enrollments at all levels of education will create demand for educational services.

Professional and business services. This group will grow by 30.4 percent and add nearly 5 million new jobs. This industry supersector includes some of the fastest growing industries in the U.S. economy.

Employment in administrative and support and waste management and remediation services will grow by 37 percent and add 2.8 million new jobs to the economy by 2012. The fastest growing industry in this sector will be employment services, which will grow by 54.3 percent and will contribute almost two-thirds of all new jobs in administrative and support and waste management and remediation services. Employment services ranks among the fastest growing industries in the nation and is expected to be among those that provide the most new jobs.

Employment in professional, scientific, and technical services will grow by 27.8 percent and add 1.9 million new jobs by 2012. Employment in computer systems design and related services will grow by 54.6 percent and add more than one-third of all new jobs in professional, scientific, and technical services. Employment growth will be driven by the increasing reliance of businesses on information technology and the continuing importance of maintaining system and network security. Management, scientific, and technical consulting services also will grow very rapidly, by 55.4 percent, spurred by the increased use of new technology and computer software and the growing complexity of business.

Management of companies and enterprises will grow by 11.4 percent and add 195,000 new jobs.

Information. Employment in the information supersector is expected to increase by 18.5 percent, adding 632,000 jobs by 2012. Information contains some of the fast growing computer-related industries such as software publishers; Internet publishing and broadcasting; and Internet service providers, Web search portals, and data processing services. Employment in these industries is expected to grow by 67.9 percent, 41.1 percent, and 48.2 percent, respectively. The information supersector also includes telecommunications; broadcasting; and newspaper, periodical, book, and directory publishers. Increased demand for residential and business land-line and wireless services, cable service, high-speed Internet connections, and software will fuel job growth among these industries.

Leisure and hospitality. Overall employment will grow by 17.8 percent. Arts, entertainment, and recreation will grow by 28 percent and add 497,000 new jobs by 2012. Most of these new job openings will come from the amusement, gambling, and recreation sector. Job growth will stem from public participation in arts, entertainment, and recreation activities—reflecting increasing incomes, leisure time, and awareness of the health benefits of physical fitness.

Accommodation and food services is expected to grow by 16.1 percent and add 1.6 million new jobs through 2012.

Job growth will be concentrated in food services and drinking places, reflecting increases in population, dual-income families, and dining sophistication.

Trade, transportation, and utilities. Overall employment in this industry supersector will grow by 14.1 percent between 2002 and 2012. Transportation and warehousing is expected to increase by 914,000 jobs, or by 21.7 percent, through 2012. Truck transportation will grow by 20.5 percent, adding 275,000 new jobs, while rail and water transportation are both projected to decline. The warehousing and storage and the couriers and messengers industries are projected to grow rapidly at 28.6 percent and 41.7 percent, respectively. Demand for truck transportation and warehousing services will expand as many manufacturers concentrate on their core competencies and contract out their product transportation and storage functions.

Employment in retail trade is expected to increase by 13.8 percent, from 15 million to 17.1 million. Increases in population, personal income, and leisure time will contribute to employment growth in this industry, as consumers demand more goods. Wholesale trade is expected to increase by 11.3 percent, growing from 5.6 million to 6.3 million jobs.

Employment in utilities is projected to decrease by 5.7 percent through 2012. Despite increased output, employment in electric power generation, transmission, and distribution and natural gas distribution is expected to decline through 2012 due to improved technology that increases worker productivity. However, employment in water, sewage, and other systems is expected to increase 46.4 percent by 2012. Jobs are not easily eliminated by technological gains in this industry because water treatment and waste disposal are very labor-intensive activities.

Financial activities. Employment is projected to grow 12.3 percent over the 2002–12 period. Real estate and rental and leasing is expected to grow by 18.4 percent and add 374,000 jobs by 2012. Growth will be due, in part, to increased demand for housing as the population grows. The fastest growing industry in the financial activities supersector will be commercial and industrial machinery and equipment rental and leasing, which will grow by 39.8 percent.

Finance and insurance is expected to increase by 590,000 jobs, or 10.2 percent, by 2012. Employment in securities, commodity contracts, and other financial investments and related activities is expected to grow 15.5 percent by 2012, reflecting the increased number of baby boomers in their peak savings years, the growth of tax-favorable retirement plans, and the globalization of the securities markets. Employment in credit intermediation and related services, including banks, will grow by 10.9 percent and add about half of all new jobs within finance and insurance. Insurance carriers and related activities is expected to grow by 7.5 percent and add 168,000 new jobs by 2012. The number of jobs within agencies, brokerages, and other insurance-related activities is expected to grow about 14.5 percent as many insurance carriers downsize their sales staffs and as agents set up their own businesses.

Government. Between 2002 and 2012, government employment, including that in public education and hospitals, is expected to increase by 11.8 percent, from 21.5 million to 24 million jobs. Growth in government employment will be fueled by growth in state and local educational services and the shift of responsibilities from the federal government to the state and local governments. Local government educational services is projected to increase 17.5 percent, adding over 1.3 million jobs. State government educational services also is projected to grow 17.5 percent, adding 388,000 jobs. Federal government employment, including the Postal Service, is expected to increase by less than 1 percent as the federal government continues to contract out many government jobs to private companies.

Other services (except government). Employment will grow by 15.7 percent. More than 4 out of 10 new jobs in this supersector will be in religious organizations, which are expected to grow by 24.4 percent. Personal care services will be the fastest growing industry at 27.6 percent. Also included among other services is private household employment, which is expected to decrease 7.2 percent.

Goods-producing industries. Employment in the goods-producing industries has been relatively stagnant since the early 1980s. Overall, this sector is expected to grow 3.3 percent over the 2002–12 period. Although employment is expected to increase more slowly than in the service providing industries, projected growth among goods-producing industries varies considerably (Chart 5).

Construction. Employment in construction is expected to increase by 15.1 percent, from 6.7 million to 7.7 million. Demand for new housing and an increase in road, bridge, and tunnel construction will account for the bulk of job growth in this supersector.

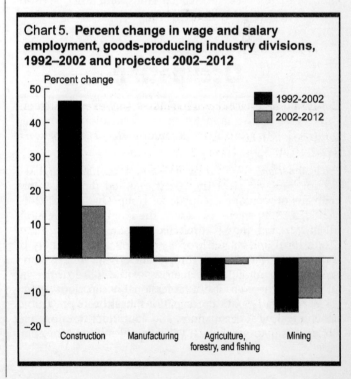

Chart 5. **Percent change in wage and salary employment, goods-producing industry divisions, 1992–2002 and projected 2002–2012**

Manufacturing. Employment change in manufacturing will vary by individual industry, but overall employment in this supersector will decline by 1 percent, or 157,000 jobs. For example, employment in plastics and rubber products manufacturing and machinery manufacturing is expected to grow by 138,000 and 120,000 jobs, respectively. Due to an aging population and increasing life expectancies, pharmaceutical and medicine manufacturing is expected to grow by 23.2 percent and add 68,000 jobs through 2012. However, productivity gains, job automation, and international competition will adversely affect employment in many other manufacturing industries. Employment in textile mills and apparel manufacturing will decline by 136,000 and 245,000 jobs, respectively. Employment in computer and electronic product manufacturing also will decline by 189,000 jobs through 2012.

Agriculture, forestry, fishing, and hunting. Overall employment in agriculture, forestry, fishing, and hunting is expected to decrease by 2 percent. Employment is expected to continue to decline due to advancements in technology. The only industry within this supersector expected to grow is support activities for agriculture and forestry, which includes farm labor contractors and farm management services. This industry is expected to grow by 18.4 percent and add 17,000 new jobs.

Mining. Employment in mining is expected to decrease 11.8 percent, or by some 60,000 jobs, by 2012. Employment in coal mining and metal ore mining is expected to decline by 30.2 percent and 38.8 percent, respectively. Employment in oil and gas extraction also is projected to decline by 27.8 percent through 2012. Employment decreases in these industries are attributable mainly to technology gains that boost worker productivity, growing international competition, restricted access to federal lands, and strict environmental regulations that require cleaning of burning fuels.

Occupation

Expansion of service-providing industries is expected to continue, creating demand for many occupations. However, projected job growth varies among major occupational groups (Chart 6).

Professional and related occupations. Professional and related occupations will grow the fastest and add more new jobs than any other major occupational group. Over the 2002–12 period, a 23.3-percent increase in the number of professional and related jobs is projected, a gain of 6.5 million. Professional and related workers perform a wide variety of duties and are employed throughout private industry and government. About three-quarters of the job growth will come from three groups of professional occupations—computer and mathematical occupations, healthcare practitioners and technical occupations, and education, training, and library occupations—which will add 4.9 million jobs combined.

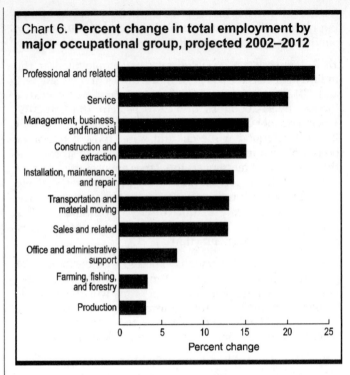

Chart 6. **Percent change in total employment by major occupational group, projected 2002–2012**

Service occupations. Service workers perform services for the public. Employment in service occupations is projected to increase by 5.3 million, or 20.1 percent, the second largest numerical gain and second highest rate of growth among the major occupational groups. Food preparation and serving related occupations are expected to add the most jobs among the service occupations, 1.6 million by 2012. However, healthcare support occupations are expected to grow the fastest, 34.5 percent, adding 1.1 million new jobs.

Management, business, and financial occupations. Workers in management, business, and financial occupations plan and direct the activities of business, government, and other organizations. Their employment is expected to increase by 2.4 million, or 15.4 percent, by 2012. Among managers, the numbers of computer and information systems managers and of preschool and childcare center/program educational administrators will grow the fastest, by 36.1 percent and 32 percent, respectively. General and operations managers will add the most new jobs, 376,000, by 2012. Farmers and ranchers are the only workers in this major occupational group whose numbers are expected to decline, losing 238,000 jobs. Among business and financial occupations, accountants and auditors and management analysts will add the most jobs, 381,000 combined. Management analysts also will be one of the fastest growing occupations in this group, along with personal financial advisors, with job increases of 30.4 percent and 34.6 percent, respectively.

Construction and extraction occupations. Construction and extraction workers construct new residential and commercial buildings and also work in mines, quarries, and oil and gas fields. Employment of these workers is expected to grow 15 percent, adding 1.1 million new jobs. Construction trades and related workers will account for more than three-fourths of these new jobs, 857,000, by 2012. Many extraction occupations will decline, reflecting overall employment losses in the mining and oil and gas extraction industries.

Installation, maintenance, and repair occupations. Workers in installation, maintenance, and repair occupations install new equipment and maintain and repair older equipment. These occupations will add 776,000 jobs by 2012, growing by 13.6 percent. Automotive service technicians and mechanics and general maintenance and repair workers will account for more than 4 in 10 new installation, maintenance, and repair jobs. The fastest growth rate will be among heating, air-conditioning, and refrigeration mechanics and installers, an occupation that is expected to grow 31.8 percent over the 2002–12 period.

Transportation and material moving occupations. Transportation and material moving workers transport people and materials by land, sea, or air. The number of these workers should grow 13.1 percent, accounting for 1.3 million additional jobs by 2012. Among transportation occupations, motor vehicle operators will add the most jobs, 760,000. Rail transportation occupations are the only group in which employment is projected to decline, by 5.4 percent, through 2012. Material moving occupations will grow 8.9 percent and will add 422,000 jobs.

Sales and related occupations. Sales and related workers transfer goods and services among businesses and consumers. Sales and related occupations are expected to add 2 million new jobs by 2012, growing by 12.9 percent. The majority of these jobs will be among retail salespersons and cashiers, occupations that will add more than 1 million jobs combined.

Office and administrative support occupations. Office and administrative support workers perform the day-to-day activities of the office, such as preparing and filing documents, dealing with the public, and distributing information. Employment in these occupations is expected to grow by 6.8 percent, adding 1.6 million new jobs by 2012. Customer service representatives will add the most new jobs, 460,000. Desktop publishers will be among the fastest growing occupations in this group, increasing by 29.2 percent over the decade. Office and administrative support occupations account for 11 of the 20 occupations with the largest employment declines.

Farming, fishing, and forestry occupations. Farming, fishing, and forestry workers cultivate plants, breed and raise livestock, and catch animals. These occupations will grow 3.3 percent and add 35,000 new jobs by 2012. Agricultural workers, including farmworkers and laborers, accounted for the overwhelming majority of new jobs in this group. The numbers of both fishing and logging workers are expected to decline, by 26.8 percent and 3.2 percent, respectively.

Production occupations. Production workers are employed mainly in manufacturing, where they assemble goods and operate plants. Production occupations will have the slowest job growth among the major occupational groups, 3.2 percent, adding 354,000 jobs by 2012. Jobs will be created

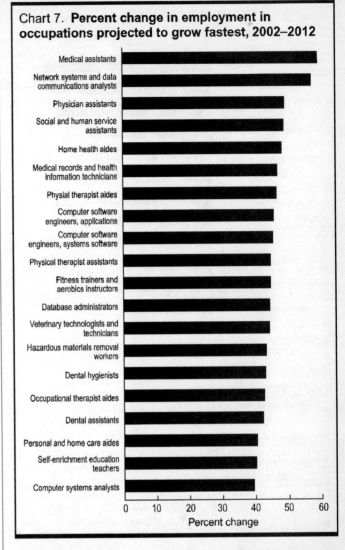

Chart 7. **Percent change in employment in occupations projected to grow fastest, 2002–2012**

for many production occupations, including food processing workers; machinists; and welders, cutters, solderers, and brazers. Textile, apparel, and furnishings occupations, as well as assemblers and fabricators, will account for much of the job losses among production occupations.

Among all occupations in the economy, computer and healthcare occupations are expected to grow the fastest over the projection period (Chart 7). In fact, healthcare occupations make up 10 of the 20 fastest growing occupations, while computer occupations account for 5 out of the 20 fastest growing occupations in the economy. In addition to high growth rates, these 15 computer and healthcare occupations combined will add more than 1.5 million new jobs. High growth rates among computer and healthcare occupations reflect projected rapid growth in the computer and data processing and health services industries.

The 20 occupations listed in Chart 8 will account for more than one-third of all new jobs, 8 million combined, over the 2002–12 period. The occupations with the largest numerical increases cover a wider range of occupational categories than do those occupations with the fastest growth rates.

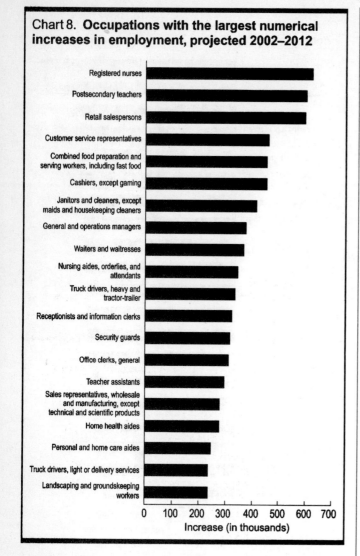

Chart 8. Occupations with the largest numerical increases in employment, projected 2002–2012

Registered nurses
Postsecondary teachers
Retail salespersons
Customer service representatives
Combined food preparation and serving workers, including fast food
Cashiers, except gaming
Janitors and cleaners, except maids and housekeeping cleaners
General and operations managers
Waiters and waitresses
Nursing aides, orderlies, and attendants
Truck drivers, heavy and tractor-trailer
Receptionists and information clerks
Security guards
Office clerks, general
Teacher assistants
Sales representatives, wholesale and manufacturing, except technical and scientific products
Home health aides
Personal and home care aides
Truck drivers, light or delivery services
Landscaping and groundskeeping workers

Increase (in thousands)

due to the proliferation of personal computers, which allows other workers to perform duties formerly assigned to word processors and typists.

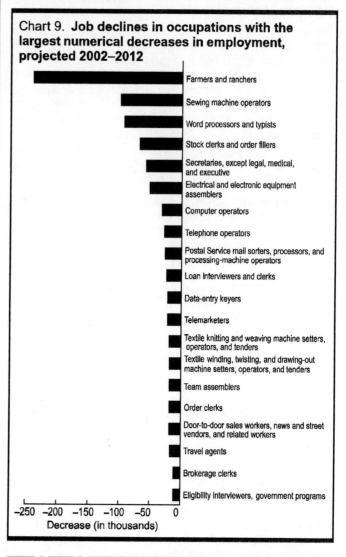

Chart 9. Job declines in occupations with the largest numerical decreases in employment, projected 2002–2012

Farmers and ranchers
Sewing machine operators
Word processors and typists
Stock clerks and order fillers
Secretaries, except legal, medical, and executive
Electrical and electronic equipment assemblers
Computer operators
Telephone operators
Postal Service mail sorters, processors, and processing-machine operators
Loan interviewers and clerks
Data-entry keyers
Telemarketers
Textile knitting and weaving machine setters, operators, and tenders
Textile winding, twisting, and drawing-out machine setters, operators, and tenders
Team assemblers
Order clerks
Door-to-door sales workers, news and street vendors, and related workers
Travel agents
Brokerage clerks
Eligibility interviewers, government programs

Decrease (in thousands)

Health occupations will account for some of these increases in employment, as well as occupations in education, sales, transportation, office and administrative support, and food service. Many of these occupations are very large and will create more new jobs than will those with high growth rates. Only 2 out of the 20 fastest growing occupations—home health aides and personal and home care aides—also are projected to be among the 20 occupations with the largest numerical increases in employment.

Declining occupational employment stems from declining industry employment, technological advancements, changes in business practices, and other factors. For example, increased productivity and farm consolidations are expected to result in a decline of 238,000 farmers and ranchers over the 2002–12 period (Chart 9). The majority of the 20 occupations with the largest numerical decreases are office and administrative support and production occupations, which are affected by increasing plant and factory automation and the implementation of office technology that reduces the needs for these workers. For example, employment of word processors and typists is expected to decline

Education and Training

Education is essential in getting a high-paying job. In fact, for all but 1 of the 50 highest paying occupations, a college degree or higher is the most significant source of education or training. Air traffic controllers is the only occupation of the 50 highest paying for which this is not the case.

Among the 20 fastest growing occupations, a bachelor's or associate degree is the most significant source of education or training for 10 of them—network systems and data communications analysts; physician assistants; medical records and health information technicians; computer software engineers, applications; computer software engineers, systems software; physical therapist assistants; database administrators; veterinary technologists and technicians; dental hygienists; and computer systems analysts. On-the-job training is the most significant source of education or training for another 8 of the 20 fastest growing occupations—medical assistants, social and human service assistants, home health aides, physical therapist aides, hazardous materials removal workers, occupational therapist aides, dental assistants, and personal and home care aides. In contrast, on-the-job training is the most significant source of education or training for 17 of the 20 occupations with the largest numerical increases; 3 of these 20 occupations—registered nurses, postsecondary teachers, and general and operations managers—have an associate or higher degree as the most significant source of education or training. On-the-job training also is the most significant source of education or training for 19 of the 20 occupations with the largest numerical decreases; one of these 20 occupations—travel agents—has a postsecondary vocational award as the most significant source of education or training.

Total Job Openings

Job openings stem from both employment growth and replacement needs (Chart 10). Replacement needs arise as workers leave occupations. Some transfer to other occupations while others retire, return to school, or quit to assume household responsibilities. Replacement needs are projected to account for 60 percent of the approximately 56 million job openings between 2002 and 2012. Thus, even occupations projected to experience little or no growth or to decline in employment still may offer many job openings.

Professional and related occupations are projected to grow faster and add more jobs than any other major occupational group, with 6.5 million new jobs by 2012. Three-fourths of the job growth in professional and related occupations is expected among computer and mathematical occupations; healthcare practitioners and technical occupations; and education, training, and library occupations. With 5.3 million job openings due to replacement needs, professional and related occupations are the only major group projected to generate more openings from job growth than from replacement needs.

Service occupations are projected to have the largest number of total job openings, 13 million, reflecting high replacement needs. A large number of replacements will be necessary as young workers leave food preparation and service occupations. Replacement needs generally are greatest in the largest occupations and in those with relatively low pay or limited training requirements.

Office automation will significantly affect many individual office and administrative support occupations. Overall, these occupations are projected to grow more slowly than average, while some are projected to decline. Office and administrative support occupations are projected to create 7.5 million job openings over the 2002–12 period, ranking third behind service and professional and related occupations.

Farming, fishing, and forestry occupations are projected to have the fewest job openings, approximately 335,000. Because job growth is expected to be slow and levels of retirement and job turnover high, more than 85 percent of these projected job openings are due to replacement needs.

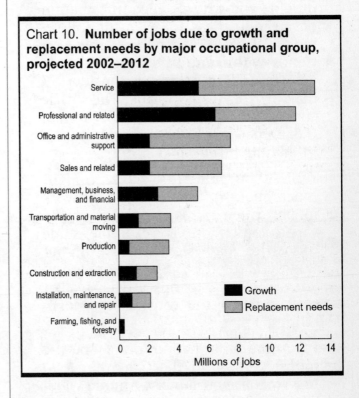

Chart 10. **Number of jobs due to growth and replacement needs by major occupational group, projected 2002–2012**

Employment Trends in Major Industries

Comments

While hundreds of specialized industries exist, about 75 percent of all workers are employed in just 42 major ones. Space limitations do not allow us to provide you with detailed information on all industries; however, the following article presents a good overview of trends within industry types. It gives you important facts to consider in making your career plans. The article comes, with minor changes, from a U.S. Department of Labor publication titled *Career Guide to Industries.*

While you may not have thought much about it, the industry you work in will often be as important as the career you choose. For example, some industries pay significantly higher wages than others. So, if you found your way back to this article, read it over carefully and consider the possibilities.

For more information on a specific industry, look for the *Career Guide to Industries* in your library. A more widely available version of the same book is published by JIST under the title *Career Guide to America's Top Industries.* It is available through bookstores and many libraries. Here are the industries covered in the *Career Guide to Industries:*

Agriculture, Mining, and Construction
Agriculture, Forestry, and Fishing
Construction
Mining
Oil and Gas Extraction
Manufacturing
Aerospace Product and Parts Manufacturing
Apparel Manufacturing
Chemical Manufacturing, Except Pharmaceutical and Medicine Manufacturing
Computer and Electronic Product Manufacturing
Food Manufacturing
Motor Vehicle and Parts Manufacturing
Pharmaceutical and Medicine Manufacturing
Printing
Steel Manufacturing
Textile Mills and Products
Trade
Automobile Dealers
Clothing, Accessory, and General Merchandise Stores
Grocery Stores
Wholesale Trade
Transportation and Utilities
Air Transportation
Truck Transportation and Warehousing
Utilities
Information
Broadcasting
Motion Picture and Video Industries
Publishing, Except Software
Software Publishers
Telecommunications
Financial Activities
Banking
Insurance
Securities, Commodities, and Other Investments
Professional and Business Services
Advertising and Public Relations Services
Computer Systems Design and Related Services
Employment Services
Management, Scientific, and Technical Consulting Services
Education and Health Services
Child Daycare Services
Educational Services
Health Services
Social Assistance, Except Child Daycare
Leisure and Hospitality
Arts, Entertainment, and Recreation
Food Services and Drinking Places
Hotels and Other Accommodations
Government
Federal Government, Excluding the Postal Service
State and Local Government, Excluding Education and Hospitals

Overview

The U.S. economy is comprised of industries with diverse characteristics. For each industry covered in the Department of Labor's publication *Career Guide to Industries,* detailed information is provided about specific characteristics: The nature of the industry, working conditions, employment, occupational composition, training and advancement requirements, earnings, and job outlook. This chapter provides an overview of these characteristics and the outlook for the various industries and economy as a whole.

Nature of the Industry

Industries are defined by the processes they use to produce goods and services. Workers in the United States produce and provide a wide variety of products and services and as a result, the types of industries in the U.S. economy range widely—from agriculture, forestry, and fishing to aerospace manufacturing. Although many of these industries are related, each industry has a unique combination of occupations, production techniques, inputs and outputs, and business characteristics. Understanding the nature of the industry is important, because it is this unique combination that determines working conditions, educational requirements, and the job outlook for each of the industries discussed in the *Career Guide.*

Industries consist of many different places of work, called *establishments,* which range from large factories and office complexes employing thousands of workers to small businesses employing only a few workers. Not to be confused with companies, which are legal entities, establishments are physical locations in which people work, such as the branch office of a bank. Thus, a company may have more than one establishment. Establishments that use the same or similar processes to produce goods or services are organized together into *industries.* Industries are, in turn, organized together into *industry groups.* These are further organized into industry subsectors and then ultimately into *industry sectors.* For the purposes of labor market analysis, the Bureau of Labor Statistics organized industry sectors into *industry supersectors* and then divided the supersectors into two broad groups: *Goods-producing industries* (natural resources and mining; construction; and manufacturing) and *service-providing industries* (trade, transportation, and utilities; information; financial activities; professional and business services; education and health services; leisure and hospitality; other services; and public administration).

Each industry subsector is made up of a number of industry groups, which are, as mentioned, determined by differences in production processes. An easily recognized example of these distinctions is in the food manufacturing subsector, which is made up of industry groups that produce meat products, preserved fruits and vegetables, bakery items, and dairy products, among others. Each of these industry groups requires workers with varying skills and employs unique production techniques. Another example of these distinc-

tions is found in utilities, which employs workers in establishments that provide electricity, natural gas, and water.

There were almost 7.8 million private business establishments in the United States in 2002. The average size of these establishments varies widely across industries.

Most establishments in the construction, wholesale trade, retail trade, finance and insurance, real estate and rental and leasing, and professional, scientific, and technical services industries are small, averaging fewer than 15 employees per establishment. however, wide differences within industries can exist. Hospitals, for example, employ an average of 712.4 workers, while physicians' offices employ an average of 9.3. Similarly, although there is an average of 13.3 employees per establishment for all of retail trade, department stores employ an average of 166.5 people.

Business establishments in the United States are predominantly small; 59.6 percent of all establishments employed fewer than 5 workers in 2002. However, the medium-sized to large establishments employ a greater proportion of all workers. For example, establishments that employed 50 or more workers accounted for only 4.7 percent of all establishments, yet employed 57.4 percent of all workers. The large establishments—those with more than 500 workers—accounted for only 0.2 percent of all establishments, but employed 18.2 percent of all workers. Table 1 presents the percent distribution of employment according to establishment size.

TABLE 1

Percent distribution of establishments and employment in all private industries by establishment size, March 2002

Establishment size (number of workers)	Establishments	Employment
Total	100.0	100.0
1 to 4	59.6	6.6
5 to 9	16.9	8.2
10 to 19	11.1	10.9
20 to 49	7.7	17.0
50 to 99	2.6	13.3
100 to 249	1.5	16.4
250 to 499	0.4	9.5
500 to 999	0.1	7.0
1,000 or more	0.1	11.2

Establishment size can play a role in the characteristics of each job. Large establishments generally offer workers greater occupational mobility and advancement potential, whereas small establishments may provide their employees with broader experience by requiring them to assume a wider range of responsibilities. Also, small establishments are distributed throughout the nation; every locality has a few small businesses. Large establishments, in contrast, employ more workers and are less common, but they play a much more prominent role in the economies of the areas in which they are located.

Working Conditions

Just as the goods and services produced in each industry are different, working conditions vary significantly among industries. In some industries, the work setting is quiet, temperature-controlled, and virtually hazard free; while other industries are characterized by noisy, uncomfortable, and sometimes dangerous work environments. Some industries require long workweeks and shift work; in many industries, standard 40-hour workweeks are common. Still other industries can be seasonal, requiring long hours during busy periods and abbreviated schedules during slower months. Production processes, establishment size, and the physical location of work usually determine these varying conditions.

One of the most telling indicators of working conditions is an industry's injury and illness rate. Overexertion, being struck by an object, and falls on the same level are among the most common incidents causing work-related injury or illness. In 2002, approximately 4.7 million nonfatal injuries and illnesses were reported throughout private industry. Among major industry divisions, manufacturing had the highest rate of injury and illness—7.2 cases for every 100 full-time workers—while finance, insurance, and real estate had the lowest rate—1.7 cases. About 5,500 work-related fatalities were reported in 2002; the most common events resulting in fatal injuries were transportation incidents, contact with objects and equipment, assaults and violent acts, and falls.

Work schedules are another important reflection of working conditions, and the operational requirements of each industry lead to large differences in hours worked and in part-time versus full-time status. In food services and drinking places, for example, 37.9 percent of employees worked part time in 2002 compared with only 1.3 percent in mining. Table 2 presents industries having relatively high and low percentages of part-time workers.

TABLE 2

Part-time workers as a percent of total employment, selected industries, 2002

Industry	Percent part-time
All industries	15.8
Many part-time workers	
Food services and drinking places	37.9
Grocery stores	30.1
Clothing, accessory, and general merchandise stores	29.2
Child day care services	29.1
Arts, entertainment, and recreation	28.1
Motion picture and video industries	24.8
Social assistance, except child day care	21.8
Educational services	21.1
Few part-time workers	
Chemical manufacturing, except drugs	3.1
Pharmaceutical and medicine manufacturing	3.1
Computer and electronic product manufacturing	2.6
Utilities	2.5
Aerospace product and parts manufacturing	2.1
Motor vehicle and parts manufacturing	1.8
Steel manufacturing	1.8
Mining	1.3

The low proportion of part-time workers in some manufacturing industries often reflects the continuous nature of the production processes that makes it difficult to adapt the volume of production to short-term fluctuations in product demand. Once begun, it is costly to halt these processes; machinery must be tended and materials must be moved continuously. For example, the chemical manufacturing industry produces many different chemical products through controlled chemical reactions. These processes require chemical operators to monitor and adjust the flow of materials into and out of the line of production. Because production may continue 24 hours a day, 7 days a week, under the watchful eyes of chemical operators who work in shifts, full-time workers are more likely to be employed. Retail trade and service industries, on the other hand, have seasonal cycles marked by various events that affect the hours worked, such as school openings or important holidays. During busy times of the year, longer hours are common, whereas slack periods lead to cutbacks in work hours and shorter workweeks. Jobs in these industries are generally appealing to students and others who desire flexible, part-time schedules.

Employment

The total number of jobs in the United States in 2002 was 144 million. This included 11.4 million self-employed workers, 140,000 unpaid workers in family businesses, and 132.3 million wage and salary workers—including primary and secondary job holders. The total number of jobs is projected to increase to 165.3 million by 2012, and wage and salary jobs are projected to account for more than 153.8 million of them.

As shown in Table 3, although wage and salary jobs are the vast majority of all jobs, they are not evenly divided among the various industries. The education and health services industry supersector is the largest source of employment, with about 26 million workers in 2002. The trade, transportation, and utilities supersector is next largest, followed by professional and business services, employing 25.5 million and 16 million workers, respectively. Wage and salary employment ranged from only 122,500 in oil and gas extraction to 12.5 million in educational services. Three industries—educational services, health services, and food services and drinking places—together accounted for 33.5 million jobs, or one quarter of the nation's wage and salary employment.

TABLE 3

Wage and salary employment in selected industries, 2002, and projected change, 2002-12

(Employment in thousands)

Industry	2002 Employment	2002 Percent distribution	2012 Employment	2012 Percent distribution	2002-12 Percent change	2002-12 Employment change
All industries	132,279	100.0	153,883	100.0	16.3	21,603
Goods-producing industries	23,766	18.0	24,539	15.9	3.2	772
Natural resources and mining	1,728	1.3	1,644	1.1	-4.9	-84
Agriculture, forestry, fishing, and hunting	1,216	0.9	1,192	0.8	-1.9	-24
Oil and gas extraction	123	0.1	88	0.1	-27.8	-34
Mining	212	0.2	180	0.1	-15.0	-32
Construction	6,732	5.1	7,745	5.0	15.1	1,014
Manufacturing	15,307	11.6	15,149	9.8	-1.0	-157
Aerospace product and parts manufacturing	468	0.4	386	0.3	-17.6	-83
Apparel manufacturing	358	0.3	112	0.1	-68.6	-245
Chemical manufacturing, except drugs	636	0.5	530	0.3	-16.7	-106
Computer and electronic product manufacturing	1,521	1.1	1,333	0.9	-12.4	-189
Food manufacturing	1,525	1.2	1,597	1.0	4.7	72
Motor vehicle and parts manufacturing	1,152	0.9	1,181	0.8	2.6	29
Pharmaceutical and medicine manufacturing	293	0.2	361	0.2	23.2	68
Printing	710	0.5	734	0.5	3.3	24
Steel manufacturing	170	0.1	136	0.1	-20.0	-34
Textile mills and products	489	0.4	338	0.2	-31.0	-152
Service-providing industries	108,513	82.0	129,344	84.1	19.2	20,831
Trade, transportation, and utilities	25,493	19.3	29,093	18.9	14.1	3,600
Automobile dealers	1,250	0.9	1,408	0.9	12.6	158
Clothing, accessory, and general merchandise stores	4,129	3.1	4,473	2.9	8.3	344
Grocery stores	2,478	1.9	2,611	1.7	5.4	133
Wholesale trade	5,641	4.3	6,279	4.1	11.3	638
Air transportation	559	0.4	626	0.4	12.0	67
Truck transportation and warehousing	1,853	1.4	2,274	1.5	22.7	422
Utilities	600	0.5	565	0.4	-5.7	-34
Information	3,420	2.6	4,052	2.6	18.5	632
Broadcasting	334	0.3	362	0.2	8.5	28
Motion picture and video industries	360	0.3	472	0.3	31.1	112
Publishing, except software	714	0.5	703	0.5	-1.5	-11
Software publishers	256	0.2	430	0.3	67.9	174
Telecommunications	1,201	0.9	1,281	0.8	6.7	80

(continued)

TABLE 3 (CONTINUED)

Wage and salary employment in selected industries, 2002, and projected change, 2002-12
(Employment in thousands)

Industry	2002 Employment	2002 Percent distribution	2012 Employment	2012 Percent distribution	2002-12 Percent change	2002-12 Employment change
Financial activities	5,815	4.4	6,405	4.2	10.1	590
Banking	1,761	1.3	1,873	1.2	6.4	112
Insurance	2,223	1.7	2,391	1.6	7.5	168
Securities, commodities, and other investments	801	0.6	925	0.6	15.5	124
Professional and business services	16,010	12.1	20,876	13.6	30.4	4,866
Advertising and public relations services	442	0.3	525	0.3	18.9	84
Computer systems design and related services	1,163	0.9	1,798	1.2	54.6	635
Employment services	3,249	2.5	5,012	3.3	54.3	1,764
Management, scientific, and technical consulting services	732	0.6	1,137	0.7	55.4	406
Education and health services	26,060	19.7	32,935	21.4	26.4	6,875
Child day care services	734	0.6	1,050	0.7	43.1	316
Educational services	12,527	9.5	15,016	9.8	19.9	2,489
Health services	12,524	9.5	16,025	10.4	28.0	3,501
Social assistance, except child day care	1,269	1.0	1,867	1.2	47.1	597
Leisure and hospitality	11,969	9.0	14,104	9.2	17.8	2,135
Arts, entertainment, and recreation	1,778	1.3	2,275	1.5	28.0	497
Food services and drinking places	8,412	6.4	9,749	6.3	15.9	1,337
Hotels and other accommodations	1,780	1.3	2,080	1.4	16.9	301
Public administration	9,774	7.4	10,582	6.9	8.3	808
Federal government, excluding the postal service	1,922	1.5	1,972	1.3	2.6	50
State and local government, except education and health	7,851	5.9	8,610	5.6	9.7	759

NOTE: May not add to totals due to omission of industries not covered in the *Career Guide*.

Although workers of all ages are employed in each industry, certain industries tend to possess workers of distinct age groups. For the previously mentioned reasons, retail trade employs a relatively high proportion of younger workers to fill part-time and temporary positions. The manufacturing sector, on the other hand, has a relatively high median age because many jobs in the sector require a number of years to learn and perfect specialized skills that do not easily transfer to other firms. Also, manufacturing employment has been declining, providing fewer opportunities for younger workers to get jobs. As a result, one-fourth of the workers in retail trade were 24 years of age or younger in 2002, compared with only 8.4 percent of workers in manufacturing. Table 4 contrasts the age distribution of workers in all industries with the distributions in five very different industries.

Employment in some industries is concentrated in one region of the country. Such industries often are located near a source of raw or unfinished materials upon which the industry relies. For example, oil and gas extraction jobs are concentrated in Texas, Louisiana, and Oklahoma; many textile mills and products manufacturing jobs are found in North Carolina, South Carolina, and Georgia; and a significant proportion of motor vehicle manufacturing jobs are located in Michigan and Ohio. On the other hand, some industries—such as grocery stores and educational services—have jobs distributed throughout the nation, reflecting the general population density.

TABLE 4

Percent distribution of wage and salary workers by age group, selected industries, 2002

Industry	Age group			
	16 to 24	25 to 44	45 to 64	65 and older
All industries	15	48	34	3
Computer systems design and related services	7	68	25	1
Educational services	10	43	44	3
Food services and drinking places	45	39	15	2
Telecommunications	10	58	32	1
Utilities	6	47	45	2

Occupations in the Industry

The occupations found in each industry depend on the types of services provided or goods produced. For example, because construction companies require skilled trades workers to build and renovate buildings, these companies employ large numbers of carpenters, electricians, plumbers, painters, and sheet metal workers. Other occupations common to construction include construction equipment operators and mechanics, installers, and repairers. Retail trade, on the other hand, displays and sells manufactured goods to consumers. As a result, retail trade employs numerous sales clerks and other workers, including more than three-fourths of all cashiers. Table 5 shows the industry sectors and the occupational groups that predominate in each.

TABLE 5

Industry sectors and their largest occupational group, 2002

Industry sector	Largest occupational group	Percent of industry wage and salary jobs
Agriculture, forestry, fishing, and hunting	Farming, fishing, and forestry occupations	61.1
Mining..	Construction and extraction occupations	33.3
Construction	Construction and extraction occupations	66.2
Manufacturing	Production occupations	52.1
Wholesale trade	Sales and related occupations...................................	24.7
Retail trade	Sales and related occupations...................................	52.5
Transportation and warehousing	Transportation and material moving occupations	56.0
Utilities	Installation, maintenance, and repair occupations....	25.6
Information...	Professional and related occupations.........................	29.1
Finance and insurance	Office and administrative support occupations..........	51.4
Real estate and rental and leasing	Sales and related occupations...................................	22.7
Professional, scientific, and technical services.............	Professional and related occupations.........................	42.6
Management of companies and enterprises	Office and administrative support occupations..........	33.6
Administrative and support and waste management and remediation services	Office and administrative support occupations..........	23.2
Educational services, private	Professional and related occupations.........................	59.6
Health care and social assistance	Professional and related occupations.........................	42.6
Arts, entertainment, and recreation............................	Service occupations	57.2
Accommodation and food services	Service occupations	84.0
Government	Professional and related occupations.........................	43.7

The nation's occupational distribution clearly is influenced by its industrial structure, yet there are many occupations, such as general manager or secretary, that are found in all industries. In fact, some of the largest occupations in the U.S. economy are dispersed across many industries. For example, the office and administrative support occupational group is among the largest in the nation since nearly every industry relies on administrative support workers. (See Table 6.) Other large occupational groups include professional and related occupations, service occupations, management, business, and financial occupations, and sales and related occupations.

TABLE 6

Total employment and projected change by broad occupational group, 2002-12

(Employment in thousands)

Occupational group	Employment, 2002	Percent change, 2002-12
Total, all occupations	144,014	14.8
Professional and related occupations	27,687	23.3
Service occupations	26,569	20.1
Office and administrative support occupations....................	23,851	6.8
Management, business, and financial occupations.................	15,501	15.4
Sales and related occupations	15,260	12.9
Production occupations	11,258	3.2
Transportation and material moving occupations....................	9,828	13.1
Construction and extraction occupations	7,292	15.0
Installation, maintenance, and repair occupations	5,696	13.6
Farming, fishing, and forestry occupations..............................	1,072	3.3

Training and Advancement

Workers prepare for employment in many ways, but the most fundamental form of job training in the United States is a high school education. Fully 88 percent of the nation's workforce possessed a high school diploma or its equivalent in 2002. However, many occupations require more training, so growing numbers of workers pursue additional training or education after high school. In 2002, 28.7 percent of the nation's workforce reported having completed some college or an associate's degree as their highest level of education, while an additional 28.7 percent continued in their studies and attained a bachelor's or higher degree. In addition to these types of formal education, other sources of qualifying

training include formal company provided training, apprenticeships, informal on-the-job training, correspondence courses, the Armed Forces vocational training, and non-work-related training.

The unique combination of training required to succeed in each industry is determined largely by the industry's production process and the mix of occupations it requires. For example, manufacturing employs many machine operators who generally need little formal education after high school, but sometimes complete considerable on-the-job training. In contrast, educational services employs many types of teachers, most of whom require a bachelor's or higher degree. Training requirements by industry sector are shown in Table 7.

Persons with no more than a high school diploma accounted for about 65.4 percent of all workers in agriculture, forestry, fishing, and hunting; 64.7 percent in construction; 63.3 percent in accommodation and food services; 56.9

TABLE 7

Percent distribution of workers by highest grade completed or degree received, by industry sector, 2002

Industry sector	High school diploma or less	Some college or associate's degree	Bachelor's or higher degree
All industries	42.5	28.7	28.7
Agriculture, forestry, fishing, and hunting.........................	65.4	21.2	13.4
Mining	57.0	23.5	19.5
Construction	64.7	25.1	10.2
Manufacturing	52.9	25.7	21.4
Wholesale trade	44.8	27.9	27.3
Retail trade	52.7	31.1	16.1
Transportation and warehousing..........................	52.9	32.1	15.1
Utilities....................................	39.8	35.3	25.0
Information	27.6	33.0	39.3
Finance and insurance............	26.1	32.0	41.9
Real estate and rental and leasing	38.9	31.5	29.6
Professional, scientific, and technical services..................	15.3	24.3	60.4
Administrative and support and waste management and remediation services	54.9	27.3	17.9
Educational services, private ..	18.9	19.5	61.6
Health care and social assistance	31.9	34.4	33.7
Arts, entertainment, and recreation...............................	41.4	30.7	27.8
Accommodation and food services..................................	63.3	26.4	10.3
Government.............................	25.6	36.7	37.8

percent in mining; 52.9 percent in manufacturing; and 52.7 in retail trade. On the other hand, those who had acquired a bachelor's or higher degree accounted for 61.6 percent of all workers in educational services, private; 60.4 percent in professional, scientific, and technical services; 41.9 percent in finance and insurance; 39.3 percent in information; and 37.8 percent in government.

Education and training also are important factors in the variety of advancement paths found in different industries. Each industry has some unique advancement paths, but workers who complete additional on-the-job training or education generally help their chances of being promoted. In much of the manufacturing sector, for example, production workers who receive training in management and computer skills increase their likelihood of being promoted to supervisory positions. Other factors that impact advancement include the size of the establishments, institutionalized career tracks, and the mix of occupations. As a result, persons who seek jobs in particular industries should be aware of how these advancement paths and other factors may later shape their careers.

Earnings

Like other characteristics, earnings differ by industry, the result of a highly complicated process that reflects a number of factors. For example, earnings may vary due to the nature of occupations in the industry, average hours worked, geographical location, workers' average age, educational requirements, industry profits, and union penetration of the workforce. In general, wages are highest in metropolitan areas to compensate for the higher cost of living. Also, as would be expected, industries that employ a large proportion of unskilled minimum-wage or part time workers tend to have lower earnings.

The difference in earnings of all wage and salary workers in computer systems design and related services, which averaged $1,112 a week in 2002, and those in food service and drinking places, where the weekly average was $359, provide a good illustration of how various factors can affect earnings. The difference is so large primarily because computer systems design and related services establishments employ more highly skilled full-time workers, while food service and drinking places employ many lower-skilled part-time workers. In addition, many workers in food service and drinking places are able to supplement their low wages with money they receive as tips, which is not included in the industry wages data. Table 8 highlights the industries with the highest and lowest average weekly earnings.

Employee benefits, once a minor addition to wages and salaries, continue to grow in diversity and cost. In addition to traditional benefits—including paid vacations, life and health insurance, and pensions—many employers now offer various benefits to accommodate the needs of a changing

labor force. Such benefits include childcare, employee assistance programs that provide counseling for personal problems, and wellness programs that encourage exercise, stress management, and self-improvement. Benefits vary among occupational groups, full- and part-time workers, public and private sector workers, regions, unionized and nonunionized workers, and small and large establishments. Data indicate that full-time workers and those in medium-sized and large establishments—those with 100 or more workers—receive better benefits than do part-time workers and those in smaller establishments.

TABLE 8

Average weekly earnings of production or nonsupervisory workers on private nonfarm payrolls, selected industries, 2002

Industry	Earnings
All industries	$610
Industries with high earnings	
Computer systems design and related services	1,112
Management, scientific, and technical consulting services	992
Securities, commodities, and other investments	971
Aerospace product and parts manufacturing	952
Pharmaceutical and medicine manufacturing	940
Software publishers	921
Computer and electronic product manufacturing	859
Telecommunications	836
Industries with low earnings	
Textile mills and products	446
Grocery stores	424
Clothing, accessory, and general merchandise stores	418
Hotels and other accommodations	410
Agriculture, forestry, fishing, and hunting	376
Food services and drinking places	359
Apparel manufacturing	348
Child day care services	348

Union penetration of the workforce varies widely by industry, and it also may play a role in earnings and benefits. In 2002, about 14.5 percent of workers throughout the nation were union members or covered by union contracts. As Table 9 demonstrates, union affiliation of workers varies widely by industry. Almost 45 percent of the workers in air transportation were union members, the highest rate of all the industries, followed by 38.5 percent in educational services and

36.9 percent in steel manufacturing. Industries with the lowest unionization rate include software publishers, 0 percent; food services and drinking places, 1.8 percent; and computer systems design and related services, 1.9 percent.

TABLE 9

Union members and other workers covered by union contracts as a percent of total employment, selected industries, 2002

Industry	Percent union members or covered by union contract
All industries	14.5
Industries with high unionization rates	
Air transportation	44.8
Educational services	38.5
Steel manufacturing	36.9
Government	35.2
Motor vehicle and parts manufacturing	32.3
Industries with low unionization rates	
Banking	2.1
Advertising and public relations services	2.0
Computer systems design and related services	1.9
Food services and drinking places	1.8
Software publishers	0.0

Outlook

Total employment in the United States is projected to increase by about 15 percent over the 2002-12 period. Employment growth, however, is only one source of job openings. The total number of openings in any industry also depends on the industry's current employment level and its need to replace workers who leave their jobs. Throughout the economy, in fact, replacement needs will create more job openings than will employment growth. Employment size is a major determinant of job openings—larger industries generally have larger numbers of workers who must be replaced and provide more openings. The occupational composition of an industry is another factor. Industries with high concentrations of professional, technical, and other jobs that require more formal education—occupations in which workers tend to leave their jobs less frequently—generally have fewer openings resulting from replacement needs. On the other hand, more replacement openings generally occur in industries with high concentrations of service, laborer, and other jobs that require little formal education and have lower wages because workers in these jobs are more likely to leave their occupations.

Employment growth is determined largely by changes in the demand for the goods and services provided by an industry, worker productivity, and foreign competition. Each industry is affected by a different set of variables that determines the number and composition of jobs that will be available. Even within an industry, employment may grow at different rates in different occupations. For example, changes in technology, production methods, and business practices in an industry might eliminate some jobs while creating others. Some industries may be growing rapidly overall, yet opportunities for workers in occupations that are adversely affected by technological change could be stagnant or even declining. Similarly, employment of some occupations may be declining in the economy as a whole, yet may be increasing in a rapidly growing industry.

As shown in Table 3, employment growth rates over the next decade will vary widely among industries. Employment in goods-producing industries is expected to increase as growth in construction is partially offset by declining employment in agriculture, forestry, fishing, and hunting; mining; and manufacturing. Growth in construction employment will stem from new factory construction as existing facilities are modernized; from new school construction, reflecting growth in the school-age population; and from infrastructure improvements, such as road and bridge construction. Employment in mining is expected to decline due to labor-saving technology and continued reliance on foreign sources of energy.

Manufacturing employment will decrease slightly—employment declines in apparel manufacturing, computer and electronic product manufacturing, and textile mills and products manufacturing will be partially offset by employment gains in food manufacturing and pharmaceutical and medicine manufacturing. Apparel manufacturing is projected to lose about 245,000 jobs over the 2002-12 period—more than any other manufacturing industry—due primarily to increasing imports replacing domestic products. Employment growth in food manufacturing is expected, as a growing and ever-more-diverse population increase the demand for manufactured food products. Employment growth in pharmaceutical and medicine manufacturing is expected as sales of pharmaceuticals increase with growth in the population, particularly among the elderly, and with the introduction of new medicines to the market. Both food and pharmaceutical and medicine manufacturing also have growing export markets.

Growth in overall employment will result primarily from growth in service-providing industries over the 2002-12 period, almost all of which are expected to have increasing employment. Rising employment in service-providing industries is expected to occur predominately in health services and educational services—the two largest industries—as well as in employment services, food services and drinking places, state and local government, and wholesale trade. When combined, these sectors will account for almost half of all new wage and salary jobs across the nation.

Health services will account for the most new wage and salary jobs, about 3.5 million over the 2002-12 period. Population growth, advances in medical technologies that increase the number of treatable diseases, and a growing share of the population in older age groups will drive employment growth. Offices of physicians, the largest health services industry group, is expected to account for about 770,000 of these new jobs as patients seek more healthcare outside of the traditional inpatient hospital setting.

Educational services is expected to grow by nearly 20 percent over the 2002-12 period, adding about 2.5 million new jobs. A growing emphasis on improving education and making it available to more children and young adults will be the primary factors contributing to employment growth. Employment growth at all levels of education is expected, particularly at the postsecondary level, as children of the baby boomers continue to reach college age and as more adults pursue continuing education to enhance or update their skills.

Employment in one of the nation's fastest-growing industries—employment services—is expected to increase by more than 50 percent, adding another 1.8 million jobs over the 2002-12 period. Employment will increase, particularly in temporary help services and professional employer organizations, as businesses seek new ways to make their workforces more specialized and responsive to changes in demand.

The food services and drinking places industry is expected to add more than 1.3 million new jobs over the 2002-12 projection period. Increases in population, dual-income families, and dining sophistication will contribute to job growth. In addition, the increasing diversity of the population will contribute to job growth in food service and drinking places that offer a wider variety of ethnic foods and drinks.

Almost 760,000 new jobs are expected to arise in state and local government, adding almost 10 percent over the 2002-12 period. Job growth will result primarily from growth in the population and its demand for public services. Additional job growth will result as state and local governments continue to receive greater responsibility for administering federally funded programs from the federal government.

Wholesale trade is expected to add almost 640,000 new jobs over the coming decade, reflecting growth both in trade and in the overall economy. Most new jobs will be in durable goods merchant wholesalers, such as professional and commercial equipment and supplies; electrical and electronic goods; and furniture and home furnishing. However, industry consolidation and the growth of electronic commerce using the Internet are expected to limit job growth to 11 percent over the 2002-12 period, less than the 15 percent projected for all industries.

Continual changes in the economy have far-reaching and complex effects on employment. Jobseekers should be aware of these changes, keeping alert for developments that can affect job opportunities in industries and the variety of occupations that are found in each industry. For more detailed information on specific occupations, consult the 2004-05 edition of the *Occupational Outlook Handbook*, which provides information on more than 275 occupations.

High-Paying Occupations With Many Openings, Projected 2002–12

Over the 2002–12 decade, career choices abound for those seeking high earnings and lots of opportunities. High-paying occupations that are projected to have many openings are varied. This diverse group includes teachers, managers, and construction trades workers.

The job openings shown in the chart represent the total that are expected each year for workers who are entering these occupations for the first time. The job openings result from each occupation's growth and from the need to replace workers who retire or leave the occupation permanently for some other reason. Not included among these openings are ones that are created when workers move from job to job within an occupation.

Median earnings, such as those listed here, indicate that half of the workers in an occupation made more than that amount and half made less. The occupations in the chart ranked in the highest or second-highest earnings quartiles for 2002 median earnings. This means that median earnings for workers in these occupations were higher than the earnings for at least 50 percent of all occupations in 2002.

Most of these occupations had another thing going for them in 2002: low or very low unemployment. Workers in occupations that had higher levels of unemployment—truck drivers, carpenters, and electricians—were more dependent on a strong economy or seasonal employment.

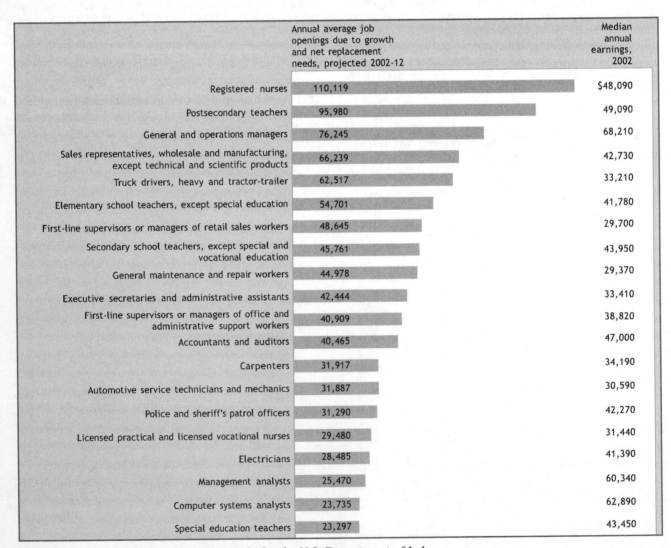

	Annual average job openings due to growth and net replacement needs, projected 2002-12	Median annual earnings, 2002
Registered nurses	110,119	$48,090
Postsecondary teachers	95,980	49,090
General and operations managers	76,245	68,210
Sales representatives, wholesale and manufacturing, except technical and scientific products	66,239	42,730
Truck drivers, heavy and tractor-trailer	62,517	33,210
Elementary school teachers, except special education	54,701	41,780
First-line supervisors or managers of retail sales workers	48,645	29,700
Secondary school teachers, except special and vocational education	45,761	43,950
General maintenance and repair workers	44,978	29,370
Executive secretaries and administrative assistants	42,444	33,410
First-line supervisors or managers of office and administrative support workers	40,909	38,820
Accountants and auditors	40,465	47,000
Carpenters	31,917	34,190
Automotive service technicians and mechanics	31,887	30,590
Police and sheriff's patrol officers	31,290	42,270
Licensed practical and licensed vocational nurses	29,480	31,440
Electricians	28,485	41,390
Management analysts	25,470	60,340
Computer systems analysts	23,735	62,890
Special education teachers	23,297	43,450

From the Occupational Outlook Quarterly *by the U.S. Department of Labor.*

Large Metropolitan Areas That Had the Fastest Employment Growth, 1998–2003

Between January 1998 and January 2003, California boasted 4 of the 7 large metropolitan areas in the United States in which employment growth was more than triple that of the nation's overall. Total U.S. nonfarm payroll employment increased 4.7 percent over the period as the nation struggled through an economic downturn. During that time, many metropolitan areas experienced little employment growth or lost thousands of jobs. As the chart shows, however, employment in 11 of the metropolitan areas with at least 300,000 jobs in January 2003 grew by at least two and a half times the national rate over the same period—and two of them increased at more than five times the national rate.

But before packing your bags for one of these metropolitan areas, remember that these data do not show the variation in the kinds of jobs added.

The Golden State shone for employment growth from 1998 to 2003, according to data from the Bureau of Labor Statistics.

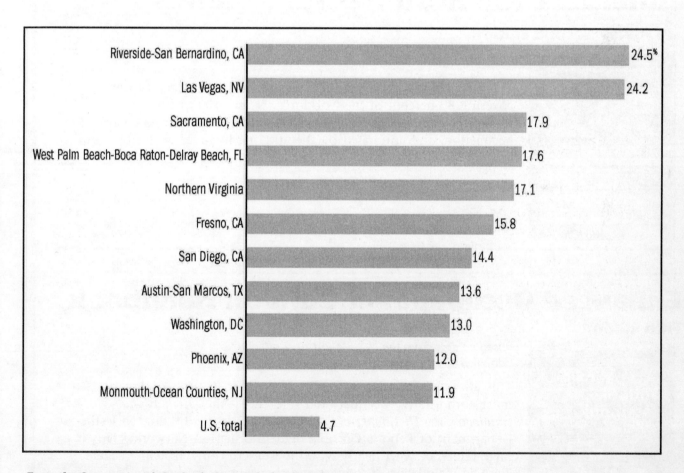

Metropolitan Area	Percent
Riverside-San Bernardino, CA	24.5*
Las Vegas, NV	24.2
Sacramento, CA	17.9
West Palm Beach-Boca Raton-Delray Beach, FL	17.6
Northern Virginia	17.1
Fresno, CA	15.8
San Diego, CA	14.4
Austin-San Marcos, TX	13.6
Washington, DC	13.0
Phoenix, AZ	12.0
Monmouth-Ocean Counties, NJ	11.9
U.S. total	4.7

From the Occupational Outlook Quarterly *by the U.S. Department of Labor.*